Watergate:

Chronology of a Crisis

CONGRESSIONAL QUARTERLY

1414 22nd STREET, N.W., WASHINGTON, D.C.

Congressional Quarterly Inc.

Congressional Quarterly Inc., an editorial research service and publishing company, serves clients in the fields of news, education, business and government. It combines specific coverage of Congress, government and politics by Congressional Quarterly with the more general subject range of an affiliated service, Editorial Research Reports.

Congressional Quarterly was founded in 1945 by Nelson and Henrietta Poynter. Its basic periodical publication was and still is the CQ *Weekly Report,* mailed to clients every Saturday. A cumulative index is published quarterly.

The CQ *Almanac,* a compendium of legislation for one session of Congress, is published every spring. *Congress and the Nation* is published every four years as a record of government for one presidential term.

Congressional Quarterly also publishes paperback books on public affairs. These include the twice-yearly *Guide to Current American Government* and such recent titles as *Energy Crisis in America* and *Congressional Districts in the 1970s.*

CQ Direct Research is a consulting service which performs contract research and maintains a reference library and query desk for the convenience of clients.

Editorial Research Reports covers subjects beyond the specialized scope of Congressional Quarterly. It publishes reference material on foreign affairs, business, education, cultural affairs, national security, science and other topics of news interest. Service to clients includes a 6,000-word report four times a month bound and indexed semi-annually. Editorial Research Reports publishes paperback books in its fields of coverage. Founded in 1923, the service merged with Congressional Quarterly in 1956.

Book Service Editor: Robert A. Diamond.

Watergate: Chronology of a Crisis **was compiled by Editor William B. Dickinson Jr.**

Contributors: Political Editor Mercer Cross and executive branch reporter Barry Polsky were responsible for much of the writing and editing of the Watergate story as it first appeared in the CQ Weekly reports from April 14, 1973 to August 1973. Virtually the entire editorial and research staffs of Congressional Quarterly Service contributed to the coverage.

Daily Chronology: Prudence Crewdson.

Cover Design: Art Director Howard Chapman.

Cover Photo: Daniel A. Devay, Photoart Studio.

Index and Editorial Assistance: Robin Meszoly.

Production Supervisor: Richard C. Young, with assistance from Richard Butler.

Library of Congress
Cataloging in Publication Data

Congressional Quarterly Inc.
Watergate: Chronology of a Crisis.

1. Watergate Affair, 1972- I. Dickinson, William B., ed. II. Title.
E859.C62 1973 364.1'32'0973 73-12792

TABLE OF CONTENTS

The organization of this book follows a chronological form, and the table of contents shows the outline and content of each chapter. Key dates are enumerated for easy recognition. A detailed *Index* is at the back of the book to further isolate facts, names and incidents.

Introduction 1
How to Use this Book 1

Backgrounding the Crisis, April 14, 1973 3
The Bugging and Break-in 4
The Money Morass 4
Biographies of Senate Select Committee Members 6
Espionage and Sabotage 8
Criminal and Civil Trials 9
Probes, Leaks, Denials 11
Partisan Repercussions 12

Chief Congressional Investigations in U.S. History 15

White House Inquiry 17
President's April 17 Statement 18

First Resignations 20

President Addresses the Nation, April 30 24
Haldeman, Ehrlichman, Dean Resignations 24
Kleindienst Resignation 26
Reaction to Nixon Speech 27
Poll on Presidential Popularity 29
Watergate Impact on Congress 33
Text of April 30 Presidential Address 34
Kleindienst, Haldeman, Ehrlichman Resignation Letters 37

Watergate's Cast of Characters 38
Occupations 38
Dwight L. Chapin 39
Charles W. Colson 39
John W. Dean III 39
John D. Ehrlichman 39
H.R. Haldeman 39
E. Howard Hunt Jr. 40
Herbert W. Kalmbach 40
G. Gordon Liddy 40
Jeb Stuart Magruder 40
James W. McCord Jr. 40
John N. Mitchell 41
Ken Rietz 41
Donald H. Segretti 41
Maurice H. Stans 41
Gordon C. Strachan 41
Ronald L. Ziegler 41

White House Staff Changes 42
Elliot L. Richardson 42
Leonard Garment 43
William D. Ruckelshaus 43

Previous White House Scandals 44
Harding: Teapot Dome 44
Truman: Vaughan and Caudle 44
Eisenhower: Sherman Adams 45

Indictments and Reorganization, May 10 46
Mitchell, Stans Indicted 46
Nixon Addresses Republican Dinner 48
Text of Nixon's May 9 Speech 49
News Media Fairness Questioned 51
Egil Krogh's Role 52
Gen. Alexander M. Haig Jr. Joins Nixon Staff 53
Impeachment in U.S. History 55
McCord Memorandum to Federal Prosecutors 57
Texts of Ellsberg Case Memos 59

President Fills Defense and CIA Posts 60
James R. Schlesinger, Defense 61
J. Fred Buzhardt Jr., Special Counsel 61
William E. Colby, CIA 61

Senate Judiciary Committee Hearings on Elliot L. Richardson 62

Senate Select Committee Opens Watergate Hearings, May 17 63
Robert C. Odle Jr. Testimony 63
James W. McCord Jr. Testimony 64
CIA Role in Coverup 66
Judge Byrne's Ruling in Ellsberg Trial 70
Excerpts From Mitchell, Stans Indictment 71
John W. Dean's Statement on Pressures 72

Proposed Reform of Election Process, May 16 73
Nixon Proposes Study Commission 73
Changes in Presidential, House Tenure 74
Electoral Reform Text 75

CQ Interview with House Majority Leader Thomas P. O'Neill Jr. . . . 77
Presidential Counterattack, May 22 . . . 79
Nixon's May 22 Statement on Coverup . . . 79
Senate Hearings, May 22-24 . . . 80
Editorial Comment by Newspapers . . . 81
CIA Role in Coverup . . . 86
White House Briefing on Watergate . . . 88
Text of President's May 22 Statement . . . 90
McCord Statement on Political Pressure, May 18 . . . 94
Selection of Special Prosecutor
Archibald Cox Accepts Position, May 18 . . . 96
Elliot L. Richardson Confirmed as Atty. Gen. . . . 96
Duty Guidelines for Special Prosecutor . . . 97
Friction Builds Over Prosecutor
Cox vs. Dash on Hearings Strategy . . . 99
Ehrlichman Testimony on CIA Role . . . 101
Haldeman Statement on CIA Activities . . . 102
Presidential Subpoena Dispute . . . 103
Fair Campaign Practices Committee Report . . . 105
Vacuum on Presidential Appointments . . . 108
Nixon Statement on San Clemente Property . . . 109
Haldeman-Ehrlichman Depositions
Effort to Blame Dean for Watergate . . . 110
Excerpts From Haldeman's Deposition . . . 113
Text of 1970 Security Recommendations . . . 122
Excerpts of CIA Memos on Watergate . . . 126
White House Reorganization . . . 130
Stans-Magruder Testify in Senate June 12, 14 . . . 132
Maurice H. Stans Denies Watergate Role . . . 132
Jeb Stuart Magruder Implicates Mitchell . . . 135
Agnew Attacks Watergate Hearings . . . 140
Text of Stans Statement . . . 141
House Committee Investigates S.E.C. . . . 144
A Week of Leaks, June 17-22 . . . 145
Hearings Postponed During Brezhnev Visit . . . 145
Dean's Committee Statements Leaked . . . 145
Republican Undercover Campaign Worker . . . 146
McGovern on Watergate . . . 147
Dean Testimony . . . 151
Damaging Charges by John W. Dean III . . . 151
White House Files Dispute . . . 151
List of 'Political Enemies' . . . 153
Text of Buzhardt Memo . . . 162
Dean Statement Excerpts . . . 163
CQ Interview with Historian Daniel J. Boorstin . . . 169
Senate Hearings Extended . . . 174
GAO Report on Agnew Campaign Dinner . . . 174
Dean Concludes Testimony . . . 174
Presidential Resignation Debate . . . 175
Presidential Testimony . . . 176
Lowell P. Weicker, Joseph M. Montoya Campaign Funds . . . 177
Mitchell Admits Coverup . . . 179
Presidential Testimony Debate . . . 179
Nixon Illness . . . 179
Mitchell Coverup Motives . . . 180
Richard A. Moore Denies Nixon Coverup . . . 184
Mitchell's Retrospect on Ellsberg . . . 185
White House Documents Dispute . . . 184
Text of Ervin Letter to Nixon . . . 186
Airline's Illegal Campaign Donation . . . 187
Text of Nixon Executive Privilege Letter . . . 189
Text of Truman Executive Privilege Letter . . . 190
Presidential Eavesdropping . . . 191
Conflict over Nixon Tapes . . . 191
Moore Concludes Testimony . . . 192
Alexander P. Butterfield Reveals Nixon Taping . . . 192
Herbert W. Kalmbach Testimony . . . 193
Butterfield's Explanation of Wiretaps . . . 194
Nixon, Ervin Letters on Tapes . . . 195
Texts of Nixon, Ervin Letters . . . 196
Fred C. LaRue Testimony . . . 197
Archibald Cox's Prosecuting Force . . . 198
Bogus Telephone Call to Ervin . . . 200
Robert C. Mardian Testimony . . . 200
LaRue Concludes Testimony . . . 201
Text of LaRue Statement . . . 204
Text of Kalmbach Statement . . . 204
Text of Moore Statement . . . 205
Senate-Nixon Deadlock . . . 208
Cox Obtains Tapes Court Order . . . 208
Mardian Concludes Testimony . . . 208
Tapes: Constitutional Issues . . . 209
Gordon C. Strachan Questioned . . . 210
Ervin, Baker Tapes Statements . . . 211
John D. Ehrlichman Testimony . . . 212
Senate Sues for White House Tapes . . . 216
Nixon Letter on Subpoenas . . . 220
Nixon Rose Garden Speech . . . 220
Ehrlichman Statement Excerpts . . . 221
Text of Cox Letter Requesting Tapes . . . 224
Text of White House Refusal Letter . . . 224
Text of Cox Subpoenas Statement . . . 225
Text of Nixon Letter to Ervin . . . 225
Text of Watergate Committee Resolution . . . 225
Text of Mardian Statement . . . 226
Text of Strachan Statement . . . 226
Haldeman Testimony at Overtime Hearings . . . 229
Hearings Accelerated . . . 229
Vernon A. Walters Testimony . . . 229
Ehrlichman Concludes Testimony . . . 230
Kalmbach Testimony . . . 230
H.R. Haldeman Testimony . . . 231
Donation to George C. Wallace . . . 232
Committee-Haldeman Showdown on Tapes . . . 233

Nixon Criticized by Adlai E. Stevenson III 234
Colson ITT Memo Disclosed 235
MacGregor Deposition 236
Richard M. Helms Testimony 238
Insult to Daniel K. Inouye 238
Robert E. Cushman Testimony 239
Poll on Nixon Popularity 240
Robert F. Drinan's Impeachment Move 242
Text of Haldeman Statement 244

Senate Hearings Recess

Tapes Battle Continues 254
Nixon Notification Discrepancies 254
Nixon Tapes Reply Text 255
L. Patrick Gray Testimony 255
Harry A. Blackmun Speech 257
Overview, Watergate Investigations 258
Kleindienst, Henry E. Petersen Testimony 260
Nixon Popularity Poll 262
Text of Gray's Opening Statement 264
Text of Walters Memo. 266
Text of Colson ITT Memo 268
Spiro T. Agnew Investigated 270
Nixon Property Expenses 271

Nixon's Watergate Reply 272

Text of Cox Tapes Subpoena Memo 273
Second Senate Hearings Background 274
Nixon Popularity Poll 274
Text of Agnew Letter Releasing Records 275
Text of Nixon Aug. 15 Speech 275
Text of Nixon Supplementary Statement 278

Index 281

INTRODUCTION

Watergate resembles nothing so much as a medieval morality play, acted out in 20th century terms on color television before the disbelieving eyes of a whole people. Because there are so many actors to sort out, with the denouement still to come, the American Everyman is understandably confused.

Nothing in the way of education or experience adequately prepared the national audience for the sorry recitation of intrigue, perjury, deception, burglary and hubris that made Watergate a generic term symbolizing the greatest political crisis since the Civil War. It can be seen as the final political holocaust in a ten-year period marked by mindless assassinations, undeclared war, and raging protest movements.

With only the first phase of the Senate's hearings completed, we cannot be wholly sure who is good and who is evil. Contradictory testimony and the public's deep respect for the office of the President combined to make the exposers of Watergate almost as suspect in the public mind as its perpetrators.

People want to be able to think well of national leaders. A scandal reaching up to—even into—the oval office of the White House has left the nation stunned and bruised. Like a patient stricken with a terrible illness, the first reaction is one of denial, followed by unstructured anger. The consensus, if any, is still to arrive.

At best, the search for Watergate's implications for the democratic process has only just begun. This book, as large and as detailed as it is, provides only one tool for following the agony in its initial stages. Watergate and it appendages could turn out to be the preoccupation of our nation for years.

Optimists will hope that out of the resulting national catharsis will come a long overdue re-examination of America's political institutions. If nothing else, Watergate reveals that we have taken our system too much for granted. More power was placed in the hands of a few than was desirable for the many.

A worry that cannot be easily dismissed centers on an unavoidable question: Does Watergate show some awful new flaw in the constitutional structure conceived by the founding fathers nearly 200 years ago? Even to ask the question is to invite suspicion in some quarters. But the tragedy of Watergate will be compounded if an aroused citizenry fails to use the occasion to change things. New protections against invasions of privacy, campaign financing irregularities and executive branch autocracy would seem to be required if confidence in self-government is to be fully restored.

How to Use This Book

The *Table of Contents* precedes this introduction. It shows the outline and content of each chapter. In general the organization of the book follows a chronological form, and key dates are enumerated for easy recognition.

A detailed *Index* is at the back of the book to further isolate a particular fact, name or incident and make it easy to find.

The first chapter summarizes the Watergate story as it was known on April 14, 1973. Subsequent major chapters follow the crisis as it unfolded until completion of the first round of Senate hearings in August 1973. Depending on later developments, *Congressional Quarterly* will issue a second volume that will carry the Watergate chronology into 1974.

The most dangerous outcome of the Watergate scandal could be the least noticed: growth in the tendency to distrust all politicians. Democracies can survive almost anything else except the loss of belief in the worthiness of elected officials.

Amid the gloom there are glimmers of light. Historian Daniel Boorstin points out *(p. 169)* that one of the distinctions between democracy and other forms of government is that while democracy is messy on the surface, other forms of government are messy underneath. We can take pride in the fact that when Watergate did surface, our society refused to bury it and made sure it reached the whole community in a highly visible way.

Disclosure, however, is not enough. If the lesson of Watergate simply teaches cynicism ("Everybody in politics acts this way"), the outcome is certain to be unfavorable to the endurance of the democratic experience. When James Madison introduced the first draft of the Bill of Rights in 1789, he observed that government is instituted and ought to be exercised for the benefit of the people, and added: "The people have an indubitable, inalienable and indefeasible right to reform or change their government, whenever it is found adverse or inadequate to the purposes of its institution." Before long we may know whether Watergate registered on the public consciousness as just another media sensation or, alternatively, set in motion fundamental rethinking and reform consistent with Madison's high vision.

WILLIAM B. DICKINSON JR.
August 1973

WATERGATE SCANDAL: A SENATE SEARCH FOR THE TRUTH

A break-in at an office building in Washington, D.C., early in the morning of June 17, 1972, has developed into one of the best-publicized pieces of political skulduggery in American history. The name of the building in which five men were arrested at 2:30 a.m. that day has become the word commonly used to describe not only the break-in itself but the widening circle of events surrounding it. The name is Watergate.

The five men were arrested in Democratic national headquarters, offices occupying a suite on the sixth floor of the Watergate office-apartment-hotel-shopping complex, one of the swankest in Washington. The men were carrying electronic surveillance equipment. They were wearing surgical gloves to prevent leaving fingerprints.

Incredulity, sometimes accompanied by cynical laughter, typified the initial public reaction to the bungled break-in. But, as one disclosure followed another, the laughter faded and the Watergate incident was recognized for what it was: one segment of a much larger political spy puzzle involving espionage and sabotage, implicating White House officials and financed with hundreds of thousands of dollars in secret campaign funds.

In a little more than seven months, the five burglars and two of their accomplices had either pleaded guilty to or been convicted of felonies. But most of the puzzle remained unsolved by early spring of 1973. A federal grand jury was continuing its investigation. Three civil suits awaited trial in U.S. District Court in Washington. A constitutional dispute over the President's right to refuse to permit his staff to testify before congressional committees cost a nominee the prestigious job of FBI director.

All the unanswered questions had created a growing uneasiness among Republican officials who feared damage to their party. An increasing number of Republicans were speaking out publicly against administration handling of the charges and were demanding candor and cooperation with investigators.

Senate Investigation

All the still-undisclosed facts, it was hoped, would be brought to light by public hearings to be conducted by a bipartisan, seven-member select committee of the Senate. The committee, chaired by Sen. Sam. J. Ervin (D N.C.), was expected to begin hearings in late April or early May. *(Committee members and staff, p. 6)*

The committee was established by a unanimous vote of the Senate Feb. 7. The resolution establishing the committee (S Res 60) provided subpoena powers and authorized $500,000 for completion of the investigation and writing of a report by Feb. 28, 1974.

Samuel Dash, a Georgetown University law professor who is chief counsel for the investigative committee, discussed a few of the committee's ground rules with

Congressional Quarterly. Without committing himself to a timetable, Dash said that public hearings would begin "as quickly as possible." Private investigation by him and minority counsel Fred Thompson was under way, he added, and "This is going to be, as far as I'm concerned, a very careful, a very thorough investigation."

Dash said he and Thompson were assembling a staff, starting with a "core team of specialists," that might number "in the 30s or 40s" when the investigation reaches its peak. Although he expects the committee to complete its work within the allotted time, he mentioned the possibility that, if necessary, the investigators might have to exercise their option for an extension of time and money to finish their job.

Arrangements must be made for a hearing room large enough to accommodate the large crowds expected to attend the hearings. One ground rule, Dash said, is that the hearings will be open to press and public. A one-day closed hearing on March 28 produced so many leaks to the press from unidentified sources that further closed hearings were canceled.

"The success of the investigation will depend on the staff," Dash said. He expects the initial public hearings to last about a month, followed by continued investigation by the staff through the summer and more extensive hearings in the fall, he said. The investigation is expected to be broad in scope, exploring not only the details of the Watergate but other charges of political wrongdoing by both the Republican and Democratic Parties.

The ultimate goal of the committee, said Dash, is to discover "what impact (all this) has on the election process in a Democratic country." The final report, he said, may contain recommendations to reform existing election laws.

The Bugging and Break-in

After the initial reports on the June 17 break-in, the Watergate incident dropped temporarily from the headlines. Not until late summer did the story of the broader scandal start to unfold. But, even during its absence from the news, a federal grand jury was conducting a secret investigation that led to the indictment of seven men. Many of the revelations that gradually came to light were the result of diligent digging by and occasional leaks to the press.

The Conspirators. These were the five men arrested by Washington police in the Democratic offices:

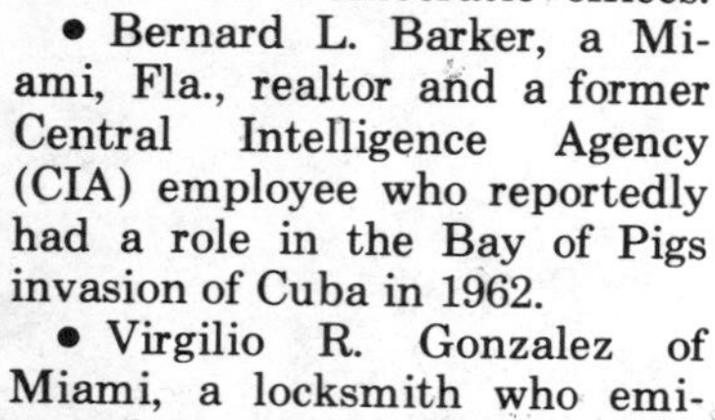

James W. McCord Jr.

- Bernard L. Barker, a Miami, Fla., realtor and a former Central Intelligence Agency (CIA) employee who reportedly had a role in the Bay of Pigs invasion of Cuba in 1962.
- Virgilio R. Gonzalez of Miami, a locksmith who emigrated from Cuba during Fidel Castro's rise to power.
- Eugenio R. Martinez, a member of Barker's real estate firm and an anti-Castro Cuban exile with CIA associations.
- James W. McCord Jr. of Washington, security coordinator for the Republican National Committee and the Committee for the Re-election of the President, a former FBI agent and CIA employee. He was fired the day after the break-in.

E. Howard Hunt Jr.

- Frank A. Sturgis of Miami, an associate of Barker who had connections with the CIA and had participated in anti-Castro activities.

The five were charged with attempted burglary and attempted interception of telephone and other communications. On Sept. 15, the grand jury indicted them and two other men for conspiracy, burglary and violation of federal wiretapping laws. The two others were:

- E. Howard Hunt Jr. of Washington, a former White House consultant, writer of spy novels and former CIA employee. Hunt's consulting work included declassification of the Pentagon Papers and intelligence work in narcotics enforcement.
- G. Gordon Liddy of Washington, counsel to the Finance Committee to Re-elect the President, former FBI agent, former Treasury Department official and former member of the White House staff. Liddy was fired for refusing to answer the FBI's questions during an investigation of the Watergate incident.

At a trial in January 1973, Hunt, Barker, Sturgis, Gonzalez and Martinez pleaded guilty. Liddy and McCord were convicted.

Partisan Reaction. Lawrence F. O'Brien, Democratic national chairman at the time of the break-in, called it "an incredible act of political espionage." John N. Mitchell, former attorney general and, until July 1, President Nixon's re-election campaign manager, said the five men arrested at the Watergate "were not operating either in our behalf or with our consent."

G. Gordon Liddy

More Bugging. On Sept. 7, O'Brien, then the campaign manager for Democratic presidential nominee George McGovern, charged that Republican-sponsored surveillance of Democratic headquarters had been going on before the June 17 arrests. He said that his phone and that of R. Spencer Oliver, executive director of the state chairmen's association of the Democratic National Committee, had been tapped for several weeks. Information from the taps had, he claimed, been monitored and transcribed in a motel across the street from the Watergate.

O'Brien said the five men arrested on June 17 had come to repair a faulty tap on his phone and to install a bugging device nearby. On May 27, he said, the presence of campaign workers had prevented some men from setting up eavesdropping equipment in McGovern campaign headquarters on Capitol Hill.

News stories on Sept. 16 identified Alfred C. Baldwin III, a former FBI agent and an alleged participant in the Watergate bugging, as the source of O'Brien's information. In a copyrighted interview published in *The Los Angeles Times* Oct. 4, Baldwin said he had delivered eavesdropping logs to the President's re-election committee less than two weeks before June 17. He said the material was sent to someone besides the seven men indicted, but he did not name that person.

The Washington Post reported on Oct. 6 that Baldwin, who was granted immunity from prosecution in return for his cooperation with investigators, told the FBI that memos describing wiretapped and bugged conversations in Democratic headquarters had been sent to three persons: William E. Timmons, Nixon's assistant for congressional relations; Robert C. Odle Jr., director of administration for the re-election committee, and J. Glenn Sedam Jr., the committee's general counsel. The charges were denied.

The Money Morass

As the grand jury was hearing witnesses throughout the summer of 1972 in connection with the Watergate bugging, reports began to appear about enormous sums of money, obtained under unusual circumstances, for use in the Republicans' intelligence operations.

GAO Investigation. An investigation by the FBI and the General Accounting Office's (GAO) Office of Federal Elections began Aug. 1 on the finances of the President's re-election committee. The investigation was started after *The Washington Post* reported that a $25,000 check intended for Nixon's campaign had been deposited to the Miami bank account of Bernard Barker, one of the men arrested at the Watergate.

Maurice H. Stans

Kenneth H. Dahlberg, midwestern finance chairman for the Nixon campaign, said he had given a cashier's check for $25,000 to Maurice H. Stans, the former secretary of commerce who was Nixon's finance chairman in 1972, as he had been in 1968.

The Washington Star-News reported on Aug. 10 that additional contributions of $89,000 had been deposited in installments in Barker's account, bringing the total to $114,000. The article quoted investigators as saying the Republicans had a "security fund" for their national convention.

A GAO report released Aug. 26 cited five "apparent" and four "possible" violations of the Federal Election Campaign Act of 1971 by the re-election finance committee. The report was turned over to the Justice Department for further action. These were among its disclosures:

• The committee failed to keep a detailed account of the $25,000 contribution. It was given anonymously, but the donor was revealed to be Dwayne Andreas, a Minneapolis, Minn., grain executive. Andreas and Dahlberg, it was later revealed, were both directors of a bank that was granted a federal charter on Aug. 22. Both denied any connection between the contribution and the charter.

• The committee did not disclose details of the $25,000 contribution in accordance with the 1971 campaign law.

• The committee failed to keep a detailed account of the money spent from the $25,000 Dahlberg check or from the four checks totaling $89,000, drawn on a Mexico City bank and eventually deposited to Barker's account. Stans told the GAO that the four checks were from donors in Texas who wished to remain anonymous by contributing before April 7—the deadline for anonymous contributions before new reporting requirements took effect under the 1971 law.

• The committee kept inadequate records, not only on the $114,000 in anonymous contributions, but on the balance of $350,000 deposited on May 25 to the credit of the Media Committee to Re-elect the President. Hugh W. Sloan, former treasurer of the finance committee, said the $350,000 had been kept in a safe in Stans' secretary's office. Only Stans and Sloan had access to the safe. Stans told the GAO that the funds had been collected before the April 7 deadline and that any records pertaining to them had been destroyed after April 7.

Indictment, Settlement. The GAO investigation led to the indictment of the re-election finance committee on eight counts of campaign spending violations. The committee was fined $8,000 on Jan. 26, 1973, in U.S. District Court in Washington after pleading nolo contendere—no contest—to the charges.

Barker Trial. Another trial that resulted from one of the Republican financial transactions was that of Barker, the Miamian in whose bank account the secretly contributed money had been deposited. Barker was indicted in Dade County (Florida) Criminal Court on a charge of fraudulently using his notary public seal to indicate that the $25,000 check from Dahlberg—the Dwayne Andreas contribution—had been endorsed in his presence.

Barker pleaded guilty on Sept. 15. He was found guilty on Nov. 1 and given a 60-day suspended sentence on the condition that he surrender his notary license.

Banking Committee Probe. But the Barker trial and conviction were only subsidiary elements in the movement of much larger amounts of money through his firm's account.

The House Banking and Currency Committee staff distributed to committee members on Sept. 12 a report claiming that finance chairman Stans knew of the transfer of $100,000 in contributions from Texas donors through a Mexican bank and into the campaign treasury. The report was leaked to the press.

According to the report, the money was delivered, along with an additional $600,000 in contributions, to the re-election committee on April 5, two days before the deadline for identifying donors. Included in the $100,000, said the report, was the $89,000 deposited to Barker's account on April 20.

The report said that Stans had denied knowledge of the Mexican bank transfer at first but later had admitted knowing about the transaction when he was confronted with conflicting testimony from a Texas fund-raiser. Stans issued a statement denying any knowledge of the Mexican transactions and calling the committee report "rubbish" and "transparently political."

By a 20-15 vote on Oct. 3, the Banking and Currency Committee rejected a probe of Nixon campaign finances. The rejection was bipartisan; six Democrats joined 14 Republicans in preventing the investigation. It was opposed by the Justice Department on grounds that it would interfere with the criminal trial of the seven Watergate defendants.

A report by Democratic members of the House committee was released Oct. 31, making additional charges of campaign fund mishandling by the Nixon re-election committee. A re-election committee spokesman said the report was a "dishonest collection of innuendo and fourth-hand hearsay." Among the allegations in the report:

• The re-election committee had developed the capability of monitoring the bank accounts of Democratic senators and representatives. The charge was attributed to a friend of Hugh Sloan, the former campaign treasurer. Sloan's attorney called it an "absolute lie."

• Alfred Baldwin, the Watergate bugger who had been granted immunity, was hired for $18,000 a year to record not only political discussions but personal conversations.

• At least $30,000 had been channeled to the Nixon committee through a Luxembourg bank before the new campaign spending law took effect.

• The campaign finance committee had committed massive bookkeeping errors and omissions, including one $800,000 discrepancy between committee records and bank records of cash on hand in April 1972.

(Continued on p. 7)

Biographies of Senate Select Committee's Members, Counsels

Sen. Sam J. Ervin Jr. (D N.C.), 76, chairman of the committee, is considered the Senate's leading constitutional scholar. In his nearly 19 years in the Senate, he has sided sometimes with the conservatives, sometimes with the liberals. He was chosen to head the committee because of his reputation for fairness and nonpartisanship. Ervin is a member of the Judiciary and Armed Services Committees and chairman of the Government Operations Committee.

When President Nixon ordered presidential aides not to honor subpoenas issued by the select committee, Ervin responded by saying, "I'd recommend to the Senate they send the sergeant at arms of the Senate to arrest a White House aide or any other witness who refuses to appear and...let the Senate try him."

Sen. Howard H. Baker Jr. (R Tenn.), 47, the committee vice chairman and ranking minority member, was elected to the Senate in 1966. His father was the late Rep. Howard H. Baker (R Tenn. 1951-64), and his father-in-law was the late Sen. Everett McKinley Dirksen (R Ill. 1951-69).

Baker unsuccessfully challenged Sen. Hugh Scott (R Pa.) for the minority leadership in 1969 and 1971 as the candidate of Senate conservatives. He serves on the Commerce and Public Works Committees, the Republican Committee on Committees and the Republican Personnel Committee.

Baker has said he favors "a full, thorough and fair investigation with no holds barred, let the chips fall where they will."

Sen. Edward J. Gurney (R Fla.), 59, elected in 1968, is the first Republican senator from Florida since Reconstruction. He is a member of the Government Operations, Judiciary and Select Small Business Committees. In 1972, Gurney was the chief defender of the Nixon administration during the Judiciary Committee's investigation of the International Telephone and Telegraph Corporation.

He has said of the Watergate investigation, "I want to see that it is as nonpartisan as possible, but I certainly want to bring out every last piece of information." When the investigation resolution was debated Feb. 7, Gurney read information from political polls indicating that the public did not have much interest in the Watergate matter.

Sen. Daniel K. Inouye (D Hawaii), 48, has represented Hawaii in Congress since the islands gained statehood in 1959. He served in the House for four years and has been a senator since 1963. He is a member of the Appropriations, Commerce and District of Columbia Committees.

In 1972, as chairman of the D.C. Appropriations Subcommittee, he conducted full-scale investigations of the District of Columbia government. He is one of four assistant majority whips and vice chairman of the Democratic Senatorial Campaign Committee.

Sen. Joseph M. Montoya (D N.M.), 57, came to the Senate in 1964 after spending eight years in the House. He is a member of the Appropriations and Public Works Committees.

When first appointed to the investigating committee, he said he expected that the members "will be able to sift through the facts and come up with a complete story of just what was involved and just who was involved, in addition, if any, to those already named."

Sen. Herman E. Talmadge (D Ga.), 59, a senator since 1957, was governor of Georgia for the nine years preceding his election to the Senate. In the Senate, he is chairman of the Agriculture and Forestry Committee and ranking Democrat on the Finance Committee. He also serves on the Veterans' Affairs, Select Standards and Conduct and Select Nutrition and Human Needs Committee and is a member of the Democratic Policy Committee.

Talmadge, considered by some senators to be one of their most intelligent colleagues, has said he plans to do no investigating on his own but will depend on the committee's hearings for his knowledge. "I see myself as a juror," he said, "and a juror doesn't background himself."

Sen. Lowell P. Weicker Jr. (R Conn.), 41, was elected to the Senate in 1970 after spending one term in the House. He is a member of the Banking, Housing and Urban Affairs and Aeronautical and Space Sciences Committees. He is also on the Republican Senatorial Campaign Committee.

Weicker has been particularly outspoken about the Watergate investigation and has said he is conducting his own studies on the matter. He has charged that offices of members of Congress were next in line to be bugged. Weicker said he sought membership on the investigating committee because "I'm a professional politician. Because of things like the Watergate, people have lost faith in politicians, and I want to see that changed. The only thing that will convince them to respect politicians is to bring dirty business like the Watergate out in the open."

Samuel Dash, 48, a Georgetown University criminal law professor, is the majority counsel for the select committee. He is director of Georgetown's Institute of Criminal Law and Procedure and is considered a leading authority on wiretapping. He is a former Philadelphia District Attorney and was a trial attorney for the Justice Department's criminal division in 1951 and 1952.

Dash has characterized the Watergate investigation as "the most important ever undertaken by the Senate because it goes to the heart of the democratic process."

Fred D. Thompson, 30, a Nashville lawyer, is the committee's minority counsel. Thompson is a former U.S. attorney for Tennessee's middle district and served as Sen. Baker's re-election campaign manager for that area in 1972. As a federal prosecutor, Thompson was known chiefly for his handling of bank robbery and moonshine whisky cases.

Thompson said he views his role as minority counsel as ensuring that the committee staff "keeps within the scope of the investigation" and does not delve into matters unrelated to political espionage.

(Watergate continued from p. 5)

Funds Returned. The contributor of the mysterious $100,000 identified himself early in 1973. He was a Texas oilman, Robert H. Allen. He acknowledged that $89,000 of his donation had been deposited to the Barker account. In a letter to Stans, he asked that the $100,000 be returned for personal reasons.

The return of Allen's $100,000 was announced on March 9 by the re-election finance committee. Also returned to its donors, the re-election committee said, was another $555,000. Of this amount, $305,000 was given back to Walter T. Duncan, a Texas land speculator, and $250,000 to Robert L. Vesco, a New Jersey financier. Duncan needed the money to pay off debts. Vesco had been accused by the Securities and Exchange Commission of a $224-million stock fraud. His contribution of $200,000 to the Nixon campaign was the object of another GAO investigation. The other $50,000 was not involved in the investigation.

Vesco's Role. The interaction of Vesco with the President's finance committee was brought to light in a court deposition made public in New York City on Feb. 27. His $200,000 contribution was delivered to the committee in cash on April 10, 1972, three days after the new reporting law took effect. But it was never reported to the GAO.

John N. Mitchell

Vesco is accused of swindling investors in IOS Ltd., an overseas mutual fund corporation. Although the $200,000 contribution and another $50,000 contribution—given after April 7 and reported as required—were returned to Vesco on Jan. 31, the finance committee claimed the law had not been violated, because Vesco had intended to contribute the money before the deadline and it was "constructively in the hands" of the committee before April 7.

The court deposition, made by an attorney who was an associate of Vesco and was Nixon's campaign manager in New Jersey in 1972, linked John Mitchell, Maurice Stans and the President's younger brother, Edward Nixon of Edmonds, Wash., to the Vesco contribution. The deposition stated that:

- Late in 1971, then Attorney General Mitchell phoned the U.S. embassy in Geneva, Switzerland, expressing interest in the jailing of Vesco on the complaint of a former IOS customer. Vesco was freed on bond within a day. Mitchell later denied any wrongdoing; he said he made the call at the request of the attorney who gave the deposition, Harry L. Sears.
- Vesco said that Stans had asked for the contribution in cash. This request was later confirmed by Edward Nixon. A re-election committee spokesman denied these statements; Stans and Edward Nixon were unavailable for comment.

More 'Apparent Violations.' A GAO report charging the President's re-election finance committee with four new "apparent violations" was referred to the Justice Department on March 12 for possible prosecution. The chief subject of the report was the $200,000 Vesco contribution. It was "undisputed," said the GAO, that the contribution was not delivered to the finance committee until after the April 7, 1972, deadline.

The committee labeled the GAO report "irresponsible" and said the committee's handling of the Vesco contribution had a "conclusive precedent." That precedent was the $25,000 Andreas contribution of April 10, 1972, which, according to the committee, had been ruled within the law in a Justice Department report on Jan. 11, 1973.

The Secret Fund. Recurrent references have been made since the fall of 1972 to a secret fund, kept in a safe in Maurice Stans' office, that allegedly was used to finance the Watergate bugging and broader espionage and sabotage operations. Press reports have said that high Republican officials in the re-election campaign and on the White House staff have had knowledge of the fund. Many of these reports have been denied, but full details on the fund and its uses have yet to be revealed.

In September 1972, *The Washington Post* quoted sources involved in the Watergate investigation as saying that John Mitchell, while attorney general, personally controlled a secret fund used to finance intelligence-gathering operations against the Democrats. Mitchell denied the charge.

Quoting federal investigators and grand jury testimony, the Post reported on Oct. 25 that H. R. Haldeman, the White House chief of staff, was one of five men authorized to approve payments from the fund. The cash fund, according to the story, fluctuated between $350,000 and $700,000. The White House said the reference to Haldeman was untrue and the report was "based on misinformation."

The first acknowledgment by a campaign official that the fund existed was made in a Washington television interview on Oct. 26 by Clark MacGregor, who had replaced Mitchell as Nixon's campaign manager on July 1. MacGregor said no money from the fund had been used for illegal purposes. And he repeated the denial of Haldeman's authority for making disbursements from the fund.

In its August report, the GAO asked the Justice Department to investigate the fund. The department took no action. In its March 12 report, the GAO repeated its request for a Justice Department investigation of the fund, which included Vesco's $200,000 contribution.

Espionage and Sabotage

Reports of an alleged widespread Republican network of espionage and sabotage against the Democrats, paid for out of the secret cash fund, began to appear in the fall of 1972. The first article, published in the Oct. 10 *Washington Post,* was dismissed as a "collection of absurdities" by a re-election committee spokesman. Information in the article was attributed to FBI and Justice Department files. Among the activities described in the Post article were:

- Following members of Democratic candidates' families and assembling dossiers on their personal lives.
- Forging letters and distributing them under Democratic candidates' letterheads.
- Leaking false and manufactured items to the press.
- Throwing campaign schedules into disarray.
- Investigating Democratic campaign workers.
- Planting provocateurs at the national political conventions.
- Seizing confidential campaign files.
- Investigating potential contributors to the Nixon campaign.

Muskie Campaign. According to the Post story, one of the targets of Republican sabotage was Sen. Edmund S. Muskie of Maine, a candidate for the Democratic presidential nomination. One of the incidents most damaging, and perhaps fatal, to his campaign was a well-publicized letter alleging his use of the pejorative word "Canuck" to describe Americans of French-Canadian descent. That incident made headlines in February 1972, before the New Hampshire primary.

The Post account said that one of its reporters had been told by Ken W. Clawson, deputy director of White House communications, that he had written the letter, which had been attributed to a man in Florida. Clawson denied the charge.

An interview with Muskie (conducted before the Oct. 10 report) was published in the Oct. 13 Post, quoting him as saying that he had been victimized by a "systematic campaign of sabotage," including:

- Theft of documents from his files.
- Middle-of-the-night telephone calls to voters from impostors claiming to be Muskie canvassers.
- False items planted in newspapers.
- Facsimiles of his envelopes used to mail embarrassing material under his name—including one assertion that two of his opponents for the nomination had engaged in illicit sexual acts.

A Tampa, Fla., secretary said that she had participated in a scheme to disrupt Muskie's primary campaign in Florida, *The New York Times* reported on Oct. 25.

Enter Segretti. The alleged recruiter of the provocateurs for the Nixon campaign was a young California lawyer and former Treasury Department attorney, Donald H. Segretti. He denied knowing anything about such an operation and called the report "ridiculous."

But that was only the first of many reports alleging that Segretti was involved in undercover rascality. The allegations of sabotage and espionage were regularly denounced as false by spokesmen for the White House and the re-election committee.

The Post reported on Oct. 15 that Segretti, one of more than 50 alleged undercover operators for the Nixon campaign, had named Dwight L. Chapin, then the President's appointments secretary, as one of his contacts. The source of the charges was a sworn statement from another California attorney, Lawrence Young. Segretti, Young and Chapin had been college classmates. Chapin said the story was "based on hearsay and is fundamentally inaccurate."

Dwight Chapin

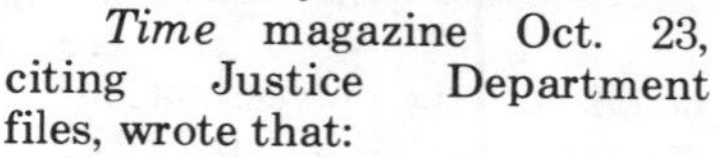

Time magazine Oct. 23, citing Justice Department files, wrote that:

•Segretti was hired by Chapin and Gordon Strachan, a White House staff assistant, and was paid by Herbert W. Kalmbach, Nixon's personal attorney.

• Segretti received more than $35,000 between Sept. 1, 1971, and March 15, 1972, "to subvert and disrupt Democratic candidates' campaigns."

• The FBI began an investigation after discovering a record of phone calls between Segretti and Howard Hunt, one of the seven Watergate defendants.

Records showed that Segretti had made calls to the White House and Chapin's home, *The New York Times* reported Oct. 18. A Times report Oct. 19 said that Segretti apparently volunteered to work for Democratic candidate McGovern in the California primary campaign in June. Although there was evidence that a man named Segretti had appeared at McGovern headquarters, there was no evidence that he actually had worked on the campaign, the Times said.

The Los Angeles Times reported on Oct. 23 that Segretti had told a San Francisco attorney that "he was trying to develop an organization to infiltrate the primary campaigns of two candidates for the Democratic nomination, Senators Muskie of Maine and Henry M. Jackson of Washington. His purpose, it was reported, was to prevent a sweep of the primaries by one candidate.

Segretti Investigation. A Justice Department investigation of Segretti was confirmed by an administration source on Feb. 11, *The New York Times* reported. Earlier, the department had said that Segretti's efforts appeared to be legal and did not warrant an investigation. But the Times quoted a source as saying that Segretti might have violated a statute making it illegal to distribute political literature that is unsigned or contains an unauthorized signature.

Attorney General Richard G. Kleindienst told reporters on Feb. 12 that his department's Watergate investigation was continuing because such an investigation is never closed. "You can just assume it's going on, and I'm not going to tell you what is," he said.

Other Incidents. James McCord, one of the defendants in the criminal case, investigated syndicated columnist Jack Anderson in the spring of 1972, *The Washington Post* reported on Sept. 27. An alleged confidential memorandum from McCord dealt with Anderson's business and social relationship with Anna Chennault of Washington, D.C., a member of the Republican National Finance Committee.

Another Watergate defendant, E. Howard Hunt Jr., had tried to recruit a government employee to investigate the private life of Sen. Edward M. Kennedy (D Mass.), the Post reported on Feb. 10. Clifton DeMotte, a General Services Administration employee at Davisville, R.I., said the incident had occurred in July 1971, when Kennedy was considered a leading contender for his party's presidential nomination.

The GAO said on March 12 that it would investigate some $150-a-week payments reportedly made to Theodore T. Brill, chairman of the Young Republicans at George Washington University. Brill told the Post that he had been paid to infiltrate radical groups in 1972 for Nixon's re-election committee.

Criminal and Civil Trials

The criminal trial of the seven Watergate defendants began on Jan. 8 and ended on Jan. 30. Sentencing was March 23. Still to be tried are three civil suits related to the Watergate. The U.S. District Court in Washington is where the criminal trial was held and where the civil suits will be tried. Chief Judge John J. Sirica tried the criminal case. Judge Charles R. Richey will try the civil cases.

John J. Sirica

Charles R. Richey

Criminal, civil trial judges

Pre-trial Activity. A federal grand jury indicted Liddy, Hunt, McCord, Barker, Martinez, Sturgis and Gonzalez on eight counts Sept. 15. The seven were charged with breaking into the Watergate offices for the purpose of stealing documents and installing electronic listening devices to intercept telephone and oral communications.

Sirica on Oct. 4 enjoined all parties connected with the bugging from making public statements about it. His injunction covered law enforcement officials, defendants, witnesses, alleged victims and attorneys. Sirica's order was greeted with a protest from several Democratic officials. He responded by amending the order to remove references to "witnesses, potential witnesses, complaining witnesses and alleged victims." And he said, "It is not the intention of this court to affect congressional activity, political debate or news media reporting."

On Oct. 11, the final day for filing motions, attorneys for Liddy, Hunt and McCord filed affidavits charging that they had been followed and their telephones had been tapped. They asked for a change of venue, which was denied.

The trial was supposed to start on Nov. 15. But on Oct. 27, Sirica postponed the trial until Jan. 8, 1973. The judge had a pinched nerve, and his doctor advised the postponement.

Trial Opening. A jury was chosen in two days. Sirica warned prospective jurors that he expected the trial to last four to six weeks. Jurors were sequestered from the start.

Defense and government attorneys made their opening statements on Jan. 10. Earl J. Silbert, the chief prosecutor, charged that a broadly ranging political espionage operation had been ordered by top officials of the Committee for the Re-election of the President in 1972. He said Liddy had received $235,000 in cash from the re-election committee to carry out various assignments. Only $50,000 of the money could be accounted for by the prosecution, Silbert said. He also described the hiring by Hunt of a Brigham Young University student, Thomas J. Gregory, to infiltrate the campaign organizations of candidates McGovern and Muskie.

Two defense attorneys, Gerald Alch and Henry Rothblatt, acknowledged in their opening statements that their clients had been in the Watergate the night of June 17. But both said their clients were innocent of the charges.

Guilty Pleas. Within a few days, the seven defendants had been reduced to two. On Jan. 11, Sirica accepted a guilty plea from Hunt on all six counts with which he was charged. On Jan. 15, Barker, Sturgis, Martinez and Gonzalez pleaded guilty. Hunt was freed after posting $100,000 bond. The other four remained in the District of Columbia jail.

Gerald Alch, McCord's attorney, made a motion for a mistrial after the guilty pleas had been made. The absence of the five men from the courtroom would lead the jurors to conclude that guilty pleas had been made and would prejudice the rights of McCord and Liddy, the two men still on trial, he argued. Sirica denied Alch's motion and advised him that he could appeal the ruling to the U.S. Court of Appeals.

Few Answers. Several times during the trial, Sirica personally questioned defendants and witnesses in an effort to get to the bottom of the Watergate affair. He interrogated Barker, Sturgis, Martinez and Gonzalez Jan. 15 about who had planned the bugging and where the money to pay for it had come from.

The four denied press reports that they had been under pressure to plead guilty, that they still were being paid by an unnamed source and that they had been promised a cash settlement as high as $1,000 a month if they pleaded guilty and went to jail.

Anti-communism and anti-Castroism figured in the testimony of the four, two of whom had been linked to the Bay of Pigs invasion. "When it comes to Cuba and the communist conspiracy involving the United States, I will do anything to protect this country," Sturgis said. Gonzalez said he had been told by Barker and Hunt that "we're solving the Cuban situation" by breaking into the Watergate.

'Law of Duress.' Alch, McCord's lawyer, wrote in a memorandum to the court Jan. 17 that his client's participation in the break-in and other activities had been justified because McCord feared violence against Nixon and other Republicans. He explained the "law of duress" to reporters in these words: "If one is under a reasonable apprehension—regardless of whether that apprehension is in fact correct—he is justified in breaking a law to avoid the greater harm..." Alch cited "potentially violent groups" that supported Democratic candidates in 1972 and might have indicated their plans to the Democrats.

Baldwin Testimony. A key government witness, Alfred Baldwin, testified in secret session Jan. 17 about the persons whose conversations he had overheard while tapping phones at the Democratic National Committee. Before the trial went into secret session, Baldwin described how McCord had hired him in May 1972 and how his wiretapping apparatus had been set up in the motel room across from the Watergate. He said he was instructed to take notes on monitored conversations through the day and into the evening, turning over his logs to McCord.

Sloan Testimony. Hugh Sloan, the former treasurer of the President's re-election finance committee, said John Mitchell and Maurice Stans had approved spending money that the government claimed was used for espionage against the Democrats.

In testimony Jan. 23, Sloan said that he had given $199,000 in cash to Liddy at the direction of Jeb Stuart Magruder, deputy campaign chairman for the President. Magruder testified that the committee budgeted about $235,000 for intelligence operations directed by Liddy. He said he knew nothing about illegal bugging activities.

Jeb. S. Magruder

Convictions. Liddy and McCord were found guilty on Jan. 30 of conspiracy, burglary and wiretapping violations. Liddy was convicted on six counts, McCord on eight. Their attorneys said they would appeal.

Alch, McCord's attorney, was bitingly critical of Sirica on the trial's last day. Sirica, he said, "did not limit himself to acting as a judge. He has become, in addition, a prosecutor and an investigator. Not only does he indicate that the defendants are guilty, but that a lot of other people are guilty. The whole courtroom is permeated with a prejudicial atmosphere." Alch claimed on Jan. 31 that Sirica had committed at least nine errors providing grounds for the reversal of McCord's conviction.

The judge had been critical of the prosecution for failing to ask more questions about the motivation of the men. He had sought to compensate for what he felt was this shortcoming by doing extensive interrogating of his own. Questions left unanswered by the trial would, he said, have to be answered by the Senate investigation.

Sentencing. Liddy was given the heaviest sentence by Sirica on March 23. He was sentenced to a minimum of six years and eight months to a maximum of 20 years in prison and was fined $40,000.

The judge left open the final sentence, pending a three-month study by the U.S. Bureau of Prisons, for Barker, Hunt, Sturgis, Martinez and Gonzalez. The five were jailed until the study was completed, at which time Sirica would, he said, uphold the "provisional" maximum sentences he had imposed, reduce the sentences or place the men on probation. For Barker, Sturgis, Martinez and Gonzalez, the potential maximum sentence was 40 years; for Hunt, 35.

One of the most unusual twists of the trial occurred the day of sentencing, when Sirica read a letter written to him by McCord earlier that week. In the letter, McCord wrote that other persons besides those convicted had been involved. Perjury had been committed, he charged. And he claimed that political pressure had been applied to make the defendants plead guilty.

Sirica postponed sentencing of McCord for one week and freed him on $100,000 bond. On March 30, Sirica deferred sentencing until June 15 so that McCord would have the opportunity to testify further before a federal grand jury and before the Senate investigating committee.

Civil Suits. Remaining to be tried before Judge Richey are three civil suits, one filed by Democrats against Republicans and two by Republicans against Democrats. The actions:

- Attorneys for the Democratic National Committee filed suit against the President's re-election committee on June 20, 1972—three days after the break-in—seeking $1-million in damages. Damages sought were increased to $3.2-million on Sept. 11 and increased again to $6.4-million on Feb. 28, 1973. Defendants were expanded to include Liddy, Hunt, former campaign treasurer Sloan, finance chairman Stans, Magruder and Herbert L. Porter, a former Nixon campaign aide.
- Stans and Francis I. Dale, chairman of Nixon's re-election committee, filed a $2.5-million countersuit on Sept. 11.
- Stans filed a $5-million libel suit against former Democratic Chairman O'Brien on Sept. 14 on the grounds that O'Brien had falsely accused him of political espionage on Sept. 11.

Probes, Leaks, Denials

The longest and most penetrating probe of the Watergate and related matters is expected to be conducted by the Senate select committee. But, in the months since the bugging arrests, other investigations as well as those by the House Banking and Currency Committee have been conducted by the FBI, the GAO, the White House and a federal grand jury. Leakage of information from these probes has led to denials, countercharges and recriminations. As the Senate committee was preparing for public hearings, Chairman Ervin and the White House appeared to be headed toward a showdown over the right of White House staff members to refuse to testify before congressional committees.

White House. At an Aug. 29 news conference, Nixon said that no one then employed in his administration had been involved in the Watergate bugging. He said that a complete investigation of the incident by John W. Dean III, his counsel, permitted him to declare "categorically that his investigation indicates that no one in the White House staff, no one in this administration, presently employed, was involved in this very bizarre incident."

John W. Dean III

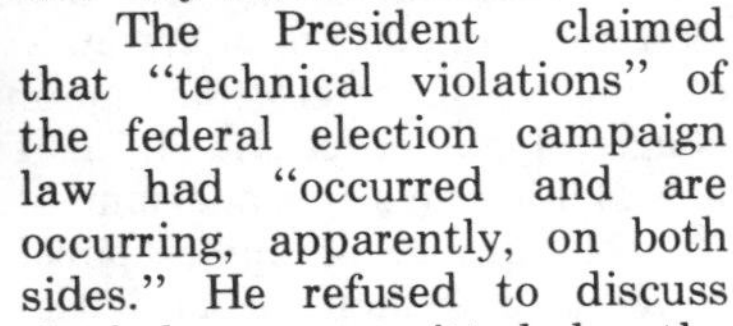

The President claimed that "technical violations" of the federal election campaign law had "occurred and are occurring, apparently, on both sides." He refused to discuss what possible violations had been committed by the Democrats, saying only that "I think that will come out in the balance of this week."

Nixon added, "What really hurts in matters of this sort is not the fact that they occur, because overzealous people in campaigns do things that are wrong. What really hurts is if you try to cover it up."

At a news conference the next day, Aug. 30, Nixon said he would not comply with a Democratic suggestion that a special, nonpartisan prosecutor instead of a Justice Department attorney be assigned to the Watergate case.

Ronald L. Ziegler, the White House press secretary, said on Sept. 8 that the report on Dean's Watergate investigation would not be released. Lawrence O'Brien, then McGovern's campaign manager, had requested its release.

Justice Department. Attorney General Kleindienst pledged on Aug. 28 that the FBI investigation of the Watergate would be "the most extensive, thorough and comprehensive investigation since the assassination of President Kennedy." When completed, he said, "no credible, fair-minded person is going to be able to say that we whitewashed or dragged our feet on it."

Nixon expressed confidence in the FBI investigation on Oct. 5. He said it made the 1948 Alger Hiss probe, which had helped him build a reputation as a young representative, look like "a Sunday school exercise."

The Washington Post reported on Oct. 11 that FBI investigators in the Watergate case had been hindered by resistance from middle- and lower-level White House officials and by witnesses who gave incorrect or incomplete information.

Judiciary Committee. The Senate Judiciary Committee began confirmation hearings Feb. 28 on L. Patrick Gray III, Nixon's nominee for permanent director of the FBI. Out of the hearings came new disclosures about espionage and the Watergate. FBI records submitted by Gray to the committee sometimes corroborated some earlier news reports. These were among the statements in the records:

- Herbert Kalmbach, Nixon's personal attorney, told the FBI he and Dwight Chapin, then the President's appointments secretary, arranged to pay between $30,000 and $40,000 to Donald Segretti, the alleged saboteur.
- Re-election committee officials tried to impede an FBI investigation of the Watergate.
- Dean, the President's counsel, sat in on all interviews of White House personnel conducted by FBI investigators. Gray told the committee on March 6 that he had opposed Dean's presence at the interviews but had permitted him to be present because the alternative would have been to have no interviews.
- Liddy and Hunt, two former White House consultants, "traveled around the United States contacting former CIA employees for the purpose of setting up a security organization for the Republican Party dealing with political espionage."
- An unnamed official of the Republican re-election committee told the FBI that Hugh Sloan "allegedly disbursed large sums to various committee officials for unknown reasons." The disbursements included $50,000 to Jeb Stuart Magruder, $100,000 to Herbert Porter and $89,000 to Liddy.

The Judiciary Committee hearings resulted in the withdrawal of Gray's nomination, at Gray's request, by the President on April 5. Confirmation of the nominee had appeared increasingly unlikely.

Among the factors that damaged Gray's chances were his testimony before the committee that he had turned over FBI files to John Dean and his statement to the committee that Dean probably had lied to the FBI in saying he did not know that E. Howard Hunt had a

White House office. Gray also was damaged by Dean's refusal to testify before the committee, claiming executive privilege.

Select Committee. The executive privilege issue is an important one in the impending hearings of the Senate investigating committee, too, and it has yet to be resolved. Chairman Ervin, considered the Senate's foremost constitutional expert, has threatened to subpoena White House staff members and have them arrested by the Senate sergeant at arms if they do not appear.

The White House has promised to cooperate with the committee by answering questions in writing. Ervin has rejected that offer and a later White House suggestion that informal testimony, not under oath, might be permitted. "That is not executive privilege," said Ervin at a news conference April 2. "That is executive poppycock."

As a result of the letter he had written to Judge Sirica, conspirator James McCord had arranged to meet with the judge several days after the sentencing. Instead, he met privately with Samuel Dash, the committee counsel, on March 23 and 24. Dash briefed reporters on the meeting on March 25 but would not discuss the substance of the conversations.

Quoting unidentified sources, *The Los Angeles Times* said that McCord had told Dash that Magruder and Dean had prior knowledge of the Watergate bugging. The report was denied—as it had been before—and Nixon reaffirmed his confidence in Dean.

McCord testified in secret before the select committee on March 28. Another leak, again attributed to an unidentified source by *The Washington Post,* quoted McCord as telling the committee that John Mitchell had approved the bugging personally and that Charles W. Colson, former special counsel to Nixon, knew in advance of the plot. More denials were forthcoming.

Charles W. Colson

The White House responded in a fury, accusing the committee of allowing "irresponsible leaks in tidal wave proportions." Responding to Ervin's rejection of the White House offer of informal testimony by its staffers, press secretary Ziegler said: "I would encourage the chairman to get his own disorganized house in order so that the investigation can go forward in a proper atmosphere of traditional fairness and due process."

Ervin announced on April 3 that the full committee would suspend closed hearings. Colson reinforced his assertion of innocence by taking a lie detector test which indicated, according to press reports April 8, that he was telling the truth.

Grand Jury. While the select committee was conducting its leaky investigation, the federal grand jury was continuing to hear witnesses in secret. E. Howard Hunt Jr. invoked the 5th Amendment (against self-incrimination) when he appeared before the jury on March 27. The next day, Judge Sirica granted the government's request to grant Hunt immunity from further prosecution, and he testified for nearly four hours.

G. Gordon Liddy, too, had been granted immunity and ordered by Sirica on March 30 to testify before the grand jury. He refused to answer the jury's questions and was sentenced to an additional jail term for contempt of court. Sirica sentenced Liddy to serve until the end of the grand jury term—the end of 1973 unless extended—or 18 months, whichever came first.

Four other conspirators—Barker, Martinez, Sturgis and Gonzalez—were ordered to testify after being given immunity. Sirica indicated their cooperation, and McCord's, would be a factor when he sentenced them and McCord in June.

Partisan Repercussions

If the Watergate scandal dropped any ominous fallout on Republican candidates in the 1972 elections, it apparently did no damage to the President, who won a second term by a landslide. Watergate simply was not an important issue in most places.

McGovern. George McGovern made several speeches about it. In a Los Angeles speech Oct. 16, he called the Republican activities "the shabbiest undercover operations in the history of American politics." On Oct. 25, in a nationwide television speech, he accused the administration of corruption and sabotage and said the nation was confronted with "a moral and a constitutional crisis of unprecedented dimensions." Earlier that day in Cleveland, McGovern had said a report linking White House staff chief Haldeman with the affair "places the whole ugly mess of corruption, espionage and sabotage squarely in the lap of Richard Nixon."

Republicans. As the Senate investigation drew closer and the administration-Congress disagreement grew sharper, Republican leaders showed more signs of worry.

Senate Republicans were becoming more concerned about the political impact, said Senate Minority Leader Hugh Scott (R Pa.) on March 29. The same day, Senators Robert W. Packwood (R Ore.) and Charles McC. Mathias Jr. (R Md.) urged Nixon to appoint a prominent outsider to head a special White House investigation. "The most odious issue since the Teapot Dome," said Packwood in describing the matter.

George Bush, the Republican national chairman, called the Watergate bugging "grubby" and said the incident should be "promptly and fully cleared up" to prevent adverse effects on the party.

But the shrillest attack on the White House was launched by Sen. Lowell P. Weicker Jr. (R Conn.), the junior Republican on the investigating committee. He said in a television interview April 1 that a paid agent of the Nixon re-election committee had spied on nine congressional offices in 1972. Two days later, he called for Haldeman's resignation because, said Weicker, he "clearly has to accept responsibility" for a broad range of alleged espionage activities during the 1972 campaign.

Senators Ervin and Howard H. Baker Jr. (R Tenn.), the select committee's vice chairman, issued a statement on April 4 saying that the committee had "received no evidence of any nature" connecting Haldeman with illegal activities. To which Weicker responded: "I concur with the statement."

Martha Mitchell's Phone Calls

Former Attorney General John N. Mitchell resigned as President Nixon's campaign manager on July 1, 1972. He said he had been spending too much time away from his wife, Martha, and their daughter.

His resignation came a week after Mrs. Mitchell had telephoned a wire service reporter twice. In both calls, she threatened to leave Mitchell if he did not give up politics.

Mrs. Mitchell phoned *The New York Times* on March 27, 1973, and said, according to the Times' report: "I fear for my husband. I'm really scared. I have a definite reason. I can't tell you why. But they're not going to pin anything on him. I won't let them, and I don't give a damn who gets hurt. I can name names.... If you hear that I'm sick or can't talk, please, please, get your reporters out to find me. Somebody might try to shut me up."

Mrs. Mitchell was quoted as saying, in another call to the wire service on March 31: "I think this administration has turned completely against my husband. In other words, they're desperate, and I will not under any circumstances let them pin it on my husband. I think my husband has become the whipping boy for the whole administration, and they want to hide who is really involved."

Newspaper Poll. A poll conducted by Political Surveys and Analyses Inc., Princeton, N.J., and commissioned by *The Wall Street Journal,* indicated that the Republicans might find the Watergate affair a serious liability. The poll, published April 6, found, in 501 telephone interviews around the country:

- Ninety-one per cent of those questioned had heard or read about the Watergate incident.
- Thirty-eight per cent believed some top Nixon aides knew in advance about the bugging; 33 per cent did not; 29 per cent were unsure.
- Seventy-one per cent said the affair would not affect their votes; 29 per cent said they would be less likely to vote Republican in 1974.
- Fifty-three per cent thought Nixon was unaware of the bugging plans; 21 per cent thought he was; 26 per cent were unsure.
- Fifty-four per cent believed the White House had tried to prevent a full investigation of the case; 23 per cent thought the White House had done "everything it should to bring out all the facts"; 23 per cent were unsure.
- Fifty-four per cent felt press coverage had been fair; 30 per cent thought the press had been "making too much" of it.
- Sixty per cent wanted the congressional investigation to continue; 26 per cent thought the case should be dropped; 14 per cent were unsure.

Bouts with the Press

Two court tests involving the press coverage have been byproducts of the Watergate affair.

Los Angeles Times. The first test resulted from the tape-recorded interview of Alfred Baldwin in October by two *Los Angeles Times* reporters, Jack Nelson and Ronald J. Ostrow. The Times had promised Baldwin that it would not divulge details of the interview without his approval.

In December, attorneys for E. Howard Hunt sought the tapes for use in the forthcoming criminal trial. Judge Sirica rejected the Times' contention that being forced to turn over the tapes would inhibit its ability to report the news and would violate the constitution's 1st Amendment protection for free press.

Sirica cited the newspaper for contempt of court and ordered its Washington bureau chief, John F. Lawrence, jailed. He was in jail for only a few hours before the impasse was broken by an agreement between Baldwin and the court. Baldwin and his attorneys agreed to make the recordings available to Sirica for private inspection, with the understanding that Sirica would edit out any remarks by Baldwin's attorneys or the two reporters.

Civil Suits. The second court action against the press occurred on Feb. 26, when attorneys for Nixon's re-election committee subpoenaed nine reporters, two newspaper executives and three other persons with knowledge of the Watergate. The publications involved were *The Washington Post, The Washington Star-News, The New York Times* and *Time* magazine.

The re-election committee attorneys sought materials such as notes, tapes and other private records from the reporters. The material was sought in connection with the three civil suits before the U.S. District Court.

Judge Richey quashed the subpoenas on March 20. "This court cannot blind itself to the possible chilling effect the enforcement of these subpoenas would have on the flow of information to the press and, thus, to the public," he said.

Steady Friction. The refusal of many potential sources of information to talk to reporters about the Watergate has forced the press to rely heavily on statements from unidentified persons. This situation has brought about frequent denials of unattributed accusations and occasional castigation of the press by administration and re-election committee spokesmen. Their favorite target has been *The Washington Post.*

One of the strongest attacks came from campaign manager Clark MacGregor on Oct. 16, just after the reports on Donald Segretti and his alleged associations with the White House. "Using innuendo, third-person hearsay, unsubstantiated charges, anonymous sources and huge scare headlines—the Post has maliciously sought to give the appearance of a direct connection between the White House and the Watergate—a charge which the Post knows—and half a dozen investigations have found—to be false," MacGregor said.

MacGregor accused the Post of "hypocrisy" for not investigating allegations that the McGovern campaign organization was responsible for isolated incidents of violence at Nixon campaign offices. The Post reported on Oct. 18 that police and both parties' campaign workers had failed to link the McGovern organization with the incidents.

After a Post report on Oct. 25 linked Haldeman, the White House staff chief, with the secret cash fund, press secretary Ziegler accused the Post of "character assassination" and "the shoddiest kind of journalism."

Later Developments

These were some of the major developments in the Watergate affair between April 5 and 13:

April 5. Judge Sirica granted McCord immunity from further prosecution, and McCord started testifying before the grand jury. McCord said that "the story should be told" and that he would hold an on-the-record press conference after he had finished testifying.

April 6. The Senate approved Sam Ervin's request to rent private office space off the Capitol grounds for the investigating committee. Space was not available on Capitol Hill, Ervin said.

April 9. Sources were quoted in *The New York Times* as saying that McCord had told the grand jury that Kenneth W. Parkinson, an attorney for the President's re-election committee, had channeled money to the Watergate defendants after their arrest. The hearsay evidence was attributed by McCord to Dorothy Hunt, the late wife of defendant E. Howard Hunt. He said Mrs. Hunt was the conduit for the money. Parkinson denied making any payments to Mrs. Hunt.

Sen. Barry Goldwater (R Ariz.), in an interview published by *The Christian Science Monitor*, warned that Republican candidates would be in trouble in 1974 unless Nixon acted to clear up the matter. Goldwater said he might not support the President if he found that Nixon had learned of the bugging but had remained silent. "All of us who support Nixon are going to be on the line in the 1974 election," he said.

April 10. *The Washington Post* quoted "reliable sources" as saying that McCord had been paid $3,000 a month and the four defendants from Miami had been paid $1,000 a month to remain silent.

McCord's attorney, Bernard W. Fensterwald, told reporters that McCord had no direct knowledge that any high-level official in the re-election committee knew of the Watergate bugging plans. G. Gordon Liddy was the source of most of McCord's information, Fensterwald said.

April 11. The Post reported that about $70,000 in cash was transferred from Nixon campaign funds to Frederick C. LaRue, one of John Mitchell's closest political aides, in July 1972. "Reliable investigative sources" were quoted in the story.

Phillip S. Hughes of the GAO said the transfer of the money, which was unreported to his office, was an apparent violation of the campaign law. The money came from the secret fund in Maurice Stans' safe, according to the Post.

Anne Armstrong, counselor to the President, said she shared Goldwater's concern at a breakfast meeting with reporters in Washington. The Watergate affair, she said, was hurting Republicans across the nation.

April 12. Sources told the Post that McCord had testified before the grand jury that Liddy had told him that transcripts of wiretapped conversations of Democrats had been hand-delivered to Mitchell. A spokesman for the re-election committee denied the charge on behalf of the former attorney general. ✓

Chief Congressional Investigations in U.S. History

Following are summaries of selected major congressional investigations conducted since 1789.

ST. CLAIR INQUIRY

The House approved the first congressional investigation in American history when it adopted on March 27, 1792, a resolution authorizing a select committee to investigate an Indian victory the previous year over troops commanded by Maj. Gen. Arthur St. Clair. The committee asked for and received War Department papers on the expedition that had sent St. Clair and about 1,500 soldiers on a road- and fort-building trip through the Northwest Territory. An Indian attack had killed about 600 men and wounded some 300.

The report of the committee completely absolved St. Clair, a former president of the Continental Congress. Blame for the disaster was placed on the War Department, particularly the quartermaster and supply contractors, who were accused of mismanagement, neglect and delay in supplying necessary equipment, clothing and munitions.

CIVIL WAR STUDY

The Joint Committee on the Conduct of the (Civil) War compiled what was widely considered, at least until the McCarthy era of the 1950s, the worst record of any congressional investigating unit. It was a political vehicle for Radical Republicans opposed to President Lincoln, and its far-ranging inquiries were used for intensely partisan purposes.

In hearings that began Dec. 24, 1861, and continued until early 1865, the committee in a sense took over partial control of Union operations. It harassed conservative and Democratic generals. Typically, when investigating a general, the committee first would interrogate his subordinate officers, searching for adverse information. With such information in hand, the committee would summon the general for interrogation, frequently without informing him of the accusations against him or the disclosures made by his subordinates. The committee's next step would be a meeting with President Lincoln at which the general's resignation or reassignment would be demanded.

CRÉDIT MOBILIER

Two House committees and one in the Senate investigated charges that arose during the 1872 presidential campaign of wholesale corruption in connection with construction by the Crédit Mobilier of America of the last 667 miles of the Union Pacific Railroad, which had been completed three years earlier. The inquiries disclosed perhaps the most serious legislative scandal in the country's history.

The charges first appeared when the *New York Sun* of Sept. 4, 1872, reported that Rep. Oakes Ames (R Mass.), a principal stockholder in both the Union Pacific and the Crédit Mobilier construction company, had used Crédit Mobilier stock to bribe Vice President Schuyler Colfax, Speaker James G. Blaine (R Maine), Rep. James A. Garfield (R Ohio) and three other members of Congress. The reported bribes represented an attempt to head off a congressional investigation of railroad transportation rates.

A House committee report filed Feb. 18, 1873, cleared Blaine but recommended that both Ames and another member be expelled from the House. The House ultimately censured the two representatives but did not expel them.

The Senate committee reported March 1, 1873, that Sen. James Patterson (R N.H.) had bought Crédit Mobilier stock from Ames at below-market prices. The committee recommended Patterson's explusion, but his term was to expire March 3, and he retired without Senate action to expel him.

Colfax, whose relation to the matter was not satisfactorily explained, had had a falling out with the regular Republicans before the scandal broke and was not renominated in June 1872 for a second term on the Grant ticket. Garfield, elected President in 1880, never was able to explain away his connection with the affair.

STUDY OF THE MONEY TRUST

The House on Feb. 24, 1912, authorized its Banking and Currency Committee to investigate the concentration of money and credit in the nation. Conducted at a time when the national interest already was turned to such industrial concentrations as the sugar trust, the meat trust and the steel trust, the new inquiry soon became known as the money trust investigation.

Conducted by a Banking and Currency subcommittee, headed by Committee Chairman Arsène P. Pujo (D La.), the inquiry brought to light previously unknown interlocking directorates among two sets of New York banks, controlled by Morgan and Rockefeller interests, and 112 of the country's largest corporations in the fields of banking, public utilities, transportation, insurance, manufacturing and trading.

The subcommittee filed its report Feb. 28, 1913, summarizing its findings and calling for corrective legislation. Within two years, Congress, prodded by President Wilson, enacted the Federal Reserve Act of 1913, the Clayton Antitrust Act of 1914 and the Federal Trade Commission Act of 1914. Each of these major measures was based on information developed during the investigation.

TEAPOT DOME

President Harding was inaugurated in 1921, and suspicions of wrongdoing grew and flourished in the first year of his administration. Oil figured importantly in many rumors. Congress in 1920 had enacted the General Leasing Act, which authorized the secretary of the Navy under certain conditions to lease naval oil reserves on public lands to private oil operators, and oil interests had been influential at the 1920 Republican convention. Harding on May 31, 1921, signed an executive order transferring jurisdiction over the naval oil reserves to the Interior Department. Early in 1922, Interior leased the Elk Hills reserve in California to Edward L. Doheny of the Pan-American Petroleum and Transport Company and the Teapot Dome reserve in Wyoming to Harry F. Sinclair's Mammoth Oil Company.

A Senate resolution authorized the Senate Committee on Public Lands and Surveys on April 29, 1922, "to investigate this entire subject of leases upon naval oil reserves...." When the hearings opened on Oct. 25, 1923, they concentrated at first on the legality and expediency of the two leases. Then the committee began probing the sudden wealth of Secretary of the Interior Albert B. Fall. In a sensational national scandal, rivaling the Crédit Mobilier, it developed that Fall had accepted enormous bribes from Doheny and Sinclair. Both Fall and Navy Secretary Edwin Denby resigned. Fall was later convicted of accepting a bribe in connection with the Elk Hills lease and was sentenced to prison and fined $100,000.

PECORA STOCK EXCHANGE PROBE

The Senate Banking and Currency Committee from 1932 to 1934 conducted an important investigation of the stock exchange and Wall Street financial manipulations, reminiscent of the Pujo hearings 20 years earlier.

As the 1933 hearings progressed under chief counsel Ferdinand Pecora, they produced spectacular accounts of dubious financial actions. Albert H. Wiggin, president of the Chase National Bank of New York, had sold short the stock of his own bank. J. P. Morgan Jr. had paid no income tax for several years because his losses offset his gains. Other witnesses recounted the operation of security flotation syndicates and stock market pools. It developed that friends of Morgan, including cabinet officers, former President Coolidge and top Republican and Democratic Party officials, had been profitably let in on the inside of some security flotations.

Practices disclosed in the hearings paved the way for such major Roosevelt administration measures as the Banking Acts of 1933 and 1935, the Securities Act of 1933 and the Securities Exchange Act of 1934.

NYE MUNITIONS INQUIRY

Riding a wave of public sentiment for a congressional investigation of the munitions industry, the Senate on April 12, 1934, established the Senate Special Committee Investigating the Munitions Industry, whose chief sponsor was Sen. Gerald Nye (R N.D.). The public was firmly convinced before the committee began hearings that the country's munitions makers were merchants of death, and the committee accepted the public's verdict and set out to find the proof.

The Nye committee, as it soon was called, opened hearings on Sept. 4, 1934. The committee investigated the munitions industry, the shipbuilding industry and business profits during World War I. The evidence, however, was thin and failed to support general conclusions about an arms conspiracy. The hearings continued until mid-1935 and were resumed briefly in early 1936.

WORLD WAR II TRUMAN COMMITTEE

The World War II Senate Special Committee to Investigate the National Defense Program came to be widely regarded as the most effective investigating group in the history of Congress. Created March 1, 1941, the committee sought to uncover and to halt wasteful practices in war preparations. Its studies were broadened to cover the entire war mobilization effort, once the country entered the conflict.

Closely identified with its first chairman, Sen. Harry S Truman (D Mo.), the committee had the broadest possible investigating authority. Studies explored camp construction and other problems of war mobilization; shortages of critical war materials, such as aluminum, rubber, petroleum products, housing and steel; the quality of materials supplied under defense contracts and the distribution of the contracts; and war frauds among contractors, lobbyists and government officials.

Succeeding Congresses continued the committee throughout the war and into the early postwar years. Its final report was submitted April 28, 1948.

KEFAUVER CRIME HEARINGS

In 1950 and 1951, the Senate Special Committee to Investigate Organized Crime in Interstate Commerce held hearings around the country, many of which were televised.

Sen. Estes Kefauver (D Tenn.) was chairman. The committee questioned governors, mayors, sheriffs and policemen and turned the spotlight on gangsters, gamblers, racketeers and narcotics peddlers. The hearings were full of names of prominent alleged racketeers, including reputed heirs of the Chicago Capone gang and leaders of the Mafia. Many of the alleged criminals proved difficult to locate. Hearings were followed by scores of citations for contempt of Congress and many local indictments for criminal activities.

McCARTHY'S INVESTIGATIONS

Under the chairmanship of Sen. Joseph R. McCarthy (R Wis.), the Permanent Investigations Subcommittee of the Senate Government Operations Committee conducted a series of wide-ranging and controversial hearings in 1953 and 1954. The hearings were the high-water mark of the McCarthy era and bore the unmistakable scars of the senator's abrasive and aggressive character. The subcommittee's activities varied from hearings on Korean war atrocities to investigation of a deal with Greek shipowners, but the State Department and the armed services were the prime targets of the probes. The subcommittee also investigated the Government Printing Office, Communist infiltration of the United Nations and the transfer to the Russians of occupation currency plates. In 1954, the subcommittee, in an unprecedented move, in effect undertook an investigation of itself.

In December 1954, the Senate adopted a resolution censuring McCarthy by a vote of 67 to 22. The resolution condemned McCarthy's abuse of the Privileges and Elections Subcommittee, which had sought to investigate questions about funds McCarthy had collected, supposedly to be used to fight communism.

SOURCE: Congressional Quarterly Guide to Congress

WATERGATE: A DRAMATIC SWITCH BY THE WHITE HOUSE

If public hearings on the Watergate scandal begin May 15 before a Senate investigating committee, as scheduled, some of the star witnesses will be members of the White House staff. Their willingness to testify was signaled by a dramatic reversal by President Nixon.

"All members of the White House staff will appear voluntarily when requested by the committee," Nixon said at a brief news conference on April 17. "They will testify under oath and they will answer fully all proper questions." *(Text of statement, box next page)*

The President also told reporters that he had begun "intensive new inquiries" into the Watergate affair on March 21 "as a result of serious charges which came to my attention." Without further elaboration, he said there had been "major new developments in the case."

Sen. Sam J. Ervin Jr. (D N.C.), chairman of the committee, indicated April 19 that the hearings may have to be postponed if key witnesses are indicted.

Magruder Statements. *The Washington Post* April 19 reported that Jeb Stuart Magruder, former deputy director of the Committee for the Re-election of the President, had accused former Attorney General John N. Mitchell and John W. Dean III, the White House counsel, of approving and helping plan the Watergate break-in and bugging of June 17, 1972. Mitchell and Dean "later arranged to buy the silence of the seven convicted Watergate conspirators," according to the Post.

Mitchell denounced the report as "nonsense" April 19. But on April 20, *The New York Times* reported that Mitchell has told friends he attended three early-1972 meetings at which Watergate bugging proposals were discussed. He reportedly said he rejected the idea.

The Post said Magruder, former special assistant to Nixon and now a Commerce Department official, made the statements to federal prosecutors April 14.

Several news accounts said that testimony by Magruder and other Republicans was expected to result in criminal indictments of high-ranking Nixon re-election campaign officials. One source was quoted by the Post as saying Mitchell and Dean would be among those indicted.

Presidential Position. Indicating that some indictments might come out of the grand jury investigation in Washington, Nixon said at his news conference: "If any person in the executive branch or in the government is indicted by the grand jury, my policy will be to immediately suspend him. If he is convicted, he will, of course, be automatically discharged."

The President did not answer questions at the hastily summoned meeting with reporters. After the conference ended, his press secretary, Ronald L. Ziegler, said that all previous statements from the White House were "inoperative...the President's statement today is the operative statement."

Ervin Response. Nixon's reversal of position apparently averted a showdown with the chairman of the Senate select committee on the Watergate, Sam J. Ervin Jr. (D N.C.). Ervin had insisted that past and present members of the White House staff be available to testify under oath before the committee. Nixon had refused to permit his staff to testify, arguing that they were protected from doing so by the doctrine of executive privilege.

Nixon said on April 17 that discussions had been going on for several weeks among Ervin; Sen. Howard H. Baker Jr. (R Tenn.), vice chairman of the investigating committee; the majority and minority counsels to the committee, and John D. Ehrlichman and Leonard Garment of the White House staff. The ground rules adopted in the discussions "totally preserve the doctrine of separation of powers," the President said. He added that "the appearance by a witness may, in the first instance, be in executive session, if appropriate," and that "executive privilege is expressly reserved and may be asserted during the course of the questioning as to any questions."

Ervin called Nixon's decision to allow his staff to testify before the committee "a victory for constitutional government." But he made clear that the committee would be the final judge of whether White House witnesses could refuse to answer questions. "Somebody has to rule on that point," Ervin said, "and these guidelines expressly say that the committee's going to do the ruling. If the committee rules adversely to the witness on any question of privilege, the committee shall require the witness to testify."

Kleindienst Withdrawal. Attorney General Richard G. Kleindienst disqualified himself from further involvement in the Watergate case on April 19 so that he would not have to put himself in the position of prosecuting present or former colleagues in the Nixon administration. His decision, he said, "relates to persons with whom I have had personal and professional relationships."

Kleindienst announced that Assistant Attorney General Henry Peterson would take full control of the Justice Department's criminal investigation of the Watergate. Petersen had been in charge of the investigation, reporting to Kleindienst.

Mitchell, who resigned as attorney general to become Nixon's campaign manager in March 1972, was quoted by *The New York Times* as praising Kleindienst's decision as "entirely appropriate and correct." Mitchell told the Times that if Kleindienst had stayed with the investigation, "no matter what he did he would be accused of playing politics, because he knew so many of the people who have been mentioned in this thing."

Dean's Role. John Dean, the President's counsel, was not involved in the discussions between the White House and the Senate committee. Nixon made no reference to him in his April 17 statement. Dean had come under attack for his refusal to testify at Senate confirmation hearings on L. Patrick Gray III as permanent FBI director, claiming executive privilege.

Watergate Announcement Text

Following is the text of President Nixon's announcement on the Watergate April 17:

I have two announcements to make. Because of their technical nature, I shall read both of the announcements to the members of the press corps.

The first announcement relates to the appearance of White House people before the Senate select committee, better known as the Ervin committee.

For several weeks, Sen. Ervin and Sen. Baker and their counsel have been in contact with White House representatives John Ehrlichman and Leonard Garment. They have been talking about ground rules which would preserve the separation of powers without suppressing the fact.

I believe now an agreement has been reached which is satisfactory to both sides. The committee ground rules as adopted totally preserve the doctrine of separation of powers. They provide that the appearance by a witness may, in the first instance, be in executive session, if appropriate.

Second, executive privilege is expressly reserved and may be asserted during the course of the questioning as to any questions.

Now, much has been made of the issue as to whether the proceedings could be televised. To me, this has never been a central issue, especially if the separation of powers problem is otherwise solved, as I now think it is.

All members of the White House staff will appear voluntarily when requested by the committee. They will testify under oath and they will answer fully all proper questions.

I should point out that this arrangement is one that covers this hearing only in which wrongdoing has been charged. This kind of arrangement, of course, would not apply to other hearings. Each of them will be considered on its merits.

My second announcement concerns the Watergate case directly.

On March 21, as a result of serious charges which came to my attention, some of which were publicly reported, I began intensive new inquiries into this whole matter.

Last Sunday afternoon, the Attorney General, Assistant Attorney General Petersen and I met at length in the EOB (Executive Office Building) to review the facts which had come to me in my investigation and also to review the progress of the Department of Justice investigation.

I can report today that there have been major developments in the case concerning which it would be improper to be more specific now, except to say that real progress has been made in finding the truth.

If any person in the executive branch or in the government is indicted by the grand jury, my policy will be to immediately suspend him. If he is convicted, he will, of course, be automatically discharged.

I have expressed to the appropriate authorities my views that no individual holding, in the past or at present, a position of major importance in the administration should be given immunity from prosecution.

The judicial process is moving ahead as it should; and I shall aid it in all appropriate ways and have so informed the appropriate authorities.

As I have said before and I have said throughout this entire matter, all government employees and especially White House staff employees are expected fully to cooperate in this matter. I condemn any attempts to cover up in this case, no matter who is involved.

In response to the attacks, Nixon had phoned Dean from Key Biscayne, Fla., on March 26 to express his personal confidence in him. In his April 17 statement, the President said he had met on April 15, as part of his investigation, with Kleindienst and Petersen. Ziegler, pressed by reporters about Dean's role, said the President "felt it was not appropriate that any member of the White House staff be involved in further investigation." Dean had conducted the first investigation for the White House in 1972.

In its April 19 story, *The Washington Post*, quoting White House sources, said that Dean's resignation was considered imminent.

But Dean himself cast doubt on that prediction when he issued this statement the same day:

"To date I have refrained from making any public comments whatsoever about the Watergate case. I shall continue that policy in the future, because I believe that the case will be fully and justly handled by the grand jury and the Ervin select committtee.

"It is my hope, however, that those truly interested in seeing that the Watergate case is completely aired and that justice is done will be careful in drawing any conclusions as to the guilt or involvement of any persons until all the facts are known and until each person has had an opportunity to testify under oath in his own behalf.

"Finally, some may hope or think that I will become a scapegoat in the Watergate case. Anyone who believes this does not know me, know the true facts nor understand our system of justice."

As early as August 1972 and as late as March 1973, the President had expressed confidence in his staff. On Aug. 29, 1972, he said at a news conference, "I can say categorically that his (Dean's) investigation indicates that no one in the White House staff, no one in this administration, presently employed, was involved in this very bizarre incident."

Civil Suits

In addition to the President's new attitude of cooperation with Senate investigators, the Republican Party reportedly was making some moves of its own toward settling one of three civil suits pending in U.S. District Court in Washington, D.C. The suit, filed just after the June 1972 break-in at Democratic national headquarters, charges the Republican Party with conspiring to violate the civil rights of Lawrence F. O'Brien, then Democratic national chairman, and other Democratic officials. The suit seeks $6.4-million in damages.

The Washington Post reported April 18 that conversations had been held between attorneys for the Democrats and Republicans concerning possible out-of-court settlement of the suit. The amount reportedly involved in the conversations was $525,000. Lawyers and party officials did not deny the report, and Democratic Chairman Robert S. Strauss confirmed that conversations had been held.

"We are not in accord," Strauss said on April 18, "but we have talked both in person and on the telephone within the last couple of weeks." Strauss was under considerable pressure from some state chairmen, it was learned, not to settle out of court for the amount reportedly discussed.

'Down at the Old Watergate'

One of the minor attractions of the Watergate affair is a song written and sung by a Democratic representative who decided to have a little fun at Republican expense.

"Down at the Old Watergate" is the name of the ditty. Its lyrics were written by Rep. William L. Hungate of Missouri, a 50-year-old attorney whose musical past dates back to saxophone-playing with bands in Missouri and Michigan and at Harvard Law School. He still puts doggerel to music occasionally for the entertainment of himself and his friends.

Rep. William L. Hungate

Hungate's latest creation has achieved considerable fame in Washington and in Missouri's 9th District, from which he has been elected six times, because it has been tape-recorded and distributed by the Democratic National Committee. Anyone who wants to hear it could call a Washington number.

What callers heard—when the line was not busy, as it usually was—was Hungate singing and accompanying himself on a piano. The tune, with modifications, is based on an old English pub song, "Down at the Olde Bull and Bush," which was adopted years ago as an American beer commercial. A national committee spokesman said some 7,000 persons had called within two weeks to hear these words:

Come, come, come and play spy with me,
Down at the old Watergate;
Come, come, come live and lie with me,
Down at the old Watergate.

See the little German band,
Ehrlichman and Haldeman;
Don't Martha Mitchell look great?
Come, come, come don't be shy with me;
I'll have the whole FBI with me;
Down at the old Water—we'll make the police blotter,
Down at the old Watergate.

Two Republican Suits. The other two civil suits were filed in 1972 by Republican officials against the Democrats. It was unclear what effect an out-of-court settlement of the O'Brien suit might have on them.

Common Cause. Negotiations directed at settlement of yet another civil suit were also reported, but the results were in doubt. The suit was filed in 1972 by Common Cause, the so-called citizens' lobby, against the President's re-election finance committee. The suit demanded that the Republicans disclose campaign contributions, estimated to total more than $10-million, made to the finance committee before a new disclosure law took effect on April 7, 1972.

John W. Gardner, chairman of Common Cause, and Maurice H. Stans, chairman of Nixon's finance committee, met on April 18. After the meeting, Gardner said that Stans continued to insist on keeping secret the names of big contributors. Stans said his committee was only trying to protect the legal rights of the contributors to remain anonymous before the April 7 deadline.

(Eight cartons of documents, including plans to bug the Watergate, were removed from the White House complex and hidden away by an unidentified employee of the Nixon campaign, Associated Press reported on April 19. The report was attributed to court papers.

(The documents were said to include lists of campaign donors and the contents of the executive office building desk of E. Howard Hunt, one of the conspirators, according to AP. The statements were contained in a petition filed with Chief Judge John J. Sirica of U.S. District Court in Washington by attorney Peter H. Wolf. The lawyer did not name his client.

(The cartons, which Wolf said were removed the day after the Watergate break-in, later were returned to the Nixon campaign. Some of them are now in the possession of the federal court that may try the Common Cause suit, AP reported.)

Other Developments

These were among the related developments in the Watergate affair:

- Judge Charles R. Richey of U.S. District Court in Washington sternly rejected on April 12 a request from the Senate committee to keep secret further pretrial testimony by James W. McCord Jr., one of the convicted conspirators. "This court will not allow either the legislative or executive branch of the government to interfere directly with the conduct of any proceedings in my court," he said.

- Harold K. Lipset, chief investigator for the Senate committee, resigned on April 13 after he learned that the press was about to disclose that he had pleaded guilty to a charge of illegal electronic eavesdropping in a 1966 New York case.

- It was reported April 15 that Ervin, chairman of the Senate Government Operations Committee, might test the executive privilege doctrine on the issue of White House refusal to reveal its records on tax-paid flights by administration officials during the 1972 election campaign. He would base his case on a 1928 law related to testimony before his committee.

- A safe was burglarized the night of April 18 in the Capitol Hill office of Sen. Lowell P. Weicker Jr. (R Conn.), a member of the investigating committee, his aides reported. It was not determined immediately whether any documents were stolen, they said.

- John Mitchell's wife, Martha, said on April 18 that she would rather testify before the Senate committee than make a deposition, "because my written word can be misinterpreted. I want to testify publicly." ✓

WATERGATE: CAPITAL'S UNWHOLESOME PREOCCUPATION

A seemingly never-ending avalanche of disclosures, charges and countercharges related to the Watergate scandal continued to dominate Washington's headlines and conversations during the week ended April 28.

The capital was rocked by the resignations of a high-ranking Nixon campaign official and the acting FBI director. The Republican national chairman and other leaders expressed alarm at the potential damage being wrought on their party. The Vice President rallied to his leader. The business of governing the nation was sidetracked by White House preoccupation with events that threatened the ruination of the President and his programs.

These were among the week's Watergate highlights:

APRIL 20

Cabinet Meeting. Before leaving Washington to spend the Easter weekend at his home in Key Biscayne, Fla., Nixon met with his Cabinet for about two hours. He was quoted as saying, in reference to the Watergate scandal, "We've had our Cambodias before." In 1970, he had been criticized bitterly for his decision to invade Cambodia. George Bush, the Republican national chairman, told reporters after the Cabinet meeting: "I came out of there with the conviction that he wants to get the truth, wants to see the criminal justice system work and work fully."

Mitchell Statements. John D. Mitchell, former attorney general and former Nixon campaign manager, testified before a federal grand jury in Washington. "I testified fully and freely and openly," he told reporters after his appearance. The former attorney general repeated that he had no prior knowledge of the bugging incident. But, when asked if he had heard discussions of such plans, he replied, "I have heard discussions of such things. They've always been cut off at all times, and I would like to know who it was that kept bringing them back and back and back." Mitchell said that he had not approved of any bugging operations "at any time or under any circumstances."

Mitchell hired as his attorney William G. Hundley of Washington, a well-known defense lawyer who was a Justice Department prosecutor for 15 years before going into private practice in 1966. Press reports described Hundley as a close personal friend of Henry E. Petersen, the assistant attorney general assigned to the Watergate investigation.

The Washington Post reported that Mitchell told the grand jury that he had approved payments of Nixon's campaign funds to the seven Watergate conspirators after their arrest on June 17, 1972. Quoting an unnamed Mitchell associate, the Post said that Mitchell testified the money was intended to pay legal fees, not to buy the silence of the defendants.

Pentagon Papers Trial

The Watergate scandal took a bizarre turn on April 27 when it was revealed that two of the convicted conspirators had been accused of stealing the psychiatric files of one of the defendants in the Pentagon Papers trial in Los Angeles.

U.S. District Court Judge Matt Byrne of Los Angeles read a secret memorandum saying that E. Howard Hunt and G. Gordon Liddy had burglarized the files of Daniel Ellsberg's psychiatrist. The name and location of the psychiatrist were not revealed. The memorandum to the court was written by Earl J. Silbert, the principal assistant to the U.S. attorney in Washington, D.C. Silbert was the chief prosecutor in the Watergate trial.

The date of the burglary was not contained in the memorandum. Neither the contents of the files nor their present location was disclosed.

Byrne ordered an immediate investigation "to determine whether this...could affect the legal or constitutional rights of any defendant in this case or the legal or constitutional rights of anyone else involved in this case." *(For aftermath, see p. 46)*

Grand Jury Leaks. Meanwhile, it was reported that the FBI was trying to learn the source of leaks from the grand jury to newspaper columnist Jack Anderson. The columnist had been printing verbatim testimony from copies of the jury's minutes.

McCord Suit. Convicted conspirator James W. McCord Jr. filed a $1.5-million suit against the Committee for the Re-election of the President, the Finance Committee to Re-elect the President and three campaign officials: Jeb Stuart Magruder, former deputy campaign director, and G. Gordon Liddy and E. Howard Hunt, two other conspirators. They had damaged his reputation, he claimed, and had caused him to suffer "severe physical, mental and emotional strain and...mental anguish."

Payments for Silence. The *New York Times* reported that John W. Dean III, the White House counsel, had supervised cash payments of $175,000 in Republican campaign funds to the seven Watergate defendants and their lawyers after the break-in. The report was attributed to sources close to the case. Purpose of the payments, the Times reported, was to silence the defendants. Robert C. McCandless of Washington, Dean's attorney, said the report that Dean had supervised the payments was "absolutely untrue."

APRIL 21

Haldeman Involvement. Unnamed sources told *The New York Times* that the federal grand jury was investigating the possibility that H. R. Haldeman, the White House chief of staff, had a role in the Watergate bugging or in later attempts to obstruct inquiry into the case. Government prosecutors were trying to learn whether a secret $350,000 fund had been used by Haldeman's office to pay off the defendants and their lawyers, the Times reported. And, the report continued, the grand jury also wanted to determine whether Haldeman had received transcripts obtained through the wiretapping of Democratic national headquarters.

According to *The Washington Post*, government prosecutors established that most of the payments to the conspirators were made by Frederick C. LaRue, an aide to Mitchell when Mitchell was Nixon's campaign manager. Gordon Strachan, Haldeman's former political aide, reportedly testified that Haldeman had ordered him to give $350,000 to LaRue to pay the conspirators.

Haldeman and John D. Ehrlichman, the President's chief counselor for domestic affairs, hired an attorney, John J. Wilson of Washington, to represent them in the Watergate case.

Common Cause Suit. A spokesman for Common Cause, the self-described citizens' lobby, said the organization would ask the U.S. District Court in Washington April 23 to force finance officials of the Nixon campaign to produce some missing records within 72 hours. A Common Cause attorney threatened to seek contempt citations against finance chairman Maurice H. Stans and two lawyers if they did not turn over the records.

The Common Cause action, one of three civil suits filed in 1972 that are related to the Watergate affair, is pending in the federal court. The purpose of the Common Cause suit was to force the Republicans to disclose the names of campaign contributors who gave money before a new disclosure law took effect on April 7, 1972.

APRIL 22

Previous Warnings. During the winter and spring of 1972-73, members of the presidential staff warned Nixon that some of his aides were involved in the Watergate bugging and its subsequent coverup, *The Washington Post* reported. Quoting highly placed sources in the executive branch, the story said that those specifically implicated were Mitchell and Dean.

The unidentified sources told the newspaper that Charles W. Colson, a former special counsel to the President, had told Nixon that some persons in his administration were obstructing justice and that action should be taken. Colson reportedly urged the President to "get rid of some people." Although associates of Colson confirmed this account, according to the Post, Colson himself denied it.

One source was quoted as saying that Ehrlichman, too, had urged the President to clear up the Watergate affair. Ehrlichman was unavailable for comment.

APRIL 23

California Fund. *The Washington Star-News*, quoting unidentified sources, disclosed the existence of a secret fund of up to $500,000, at least part of which reportedly had been used to pay for Republican sabotage and espionage operations in the 1972 campaign. The fund, said the Star-News, was controlled by the President's personal lawyer, Herbert W. Kalmbach, and was kept in banks in Newport Beach, Calif. Payments from this fund, not from a previously reported $350,000 fund kept in Maurice Stans' safe, were used to pay accused saboteur Donald H. Segretti, the Star-News reported.

It was the third secret fund reported in the President's re-election campaign. The other one was a $350,000 cash fund kept in Haldeman's White House office.

Vesco Investigation. The U.S. government sought to have Robert L. Vesco cited for contempt of court for failing to appear before a federal grand jury in New York on April 18. Vesco, a financier who gave $250,000 to the Nixon campaign in 1972—the money was later returned to him—has been charged by the Securities and Exchange Commission (SEC) with a $224-million mutual fund swindle.

The New York grand jury is investigating why Vesco made a $200,000 secret cash payment to the Nixon campaign April 10, 1972, during the SEC investigation. According to *The Wall Street Journal*, Vesco met with Stans in March 1972 and offered to give the Nixon campaign as much as $500,000. The Journal quoted sources close to the New York grand jury proceedings.

After the meeting with Stans, according to the Journal, Vesco met with Mitchell. Vesco expressed hope to Stans that his $200,000 contribution would result in some "help" with his SEC problems, the story continued. And, it added, Mitchell phoned Vesco's lawyer in May 1972—after the donation had been made —to arrange a meeting between the lawyer and William Casey, then chairman of the SEC.

Common Cause Suit. Three more cartons of Republican finance records were turned into U.S. District Court in Washington in connection with the civil suit filed by Common Cause. But a Common Cause lawyer, Mitchell Rogovin, was skeptical about the completeness of the records. "They should be bringing in carloads of stuff," he said. Another lawyer for Common Cause, Kenneth J. Guido, said he would press for contempt citations against Stans and otheres if complete records were not turned in within 72 hours.

Jury Leaks. The 15-judge U.S. District Court in Washington, after meeting in executive session, ordered the U.S. attorney to conduct a grand jury investigation into the "unauthorized disclosure" of secret testimony before the Watergate grand jury.

Kissinger Remarks. Henry A. Kissinger, the President's chief foreign policy adviser, said at a luncheon of the American Newspaper Publishers Association in New York: "I have no question that the President will insist on the full disclosure of the facts and that when that is accomplished and the human tragedies are completed, the country will go on. Then we have to ask ourselves whether we can afford an orgy of recriminations or whether we should not keep in mind that the United States will be there longer than any particular crisis—whether all of us do not have an obligation to remember that faith in the country must be maintained and its promise should be eternal."

APRIL 24

Ehrlichman-MacGregor Split. Two key Republican officials differed sharply in their accounts of reported efforts in the summer of 1972 to investigate whether members of the campaign staff were involved in the Watergate affair, *The Washington Star-News* said. White House Assistant John Ehrlichman was quoted as saying: "I proposed not only to the campaign manager but to the whole campaign planning group that the time was right to make the fullest disclosure about Watergate." But Clark MacGregor, who became campaign manager July 1 after Mitchell left, said: "It may be that John (Erhlichman), in his own individual circles, was talking with some anxiety about Watergate, but that concern was never communicated to me."

Wiretap Information. *The New York Times* said that federal investigators had determined that significant political information obtained from the Watergate wiretaps was turned over to White House officials. Who processed the material and who received it were not revealed, the Times reported.

Rietz Resignation. Kenneth Rietz, 31, who ran the Nixon youth campaign in 1972, resigned unexpectedly from his job as director of the Republican National Committee's "new majority" campaign for the 1974 mid-term congressional elections.

National Chairman George Bush announced Rietz's resignation with a brief statement saying that Rietz had accepted a "quite extraordinary" job offer in private industry. But it was later disclosed that Rietz had informed Bush on April 23 that he might be implicated further in the Watergate scandal.

In March, it had been reported that George K. Gorton, Rietz's deputy on the campaign staff, had hired a George Washington University student for $150 a week to spy on peace demonstrators. But Bush had been assured that Rietz himself had not been involved in espionage. Later reports indicated, however, that Rietz had recruited a group of young people to spy on Democratic campaign headquarters.

Presidential Involvement. Nixon met for an hour on April 19 with John J. Wilson, the lawyer for Haldeman and Ehrlichman, deputy press secretary Warren said at Key Biscayne. He did not give details of the discussion.

Reports had emerged from the Jack Anderson publication of grand jury transcripts that conspirator James McCord had been offered executive clemency if he would remain silent. "The President has not made such an offer, nor have there been any discussions with the President about executive clemency," Warren said.

Grand Jury. Nixon told Attorney General Richard G. Kleindienst on April 20 that the grand jury leaks to columnist Anderson apparently were coming from the federal prosecutors of the case, the Times reported. The three-man prosecution team reportedly was castigated by Justice Department officials.

APRIL 25

Haiphong Publicity. The President's re-election committee spent at least $8,400 in May 1972 on a campaign to give a distorted view of public reaction to the President's decision to mine Haiphong harbor, *The Washington Post* reported. Jeb Stuart Magruder, deputy campaign director, authorized the expenditures, the story said. According to the Post, the campaign included paying for telegrams to be sent to the White House in support of the mining and a $4,400 ad in *The New York Times.* The expenditure for the ad was not reported to the General Accounting Office, as required by law, the Post said.

Housecleaning. Capitol Hill sources told the Post that former Secretary of Defense Melvin R. Laird had turned down an offer by Nixon to replace Haldeman as chief of staff and "clean house." Earlier reports said the President had made a similar offer to Secretary of State William P. Rogers. Both reports met with denials from the White House.

Agnew Statement. Vice President Agnew, who earlier had been reported to be appalled by the Watergate scandal, held a news conference to express his support for Nixon and to discount the earlier reports. "I have full confidence in the integrity of President Nixon and in his determination and ability to resolve the Watergate matter to the full satisfaction of the American people," he said.

Grand Jury Testimony. After a meeting with federal prosecutors, columnist Anderson said that he had agreed to their request to stop publishing verbatim testimony from grand jury transcripts. Anderson said he made the decision voluntarily after learning of anonymous phone calls to a prosecutor's office from potential witnesses who refused to testify for fear that their testimony might be leaked to the press.

Vesco Investigation. In the federal grand jury investigation of the $200,000 Vesco contribution to the Nixon campaign, according to *The Washington Star-News*, a Vesco business aide was quoted as asking Stans, as he delivered the cash to him, for "help somewhere along the line." The story also said that numerous calls were made from Vesco's New Jersey headquarters to Nixon campaign headquarters in Washington in the summer of 1972. Some of the calls were made to the phone of the President's brother, Edward, the report continued.

Attorney General Kleindienst, who earlier had withdrawn from the Watergate investigation, also withdrew from the Vesco grand jury investigation for similar reasons —the possible indictment of present or former associates.

APRIL 26

Destroyed Documents. L. Patrick Gray III, acting director of the FBI, destroyed documents belonging to conspirator E. Howard Hunt early in July 1972, according to press reports. The story was first reported by *The New York Daily News* and was later verified by other newspapers. Gray announced his resignation, effective immediately, on April 27. *(See p. 23)*

Gray, whose name had been withdrawn as Nixon's nominee for permanent FBI director, was told to destroy the documents by Ehrlichman and Dean, who said they "should never see the light of day," the reports said. One dossier, according to the reports, included phony State Department cables fabricated by Hunt to implicate the late President Kennedy in the 1963 assassination of South Vietnamese President Ngo Dinh Diem. Another dossier contained material that Hunt had collected on the automobile accident involving Sen. Edward M. Kennedy (D Mass.) at Chappaquiddick Island in 1969.

Ehrlichman issued a statement denying both that he knew the contents of the files and that he had told Gray what to do with them. Gray said that he had not examined the papers and did not know their contents until April 16, when he was questioned about the incident by Assistant Attorney General Petersen.

Magruder Resignation. The first former White House or campaign official to resign from the administration was Jeb Stuart Magruder. He quit his $36,000-a-year job as director of policy development at the Commerce Department.

Bush Statement. Republican Chairman Bush told employees at national headquarters that he and the party organization were in danger of being compromised by Watergate. He said that "no one connected with that whole mess" would work in future campaigns.

Haiphong Publicity. Charles W. Colson, a former special assistant to Nixon, wrote the ad for *The New York Times* supporting the mining of Haiphong Harbor, *The Washington Post* reported. Another part of the publicity effort, according to the Post, was the stacking of a poll conducted by Washington television station WTTG, by sending in 2,000 to 4,000 phony ballots supporting the President's action.

Gorton Dismissal. The Post reported that George Gorton, the Rietz deputy who had paid the Washington student to spy, was fired from his job at the Interior Department. A department spokesman was quoted as saying Gorton was told to leave because of adverse publicity surrounding his role as national college director of the President's re-election campaign.

Gray's Resignation Statement

Following is the text of a statement by L. Patrick Gray III announcing his resignation on April 27 as Acting Director of the Federal Bureau of Investigation:

Serious allegations concerning certain acts of my own during the ongoing Watergate investigation are now a matter of public record. As a consequence, I have today tendered my resignation as Acting Director of the Federal Bureau of Investigation, effective immediately.

This action is required to preserve in both image and fact the reputation, the integrity and the effectiveness of the FBI.

This superb investigative agency has been in no way involved in any of those personal acts or judgments that may now be called into question—and my own continued presence at the helm must not be permitted to create even the hint or implication of involvement, false though it is.

The FBI deserves the full trust of the American people: that is bedrock and must always remain so.

I depart from the FBI with a clear conscience, the knowledge that I have done my duty as best I have been able to see that duty and with an admiration and respect for the men and women of the FBI that only one who has led them and served with them can ever fully understand.

Senate Committee Funding

It took less than five months for the Senate Select Committee on Presidential Campaign Activities to decide that it needed more money.

The original budget, approved Feb. 7 in S Res 60—the resolution creating the committee—was $500,000. Chairman Sam J. Ervin (D N.C.) returned to the Senate on June 25 with S Res 132, doubling the authorization to $1-million. The funds were approved on a voice vote without debate. √

Poll Report

President Nixon's popularity has declined as the Watergate scandal has unfolded, according to the Gallup Poll. The issue, said Gallup, "has become of such widespread concern that it could seriously affect GOP fortunes in next year's congressional races."

The latest Gallup surveys were conducted April 6-9, before Nixon's April 17 news conference at which he said he had discovered "major developments" in the Watergate case. The surveys included 1,528 adults interviewed nationwide.

Popularity. The President's popularity, Gallup found, has dropped 14 percentage points from its high point of 68 per cent approval in late January, after the Vietnam peace settlement. The approval rating dropped five points in a week. Persons interviewed were asked, "Do you approve or disapprove of the way Nixon is handling his job as President?"

	Latest	March 30-April 2
Approve	54%	59%
Dissapprove	36	33
No opinion	10	8

Gallup noted that Nixon's popularity rating since January was down 16 points among independents, 13 points among Democrats and six points among Republicans.

Public Attitudes. The Gallup survey found that 83 per cent of those interviewed said they had heard or read about the Watergate, an increase of 31 per cent since October 1972. "This is a surprisingly high awareness figure, even considering the attention given Watergate by the media," Gallup concluded.

More than four in 10 persons interviewed said they thought Nixon knew about Watergate in advance. "Do you think President Nixon knew about the Watergate situation in advance, or not?" they were asked.

Yes	41%
No	32
No opinion, not heard	27

Nearly one-third said they thought the Watergate indicated administration corruption. The question: "Which of these two statements comes closer to your point of view about Watergate?—It's a very serious matter because it reveals corruption in the Nixon administration; or, it's just politics—the kind of thing that both parties engage in."

Reveals corruption	31%
Just politics	53
No opinion, not heard	16

WATERGATE: TRAUMATIC WEEK FOR THE ADMINISTRATION

The burgeoning Watergate scandal unreeled with breathtaking speed in the week ended May 5. The week's developments in the many-faceted drama led to partial paralysis of the Nixon administration. The President himself publicly accepted responsibility for any wrongdoing in the affair. A cabinet officer and three of Nixon's top assistants resigned. The taint of corruption reached into the Pentagon Papers trial in Los Angeles.

There were the highlights of the week's climactic events:

- The President April 30 announced the resignation of four men: H. R. Haldeman, White House chief of staff, John D. Ehrlichman, chief counselor for domestic affairs; John W. Dean III, presidential counsel, and Attorney General Richard G. Kleindienst. At the same time, Nixon announced the nomination of Defense Secretary Elliot L. Richardson as attorney general and the appointment of Leonard Garment as presidential counsel.
- Alexander M. Haig Jr., Army vice chief of staff and former chief deputy to Henry A. Kissinger, Nixon's national security adviser, was appointed interim White House chief of staff May 4.
- Addressing the nation the night of April 30, Nixon said he took full responsibility for any improper activities connected with his 1972 presidential campaign and pledged that "justice will be pursued fairly, fully and impartially." The President said Richardson would have full charge of the administration's Watergate investigations and would have authority to appoint a special prosecutor in the case.
- A Gallup Poll published May 4 found that 40 per cent of the 456 persons questioned did not think Nixon had told the whole truth in this speech. Fifty per cent said they thought he had participated in a coverup.
- It was disclosed on May 1 that Ehrlichman had told FBI interviewers on April 27 that the President had directed him in 1971 to undertake an independent investigation of the Pentagon Papers leak. Ehrlichman hired E. Howard Hunt and G. Gordon Liddy—convicted conspirators in the Watergate break-in—to conduct the probe, which led to the burglary of the office of Pentagon Papers defendant Daniel Ellsberg's psychiatrist. Ehrlichman said he had not authorized the burglary and that when he learned about it, he instructed Hunt and Liddy "not to do this again."

White House Resignations

"Today, in one of the most difficult decisions of my Presidency, I accepted the resignations of two of my closest associates in the White House—Bob Haldeman, John Ehrlichman—two of the finest public servants it has been my privilege to know.

"I want to stress that in accepting these resignations, I mean to leave no implication whatever of personal wrongdoing on their part, and I leave no implication tonight of implication on the part of others who have been charged in this matter. But in matters as sensitive as guarding the integrity of our democratic process, it is essential not only that rigorous legal and ethical standards be observed, but also that the public, you, have total confidence that they are both being observed and enforced by those in authority and particularly by the President of the United States. They agreed with me that this move was necessary in order to restore that confidence.... The Counsel to the President, John Dean has also resigned.

—President Nixon in address to the nation, April 30, 1973

- The judge in the Pentagon Papers trial, W. Matthew Byrne Jr., confirmed May 2 that he had discussed a possible job offer as FBI director with Ehrlichman on April 5 and April 7. Byrne said he refused to "discuss or consider" the offer until the Pentagon Papers trial had been concluded.

- Ehrlichman's name had surfaced April 27 in connection with allegations that he had promised on at least two occasions to help accused mutual fund swindler Robert L. Vesco, a big contributor to the 1972 Nixon campaign, take over a scandal-ridden Lebanese bank. Ehrlichman said he had met once with Vesco's representatives, but he denied providing any assistance.

A similar intercession on behalf of Vesco by John N. Mitchell was reported May 1. The intercession allegedly took place while Mitchell was still attorney general; it was the third alleged intercession by Mitchell on behalf of Vesco.

"In any organization, the man at the top must bear the responsibility. That responsibility, therefore, belongs here, in this office. I accept it."

"It has become virtually impossible... to carry on my regular responsibilities in the White House."

—H. R. Haldeman

"My present usefulness to you and ability to discharge my duties have been impaired by these attacks, perhaps beyond repair."

—John D. Ehrlichman

"Some may hope or think that I will become a scapegoat in the Watergate case."

—John W. Dean III

The Justice Department May 2 filed criminal charges against the Finance Committee to Re-elect the President for allegedly concealing a $200,000 contribution made by Vesco.

• *The New York Times* reported May 2 that government investigators had gathered evidence implicating high-ranking officials in the White House and the President's re-election committee in an elaborate coverup of White House involvement in the June 17, 1972, Watergate break-in.

• Donald H. Segretti, a California lawyer, was indicted by a grand jury in Orlando, Fla., May 4 on charges of distributing a phony letter on the stationery of Sen. Edmund S. Muskie (Maine), a 1972 candidate for the Democratic presidential nomination. The letter accused two other candidates, Senators Henry M. Jackson (Wash.) and Hubert H. Humphrey (Minn.), of sexual misconduct.

Following is a day-to-day chronology of the week's events:

APRIL 27

Dean Urges Disclosure. White House counsel John W. Dean III reportedly told Nixon on March 20 that "to save the presidency," Dean, Ehrlichman and Haldeman would have to disclose all they knew about the Watergate case. As reported by *The Washington Post* April 27, three unnamed sources said Dean had told federal prosecutors April 6 all he knew about the bugging in the hope that Ehrlichman and Haldeman would follow suit.

According to the sources, Dean reportedly told Nixon March 20 that Ehrlichman and Haldeman had detailed knowledge of the coverup of involvement by presidential aides—some of whom had not yet been named in connection with the affair—and that the two advisers had authorized Dean's activities.

The Post April 29 quoted two high-level White House officials as saying that Dean had been directed by Ehrlichman and Haldeman to ensure that the Watergate bugging would never be linked to White House aides. In addition, the sources said, Dean was directed to prevent the disclosure of other campaign espionage activities.

Ruckelshaus Appointment. William D. Ruckelshaus, administrator of the Environmental Protection Agency since its establishment in 1970, was named acting director of the FBI, succeeding L. Patrick Gray III, who resigned as a result of his involvement in the attempted coverup of the Watergate case. Ruckelshaus promised "honest, fair and vigorous" administration of the FBI during his tenure, but added, "I don't anticipate that I will be in this position much longer than two months."

GAO Report. The General Accounting Office (GAO) urged "in the strongest terms" that the Justice Department move quickly on GAO reports charging the Nixon campaign finance committee with "apparent violations" of the Federal Election Campaign Act. The GAO report included new charges that former finance committee treasurer Hugh W. Sloan Jr. "knowingly and willfully" submitted false financial reports to the GAO Office of Federal Elections.

Vesco Investigation. An unnamed source told *The Washington Post* that presidential aide John D. Ehrlichman promised on at least two occasions to help accused swindler Robert L. Vesco buy the U.S. government's interest in a scandal-ridden Lebanese bank.

Ehrlichman issued a statement conceding that he had met once with three Vesco representatives, but he denied any "White House support for, or interest in, the Vesco activities" in Lebanon. The meeting was held Dec. 17, 1971, in the Executive Office Building; according to the Post report, however, this was the second time Ehrlichman had met to discuss the bank purchase.

Staff Changes. White House sources told *The Washington Post* that special presidential consultant Leonard Garment and presidential counsel Richard Moore had taken on special advisory functions for Nixon on the Watergate case. *(Background on Garment, p. 43)*

Republican Protest. In statements and speeches throughout the country, several Republican party and congressional leaders joined in the rising chorus of demands for presidential action to clear up the Watergate case.

"Right now the credibility of the administration is zilch, zero," said Sen. Robert Dole (Kan.), former party chairman. Dole called for the resignation of Haldeman and Ehrlichman. His relations with some White House staffers had long been bitter.

Sen. Milton R. Young (R N.D.) called the Watergate "one of the worst incidents of its kind" and said "it can't help but hurt some" on forthcoming legislative votes. Also warning of the potential impact on the administration's legislative proposals, Sen. Robert W. Packwood (R Ore.) said the affair was reaching "disastrous proportions."

Sen. Richard S. Schweiker (R Pa.) called the Watergate "an albatross around the party's neck" and said the case would have a "very serious impact" on the 1974 elections. *(Watergate's impact on Congress, p. 33)*

George Romney, former secretary of housing and urban development in the Nixon administration, warned that Nixon was "likely to lose his capacity for leadership" unless he aggressively "proceeds to the truth" of the Watergate scandal.

Vacancy Rates. Government officials contacted in an Associated Press survey cited the Watergate scandal as one reason for the White House's inability to fill nearly 59 top-level federal jobs. According to the AP survey, 26 sub-cabinet posts remained unfilled three months after Nixon began his second term, while 23 ambassadorships had not been filled. A White House breakdown showed the vacancy rate exceeded 25 per cent in the upper levels of some departments. *(Related story p. 42)*

APRIL 28

As Watergate disclosures continued to mount, Nixon was reported to be in virtual seclusion at his mountain retreat at Camp David, Md. It was later learned that Secretary of State William P. Rogers, Secretary of Defense Elliot L. Richardson, White House press secretary Ronald L. Ziegler and presidential consultant Leonard Garment had visited the President over the weekend. On April 29, the President met at Camp David with Haldeman and Ehrlichman at their request. A presidential aide said the two reportedly told Nixon they did not want to resign, but would accept whatever decision he reached. The President also met with Kleindienst. He did not meet with Dean.

APRIL 29

Colson Implication. Former special presidential counsel Charles W. Colson allegedly knew of the Watergate bugging plans and urged that the surveillance be expedited, according to "highly reliable sources" cited in *The Washington Post.* The sources said two officials of Nixon's re-election campaign—former White House aides Jeb Stuart Magruder and Frederick C. LaRue—told U.S. prosecutors in the Watergate case that Colson telephoned Magruder in early 1972 expressing dissatisfaction that the bugging had not yet been carried out. Colson, who resigned from his White House post in March, had denied any advance knowledge of the bugging.

Coverup Fund. The Post reported that the President's personal attorney, Herbert W. Kalmbach, was under investigation by the Watergate grand jury on

Kleindienst Resignation

Richard G. Kleindienst, son of a railroad brakeman, had attained the peak of the legal profession before his 49th birthday. On June 9, 1972, after one of the longest confirmation controversies in history, he was confirmed as attorney general of the United States. At his swearing-in three days later, President Nixon praised him as "a great ship...tested by... rough seas."

But within the year—and before his 50th birthday—Kleindienst had resigned, apparently an innocent victim of the Watergate scandal which implicated, as he noted in his letter of resignation, many persons with whom he had "close personal and professional associations."

"Fair and impartial enforcement of the law requires," wrote Kleindienst to Nixon, "that a person who has not had such intimate relationships be the attorney general." Kleindienst, national director of field operations for the 1968 Nixon campaign, had worked then and later with John N. Mitchell, campaign manager; John D. Ehrlichman, campaign "tour director," and H.R. Haldeman, Nixon's personal chief of staff. Kleindienst, after the election, had served under Mitchell as deputy attorney general from early 1969 until Mitchell's resignation to head the 1972 campaign early in 1972. Also at the Justice Department, Kleindienst had worked with John W. Dean III, who spent a year and a half as one of Kleindienst's associates before moving over to the post of White House counsel. *(Text of resignation letter, p. 37)*

During Senate hearings on Kleindienst's nomination to the post of attorney general, there were charges that Nixon administration officials in the Justice Department had agreed to settle antitrust charges against the International Telephone and Telegraph Corp. (ITT) out of court in return for a $400,000 contribution to the cost of the 1972 Republican national convention. Kleindienst denied such charges; the evidence presented at the confirmation hearings was inconclusive. *(1972 Almanac p. 207)*

Post-election rumors in 1972 pointed to Kleindienst as one of the first cabinet members whose resignation would be accepted. The basis for the supposition was the feeling that the Nixon administration had been badly embarrassed by the airing of the ITT charges. But intervention by Kleindienst's old friend and patron, Sen. Barry Goldwater (R Ariz.), apparently saved Kleindienst his post—for a time. It was expected, nevertheless, that Kleindienst would resign during 1973.

Kleindienst practiced law in Phoenix, Ariz., before joining the Nixon administration in 1969.

Reaction to Nixon's Speech

Comments made by members of Congress after President Nixon's April 30 television speech ranged from laudatory to hostile. In general, there was relief that he had broken his long-standing silence. There was widespread feeling in both parties, however, that he had not gone far enough toward appointing an outside investigator, even though he gave such authority to Attorney General-designate Elliot L. Richardson. *(Speech text, p. 34)*

Republicans. The most enthusiastic response came from members of Nixon's own party. House Republican Leader Gerald R. Ford (Mich.) said the President "fully deserves the trust and confidence of the American people.... I have the greatest confidence in the President and am absolutely positive he had nothing to do with this mess."

Rep. John B. Anderson (Ill.), chairman of the House Republican Conference, had some qualifications about the firing and resignations of high administration officials. "Until it has been amply demonstrated to the American public that the last shadowy element in this tragedy has been brought to light, that every possible question has been asked and answered satisfactorily, our institutions of government will remain under a cloud," he said.

Sen. Barry Goldwater (Ariz.), the Republican presidential nominee in 1964, said at a news conference that he did not think Nixon had withheld information but that he would like to know more about the case. "If it's been shown that the President did know about it, then it's done real damage," he said. "And if it goes that far, I would expect impeachment proceedings."

Sen. Carl. T. Curtis (R Neb.), who had just returned from a trip to Australia and New Zealand, said the scandal "has damaged the credibility of the United States worldwide." He called for an independent investigation headed by former Sen. John J. Williams (R Del.) 1947-71).

Democrats. Robert C. Byrd (W.Va.), the Senate Democratic whip, expressed disappointment that Nixon did not say that appointment of a special prosecutor was "imperative and was definitely going to be done." Such a prosecutor, Byrd added, was necessary "to avoid any suspicion of a whitewash."

"The President didn't tell us very much that we didn't already know," said Sen. Edmund S. Muskie (Maine), a contender for the Democratic presidential nomination in 1972. The nominee, Sen. George McGovern (S.D.), had no comment.

The strongest language came from Rep. John E. Moss (D Calif.), who urged Democratic leaders of the House to start a formal inquiry into possible impeachment of the President. "I'm not saying we should do it," said Moss, "but we should prepare ourselves to have all the facts."

Thomas P. O'Neill Jr. (Mass.), House Democratic floor leader, said the House leadership "feels, at this time, that the Moss idea is a bit premature. The time could come when such a committee should be set up."

allegations of obstructing justice by providing money that was used to buy the silence of the seven defendants in the Watergate bugging case. Sources from the Committee for the Re-election of the President said between $500,000 and $1-million left over from Nixon's 1968 campaign provided the money for the secret fund maintained by Kalmbach to pay the Watergate defendents.

Special Prosecutor. Appearing on ABC's "Issues and Answers," Sen. Charles H. Percy (R Ill.) said the Watergate investigation "should be taken out of the Justice Department." Percy said he intended to urge the Senate to pass a resolution calling on the President to appoint a special independent prosecutor.

Appointment of a special prosecutor was also urged by the Ripon Society, a progressive Republican research and policy organization. The idea was endorsed by American Bar Association president Robert W. Meserve.

On April 26, Orville H. Schell Jr., president of the prestigious 10,000-member New York City Bar Association, had released a letter sent to President Nixon with the unanimous support of the group's executive committee urging appointment of an independent lawyer to conduct the Watergate investigation.

Agnew Remarks. "There can be little doubt that it (Watergate) will have some effect" on Republican electoral chances in 1974, "but I don't think it's going to be the factor anticipated by the opposition," predicted Vice President Spiro T. Agnew in an interview with *U.S. News and World Report.* "The President is moving in a determined way to resolve the matter to the full satisfaction of the American people, and I am confident of his ability to do so."

The Vice President expressed strong objections to the planned public Senate Watergate investigation while the grand jury probe was continuing. A televised Senate probe was "not a forum that produces enlightenment," he said. "This is a forum that produces emotion, and we don't need that right now in this matter."

APRIL 30

Resignations Announced. In a dramatic turn of events, the President announced the resignations of four of his closest aides: Haldeman, Ehrlichman, Dean and Attorney General Kleindienst. At the same time, he announced he was immediately nominating Secretary of Defense Elliot L. Richardson as attorney general.

The announcements were made by White House press secretary Ziegler while the President remained at his Camp David retreat working on his televised speech. Effective immediately, Ziegler said, the President asked special consultant Leonard Garment, who had been investigating White House aides' involvement in the Watergate case, to assume the additional duties of presidential counsel, the post held by Dean.

Kleindienst, who submitted his resignation "after long and searching thought," said disclosures made to him on April 15 by Assistant Attorney General Henry Peterson and U.S. prosecutors "dictate this decision at this time." The President said he accepted Kleindienst's resignation "with regret" and added, "in making this decision, Mr. Kleindienst has acted in accordance with the highest standards of public service and legal ethics." ***(Resignation text, p. 37)***

In his letter of resignation, Haldeman said he had "hoped and expected to have had an earlier opportunity to clear up various allegations and innuendos that have been raised." But, he said, it was imperative that the work of the President's office continue unimpeded "rather than being diverted by the daily rumors and developments in the Watergate case." It has become "virtually impossible...for me to carry on my regular responsibilities in the White House," he said. *(Text, p. 37)*

Haldeman said he intended "to cooperate fully with the investigation" and would soon meet, at his request, with U.S. attorneys and with the counsel to the Senate select committee investigating the case.

Ehrlichman's stated reasons for resigning were similar to those of Haldeman. "For the past two weeks, it has become increasingly evident that, regardless of the actual facts, I have been a target of public attack," Ehrlichman wrote. "I have to conclude that my present usefulness to you and ability to discharge my duties have been impaired by these attacks, perhaps beyond repair." *(Text, p. 37)*

In accepting the resignations "of two of my closest friends and most trusted assistants," Nixon said, "I emphasize that neither the submission nor the acceptance of their resignations at this time should be seen by anyone as evidence of any wrongdoing by either one." Of his counsel, the President only stated, "I have requested and accepted" Dean's resignation. *(Text, p. 34)*

Nixon Address. After the announcement of the four resignations, Nixon took his case to the nation in a televised address. During the 24-minute address, the President said he took full responsibility for any improper activities connected with his 1972 presidential campaign, and he pledged that "justice will be pursued fairly, fully and impartially, no matter who is involved."

"There can be no whitewash at the White House," the President declared. He said Richardson would have full charge of the case and would have authority to appoint a special supervising prosecutor if Richardson considered it appropriate. In turning over the administration investigation to Richardson, the President said he had devoted far too much time to the Watergate case in recent weeks and "must now turn my full attention once again to the larger duties of this office."

Declaring that he was "appalled" when he learned of the "senseless, illegal" Watergate break-in on June 17, 1972, Nixon said he was unaware of the real proportions of the case until March 1973. In March, he said, "new information...came to me...suggesting there had been an effort to conceal the facts both from the pub-

Senate Backs Special Prosecutor for Watergate

Reflecting sentiment on Capitol Hill that the Watergate investigation should be supervised by someone independent of the Nixon administration, the Senate May 1 approved by voice vote a resolution (S Res 105) requesting the President to appoint a special prosecutor, subject to Senate confirmation, to head the investigation.

Passage of the "sense of the Senate" resolution, which did not have the force of law, came only one day after President Nixon announced to the nation that he had appointed Secretary of Defense Elliot L. Richardson to take charge of all aspects of the case. *(Text of resolution, p. 34)*

Sen. Charles H. Percy (R Ill.)

The resolution, introduced by Charles H. Percy (R Ill.) and cosponsored by seven Democrats and 11 Republicans, was passed with only five senators present on the floor. Percy's initiative was reported in the press to have angered President Nixon, and it drew sharp criticism from three Republican senators who objected that the resolution had not been considered in committee and that senators had not been given notice that the bill was going to be considered on the floor.

According to a report in the *Chicago Tribune* May 2, Nixon told a closed meeting of his cabinet that Percy would never be President "as long as I have anything to say about it." The Tribune said the remark was attributed to Nixon by "persons who were at the meeting."

In the House, John B. Anderson (R Ill.) and 19 cosponsors May 1 introduced a bill (H Res 367) calling on Richardson to appoint a special prosecutor from outside the executive branch and to give him the authority necessary to fully investigate the case. H Res 367 was referred to the House Judiciary Committee.

Senate Debate. Introducing his bill May 1, Percy said he in no way questioned the integrity or ability of Richardson. But the basic question was simple, he said: "Should the executive branch investigate itself? I do not think so."

Later the same afternoon, Carl T. Curtis (R Neb.) asked unanimous consent that passage of S Res 105 be reconsidered. Curtis said he wanted to offer an amendment allowing the President to appoint an investigator, if he so desired, rather than a prosecutor. The amendment, he added, would allow Nixon to appoint former Sen. John J. Williams (R Del. 1947-71), known during his Senate years for his integrity and impartiality, as the investigator. Williams is not an attorney and presumably would be barred from becoming a prosecutor.

Curtis and Senators Norris Cotton (R N.H.) and George D. Aiken (R Vt.) also criticized the procedure used to pass S Res 105. "This resolution is not the sense of the Senate," Curtis said. "It's the sense of five senators."

Percy said he has obtained permission for floor consideration from the leadership of both parties, adding that it was routine for resolutions with little opposition to be brought up in this manner.

On May 2, Percy asked unanimous consent to allow the Senate to reconsider S Res 105, with a final vote to occur not later than May 8. Cotton objected to his request, and S Res 105 stood as approved May 1.

lic...and from me. As a result," he continued, "on March 21, I personally assumed the responsibility for coordinating intensive new inquiries into the matter." *(Text p. 34, congressional reaction, box p. 27)*

Pentagon Papers Affidavits. U.S. district Court Judge W. Matthew Byrne Jr., judge in the Pentagon Papers trial, said he would order affidavits from several persons involved in the Watergate case regarding their possible involvement in the trial. Lawyers for the defense had requested that the individuals be subpoenaed to testify at a special hearing.

Byrne's action resulted from an April 27 revelation that Hunt and Liddy, two of the convicted Watergate conspirators, had burglarized the files of defendant Daniel Ellsberg's psychiatrist.

In another development, Byrne acknowledged that he had met with the President and Ehrlichman "about a month ago" to discuss the possibility of a high administration post (reportedly the FBI directorship) for Byrne. The judge said he told Ehrlichman he would refuse to consider a government position until the Pentagon Papers trial was completed. He added, "I did not discuss with the President or Mr. Ehrlichman any aspect of this case."

Governors' Meeting. Meeting near Huron, Ohio, a group of the nation's 31 Democratic governors April 30 adopted a resolution calling for "full and total disclosure of all the facts surrounding the Watergate affair" and for appointment of an independent prosecutor to conduct the investigation.

Poll Report: Damage to Nixon from Watergate Affair

Watergate has taken a serious toll with the public in President Nixon's popularity and credibility ratings, according to the latest Harris Survey. The survey was conducted among 1,537 households April 18-23, before the President's television speech April 30.

These were the questions and responses in the Harris poll, published April 29:

"Do you feel that the White House has been frank and honest on the Watergate affair, or do you feel they have withheld important information about it?"

Frank and honest	9%
Withheld important information	63
Not sure	28

"How would you rate President Nixon on his handling of the Watergate political spying case—excellent, pretty good, only fair, or poor?"

Excellent to pretty good (positive)	17%
Only fair to poor (negative)	61
Not sure	22

"How would you rate President Nixon on his handling of corruption in government—excellent, pretty good, only fair, or poor?"

	April	February	October 1972
Positive	25%	32%	32%
Negative	64	55	55
Not sure	11	13	13

"How would you rate President Nixon on inspiring confidence personally in the White House—excellent, pretty good, only fair, or poor?"

	April	March	February	January
Positive	50%	59%	60%	53%
Negative	49	39	39	45
Not sure	1	2	1	2

Agnew vs. Reagan. Two Gallup Polls were conducted that were unrelated to the Watergate affair. One, published April 29, found Vice President Agnew the favorite choice of Republicans for their presidential nomination in 1976. The poll was taken before former Texas Gov. John B. Connally announced his switch from the Democratic to the Republican Party on May 2.

Gallup interviewers asked 798 persons who classify themselves as Republicans March 30-April 2: "Here is a list of people who have been mentioned as possible presidential candidates for the Republican Party in 1976. Which one would you like to see nominated as the Republican candidate for President in 1976? And who would be your second choice?"

	1st Choice	2nd Choice	Combined Total
Vice President Agnew	35%	21%	56%
Gov. Ronald Reagan (Calif.)	20	21	41
John B. Connally	15	12	27
Gov. Nelson A. Rockefeller (N.Y.)	11	14	25
Sen. Charles H. Percy (Ill.)	8	9	17
Sen. James L. Buckley (N.Y.)	2	5	7
Sen. Edward W. Brooke (Mass.)	1	3	4
Sen. Howard H. Baker Jr. (Tenn.)	1	2	3
Gov. Daniel J. Evans (Wash.)	1	—	1
Sen. Bill Brock (Tenn.)	—	1	1
No answer	6	12	18

Kennedy vs. Agnew. In a trial heat published April 30, Gallup found Sen. Edward M. Kennedy (D Mass.) defeating Agnew in 1976. The results were based on interviews with 1,162 registered voters April 6-9.

	Latest	November 1972
Kennedy	51%	49%
Agnew	38	43
Other, undecided	11	9

MAY 1

Ehrlichman Role. A two-page summary of an April 27 FBI interview of Ehrlichman disclosed that the President had directed his domestic affairs adviser to undertake the independent investigation of the Pentagon Papers case that led to the burglary of the office of Ellsberg's psychiatrist.

In the summary of the FBI interview, made available to the defense by Judge Byrne, Ehrlichman said he did not know about or authorize the burglary, and that when he learned about it, he instructed Hunt and Liddy "not to do this again." *(Text, p. 34)*

Ehrlichman was said to have told the FBI that Nixon had asked him sometime in 1971 to make "inquiries independent of concurrent FBI investigation" of the Pentagon Papers case. Ehrlichman hired Hunt and Liddy to conduct the probe "directly out of the White House."

"The efforts of Liddy and Hunt were directed toward an 'in-depth investigation of Ellsberg to determine his habits, mental attitudes, motives, etc.,' " Ehrlichman was said to have told the FBI.

With disclosure of the FBI report, Ellsberg's lawyers moved for a dismissal of the case. They pointed out that Ehrlichman apparently had known long in advance about the burglary and secret investigation but did not make the information available to the judge or the defense. They also pointed out that, knowing about the Liddy-Hunt investigation, Ehrlichman April 5 had summoned Byrne to discuss a possible government job.

Responding to the defense arguments for dismissal, Byrne said he intended "to get the full story.... This case is not going to any jury until I've had the opportunity to evaluate all the information."

FBI Guards. Before Haldeman and Ehrlichman moved out of their offices, FBI agents moved into the White House to keep a 24-hour watch over the files of the two former presidential sides. Press secretary Ziegler said the agents were detailed to the offices of Ehrlichman, Haldeman and Dean "to physically protect the files to make sure that access and removal of any files were supervised in accordance with very strict procedure."

Senate Vote. By a voice vote, the Senate passed a resolution (S Res 105) requesting the President to appoint a special outside prosecutor in the Watergate case. The resolution was sponsored by Sen. Charles H. Percy (R Ill.) and was endorsed by a bipartisan group of Senators. *(Story, p. 28)*

Meanwhile, Nixon was reported to have told members of his Cabinet that he was leaving the decision to appoint a special prosecutor up to Attorney General-designate Richardson. Press secretary Ziegler said Richardson alone would determine the powers of any such prosecutor.

Vesco Investigation. *The Los Angeles Times* reported that reliable sources had said John N. Mitchell interceded on behalf of financier Robert L. Vesco in Vesco's attempt to gain control of Intra Bank, a large Lebanese bank. Mitchell's alleged action reportedly occurred in January 1972, while he was still attorney general.

Mitchell was said to have either cabled or telephoned the legal section of the U.S. embassy in Beirut. Although details of the action were unclear, Mitchell was said to have expressed confidence in Vesco and indicated there was top-level interest in assisting his attempt to take over the bank. Later, however, embassy officials were instructed that Vesco was to receive no special treatment; and when the U.S. ambassador sought instructions, Mitchell reportedly said there had been some misunderstanding.

The alleged bank intercession was the third reported action by Mitchell on behalf of Vesco. In November 1971,

1962 Campaign Incident

During the 1962 California gubernatorial campaign, Richard M. Nixon and H. R. Haldeman were directly involved in an attempt to disrupt the campaign of Nixon's Democratic opponent, Edmund G. Brown. According to a judgment filed by a California judge in 1964, Nixon and campaign manager Haldeman personally authorized and approved efforts to sabotage Brown's credibility with registered Democrats.

According to the judgment, the 1962 sabotage effort involved the solicitation of contributions from registered Democrats, purportedly to change the ideological base of the state Democratic Party, when in fact the funds went directly to the support of the Nixon candidacy. The judgment was signed by Judge Byron Arnold, who then sat on the San Francisco County Superior Court.

As outlined in the judgment, a dummy Nixon organization called the "Committee for the Preservation of the Democratic Party in California" conducted a postcard poll of Democrats which criticized the candidates endorsed by the California Democratic Council. The poll asked for views on how the council should be changed and for money to carry out these views.

Arnold noted that nowhere on the postcard was it stated that the dummy committee and the mailing were supported and paid for by a Nixon election committee. The poll gave the false impression that Democrats were appealing to Democrats, an act in violation of the California election laws.

Although neither Nixon nor Haldeman was a defendant in the suit brought by the state Democratic Party after the 1962 election, the judge ruled that the poll "was reviewed, amended and finally approved by Mr. Nixon personally." Payment statements from a company hired to conduct the postcard poll were sent directly to Haldeman, the judgment added.

Arnold concluded that "the activities of the defendant committee including its postcard poll, its letters and its publicity releases were instigated, financed, prepared, implemented, supervised and executed" by two Nixon campaign committees. The "paramount purpose" of these activities was "to obtain from registered Democrats votes and money for the campaign of Richard M. Nixon."

The court enjoined several defendants who had worked for Nixon election committees and the dummy organization from every using such tactics again. The case never was appealed by the defendants.

Mitchell reportedly telephoned the U.S. embassy in Bern, Switzerland, to aid Vesco's release from a Swiss jail. In May 1972, Mitchell reportedly arranged a meeting with Securities and Exchange Commission (SEC) officials to discuss Vesco's pending investigation by the SEC on charges of a mutual fund swindle.

Faked Documents. Former presidential special counsel Charles W. Colson told a former *Life* magazine reporter that he knew as early as February 1972 that convicted Watergate conspirator E. Howard Hunt Jr. had fabricated a cable implicating President Kennedy in the 1963 assassination of South Vietnam President Ngo Dinh Diem. According to reporter William Lambert, Colson said he made the discovery four months before the Watergate break-in but apparently had not told his superiors about the phony cable.

Newspapers April 26 had reported that L. Patrick Gray III, then acting director of the FBI, had been told by Ehrlichman and Dean to destroy documents belonging to Hunt—including the fabricated cables. Gray destroyed the documents early in July 1972. On April 27, 1973, Gray announced his resignation as acting FBI director. *(Story, p. 22)*

MAY 2

Coverup Implications. *The New York Times* reported that government investigators had gathered evidence implicating high-ranking officials in the White House and the Committee for the Re-election of the President in an attempt to obstruct justice after the June 1972 Watergate break-in. The investigators reportedly said that a careful cover story was arranged at secret meetings in the re-election headquarters in late June. The basic scheme was said to have called for all those involved in the operation to deny any knowledge of it, and for the re-election committee to issue public statements to that effect.

The cover-up operation reportedly was coordinated by Ehrlichman and Haldeman—the President's closest aides at the time—as well as former Attorney General John N. Mitchell, who was then head of the re-election committee. Three other former White House aides—Dean, Magruder and LaRue—also reportedly were involved. The Times quoted sources close to the case as saying that all six men were expected to be indicted by the Watergate grand jury.

"And I think after the history of this first term is written and you look back, you're going to see that compared to other administrations or by any standard you'd want to apply, that it has been an extraordinarily clean, corruption-free administration because the President insists on that."

—John D. Ehrlichman, Sept. 7, 1972, PBS's "Thirty Minutes With..."

The sources reportedly said that at least four other persons also were involved in the coverup and were under grand jury investigation. They were Dwight L. Chapin, the President's former appointments secretary; Gordon C. Strachan, an assistant to Haldeman; Herbert L. Porter, who worked in the White House information office, and Kenneth W. Parkinson, a lawyer hired by the re-election committee shortly after the break-in.

Mitchell issued a statement saying the Times report of his role in the coverup was "absolutely false and without factual foundation."

Criminal Charges. Acting on a General Accounting Office (GAO) recommendation, the Justice Department filed criminal charges against the Finance Committee to Re-elect the President for allegedly concealing a $200,000 contribution from financier Robert L. Vesco. The action was announced by departing Attorney General Kleindienst.

In the three-count information filed in U.S. District Court, the department said the committee was acting through chairman Maurice H. Stans and treasurer Hugh P. Sloan Jr. but named neither as a defendant. The department charged that the committee, acting through Stans, failed to give Sloan a detailed account of the contribution, as required by the Federal Elections Campaign Act. In addition, said the information, the committee, acting through Sloan, neglected to keep records on the contribution and to report it to the GAO, as required.

The Vesco charge marked the second time the Justice Department had filed criminal charges against the committee.

Ehrlichman FBI Interview. After the May 1 disclosure that he had directed a secret White House investigation of the Pentagon Papers trial, former presidential aide Ehrlichman had a second interview with the FBI. The interview took place May 2. In that discussion, Ehrlichman contended that he had not seen anything about the secret probe for more than a year and that the results of the investigation were probably in the hands of former White House aides Egil Krogh Jr. and David Young.

Ehrlichman also said he had seen FBI reports on Ellsberg's wife and on *New York Times* reporter Neil Sheehan, who originally broke the Pentagon Papers story.

Meanwhile, it was reported that Krogh had taken sudden leave from his job as under secretary of transportation after Secretary of Transportation Claude S. Brinegar had requested Krogh to explain publicly his role in the White House probe. Krogh was an assistant to Ehrlichman at that time.

The White House press office announced that Young had resigned April 30 from his post on the National Security Council staff. Both Krogh and Young were members of a group known at the White House as "the plumbers." Liddy and Hunt were also members of the group, which worked out of basement offices in the Executive Office Building. The group was set up on orders from Nixon in July 1971, after publication of the Pentagon Papers in several newspapers, with the publicly announced mission of stopping any more such leaks. Krogh has said he exercised general supervision of "the plumbers."

Judge Byrne made available to defense attorneys in the Pentagon Papers case results of FBI interviews conducted with former White House chief of staff Haldeman and Bruce A. Kehrli, a staff secretary to the President, as well as the results of the second Ehrlichman interview. Both denied any prior knowledge of the White House investigation or of the results. However, according to earlier disclosures, Kehrli had opened Hunt's White House safe after the Watergate break-in and had removed documents, some of which were related to the Pentagon Papers case.

Byrne Meeting. Speaking from the bench during the Ellsberg trial, Byrne confirmed that he had held a second meeting with Ehrlichman to discuss a possible government post. Byrne previously had acknowledged meeting with Nixon's aide on April 5; the second meeting took place April 7. Byrne revealed that the specific post under consideration was that of FBI director. The judge reiterated that at both meetings he had refused to "discuss or consider" the offer until the Pentagon Papers trial had been concluded.

Ellsberg's defense lawyers said they would use the disclosure to press for an "immediate dismissal" of the charges against Ellsberg and codefendent Anthony J. Russo Jr.

Senate Committee. Challenging a previous ruling by Kleindienst, the Senate select committee investigating the Watergate voted to request Attorney General-designate Richardson to make FBI files in the case available to all members of the committee. On March 16, Kleindienst and the committee had reached an agreement whereby only four persons would have access to the files: the chairman and vice chairman and the majority and minority counsels.

After the May 2 committee meeting—during which members unanimously confirmed their intention to begin public hearings about May 15—Ervin told reporters that the panel had not reached a decision regarding granting immunity to prospective witnesses. Asked whether the committee would probe the roles of Hunt and Liddy in the Pentagon Papers case, Ervin said the committee was not authorized to investigate that matter.

Special Prosecutor. Several members of the Senate Judiciary Committee said they would press for appointment of a special Watergate prosecutor before approving the nomination of Richardson as attorney general. The committee was scheduled to begin hearings on the nomination May 9. Senators Robert C. Byrd (D W.Va.) and Philip A. Hart (D Mich.) said they expected Richardson to appoint a special prosecutor before that time. Sen. John V. Tunney (D Calif.) said he would try to block approval of Richardson's nomination unless Richardson agreed in advance to name such a prosecutor.

Several Republican senators demanded reconsideration of a resolution sponsored by Sen. Charles H. Percy (R Ill.) urging the President to appoint a special prosecutor totally unconnected with the administration. The resolution passed the Senate May 1, with only five senators present.

Nixon was reported to have expressed his anger at Percy's move during a May 1 cabinet meeting. He reportedly said the action implied lack of confidence in Richardson and was motivated by presidential ambitions. Nixon was quoted as saying the Illinois senator never would become President "if I have anything to say about it."

MAY 3

Wiretaps on Reporters. *The Washington Post* reported two highly placed but unnamed administration sources as saying the Nixon administration had tapped the telephones of at least two reporters in 1971 as part of the investigation reportedly ordered by the President into the Pentagon Papers leaks. According to one source, the wiretapping was conducted by a so-called "vigilante squad" and not by the FBI, the agency usually responsible for performing legal electronic surveillance operations. The source said the wiretapping was supervised by Hunt and Liddy from their White House offices and was authorized by then Attorney General Mitchell.

One of the sources named said two *New York Times* reporters were among those whose phones were tapped. The sources also said the White House had ordered wiretaps of other reporters concerning leaks of information about the strategic arms limitation talks (SALT). At least 10 White House staff members had their phones tapped as well, the story said.

One of the sources told the Post that in late 1971 or early 1972, Nixon campaign strategists decided to use some members of the "vigilante squad" to tap the phones of Democratic presidential candidates. According to the Post's sources, all records of the "vigilante squad's" activities have been destroyed.

Nixon Notification. Justice Department officials said Nixon had received advance information on the burglary of Ellsberg's psychiatrist's office before that information was sent to Judge Byrne April 27. The advance notification was reported in *The Washington Post.* The Post quoted Justice Department officials as saying that once Nixon received the information, he "endorsed without hesitation" the decision to transmit it to Byrne.

According to the Post's sources, the Justice Department was completely unaware of the burglary until it was disclosed to chief Watergate prosecutor Silbert in an April 15 interview with an unidentified person. Silbert then sent a memo on the subject to Assistant Attorney General Petersen, and the memo was passed on to Byrne more than a week later.

The Post said it was unclear exactly when the President reportedly had been told about the burglary, or whether he had been consulted before the summary of the April 27 FBI interview with Ehrlichman was submitted to Byrne.

Scope of Sabotage. Government investigators told *The New York Times* that Republican sabotage and espionage efforts during the 1972 presidential campaign were more widespread than previously known. The Times quoted sources as saying that the Watergate bugging was only part of an over-all effort directed toward promoting the nomination of Sen. George McGovern (S.D.), whom Republican strategists felt was the weakest Democratic presidential candidate.

According to the Times' sources, the Republican espionage efforts initially were directed toward the campaign of Sen. Edmund S. Muskie (D Maine), the presidential front-runner in early 1972. After Muskie's campaign setbacks, attention focused on the other candidates, one source said. The over-all espionage program initially had been authorized by former White House chief of staff Haldeman, the Times reported. ✓

Watergate's Impact on Congress: Presumably Brief

Dramatic as Watergate may be, the consensus at the Capitol is that it will take a lot more than that to make any lasting difference in congressional decision-making or in national elections. Republicans insist—and most Democrats agree—that whatever problems the scandal causes for the Republican Party in the short run, the political facts of life remain the same.

"Nixon will heap on the coals about fighting inflation and getting the most for the dollar," predicted Rep. Hugh L. Carey (D N.Y.). "He will attempt to show that even without his henchmen he still has a lot of clout around here. And the fact is, he does. The coalition of Republicans and southern Democrats will still be a potent combination."

Few members of either party were willing to predict that Congress would be more successful in overriding the President's vetoes and fighting his budget priorities than they were before the scandal exploded. A few said they felt, along with Robert C. Byrd (D W.Va.), the Senate majority whip, that "it will probably impair his influence in the short run." But the consensus was that the long-range effect on executive-congressional relations would be slight.

There was some feeling that the President would find it easier to rally Republicans around him. "It may make it more difficult to override vetoes," said Rep. George E. Danielson (D Calif.). "The Republicans will feel that this is an emergency, the going is rough and we have to get behind the President."

Danielson went beyond saying that it would be hard for Congress to act against the President. He said he felt it would be hard for Congress to act on anything. "I think the effect is going to be one of impairing the legislative process," Danielson told Congressional Quarterly. "People are going to be looking for mousetraps. They will be super-cautious, and that will slow things down."

A Long Time. Danielson predicted that the Senate would take a long time to approve the President's new cabinet choices, no matter how qualified the individuals might be.

Members interviewed said they felt this legislative slowdown would be complicated by the vacuum in the White House staff following the resignations of John D. Ehrlichman and H.R. Haldeman. "His whole organization has fallen apart, and his contacts with Congress will be new people," said Rep. Tom S. Gettys (D S.C.). "They will have difficulty establishing a rapport, especially when relations are already strained.... Who will believe anything they say?"

"Nixon will attempt to show that even without his henchmen he still has a lot of clout around here. And the fact is, he does."

Rep. Hugh L. Carey (D N.Y.)

"I'm going to try not to let this affect my judgment too much."

Rep. Alan Steelman (R Texas)

Few Republicans interviewed by Congressional Quarterly gave any indication that Watergate would affect their own legislative work. Most of them expressed sentiments such as those of John Ware (R Pa.), who said, "I believe in supporting the chief executive no matter who he is, as much as you can. The two branches have to cooperate, or the country suffers."

Some took a more independent position. "I'm going to try not to let this affect my judgment too much," said Rep. Alan Steelman (R Texas), a freshman. "But in a benefit-of-the-doubt type of case, it would have an effect on me."

But both friends and foes of Nixon cautioned against a simplistic argument that Watergate is a victory for those who oppose Nixon's legislative goals. "This strengthens Congress," conceded one Democrat, "but it doesn't necessarily strengthen the liberal forces within Congress. There may be a lot of sentiment that if the federal government is this corrupt, let's stop giving them money to waste."

Same Answers. The answers were the same when the subject turned to national elections. "I don't think people feel the way to resolve this is to turn to the Democratic Party," said Democrat Carey of New York. "We're still looked on as the big-city machine party. We're not exactly seen as a symbol of puritan integrity. So I don't see any benefit for us. We'll have to come forward and show that we're deserving of it."

Gettys, a more conservative Democrat, agreed that voters in his state were unlikely to base their long-term voting behavior on reaction to Watergate. "I don't think this is going to hurt the Republicans in South Carolina, assuming they have a future there otherwise," he said. "There will be some rub-off on Republican candidates in some parts of the country, but this goes to the integrity of individuals, rather than a party."

Steelman noted a financial problem, saying that big Republican contributors in his Dallas district claimed they did not want to give if their money would be used for espionage. Some feared it might actually end up in Democratic coffers, as part of the settlement Republican officials are trying to make in a civil suit brought by the Democratic Party in the aftermath of Watergate, he said. But he too emphasized the short-range nature of these problems.

SENATE RESOLUTION TEXT

Following is the text of the resolution passed by the Senate May 1 calling on President Nixon to appoint an independent prosecutor to handle the Watergate case. (Story, p. 28)

Resolved, that it is the sense of the Senate that:

1. the President immediately designate an individual of the highest character and integrity from outside the executive branch to serve as special prosecutor for the government of the United States in any and all criminal investigations, indictments, and actions arising from any illegal activity by any persons, acting individually or in combination with others, in the Presidential election of 1972, or any campaign, canvass, or other activity related to it;

2. the President should grant such special prosecutor all authority necessary and proper to the effective performance of his duties; and

3. the President should submit the name of such designee to the Senate, requesting a resolution of approval thereof. √

FBI EHRLICHMAN INTERVIEW

Following is the text of an FBI report on an interview on April 27 with presidential adviser John D. Ehrlichman in connection with the alleged burglary of the offices of Daniel Ellsberg's psychiatrist:

John D. Ehrlichman, adviser to the President, was contacted in his office at the executive office of the President.

It was explained to Mr. Ehrlichman that this interview was being conducted at the specific request of the Justice Department. He was told that information had been received alleging that on an unspecified date the offices of an unnamed psychiatrist retained by Daniel Ellsberg had been burglarized, apparently to secure information relating to Ellsberg. Mr. Ehrlichman was advised that the purpose of this interview was to learn what knowledge he might have concerning this alleged burglary.

Mr. Ehrlichman recalled that sometime in 1971 the President had expressed interest in the problem of unauthorized disclosure of classified government information and asked him to make inquiries independent of concurrent FBI investigation which had been made relating to the leak of the Pentagon papers. Mr. Ehrlichman assumed this responsibility and was assisted in this endeavor by Egil Krogh, a White House assistant, and David Young of the National Security Agency. A decision was made by them to conduct some investigation in the Pentagon Papers leak matter "directly out of the White House." G. Gordon Liddy and E. Howard Hunt were "designated to conduct this investigation."

Mr. Ehrlichman knew that Liddy and Hunt conducted investigation in the Washington, D.C., area and during the inquires were going to the West Coast to follow up on leads. There was information available that Ellsberg had emotional and moral problems and Liddy and Hunt sought to determine full facts relating to these conduct traits. Hunt endeavored to prepare a "psychiatric profile" relating to Ellsberg. The efforts of Liddy and Hunt were directed toward an "in-depth investigation of Ellsberg to determine his habits, mental attitudes, motives, etc."

Although Mr. Ehrlichman knew that Liddy and Hunt had gone to California in connection with the above inquiries being made by them, he was not told that these two individuals had broken into the premises of the psychiatrist for Ellsberg until after this incident had taken place. Such activity was not authorized by him, he did not know about this burglary until after it had happened. He did not "not agree with this method of investigation" and when he learned about the burglary he instructed them "not to do this again."

Mr. Ehrlichman does not recall who specifically reported to him about the above mentioned burglary but it was verbally mentioned to him. He does not know the name of the psychiatrist involved nor the location of this individual. He does not know whose idea it was to commit this burglary. Mr. Ehrlichman has no knowledge whether anything was obtained as a result of this activity.

"I was determined that we should get to the bottom of the matter, and that the truth should be fully brought out—no matter who was involved."

—President Nixon, April 30

WATERGATE TEXT

Following is the White House text of the President's April 30 television address on the Watergate affair:

I want to talk to you tonight from my heart on a subject of deep concern to every American.

In recent months, members of my Administration and officials of the Committee for the Re-election of the President—including some of my closest friends and most trusted aides—have been charged with involvement in what has come to be known as the Watergate affair. These include charges of illegal activity during and preceding the 1972 Presidential election and charges that responsible officials participated in efforts to cover up that illegal activity.

The inevitable result of these charges has been to raise serious questions about the integrity of the White House itself. Tonight I wish to address those questions.

Last June 17, while I was in Florida trying to get a few days' rest after my visit to Moscow, I first learned from news reports of the Watergate break-in. I was appalled at this senseless, illegal action, and I was shocked to learn that employees of the Reelection Committee were apparently among those guilty. I immediately ordered an investigation by appropriate government authorities. On September 15, as you will recall, indictments were brought against seven defendants in the case.

As the investigations went forward, I repeatedly asked those conducting the investigation whether there was any reason to believe that members of my Administration were in any way involved. I received repeated assurances that there were not. Because of these continuing reassurances—because I believed the reports I was getting, because I had faith in the persons from whom I was getting them—I discounted the stories in the press that appeared to implicate members of my Administration or other officials of the campaign committee.

Until March of this year, I remained convinced that the denials were true and that the charges of involvement by members of the White House staff were false. The comments I made during this period, and the comments made by my Press Secretary on my behalf, were based on the information provided to us at the time we made those comments. However, new information then came to me which persuaded me that there was a real possibility that some of these charges were true, and suggesting further that there had been an effort to conceal the facts both from the public, from you, and from me.

New Investigation

As a result, on March 21, I personally assumed the responsibility for coordinating intensive new inquiries into the matter, and I personally ordered those conducting the investigations to get all the facts and to report them directly to me, right here in this office.

I again ordered that all persons in the Government or at the Re-election Committee should cooperate fully with the FBI, the prosecutors and the Grand Jury. I also ordered that anyone who refused to cooperate in telling the truth would be asked to resign from government service. And, with ground rules adopted that would preserve the basic constitutional separation of powers between the Congress and the Presidency, I directed that members of the White House staff should appear and testify voluntarily under oath before the Senate Committee investigating Watergate.

I was determined that we should get to the bottom of the matter, and that the truth should be fully brought out—no matter who was involved.

At the same time, I was determined not to take precipitate action, and to avoid, if at all possible, any action that would appear to reflect on innocent people. I wanted to be fair. But I knew that in the final analysis, the integrity of this office—public faith in the integrity of this office—would have to take priority over all personal considerations.

Resignations

Today, in one of the most difficult decisions of my Presidency, I accepted the resignations of two of my closest associates in the White House—Bob Haldeman, John Ehrlichman—two of the finest public servants it has been my privilege to know.

I want to stress that in accepting these resignations, I mean to leave no implication whatever of personal wrongdoing on their part, and I leave no implication tonight of implication on the part of others who have been charged in this matter. But in matters as sensitive as guarding the integrity of our democratic process, it is essential not only that rigorous legal and ethical standards be observed, but also that the public, you, have total confidence that they are both being observed and enforced by those in authority and particularly by the President of the United States. They agreed with me that this move was necessary in order to restore that confidence.

Because Attorney General Kleindienst—though a distinguished public servant, my personal friend for 20 years, with no personal involvement whatever in this matter—has been a close personal and professional associate of some of those who are involved in this case, he and I both felt that it was also necessary to name a new Attorney General.

The Counsel to the President, John Dean, has also resigned.

As the new Attorney General, I have today named Elliot Richardson, a man of unimpeachable integrity and rigorously high principle. I have directed him to do everything necessary to ensure that the Department of Justice has the confidence and trust of every law abiding person in this country.

I have given him absolute authority to make all decisions bearing upon the prosecution of the Watergate case and related matters. I have instructed him that if he should consider it appropriate, he has the authority to name a special supervising prosecutor for matters arising out of the case.

Whatever may appear to have been the case before—whatever improper activities may yet be discovered in connection with this whole sordid affair—I want the American people, I want you to know beyond the shadow of a doubt that during my terms as President, justice will be pursued fairly, fully, and impartially, no matter who is involved. This office is a sacred trust and I am determined to be worthy of that trust.

Watergate Questions

Looking back at the history of this case, two questions arise: How could it have happened? Who is to blame?

Political commentators have correctly observed that during my 27 years in politics I have always previously insisted on running my own campaigns for office.

But 1972 presented a very different situation. In both domestic and foreign policy, 1972 was a year of crucially important decisions, of intense negotiations, of vital new directions, particularly in working toward the goal which has been my overriding concern throughout my political career—the goal of bringing peace to America and peace to the world.

That is why I decided, as the 1972 campaign approached, that the Presidency should come first and politics second. To the maximum extent possible, therefore, I sought to delegate campaign operations, and to remove the day-to-day campaign decisions from the President's office and from the White House. I also, as you recall, severely limited the number of my own campaign appearances.

Who, then, is to blame for what happened in this case? For specific criminal actions by specific individuals, those who committed those actions, must, of course, bear the liability and pay the penalty.

For the fact that alleged improper actions took place within the White House or within my campaign organization, the easiest course would be for me to blame those to whom I delegated the responsibility to run the campaign. But that would be a cowardly thing to do.

I will not place the blame on subordinates—on people whose zeal exceeded their judgment, and who may have done wrong in a cause they deeply believed to be right.

Accepts Responsibility

In any organization, the man at the top must bear the responsibility. That responsibility, therefore, belongs here, in this office. I accept it. And I pledge to you tonight, from this office, that I will do everything in my power to ensure that the guilty are brought to justice, and that such abuses are purged from our political processes in the years to come, long after I have left this office.

Some people, quite properly appalled at the abuses that occurred, will say that Watergate demonstrates the bankruptcy of the American political system. I believe precisely the opposite is true. Watergate represented a series of illegal acts and bad judgments by a number of individuals. It was the system that has brought the facts to light and that will bring those guilty to justice—a system that in this case has included a determined Grand Jury, honest prosecutors, a courageous Judge, John Sirica, and a vigorous free press.

It is essential now that we place our faith in that system—and especially in the judicial system. It is essential that we let the judicial process go forward, respecting those safeguards that are established to protect the innocent as well as to convict the guilty. It is essential that in reacting to the excesses of others, we not fall into excesses ourselves.

It is also essential that we not be so distracted by events such as this that we neglect the vital work before us, before this Nation, before America, at a time of critical importance to America and the world.

Since March, when I first learned that the Watergate affair might in fact be far more serious than I had been led to believe, it has claimed far too much of my own time and attention.

Whatever may now transpire in the case—whatever the actions of the Grand Jury, whatever the outcome of any eventual trials—I must now turn my full attention once again to the larger duties of this office. I owe it to this great office that I hold, and I owe it to you—to our country.

I know that as Attorney General, Elliot Richardson will be both fair and fearless in pursuing this case wherever it leads. I am confident that with him in charge, justice will be done.

Work to be Done

There is vital work to be done toward our goal of a lasting structure of peace in the world—work that cannot wait. Work that I must do.

Tomorrow, for example, Chancellor Brandt of West Germany will visit the White House for talks that are a vital element of "The Year of Europe" as 1973 has been called. We are already preparing for the next Soviet-American summit meeting, later this year.

This is also a year in which we are seeking to negotiate a mutual and balanced reduction of armed forces in Europe, which will reduce our defense budget and allow us to have funds for other purposes at home so desperately needed. It is the year when the United States and Soviet negotiators will seek to work out the second and even more important round of our talks on limiting nuclear arms, and of reducing the danger of a nuclear war that would destroy civilization as we know it. It is a year in which we confront the difficult tasks of maintaining peace in Southeast Asia, and in the potentially explosive Middle East.

There is also vital work to be done right here in America—to ensure prosperity, and that means a good job for everyone who wants to work, to control inflation, that I know worries every housewife, everyone who tries to balance a family budget in America, to set in motion new and better ways of ensuring progress toward a better life for all Americans.

When I think of this office—of what it means—I think of all the things that I want to accomplish for this nation—of all the things I want to accomplish for you.

Second Term Goals

On Christmas Eve, during my terrible personal ordeal of the renewed bombing of North Vietnam, which after 12 years of war, finally helped to bring America peace with honor, I sat down just before midnight. I wrote out some of my goals for my second term as President.

Let me read them to you.

"To make it possible for our children, and for our children's children, to live in a world of peace.

"To make this country be more than ever a land of opportunity—of equal opportunity, full opportunity for every American.

"To provide jobs for all who can work, and generous help for all who cannot.

"To establish a climate of decency, and civility, in which each person respects the feelings and the dignity and the God-given rights of his neighbor.

"To make this a land in which each person can dare to dream, can live his dreams—not in fear, but in hope—proud of his community, proud of his country, proud of what America has meant to himself and to the world."

These are great goals. I believe we can, we must work for them. We can achieve them. But we cannot achieve these goals unless we dedicate ourselves to another goal.

We must maintain the integrity of the White House, and that integrity must be real, not transparent. There can be no whitewash at the White House.

We must reform our political process—ridding it not only of the violations of the law, but also of the ugly mob violence, and other inexcusable campaign tactics that have been too often practiced and too readily accepted in the past—including those that may have been a response by one side to the excesses or expected excesses of the other side. Two wrongs do not make a right.

I have been in public life for more than a quarter of a century. Like any other calling, politics has good people, and bad people. And let me tell you, the great majority in politics, in the Congress, in the Federal Government, in the State Government, are good people. I know that it can be very easy, under the intensive pressures of a campaign, for even well-intentioned people to fall into shady tactics—to rationalize this on the grounds that what is at stake is of such importance to the Nation that the end justifies the means. And both of our great parties have been guilty of such tactics in the past.

New Standards

In recent years, however, the campaign excesses that have occurred on all sides have provided a sobering demonstration of how far this false doctrine can take us. The lesson is clear: America, in its political campaigns, must not again fall into the trap of letting the end, however great that end is, justify the means.

I urge the leaders of both political parties, I urge citizens, all of you, everywhere, to join in working toward a new set of standards, new rules and procedures—to ensure that future elections will be as nearly free of such abuses as they possibly can be made. This is my goal. I ask you to join in making it America's goal.

When I was inaugurated for a second term this past January 20, I gave each member of my Cabinet and each member of my senior White House staff a special four-year calendar, with each day marked to show the number of days remaining to the Administration. In the inscription on each calendar, I wrote these words: "The Presidential term which begins today consists of 1,461 days—no more, no less. Each can be a day of strengthening and renewal for America; each can add depth and dimension to the American experience. If we strive together, if we make the most of the challenge and the opportunity that these days offer us, they can stand out as great days for America, and great moments in the history of the world."

I looked at my own calendar this morning up at Camp David as I was working on this speech. It showed exactly 1,361 days remaining in my term. I want these to be the best days in America's history, because I love America. I deeply believe that America is the hope of the world, and I know that in the quality and wisdom of the leadership America gives lies the only hope for millions of people all over the world, that they can live their lives in peace and freedom. We must be worthy of that hope, in every sense of the word. Tonight, I ask for your prayers to help me in everything that I do throughout the days of my Presidency to be worthy of their hopes and of yours.

God bless America and God bless each and every one of you. ✓

RESIGNATION LETTERS

Following are White House texts of the President's April 30 statement on the resignations of Attorney General Richard G. Kleindienst and presidential assistants H. R. Haldeman and John D. Ehrlichman, and the texts of their resignation letters.

Statement by the President

I have today received and accepted the resignation of Richard G. Kleindienst as Attorney General of the United States. I am appointing Elliot L. Richardson to succeed him as Attorney General and will submit Mr. Richardson's name to the Senate for confirmation immediately.

Mr. Kleindienst asked to be relieved as Attorney General because he felt that he could not appropriately continue as head of the Justice Department now that it appears its investigation of the Watergate and related cases may implicate individuals with whom he has had a close personal and professional association. In making this decision, Mr. Kleindienst has acted in accordance with the highest standards of public service and legal ethics. I am accepting his resignation with regret and with deep appreciation for his dedicated service to this Administration.

Pending Secretary Richardson's confirmation as Attorney General, I have asked him to involve himself immediately in the investigative process surrounding the Watergate matter. As Attorney General, Mr. Richardson will assume full responsibility and authority for coordinating all Federal agencies in uncovering the whole truth about this matter and recommending appropriate changes in the law to prevent future campaign abuses of the sort recently uncovered. He will have total support from me in getting this job done.

In addition, I have today accepted the resignations of two of my closest friends and most trusted assistants in the White House, H. R. Haldeman and John D. Ehrlichman.

I know that their decision to resign was difficult; my decision to accept it was difficult; but I respect and appreciate the attitude that led them to it. I emphasize that neither the submission nor the acceptance of their resignations at this time should be seen by anyone as evidence of any wrongdoing by either one. Such an assumption would be both unfair and unfounded.

Throughout our association, each of these men has demonstrated a spirit of selflessness and dedication that I have seldom seen equalled. Their contributions to the work of this Administration have been enormous. I greatly regret their departure.

Finally, I have today requested and accepted the resignation of John W. Dean III from his position on the White House staff as Counsel.

Effective immediately, Leonard Garment, Special Consultant to the President, will take on additional duties as Counsel to the President, and will continue acting in this capacity until a permanent successor to Mr. Dean is named. Mr. Garment will represent the White House in all matters relating to the Watergate investigation and will report directly to me.

Kleindienst Letter

Dear Mr. President:

It is with deep regret and after long and searching thought that I hereby submit my resignation as Attorney General, to take effect upon the appointment and qualification of my successor.

Even though, as you know, I had previously indicated a desire to leave the government this year for family and financial reasons, the circumstances surrounding the disclosures made to me on Sunday, April 15, 1973 by Assistant Attorney General Petersen, United States Attorney Titus, and Assistant United States Attorney Silbert, dictate this decision at this time.

Those disclosures informed me, for the first time, that persons with whom I had had close personal and professional associations could be involved in conduct violative of the laws of the United States. Fair, and impartial enforcement of the law requires that a person who has not had such intimate relationships be the Attorney General of the United States.

It is not for me to comment now on the tragedy that has occurred. However, I will always be mindful of your charge to me from the very beginning that the entire matter be fully investigated and that the full effect of the law be administered no matter who it might involve or affect. You can be proud of the Department of Justice for the manner in which it, from the beginning, has responded to that charge.

Finally, let me express my deep personal appreciation to you for having appointed me the 68th Attorney General of the United States. It is the greatest honor I shall ever have. I shall always be humbly proud to have been a part of the Department of Justice and to have had the opportunity to serve my country as a part of your Administration.

Haldeman Letter

Dear Mr. President:

As you know, I had hoped and expected to have had an earlier opportunity to clear up various allegations and innuendos that have been raised in connection with matters related to the Watergate case. It now appears that this process may consume considerable time. Meanwhile, there is apparently to be no interruption in the flood of stories arising every day from all sorts of sources.

I fully agree with the importance of a complete investigation by the appropriate authorities of all the factors that may be involved; but am deeply concerned that, in the process, it has become virtually impossible under these circumstances for me to carry on my regular responsibilities in the White House.

It is imperative that the work of the Office of the President not be impeded and your staff must be in a position to focus their attention on the vital areas of domestic and international concern that face you, rather than being diverted by the daily rumors and developments in the Watergate case. For these reasons, I submit my resignation as Assistant to the President.

I intend to cooperate fully with the investigation—and will at my request be meeting this week for that purpose with the U.S. Attorneys and with the counsel to the Senate Select Committee.

I am convinced that, in due course, I will have the opportunity not just to clear up any allegations or implications of impropriety but also to demonstrate that I have always met the high and exacting standards of integrity which you have so clearly and properly demanded of all who serve on the White House staff.

I have full confidence that when the truth is known the American people will be totally justified in their pride in the Office of the President and in the conduct of that office by President Nixon.

Ehrlichman Letter

Dear Mr. President:

For the past two weeks it has become increasingly evident that, regardless of the actual facts, I have been a target of public attack. The nature of my position on your staff has always demanded that my conduct be both apparently and actually beyond reproach. I have always felt that the appearance of honesty and integrity is every bit as important to such a position as the fact of one's honesty and integrity.

Unfortunately, such appearances are not always governed by facts. Realistically, they can be affected by repeated rumor, unfounded charges or implications and whatever else the media carries. For instance, this week totally unfounded stories appeared in the *Los Angeles Times* claiming I had asked our Embassy in Lebanon to help the Vesco group in a banking deal. I not only did not do so but, in actual fact, I caused the State Department to cable the Embassy that no one at the White House had any interest in the Vesco dealings.

Since I have already reported to you many of the facts in the Gray case, I need only say that at no time did I directly or indirectly suggest that Mr. Gray should do other than keep the Hunt documents, although there have been reports to the contrary. Equally without merit are the source stories about some alleged involvement in the Watergate matter.

As I analyze my situation, I have to conclude that my present usefulness to you and ability to discharge my duties have been impaired by these attacks, perhaps beyond repair.

It is not fair to you and my staff colleagues for me to try to do my job under these circumstances. Too much of my time and attention is and will be consumed in concern for and straightening out such allegations. At my request, I am going to have separate interviews this week with the District Attorney and the Senate Committee Counsel. Thus, I am looking forward to an early review of the facts and evidence with the appropriate authorities, and I should spend the time necessary in relation thereto.

One of the toughest problems we have in this life is in seeing the difference between the apparent and the real, and in basing our actions only on that which is real. We all must do that more than we do. I have confidence in the ultimate prevalence of truth; I intend to do what I can to speed truth's discovery.

Therefore, Mr. President, I submit to you my resignation. There are on the Domestic Council staff so many good people of ability that I am confident a transition of my responsibilities can be affected without loss of progress. I will do all I can to assist in accomplishing the transition.

WATERGATE CAST OF CHARACTERS: SIMILAR BACKGROUNDS

Lawyers, businessmen, media specialists, non-politicians—these are the words that characterize the men whose names have been prominently mentioned in news accounts of the Watergate case. *(Biographies next page)*

The common denominator appears to be lack of experience as candidates for public office. With the exception of convicted conspirator G. Gordon Liddy, not one ever sought office. Liddy made an unsuccessful try for the Republican nomination for the U.S. House from New York in 1968—on a law-and-order theme.

The only political background attributable to any of the other Watergate personalities comes from managing or participating in the campaigns of others—particularly President Nixon. Former Attorney General John N. Mitchell was Nixon's campaign manager in 1968. White House aides H. R. Haldeman and John D. Ehrlichman were advance men in past Nixon campaigns, as was Dwight L. Chapin, the President's former appointments secretary. Maurice H. Stans was Nixon's chief fund-raiser in 1968 as well as 1972.

Occupations. The legal profession claims Ehrlichman; Liddy; Mitchell; John W. Dean III, the President's former counsel; Gordon C. Strachan, Haldeman's former deputy, and Charles W. Colson, the President's former special counsel.

From business come Maurice Stans, a former commerce secretary; Jeb Stuart Magruder, a former Haldeman deputy, and James W. McCord Jr., another convicted conspirator.

Media specialists have been plentiful in the Nixon White House, most of them former colleagues of Haldeman at the Los Angeles office of the J. Walter Thompson advertising agency, which he managed. Among them are Ronald L. Ziegler, the President's press secretary, and Chapin. Magruder also has a background in advertising and business.

Recruitment. Haldeman, one of the prime recruiters of White House talent, was responsible for bringing in Ziegler, Chapin, Magruder and Ehrlichman. Mitchell's efforts brought Dean and Strachan to the executive mansion.

The ages of the Watergate personalities range from Strachan (29) to Stans (65). Most of them are in their 40s and 50s.

Liddy, McCord and E. Howard Hunt are three of seven men convicted in the Watergate affair. None of the men subsequently linked to Watergate or other campaign excesses has been indicted, but all have been or are likely to be called before the Watergate grand jury to explain their roles.

(Ziegler is not a suspect in the affair, nor has his name been mentioned in connection with any other campaign efforts that might come under the grand jury's scrutiny. He is included in the biographical sketches because of his prominence as the White House's spokesman.)

Accusations. According to testimony leaked from the grand jury probe, Haldeman kept a $350,000 fund in his White House office, some of which allegedly was channeled to convicted Watergate conspirators through Strachan to buy their continued silence. He has denied such charges.

Watergate and Fund-raising

The Watergate scandal is having a damaging effect on Republican fund-raising. One measure of the effect is the shortage of money being collected for the "New Majority" dinner May 9 in Washington, D.C.

Originally, the goal for the $1,000-a-plate dinner was $2-million. That figure has been cut in half. Proceeds from the annual fund-raiser are divided equally among the three sponsors, the Republican campaign finance committees of the House, Senate and national committee.

The man in charge of the dinner, at which President Nixon and Vice President Agnew are scheduled to speak, is Buehl Berentson, executive director of the party's Senatorial Campaign Committee. "It's slow," he told Congressional Quarterly. "We still hope we'll crack a mil, but we're not sure. All the rules and criteria are out this year."

Berentson did not attribute this year's tight-fistedness solely to Watergate. Few prospective contributors, he said, have cited the affair as a reason for not giving. "It may be that our answer is their silence," he added.

Campaign Surplus. Another reason mentioned for the reluctance of Republican givers is the surplus of some $4.9-million left over from the 1972 presidential campaign. Berentson emphasized that this money does not belong to the House and Senate campaign committees. "We've got no money in our till," he said.

He added, however, that he hopes the Republican National Committee will be generous in using its resources to help congressional candidates in 1974. The "New Majority" campaign for the mid-term elections was sidetracked April 24 by the resignation of its director, Kenneth Rietz, who had been implicated in a 1972 plan to hire youths to spy on Democratic activities.

Widespread Uneasiness. A random sampling of state officials by Congressional Quarterly found mixed reactions to the impact of Watergate on Republican fund-raising. "It has to come from the faithful, and the faithful are mad," said Clarke Reed, the party chairman in Mississippi. But, he continued, "Even without Watergate we'd be having trouble."

"Until Watergate gets cleared up, we're going to have a tough time collecting any money," said John Pierson of St. Paul, state finance chairman of the Minnesota Republican Party.

More optimistic was a Colorado Republican working on her state's annual "neighbor to neighbor" fund drive. She said she had come across only two or three persons who had refused to give because of Watergate. Many, she added, said they believed that Nixon was a victim of circumstances he could not control.

Ehrlichman was not publicly connected to Watergate until April 26, when it was disclosed that he had been present when Dean gave former acting FBI Director L. Patrick Gray III documents allegedly taken from E.

Howard Hunt's White House office. The documents later were destroyed by Gray, it was reported. Ehrlichman has confirmed that he was present when the documents were turned over to Gray, but insists that he did not know their contents and did not order their destruction.

Mitchell has admitted attending three meetings at which the Watergate bugging was discussed, but has insisted that he did not approve such plans. Magruder reportedly told the grand jury that Mitchell and Dean approved the bugging and that Colson knew about it.

Kalmbach reportedly controlled a $500,000 fund that helped pay for alleged sabotage activities by Donald L. Segretti. Chapin, in turn, has been named as Segretti's contact in the White House.

Stans, according to testimony at the Watergate trial, kept large sums of cash in his safe at the re-election committee, some of which helped pay for the bugging.

Dwight L. Chapin

Dwight Lee Chapin, 32, had worked on and off for Nixon ever since his graduation from the University of Southern California in 1962. As the President's appointments secretary from 1969 until his Feb. 28 departure for private business, Chapin was one of the few White House staff members with easy access to the President. He charted the President's schedule and coordinated all trips, including the 1972 China visit. He was born Dec. 2, 1940, in Wichita, Kan.

Described as utterly loyal to the President, Chapin worked as an advance man for Nixon in his 1964 and 1968 presidential campaigns. From 1963 to 1966, he worked under H. R. Haldeman at the J. Walter Thompson advertising agency in Los Angeles. Although unofficially involved in the 1972 campaign, Chapin has been named as a contact for Donald H. Segretti, an alleged operative in undercover espionage activities for the Republicans.

Charles W. Colson

Special counsel to the President from late 1969 until last February, Charles Wendell Colson, 41, was known in White House circles as a tough troubleshooter and key political adviser. In charge of liaison with outside groups, Colson hammered out agreements between administration officials and lobbies and took charge of public relations efforts to garner support for presidential policies.

He was born Oct. 16, 1931, in Boston, graduated from Brown University and took a law degree from George Washington University. From 1956-61, Colson was administrative aide to former Sen. Leverett Saltonstall (R Mass. 1945-67), and after several years in private law practice, he played a marginal role in Nixon's 1968 presidential campaign.

During the 1972 campaign, Colson rode herd on the campaign efforts of White House staff members, while reportedly trying to influence re-election committee activities. Watergate conspirator E. Howard Hunt worked as a consultant for Colson in early 1972. In an August 1972 memo to White House staffers, Colson wrote that it was correct he once said "I would walk over my grandmother if necessary" to assure the President's re-election.

John W. Dean III

John Wesley Dean, 34, the President's counsel since July 1970, is one of the bright, young—but politically inexperienced—aides Nixon surrounded himself with since taking office. Dean was largely responsible for the legal work on the unprecedented positions the President has taken on executive privilege and impoundment of funds voted by Congress.

It was Dean who conducted the first Watergate investigation for the President in the summer of 1972 and reported that no one then at the White House was involved. Later events, however, led Nixon to ask for Dean's resignation, which he received and accepted April 30. Dean was born Oct. 14, 1938, in Akron, Ohio. He attended three undergraduate schools and graduated from Georgetown University Law School in 1965.

Dean's rise to the important job of the President's White House lawyer was rapid. He was minority counsel for the House Judiciary Committee in 1967, associate director of the National Commission on Reform of the Criminal Laws from 1967 to 1969, and associate deputy attorney general from 1969 to 1970 before replacing John D. Ehrlichman as counsel to the President.

John D. Ehrlichman

John Daniel Ehrlichman, 48, directed the White House organization for domestic policy that parallels Dr. Henry Kissinger's foreign affairs staff. Described as efficient, brusque and a stickler for punctuality, Ehrlichman rose rapidly in the Nixon administration. He was counsel to the President from January to November 1969, when he became assistant to the President for domestic affairs. He was born in Tacoma, Wash., on March 20, 1925.

Ehrlichman—like White House staff chief H. R. Haldeman, another principal in the Watergate case who also resigned April 30—was an advance man during Nixon's 1960 presidential campaign. He was a classmate of Haldeman at the University of California at Los Angeles.

Ehrlichman served as Nixon's "tour director" during the 1968 campaign. Before joining the campaign, he was associated with the law firm of Hullin, Ehrlichman, Roberts and Hodge in Seattle, Wash. He held no official post in the 1972 Nixon re-election campaign.

H. R. Haldeman

Harry Robbins Haldeman, 46, was generally considered the most powerful man in the White House after the President until his resignation April 30. The crew-cut Haldeman, who had been an assistant to the President since 1969, was charged with running the White House, passing the President's ideas to subordinates and jealously guarding the President's schedule. He was born Oct. 27, 1926, in Los Angeles, and graduated from the University of California at Los Angeles.

Haldeman was an advance man in Nixon's 1960 presidential campaign, managed his 1962 try for the governorship of California and was chief of staff in Nixon's 1968 presidential campaign. Although he took no official part in the 1972 campaign, it has been reported Haldeman played a major role in directing the Committee for the Reelection of the President from the White House.

Many of the personalities connected to the Watergate affair either worked for Haldeman when he managed the J. Walter Thompson advertising agency's Los Angeles office in the 1960s or were recruited by him. Among them are John D. Ehrlichman, Haldeman's college classmate, and Dwight Chapin and Ronald Ziegler from the advertising firm.

E. Howard Hunt Jr.

Everette Howard Hunt Jr., 54, is a former Central Intelligence Agency operative who pleaded guilty to all charges against him in the Watergate break-in and bugging trial. He served as White House consultant to his friend, Charles W. Colson, one of President Nixon's chief aides.

Born in Hamburg, N.Y., Oct. 9, 1918, he graduated from Brown University in 1940. After graduation he worked as a war correspondent, editorial writer and screenwriter before beginning a 21-year global career as a CIA agent. Over the years he also wrote 42 short stories and spy novels under several pseudonyms. He faces a maximum possible sentence of 35 years in jail and a $40,000 fine as a result of his Watergate conviction.

Hunt's wife died in a Dec. 8, 1972, plane crash in Chicago. Authorities examining the wreckage found $10,000 in $100 bills in Mrs. Hunt's purse.

Herbert W. Kalmbach

Herbert Warren Kalmbach, 51, is President Nixon's personal attorney. A partner in the Los Angeles firm of Kalmbach, De Marco, Knapp and Chillingsworth, Kalmbach is a longtime associate of Nixon and Robert H. Finch, the former Nixon aide. He was born Oct. 19, 1921, in Port Huron, Mich., and graduated from the University of Southern California and its law school.

Kalmbach was the associate finance chairman of the 1968 Nixon for President campaign under Maurice H. Stans and acted as an unofficial fund-raiser for President Nixon until the Committee for the Re-election of the President was organized.

G. Gordon Liddy

George Gordon Liddy, 42, is probably the most flamboyant personality known to have been involved in the break-in at Democratic party headquarters. A former FBI agent, assistant district attorney and law-and-order candidate for Congress, Liddy was at one time considered to be the organizer of the ill-fated bugging attempt. He was convicted Jan. 3 by a U.S. district court jury of conspiracy, burglary and illegal wiretapping, and later refused to testify before the Watergate grand jury.

Born in New York City Nov. 30, 1930, Liddy is a graduate of Fordham University and Fordham law school. He spent five years with the FBI before joining the Dutchess County, N.Y., district attorney's office in 1965. In 1968 Liddy ran unsuccessfully for the Republican nomination in what was then New York's 28th congressional district.

After practicing law in his father's New York firm, Liddy became special assistant in the Treasury Department in 1969, where he gained his reputation for stubborn independence. An unauthorized speech on gun control led to his dismissal in 1971. Liddy joined the staff of the White House Domestic Council under John D. Ehrlichman in June 1971, but left that post in December 1971 to become general counsel to the Committee for the Re-election of the President. Four months later he moved to the finance committee as counsel.

Jeb Magruder

Jeb Stuart Magruder, 38, the first administration official to resign over the Watergate affair, was another of the California advertising and management types who populated the White House in the first Nixon term. He was in line for a high administration job in the second term, but assumed the vague position of planning director for the Commerce Department after being tainted by the Watergate trial. He testified at the trial that he helped establish what he thought to be a "legal" intelligence-gathering operation.

At the White House, which he joined in 1969, Magruder worked for Haldeman and Herbert G. Klein, communications director for the executive branch. He left the executive mansion in late 1971 to become deputy director of the Committee for the Re-election of the President.

The boyish-looking Magruder was born Nov. 5, 1934, in New York City. He graduated from Williams College and attended the University of Chicago's business school. He was regarded as a top-notch administrator, having worked in advertising and management before heading a small cosmetics firm in Santa Monica, Calif. He was a volunteer for Nixon, Sen. Barry Goldwater (R Ariz.) and former Rep. Donald Rumsfeld (R Ill.).

James W. McCord Jr.

When James Walter McCord Jr. was arrested along with four other men inside the Democratic headquarters last June 17, he was serving as security co-ordinator for the Nixon re-election committee and the Republican National Committee. He was fired the next day.

From 1951 until his retirement in 1971 McCord worked for the CIA, and before that, as a clerk and special agent at the FBI.

At his arrest McCord listed his birthday as Oct. 9, 1918, but *The New York Times* reported that bail records showed it to be July 26, 1924. News reports have quoted sources as saying he was born in Texas, and that he holds degrees from the University of Texas and George Washington University.

After retiring from the CIA, McCord started his own security consulting business, McCord Associates Inc., in Rockville, Md. In 1971 he taught a seminar entitled "Industrial and Retail Security" at Montgomery College in Maryland.

McCord was convicted Jan. 30 on eight counts of conspiracy, burglary and wiretapping. On March 23 Judge John J. Sirica read in court a letter McCord had written him charging that persons besides those convicted were involved in the Watergate case, that perjury had been committed during the trial and that political pressure had been applied to make the defendants plead guilty. On March 30 Sirica deferred McCord's sentencing until June 15. McCord testified March 28 in closed session before the Ervin committee investigating the Watergate.

John N. Mitchell

John Newton Mitchell, 59, the President's former law partner, was Nixon's closest adviser on domestic and political affairs during his term as attorney general (1969-72) and director of the Committee for the Re-election of the President (March 1-July 1, 1972). Mitchell left the re-election committee after his wife, Martha, demanded publicly that he leave politics and "all those dirty things that go on."

Mitchell and Nixon were partners in the New York law firm of Mudge, Rose, Guthrie, Alexander and Mitchell, which Nixon joined after losing the 1962 California governor's race. Mitchell specialized in municipal bonds. He was born Sept. 5, 1913, in Detroit, and graduated from Fordham University and its law school.

Mitchell ran Nixon's 1968 campaign and served as an unofficial adviser in the 1972 campaign after he left the re-election committee. Mitchell was credited with developing the tough law-and-order stance which was a major campaign issue for Nixon in 1968. His famous watchword to reporters in the early days of Nixon's first term was, "Watch what we do, not what we say."

Ken Rietz

Kenneth S. Rietz, 32, headed President Nixon's youth campaign in 1972. On March 1, 1973, he was named director of the Republican National Committee's "New Majority Campaign for 1974," a position he resigned from April 23, 1973. He was born May 3, 1941, in Oshkosh, Wis., and graduated from George Washington University.

Rietz first gained prominence as Sen. Bill Brock's (R Tenn.) campaign manager in 1970. Prior to that, he was active with the Wisconsin Republican organization in 1965 and 1966 and served as campaign director in 1966 and 1968 and legislative assistant 1966-68 to Rep. William A. Steiger (R Wis.). In 1969, he was named assistant communications director and information director of the Republican National Committee.

Reitz's deputy on the campaign staff, George K. Gorton, reportedly has admitted that he hired and paid a George Washington University student last year to infiltrate radical groups. Gorton, 25, was hired March 19 by the Interior Department's Bicentennial Commission, but was removed from the job April 21. The appointment had been temporary, a department spokesman said.

Donald H. Segretti

Donald H. Segretti, 31, a California lawyer, has been under Justice Department investigation for reportedly directing a campaign of political sabotage on behalf of the Republican party during the 1972 presidential campaign. Segretti reportedly was paid at least $20,000 by the President's personal attorney, Herbert Kalmbach, with money from a secret fund kept in the office of former Secretary of Commerce Maurice Stans.

Born Sept. 17, 1941, in San Marino, Calif., a Los Angeles suburb, Segretti received a degree in finance from the University of Southern California in 1963. At USC he met Dwight Chapin, former appointments secretary to President Nixon and a Watergate figure.

After graduation, Segretti studied in Cambridge, England, for a year and then graduated from University of Southern California law school. After a brief stint with the Treasury Department in Washington, he served as a captain in the army Judge Advocate General's Corps and was discharged in 1971

Maurice H. Stans

Maurice Hubert Stans, 65, was the chief fund-raiser for the 1968 and 1972 Nixon-Agnew campaigns and is currently chairman of the Finance Committee to Re-elect the President. From Aug. 23, 1972, to Jan. 17, Stans served concurrently as chairman of the Republican National Finance Committee.

Stans resigned Feb. 15, 1972, as secretary of commerce, a post he had held since the start of the Nixon administration. He was born March 22, 1908, in Shakopee, Minn., and attended Northwestern and Columbia Universities.

Stans held several positions in the Eisenhower administration including director of the Bureau of the Budget from 1958-60. Before heading the 1968 fundraising campaign, Stans was a New York investment banker.

Gordon C. Strachan

Gordon C. Strachan, 29, was staff assistant to presidential aide H. R. Haldeman from August 1970 till December 1972. In January 1973, Strachan became general counsel of the United States Information Agency. He resigned April 30, the same day as Haldeman. He was born July 24, 1943, in Berkeley, Calif., graduated from the University of Southern California and received his law degree from the University of California.

Strachan was an associate with Nixon's law firm of Mudge, Rose, Guthrie & Alexander from 1968 to 1970.

Strachan was an associate with Nixon's law firm of political aides and served as the liaison between Haldeman's office and the Committee for the Re-election of the President.

Ronald L. Ziegler

Ronald Louis Ziegler, 33, the President's press secretary since 1969, has taken much of the heat from reporters over the Watergate affair—mainly because he is the only administration spokesman on the subject. His credibility was damaged badly by 10 months of denials of Watergate news stories as "fiction," "shabby journalism" and "character assassination," only to turn around after the President's April 17 statement and declare his past remarks "inoperative."

But Ziegler always did a good job of fending off the press and is believed to be a favorite of the President. The press secretary is a protege of H.R. Haldeman, for whom he worked at the J. Walter Thompson advertising agency in Los Angeles.

Ziegler was born May 12, 1939, in Covington, Ky. He graduated from the University of Southern California in 1961 and immediately went to work as press secretary to California Republican legislators. He worked on Nixon's unsuccessful gubernatorial campaign in 1962 and was campaign press secretary for Nixon in 1968. He also aided in the 1964 campaign of former Sen. George Murphy (R Calif. 1965-71) ✓

RESIGNATIONS IMPEDE WHITE HOUSE WORK AND INITIATIVES

The departure of presidential aides H. R. Haldeman and John D. Ehrlichman in the wake of Watergate was not only a personal blow to their friend Richard Nixon, but put a severe crimp in executive branch operations.

Haldeman, Nixon's chief of staff, and Ehrlichman, his assistant for domestic policy, were indispensible adjuncts of presidential power. Through their toughness, strong will and unswerving loyalty to the President, they were able to get things done.

If they ruffled a few feathers along the way, they apparently felt it was worth it and so did Nixon. Haldeman once said Nixon told him "there has to be a few SOB's in any organization, and I'm his." *(Congressional reaction to departures favorable, p. 27)*

Their departures placed in question a whole range of Nixonian initiatives and policies, from executive reorganization to impoundment of appropriated funds. And it raised the question of whether staff changes would result in a different style of dealing with Congress and the press.

Slowdown Evident

White House spokesman Ronald L. Ziegler, while not downplaying the importance of the pair, insisted publicly that the work of the White House went on without them. "The White House staff is operating and functioning very well today," he said May 1, the day after Ehrlichman, Haldeman and presidential counsel John W. Dean III announced their resignations. "Work is continuing under various department heads," he stated.

But another White House aide told Congressional Quarterly the effect of the resignations depended on how often one had to deal with Ehrlichman or Haldeman. He said he personally was not affected greatly, but implied others were. The general feeling after Nixon's April 30 television address was that "we've got to get on with our business," he said. *(Nixon address text, p. 34)*

Still, there was evidence of a slowdown:

- Office of Management and Budget director Roy L. Ash said on "Face the Nation" April 29 that Watergate had delayed some executive decisions because it preempted the time of Ehrlichman and Haldeman. This was before they resigned.
- Meetings between the President and his economic advisers on the inflation subject, scheduled for April 25 and 28, were canceled as the President wrestled with the problem of what to do about Watergate.
- Ehrlichman and Haldeman, in their resignation letters, admitted that Watergate developments were taking up too much of their time.

The President quickly replaced Dean by naming his former law partner, Leonard Garment, to the counsel's post. But replacements for Haldeman and Ehrlichman, his long-time friends and advisers, will be more difficult to come by.

The President, in his statement on their resignations, described them as "two of my closest friends and most trusted assistants." *(Resignation letters, Nixon's statement, p. 36)*

Expected to move into positions of added importance in the White House, though not necessarily replacing Haldeman and Ehrlichman, are Ash, Garment, speech writer Patrick J. Buchanan, special counsel Richard A. Moore, and domestic council executive director Kenneth R. Cole. Nixon May 2 named Vice President Agnew vice-chairman of the domestic council (a new position; Agnew previously had been listed as a member). Ziegler said Agnew generally would have a "broadened role" in domestic policy formulation.

Despite stories that former cabinet members Robert Finch (HEW) and Melvin Laird (Defense) and others had offered their services to Nixon, Ziegler maintained that the President had had no discussions with them and had made no decisions on re-aligning his personal staff.

Beyond the White House, Nixon is faced with the task of selecting replacements for Elliot L. Richardson at Defense, William D. Ruckelshaus at the Environmental Protection Agency and L. Patrick Gray at the FBI. Ruckelshaus has been named acting director of the FBI, but says he won't stay at the job more than a month or two. Sub-cabinet jobs are also vacant.

Richardson: Third Cabinet Post

Elliot Lee Richardson, 52, who has served three months as secretary of defense, once told a reporter that "Every time I've spent some time on a job and I get to the point that I think I know what I'm talking about, somebody always makes me (another) offer."

President Nixon's announcement April 30 that Richardson would replace Richard Kleindienst as Attorney General and be given the responsibility for "uncovering the whole truth" about Watergate marked the third time in Richardson's career that he has been asked to assume a Nixon cabinet post. Only one other man in this century has served in as many cabinet posts under one President. (George Cortelyou served in three cabinet posts in Theodore Roosevelt's administration.)

The appointment of Richardson to the Justice Department came as a surprise. A Massachusetts lawyer with a wide range of government experience, Richardson's background differs from those of former high level Nixon aides.

Career in Government. Following his graduation from Harvard law school in 1947, Richardson chose to pursue a career in government and politics. He served as a law clerk to Supreme Court Justice Felix Frankfurter and was an assistant to Massachusetts Senator Leverett Saltonstall (R 1945-67) during the early 1950s.

In 1956, Richardson was appointed assistant secretary of the newly created department of Health, Education and Welfare by President Eisenhower. He left HEW in 1959 to become the U.S. Attorney for Massachusetts.

In his first bid for political office in 1962, Richardson was defeated in the Republican primary for state attorney general by Edward W. Brooke, who later was elected to the Senate and is now a close friend of Richardson's.

In 1964, Richardson was elected lieutenant governor of Massachusetts and, two years later, he was elected state attorney general.

Richardson joined the Nixon administration early in 1969. In the four years since, he has served as under secretary of state, secretary of HEW and, for three months in the second administration, as secretary of defense.

Richardson seldom attracted controversy in the first Nixon administration, assuming the role of a tactful spokesman for administration policies.

Nevertheless, he was reported to be close to resigning his HEW post in August 1971 after Nixon had disavowed a busing plan proposed by HEW for desegregation of the Austin, Texas public schools. But after a private meeting with the President, Richardson said Aug. 25 that they agreed that busing for the purpose of racial balance in schools could be educationally counterproductive and denied that he had considered resigning over the matter.

Garment: Representing Nixon

The official White House biography of Leonard Garment (no middle name) is brief—12 lines—and only three lines are devoted to his White House duties. But that biography is dated Dec. 2, 1972. The next one, when it's issued, undoubtedly will be more generous in content and job description.

Garment on April 30 emerged from relative obscurity to replace John W. Dean III as President Nixon's White House counsel and chief Watergate troubleshooter. The President said Garment "will represent the White House in all matters relating to the Watergate investigation and will report directly to me."

Garment is a liberal and a Jew in a conservative, Protestant, White House. Initially he was given little of significance to do. He spent four years as a special consultant to the President, assisting, as his biography states, "on a variety of various (sic) projects, with special emphasis on civil and human rights, voluntary action and the arts."

Nixon turned to Garment, 48, because he was a loyal friend and confidant, and—most importantly—he was not tainted by Watergate.

Nixon first met Garment when the President joined the Wall Street law firm of Mudge, Rose, Guthrie and Alexander in 1965. Garment had been with the firm since 1957 and was a partner and head of its litigation section when he and Nixon became acquainted.

Garment was born May 11, 1924, in Brooklyn, of immigrant parents. He attended Brooklyn College and graduated from its law school. An accomplished jazz clarinetist, he once played in Woody Herman's band.

Garment was one of Nixon's inner circle of associates in 1966 and 1967 when Nixon was gearing up for his 1968 try for the presidency. He worked primarily as a recruiter and, according to one account, suggested John N. Mitchell to Nixon as a possible campaign head.

After the campaign, Garment returned to his law firm, but joined the White House May 28, 1969. His liberal views and good relations with the press, however, kept him outside the corridors of power in the executive mansion.

Some of his assignments included liaison with black groups, war protestors and militant Indians. He reportedly objected to the nominations of Clement F. Haynsworth and G. Harrold Carswell to the Supreme Court, and to the firing of the Rev. Theodore Hesburgh from the chairmanship of the U.S. Commission on Civil Rights—all to no effect.

Ruckelshaus: 'Mr. Clean' to the FBI

Within hours of the resignation of acting FBI Director L. Patrick Gray III April 27, Nixon had chosen the man to fill that temporary post—William D. Ruckelshaus, chief of the two-year-old Environmental Protection Agency (EPA).

Ruckelshaus, whose mild-mannered demeanor and tough enforcement of federal anti-pollution laws have won him the nicknames of Clark Kent—Superman's alter-ego—and 'Mr. Clean', made clear that he was assuming the post only until a permanent director could be selected and confirmed, a process which he indicated should consume only a few months.

Gray had been named permanent director, but the nomination was withdrawn at his request, after his testimony before a Senate committee aroused concern about his lack of independence in the face of White House pressures and his involvement in the Watergate investigation.

Gray said that, ordered by Dean and Ehrlichman, he destroyed documents which included cables forged by E. Howard Hunt in an effort to link President Kennedy to the assassination of Ngo Dinh Diem.

To ensure that his performance at the FBI be free from political connotations, Ruckelshaus, who resigned April 30 from his EPA post, also renounced any ambitions to return to his homestate of Indiana to run for the Senate in 1974. Ruckelshaus came to the Nixon administration after an unsuccessful 1968 challenge to Sen. Birch Bayh (D Ind.), and it had been rumored that he was interested in a rematch in 1974.

Ruckelshaus assumed his third post in the Nixon administration with a solid reputation for independence, competence and skillful administration. As assistant attorney general, civil division, from 1969 until late 1970, he won commendation especially for his dealings with student demonstrators during the spring 1970 protests of the Cambodian incursion. As chief of the new environmental agency from late 1970 until his move to the FBI, Ruckelshaus demonstrated his independence of White House influence; reports were common—especially in 1972—of campaign officials' concern that the EPA was a little too vigorous in prosecuting polluting companies which were also Republican campaign contributors.

SCANDALS FOR HARDING, TRUMAN, EISENHOWER

Scandals involving cabinet officers or high level presidential assistants have shaken at least three previous administrations in this century. In contrast to the Watergate affair, the earlier affairs involved allegations of bribery or influence peddling for economic favors.

Presidents Warren G. Harding, Harry S Truman, and Dwight D. Eisenhower all faced crises involving alleged wrongdoing by those close to them. Harding died just as the massive scandals which became the hallmark of his administration were beginning to break into the open. His Vice President and successor, Calvin Coolidge, moved quickly to deal with the corruption and his actions have been credited with saving his new administration and the Republican Party from much of the onus.

But Presidents Truman and Eisenhower attempted for a time to defend their aides, thereby incurring political damage for seeming to be reluctant to take corrective actions. Republican promises to clean up the Truman administration's "mess in Washington" were used effectively in the 1952 presidential campaign. And the huge Democratic gains in the 1958 mid-term elections have been attributed in part to the influence-peddling charges made against President Eisenhower's chief assistant, Sherman Adams.

Key elements in all the scandals were vigorous congressional investigations and widespread press coverage.

Following is an account of the three major episodes of scandal in modern American political history.

Harding: Teapot Dome

The Harding administration scandals—which actually broke in full force after the President's death on Aug. 2, 1923—resulted in the resignations of Attorney General Harry M. Daugherty and Secretary of the Navy Edwin Denby, the dismissal of William J. Burns as head of the Bureau of Investigation (subsequently renamed the Federal Bureau of Investigation), and the later conviction and imprisonment of Secretary of the Interior Albert B. Fall.

The central scandal, known as Teapot Dome, involved leases of naval oil reserves. Congress in 1920 had enacted the General Leasing Act, which authorized the secretary of the Navy under certain conditions to lease naval oil reserves on public lands to private oil operators.

Harding on May 31, 1921, signed an executive order at the urging of Interior Secretary Fall and Navy Secretary Denby transferring jurisdiction over the naval oil reserves from the Navy to the Interior Department. Then, early in 1922, Fall leased the Elk Hills reserve in California to Edward L. Doheny of the Pan-American Petroleum and Transport Company and the Teapot Dome reserve in Wyoming to Harry F. Sinclair's Mammoth Oil Company. The leases were granted without public notice or competitive bidding.

When Senate hearings opened on Oct. 25, 1923, they concentrated at first on the legality and expediency of the two leases. Then Sen. Thomas J. Walsh (D Mont. 1913-33) began probing the sudden wealth of former Interior Secretary Fall, who had resigned in March 1923. The investigation revealed that Fall had accepted bribes from Doheny and Sinclair. Doheny had given Fall at least $100,000 and Sinclair had given the interior secretary at least $300,000. Fall was later convicted of accepting a bribe in connection with the Elk Hills lease and was sentenced to prison and fined $100,000.

Fall became the first cabinet officer to serve a prison term for illegal activities connected with government service. Navy Secretary Denby also resigned, but was never charged with criminal acts.

Justice Department Inaction. The Justice Department also came under fire for its handling of Teapot Dome. Attorney General Harry M. Daugherty's failure to prosecute Fall, Sinclair, Doheny and others led President Coolidge on March 28, 1924, to demand Daugherty's resignation.

To replace Daugherty as attorney general, Coolidge appointed Harlan Fiske Stone, former dean of Columbia University's Law School, with instructions to clean up the Justice Department. Stone later went on to become an associate justice of the United States Supreme Court, and served as chief justice from 1941 to 1946.

One of Stone's first moves as attorney general was to revamp the Bureau of Investigation. William J. Burns, founder of the detective agency that bears his name, was serving as head of the bureau. Stone later wrote, "When I became attorney general, the Bureau of Investigation was...in exceedingly bad odor.... The head of the Bureau...had himself participated in serious infractions of the law and obstructions of justice." As a replacement, Stone appointed the young assistant director, J. Edgar Hoover.

References on Scandals

Adams, Samuel Hopkins, *Incredible Era: The Life and Times of Warren G. Harding,* 1939.

Congressional Quarterly, *Guide to the Congress of the United States,* 1971.

Noggle, Burl, *Teapot Dome: Oil and Politics in the 1920s,* 1965.

Phillips, Cabell, *The Truman Presidency: The History of a Triumphant Succession,* 1966.

Russell, Francis, *The Shadow of Blooming Grove: Warren G. Harding in His Times,* 1968.

Truman: Vaughan and Caudle

The last years of President Harry S Truman's administration were rocked by a series of scandals involving White House aides and Justice Department officials. The abrupt dismissal of Attorney General J. Howard McGrath and his replacement by Federal Judge James P. McGranery of Philadelphia in the spring of 1952 was the most dramatic event in a string of events that began in 1949.

The first Truman aide to come to public attention in connection with possible wrongdoing was Gen. Harry Vaughan, the President's military aide as well as a personal friend. Charges were made before a special Senate investigating subcommittee that Vaughan had used his influence to gain quick action on a number of

"In this job I am not worried about my enemies. It is my friends that are keeping me awake nights."

Warren G. Harding, 1923

projects for clients of friends. Vaughan came under congressional fire for accepting a present of a deep freeze from a Chicago company, a gift that became widely used by editorial cartoonists as a symbol of corruption in Washington. Despite the allegations, Vaughan remained in Truman's favor throughout the administration.

A second scandal involved the Reconstruction Finance Corporation (RFC) and Donald Dawson, special assistant to President Truman for personnel affairs. The RFC, established in 1932 under the Hoover administration to provide easy credit terms to failing businesses, was kept going after World War II as a hedge against a possible recession. A subcommittee of the Senate Banking and Currency Committee headed by freshman Sen. J. William Fulbright (D) of Arkansas cited Dawson as wielding undue influence on who received loans from the RFC. No criminal charges were brought, and like Vaughan, Dawson was kept on in the White House despite implications of questionable activities.

The most serious corruption in Truman's presidency, and the one which led to large-scale resignations and eventual jail terms for some of those implicated, involved the Justice Department and the Bureau of Internal Revenue (now known as the Internal Revenue Service). Among the senior officials implicated in charges of fixing tax cases were T. Lamar Caudle, assistant attorney general in charge of the Tax Division; Charles Oliphant, general counsel to the Bureau of Internal Revenue; George J. Schoenman, Internal Revenue Commissioner; Joseph Nunan, a former Internal Revenue Commissioner; Jess Larson, chief of the General Services Administration, and Matthew H. Connelly, Truman's appointments secretary. Much of the evidence in the cases was uncovered by a special investigating subcommittee of the House Ways and Means Committee. Altogether, 66 persons in the Bureau of Internal Revenue and the Justice Department were ousted, and nine—including Caudle and Connelly—ended up in prison.

In the face of these charges, Truman appointed Attorney General McGrath to head a cleanup drive. Truman's announcement met with opposition because McGrath was a former chairman of the Democratic National Committee (1947-49) and was the head of the Justice Department when much of the alleged activity had occurred. The House Judiciary Committee reacted by voting to investigate McGrath and the Justice Department.

Independent Prosecutor Appointed. Truman finally appointed Newbold Morris, a prominent liberal Republican lawyer from New York, as a special prosecutor. When McGrath and Morris feuded, the attorney general let the special prosecutor go, and was in turn fired by Truman. Truman brought in Judge McGranery as his new attorney general, but no successor to Morris was named. The Justice Department's handling of the case, concluded a House Judiciary subcommittee, raised "additional doubts in the public mind as to the honesty of those in public office."

Eisenhower: Sherman Adams

In 1958, President Eisenhower's White House chief of staff, Sherman Adams, stood accused of interference in the activities of federal regulatory agencies. The controversy culminated in Adams' resignation.

On Feb. 17, 1958, evidence was presented to a special House Legislative Oversight Subcommittee that Adams had attempted to influence a case pending before the Civil Aeronautics Board in 1953. On May 26, the subcommittee heard testimony regarding a 1953 letter sent by then FCC Chairman Rosel H. Hyde to Adams reporting on the status of contests for TV licenses in St. Louis, Mo., and Flint, Mich.

Then on June 5, acting Chairman John Bell Williams (D Miss. 1947-68) said the subcommittee had authenticated information that Adams had occupied hotel rooms in Boston paid for by Bernard Goldfine, a Boston textile magnate who was involved in cases before the Federal Trade Commission and the Securities and Exchange Commission. Revelations followed concerning gifts of a $700 vicuna coat and a $2,400 oriental rug Adams had received from Goldfine.

Press coverage of the relationship between Adams and Goldfine prompted President Eisenhower to issue a statement of support for Adams on June 18, 1958. While admitting that Adams may have been "imprudent" in his relations with Goldfine, the President said Adams was an "invaluable public servant, doing a difficult job efficiently, honestly, and tirelessly." "I need him," the President said.

But the furor did not subside. Republicans concerned about the impact of the Adams affair on the upcoming mid-term election began voicing their fears. Senate Republican leader William F. Knowland (R Calif. 1945-59) said Adams "has so hurt his usefulness in his position that it will be harmful to the broad policies" of the President.

Rep. Richard M. Simpson (R Pa.), chairman of the Republican Congressional Campaign Committee, said Adams' activities "can only be harmful" to the GOP at election time.

Throughout the summer, the subcommittee's investigations continued to keep the case in the public mind.

On September 22, 1958, Adams resigned his position in a nationwide radio and television address. He said he "must give full consideration to the effect of (his) continuing presence on the public scene." He referred to "a campaign of vilification by those who seek personal advantage by my removal from public life." Adams said testimony before the subcommittee had established that he had done "no wrong."

President Eisenhower, in a letter accepting his assistant's resignation, commended Adams for his "selfless and tireless devotion to the work of the White House and to me personally...."

Goldfine served a jail sentence for contempt of court and income tax evasion. Adams continued to deny any wrongdoing and retired to New Hampshire. No charges were ever pressed against him.

"The trouble with Republicans is that when they get in trouble they start acting like cannibals."

Richard M. Nixon, 1958

WATERGATE: INDICTMENTS, HIGH-LEVEL REORGANIZATION

Two former Republican cabinet officers were indicted for obstructing justice. President Nixon ordered a major reorganization of his top advisers. The Pentagon Papers trial in Los Angeles ended in a mistrial, and all charges were dismissed after disclosures that one of the defendants had been wiretapped by the FBI and that the records of the taps had been destroyed. A Senate select committee was preparing to start public hearings on 1972 campaign activities.

These were some of the events surrounding the Watergate scandal during the week ended May 12. Highlights:

• A federal grand jury in New York City May 10 indicted four men, including former Attorney General John N. Mitchell and former Secretary of Commerce Maurice H. Stans. Mitchell was President Nixon's re-election campaign manager for three months in 1972. Stans is chairman of the Finance Committee to Re-elect the President, which continues to exist.

Mitchell and Stans were accused of obstructing justice by interfering with a federal investigation and lying to the grand jury. They were charged with obtaining a secret $200,000 cash contribution to the Nixon campaign in return for promises to intercede with the government on behalf of the contributor, financier Robert L. Vesco, who already was in trouble with the Securities and Exchange Commission (SEC) over an alleged mutual fund swindle.

Committee's Mandate

Following is the language of Section 1 (a) of S Res 60, the resolution creating the committee usually referred to as the Senate select committee on the Watergate:

"(Resolved), That there is hereby established a select committee of the Senate, which may be called, for convenience of expression, the Select Committee on Presidential Campaign Activities, to conduct an investigation and study of the extent, if any, to which illegal, improper, or unethical activities were engaged in by any persons, acting either individually or in combination with others, in the presidential election of 1972, or in any related campaign or canvass conducted by or in behalf of any person seeking nomination or election as the candidate of any political party for the office of President of the United States in such election, and to determine whether in its judgment any occurrences which may be revealed by the investigation and study indicate the necessity or desirability of the enactment of new congressional legislation to safeguard the electoral process by which the President of the United States is chosen."

Vesco, a New Jerseyite who left the United States two months before the grand jury indictment, also was indicted, along with Harry L. Sears, a New Jersey lawyer and Republican politician. They were charged with attempting to obstruct the SEC investigation.

If convicted of all charges, Mitchell and Stans each could be sentenced to 50 years in prison and fined $85,000. Vesco and Sears, if convicted of all charges, could be sent to prison for 20 years each and fined $25,000. The four were scheduled to enter pleas on May 21. All but Vesco issued denials of the charges.

• As a result of White House resignations and firings resulting from the Watergate affair, the President brought his former treasury secretary, John B. Connally, back to the administration as an unpaid, part-time presidential adviser on foreign and domestic matters. James R. Schlesinger, director of the Central Intelligence Agency (CIA), was nominated to be secretary of defense. William E. Colby, CIA deputy director for operations, was nominated to succeed Schlesinger. J. Fred Buzhardt Jr., the Defense Department's general counsel, was named special counsel to Nixon to handle all Watergate matters affecting the White House. *(Story, p. 60)*

• In the Pentagon Papers trial, all charges of espionage, theft and conspiracy against Daniel Ellsberg and Anthony J. Russo were dismissed on May 11 by Judge W. Matthew Byrne of U.S. District Court in Los Angeles. Byrne said he was both dismissing the charges and declaring a mistrial because of government misconduct. *(Text, p. 70)*

Byrne said the misconduct began early in the trial but culminated in the involvement of White House officials and Watergate conspirators in the burglary of Ellsberg's psychiatrist's office and in the May 10 disclosure of an FBI wiretap on Ellsberg's telephone. "The conduct of the government has placed this case in such a posture it precludes the fair and dispassionate consideration of issues by the jury," he said. His decision, he added, was influenced by the "bizarre events" revealed in the last two weeks of the trial.

The judge had suspended the trial on May 10 and ordered prosecutors to supply full details of the surveillance of Ellsberg.

• The Senate select committee on the Watergate, chaired by Sam J. Ervin Jr. (D N.C.), scheduled its first public hearings for May 17. Ervin on May 10 called the hearings "the most important investigation ever entrusted to the Congress."

But the hearings were to begin against a background of increasing friction between the investigators for the Senate committee and the prosecutors working on the Watergate grand jury investigation. *The New York Times* quoted a source close to the prosecutors as saying, "The Senate is dismantling the criminal case before our eyes." Samuel Dash, chief counsel to the Senate committee, was

Executive Privilege Guidelines

The following statement on executive privilege was issued by the White House on May 3:

"The President desires that the invocation of Executive Privilege be held to a minimum. Specifically:

"1. Past and present members of the President's staff questioned by the FBI, the Ervin Committee, or a Grand Jury should invoke the privilege only in connection with conversations with the President, conversations among themselves (involving communications with the President) and as to Presidential papers. Presidential papers are all documents produced or received by the President or any member of the White House staff in connection with his official duties.

"2. Witnesses are restricted from testifying as to matters relating to national security not by executive privilege, but by laws prohibiting the disclosure of classified information (e.g., some of the incidents which gave rise to concern over leaks). The applicability of such laws should therefore be determined by each witness and his own counsel.

"3. White House Counsel will not be present at FBI interviews or at the Grand Jury, and, therefore, will not invoke the privilege in the first instance. (If a dispute as to privilege arises between a witness and the FBI or the Grand Jury, the matter may be referred to White House Counsel for a statement of the President's position."

The following supplement to the May 3 memorandum was issued on May 4:

"White House Counsel will be present at informal interviews of White House personnel by Ervin Committee Staff, but only for the purpose of observing and taking notes. Privilege will be invoked by White House Counsel, if at all, only in connection with formal hearings before the Ervin Committee."

quoted as saying, "I'm cooperating with them. You ask if they're cooperating with us."

One source of friction was the committee's decision on May 8 to subpoena former White House counsel John W. Dean III in return for a grant of immunity from further prosecution for him. A day earlier, it was reported, federal prosecutors had decided not to give him immunity because they felt it was unnecessary to their case.

Another problem confronting the Senate committee is the prospective appearance of indicted persons. Stans and Mitchell are on the list of the first 20 prospective witnesses, and more indictments are expected eventually to come out of the Watergate grand jury investigation. *(Witness list, p. 57)*

"There's no law that says we can't subpoena a man to testify who's been indicted, and in some cases we might," Sen. Howard H. Baker Jr. (R Tenn.), vice chairman of the committee, told Congressional Quarterly on May 7. "But there is an appeal to reason, an appeal to the sensibilities, that would make it very difficult for us to decide to subpoena a man who'd been indicted on a criminal charge and not yet tried."

Late Developments. There were these other late developments in the Watergate scandal:

- Former counsel Dean, fired by Nixon on April 30, issued a statement through his lawyer on May 10 denying that he had been the source of earlier news reports that he was prepared to testify Nixon knew about the alleged Watergate coverup. (Further investigation found the Dean assertion to be inaccurate, *The New York Times* reported on May 10.)

Dean's statement said he was "not willing to see the truth distorted further, nor am I willing to shoulder the blame for those unwilling to accept the truth." He said he was "very aware that there is an ongoing effort to limit or prevent my testifying fully and freely." And he said he had learned from friends "that there is a concerted effort to 'get me.' "

- Charles W. Colson, former special counsel to Nixon, said he was told twice by John D. Ehrlichman, the President's former chief assistant for domestic affairs, and once by Dean to keep quiet about the burglary of the office of Ellsberg's psychiatrist.

Colson's statement was part of an interview with the FBI on May 8. The statement was made available to defense attorneys in the Pentagon Papers trial on May 10.

- Hugh W. Sloan Jr., former treasurer of the President's re-election finance committee, said under oath that he had repeatedly warned in 1972 that re-election committee officials might have been involved in the Watergate bugging and its coverup. Sloan also said he had expressed concern over the use of large sums of money given to G. Gordon Liddy, one of the conspirators. The statement was contained in a pretrial deposition given by Sloan in civil suits arising from the Watergate affair. It was made public on May 10.
- Quoting sources familiar with the operation, *The New York Times* May 11 said the Nixon administration had, for a two-year period starting in 1969, tapped the phones of reporters and government officials in an attempt to discover the sources of security leaks. Three newspapers were mentioned: The Times, *The Sunday Times of London* and *The Washington Post.*

Baker Interview. In his interview with Congressional Quarterly, Sen. Baker played down the interrelationship of the Senate investigating committee and other Watergate investigations conducted by the FBI and grand juries. "I don't think they interrelate at all," he said. "They're parallel and complementary."

He noted the "marked distinctions between the judicial and the executive undertakings," starting with the presumption of innocence in a court trial. "Obviously," he said, "we (the committee) aren't going to start with the presumption of guilt. But we also don't start with any presumption of innocence. We just start on a fact-finding expedition to find out what the facts are."

The goal of the committee, Baker continued, is to try to "string together the subject matter and to present a coherent story and to produce a mosaic from all this that will identify faces and things and places." From the investigation, he said, he expects legislative recommendations to emerge that will prevent future Watergates.

Baker said the committee will be "the most effective forum for the presentation of coherent and sequential declamation of what happened in all this." The committee will, he thinks, "have a far wider range of opportunities than the courts or the executive, to be free of the responsibility to determine guilt or innocence, to probe assertions and allegations for whatever they may be worth."

In an indirect reference to the other investigations, Baker said the Senate committee is "doing the most thorough job in town, and clearly the most even-handed job in town." Information leaks left something to be desired when the committee staff began its work, he acknowledged, "but I'm not even upset about that. This committee is doing an extraordinarily good job. Our work product is going to be the best product of our performance, so let's just wait and see how it works."

Sources on the committee staff said the staff now has 35 employees, including Samuel Dash, the majority counsel, and Fred D. Thompson, the minority counsel. Baker said that a much larger staff would be necessary only if information from previous investigations had to be retraced, and "I see no evidence of that."

But, Baker added, "I don't exclude that possibility in some instances, not because I'm being critical of the FBI but because some of the material may be so important that it simply has to be retracked. But right now, I don't see the necessity to staff up for a brand-new, independent investigation. I think that we can, by and large, depend on the rather voluminous body of information that's already been assembled."

In the beginning, at least, Baker said that partisanship among members of the seven-member committee—four Democrats and three Republicans—is "totally absent." He would not speculate on whether or not it would remain absent. "It would be the political miracle of the century if we could keep it completely absent, but it's a minor miracle that it's absent at this point."

There is a great incentive to keep partisanship out of the committee proceedings, Baker said. "The Republicans have got a lot more to gain by getting this thing ventilated and cleared up than the Democrats do, really."

Still unresolved by the committee is the question of making FBI files available to all seven members. The original agreement was that the files would be available to Ervin, Baker and the Democratic and Republican counsels. This agreement, worked out with the FBI, angered some other members of the committee, who felt they should have the same access as the chairman and vice chairman.

Baker said he thought the problem would be resolved by giving all seven members equal access. He does not want to see any "raw" FBI files of unprocessed investigative data, he added, but does not have the same misgivings about FBI summaries. He indicated that he would not like to have everyone on the committee going through raw data.

"I have confidence that the committee will treat it with utmost and highest confidence," Baker said of the data. He has urged both committee members and staff to keep records if they do see raw data, in order to protect themselves in the event of future leakage of information.

Committee Procedures. The Senate committee, under the resolution creating it (S Res 60), has until Feb. 28, 1974, to finish its job. Baker and others said they expect the first round of hearings to last three or four weeks. Two other rounds are expected later in 1973. *(Committee mandate, box p. 46)*

The hearings will be held mornings and afternoons three days a week. Between hearings, the investigative staff will continue its compilation of information.

Witnesses will be heard in public, in front of television cameras. More than 100 are on the list already, and the list continues to grow. The full list has not been released because, in Baker's words, "You start bandying about names of people who are going to be witnesses or people who aren't going to be witnesses, you end up inevitably with an implication that they are or are not involved, and I'm determined not to do that."

Baker and other committee members are also determined to maintain as much decorum as possible in what is bound to be the best-publicized congressional hearing in years. The caucus room in the Russell Senate Office Building, where the hearings will be conducted, is the site of many a past flamboyant performance.

"We're not out to produce a TV spectacular," said Baker. "We're not there to see who can have Martha Mitchell first. We're not there to see who can get Ehrlichman and Haldeman before the TV cameras first. Contrary to what is suggested from time to time in the press, we literally are not in a race with anybody."

The nerve center of the committee's pre-hearings investigation is a small, crowded suite of offices in a narrow corridor of the Dirksen Senate Office Building. A hand-written request is stuck to the door: "Please knock." Below that is an apologetic letter from Chairman Ervin explaining that the committee's "crowded condition" and the "highly sensitive nature of its work" require newsmen to wait in the hall.

The rapid buildup of the staff has led to some makeshift arrangements. Part of the staff is working in an old residence behind the Senate office buildings. Secre-

(Continued on p. 50)

'New Majority' Dinner

Despite a speech by President Nixon, the Republican "New Majority" fund-raising dinner May 9 in Washington, D.C., fell far short of expectations and far short of past fund-raising goals. Sponsors of the annual event—the party's Senate, House and national committee's campaign finance committees—said the $1,000-a-plate banquet brought in gross receipts of $750,000, with expectations of a net of some $600,000.

Officials estimated the crowd at 1,500, of whom about 500 had been given complimentary tickets to fill the large ballroom at the Washington Hilton hotel.

In his 15-minute speech, the President pledged that Attorney General-designate Elliot L. Richardson and his special prosecutor "will have the total cooperation of the executive branch of this government" in investigating the Watergate scandal. "They will get to the bottom of this thing. They will see to it that all of those who are guilty are prosecuted and are brought to justice." *(Text, p. 49)*

WATERGATE SPEECH

Following is a text of excerpts from President Nixon's speech to a May 9 Republican fund-raising dinner in Washington, as recorded by ABC News. (Background on dinner, p. 38)

I have been hearing that this would be less than an enthusiastic dinner tonight; and I must say that you have proved that perhaps the critics were wrong.

Now as is always my custom before speaking before any audience, such a distinguished group as this, I ask the chairman what I should talk about. And it just happened this afternoon I met with the chairman—Chairman (George) Bush...and we had a discussion about this dinner tonight and what you would like to hear about.

You've already heard the Vice President praise the accomplishments of the Administration and so for me to add to that would simply be, of course, adding praise for what he says I have done; but which you have made possible. And all of us working together have made possible.

And I will have something to say about that as I conclude tonight.

But it's always been my practice before any kind of an audience to take on those subjects that some people think you don't want to take on because they're difficult ones.

Let me say, I didn't get where I am by ducking tough issues. And I believe—

I'm keenly aware of the fact that many Americans—everybody in this room, for example—are concerned about the developments that we've been reading about and hearing about in recent weeks and recent months. I expressed my concern just a few days ago on national television. I will not add to what I said then except to make some comments that I think are quite appropriate at this time.

Challenge

In the American political process one of the most difficult tasks of all comes when charges are made against high officials in an Administration. That's a very great test of an Administration and many times in the history of our country, Administrations have failed to meet the test of investigating those charges that might be embarrassing to the Administration because they were made against high officials in an Administration.

We have had such a situation, we have been confronted with it, we are dealing with it, and I will simply say to you tonight that this nation—Republicans, Democrats, Independents, all Americans—can have confidence in the fact that the General, Elliot Richardson, and the special prosecutor that he will appoint in this case will have the total cooperation of the executive branch of this Government.

They will get to the bottom of this thing. They will see to it that all of those who are guilty are prosecuted and are brought to justice. That is the pledge I make tonight, and that I think the American people are entitled to it.

But I would add that the place where that should happen is in the courts of law. Charges are these days made rather easily, as we know, in our political process, and there is sometimes a tendency for us to convict the innocent in our own mind before they have the opportunity to be heard—before they had the opportunity, even if charges are made, to be tried. And let us resolve tonight that until we hear the evidence, until those who had been charged have had a change to present their case in a court of law, let's uphold the great American tradition that an individual even a government official, is innocent until he's proven guilty.

I also want to add a word with regard to what all this is goint to mean to the next three-and-a-half and a bit more years that we have in office as a result of the election last November.

I can assure that we will get to the bottom of this very deplorable incident. We should do everything that we can to develop new legislative tools which will deal with this kind of abuse and other abuses as practiced too often in many campaigns by both parties over the years.

But the most important thing I want to say tonight is this: We are not going to allow this deplorable incident to deter us or deflect from going forward toward achieving the great goals that an overwhelming majority of the American people elected us to achieve in November of 1972.

We received the greatest popular majority in history for a good reason. The American people had a clear choice. And the same reasons and the same choice exist today as it did exist then. And when we look at those goals, some of which the Vice President has referred to so eloquently, when we look at those goals, it is our responsibility at this time to go forward now and achieve them. And that is what we do intend to do.

And I can assure you that whether it's at a Cabinet meeting that we will be having in the morning, or whether it's a meeting with legislative leaders that we will be having next week, that you can be sure the business of your Government is going forward and we're going to make the next four years better than the last four years—and that's something Americans are entitled to.

Peace

As you know, in a few weeks I shall probably be meeting with the leader of the Soviet Union in the return visit that he will be making to the United States.

And as the Vice President has indicated, we have had great progress over the past year, particularly in trying to work toward not just ending a war that had gone on much too long—12 years as a matter of fact—but in building a more peaceful world so that, for example, the leaders of one-fourth of all the people in the world wouldn't be out there isolated from the rest of the world, with the danger of a confrontation 15 to 20 years from now being inherited by our children....

What I would like to say to you, my friends, is this: Every individual, I'm sure, who occupies the office of the President tries to think of one thing he wants more than anything else. And I could name many goals tonight that I want more than anything else.

But, more important than anything else for the present President of the United States is the goal of building a new structure of peace in the world. And the reason that is the most important role is that unless the President of the United States, backed by the people of the United States, and the Congress, takes the leadership in this field, we will not have peace. That is the truth of the matter.

Because there is no other free nation that is strong enough, and there is no other group of nations that has the will to provide that leadership.

We have tried to meet that responsibility over the past four years. And we have made progress. We are going to continue to make it—meet that responsibility over the next three and a half years. As I have indicated.

But in order to meet it, it is essential that we concentrate our minds and our hearts and our souls and our energy toward achieving that goal, as well as the others that I mentioned in my speech a few days ago and that the Vice President referred to in his introduction today.

And that brings me to a personal note, referring to everybody here. I have had, as you know, some political ups and downs my 27 years in politics; and I have known times when I wondered if I had very many friends. And every man or woman who has been in politics knows that when you win, they're all your friends, and when you lose, it's pretty hard to find them except when you lose and they're still there, they're the real friends.

Let me say, I don't stand here tonight as a loser. We stand here tonight as winners and we're going to win again.

Poll Report

The Harris Survey conducted a telephone poll of 892 persons nationwide on May 1-3 to measure public reaction to President Nixon's April 30 television address. *(Earlier poll report, p. 29)*

These were among the survey's findings:

- Do you "think President Nixon should resign?" No, 77 per cent; yes, 13 per cent.
- Do you think Nixon "has lost so much credibility that it will be hard for him to be an effective President again?" Yes, 54 per cent; no, 37 per cent.
- Do you feel that "there are so many unanswered questions still left about Watergate that only a completely independent investigation of the affair by people not controlled by the President will get at the truth?" Yes, 78 per cent; no, 14 per cent.
- Do you think Attorney General-designate Elliot Richardson, who is in charge of the investigation, "will really get at the truth?" Yes, 41 per cent; no, 29 per cent.
- Do you agree with the statement that "President Nixon still has most of his second term in the White House to go, so it is best to give him the benefit of the doubt in the Watergate bugging and the coverup."? Agree, 59 per cent; disagree, 31 per cent.
- Seventy per cent of the public watched or listened to the speech. Of those who did, 41 per cent gave the President a positive rating and 36 per cent gave him a negative rating.

Nixon Popularity. On the eve of the President's speech, the Gallup Poll completed a survey that showed Nixon's popularity matching his all-time low of 48 per cent. It was down 20 points from its high point in January after he announced the Vietnam peace settlement. The Gallup sample was asked: "Do you approve or disapprove of the way Mr. Nixon is handling his job as President?"

Approve	48%
Disapprove	40
No opinion	12

The same poll also found the Watergate scandal to be damaging Republican prospects in the off-year elections of 1974. This question was asked persons who said they had heard or read about Watergate: "Does the Watergate affair make you less likely than before to vote for a Republican candidate in next year's congressional election, or not?"

Yes, less likely	31%
No	56
No opinion	13

taries are banging on typewriters in the Dirksen building's auditorium.

All this is being done on a budget of $500,000—a figure that persons involved in the investigation admit may have to be supplemented before the committee completes its job.

Daily Chronology

Following is a day-to-day chronology of the week's events:

MAY 4

Ellsberg Burglary. E. Howard Hunt, a convicted Watergate conspirator, told a federal grand jury that White House and Central Intelligence Agency (CIA) officials paid for and supervised the September 1971 burglary of the office of Daniel Ellsberg's former psychiatrist. Ellsberg is one of two defendants in the Pentagon Papers trial.

Hunt said in testimony released by U.S. District Court in Los Angeles that the project was supervised by Egil (Bud) Krogh, then an assistant to John D. Ehrlichman, chief domestic affairs adviser to the President. Hunt, a former CIA agent, told the grand jury of a scheme wherein the CIA provided logistical aid, disguises and equipment used in breaking into the Beverly Hills office of Dr. Lewis Fielding. *(Krogh biography, box p. 52; texts of CIA memos, p. 59; earlier story, p. 20)*

Dean Files. Former White House Counsel John W. Dean III asked Chief U.S. District Judge John G. Sirica of Washington, D.C., to accept custody of nine documents Dean said were related to the Watergate affair. Lawyers for Dean turned over to the court two keys to safe deposit boxes in which Dean placed the documents. White House sources were quoted as saying that Dean believed the documents contained circumstantial evidence that H. R. Haldeman, former White House chief of staff, and Ehrlichman directed a coverup of the Watergate affair.

Executive Privilege. New White House guidelines on the use of executive privilege were issued the day after Haldeman and Ehrlichman testified before the Watergate grand jury in Washington. The former White House assistants spent a total of seven hours testifying. The new guidelines ordered that use of executive privilege be kept to a minimum; this position contrasted with earlier White House refusal to allow present and former members of the executive branch to testify.

Secret Campaign Funds. Hugh W. Sloan Jr., former treasurer of the Finance Committee to Re-elect the President, said in a deposition that a secret cash fund of $1-million to $2-million in campaign contributions was never reported publicly. The deposition was taken in connection with a civil suit filed by Common Cause against the President's re-election committee to force disclosure of contributors' names. Sloan said he had destroyed a book recording the source of the contributions prior to April 7, 1972, the effective date of a new federal law ordering public reports of campaign finances, in order to protect the anonymity of the donors. *(Story, p. 21)*

A bench warrant was issued for financier Robert L. Vesco to force him to appear before a federal grand jury in New York that is probing fraud allegations and a secret $200,000 donation he made to the Nixon campaign. *The New York Times* reported that Vesco wanted a special independent prosecutor and total immunity before he would testify. *(p. 25)*

MAY 5

Krogh Role. Former White House aide Egil Krogh took full responsibility for the September 1971 burglary

(Continued on p. 52)

The Press and Watergate: How Fair Has It Been?

The role of the press in covering the Watergate scandal came in for both praise and censure during the week ended May 12. Of greatest significance was the award of a Pulitzer Prize to *The Washington Post* for its leadership in the coverage. But the same day the prizes were announced, the Vice President, several senators and a leading political columnist were among those who had critical things to say about the performance of the press.

Pulitzer Award. The Post won a gold medal "for a distinguished example of meritorious service" from the trustees of Columbia University, who issue the Pulitzer Prizes. "*The Washington Post* from the outset refused to dismiss the Watergate incident as a bad political joke, a mere caper," said the material accompanying the award, announced May 8.

"It mobilized its total resources for a major investigation, spearheaded by two first-rate investigative reporters, Carl Bernstein and Robert Woodward. As their disclosures developed the Watergate case into a major political scandal of national proportions, the Post backed them up with strong editorials, many of them written by Roger Wilkins, and editorial cartoons drawn by the two-time Pulitzer Prize winner, Herbert A . Block (Herblock)."

Agnew Criticism. Vice President Agnew, long an outspoken critic of media performance, attacked some of the press, including the Post, on May 8 in a speech at the University of Virginia in Charlottesville. While acknowledging a contribution from "some elements of the press," he went on to say that the contribution had been "overblown by self-adulating rhetoric."

Among Agnew's complaints, according to the news coverage of his speech, were these: Some of the media had "transgressed the boundaries of propriety"...it is a "very short jump to McCarthyistic techniques from What's going on now"...some of the press has been guilty of "double hearsay," "undisclosed source rumor" and "character assassination."

Proxmire Attack. Democrat William Proxmire, the man who replaced the late Republican Joseph McCarthy as the senator from Wisconsin, took the Senate floor on May 8 to denounce "the McCarthyistic destruction of President Nixon that is now going on with increasing vehemence daily in the in the press." While giving the media credit for doing "a tremendous job in covering one of the most important scandals in American history," Proxmire, a former newspaperman, said that some statements about Nixon had become "grossly unfair" to the President.

Sen. William Proxmire

Proxmire was especially critical of reports that former White House counsel John W. Dean III had privately charged the President with being directly involved in a coverup of Watergate. "President Nixon is being tried, sentenced and executed by rumor and allegation," said Proxmire. Such unattributed information—"a reckless momentum of reporting innuendo and rumor," Proxmire called it—"may well have gone a long way toward destroying the President of the United States," he said.

Scott, Mansfield. Proxmire was joined by the Senate's two floor leaders, Republican Hugh Scott (Pa.) and Democrat Mike Mansfield (Mont.). "The media, when they are responsible, are the finest press in the world," said Scott. "But when they ride momentum and suddenly decide that a whisper can be turned into a charge, or a rumor into a fact, or a wrongful deed by one person into an alleged wrongful deed by another, up to that point unconnected, then the media are acting irresponsibly as well."

Mansfield noted that "rumors and innuendos flourish and take hold. From the seed comes plants of various kinds. But rumors, innuendos and the like are not facts, and the innocence or guilt of any individual involved in this messy, sordid situation will have to be determined on that basis and that basis only."

Reston's Rebuttal. *New York Times* columnist James Reston, in his column May 9, challenged Proxmire to come up with a solution to stem the flow from the "underground geyser" of Watergate information.

"There is obviously a serious problem here," he wrote, "but it raises some fundamental questions: Would this scandal have reached the present point of disclosure if the press had not reported the secret testimony of witnesses in this case? Is a government which had knowledge of this kind of political espionage and sabotage, and then tried to conceal the facts, entitled to bar reporters from getting beyond the screen of secrecy?"

Broder's Advice. Another columnist to discuss the issue of the press and Watergate was David S. Broder, a political reporter for *The Washington Post*, who had just won a Pulitzer Prize for his 1972 commentary.

Broder was critical in his May 8 column of his Washington colleagues for their general failure to pursue the Watergate story. He quoted Ben H. Bagdikian, a press critic who had told the newspaper editors' convention in Washington the week before that no more than 14 of the 2,200 regularly employed reporters in the capital "did any substantial work on the Watergate case, and the number of publications that pursued it with any vigor can be counted on one hand."

Broder remarked that only nine easily deflected questions about campaign practices had been asked the President at press conferences between the break-in and the White House resignations. He called for the revival of the presidential press conference "—a vital, irreplaceable institution—which the press itself has allowed to wither into disuse under the antagonism of the last two Presidents."

Egil Krogh Jr.

Egil (Bud) Krogh Jr., 33, was one of the bright young men the White House placed in various departments and agencies in order to make the federal bureaucracy more responsive to President Nixon's leadership during his second term. He took indefinite leave from his job as under secretary of transportation May 2 and resigned May 9. In his letter of resignation, Krogh took "full responsibility" for the burglary of Daniel Ellsberg's psychiatrist's office by two Watergate conspirators.

Krogh joined the White House in May 1969 as an aide to then presidential counsel John D. Ehrlichman, for whom he had worked briefly in a Seattle law firm. He followed Ehrlichman to the domestic council in 1970 and worked in areas such as transportation, narcotics control, corrections, legal services and District of Columbia affairs.

President Nixon nominated Krogh as transportation under secretary in December 1972. Krogh was born Aug. 3, 1939, in Chicago. He graduated from Principia College, Elsah, Ill., in 1961, served in the Navy from 1962 to 1965 and graduated from the University of Washington law school in 1968.

Krogh was named by Ehrlichman as a participant in a White House-ordered probe of Pentagon Papers leaks involving Ellsberg. He took leave after Transportation Secretary Claude S. Brinegar urged him to publicly explain his role in the burglary. Krogh wrote in his letter of resignation to the President that he acted without knowledge of any superior. He admitted making an error of judgment.

David R. Young

David Young, 36, was assigned, with Krogh, to investigate the Pentagon Papers leak. He resigned as a presidential assistant on the domestic council, headed by Ehrlichman, April 30.

A lawyer, Young joined the White House Jan. 5, 1970, as an assistant on Henry A. Kissinger's national security council staff. He was detailed July 1, 1971, to the domestic council to help conduct a study of document classification procedures.

According to Kissinger, Young remained on the domestic council—although he was being paid by national security council funds—because of a greater interest in domestic affairs. Young was born Nov. 10, 1936.

According to state department spokesman Charles W. Bray, it was Young who, around Sept. 20, 1971, requested permission for E. Howard Hunt to examine state department documents.

(Continued from p. 50)

of the office of Dr. Lewis Fielding. Krogh's statement was part of an affidavit filed in the Pentagon Papers trial.

Krogh said that neither John Ehrlichman nor President Nixon had advance knowledge of the burglary, which reportedly was carried out by Watergate conspirators E. Howard Hunt and G. Gordon Liddy. *(Story, p. 29)*

Prosecution Probed. The Senate select committee on the Watergate was reported in *The Washington Post* to be actively probing the handling of the Watergate prosecution by the Justice Department. There were questions about the prosecution's insistence throughout the trial of seven accused conspirators that there was no evidence to indicate the Watergate conspiracy extended beyond the seven men who were convicted or pleaded guilty, the Post reported. The committee reportedly was concerned over why the prosecutors did not pursue leads indicating that there might have been a coverup of high-level involvement, although they received evidence of it six months before the trial. The Post quoted one government source as saying, "It adds up to a sloppy job." *(Trial summary, p. 9)*

MAY 6

Marine Commandant. Gen. Robert E. Cushman Jr., Marine Corps commandant and former deputy director of the CIA, was reported by *The New York Times* to have authorized the use of CIA material and research in the burglary of Ellsberg's former psychiatrist. His actions were at Ehrlichman's request, according to the Times' sources.

MAY 7

Alleged Nixon Knowledge. *Newsweek* magazine reported that former presidential counsel Dean was prepared to give testimony regarding two incidents that led him to believe Nixon had knowledge of an effort to cover up White House involvement in the Watergate affair.

Dean claimed, according to the magazine report, that Haldeman and later Nixon himself congratulated him for doing a good job shortly after the Watergate burglars were indicted on Sept. 15, 1972. Dean felt that they were pleased with his success in "keeping the lid on" and because no one higher up in the administration had been indicted, according to *Newsweek*.

Dean also said that a lawyer for Watergate defendant E. Howard Hunt Jr. had approached former White House special counsel Charles W. Colson to see what could be done to avoid a long jail term for Hunt. Colson reportedly passed the request on to Dean and Ehrlichman. Ehrlichman went to the President's office, returned and told Colson to tell Hunt's lawyer, William O. Bittman, that "everything was okay" and the President had agreed to executive clemency, according to the *Newsweek* account.

News reports quoted government sources as saying that Dean was desperate to gain assurances of immunity from prosecution through the exclusive disclosures.

Denials. White House spokesman Gerald Warren announced that "any suggestion that the President participated in any coverup activities is untrue." Warren also denied that the President ever authorized an offer of clemency to Watergate conspirators. Colson, too, denied the report of his dealings with Hunt.

Phony Cables. Hunt said in secret grand jury testimony released by Judge Byrne in Los Angeles that he had been authorized by Colson to prepare fabricated cables. The counterfeit cables embellished the Kennedy administration's association with the assassination of South Vietnam President Ngo Dinh Diem in September 1963.

Special Prosecutor. Attorney General-designate Elliot L. Richardson announced that he soon would select a special prosecutor to investigate Watergate. He offered the Senate the opportunity to evaluate and informally confirm his choice before it became final. Richardson's authority to appoint a special prosecutor was spelled out in Nixon's speech April 30. *(Story, p. 24)*

White House View. According to *The New York Times,* White House aides said privately that Nixon was dismayed by a series of leaks to the press in 1970 and 1971 involving information deemed to be vital to national security. His dismay, combined with his lack of confidence in the FBI, led to the creation of a special White House investigative unit and created an atmosphere in which his subordinates authorized Hunt to break into Ellsberg's psychiatrist's office, the sources were quoted as saying.

Security Concern. The Times reported that Nixon on two occasions invoked national security as the reason when he attempted to prevent releasing to the Los Angeles court the details of the burglary of Ellsberg's psychiatrist. Richardson and Assistant Attorney General Henry E. Petersen, who had been supervising the Watergate probe, reportedly rejected the President's advice and released the documents to the court.

The Times quoted high White House officials as saying reports that the President had at first opposed the release of the details of the break-in were "irresponsible." *The Washington Post* reported that both Richardson and Petersen were shocked at the President's idea.

MAY 8

Immunity. The Senate Watergate committee announced that it would begin televised public hearings on May 17 and would move to compel testimony by John W. Dean III, former White House counsel, by granting him immunity from prosecution.

In a turnabout from the President's April 17 statement, the White House announced that Nixon no longer would advise prosecutors in the Watergate case not to grant immunity to present or former members of the administration. Dean was understood to have bargained with the government prosecutors for immunity from prosecution in exchange for his grand jury testimony. But it was reported that the prosecutors felt they did not need his testimony to build their case.

McCord Memo. James W. McCord Jr., convicted Watergate conspirator, charged that he was pressured by his attorney on two occasions before his trial to say that

Alexander M. Haig Jr.

Like President Eisenhower before him, Richard Nixon has turned to a military man to repair a White House staff structure that has been badly damaged by a major political scandal.

Nixon May 4 picked Gen. Alexander Meigs Haig Jr., 48, as an interim replacement for H.R. Haldeman, his former chief of staff, who resigned in the wake of Watergate disclosures. Eisenhower, faced with a similar problem when Sherman Adams resigned in 1958, turned to Army Maj. Gen. Wilton B. Persons to put the White House back in order. *(1958 Almanac p. 699)*

In each case, the military man was a trusted friend of the President and the appointment was aimed at helping restore public confidence in an executive office caught in a credibility crisis.

In announcing Haig's appointment, presidential press secretary Ronald L. Ziegler said the replacement for Haldeman was not permanent. Haig has been Army vice chief of staff since Jan. 4 and presumably will keep that post. Ziegler said the President felt someone had to handle Haldeman's duties while Nixon reviews the entire White House staff structure.

Unlike Haldeman, who was generally regarded as arrogant and contemptuous of Congress and cabinet officers, Haig is said to be tactful, soft-spoken and diplomatic with his subordinates and superiors.

Ziegler told reporters that cabinet members would not have to go through Haig to get to the President as they had to with Haldeman. He described Haig's duties as those of a White House staff coordinator and administrator.

Haig first caught the President's eye in January 1969 when he entered the White House as a colonel and senior military adviser to Henry A. Kissinger, assistant to the President for national security affairs. By the time he left the White House four years later, Haig was a full general and was second only to Kissinger in the President's esteem as an international trouble shooter.

As deputy assistant to the President for national security affairs from June 1970 to January, Haig played a major role in the Vietnam peace settlement for which Kissinger is given chief credit. He made several fact-finding missions to Southeast Asia that led to the peace accord and personally got President Thieu of South Vietnam to agree to the terms.

As recently as April 7, Nixon sent Haig to Indochina for a first-hand assessment of conditions in Laos, Cambodia, Thailand and South Vietnam.

Haig was born Dec. 2, 1924, in Philadelphia, Pa. He graduated from West Point in 1947 and in 1962 earned a master's degree in international relations from Georgetown University in Washington.

Grand Juries: Sword or Shield

"No person shall be held to answer for a capital, or otherwise infamous, crime, unless on a presentment or indictment of a grand jury...." The 5th Amendment.

Central to disclosure of much information concerning the Watergate burglary and related charges of political espionage has been the work of three federal grand juries:

- In Washington, the grand jury which in September 1972 indicted the original seven Watergate defendants, was reconvened March 26 to consider the new charges related to the Watergate affair.
- In Orlando, Fla., a grand jury May 4 indicted California lawyer Donald H. Segretti on charges of distributing a fraudulent campaign letter, an action thought to be part of a political espionage effort. *(Story, p. 25)*
- In New York City, a grand jury investigating a possible link between a secret $200,000 contribution to the 1972 Nixon campaign and possible government favors in return indicted the contributor, financier Robert L. Vesco, and three other men, including former cabinet officers John N. Mitchell and Maurice H. Stans.

The grand jury was an English institution adopted by the New World colonists, who retained its use—in all federal districts and many states—after its abolition in Britain. It was initially conceived as a shield for citizens against unwarranted prosecution by over-zealous or biased prosecutors. The federal grand jury is composed of 23 persons drawn from the voter registration lists of a federal judicial district. It listens to the prosecutor present the evidence he has formulated and evaluates it—and the testimony of witnesses it can require, by subpoena, to appear before it—and determines whether the evidence warrants an indictment. An indictment is a formal accusation of a crime, framed by the prosecutor and presented—after approval—by the grand jury to the court which impaneled the jury. A presentment is an indictment originated by the grand jury.

In recent years, the federal grand jury has been used increasingly as an investigatory tool, a role facilitated by the Organized Crime Control Act of 1970. Critics have charged that the grand jury is being perverted from the citizens' shield into the prosecutors' sword. They say the prosecutor—who does not have power to compel witnesses to appear and testify—makes use of the grand jury's powers of subpoena and contempt to conduct its own investigation.

Grand jury proceedings are not a formal trial, and therefore many of the safeguards for a fair trial are not in operation: the witnesses called are not informed of the reason for the summons, they are compelled to testify under threat of a contempt sentence, they are not allowed to have counsel present during the grand jury proceedings, and no judge is present during the proceedings.

he and his co-conspirators were working on a covert CIA operation when they were arrested.

The New York Times printed the text of a McCord memorandum to investigators indicating that his lawyer said that CIA records could be changed to show he was still an agent despite the fact that he had retired in 1970.

McCord's lawyer, Gerald Alch, was quoted in the memorandum as saying that James R. Schlesinger, the newly designated CIA director, "could be subpoenaed and would go along with it." McCord refused to sanction the plan to blame the CIA for Watergate and wrote that he was convinced the White House was behind the idea. There was no immediate comment from either the CIA or Alch, who said only that "it would be inappropriate to comment because of the attorney-client relationship." *(Memorandum text, p. 57)*

CIA Memos. CIA memorandums made public in the Pentagon Papers trial revealed that the agency canceled its assistance to E. Howard Hunt—but not until five weeks after Gen. Robert Cushman Jr., then CIA deputy director and now Marine Corps commandant, had met with and agreed to help Hunt in the plot to steal Daniel Ellsberg's psychiatric records. The CIA cancelled the aid when it learned it was participating in a "domestic clandestine operation." *(Texts of memos, p. 59)*

State Department. *The Washington Post* reported that officials had acknowledged that Hunt had obtained copies of 240 classified diplomatic cables from the State Department in 1971 on a "routine" request from White House aide David Young, apparently with no check on his security status.

MAY 9

Krogh Resignation. Egil (Bud) Krogh Jr., the former White House aide who had admitted organizing an attempt to steal records from Daniel Ellsberg's psychiatrist, resigned as under secretary of transportation. In his resignation letter to the President, Krogh wrote that the assignment of two Watergate conspirators "was my responsibility, a step taken in excess of instructions and without the knowledge or permission of any superior.... I believed that my decision was dictated inescapably by the vital, national security interest of the United States. I now see that this judgment may well have been in error, though prompted by what was then my highest sense of right."

Labor Doubts. The AFL-CIO Executive Council, questioning the administration's ability to investigate itself adequately, called for a probe by an "outside citizen's commission who are of unquestioned stature."

Dean Files. *The Washington Post* reported that the new presidential counsel, Leonard Garment, had begun legal proceedings to retrieve documents that his predecessor, John Dean, had placed in a safe deposit box. A White House source told the Post, "We want the originals back. They're our papers... (if) anyone is concerned that we're going to do anything sneaky, let the court hang on to a copy."

CIA Role. The director of the CIA, James L. Schlesinger, conceded that the agency cooperated with former CIA agent E. Howard Hunt in the burglary of Ellsberg's former psychiatrist. In testimony before a

(Continued on p. 56)

Impeachment: An Infrequent and Often Political Move

Despite revelations, accusations and denials surrounding the Watergate scandal and alleged coverup attempts, congressional leaders of both parties have been reluctant to discuss the subject of presidential impeachment. This reluctance may in part reflect an awareness of the sensationalism and partisan politics that have historically been associated with impeachment proceedings.

Senate Majority Leader Mike Mansfield (D Mont.) May 8 expressed hope that both the press and members of Congress would not make hasty judgments, adding that "rumors, innuendos and the like are not facts." He pointed out that broad investigations were in progress.

Rep. John E. Moss (D Calif.) April 30 urged House Democratic leaders to start a formal inquiry into possible impeachment of President Nixon. (The House must initiate impeachment proceedings.) But House Democratic floor leader Thomas P. O'Neill (Mass.) publicly termed the Moss proposal "premature." *(p. 27)*

CONSTITUTIONAL PROVISIONS

Impeachment, the process by which legislatures may remove public officials from office for certain proscribed actions, dates from 14th century England. The subject of much controversy at the Constitutional Convention in 1787, the impeachment provisions of the U.S. Constitution are scattered in the first three articles:

- The House of Representatives...shall have the sole power of impeachment. *(Article I, section 2.)*
- The Senate shall have the sole power to try all impeachments. When sitting for that purpose, they shall be on oath or affirmation. When the President of the United States is tried, the Chief Justice shall preside. And no person shall be convicted without the concurrence of two-thirds of the Members present. Judgment in cases of impeachment shall not extend further than to removal from office, and disqualification to hold and enjoy any office of honor, trust or profit under the United States; but the party convicted shall, nevertheless, be liable and subject to indictment, trial, judgment and punishment, according to law. *(Article I, section 3.)*
- The President...shall have power to grant reprieves and pardons for offenses against the United States, except in cases of impeachment. *(Article II, section 2.)*
- The President, Vice President and all civil officers of the United States shall be removed from office on impeachment for, and conviction of, treason, bribery or the other high crimes and misdemeanors. *(Article II section 4.)*
- The trial of all crimes, except in cases of impeachment, shall be by jury.... *(Article III, section 2.)*

Congressional Procedures. Congress has dealt with impeachment under such widely varying circumstances that few uniform procedures have been established. The House, which must initiate the process, usually refers a resolution proposing impeachment of an official to its Judiciary Committee or to a special investigating committee. If the committee approves the resolution and reports it to the floor, the House must adopt it by a majority vote in order to impeach the official.

The House then selects several managers from its membership to present the articles of impeachment to the Senate, and to serve as prosecutors during the Senate trial proceedings.

Senate rules adopted in 1868 allow both sides to present witnesses and evidence, and the defendant to have benefit of counsel and the right of cross-examination.

IMPEACHMENT IN U.S. HISTORY

Impeachment proceedings have been initiated more than 50 times in the House since 1789, but only 12 cases have reached the Senate. Of these 12 cases, only one involved a President. Two of the cases were dismissed on jurisdictional grounds, six ended in acquittal and four in conviction. Nine of the 12 cases, including the four convictions, involved federal judges.

In 1805, Supreme Court Justice Samuel Chase was impeached on charges of partisan conduct on the bench but was acquitted by the Senate after a sensational trial.

The three nonjudicial officials impeached and then acquitted were Sen. William Blount (D Tenn. 1796-97) in 1797; William W. Belknap, President Grant's secretary of war, in 1876; and President Andrew Johnson in 1868.

Andrew Johnson. The only President to be impeached, Andrew Johnson, survived several Senate roll calls on conviction by a one-vote margin.

The first of two impeachment attempts came as the culmination of a post-Civil War battle between Johnson, who favored a lenient attitude toward the Confederate states, and Radical Republicans in Congress, who favored more repressive policies. In 1867 the House rejected a Judiciary Committee resolution impeaching Johnson.

Johnson's dismissal of his secretary of war without Senate concurrence in 1868, however, gave his enemies another opportunity. A few days later the House voted to impeach the President on charges of violating the Tenure of Office Act and attacking Congress in a series of political speeches.

After weeks of argument and testimony, the Senate took a test vote on one of the 11 articles of impeachment, falling one vote short of conviction. After two more votes produced the same result, the Senate adjourned *sine die*, abruptly ending the trial.

Other Presidents. Resolutions to impeach or investigate the possibility of impeaching at least five Presidents had been introduced in the House prior to 1973. The resolutions named Nixon (1972), Harry S Truman (1952), Herbert Hoover (1932 and 1933), Grover Cleveland (1896) and John Tyler (1843).

12 Resigned or Fired

While the Watergate affair has had its most direct effect on the White House staff, other federal departments and agencies are feeling the impact of firings and resignations of persons whose names have been connected with the case.

One of the President's goals affected by the non-White House resignations was closer control of the government through trusted aides placed in top policy-making positions to help cut through bureaucratic red tape.

The earlier resignations of H. R. Haldeman and John D. Ehrlichman and the firing of John W. Dean III were severe blows to White House operations. Haldeman, Nixon's chief of staff, and Ehrlichman, his chief domestic adviser, were the two most powerful men in the White House after Nixon himself.

The resignation May 9 of Egil Krogh Jr., transportation under secretary, was the 12th by former White House aides or members of the Committee for the Re-election of the President, some of whom had graduated to top bureaucratic posts.

The first to fall from grace was Jeb S. Magruder, who resigned April 26 as director of policy development in the Commerce Department. Magruder, deputy re-election campaign director, had been slated for a more prestigious job, but his testimony at the Watergate trial, that he had established what he thought was a legitimate espionage operation for the committee, meant his chances for a post requiring Senate confirmation were slim.

Next to resign was Gordon C. Strachan, a former Haldeman deputy, who quit as general counsel of the U.S. Information Agency April 30, the same day Haldeman, Ehrlichman and Dean left. Strachan was Haldeman's link to the re-election committee.

In his letter of resignation, Krogh accepted responsibility for a buglary connected with the Pentagon Papers trial in Los Angeles.

On May 7, Robert C. Odle Jr., former director of administration for the re-election committee, was fired from his consultant's job at the Agriculture Department. He had been named by the General Accounting Office as one of several people who handled "unrecorded" campaign funds.

Following are names of other Nixon administration officials who left the government in the wake of Watergate or other campaign excesses (Weekly Report page numbers in parentheses):

Dwight L. Chapin, presidential appointments secretary, resigned February 28. *(p. 39)*

L. Patrick Gray III, acting director of the FBI, resigned April 27. *(p. 22)*

Richard G. Kleindienst, attorney general, resigned April 30. *(p. 24)*

Kenneth Rietz, director of the Republican National Committee's "new majority" campaign for the 1974 elections, resigned April 24. *(p. 22)*

David R. Young, presidential assistant for domestic affairs, resigned April 30. *(p. 31)*

(Continued from p. 54)

Senate investigating committee, Schlesinger described the agency's role as an "ill-advised act." He said John Ehrlichman made the initial contact with Gen. Cushman, then CIA deputy chief. Schlesinger said the CIA had no knowledge of the burglary itself but did assist Hunt with materials in the belief that Hunt was trying to halt security leaks.

Hunt's name was also mentioned when the Pentagon disclosed that the convicted conspirator had tried several times in the fall of 1971 to see classified Defense Department documents on the Pentagon Papers. His requests were turned down. A Pentagon spokesman said Hunt was rejected "because of a firmly established policy of the secretary of defense that in legal matters we respond only to the Department of Justice."

This contrasted with reports of Hunt's experience at the State Department, where it was learned that, on the strength of his status as a White House aide, he was able to copy some 240 classified diplomatic cables on Vietnam policy.

Denial of Suppression. White House press secretary Ziegler declared unfounded the reports that Nixon had tried to prevent the Justice Department from giving information on the Ellsberg burglary to the Pentagon Papers trial court.

Special Prosecutor. Attorney General-designate Richardson told the Senate Judiciary Committee that it should reject his nomination unless it was willing to trust him with final authority over the Watergate investigation. Richardson disagreed with a suggestion from Sen. Philip A. Hart (D Mich.) that the proposed special Watergate prosecutor's independence in conducting the investigation be assured before the committee acted to confirm Richardson's appointment. *(Story, p. 62)*

Another Grand Jury. Los Angeles County District Attorney Joseph Busch said a grand jury would hold four days of hearings beginning June 5 to investigate the burglary of Ellsberg's psychiatrist.

MAY 10

New York Indictments. Four men, including two former Nixon cabinet officers, were indicted by the federal grand jury in New York on charges of conspiring to arrange a secret $200,000 contribution to the President's 1972 re-election campaign. Indicted were John N. Mitchell, former attorney general who later became Nixon's campaign manager; Maurice H. Stans, former commerce secretary who became Nixon's finance chairman; Robert L. Vesco, the New Jersey financier who made the contribution, and New Jersey attorney Harry L. Sears, state chairman of the Nixon re-election campaign in 1972.

The grand jury had investigated the contribution in connection with a larger investigation related to Securities and Exchange Commission charges that Vesco and others had looted four overseas mutual funds directed by IOS Ltd. of $224-million. Vesco's $200,000 contribution to the Republicans, and another $50,000 not in question, were returned to him after the re-election committee learned of the grand jury investigation.

Administration Shifts. Former Treasury Secretary John B. Connally was appointed as a special

First 20 Senate Witnesses

These are the first 20 prospective witnesses, listed May 9 in their tentative order of appearance, who are scheduled to testify at the first round of hearings before the Senate select committee investigating the Watergate affair:

Robert C. Odle Jr., former office manager of the Committee for the Re-election of the President.

District of Columbia Police Sgt. Paul Leeper, who participated in the arrest of five suspects in the June 17, 1972, break-in.

James W. McCord, Jr., convicted conspirator and former security director for the re-election committee.

Sally Harmony, former secretary to convicted conspirator G. Gordon Liddy.

Robert Reisner, a former aide to Jeb Stuart Magruder, former deputy director of the Nixon campaign.

E. Howard Hunt Jr., a former White House aide and a convicted conspirator.

G. Gordon Liddy, former counsel to the re-election finance committee.

Hugh W. Sloan Jr., former re-election committee treasurer.

Herbert L. Porter, former scheduling director for the committee.

Powell Moore, a former committee press aide.

Jeb Stuart Magruder, a former White House aide and Commerce Department official.

Charles W. Colson, former special counsel to the President.

John W. Dean III, former presidential counsel.

Herbert W. Kalmbach, Nixon's former personal lawyer.

Frederick C. LaRue, former aide to the re-election committee director.

Maurice H. Stans, former secretary of commerce and director of fund-raising for the re-election committee.

John N. Mitchell, former attorney general and Nixon campaign manager.

L. Patrick Gray III, former acting director of the FBI.

John D. Ehrlichman, former assistant to the President for domestic affairs.

H. R. Haldeman, former White House chief of staff.

part-time, unpaid adviser to Nixon. The previous week he had announced his switch from the Democratic to the Republican Party.

"Connally is a man whose judgment the President values," said press secretary Ziegler. "He has agreed to assist and advise the President in any way that he can. The President appreciates that very much. He looks forward to sitting down and talking to him on a more frequent basis."

Other high-level changes announced by the White House included the nomination of CIA Director Schlesinger as secretary of defense and the appointment of J. Fred Buzhardt, general counsel of the Defense Department, as a special counsel to the President. *(Story, p. 61)*

Dean Evidence. *The New York Times* reported that on the basis of extensive interviews, Senate and federal investigators said they believe that former White House counsel Dean has no evidence linking Nixon either to the Watergate bugging or any coverup. Prosecutors and the Senate were reported to be in conflict over a Senate decision to seek immunity for Dean before the Senate select committee begins public hearings. ✓

McCORD MEMO TEXT

Following is the text of a memorandum submitted May 7 to the Senate Watergate investigating committee and federal prosecutors by James W. McCord Jr., one of the seven convicted conspirators involved in the June 1972 break-in:

Subject: Pressure on the defendants to blame the Watergate operation on CIA;

I have previously referred to political pressure which was applied to the seven Watergate defendants.

One area of pressure which was applied was that of December, 1972, in which intense pressure was applied on some of the defendants to falsely claim for purposes of a defense during the trial in January, 1973, that the Watergate operation was a CIA operation. This would have had the effect of clearing the Committee for the Re-election of the President and the White House of responsibility for the operation.

In two separate meetings in December, 1972, it was suggested that I use as my defense during the trial the false story that the operation was a CIA operation. I refused to do so.

I was subsequently informed by Bernard Barker just before the trial began in January, 1973, that E. Howard Hunt and other unnamed persons in Miami had brought intense pressure to bear against the Cuban-Americans who were defendants to use the same story as their defense, that my stand taken against it had been the decisive factor causing this ploy to be dropped, and that Hunt was very bitter about it. Hunt's bitterness was later revealed early in the trial when the Cubans advised that Hunt had said that I "was responsible for our being in the plight we were in for not going along with the CIA thing."

At a later time, I heard from Barker that he had been told that Cuban money was suspected of being funneled into the McGovern campaign. I have no knowledge that this suspicion was ever verified.

DECEMBER MEETINGS

The two December, 1972, meetings with me were on December 21, 1972 and on December 26, 1972. Present at the first meeting with me at the Monocle Restaurant in Washington, D.C., were Gerald Alch and Bernard Shankman, my attorneys. Present at the second meeting was Gerald Alch, and the meeting was at his offices in Boston, Mass.

In the first meeting, Alch stated that he had just come from a meeting with William O. Bittman, attorney for E. Howard Hunt, and I received the impression in the discussion that followed that Alch was conveying an idea of request from Bittman. There followed a suggestion from Alch that I use as my defense during the trial the story that the Watergate operation was a CIA operation.

I heard him out on the suggestion, which included questions as to whether I could ostensibly have been recalled from retirement from CIA to participate in the operation. He said that if so, my personnel records at CIA could be doctored to reflect such a recall. He stated that Schlesinger, the new director of CIA whose appointment had just been announced, "could be subpoenaed and would go along with it."

I had noted in the newspapers of that day, Dec. 21, 1972, that it had been announced by the White House that Schlesinger would take over as director of CIA, and that it had been decided that Pat Gray would be supported by the White House to be permanent director of the FBI.

PERJURY CHARGED

Alch went on to mention testimony, or a statement, made to Federal authorities by Gary Bittenbender, a metropolitan police department undercover police officer, whom I had seen at the courthouse on June 17, 1972, when the five of us who were arrested were arraigned, in which Bittenbender purportedly claimed that I had told him that day that the Watergate operation was a CIA operation. I advised Alch that if Bittenbender had made such a statement under oath that he had perjured himself, and that I had not made such a claim.

Bittenbender can be interviewed to determine the circumstances under which he had made such a statement, and whether his statement was in fact an honest error of impressions based on events which occurred in court on that day, which could have misled him. Those were that some of us were identified in the hearing in court as formerly connected with CIA.

Alch went on to mention the name of Victor Marchetti whom he was considering calling to describe CIA training in which its employees were trained to deny CIA sponsorship of an operation if anything went wrong and its participants were arrested. He also requested that I meet with him in Boston on Dec. 26, 1972, which I did. There he opened the discussion by showing me a written statement of an interview with Bittenbender in which Bittenbender claimed that on June 17, 1972, I had told him that the Watergate operation was a CIA operation. I repeated to Alch my earlier statement, that Bittenbender had either perjured himself, or had made a false statement to Federal authorities. I told Alch that I would not use as my defense the story that the operation was a CIA operation because it was not true.

In addition, I told him that even if it meant my freedom, I would not turn on the organization that had employed me for 19 years, and wrongly deal such a damaging blow that it would take years for it to recover from it, and finally that I believed that organization to be one of the finest organizations of any kind in the world and would not let anyone wrongly lay the operation at the feet of CIA.

WHITE HOUSE SUSPECTED

By now, I was completely convinced that the White House was behind the idea and ploy which had been presented, and that the White House was turning ruthless, and would do whatever was politically expedient at any one particular point in time to accomplish its own ends.

In addition, I earlier had determined to tell the true story of the Watergate operation, and it was now only a matter of a propitious time to do so.

On Friday, Dec. 29, 1972, I visited Bernard Shankman's office in Washington, D. C., and let him read a statement which I had prepared, which I proposed to read to the press on Dec. 30, 1972, releasing Alch as my attorney. I believed that although Shankman had been present at the first meeting he was not a party to the events previously described. Shankman suggested that I give Alch an opportunity to meet with me and explain why he had undertaken the course which he had, and such a meeting was set up for Tuesday, Jan. 2, 1973 in Washington.

Alch failed to appear, and I delivered a letter to Judge Sirica, releasing Alch as my attorney. Alch immediately called, asked to meet with me on Jan. 3, 1973, and asked to continue as my attorney. We met and Alch stated that he, in conveying the request made of me on Dec. 21 and Dec. 26, 1972, was acting out of what he felt to be was my own best interests. By this time, I was convinced that the ploy to lay the operation at CIA's doorstep had been headed off, and agreed to give him a second chance.

By this time, I was also convinced that the White House had fired Helms in order to put its own man in control at CIA, but as well to lay the foundation for claiming that the Watergate operation was a CIA operation, and now to be able to claim that "Helms had been fired for it." There had been indications as early as July that the Committee for the Reelection of the President was claiming that the Watergate operation was a CIA operation.

Mrs. Hunt had told me in late July, 1972, that Paul O'Brien had told Howard Hunt in July that the Committee to Re-elect the President had originally informed him that the Watergate operation was a CIA operation. Mrs. Hunt said that her husband had denied to O'Brien that it was a CIA operation. By early December, 1972, it appeared that the White House was beginning to make its move. The events of Dec. 21, and Dec. 26, 1972, only confirmed this in my mind.

CIA, FBI CONTROL

Further, based on an earlier discussion with Robert Mardian in May, 1972, it appeared to me that the White House had for some time been trying to get political control over the CIA assessments and estimates, in order to make them conform to "White House policy." One of the things this meant to me was that this could mean that CIA estimates and assessments could then be forced to accord with DOD (Department of Defense) estimates of future U.S. weapons and hardware needs. This could be done by either shifting an intelligence function to DOD from CIA, or by gaining complete political control over it at CIA.

Among other things, this also smacked of the situation which Hitler's intelligence chiefs found themselves in, in the 1930s and 1940s, when they were put in the position of having to tell him what they thought he wanted to hear about foreign military capabilities and intentions, instead of what they really believed, which ultimately was one of the things which led to Nazi Germany's downfall.

When linked with what I saw happening to the FBI under Pat Gray—political control by the White House—it appeared then that the two Government agencies which should be able to prepare their reports, and to conduct their business, with complete integrity and honesty, in the national interest, were no longer going to be able to do so. That the nation was in serious trouble, has since been confirmed by what happened in the case of Gray's leadership of the FBI.

E. Howard Hunt has additional information relevant to the above. Hunt stated to me on more than one occasion in the latter part of 1972, that he, Hunt, had information in his possession which "would be sufficient to impeach the President."

ALLEGED HUNT LETTER

In addition, Mrs. E. Howard Hunt, on or about Nov. 30, 1972, in a personal conversation with me, stated that E. Howard Hunt had just recently dictated a 3-page letter which Hunt's attorney, William O. Bittman, had read to Kenneth Parkinson, the attorney for the Committee to Re-elect the President, in which letter, Hunt purportedly threatened "to blow the White House out of the water." Mrs. Hunt at this point in her conversation with me, also repeated the statement which she, too, had made before, which was that E. Howard Hunt had information which could impeach the President.

I regret that this memorandom has taken this length to set forth. In view of the nature of the information which I had to furnish, however, it appeared that there was no other way to adequately set this material forth, and to do so in the proper context, without deleting material highly relevant to the events being reported. I shall be glad to appear and answer questions under oath on the material which appears in this memorandum.

TEXTS OF ELLSBERG CASE MEMOS

Following are the texts of two Central Intelligence Agency (CIA) memorandums in the Pentagon Papers trial in Los Angeles. The Justice Department gave the memos to the U.S. District Court in which the case was being tried. The court gave the memos to attorneys for the defendants, Daniel Ellsberg and Anthony J. Russo Jr., who made them public on May 8. Judge W. Matthew Byrne Jr. blanked out the names of CIA officials for security reasons.

FIRST MEMORANDUM

Memorandum for the record (1)
Subject: Summary of contacts
by Mr. (Blank) with Mr. E.
Howard Hunt.

1. On 4 December 1972 Mr. (Blank 1) was interviewed for the purpose of obtaining full details on his contacts with "Edward" and an associate during the summer months of 1971. Mr. (Blank 1) has now identified "Edward" as being E. Howard Hunt.

2. Mr. (Blank 1) advised that in the summer of 1971 he and his section chief were called into the office of the deputy division chief, who briefed them to the effect that a disguise, documentation and other support were to be provided to an individual identified as "Edward."

(Blank 1) met with "Edward" the following day and made all the necessary arrangements to immediately provide him with a disguise and alias documentation. "Edward" was observed signing his name to those items which required a signature, and he tried a mouth device that was utilized in connection with the operations.

3. Approximately two weeks later, "Edward" called to indicate that he needed some help with the disguise's glasses. (Blank 1) is not sure of timing, but he recalls that Mr. (Blank 2) accompanied him to the meeting because (Blank 2) had been asked to provide "Edward" with a tape recorder. (Blank 2) showed "Edward" how the tape recorder worked, and then departed from the house without waiting for (Blank 1).

The latter individual made some adjustment to the glasses. And it was probably at this meeting that "Edward" inquired about a back-stopped telephone number and address in New York. (Blank 1) indicated that he would have to check with his superiors. Mr. (Blank 1) is not absolutely certain, but it is his best recollection that "Edward" also requested a disguise and alias documentation for an associate.

4. At the next meeting, "Edward" was accompanied by an unknown associate, who expressed a requirement for a disguise, alias documentation and a camera. (Blank 1) immediately made all the necessary arrangements for this support, and the associate was appropriately briefed on the use of the camera.

"Edward" and his unknown friend talked about having to stop by the Pentagon before going to the airport, and it was indicated that further assistance would be required immediately upon their return from the trip. "Edward" did not indicate where he was going, but he left the impression that it had something to do with the investigation of drugs.

5. In what was assumed to be a long-distance telephone call, Mr. (Blank 1) was contacted at his home in less than three weeks. At this time "Edward" asked that he be met at Dulles Airport at about 6:00 A.M. the following day. Mr. (Blank 1) met "Edward" and his associate at Dulles Airport early the following morning, when he was given some film and asked to have it developed later in the afternoon. Mr. (Blank 1) is "certain that the pictures were developed and delivered to "Edward" in accordance with his priority request.

It was also at about this time that Mr. (Blank 1) was informed by his supervisor that additional operational support was to be curtailed because "Edward's" requests were beyond what was authorized. In this last meeting with "Edward," (Blank 1) delivered the photographs and indicated that additional operational support would not be forthcoming without specific authorization. However, "Edward" was obviously in a hurry, apparently having some type of appointment, and the meeting lasted less than 10 minutes.

6. Mr. (Blank 1) stated that he cannot be sure, but he estimates that he met with "Edward" on about five different occasions. In response to inquiry, Mr. (Blank 1) advised that he is now reasonably certain that "Edward" is E. Howard Hunt, based upon 1972 publicity relating to the Watergate incident. With respect to the second individual "Edward's" associate, Mr. (Blank 1) stated that he was a "similar type" to Gordon Liddy. Mr. (Blank 1) does not recall the use of the name "Tom," and it is his best recollection that the second individual used the name "George."

SECOND MEMORANDUM

Memorandum for the Record (2)
Subject: Summary of
Mr. (Blank) knowledge of
CIA assistance to
Mr. E. Howard Hunt

1. On 22 July 1971, Mr. E. Howard Hunt, known to be working at the White House, visited General Cushman. He stressed that he had been authorized to conduct a very sensitive operation by the White House and that it should be held as a very secret matter. Mr. Hunt stated that he had a requirement to elicit information and in order to accomplish this he would like some false alias documentation and physical disguise. General Cushman responded that he would look into it and get in touch with Mr. Hunt at his White House office.

2. Pursuant to General Cushman's instructions, Mr. Hunt was met by technical personnel on 23 July and provided with a set of alias documents and a disguise (wig, glasses, and a speech alteration device).

3. Thereafter, Mr. Hunt requested certain additional support, on 20 August, Mr. Hunt was given a recorder and business cards. He arranged for an associate to be documented and disguised. He asked for a back-stopped address and phone in New York, but they were not provided.

4. Mr. Hunt was later given a concealed camera. On 26 August Mr. Hunt telephoned a CIA officer and asked to be met at the airport to pick up and develop certain film. This was done, and Mr. Hunt was met later in the day when the developed film was returned.

5. On 27 August Mr. (Blank) instructed the technical personnel to withhold further assistance to Mr. Hunt because his requests had gone beyond the original understandings. Furthermore, they appeared to involve the agency in domestic clandestine operation. Mr. (Blank) immediately reported these facts to General Cushman and sought guidance. General Cushman called the appropriate individual in the White House with these concerns and explained that the agency could not meet the kinds of requests Mr. Hunt was levying. The White House official stated he would restrain Mr. Hunt. Since 27 August, 1971, neither General Cushman nor Mr. (Blank) had any further contact with Mr. Hunt on this subject. ✓

APPOINTMENTS: PRESIDENT FILLS DEFENSE AND CIA POSTS

President Nixon, acting to plug gaping holes in his cabinet and White House staff, May 10 selected a nominee for secretary of defense and appointed two new advisers.

The changes announced by the White House included:

- James R. Schlesinger, director of the Central Intelligence Agency (CIA), to be nominated to replace Elliot L. Richardson as defense secretary.
- William E. Colby, the CIA's deputy director for operations, to succeed Schlesinger.
- Former treasury secretary John B. Connally named a special adviser to the President.
- J. Fred Buzhardt, defense department general counsel, named a special counsel to the President to work on Watergate and campaign practices reform.
- The presidential counselor responsibilities of three cabinet officers to be suspended.

Administration Vacancies

The changes were made to fill cabinet and White House staff vacancies left by the resignations April 30 of Attorney General Richard Kleindienst and presidential aides H.R. Haldeman, John D. Ehrlichman and John W. Dean III. In addition, Defense Secretary Elliot L. Richardson was appointed as attorney general. *(Story, p. 24)*

The only major surprise among the announcements was that of Schlesinger. David L. Packard, a former under secretary of defense, had been rumored in line for the job. Presidential press secretary Ronald L. Ziegler said Packard met with the President several times to discuss the offer, but ultimately turned it down.

Connally's selection as a special adviser was expected, especially since he bolted the Democratic Party to join Republican ranks May 2.

The changes were announced by Ziegler after the President first discussed them with Republican congressional leaders and the cabinet in separate meetings the morning of May 10.

Defense Post. Technically, Richardson remains the secretary of defense, even though he has been nominated as attorney general. The question of when he will give up his defense post was unanswered. The Senate is not expected to vote on his confirmation for the Justice Department job for a week or more.

Ziegler expressed the White House's "confidence" that Richardson will be confirmed soon. Schlesinger's nomination will be sent to the Senate next week. *Richardson confirmation hearings, p. 62; Schlesinger biography, below)*

Connally Appointment. Connally will serve as a part-time adviser without pay, and will have an office in the old Executive Office Building. He will be available to the President for a wide variety of assignments in the domestic and foreign fields, Ziegler said. He added "we assume (requests for Connally's advice) will be frequent."

Ziegler asserted there would be no conflict of interest regarding Connally's law practice, which he will maintain, and his new duties as a presidential adviser. He explained that the former Texas governor's duties would not be in operational field, only in advisory areas.

In answer to a question about how Connally could advise the President on energy matters when some of his law firm's biggest clients are oil companies, Ziegler answered that on oil matters the President would turn to White House experts on the subject.

He also said there would be no conflict between Connally's foreign affairs advisory duties and those of national security adviser Henry A. Kissinger.

Buzhardt Appointment. Ziegler said Buzhardt will join the White House staff in an interim capacity, pending resolution of Watergate matters and the drawing up of a new campaign practices law. The President had promised in his April 30 television address that he would work for reform of the campaign laws to prevent future election abuses. *(p. 43)*

Buzhardt was selected to help out Leonard Garment who, since the April 30 firing of Dean as Counsel to the President, has taken over Dean's duties plus White House responsibility for Watergate matters.

It was unclear from Ziegler's explanations of Buzhardt's functions just who—Buzhardt or Garment—would be in overall charge of Watergate for the White House. He said Buzhardt would have "full responsibility" on Watergate matters, but that Garment also will continue to work on Watergate and will report, with Buzhardt, to the President on the subject.

Garment, in addition to his duties as the president's counsel, will take the "lead role" on campaign reform, with assistance from Buzhardt, Ziegler said.

Counselors Shelved. While Ziegler would not concede it, the President's highly touted plan to reorganize the executive branch by making three cabinet officers counselors to the President—with other domestic affairs cabinet officers reporting to them—appears to have been scrapped.

The plan, ordered by the President January 5, was one of the most sweeping executive branch chages in history. Appointed as counselors were Earl L. Butz, agriculture secretary (for natural resources), Caspar W. Weinberger, secretary of health, education and welfare (for human resources) and James T. Lynn (secretary of housing and urban development (for community development).

Under the plan, all domestic affairs cabinet officers, except the attorney general, would report to the White House through the counselor responsible for their subject area. The counselors would, in turn, have to report to

John D. Ehrlichman, the President's former assistant for domestic affairs.

Ziegler said the counselor plan would be "moved aside" until Congress acted on the reorganization. That, plus remarks by the press secretary that the President wanted "more direct contacts with his cabinet" officers, plus no congressional action on the plan, appeared to signal the end of the "super-cabinet" idea, as it was known.

Asked for a further explanation of the change, Ziegler replied that the "existing members of the White House staff who were here...when it was devised have left." This was a reference to Haldeman and Ehrlichman, who were believed to have originated the counselor plan.

James R. Schlesinger

The President's announcement May 10 that he had picked James R. Schlesinger, 44, to become Secretary of Defense came barely five months after Nixon appointed Schlesinger to head the Central Intelligence Agency (CIA). As Secretary of Defense, Schlesinger succeeds Elliot L. Richardson who has been nominated to the post of Attorney General.

Schlesinger joined the Nixon administration in 1969 as an assistant Director of the old Budget Bureau. Following the administration's reorganization of the Budget Bureau into the new Office of Management and Budget (OMB), Schlesinger was appointed assistant director of OMB with responsibilities in the areas of national security.

AEC Chairman. In 1971 Nixon appointed Schlesinger chairman of the Atomic Energy Commission. As chairman of the AEC Schlesinger earned a reputation as a conscientious administrator intent on opening up the agency's operations to public scrutiny whenever possible. Schlesinger remained chairman of the AEC until late December 1972. It was at that time that Nixon once again reached into his administration ranks to appoint Schlesinger director of the CIA.

During the first four months of 1973, Schlesinger had been reorganizing the CIA's upper staff levels in what was regarded as a major shakeup of the agency. He had reportedly encouraged many older employees to seek an early retirement and had appeared before Congress to push for fewer restrictions on CIA retirement standards.

Schlesinger's background in national security matters, first as an economics professor and later as an associate of the Rand "think tank" Corporation, make him particularly suited to run the vast Defense bureaucracy. He is the author of two books on the economics of national defense and security issues. Schlesinger directed a study of ways to reduce the defense budget while serving as Nixon's assistant at OMB.

In making the announcement of Schlesinger's new appointment, White House Press Secretary Ron Ziegler said Nixon considered Schlesinger "exceptionally well-equipped to provide the strong leadership needed at the Department of Defense" in the months following the end of the Vietnam war.

Schlesinger is a native of New York City. He received his undergraduate and graduate degrees from Harvard.

J. Fred Buzhardt Jr.

Joseph Fred Buzhardt, 49, who was named May 10 as a special counsel to the President, is also general counsel of the Defense Department. He will hold the two posts simultaneously for an indefinite period, the White House said.

Buzhardt joined the Defense Department in February 1969 as a special assistant to the assistant secretary of defense for administration. He has held the post of the department's chief legal officer since Aug. 18, 1970.

The new presidential aide was born Feb. 21, 1924, in Greenwood, S.C. He served in the army air corps in 1942 and 1943 before entering West Point, from which he graduated in 1946. He served as an air force officer from 1946 to 1950, and earned a law degree from the University of South Carolina in 1952.

Buzhardt practiced law in McCormick, S.C., from 1952 to 1958 and from 1966 to 1969. He spent the in-between years as an aide to Sen. Strom Thurmond (R S.C.). While Defense Department general counsel, Buzhardt denied a request from G. Gordon Liddy, a convicted Watergate conspirator, to see classified defense documents on the Pentagon Papers.

William E. Colby

William Egan Colby, 53, who will be nominated by the President to head the Central Intelligence Agency (CIA), has had a background conforming to the cloak and dagger image of the agency. During World War II he was parachuted behind enemy lines in France to work with a resistance unit and toward the end of the war he headed a demolition team dropped in Norway to destroy a railroad line used by the Germans.

Colby had been the CIA's deputy director of operations only since March 3 when the President selected him to head the agency. He was CIA comptroller from Jan. 10, 1972, to March. Colby was born Jan. 4, 1920, in St. Paul, Minn. He spent three years of his early life in Tientsin, China, where his father, an army officer, was assigned.

Colby graduated from Princeton University in 1941 and earned a law degree from Columbia. Before entering the government, he worked for a law firm of William J. Donovan, former head of the Office of Strategic Services (OSS), a CIA predecessor. Colby has worked for the National Labor Relations Board, the State Department and the Agency for International Development, in addition to the CIA. √

RICHARDSON: A QUESTION OF ULTIMATE RESPONSIBILITY

Hearings—Senate Judiciary Committee May 9-10 on the nomination of Elliot L. Richardson as attorney general.

"Did you ever hear of the Watergate affair?" asked Senate Judiciary Committee Chairman James O. Eastland (D Miss.) May 9.

"Yes," responded Secretary of Defense Elliot L. Richardson, as hearings began on his nomination as attorney general, the third cabinet post he would hold in the Nixon administration.

"If you're attorney general," asked Eastland, "what are you going to do about it?"

Richardson's answer was that he was determined to pursue the truth wherever it might lead without fear or favor and with regard solely to the public interest. *(Final Action, p. 96)*

Richardson responded further to Eastland's question by restating his May 7 announcement that he would, if confirmed, appoint a special prosecutor to conduct the Watergate investigation. Committee members used the opportunity to question Richardson thoroughly about the details of his plans.

Richardson was formally introduced to the committee May 9 by Massachusetts Senators Edward M. Kennedy (D) and Edward W. Brooke (R) who described him as a man of "integrity...independence of judgment...toughness of mind"—the same adjectives applied to the yet-unnamed prosecutor whom they hoped to find. Without Watergate, there would be no doubt of Richardson's speedy confirmation.

But because as attorney general Richardson would insist upon retaining ultimate responsibility for the work of the special prosecutor, Watergate was the crucial issue in his confirmation. Lacking close ties to any men named to date in the scandal, Richardson had nonetheless been a key figure in the Nixon administration from its beginning, a fact which raised questions about the appropriateness of his heading the Department of Justice at this particular time. *(Biography, p. 42)*

Meeting head-on this concern which he saw reflected in some of the committee questions, Richardson May 10 declared: "I am among the Republicans who feel betrayed by the shoddy standards of morals of the activities of persons which have recently come to light." That should at least neutralize, he said, any fear "that... as part of the administration I might be tempted to go easy" on persons involved both with the administration and Watergate.

There would be an "arm's length" distance relationship between the Justice Department, including himself as attorney general and the special prosecutor, and the White House, Richardson said. Nixon had told him that he did not wish to be kept informed of the progress of the investigation, said Richardson.

Authority of Prosecutor

A virtual veto over the selection of the special prosecutor was granted by Richardson to the Senate and its judiciary committee May 9. One primary element in his decision to seek such a figure, he said, was the hope that he might thus restore public confidence in government; this purpose would not be served by choosing a man who failed to win approval from the Senate.

Sam J. Ervin Jr. (D N.C.), chairman of the select committee investigating the Watergate matter, asked Richardson's reaction to the powers and "final authority" delineated for the special prosecutor in a resolution (S Res 109) introduced May 8 by Sen. Adlai E. Stevenson III (D Ill.) and 29 other senators.

"The special prosecutor should have all the responsibility and support set forth in the Stevenson resolution," Richardson replied, "but it is important for the attorney general to retain the ultimate responsibility."

Before confirmation of an attorney general, said Philip A. Hart (D Mich.), May 9, ground rules should be agreed upon to ensure the prosecutor's independence: "Appearance demands that the investigation be insulated... from any hint of coverup through control by the Republican administration." Hart doubted that this appearance could be satisfied if Richardson retained ultimate responsibility for the investigation of the administration of which he was a part. The prosecutor's independence would be guaranteed to the public, said Richardson, by its faith in that individual's character and in Richardson himself.

Responding to the suggestion that, like former Attorney General Richard G. Kleindienst, he remove himself from any responsibility for the prosecutor's investigation, Richardson said that if he had to do that, "no purpose would be served by my becoming attorney general."

Immunity

Probing an area of potential conflict between the Senate select committee and the Justice Department, Ervin asked Richardson what his attitude would be toward waiving the requirement that the Senate committee give 10 day's notice to the attorney general of its intention to grant a witness before it immunity from prosecution in order to persuade or compel him to testify to the committee. Ervin also inquired whether Richardson would be inclined to exercise the attorney general's authority to delay, for up to 20 days, the granting of such immunity.

Richardson said he would like for the special prosecutor to have some notice of any immunity grant and that the prosecutor should also have the opportunity to consider delaying such a grant. "This could be a very serious problem," he said; "The Senate could foreclose prosecution of a key man" by granting him immunity from any prosecution based on his testimony before the committee. "It is more important for the country for this matter to be clarified," said Ervin, "than whether two or three persons go to jail." √

WATERGATE: COMMITTEE HEARINGS OF 'UTMOST GRAVITY'

Exactly 11 months after the break-in and bugging of Democratic national headquarters, a Senate committee opened hearings on the Watergate scandal "in an atmosphere of the utmost gravity." The incident on June 17, 1972, was only a pebble at the center of a still-widening circle of disclosures of governmental and political corruption. The seven-member Senate Select Committee on Presidential Campaign Activities began its public hearings on May 17.

Chairman Sam J. Ervin Jr. (D N.C.) described the atmosphere as testimony began in front of the television floodlights that filled the pillared, chandeliered, marble-walled caucus room of the Russell Senate Office Building. "If the allegations that have been made in the wake of the Watergate affair are substantiated, there has been a very serious subversion of the integrity of the electoral process," he said, "and the committee will be obliged to consider the manner in which such a subversion affects the continued existence of this nation as a representative democracy, and how, if we are to survive, such subversions may be prevented in the future."

The hearings got off to a slow start the first day. But they sprang vividly to life on the second day with testimony from convicted Watergate conspirator James W. McCord Jr. His testimony implicated President Nixon himself in alleged offers of executive clemency in return for a guilty plea by McCord at the January criminal trial of seven Watergate defendants.

McCord, a stocky, balding veteran of 19 years with the Central Intelligence Agency (CIA), read a statement to the committee. The presidential pressure, he said, was conveyed to him in January by John J. Caulfield, a former presidential staff assistant whose immediate supervisor was former White House counsel John W. Dean III. At midnight May 18, Caulfield went on administrative leave from the Treasury Department.

Caulfield told him, McCord said, "to remain silent, take executive clemency by going off to prison quietly, and I was told that while there I would receive financial aid and later rehabilitation and a job. I was further told in a January meeting in 1973 with Caulfield that the President of the United States was aware of our meeting, that the results of the meeting would be conveyed to the President, and that a future meeting there would likely be a personal message from the President himself."

Witnesses May 17

The first round of hearings dealt with the planning and execution of the wiretapping and break-in and the alleged coverup of the incident. A second round of hearings was to explore allegations of broader campaign espionage and sabotage. And a third will probe alleged violations of campaign spending laws. *(Earlier story, p. 46)*

Watergate Prosecutor: Archibald Cox

Attorney General-designate Elliot L. Richardson May 18 picked former Solicitor General Archibald Cox as the special prosecutor for the Watergate case. Cox, who served under Presidents Kennedy and Johnson, is a Harvard law school professor. The solicitor general represents the federal government before the Supreme Court.

Odle. The lead-off witness May 17 was Robert C. Odle Jr., 28-year-old former director of administration for the Committee for the Re-election of the President. He informed the senators and the standing-room-only crowd of press and public:

- H. R. Haldeman, former White House chief of staff, and former Attorney General John N. Mitchell had a great deal to do with hiring the re-election committee staff, many of whom were recruited from the White House and the executive branch.
- As early as May 1971, soon after the nucleus of a campaign organization had been formed and 10 months before he left the Justice Department to become President Nixon's re-election campaign director, Mitchell was involved in major campaign decisions. A confidential White House memorandum dated Feb. 9, 1972, was released at the hearing by Samuel Dash, the Senate committee's chief counsel. The memo indicated that Mitchell had final decision-making authority on the re-election committee.
- Odle and Robert Reisner, then an aide to Jeb Stuart Magruder, deputy director of the re-election committee, took some committee files home, on Magruder's orders, for safekeeping the weekend after the break-in and returned them to Magruder the next Monday. Sen. Howard H. Baker Jr., vice chairman of the investigating committee, questioned whether the file taken by Odle contained records of "Operation Gemstone," the code phrase for alleged espionage and sabotage plans.

Odle, who admitted repeatedly that he had "a very hard time reconstructing the chronology of that day," said he had not looked at the file, knew nothing in advance about the break-in and did not learn until later that "things which have no place in a political campaign were in it (the files)."

- Odle's first hint of the break-in came in a phone call the afternoon of June 17 from Mrs. James W. McCord Jr., wife of one of five men arrested at the Watergate office building early that morning. According to Odle, she told him, "Jim has been involved in a project that's failed. He's in jail."

• The other man convicted—five others pleaded guilty—G. Gordon Liddy, former re-election committee counsel, approached Odle the afternoon of June 17 and, according to Odle, "asked where the paper shredder was. I said, 'It's in there.' " After being told how to work the machine, said Odle, Liddy returned with a foot-high stack of papers. Odle said he presumed Liddy shredded the papers.

• In May 1972, at the time of Nixon's decision to bomb Haiphong harbor, Odle was given between $3,000 and $4,000 to finance a public demonstration of support. The money was spent partly to bring people to Washington in buses for rallies, he said.

Dismissing criticisms of the tactics used, Odle told the Senate committee that the re-election committee "did it publicly; they did it overtly and they did it honestly." The committee of 400 employees "kind of came together that week," he said. "Everybody worked hard."

Other Witnesses. Three other witnesses appeared before the select committee on May 17. They were Bruce A. Kehrli, special assistant to the President, and Sgt. Paul W. Leeper and Officer John Barrett of the Metropolitan Police Department in Washington.

Witnesses May 18

McCord, the former security coordinator for the President's re-election committee, dominated the May 18 hearing with his electrifying allegations of White House involvement. In his statement, he described not only the alleged approaches by Caulfield, but a series of cloak-and-dagger conversations with an unidentified person from a highway telephone booth near his Rockville, Md., home.

On Jan. 8, the first day of the criminal trial, McCord said his attorney, Gerald Alch, told him that William O. Bittman, the attorney for another defendant, E. Howard Hunt Jr., wanted to meet with him and with a third defendant, Bernard Barker, to discuss clemency. "I had no intention of accepting executive clemency," McCord said. "But I did want to find out what was going on, and by whom, and exactly what the White House was doing now."

McCord said that Alch, not he himself, met with Bittman. Alch, he added, informed him that Bittman had sent word that McCord would be called that night by "a friend I had known from the White House."

That night, McCord continued, he was phoned by an unidentified person—he later said the caller had a New York accent—who instructed him to go to a pay phone booth near an inn on a highway. McCord said he followed the instructions and was advised by the same person in the second telephone conversation to plead guilty and not to accept immunity from a grand jury in exchange for his testimony. The voice, according to McCord, promised him executive clemency, care for his family, "rehabilitation" after his release from prison, and a job.

McCord described later meetings and conversations with Caulfield. He said he refused to discuss clemency or pleading guilty but was glad to talk with him in order to make his position clear.

Caulfield, according to McCord, said the clemency offer came "from the very highest levels of the White House." He quoted Caulfield as saying that the President, who was in Key Biscayne, Fla., at that time, "had been told of the forthcoming meeting with me and would be immediately told of the results of the meeting... I may have a message to you at our next meeting from the President himself."

Earlier in his testimony before the Senate committee, McCord had reported that he had been told of strategy meetings on bugging and espionage by the re-election committee that had been held in the office of then Attorney General John N. Mitchell, who resigned on March 1, 1972, to become Nixon's campaign director. Also involved in the meetings, he said, were Jeb Stuart Magruder, deputy campaign director, and presidential counsel Dean. The source of McCord's information on the meetings, he said, was G. Gordon Liddy, another Watergate conspirator.

Clemency offers were made to him by Caulfield several times, at meetings on a parkway near Washington and on a drive into the country, McCord said. He quoted Caulfield as telling him that "the President's ability to govern is at stake. Another Teapot Dome scandal is possible and the government may fall. Everybody else is on track but you. You are not following the game plan. Get closer to your attorney."

At their final meeting, a Jan. 25 drive into the countryside near Warrenton, Va., McCord said he was told when he repeated his refusal to plead guilty: "You know that if the administration gets its back to the wall, it will have to take steps to defend itself." And, according to McCord, Caulfield offered White House assistance in providing $100,000 in cash to bail him out of jail.

"The testimony of Mr. McCord as to what was told him by John Caulfield would not be accepted in a court of law, to connect the President with what Mr. Caufield was doing," Ervin said. "But it is admissible to show whether or not Mr. Caufield is a party to any agreement to attempt to suppress information about what is popularly known as the Watergate affair at this stage," Ervin continued.

Policeman's Testimony. A second witness, who testified briefly at the opening of the May 18 hearing, was Washington policeman Carl M. Shoffler. He described his part in apprehending five men in the Watergate building at the time of the June 1972 break-in.

Daily Chronology

Following is a day-to-day chronology of the week's events:

MAY 10

Dean Statement. In a statement issued through his lawyer, former presidential counsel John W. Dean III said he was "very aware that there is an ongoing effort to limit or prevent my testifying fully and freely." Dean also denied that he had been the source of earlier news reports that he was prepared to testify that Nixon knew about the alleged Watergate coverup. *(Statement text, p. 72; earlier story, p. 47)*

Colson on Break-in. Information released to defense attorneys in the Pentagon Papers trial revealed that

Charles W. Colson, a former special presidential counsel, said during a May 8 FBI interview that he was told twice by former White House aide John D. Ehrlichman and once by Dean to keep quiet about the break-in at the office of Daniel Ellsberg's psychiatrist. *(p. 20)*

Sloan Warning. Hugh W. Sloan Jr., former treasurer of the President's re-election finance committee, said under oath that he had repeatedly warned White House officials in 1972 that re-election committee officials might have been involved in the Watergate bugging and its coverup, it was learned. Sloan made the statement in a pretrial deposition in a civil suit connected with the Watergate affair. *(p. 47)*

Richardson Testimony. Elliot L. Richardson told the Senate Judiciary Committee, which was considering his nomination as attorney general, that he felt "betrayed by the shoddy standards" of administration officials implicated in the Watergate case. Richardson added that "the President has told me he does not want to be informed" about the government's Watergate investigation. *(Hearings, p. 62)*

MAY 11

Pentagon Papers Trial. The Pentagon Papers trial ended abruptly, as Judge W. Matthew Byrne Jr. of U.S. District Court in Los Angeles dismissed all charges of espionage, theft and conspiracy against Daniel Ellsberg and Anthony J. Russo and declared a mistrial because of government misconduct. *(p. 46)*

Phone Taps. Quoting sources familiar with the operation, *The New York Times* said the Nixon administration had, for a two-year period starting in 1969, tapped the phones of reporters and government officials in an attempt to discover the sources of security leaks. *(Weekly Report p. 47)*

Immunity Granted. Chief Judge John J. Sirica of U.S. District Court in Washington, D.C., the judge in the Watergate criminal case, granted immunity from further prosecution to four men who pleaded guilty to the Watergate burglary, in order to allow them to testify before the Senate investigating committee. They are Bernard L. Barker, Eugenio R. Martinez, Frank Sturgis and Virgilio R. Gonzalez.

Finance Committee Plea. The Finance Committee to Re-elect the President pleaded not guilty in Federal District Court in Washington to a charge that it failed to report a $200,000 campaign contribution made in 1972 by financier Robert L. Vesco *(p. 46)*

Connally Move. John B. Connally, newly named special adviser to the President, announced that he would take a leave of absence from his law firm and resign from all corporate boards while serving in the White House. The announcement came in the wake of press reports that Connally's law firm was representing Gulf Resources and Chemical Corporation, which was under investigation by a federal grand jury in connection with campaign contributions to the Nixon re-election committee.

MAY 12

Gray-Nixon Conversation. L. Patrick Gray III told investigators working for the Senate select committee that he called Nixon July 6, 1972, to express concern over the interference of White House aides in the FBI's Watergate investigation, according to committee sources quoted by *The New York Times* and *The Washington Post.* Gray, who was acting FBI director when he made the call, reportedly told the investigators that Nixon told him to "go ahead and do your job," but did not press Gray for details of his complaint.

Vesco Threat. Citing "sources close to the case," *The New York Times* reported that Robert L. Vesco, the financier indicted in connection with a $200,000 cash contribution to the Nixon campaign, believed that the case against his co-defendants, John N. Mitchell and Maurice H. Stans, probably would fail without his testimony. Vesco, who was out of the country in spite of a warrant for his arrest, was seeking total immunity from prosecution and appointment of a special prosecutor as conditions for his testimony. *(Indictment, p. 46)*

Kalmbach Investigation. Federal investigators in Los Angeles were looking into possible election finance law violations by Herbert W. Kalmbach, Nixon's former personal lawyer and a principal Nixon re-election fundraiser, *The New York Times* said. The Times story also quoted campaign aides of Sen. Hubert H. Humphrey (D Minn.) as saying that unexplained acts of sabotage were directed against Humphrey in the 1972 California presidential primary.

MAY 13

Dean Offer. Government sources, quoted in *The New York Times,* said that former presidential counsel John W. Dean III offered to pay an Interior Department official to participate in or direct an undercover political espionage network. The official, Kenneth C. Tapman, told the Times that Dean had made the offer, but was said by the sources to have rejected it. Dean's alleged proposal involved an effort to infiltrate anti-war protest groups before the 1972 Democratic and Republican national conventions.

Baker Interview. Sen. Howard H. Baker Jr. (R Tenn.), senior minority member of the Senate Watergate investigating committee, said on NBC-TV's "Meet the Press" that Nixon might be given an opportunity to "state his side of the case" to the committee, "through counsel, by statement or otherwise." But Baker said it probably would be impossible to subpoena Nixon to appear in person before the committee.

Caulfield Departure. John J. Caulfield, a Treasury Department law enforcement official, went on annual leave after being mentioned in connection with the Watergate case. *The Los Angeles Times* reported the same day that, according to its sources, Caulfield met with Watergate conspirator James W. McCord Jr. twice during the criminal trial in January and promised him executive clemency if he would remain silent throughout the trial. *(Previous resignations, p. 56)*

Butz Attack. Speaking in Charlotte, N.C., Secretary of Agriculture Earl L. Butz charged that the Senate Watergate committee's investigation was a "very improper...political inquisition" conducted "largely for political reasons." Butz labeled the committee's chairman, Sen. Sam J. Ervin Jr. (D N.C.), a "publicity-seeking senator."

CIA Says White House Pressured It To Assume Role

In testimony before the Senate Armed Services Committee May 14, Lt. Gen. Vernon Walters, deputy director of the Central Intelligence Agency (CIA), revealed that the White House tried to pressure the CIA into assisting in a coverup of the Watergate scandal.

During a closed session of the committee, the CIA deputy told members that he had twice threatened to resign and seek a private meeting with the President if the pressure from top Nixon aides on the CIA to assist in the coverup did not stop.

Walters' testimony was revealed by acting Armed Services Committee Chairman Stuart Symington (D Mo.). Symington said that it was "very clear...that there was an attempt to unload major responsibility for the Watergate bugging and coverup on the CIA."

Symington said that former Nixon aides H. R. Haldeman, John D. Ehrlichman, John W. Dean III and former acting director of the FBI, L. Patrick Gray, were directly involved in the attempts to pressure the CIA into assisting with a coverup of the Watergate break-in and its connection with the Nixon re-election committee.

The three White House aides, Symington said, "were doing everything in the world to obstruct justice." According to Symington, Walters was summoned on numerous occasions to White House meetings designed to pressure the CIA deputy into obligating the agency in efforts to coverup the Watergate scandal.

Symington said in a statement issued after Walters appeared before the committee that "under these difficult circumstances and heavy pressures, I believe that (CIA) Director (Richard M.) Helms and General Walters...behaved very well with respect to this attempt."

Helms. Meanwhile, former CIA Director Helms appeared before a Senate appropriations subcommittee May 16 and reportedly told the committee that several White House aides used Nixon's name in requesting CIA help in the Watergate coverup.

Following the closed hearing, Sen. John L. McClellan (D Ark.) told reporters that Helms resisted the attempts to involve the CIA in a coverup, but did not disclose the attempts to Congress or the President because the requests came from top levels in the White House.

The CIA "wanted to go as far as they could to accommodate the President," McClellan said, but "some things went too far and they put a stop to it."

McClellan accused the White House of violating the 1947 National Security Act which prohibits the CIA from engaging in domestic intelligence operations. The conservative Democrat called the attempts by Haldeman, Ehrlichman and Dean to involve the CIA in the coverup "beyond impropriety."

Ellsberg. On May 16, Daniel Ellsberg told a joint subcommittee looking into government secrecy that the Pentagon Papers case was "part of a scheme to re-elect the President."

Ellsberg, recently acquitted of charges in the case, told the subcommittee that the scheme involved an attempt to associate certain Democratic presidential candidates with the release of the Pentagon Papers and Ellsberg.

Acting Subcommittee Chairman Edmund S. Muskie listened as Ellsberg said the Nixon administration had hoped to "establish a link between me and the Democratic candidates, specifically you, Mr. Muskie."

Ellsberg's statement prompted a heated exchange between Muskie and Sen. Strom Thurmond (R S.C.). Thurmond accused Muskie of using the subcommittee and Ellsberg's appearance as a political forum.

"You brought him (Ellsberg) here to criticize the President...," Thurmond shouted at Muskie. "You are not fit to be a presidential candidate."

Muskie apologized to Ellsberg for the "senatorial temper" displayed at the hearing. Thurmond declined comment on the exchange with Muskie.

MAY 14

Ruckelshaus Announcement. William D. Ruckelshaus, acting FBI director, reported at a news conference that records of 17 wiretaps of newsmen and government officials from May 1969 to February 1971 had been found in the White House safe of former presidential adviser John E. Ehrlichman. Ruckelshaus said he located the records, which had been taken from the FBI in September 1971, only hours after a mistrial was declared in the Pentagon Papers case May 11. He said the documents included transcripts of wiretapped conversations involving Daniel Ellsberg, a defendant in the trial.

Dean Denial. In an interview with *Newsweek* magazine, former presidential counsel John W. Dean III claimed that he never wrote a report on the Watergate case and was never asked to do so by the President. Dean reportedly said he was "flabbergasted" when Nixon referred to such a report in a news conference on Aug. 29, 1972.

Quoting a close associate of Dean, *Time* magazine reported that Dean and his wife had been gathering evidence to prove that he did not meet with the President between the time of the Watergate arrests and Nixon's Aug. 29 press conference, when the President stated that Dean had "conducted a complete investigation" of the case and that the results showed no member of the administration was involved.

Gray Warned. Former acting FBI Director L. Patrick Gray III was warned by FBI officials of coverup attempts several weeks after the Watergate burglary, *The Washington Post* reported. Citing "two reliable sources," the Post said that Gray told the officials he could not relay the warning to Nixon because it would be improper to involve the President in an FBI investigation.

Dean Papers. Judge John J. Sirica took custody of secret papers turned over to the court by John W. Dean III and ordered that copies of the documents be given to federal prosecutors in the Watergate case and to the Senate invesigating committee. The papers, which Dean took with him when he was fired as presidential counsel, had been claimed by the White House as the property of the President. *(p. 50)*

Federal Prosecutor. In testimony before the Senate Judiciary Committee, Attorney General-designate Elliot L. Richardson said two new members of the White House staff, Gen. Alexander M. Haig Jr. and Leonard Garment, had suggested to him the names of two possible candidates for the job of special prosecutor in the Watergate case, but that he had disregarded their suggestions. Richardson named four men he was still considering for the position: Harold R. Tyler Jr. and David Peck, both federal judges in New York City; Judge William Erickson of the Colorado Supreme Court, and Warren Christopher, a Los Angeles attorney and former deputy attorney general. *(Hearings, p. 63)*

SEC Investigation. G. Bradford Cook, chairman of the Securities and Exchange Commission (SEC), testified under oath at a closed hearing of a Senate Appropriations subcommittee about the agency's investigation of financier Robert L. Vesco. Cook had told the subcommittee earlier that he had not discussed the case with former Commerce Secretary Maurice H. Stans until after the SEC had filed its lawsuit against Vesco.

Sen. William Proxmire (D Wis.), chairman of the subcommittee, said Cook later had "corrected" his testimony, saying he had discussed the case with Stans before the lawsuit was filed. Proxmire called Cook back to explain allegations that he had failed to mention in the lawsuit—at Stans' request—Vesco's $200,000 contribution to the Nixon campaign.

CIA Involvement. Sen. Stuart Symington (D Mo.) told reporters that former White House aides H. R. Haldeman, John D. Ehrlichman and John W. Dean III attempted to involve the CIA in domestic activities on behalf of the Nixon administration in 1971 and 1972. Symington based his remarks on testimony by the CIA deputy director, Lt. Gen. Vernon A. Walters, before the Senate Armed Services Committee. *(Box, p. 66)*

MAY 15

Dean Immunity The Senate Watergate investigating committee met privately and voted unanimously to apply for limited immunity from prosecution for John W. Dean III and Roy H. Sheppard, a lesser-known witness who allegedly moved some cartons of documents from the White House after the June 17 break-in. If the request were granted, Dean and Sheppard could not be prosecuted on the basis of their testimony before the committee.

CIA Hearings. The CIA's deputy director said John W. Dean III asked the agency in 1972 to help cover up the Watergate case by paying bail and salaries for those involved. The deputy director, Lt. Gen. Vernon A. Walters, also testified in a May 14 closed hearing of the Senate Armed Services Committee that former White House aides H. R. Haldeman and John D. Ehrlichman tried to get the CIA to cut off an FBI inquiry into Nixon re-election funds that came through a Mexican bank, according to a statement issued by Sen. Stuart Symington (D Mo.). "It is very clear to me," Symington said, "that there was an attempt to unload major responsibility for the Watergate bugging and coverup on the CIA."

G. Bradford Cook

Scandals growing out of President Nixon's 1972 re-election campaign May 16 claimed another promising government career with the resignation of G. Bradford Cook, the 36-year-old chairman of the Securities and Exchange Commission (SEC).

Cook, the youngest man ever to head a federal regulatory agency, quit slightly more than 10 weeks after President Nixon swore him in on March 3 as successor to William J. Casey. Cook had served under Casey since 1971 as the commission's director of market regulation and general counsel.

His departure may threaten the SEC's efforts to reorganize stock markets, to restore investor confidence and securities industry profitability and to pursue enforcement cases—projects that Cook had pushed energetically after taking over from Casey, who was appointed under secretary of State for economic affairs.

Although charged with no illegal activity, Cook was forced out by congressional reaction to a grand jury's disclosure that he had altered an SEC complaint against financier Robert L. Vesco after discussions with Maurice Stans, the President's chief campaign fund-raiser. *(p. 68)*

A Nebraska native, Cook is the son of George Cook, a Lincoln, Neb., insurance company founder who was chief fund-raiser in that state for Nixon's presidential campaigns in 1968 and 1972. Educated at Stanford University and the University of Nebraska Law School, Cook practiced corporate and securities law as a partner of Winston and Strawn, a prestigious Chicago law firm, for 10 years before joining the SEC.

Election Commission. At a White House meeting with congressional leaders, Nixon proposed establishing a 17-member bipartisan election reform commission.

Special Prosecutor. Judge Harold R. Tyler Jr. of U.S. District Court in New York turned down the post of special prosecutor in the Watergate case, Elliot L. Richardson revealed during continued Senate Judiciary Committee hearings on his nomination as Attorney General.

The same day, Robert W. Meserve, president of the American Bar Association, said the special prosecutor should be independent of the attorney general and that a special federal agency should be created to conduct the investigation and prosecution.

Nixon Role. Jeb Stuart Magruder, former deputy campaign director at the Nixon re-election committee, had said that the President played an active role in run-

Caucus Room

Room 318 of the Old (Russell) Senate Office Building has witnessed the making or breaking of many political careers during its 62 years. Scene of numerous historic investigations, the high-ceilinged, neoclassical Caucus Room is serving once again as the stage for a drama that will be seen by television viewers throughout the nation. *(Previous major congressional investigations, p. 15)*

It was in the Caucus Room 50 years ago that the Senate Committee on Public Lands and Surveys held its hearings on leases of naval oil reserves, investigating what became known as the Teapot Dome affair, one of the most celebrated government scandals in the nation's history.

In 1950 and 1951, a national television audience was able to tune in on the now-famous investigations of organized crime conducted by the late Sen. Estes Kefauver (D Tenn.). The hearings propelled Kefauver into the political spotlight, and he ran for the Democratic presidential nomination in 1952.

During 1953 and 1954, the Caucus Room again provided the stage for a controversial drama—this time, the abrasive investigations of Sen. Joseph R. McCarthy (R Wis.) into alleged Communist infiltration of the State Department and armed services. Unlike Kefauver's probe, however, the televised hearings led to McCarthy's undoing and ultimate censure by the Senate.

It was in the Caucus Room that the 1957 Senate hearings on labor union malpractices and Teamsters' rackets were held. Television viewers saw Teamster union president Jimmy Hoffa confronted with sharp questioning by a young committee staff member named Robert F. Kennedy. In 1968, Kennedy, like his brother John in 1960, announced his presidential candidacy from Room 318 of the Old Senate Office Building.

Public and congressional opposition to the Vietnam war was spurred by the 1966 televised hearings held in the Caucus Room by Foreign Relations Committee Chairman J. W. Fulbright (D Ark.). Two years later, faced with deepening divisions within the nation over U.S. involvement in Southeast Asia, Lyndon Johnson announced he would not seek re-election to a second term as President.

ning his campaign until a month after the Watergate burglary, *The New York Times* reported. The story was based on a transcript of a Harvard University political science seminar Magruder attended in January 1973.

MAY 16

Cook Resigns. G. Bradford Cook resigned as chairman of the Securities and Exchange Commission amid allegations that he yielded to pressure in his handling of an SEC lawsuit against indicted financier Robert L. Vesco. *(Box, p. 67)*

White House Report. Presidential Press Secretary Ronald L. Ziegler confirmed a *New York Times* report that President Nixon did not talk with John W. Dean III before making his Aug. 29 statement clearing all White House staff of connection with Watergate on the basis of a report by Dean. The Times story asserted that Nixon based his remarks on information provided by his former chief of staff John D. Ehrlichman.

Ziegler told reporters at a briefing that "the President called for an investigation" and that "the responsibility for conducting that investigation clearly fell in the counsel's office," then occupied by Dean.

Wiretaps. The White House confirmed a *New York Times* report that President Nixon personally authorized the wiretapping of officials in the National Security Council and the Pentagon beginning in 1969, after the paper had revealed that the United States was bombing Cambodia.

Helms Testimony. Richard Helms, former CIA director, testified at closed hearings of the Senate appropriations subcommittee investigating CIA involvement in the Watergate and Pentagon Papers cases. Chairman John L. McClellan (D Ark.) said Helms admitted knowing of White House requests for CIA help in the Watergate affair, but did not tell the President of them. *(Box p. 66)*

Clemency Offer. John J. Caulfield, the Treasury Department official who went on administrative leave May 13, told federal authorities April 30 that John W. Dean III instructed him to offer James W. McCord Jr. executive clemency in exchange for silence on the Watergate case, *The Los Angeles Times* reported.

Special Prosecutor. Warren Christopher, a Los Angeles attorney, became the second to turn down the job of special Watergate prosecutor, saying it would not allow enough independence. Democratic members of the Senate Judiciary Committee continued to warn that Elliot L. Richardson's refusal to grant total autonomy to a prosecutor was jeopardizing his confirmation as Attorney General.

Supreme Court Pressure. A former Justice Department official said he had conveyed then-Attorney General John N. Mitchell's objections to a Supreme Court wiretap decision to two of the justices. Jack C. Landau, director of information at the Justice Department in 1969 and 1970, said he delivered the message after the court's March 10, 1969, ruling that accused persons are entitled to see records of illegal surveillance against them. One week later, the Justice Department asked the court to rehear the case. Mitchell issued a statement denying Landau's story.

Ervin Statement. At a news conference in Brunswick, Maine, Sen. Sam J. Ervin Jr. (D N.C.) said he expected "some startling revelations" from the Senate committee hearings, and that the committee would probably complete its investigation by the end of the year.

Liddy Immunity. Federal Judge John J. Sirica granted limited immunity for testimony by Watergate conspirator G. Gordon Liddy before the Senate investigating committee, as the committee had requested.

Election Commission. In a special message to Congress and in a five-minute radio broadcast, President Nixon proposed establishment of a 17-member nonpartisan election reform commission to report recommendations by Dec. 1. *(Text of statement, and radio address, p. 75)*

The President said "recent disclosures of widespread abuses during the presidential campaign of 1972" made election reform urgent.

Republican Fallout. Republican leaders continued to express concern about Nixon's handling of Watergate. Sen. Barry Goldwater (R Ariz.) issued a statement calling on the President to "start making moves in the direction of leadership which has suffered from lack of attention because of an understandable concern about Watergate." Sen. Hugh Scott (R Pa.), minority leader, issued his own statement supporting Goldwater's.

In a CBS radio interview, Sen. Robert Dole (R Kan.) said, "I think there is still a lot of doubt in the eyes of the public," about Watergate.

Loeb Charge. The federal government filed a criminal information in U.S. district court in New York against John L. Loeb, an investment banker, for making $48,000 in illegal, indirect contributions to Sen. Hubert H. Humphrey's presidential primary campaign.

Ellsberg Testimony. Former Pentagon Papers defendant Daniel Ellsberg, testifying before a group of Senate subcommittees investigating government secrecy, portrayed the government's unsuccessful prosecution as "part of a scheme" to influence the Democrats' selection of a presidential candidate in 1972.

MAY 17

Hearings Open. The seven-member Senate Select Committee on Presidential Campaign Activities, chaired by Sen. Sam J. Ervin Jr. (D N.C.), opened its hearings on the Watergate case and related events at 10 a.m. EST. After opening statements by committee members, Robert C. Odle Jr., former office manager of the Nixon re-election committee, was the first witness to testify. He was followed by Bruce Kehrli, a White House aide, and Sgt. Paul W. Leeper, an arresting officer in the June 17 break-in.

Undercover Network. Citing "highly placed sources in the executive branch," *The Washington Post* reported that the Watergate bugging and the break-in at Daniel Ellsberg's psychiatrist's office were "part of an elaborate, continuous campaign of illegal and quasi-legal undercover operations conducted by the Nixon administration since 1969."

Kissinger Wiretaps. Henry A. Kissinger, the President's national security adviser, requested that some of his aides be wiretapped between 1969 and 1971, *The New York Times* reported. The Times story, quoting Justice Department sources, said Kissinger requested a tap on the phone of Helmut Sonnenfeldt, a top official at the National Security Council, and others, in order to trace leaks of secret information. Kissinger previously had told the Times he saw summaries of several wiretaps, but that he did not request their placement.

Segretti Plea. Donald H. Segretti, a Los Angeles attorney implicated in alleged Republican political sabotage, pleaded innocent to two charges of violating federal election laws before a U.S. magistrate in Tampa, Fla. Segretti and Tampa accountant George Hearing were indicted by a federal grand jury in Orlando, Fla., May 4 on charges of distributing a bogus letter under the letterhead of 1972 Democratic presidential candidate Edmund S. Muskie.

Republican Task Force

Bill Frenzel (Minn.) is chairman of a 15-member task force on election reform that was announced on May 12 by the House Republican Research Committee. The task force will study and make recommendations on campaign contributions and spending, reporting procedures and enforcement, voter registration laws, election fraud, electoral college reform, vice presidential selection procedures and presidential primaries.

The other 14 members are Representatives Edward G. Biester Jr. (Pa.), Clarence J. Brown (Ohio), Clair W. Burgener (Calif.), M. Caldwell Butler (Va.), Philip M. Crane (Ill.), David W. Dennis (Ind.), Louis Frey Jr. (Fla.), Harold V. Froehlich (Wis.), James F. Hastings (N.Y.), John E. Hunt (N.J.), Edward Hutchinson (Mich.), William J. Keating (Ohio), Trent Lott (Miss.) and Matthew J. Rinaldo (N.J.).

RUCKELSHAUS STATEMENT

Following is the text of a statement read on May 14 by William D. Ruckelshaus, acting director of the FBI, on the results of an investigation into missing records relating to electronic surveillances of certain individuals:

Shortly after assuming this job, my attention was drawn to several newspaper and periodical accounts of electronic surveillances—wiretaps—having been placed on telephones of government employees and newsmen in an effort to stem the leaks of information related to highly sensitive foreign policy issues. Upon inquiry, I was informed by FBI employees that these surveillances had been performed and that the records relating to them were missing from the FBI files. Also the question had been raised in the Ellsberg trial whether information from these alleged taps had been used by the prosecution in any way and thus tainted the evidence.

As a result of this information, I immediately ordered an investigation into the facts surrounding the taps and the missing records. This investigation was started Friday, May 4, 1973, and was conducted under my personal supervision by highly skilled FBI personnel at Headquarters. Forty-two separate interviews were conducted, all by Headquarters personnel, and included travel to Phoenix, Arizona; Tampa, Florida; Savannah, Georgia; New York City; and Stamford, Connecticut.

The investigation revealed that from May 1969, to February, 1971, based on consultations between the Director of the FBI and the White House, certain wiretaps were instituted in an effort to pinpoint responsibility for leaks of highly sensitive and classified information which, in the opinion of those charged with conducting our foreign policy, were compromising this Nation's effectiveness in negotiations and other dealings with foreign powers.

There was a total of 17 wiretaps placed for this purpose. Four were placed on newsmen as the potential recipients of leaks and thirteen on government employees as the potential sources. The taps were on for varying lengths of time during the period in question; two for as little as 30 days and one for as long as 21 months.

These requests were handled in the same way as other requests involving national security for a number of years. When a government agency or the White House requests surveillance the request is studied by the senior officials of the FBI, and if the Director approves, authority is then requested from the Attorney General. If he approves, as was done in this case, the surveillance commences, summaries are prepared from the logs, which are transmitted to the interested agency, or as in this case, the White House.

Because of the sensitivity of these particular surveillances, the records were very closely held; first in the Director's Office and then on the Director's orders under the custody of Mr. W. C. Sullivan who was an Assistant to the Director.

The investigation indicates that sometime in the summer of 1971, after the taps were all taken off, Mr. Sullivan contacted Mr. Robert Mardian, who was then Assistant Attorney General in charge of the Internal Security Division, and informed him of the nature of these records and recommended that they be transferred to The White House. According to Mr. Mardian, the recommendation was made on the claim by Mr. Sullivan that Mr. Hoover might use the records in some manner against the Attorney General or the President. Mr. Sullivan does not affirm Mr. Mardian's claim. There is certainly no proof that Mr. Hoover had such intention but the charge had its desired effect. According to Mr. Mardian, he informed Mr. Mitchell, who in turn informed The White House. The records were taken from the files by Mr. Sullivan, who ordered them given to Mr. Mardian, who delivered them to The White House.

When the FBI discovered the records were missing upon Mr. Sullivan's retirement in the fall of 1971, it commenced an inquiry which ended when Mr. Hoover was informed by Mr. Mitchell that the records had been destroyed. It should be noted that Mr. Mitchell has denied making such a statement to Mr. Hoover. This conflict cannot be resolved because of Mr. Hoover's death. Mr. Mitchell, however, confirmed that the records were moved to The White House.

In any event, the FBI accepted the premise that the records had been destroyed, and when I assumed my present position, I also had no reason to believe that the records were still intact. It was not until last Thursday night that our investigation revealed, during an interview with Mr. Mardian in Phoenix, that the records probably still existed and might be in The White House.

The next day the records were located in The White House, having been filed in a safe in Mr. Ehrlichman's outer office.

Unfortunately, the records were not located in time to respond to Judge Byrne's inquiries about the potential taint of evidence in the Ellsberg trial. The interceptions of Ellsberg's conversations all occurred when he was either a guest of Morton Halperin, National Security Council, or conversing with him. It was one of these conversations of Mr. Ellsberg which I had informed the Judge on Wednesday, May 9, 1973, had been remembered by one of our employees who had monitored the tape. Of course whether the location of the records would have had any affect on the Judge's decision is not for me to say.

On Saturday an FBI Agent and I went to The White House, identified and retrieved the records. They now rest in the FBI files.

The investigation was conducted with skill, speed, and effectiveness by the FBI and resulted in the full retrieval of the records. I believe it is in the public interest to reveal these facts so that this story can be put in proper perspective.

EXCERPTS FROM BYRNE RULING

Following are excerpts from the May 11 ruling of Judge W. Matthew Byrne Jr. of U.S. District Court in Los Angeles, in which he dismissed all charges in the Pentagon Papers trial of Daniel Ellsberg and Anthony J. Russo Jr. (Earlier story, p. 46)

...Commencing on April 26, the Government has made an extraordinary series of disclosures regarding the conduct of several governmental agencies regarding the defendants in this case. It is my responsibility to assess the effect of this conduct upon the rights of the defendants. My responsibility relates solely and only to this case, to the rights of the defendants and their opportunities for a fair trial with due process of law.

As the record makes clear, I have attempted to require the government and to allow the defendants to develop all relevant information regarding these highly unusual disclosures. Much information has been developed, but new information has produced new questions, and there remain more questions than answers.

The disclosures made by the government demonstrate that governmental agencies have taken an unprecedented series of actions with respect to these defendants. After the original indictment, at a time when the government's rights to investigate the defendants are narrowly circumscribed, White House officials established a special unit to investigate one of the defendants in this case. The special unit apparently operated with the approval of the FBI, the agency officially charged with the investigation of this case.

We may have been given only a glimpse of what this special unit did regarding this case, but what we know is more than disquieting. The special unit came to Los Angeles and surveyed the vicinity of the offices of the psychiatrist of one of the defendants. After reporting to a White House assistant and apparently receiving specific authorization, the special unit then planned and executed the break-in of the psychiatrist's office in search of the records of one of the defendants.

From the information received, including the last document filed today, it is difficult to determine what, if anything, was obtained from the psychiatrist's office by way of photographs.

CIA PARTICIPATION

The Central Intelligence Agency, presumably acting beyond its statutory authority, and at the request of the White House, had provided disguises, photographic equipment and other paraphernalia for covert operations.

The government's disclosure also revealed that the special unit requested and obtained from the CIA two psychological profiles of one of the defendants.

Of more serious consequences is that the defendants and the court do not know the other activities in which the special unit may have been engaged and what has happened to the results of these endeavors. They do not know whether other material gathered by the special unit was destroyed, and though I have inquired of the government several times in this regard, no answer has been forthcoming...

These recent events compound the record already pervaded by incidents threatening the defendants' right to a speedy and fair trial. The government has time and again failed to make timely productions of exculpatory information in its possession requiring delays and disruptions in the trial.

Within the last forty-eight hours, after both sides had rested their case, the government revealed interception by electronic surveillance of one or more conversations of defendant Ellsberg. The government can only state and does only state that the interception or interceptions took place.

Indeed, the government frankly admits that it does not know how many such interceptions took place or when they took place or between whom they occurred or what was said...

Of greatest significance is the fact that the government does not know what has happened to the authorizations for the surveillance, nor what has happened to the tapes nor to the logs nor any other records pertaining to the overheard conversations. This lack of records appears to be present not only in the Justice Department, but in the Federal Bureau of Investigation, from the response of both FBI and the Justice Department appear to have been missing...

There is no way the defendants or the court or, indeed, the government itself can test what effect these interceptions may have had on the government's case here against either or both of the defendants. A continuation of the government's investigation is no solution with reference to this case. The delays already encountered threaten to compromise the defendants' rights, and it is the defendants' rights and the effect on this case that is paramount, and each passing day indicates that the investigation is further from completion as the jury waits...

INCOMPLETE ISSUES

The charges against these defendants raise serious factual and legal issues that I would certainly prefer to have litigated to completion... However, while I would prefer to have them litigated, the conduct of the government has placed the case in such a posture that it precludes the fair dispassionate resolution of these issues by a jury.

In considering the alternatives before me, I have carefully weighed the granting of a mistrial, without taking any further action. The defendants have opposed such a course of action, asserting their rights, if the case is to proceed, to have the matter tried before this jury. I have concluded that a mistrial alone would not be fair.

Under all the circumstances, I believe that the defendants should not have to run the risk, present under existing authorities, that they might be tried again before a different jury.

The totality of the circumstances of this case which I have only briefly sketched offend "a sense of justice." The bizarre events have incurably infected the prosecution of this case. I believe the authority to dismiss this case in these circumstances is fully supported by pertinent case authorities...

I have decided to declare a mistrial and grant the motion to dismiss.

I am of the opinion, in the present status of the case...that the only remedy available that would assure due process and the fair administration of justice is that this trial be terminated and the defendants' motion for dismissal be granted and the jury discharged.

The order of dismissal will be entered; the jurors will be advised of the dismissal, and the case is terminated.

INDICTMENT EXCERPTS

Following are excerpts from the indictment by a federal grand jury in New York City on May 10 of former Attorney General John N. Mitchell, former Secretary of Commerce Maurice H. Stans, financier Robert L. Vesco and attorney Harry L. Sears. (Earlier story, p. 46)

From on or about March 1, 1971, up to and including the date of the filing of this indictment, the defendants, and other persons to the Grand Jury known and unknown, unlawfully, wilfully, and knowingly did combine, conspire, confederate and agree together and with each other to commit offenses against the United States...by interfering with and obstructing ...lawful governmental functions by deceit, craft, trickery and means that are dishonest.

It was a part of said conspiracy that the defendants and co-conspirators would and did corruptly and by threats and by threatening communications, endeavor to influence, obstruct and impede the due administration of justice in connection with an investigation of and subsequent legal proceeding against Robert L. Vesco...and others by the Securities and Exchange Commission....

The defendants and co-conspirators would and did willfully endeavor by means of misrepresentation and intimidation to obstruct, delay and prevent the communication of information relating to violations of criminal statutes of the United States by persons to attorneys and investigators duly authorized by the Securities and Exchange Commission to conduct or engage in investigations of violations of criminal laws of the United States....

The defendants and co-conspirators would and did interfere with and obstruct the lawful governmental functions of the SEC and GAO by concealing and attempting to conceal by deceit, craft, trickery and dishonest means, the true facts relating to a secret cash campaign contribution by the defendant Robert L. Vesco.

It was further a part of said conspiracy that...Vesco would and did make a secret contribution of $200,000 in cash for the use of the Committee for the Re-election of the President, the largest cash contribution ever received by the committee...

Following the receipt of said contribution by the committee, its chairman,...Mitchell, would and did arrange for...Sears to meet with William Casey, chairman of the SEC, to discuss the SEC's investigation...without advising Casey of the fact that such a secret cash contribution had been made....

Stans would and did conceal the origin of the Vesco contribution from members of the finance committee staff, would and did cause incomplete records to be made, would and did thereafter cause such records to be destroyed, and would and did cause false and fraudulent reports to be filed with GAO in order to conceal the Vesco cash contribution and the uses to which it was put.

INFLUENCES ON SEC

It was further a part of said conspiracy that...Mitchell would and did cause John W. Dean III, the counsel to the President of the United States, to communicate with Casey ...to seek postponement of the return date of SEC subpoenas served on employees of International Controls Corp. in order to prevent or delay disclosure by them of facts relating to the secret Vesco contribution.

...Stans would and did cause G. Bradford Cook, counsel to the SEC, to delete all specific references to the $250,000 in cash delivered to Vesco's office on April 6, out of which the secret Vesco contribution was made, from the draft of the proposed SEC civil complaint....

...Stans would and did cause Cook...to request the SEC staff not to file transcripts of testimony relating to the said $250,000 with the United States District Court for the Southern District of New York.

Among the means by which the defendents and co-conspirators would and did carry out the aforesaid conspiracy were the following:

...Vesco would and did arrange with...Sears to have Sears speak with the Attorney General of the United States, defendant John N. Mitchell, about the SEC investigation of Vesco with the intent of having Mitchell exert his influence on the SEC on behalf of Vesco, ICC, IOS and others.

...Sears would and did ask...Mitchell to speak with Casey ...about the SEC investigation of Vesco.

...Vesco would and did pay and promise to pay...Sears substantial sums of money in return for Sears requesting... Mitchell to exert his influence on the SEC on behalf of Vesco, ICC, IOS and others...

...Sears would and did ask...Mitchell to arrange a meeting between Sears and...Casey to discuss the SEC investigation of Vesco.

...Vesco would and did meet with...Stans and discuss the SEC investigation of Vesco. At that meeting...Vesco would and did offer to give at least $250,000 and possibly $500,000 to the Committee for the Re-election of the President with the intent of having...Stans,...Mitchell and others exert their influence on the SEC on behalf of Vesco, ICC, IOS and others. At that meeting...Vesco would and did accede to Stans' request to give $250,000 in cash before April 7, 1972.

On or about March 8, 1972, immediately after his meeting with...Stans...Vesco went to the office of the chairman of the Committee for the Re-election of the President, defendant... Mitchell, to discuss the SEC investigation.

MONEY DELIVERED

Shortly thereafter,...Stans and...Mitchell discussed the proposed contribution from...Vesco.

At about 11:00 a.m. on April 10, 1972...Sears and Laurence B. Richardson would and did deliver $200,000 in cash to... Stans at which time Richardson gave Stans a message from Vesco to the effect that Vesco wanted help on the SEC investigation.

At or about 1:00 p.m. on April 10...Sears would and did meet with ...Mitchell to advise Mitchell that Vesco's $200,000 had been delivered to Stans that day.

At or about 4:00 p.m. on April 10...Sears would and did discuss the SEC investigation of Vesco, ICC, IOS and others with (Casey and Cook) at a meeting arranged by...Mitchell earlier that day.

From on or about April 10, 1972, and continuously thereafter...Stans would and did fail to report or cause any report to be made to GAO of the fact of...Vesco's $200,000 cash contribution or of expenditures made there from as required by federal law.

In May, June, July and August...Sears would and did attend additional meetings with Casey and Cook to discuss the investigation...

In July...Vesco would and did instruct Laurence B. Richardson to arrange a meeting with...Stans to determine what Stans was doing to help Vesco in the SEC investigation.

Vesco would and did cause the President of Costa Rica, Jose Figueres, to send a letter addressed to Richard M. Nixon, the President of the United States, specifically referring to the SEC investigation of Vesco and indicating his concern that adverse publicity emanating from the SEC against Vesco might jeopardize the development of Costa Rica as "a showpiece of democratic development" in the Western Hemisphere.

In August...Sears would and did meet privately during the Republican National Convention at Miami, Florida, with Casey to discuss the SEC investigation of Vesco, ICC, IOS and others.

In October...Vesco would and did threaten to disclose the facts surrounding the secret $200,000 cash contribution delivered to...Stans on April 10, 1972, unless an SEC subpoena issued to Vesco was withdrawn...(and) Sears would and did relay Vesco's threat to...Mitchell.

In October Sears would and did discuss with Mitchell having Mitchell arrange to cancel or defer the appearances of ICC employees who had been subpoenaed to testify in connection with the SEC investigation.

MEMO TO DONALD NIXON

In November Vesco would and did attempt to submit a written memorandum to Donald Nixon, the brother of the President of the United States, the purport and tenor of which was to threaten disclosure of the secret cash contribution and other adverse consequences unless the SEC was directed to drop all legal proceedings against Vesco. When the memorandum came to the attention of Mitchell, he turned it over to Sears and concealed its existence and contents from the SEC and other law enforcement agencies who properly should have been made aware of it.

From October 1972 through April 1973...Sears and Mitchell discussed various methods to avoid having the defendant Sears testify before the SEC or any other investigative body about the facts relating to the defendant Vesco's $200,000 cash contribution.

In November...Sears attempted to persuade G. Bradford Cook to limit any SEC inquiry of Sears so as to conceal the facts relating to...Vesco's $200,000 cash contribution.

On November 15...Mitchell and Stans met in New York and discussed efforts by Stans to cause...Cook...to change a paragraph in the proposed SEC complaint...in such a way as to delete specific references to any transactions involving the $250,000....

In January and February...Stans asked Cook to limit the SEC inquiry relating to Vesco's receipt of $250,000 cash on April 6 to facts concerning only the source and not the disposition of the money.

The Grand Jury further charges:

From in or about March, 1971, up to and including the date of the filing of this indictment, Mitchell...Stans...Sears... Vesco and other persons to the Grand Jury known and unknown, unlawfully, willfully and knowingly, did endeavor, by means of misrepresentations and intimidation, to obstruct delay and prevent...Vesco...Sears, Richard Clay, Laurence B. Richardson, Shirley Bailey, Helen Force and other persons from communicating information relating to criminal violations of the federal securities law to attorneys and investigators duly authorized by the Securities and Exchange Commission to engage in investigations of criminal violations of the securities laws.

DEAN STATEMENT

*Following is the text of a statement issued on May 10, through his attorney, by John W. Dean III, former presidential counsel. (*Earlier story, p. 47)

In light of unfounded reports and persistent rumors concerning me and my testimony, I feel compelled to present what I earnestly hope will be kept in mind by all who are interested in the complete truth concerning the Watergate case.

The news stories quoting unidentified sources and speculating on the nature of my testimony do not come from me, have not been authorized by me, nor have they come from my attorneys.

The information contained in these stories is neither complete nor accurate. I have not, and will not, leak my testimony to the media.

There have been discussions within the White House during the past four to five months as to how to end the Watergate matter, but these discussions always ended with an unwillingness to accept the truth for what it meant.

That unwillingness to accept the truth still prevails among some who are affected by the truth. I have always been —as I am now—prepared to have the truth emerge, but I am not willing to see the truth distorted further, nor am I willing to shoulder the blame for those unwilling to accept the truth.

I am very aware that there is an ongoing effort to limit or prevent my testifying fully and freely.

Efforts have been made to prevent me from obtaining relevant information and records; attempts have been made to influence the handling of my testimony by the prosecutors; restrictions have been placed on the scope of my testimony as it relates to the White House; and blatant efforts have been made to publicly intimidate me.

Finally, I am, of course, aware of efforts to discredit me personally in the hope of discrediting my testimony.

In fact, I have learned from several good friends that there is a concerted effort to "get me." Indeed, this is a most unfortunate attitude, for I seek to "get" no one, rather, I seek to get only the truth.

This infamous matter has already lingered too long and done too much damage to the processes of government. It will only end when the truth is told.

Those who believe that they can "get me" and discredit my testimony with absurd or personal attacks are forgetting what I believe is a basic fact of life—ultimately the truth always emerges. The truth will emerge in the Watergate case.

I am a lawyer and have full faith in our judicial process. The taxpayers, who have been my employers for the last several years, deserve from me the full facts as I know them.

And I, too, believe that justice must be pursued fairly, fully, and impartially no matter who is involved. ✓

NIXON: A COMMISSION TO REFORM THE ELECTION PROCESS

President Nixon May 16 asked Congress to create an independent commission to propose ways of reforming the federal election process.

In both a message to Congress and a taped radio address to the nation, the President said the commission's mandate should be "as broad as the federal election process itself. Nothing would be excluded." *(Texts of message, radio address, p. 75)*

Among the proposals the President said the commission might consider were constitutional amendments changing House members' terms to four years from two and the President's term to six years without the possibility of re-election. *(Box, p. 74)*

In his message, the President also suggested that the commission examine campaign costs and financing, reporting and disclosure laws, the length of campaigns, use of television and methods of combatting unfair campaign practices.

"I believe that reform is essential and urgent," the President told Congress. "I also believe it is vital that these proposed reforms be carefully considered not singly, but in their relations to each other...."

Watergate. There were reports that Nixon's proposals stemmed from reaction against the Watergate scandal. On April 30, when Nixon discussed the Watergate affair on national television, he said he planned to urge both parties to work for new rules that would ensure clean campaigns in the future. He contended that both parties had been guilty in the past of "shady tactics."

Leonard Garment, the acting counsel to the President, briefed reporters on the proposals at the White House. Asked if the President, by his proposals, meant to imply that the entire political system was sick, Garment answered that there was no "systematic problem," but that Watergate presented a "unique opportunity" for bipartisan action on federal campaign practices.

Watergate revelations have included allegations of illegal contributions and handling of finances by the Finance Committee to Re-elect the President.

Nixon, in his radio message, said he personally favored a four-year term for members of the House, with half the membership elected every two years. Under the existing two-year terms, the President said, members spend their second year running for re-election, thus placing a great burden on the member, to the disadvantage of his constituents.

The President said he hoped the commission would make its report by December 1, so that reforms might be enacted by Congress for the 1974 elections. He recommended that the commission have 17 members, eight chosen by Congress and seven by himself, with automatic membership for the chairmen of the Democratic and Republican National Committees.

Nixon did not specifically endorse the six-year, nonrenewable presidential term, but simply noted that many political scientists had suggested it. Senators Mike Mansfield (D Mont.) and George Aiken (R Vt.) are among those who favored such a change in the past.

Democratic National Chairman Robert S. Strauss and Common Cause director John W. Gardner reacted negatively to the President's proposals. Both said they saw it as a delaying tactic when what was needed was presidential action to restore integrity to the executive branch.

Nixon briefed congressional leaders on the proposal May 15, the day before it was officially announced. Attending the meeting between the leaders and Nixon

(Continued on p. 75)

Executive Privilege

Presidential counsel Leonard Garment May 16 characterized the President's new executive privilege guidelines as less than rigid and promised that they would not be used to cover up the Watergate scandal.

The guidelines, as released May 3 by the White House, said past and present presidential aides questioned regarding Watergate should invoke the privilege in connection with conversations with the President, conversations among themselves involving communications with the President and as to presidential papers. *(Text of guidelines, p. 47)*

Asked by White House reporters if the guidelines effectively barred past and present presidential aides from testifying about Watergate, Garment replied that the application of the guidelines in individual cases could not be predicted.

"We're not dealing with a static set of rules," he said, emphasizing that the guidelines offered only "general guidance," and their adequacy would become clear as the investigations by the Senate special committee and the grand jury moved forward.

He noted that there was no way to force an aide to invoke executive privilege if he did not want to, and pointed out that certain former aides already had violated the guidelines in talks with the press.

If the guidelines prove unworkable, "they'll be addressed again, reviewed and appropriate changes will be made," Garment said. The guidelines "do not represent attempts to restrict or suppress information," he said.

Asked if he could give assurances that executive privilege would not be used to cover up the Watergate affair, Garment replied, "I think you can be sure of that."

Background On Changes in Presidential, House Tenure

The President's term in office was one of the most controversial topics at the nation's Constitutional Convention in 1787. The arguments have yet to cool off, for since the Constitution was adopted in 1788, hundreds of amendments have been proposed to alter the provision on presidential tenure.

Nearly 160 amendments have been offered in Congress expressly ordering a change in the presidential term to six years from four with most making a President ineligible for re-election. Action to amend the Constitution's provisions on Presidential terms has been successful only once, in 1951 when the 22nd Amendment was ratified limiting Presidents to two four-year terms.

Though not as widespread through the years, the movement to change the term of office in the House of Representatives from two to four years has had recent presidential support: Dwight D. Eisenhower; Lyndon B. Johnson, who endorsed it in his 1966 State of the Union message; and Richard Nixon are on record in favor of the change.

Presidential Term. Supporters of the single six-year presidential term argue that, under the existing system, Presidents make decisions with a view to the effect a given course of action may have on the next election.

Senate Majority Leader Mike Mansfield (D Mont.), who with Sen. George D. Aiken (R Vt.) in 1971 cosponsored a resolution (S J Res 77) proposing a single six-year presidential term, said in support of the proposal: "Six years could be devoted, free of the burdens of seeking—however unavoidably—partisan political objectives and free of any potential conflicts inherent in such endeavors."

Historically, such a move has had the support of Presidents Andrew Jackson, James Buchanan, Andrew Johnson, Rutherford B. Hayes and Lyndon B. Johnson.

Opponents, however, doubt the efficacy of a single six-year term in correcting the supposed evils in the existing presidential term of office. They charge that a six-year President would be a "lame duck" at once.

In testimony opposing the 1971 Mansfield-Aiken proposal, George Reedy, former press secretary to President Johnson, remarked, "Presidents politic all the time, not just to be re-elected but because there is no other way they can gain support for their programs. Effectiveness and political support are tied together and any effort to separate them will work against the interest of our nation."

The framers of the Constitution had strong sentiments on the issue. According to a Library of Congress report, it took at least 60 ballots before the method of selecting the President was determined. Two alternatives were possible: election by the people or by the Congress. If the Congress was to choose the President, a long term with no re-election was favored by most. If choice was by some other method, a short term with the possibility of re-election was generally favored. Popular election was not considered with great favor during the proceedings. However, the proposals for selection of the President by the Congress gave rise to fears that the legislature would control the executive, thus destroying the principle of separation of powers. Popular election was the form agreed to.

Dissatisfaction with the method has led to suggestions from time to time that the burdens and powers of the presidency be reduced by adopting some sort of parliamentary government.

An amendment providing for a single six-year term was first introduced by Rep. Joseph Hemphill of Pennsylvania in 1826 and has been advocated at different periods ever since. In the last 5 years Senators Mansfield and Aiken have proposed a total of three amendments.

House Term. Proposals for a four-year House term have been considered sporadically by Congress. A committee of the American Political Science Association supported the proposal in 1950, and hearings on the subject were held by the Senate Judiciary Subcommittee on Constitutional Amendments in 1954. President Eisenhower endorsed it at a March 2, 1955, news conference and supported it again in January 1963, after leaving office.

The move for a new House term of four years gained temporary momentum early in 1966 after President Johnson urged it in his State of the Union message. After brief hearings, however, the proposal failed to emerge from House and Senate committees and died in the 89th Congress.

Enthusiasm weakened as opponents criticized President Johnson's insistence that four-year terms coincide with the presidential term. This would create a House of "coattail riders," critics said, and end the minority party's traditional gains in non-presidential election years. The fear of diminishing the independence of the House appeared to be the principal factor that killed the proposal.

The amendment proposed by the President would have taken effect in the November 1972 elections if approved by Congress and three fourths of the states. Johnson, if he were then still President, would have been ineligible to seek another term. His proposal also specified that representatives in mid-term could not run for the Senate without resigning from the House 30 days before the election. This was to allay senators' fears that representatives who were in the middle of a four-year term could seek to unseat a senator without jeopardizing their House seats if unsuccessful.

Supporters argued a four-year term would cut mounting campaign costs and improve legislative expertise. Opponents said the two-year term was designed by the founding fathers with the specific intent of keeping the representatives responsive to the people's wishes and that midterm elections serve as a kind of national referendum on presidential policies. ✓

(Continued from p. 73)
were Vice President Spiro T. Agnew and Attorney General-designate Elliot L. Richardson. Senate Minority Leader Hugh Scott (R Pa.) later told reporters the President was very firm about the need for a commission to recommend ethical standards for future national election campaigns. √

ELECTORAL REFORM TEXT

Following is the White House text of President Nixon's May 16 message to Congress asking for creation of a federal election reform commission:

TO THE CONGRESS OF THE UNITED STATES:

A thorough-going reform of campaign practices in our Federal elections ranks high on our list of national priorities.

Many separate proposals for such reform are now pending before the Congress, in light of recent disclosures of widespread abuses during the Presidential campaign of 1972, many more will doubtless soon be made.

I believe that reform is essential, and urgent; I also believe it is vital that these proposed reforms be carefully considered not singly, but in their relation each to the others, and that this be done in a nonpartisan context.

Therefore, I recommend creation of a Non-partisan Commission on Federal Election Reform, to be established as quickly as possible and to be charged with examining our entire pattern of campaign practices and with recommending a comprehensive set of reforms. A proposed Joint Resolution to accomplish this accompanies this Message.

The Commission I propose would be composed of seventeen members. Eight of these would be chosen by and from the Congress, two Democrats and two Republicans from the Senate and two Democrats and two Republicans from the House of Representatives. It would also include the national chairmen of the two principal political parties, and seven other, public members, to be selected by the President. No more than four of seven public members shall be members of the same political party. To further ensure its complete independence, the chairman and vice-chairman would be selected from among the members of the Commission, by the Commission itself.

The Commission's mandate would be as broad as the Federal election process itself. Nothing would be excluded. It would be authorized to examine the cost and financing of campaigns, including proposals for alternative methods of financing; laws on reporting and disclosure; the elimination from campaigns of violence and the threat of violence, and infringements on the right of privacy, curbing vote frauds, the length of political campaigns; the use and abuse of techniques such as television commercials, polling and computerized direct mail; methods of curbing the entire range of unfair or unsavory campaign practices; and anything else the Commission might consider desirable for a comprehensive reform of Federal elections and campaign practices.

It would be directed to make its final report to the Congress and the President no later than December 1, 1973. It would also be encouraged to make interim recommendations during the course of its work, in order to expedite their consideration by the Congress.

Because it bears an intimate and vital relationship to campaign reform, I recommend that the Commission also consider the question of whether the length of the terms of office of members of the Senate, of the House of Representatives or of the President should be changed.

If the Commission is to complete its work promptly, in order to allow the Congress time to consider and possibly to act on its recommendations prior to the 1974 Congressional campaigns, it is, of course, essential that the Commission begin its work soon and pursue it expeditiously. For my part, I shall do all that I can to facilitate this, and I urge the Congress to take swift and favorable action on this proposal.

RICHARD NIXON

RADIO MESSAGE

Following is the White House text of President Nixon's taped radio address of May 16 on his proposal for a federal election reform commission:

In my televised address to the Nation two weeks ago, I called on the leaders of both political parties, and on citizens everywhere, to join in working toward new ways of ensuring that future elections would be as nearly free of abuse as possible.

To achieve this goal, I have today proposed to the Congress the establishment of a non-partisan, top-level, independent commission charged with making concrete proposals for reform—not only to examine our laws and see what new ones are needed, but also to examine the observance and enforcement of our laws, and those campaign standards and practices not governed by law but rooted in common usage.

This Commission would be composed of seventeen members. Eight would be chosen by and from the Congress—two Democrats and two Republicans from the House, and two Democrats and two Republicans from the Senate. Seven public members would be chosen by the President for their experience, knowledge and perspective in this field—of whom no more than four could be from the same political party. The chairman of the Democratic and Republican National Committees would also serve on the panel. To further ensure the Commission's complete independence, its chairman and vice chairman would be selected from among the members of the Commission by the Commission itself.

Quick Action Asked

I trust the Congress will act swiftly to establish the Commission. Yesterday I met with the bipartisan leadership of the Congress to discuss this matter. The proposal I am making today incorporates suggestions made by them; and my discussions with them have given me reason to believe that swift action is possible. If the Congress does give this proposal its quick approval, then the Commission's report and recommendations can provide the basis for reforms that could be in place in time for the 1974 Congressional elections.

The mandate of the Commission I have proposed will be as broad as the Federal election process itself. Nothing will be excluded.

It will be authorized to examine the costs and financing of campaigns, and look into the various ways in which the costs can be kept down and improper influence or influence-seeking through large campaign contributions can be ended. It can consider limitations on the total amounts candidates can spend, recognizing both the potential for abuse and the heavy burden that high campaign costs impose on both parties. It can look into the laws governing disclosure of campaign funds and how they are spent, and how both those laws and their enforcement might be improved. It can review the tax laws as they relate to the financing of political campaigns and can look into the question of possible public funding of campaigns.

Other areas for inquiry would include the elimination from our election campaigns of violence and the threat of violence; of intimidation; of frauds in the casting and counting of ballots; of the throwing about of misleading or malicious charges; of sabotage and espionage and other infringements on the rights of privacy; and of the whole range of improper campaign practices.

Beyond measures to curb these clearly evident abuses, the Commission will be authorized to examine such matters as the length and structure of our political campaigns, the purposes for which campaign funds are spent, the use and abuse of techniques such as television commercials, polling and computerized direct mail—and whatever else it may consider appropriate to a thorough-going campaign reform.

Terms for Officeholders

There is another matter of crucial importance to our election process, which I am also asking that the Commission consider. That is whether the Constitution should be amended to change the length of the terms of office of members of the House, of the Senate or of the President.

Many political scientists have suggested, for example, that the President should be elected for a single, non-renewable six-year term, instead of being eligible for two four-year terms. The Commission could well consider the merits of this proposal.

Another change it might consider is whether members of the House of Representatives should be elected for terms of four years instead of two.

Personally, I have long favored the four-year term for members of the House, with half of the members elected every two years. Members serving for two-year terms have to spend one of every two years running for re-election, with the result that they serve one year and run one year. This not only places an enormous burden on the member himself; it also can work to the disadvantage of his constituents and of the country. By reducing the extraordinary campaign burden on its members, I believe the House of Representatives could be made a more effective instrument of government.

The Commission will be directed to come up with a comprehensive set of legislative recommendations. It will also be directed to examine whether additional measures, such as voluntary agreements between candidates or party organizations, may be desirable to extend into those areas where legislation cannot appropriately reach.

Because time is of the essence, the Resolution I have proposed would direct the Commission to file a public report no later than December 1 of this year. I believe that with hard work, the members of the Commission can complete their study even before then.

Commission Independence

The Commission will have complete, independent authority to choose its own priorities among the matters to be considered—and, as it proceeds, it will be encouraged to make interim recommendations for action by the Congress without waiting for its final report.

One option I considered was for the Administration itself to prepare a set of proposed reforms and present them at this time. I rejected that course for two reasons:

First, a really comprehensive campaign reform, which I believe we need, must thread its way through enormous complexities, high sensitivities, entrenched interests, and a careful assessment of the possibilities of enactment by the Congress. This will take time. It can be done, but it cannot be done overnight.

Second, I feel it is essential that proposals for reform come not from one political party, not from one Administration, not from one Congress, but from a bipartisan group of recognized experts, working in a non-partisan atmosphere and broadly enough based to give their recommendations the full authority of manifest impartiality.

Let me stress that this new Commission is in no way competitive with the Senate's Ervin Committee. The new Commission will draw on information being developed by the Ervin Committee, and also on other studies of past campaign abuses. But its own central focus will be on the future—on how not only Presidential elections, but also Congressional elections, can most effectively be reformed.

Campaigns have changed drastically in the past century, and even in the past generation. Television, the rise of professional campaign management firms, jet air travel, sophisticated polling techniques, skyrocketing costs, all have had a powerful impact on the way campaigns are conducted. As in so many other areas of our life, the sheer size of modern campaigns has contributed to the size of the problem and to the magnitude of the abuses.

'Sweeping' Reforms Needed

There will be a temptation to attempt reforms piecemeal; this, I believe, would be a mistake. The reforms needed are sweeping rather than scattered, and each should be considered in relation to the others. We should think in terms of nothing less than a complete re-examination of our system of elections and campaign practices.

Scores, perhaps hundreds, of ideas for various election reforms have already been seriously and responsibly put forward. Many are now pending before the Congress. The principal need is to sort through these ideas, to develop such additional ones as may be appropriate, and to design a comprehensive reform of the campaign system so that in its totality it will work, and work fairly and honestly.

It would be premature to predict what a Commission such as the one I propose might recommend. But these are a few examples of the kinds of reform it would certainly consider:

- strict limits on cash contributions;
- strict limits on the size of campaign contributions or the amount of campaign assistance that can be given by business, labor or professional organizations;
- strict limits on the size of individual campaign contributions;
- tightened control over the activities of multiple organizations working for the same candidate;
- shorter election campaigns;
- new disclosure rules that would simplify not only the filing of reports, but also the public discovery of what was important in those reports;
- reducing the cost of reaching the public, as, for example, by making free radio and television time available to candidates, or by revision of the equal time requirements that now restrict broadcasters in their campaign coverage;
- new Federal laws that would make illegal, practices that are now only unethical; and
- the establishment of an independent Federal Elections Commission, with its own enforcement powers.

It is important that these reforms stay within the spirit as well as the letter of the Constitution; that they not unduly infringe either the rights of the States or the First Amendment rights of individuals to freedom of expression and freedom of assembly. It is important that they be fair, effective, realistic and enforceable. Devising such a system of campaign reform will be difficult, but not impossible.

I am convinced a route can be charted that will avoid the obstacles; that wide-ranging reforms are possible and desirable; and that persons of the caliber of those who would be named to this Commission, given a reasonable period of time and also a firm deadline, can come up with a set of proposals that will work, and that will help to restore the faith of the American people in the integrity of their political processes. ✓

O'NEILL: WATERGATE MAY HELP FREE REPUBLICAN VOTES

House Democratic leaders are hopeful that recent Republican defections from the President on the Cambodia issue in Congress are an omen of a new Republican independence spawned by the Watergate disclosures.

"As I look at Watergate, it is releasing pressure that has been on the liberal and progressive Republicans," House Majority Leader Thomas P. O'Neill Jr. (D Mass.) said in an interview with Congressional Quarterly. "It is going to allow them to vote the will of their particular areas. There is no time for us to settle back. Now is the time for us to keep moving."

O'Neill and Speaker Carl Albert (D Okla.) plan to continue their strategy of working to override the President every time he vetoes a piece of legislation because he considers it too expensive. That strategy was a disaster the first time it was tried; the House fell 51 votes short of the two-thirds majority it needed to override a veto of a rural water and sewer grant bill.

Bad Choice. O'Neill concedes that the water-sewer bill wasn't a particularly good bill to use as a test vote. But he said he believes true sentiment on the issue was closer to a two-thirds majority than the actual vote made it appear. In his view, a sizable number of Republicans wanted to vote for the bill but didn't do so because the White House was putting on the squeeze. Now he doesn't think there will be that kind of squeeze.

As evidence, O'Neill cites the April 30 vote on the final version of a bill extending the President's wage and price controls for one more year. The President was dissatisfied with portions of the bill permitting gasoline rationing and calling for disclosure of information about companies that raise prices. But the administration made no attempt to oppose it actively on the floor, and it passed by a 267-115 vote.

"We got some Republican votes on it," O'Neill said, "and I have an idea Watergate may have had something to do with it. We didn't have the usual White House arm-twisting among conservatives."

O'Neill said the same factor was evident the following day when the House voted 229-171 in favor of a bill making the President's budget director subject to Senate confirmation.

Bigger Margin. "We had taken a whip count," O'Neill recalled, "and we were going to win the vote by 12 and 18 votes. We finally won it by 58 votes.... We got a tremendous surge of Republicans who voted along with us.... I feel the Republican members are going to yield and the White House will bend and yield."

The point was made much more dramatically on May 10, when the House voted 219-188 to bar the transfer of funds in a supplemental appropriations bill to pay for U.S. bombing in Cambodia. It was the first anti-war legislation passed in the House since the Vietnam war began, and it passed with the help of 35 moderate Republicans who broke with the President and Minority Leader Gerald R. Ford to support it.

"I think you will see Mr. Nixon moving back toward the middle...I believe we can expect fewer vetoes."

—House Majority Leader Thomas P. O'Neill Jr. (D Mass.)

The majority leader is hopeful that President Nixon, his strength among Republicans seriously weakened by Watergate, will temper the aggressive posture he has maintained toward this Congress.

"I think you will see Mr. Nixon moving back toward the middle. I don't think those who will be advising him are going to be as stringent as those who have been advising him in the past. I believe we can expect fewer vetoes."

Democratic Defectors. But Republicans have not been the only source of worry for the Democratic leadership in recent months. Conservative southern Democrats, under the direction of Rep. Joe D. Waggonner Jr., of Louisiana, have been voting with the Republicans an increasing percentage of the time, even on procedural matters. The Democratic leadership has sought to counter this by getting help from other senior members within the south.

O'Neill said he believes the southerners are not as effective in working together as they were in the days of Rep. Howard W. Smith (D Va. 1931-67). "Smith was quite a leader within the southern bloc," O'Neill recalled, "and he had a staff of people who wrote speeches and were constantly prepared to furnish them to conservative members on a moment's notice. There is nobody of his caliber around today, and I don't think there is anything really cohesive and organized like there was in the past."

Following are excerpts from the transcript:

CQ: There has been a lot of talk about a separate Democratic program to counter some of the President's legislative plans. Are there signs that Democrats in Congress are moving toward their own program of social legislation?

O'NEILL: There will definitely be a strong push for a tax reform bill. There is no question in my mind, after the discussion that took place in our Democratic Steering and Policy Committee, that we have to have legislation of that type, and the leadership is going to sit down with Mr. Mills [Wilbur D. Mills (D Ark.)] and discuss it. That was just one of the items of discussion at the policy meeting.

Somewhere between now and the end of this Congress—not necessarily this year but by the end of 1974—we will have some kind of a health insurance program. There has been a group working on it in the Senate for a year, and Mr. Mills has been cooperating in the House. He has a staff working on it. A health bill isn't something you can put together overnight. They have been working on it for about three years.

We have manpower legislation which we are going forward with, and there is a new elementary and secondary education bill that is being put together by our staff on the Democratic side of the Education and Labor Committee.

We are working on pension reform, too. As I traveled around the country last year to help our Democratic candidates, going to various meetings they had all over the country, frequently people told me about a situation in which some plant in their neighborhood had just gone out of business. They had 18 or 20 years in, and they were only 40 years old, but they had lost their pension rights. The Senate Committee, I believe, is working on that particular legislation.

So I have to say very definitely we do have our own program in mind. The policy committee is meeting now for the first time. We will be meeting twice a month, at least, and new ideas will crop up.

Value of Old Programs

CQ: Would you give much validity to the President's arguments that the Great Society programs have expanded the bureaucracy and often failed to reach the people they were aimed at?

O'NEILL: You have to look at individual programs. If one or two pilot programs have not reached all the way down to the bottom, you cannot condemn all of them.

For example, take the Community Action Programs (CAP). I was amazed, when I went out to South Dakota, and spent three days out there, at how well CAP had worked. It had done so much to aid and stimulate the senior citizens. The programs were tremendous. The senior citizens were becoming much more interested in their own communities.

When I entered major cities I heard the CAP wasn't reaching all the way through to all the people. There were too many persons on the payroll and the money wasn't getting to the roots where it was supposed to be going. So what is good for one area is not good for another. Where there are inequities, we should correct them. But I think the bulk of the programs have done tremendous good.

Presidential Vetoes

CQ: How was the President able to sustain his vetoes?

O'NEILL: It was early in the year. It was a new Congress. Last year the President won one of the most massive victories in the history of the country. There was good discipline in his party.

You have to look at the specific votes. We lost the rural water and sewer bill by a substantial margin. Once the President's supporters reached the magic number of 145 during the roll call and it was known that the President's veto was going to be sustained, we lost 20 to 25 more votes we normally would have had.

If the President vetoes more bills, we will bring them before the Congress, and see what happens. I think you will see Mr. Nixon moving back toward the middle. I do not think those who will be advising him are going to be as stringent as those who have been advising him in the past. I believe we can expect fewer vetoes.

Look at the vote on the bill making the director of the Office of Management and Budget subject to Senate confirmation. We had taken a whip count and we were going to win by 12 to 18 votes. We finally won it by 58 votes. We got a tremendous surge of Republicans who voted along with us. I feel the Republican members are going to yield and the White House will bend.

The Republicans appreciate that if a congressional election were to be held now, we would gain 25 to 30 new seats here. Instead of being beholden to the pressure of the White House, they are going to start voting the feeling of their districts.

Impact of Watergate

CQ: Some members have said that the effect of Watergate would be to slow things down legislatively and create a kind of lethargy around here for the next few months.

O'NEILL: I don't see it that way at all. As I look at Watergate, it is releasing pressure that has been on the liberal and progressive Republicans. It is going to allow them to vote the will of their particular areas. There is no time for us to settle back. Now is the time for us to keep moving.

Campaign Spending

CQ: Will the Democrats push for further amendments to the campaign spending act, perhaps to make it a crime to bug a congressional candidate?

O'NEILL: I don't really think it's got to that point around here. There has been some comment about further progress in correcting the inequities of last year's bill. Mr. Udall (Morris K. Udall (D Ariz.)) put that bill together, for the most part, and he is making a study of how it worked. There is always the opportunity for improvement when legislation is comparatively new.

CQ: Do you expect any specific proposals from the administration as a result of the President's speech the other night, in which he said he wanted to clean up campaigning.

O'NEILL: Not at this particular time. First you have to bring in the independent prosecutor for Watergate, give the man adequate appropriations, access and the ability to subpoena witnesses, and give them immunity. Until that is out of the way, it is too soon to talk about any reform to prevent these things coming about in the future.

White House Staff

CQ: Republicans have complained consistently about their relations with the White House when Haldeman and Ehrlichman were there. Did you deal with them very much?

O'NEILL: I have been to the White House this year seven times on leadership meetings. I missed one because I was out of town.

Normally, we receive a telephone call informing us that the President is going to send up a message or make appointments or something of that nature. On Monday, for example, we received a notification that Haldeman and Ehrlichman were through. This was before the announcement to the press.

When the President has a major problem, a trade or foreign aid bill, he will talk to the leadership on both sides of the aisle and to the ranking members of the committee that would be affected. He did that on foreign aid the other day.

Mr. Kissinger gave a briefing for about 10 minutes and Mr. Rogers gave a briefing for about 10 minutes and the head of the Agency for International Development gave one. Then it went into general questions, with the President putting in his point of view as we went along. That is the usual procedure.

We can ask them the questions that we desire, but they tell us what they are going to send up, and usually it is a message. The problem has been that they send the messages up but not the legislation. The practice has been for the last couple of years that the Nixon administration sends up a message and six weeks later someone within their regime screams that Congress has taken no action. They don't admit to the public that they haven't sent up the legislation.

WATERGATE: A PRESIDENTIAL COUNTERATTACK

President Nixon issued a statement denying any personal complicity in the Watergate scandal but admitting for the first time that some persons in the White House had attempted to cover it up. As talk of his possible resignation increased, the President said he would "continue to do the job I was elected to do."

Nixon did not read the 4,000-word May 22 statement himself. Several members of his staff submitted to an intensive and occasionally acrimonious grilling by reporters.

The Central Intelligence Agency (CIA) was at the forefront of Watergate developments during the week ended May 26. It turned up as a focal point of interest at the second week of hearings by the Senate Watergate investigating committee and in several other committees of both the House and Senate.

As Watergate disclosures continued to unreel on several fronts, U.S. Attorney Harold H. Titus Jr. said in Washington May 24 that more indictments were expected in two to three months. A key figure in the case had agreed to plead guilty and become a government witness, he said. Government sources identified the witness as former White House aide Jeb Stuart Magruder, according to press reports.

Nixon and National Security

President Nixon made a ringing defense of government secrecy in national security affairs May 24 before an audience of more than 500 cheering former Vietnam POWs. Confidentiality and secrecy were essential to the conduct of administration policies aimed at promoting world peace, the President said.

"It is time to quit making national heroes out of those who steal national secrets and publish them in the newspapers," Nixon said in a remark that drew a standing ovation at a reception in the State Department auditorium. "If a document is classified, keep it classified."

The President did not mention his current troubles over the Watergate affair, but the issue of governmental secrecy has been central to Watergate and related activities that have caused him much embarassment. On May 22, the President issued a statement saying his intervention in the Watergate scandal was aimed at protecting national security information from leaks to the press.

Nixon's Statement on Coverup

President Nixon admitted May 22 that there had been a White House coverup in the Watergate affair, but asserted he was innocent of any planning or knowledge of it.

The White House had been buffeted for weeks by charges of complicity in the Watergate break-in and coverup, particularly from grand jury testimony, the Senate special Watergate committee and other congressional hearings. As a result, there were calls for Nixon's resignation.

The President, in a 4,000-word statement and another summary statement, his first public remarks on Watergate since May 9, sought to explain his and the White House's roles in the Watergate affair and related activities. *(Texts, p. 90)*

Nixon did not meet with reporters on the statements. They were released by his press office and questions were taken by presidential aides. *(Excerpts, p. 88)*

Discussing his actions that may have led to the coverup, Nixon said that in 1971, after publication of the Pentagon Papers, he had organized a Special Investigations Unit in the White House headed by John D. Ehrlichman and Egil Krogh, to probe leaks to newsmen.

When the Watergate scandal broke in June 1972, Nixon said he feared that a Watergate investigation might lead to a probe of the Special Investigations Unit (also known as the "plumbers") and from there to the CIA, which he said he mistakenly believed may have been involved in Watergate.

"In this area," Nixon said, "I felt it was important to avoid disclosure of the details of the national security matters with which the group was concerned. I knew that once the existence of the group became known, it would lead inexorably to a discussion of these matters, some of which remain, even today, highly sensitive.

"I wanted justice done with regard to Watergate; but in the scale of national priorities with which I had to deal—and not at that time having any idea of the extent of political abuse which Watergate reflected—I also had to be deeply concerned with ensuring that neither the covert operations of the CIA nor the operations of the Special Investigations Unit should be compromised.

"Therefore, I instructed Mr. (H.R.) Haldeman and Mr. Ehrlichman to ensure that the investigation of the break-in not expose either an unrelated covert operation of the CIA or the activities of the White House investigations unit—and to see that this was personally coordinated between General (Vernon A.) Walters, the deputy director of the CIA, and Mr. (L. Patrick) Gray of the FBI. It was certainly not my intent, nor my wish, that the investigation of the Watergate break-in or of related acts be impeded in any way.

"It now seems that later, through whatever complex of individual motives and possible misunderstandings, there were apparently wide-ranging efforts to limit the investigation or to conceal the possible involvement of members of the administration and the campaign committee."

In a tone of contrition, the President said that hindsight made it apparent he "should have given more heed to the warning signals I received along the way about a Watergate coverup and less to the reassurances.

"To the extent that I may in any way have contributed to the climate in which they (the Watergate and other illegal campaign activities) took place, I did not intend to; to the extent that I failed to prevent them, I should have been more vigilant.

In order to assure that justice is done, Nixon said, he was amending his earlier positions on executive privilege. Henceforth, he said, the doctrine will not be invoked in any matter concerning criminal conduct, and he specifically mentioned Watergate and the coverup.

Concerning the Dean documents, Nixon said they included "authorization for surreptitious entry—breaking and entering, in effect—on specified categories of targets in specified situations related to national security."

Nixon said the plans were drawn up in 1970 under his supervision by the directors of the FBI, CIA, Defense Intelligence Agency and National Security Agency.

The President said the plans were approved July 23, 1970, but five days later, on July 28, approval was rescinded because FBI Director J. Edgar Hoover in the meantime had objected to them.

"It was this unused plan and related documents that John Dean removed from the White House and placed in a safe deposit box," Nixon said. He added that the documents were "extremely sensitive" because they were based upon and included assessments of foreign intelligence capabilities which must remain secret.

Nixon said he organized the "plumbers" in 1971 after publication of the Pentagon Papers. "It created a situation in which the ability of the government to carry on foreign relations...could have been severely compromised," he said.

When Daniel Ellsberg was identified as the papers "leak," Nixon said he told Krogh that the unit "should find out all it could about Mr. Ellsberg's associates and his motives. I did impress upon Mr. Krogh the vital importance to the national security of his assignment," Nixon said.

But the President denied any authorization or knowledge of the break-in at the office of Ellsberg's psychiatrist that later resulted in the dismissal of espionage charges against Ellsberg.

"Because of the emphasis I put on the crucial importance of protecting the national security, I can understand how highly motivated individuals could have felt justified in engaging in specific activities that I would have disapproved had they been brought to my attention," Nixon said. He added that he had to assume responsibility for those actions.

The work of the unit "tapered off" at the end of 1971, but its activities cannot be revealed because of the "highly sensitive" nature of its efforts, Nixon said.

Witnesses May 22

When the Senate Watergate committee opened its third day of hearings on May 22, conspirator James W. McCord Jr. resumed the testimony he had begun the previous week. Also testifying later in the day was James J. Caulfield, a Treasury Department official and former White House aide who described his role in conveying offers of executive clemency from the White House to McCord. *(p. 63)*

McCord had testified earlier that he believed President Nixon had direct knowledge of the clemency negotiations. This was contradicted by Caulfield's testimony, as were several other points in the original McCord statement. But in general, the statements of the two men corroborated each other. *(Text of May 18 McCord statement, p. 94)*

McCord Testimony. In his second day before the committee, McCord described what he called White House-inspired attempts to blame the Watergate operation on the CIA, his employer for 19 years, and to clear the President's re-election committee of any involvement. He read from a memorandum he had submitted to the committee on May 4.

Implicated by McCord was his former attorney, Gerald Alch. The lawyer suggested, McCord said, that McCord's records could be "doctored" to show that he had come out of retirement from the CIA to participate in the Watergate affair.

McCord quoted Alch as telling him that James R. Schlesinger, then the newly announced CIA director, "could be subpoenaed and would go along with it." (Alch denied McCord's allegations concerning his role and said he had asked to testify before the Senate committee. Sen. Henry M. Jackson (D Wash.) issued a statement May 22 which denied Schlesinger's involvement in the alleged scheme.) *(Other CIA developments, box p. 86)*

"I told Alch that I would not use as my defense the story that the operation was a CIA operation, because it was not true," McCord told the committee, reading from one of several written statements he had prepared. "By now," he continued, "I was completely convinced that the White House was behind the idea and ploy which had been presented, and that the White House was turning ruthless and would do whatever was politically expedient at any one particular point in time to accomplish its own ends."

McCord said he was convinced that the White House had fired the former CIA director, Richard Helms, "in order to put its own man in control at CIA," later to pin the operation on the CIA and claim that Helms had been fired for it.

Because of the pressure to blame Watergate on the CIA, said McCord, he had become angry and had written an unsigned letter to Caulfield the week of Dec. 25, 1972. It said:

"I am sorry to have to write you this letter. If Helms goes and the Watergate operation is laid at CIA's feet where it does not belong, every tree in the forest will fall. It will be a scorched desert. The whole matter is at the precipice right now. Pass the message that if they want it to blow, they are on exactly the right course. I'm sorry that you will get hurt in the fallout."

Reading from another statement, McCord said that in September and October 1972 he had phoned the Chilean and Israeli embassies in Washington. He assumed their phones were tapped, he said.

McCord told the committee that he had asked his attorney to file a motion for government disclosure of interceptions of the calls. The attorney, according to McCord's statement, reported that the government had found no evidence of the calls. "I did believe that such

(Continued on p. 82)

Editorial Comment on Nixon's May 22 Statement

Following are excerpts from editorials commenting on President Nixon's May 22 statement on the Watergate situation:

The Washington Evening Star and News, May 23:

Mr. Nixon would have us believe that, in actions he may have taken as regards Watergate, he was motivated by nothing but concern for the national security.

It may be so. But there are a few matters which still confuse us and upon which we would welcome further presidential elucidation. For example, Mr. Nixon admits that the White House Special Investigations Unit ("The Plumbers") was set up on June, 1971, with his approval. He describes it as "a small group" under John Ehrlichman, consisting of Egil Krogh, David Young, E. Howard Hunt and G. Gordon Liddy, a unit known only to "a very few persons at the White House."

Mr. Nixon says the task of The Plumbers was two-fold: to stop security leaks and to "investigate other sensitive security matters." We can understand the group's first function. But we dinf it a trifle hard to understand that, with a huge federal intelligence establishment at his beck and call, Mr. Nixon felt compelled to turn to this small group of buccaneers to undertake tasks of grave national security. Was the FBI really that useless? Could no one in the Secret Serviece be trusted? What about the National Security Agency, the CIA, the Department of Justice, The Treasury, the Defense Department? What qualities had Hunt and Liddy that were lacking in these great departments and agencies?

The New York Times, May 24:

President Nixon's lengthy statement on the Watergate scandals reveals more of the truth than he or any of his senior associates had previously been willing to put on the record. The involvement of the President and of his White House aides in the tangled events that led to these assorted crimes and conspiracies and the subsequent attempt to cover them up is much more extensive than had previously been acknowledged.

The President attempts to justify this involvement by asserting the claims of national security and internal security, but what comes through is the picture of Government frighteningly out of control and directed by men seemingly incapable of making the most elementary distinctions between foreign affairs and domestic affairs, between the interests of the nation and the interests of a particular President or political party, between what is legal and illegal and between what might be permissible in a grave emergency and what is routine procedure....

Although the President's latest statement discloses more of the truth, only the statements of other principals can show whether the whole truth has yet been revealed. Mr. Nixon has reiterated several specific denials about the extent of his knowledge of and therefore his culpability for various misdeeds. Those denials have to stand the test of time. Meanwhile, it is abundantly clear that an inflated and erroneous conception of "national security" led to criminal behavior which has brought the office of the President into grave disrepute.

The Wall Street Journal, May 24:

President Nixon's latest statement on Watergate offers a plausible and even persuasive explanation of events leading up to the break-in and bugging. His explanation of events after the bugging is far less persuasive, and most of all it's a pity the same statement was not made long ago. Coming as it does it reinforces an impression of Greek tragedy, with the President carried by the Fates and the nation dragged along.

We find it absolutely fascinating, in fact, to read of how the Watergate conspirators were first hired to plug the leaks that led to the Pentagon Papers and other disclosures of classified information. And how once started, this rather seamy business became steadily more so, escalating first into illegality in the name of national security, then into illegality in the name of partisan politics.

It in no way excuses any of the offenses, or ignores that those in charge of enforcing laws have a special responsibility to observe them, to note that in this chain of events the Watergage conspirators were neither the only ones nor the first ones to conclude that their purposes were more important than the law. It is a lesson in how much the law depends on a climate of civility, on a consensus that certain offenses are unthinkable, that erodes when the nation becomes politically polarized.

A certain teleology is evident in the sequence leading to the bugging, and one suspects something similar prevailed after the arrests as well. But the President was far less detailed and specific in describing how the coverup came about, though he was more willing than before to admit personal failing, as opposed to mere institutional responsibility. But this admission was wrung out under tremendous pressure, and after one supposedly final explanation. The context can only add to the impression that the President is acting like a man with something to hide.

The Washington Post, May 24:

On Tuesday the President suddenly issued (via Mr. Ziegler) a document of several thousand words seeking to clarify his role in the Watergate crime and coverup and in the related squalors that have come to public attention. It is interesting—and it is also heartbreaking. For appalling as many of the revelations have been that have come to us through the press, the courts and the Ervin Committee hearings, none has provided do damning an indictment of the Nixon presidency as does Mr. Nixon's own attempt to defend it. The President's lengthy statement is—by turn—pathetic, unconvincing, confused. What emerges, however, is all too clear. If you take Mr. Nixon's explanations at face value, there emerges the picture of a kind of incompetence bordering on the criminally negligent, a failure of authority and responsibiility and plain sense that all but defies belief....

Presidents of the United States, over the past couple of decades have been granted by the people considerable license to invoke national security needs as a justification for all manner of activities that otherwise would not be permitted and which certainly would not be permitted to go on in secrecy. This is an enormous trust, and from time to time, our Presidents have abused it. You could argue—and many people do—that President Johson abused it in the course of escalating the American Vietnam involvement. But nobody argues that he abused it for small or personal or political reasons: the dissembling was undertaken, he believed, to fulfill a genuine, if unpopular, national security imperative abroad. Whether he was right or wrong, that is a distinction of some importance. For what we must reluctantly suspect now is not just that Mr. Nixon's campaign and government appointees abused the prerogatives of White House power, but that the President himself is invoking the sacred and serious national security claim frivolously and to ends for which it was never intended. Trust me, the President says. With every effort of his own to maintain such trust, he makes it harder.

Profile of a 'Wireman': He Doesn't Need an Army

Following is the transcript of a brief exchange between Anthony T. Ulasewicz, a former New York City policeman, and Sen. Howard H. Baker Jr. (R Tenn.) at the Senate Watergate committee hearings May 23:

BAKER: I am not familiar with the term. What do you mean a pretty good wireman?

ULASEWICZ: Well, a wireman in police parlance would be anyone who is familiar with applying wiretaps, any type of surveillances by electrical means, and so forth in a room, on a person, in an automobile, in a tire or any place, and I would say he was a good man.

BAKER: Is that a term of general usage in your trade?

ULASEWICZ: Yes, sir. However, I was never a wireman. (laughter) While I was in the Police Department, many of the functions that we did, of course, they were all legal with proper papers, et cetera, and judicial permission. We have some of the finest wiremen in the department. (laughter) So it would be a thing of common knowledge to myself or anyone else.

BAKER: You think your wiremen were better than McCord's wiremen? (This was a reference to James W. McCord Jr., a Watergate conspirator.)

ULASEWICZ: I will tell you, any old retired man in the New York City Police Department who would become involved in a thing like that, he thought he had to for whatever reason it was, he would not have walked in with an army, that is for sure. (laughter)

BAKER: He would not have walked in with an army. Would he have walked in with identification papers and serial-numbered $100 bills and (an) address book?

ULASEWICZ: He probably would have walked in like any decent, common-looking citizen, laid something in the right place and walked right out, and that would have been the end of it for a long time. (laughter) You see, I must be honest here, Senator. (laughter)

BAKER: How could you have gained the information, how could you have gained the information that Mr. McCord obviously or apparently was seeking—that is, a telecommunication link with what was going on in the Democratic National Committee—without going in there with an army and taping the doors and all the rest? Describe to us how else that might have been done by a good man.

ULASEWICZ: Well, a wireman would only do wires. He might not necessarily be a good man for a different type of investigation. If it is a question of obtaining information from the Democratic Party, Republican Party or anybody else, the easiest way is to write a postal card asking them to mail you all their leaflets. They will put you on their mailing list, and you will have everything. If it is all written, they will do it.

BAKER: Politicians are pretty anxious to add to their mailing list.

ULASEWICZ: Politicians are the most vulnerable people in the world, in my last three years of experience, to any kind of scandal, et cetera. I do not say they are guilty of it, because I still have to come back here. (laughter) But because of the type—

BAKER: The last thing on earth I would want to do is to convert your testimony into self-serving purposes for this committee, but you do not have any good wiremen on us, do you? (laughter)

ULASEWICZ: It looks like there are plenty of them here. (He pointed to the television lights overhead.) (laughter)

BAKER: You know that is not a very good answer. You are heightening my concern. (laughter)

ULASEWICZ: I have none on anybody. Thank you.

BAKER: Thank you. (laughter)

disclosure would be a way of testing the truthfulness of the government regarding such illegal interceptions," said McCord.

In another statement read to the committee, McCord explained his reasons for becoming involved in the Watergate matter. He said that former Attorney General John N. Mitchell and former presidential counsel John W. Dean III had given "sanction" to the operation.

McCord said he thought violence was possible at both 1972 national political conventions and that he made some 30 recommendations to protect against violence at the Republican convention in Miami Beach, Fla. "In hindsight," McCord concluded, "I do not believe that the operation should have been sanctioned or executed. However, you asked about my motivations at the time."

McCord also read a statement, the most bizarre of the day, about alleged—but apparently never fulfilled—plans to steal papers from the office of Hank Greenspun, editor of the Las Vegas (Nev.) *Sun.* McCord stated the information came from fellow conspirator G. Gordon Liddy. The incident as reported by McCord occurred in January or February 1972.

Liddy said, according to McCord, that Mitchell wanted some "blackmail-type information" involving a Democratic candidate for President.... Liddy said that this information was in some way racketeer-oriented, racketeer-related, indicating that if this candidate became President, the racketeers or national crime syndicate could have a control or influence over him as President."

Billionaire industrialist Howard Hughes entered into McCord's testimony. McCord quoted Liddy as saying that after the planned break-in at Greenspun's office, "a Howard Hughes plane would be standing by to fly the team directly into a Central American country so that the team would be out of the country before the break-in was discovered."

Also involved, according to McCord's testimony were a prospective job offer (which never materalized) from Hughes after the election, and some alleged contributions by Hughes to the Nixon campaign. "My inclination at this point," said McCord, "is to disbelieve the allegation against the Democratic candidate referred to above and to believe that there was in reality some other motive for wanting to get into Greenspun's safe."

Caulfield Testimony. The chief discrepancy between McCord's and Caulfield's testimony was over presidential knowledge of the clemency offer. According to Caulfield, he never referred to the President himself but to "the highest levels of the White House." His White House contact, he said, was counsel John Dean.

"I specifically never spoke to the President of the United States and have no knowledge of my own as to whether he personally had endorsed this offer or indeed whether anyone had ever discussed it with him," said Caulfield. The 44-year-old former New York City undercover policeman spent an hour and 10 minutes reading a 26-page statement to the committee.

"Since I had worked extensively for Mr. Dean and Mr. Ehrlichman (John D. Ehrlichman, former presidential adviser on domestic affairs), and had formed an impression that Mr. Dean rarely made decisions on matters of consequence without speaking to Mr. Ehrlichman, my guess was that when Mr. Dean referred to 'high White House officials' he at least meant Mr. Ehrlichman," Caulfield testified.

Caulfield differed with McCord's explanation of his reasons for calling the two embassies: "It was Mr. McCord's theory that if the government searched its wiretap records, it would find records of these two calls. Meanwhile, Mr. McCord and his attorneys would make a motion in court, aimed at dismissing the case against Mr. McCord because of the use of wiretap evidence by the prosecution. Mr. McCord's idea was that when the U.S. attorney was told that at least two of Mr. McCord's conversations had been intercepted over a national security wiretap, he would be forced to dismiss the case rather than reveal that the two embassies in question were the subject of a national security wiretap."

Caulfield denied McCord's assertion that he had told McCord to remain silent if called before a grand jury or a congressional committee.

He said that at no time did he "advise, pressure or threaten" McCord "in an attempt to make him accept the offer of executive clemency," adding that he viewed his role as "one of a messenger." At the time of his first conversation with McCord in January, he said, he realized that "I was involved in questionable activity, but I felt that it was important for me to carry this message for the good of the President."

Witnesses May 23

John Caulfield concluded his testimony before the Senate select committee May 23, saying he thought Nixon might have known about attempts to blame the Watergate bugging on the CIA. Caulfield was followed by Anthony T. Ulasewicz, a former New York City detective who enlivened the generally sober proceedings with some unintentional hilarity about the craft of electronic surveillance. *(Box, p. 82)*

But the high points of the day's testimony came later from Boston lawyer Gerald Alch, McCord's former attorney, who had been accused earlier by his former client of pressing McCord to plead guilty and serve a short prison term in return for executive clemency, care for his family and job rehabilitation after his release from prison.

Caulfield Testimony. Persistent questioning by Sen. Lowell P. Weicker Jr. (R Conn.) elicited from Caulfield a comment in which he referred to his humble background as a policeman and said, "I felt extremely strongly about the President." He was loyal to Nixon and his staff, he added, and "I place a high value on loyalty."

This loyalty overrode other considerations, Caulfield admitted in answering a later question from Weicker. The senator quoted from a statement contained in Caulfield's testimony the previous day in which he said he advised McCord, who had resisted alleged overtures from the White House: "Jim, I have worked with these people, and I know them to be as tough-minded as you and I. When you make your statement, don't underestimate them. If I were in your shoes, I would probably do the same thing." Weicker asked Caulfield if this statement did not conflict with his theretofore successful career in law enforcement.

"There's a definite conflict," Caulfield responded. "I know when wrongdoing is occurring. I knew the offer of executive clemency was wrong." As for conflict between the good of the President and the good of the country, Caulfield answered Weicker: "That's a tough question. All I can say is that I did what I did for the reasons I have stated."

He acknowledged that, despite his disclaimers of personal awareness of presidential involvement, "In my mind I felt that the President probably did know about it.... It crossed my mind that this was conceivable for the President."

Ulasewicz Testimony. Ulasewicz, who formerly had worked with Caulfield on investigative matters, had been identified several days before he testified as the man who had made telephone contact with McCord, on Caulfield's behalf, regarding executive clemency. In his committee testimony, he added further corroboration to the stories McCord and Caulfield had told.

In 1971 and 1972, he said in response to questions from Sen. Daniel K. Inouye (D Hawaii), he was paid an annual salary of $22,000 plus expenses by the law firm of Herbert W. Kalmbach, Nixon's former personal lawyer and a Republican fund-raiser, for his investigative activities. "I was no spy, of course, at any time," he said. But he admitted, when asked about his part in calling McCord for Caulfield, "I knew that it was wrong."

Alch Testimony. Alch, an associate of famed defense attorney F. Lee Bailey, read a long statement—backed up by letters and memos submitted to the committee—to attempt to tear down the case McCord had tried to build against him. "These allegations are in some instances completely false and, in other instances, have been twisted out of context into untruths, presumably to serve his present purpose, whatever that may be, but which impugn my personal standards of ethical and legal behavior," he said.

Scattered throughout Alch's testimony were numerous references to the praise he said McCord had heaped on him for his excellence as a lawyer all the way through the criminal trial. McCord and Bernard Fensterwald, another lawyer hired by McCord after his conviction, were present in the hearing room for most of Alch's testimony.

These were the chief points, some of which differed from McCord's statements, of Alch's testimony:

- At no time, said Alch, did McCord tell him that he regarded the Watergate operation as legal because of the alleged involvement of former Attorney General Mitchell or former White House counsel Dean. Alch advised the legal defense of "duress"..."wherein the perpetrator felt compelled to break a law in order to prevent a greater evil." McCord agreed, he said. (The defense was rejected by the court.)
- McCord did not tell his attorney that his phone calls to the Chilean and Israeli embassies in the fall of 1972 were not of relative substance to the case, Alch said. "His theory was that the government, rather than

reveal such (embassy wiretapping) activity, would dismiss the case against him."

• Government prosecutors and the trial judge offered McCord three pre-trial opportunities to plead guilty in return for a recommendation of leniency (but not freedom), said Alch. The attorney made this point to counter what he called McCord's implications that Alch had pressured him to plead guilty and remain silent.

• "At no time did I suggest to Mr. McCord that the so-called CIA defense be utilized.... Mr. McCord's allegation that I announced my ability to forge his CIA personal (sic) records with the cooperation of then acting CIA Director Schlesinger is absurd and completely untrue."

• It was not true, according to Alch, that he told McCord that the lawyer for codefendant E. Howard Hunt Jr. wanted to discuss an executive clemency offer. "At this point, I mentioned to Mr. Bittman (William O. Bittman, Hunt's lawyer) that I felt my client was becoming a bit paranoid, that he felt he was being made the 'patsy' or 'fall guy....' "

Alch said Bittman advised him to "tell McCord he will receive a call from a friend of his." No mention of the White House was made, as alleged by McCord, Alch added. The phone calls and meetings described earlier by McCord resulted from the initial call from Ulasewicz.

• Contrary to McCord's allegation, executive clemency was discussed with Alch only once, late in 1972, the lawyer said. "Jim, it can be Christmas, Easter and Thanksgiving all rolled up into one, but in my opinion, the President wouldn't touch this with a 10-foot pole," Alch said he told McCord. His client "laughed and agreed with me," Alch added.

• Attorney Fensterwald was recommended as a man who could help raise McCord's $100,000 bail after his conviction, Alch said. Fensterwald's efforts to raise the money were unsuccessful, and he later said he had never met McCord, Alch continued. "This seemed unusual to me, to say the least, that a man would be doing what Mr. Fensterwald said he was trying to do for someone he had never met, but I was not about to look a gift horse in the mouth." McCord's wife, said Alch, was able to raise $60,000 for bail, and Fensterwald produced the remaining $40,000.

• Alch said he did not know until March, when it was read in open court, that McCord had written a memo to Judge John J. Sirica charging political pressure against the defandants and perjury by unnamed persons.

• He and Fernsterwald agreed to represent McCord—Fensterwald while Alch was at a trial in Chicago for several weeks—at the end of March, said Alch. He said he has talked by phone with Fensterwald several times since, but has seen neither him nor McCord.

He quoted Fensterwald as saying in one conversation, "We're going after the President of the United States." When he retorted that he was not interested in a vendetta against the President, said Alch, Fensterwald responded, "Well, you'll see; that's who we're going after, the President."

• Alch quoted Fensterwald as telling him, when notified of a May 7 McCord memorandum to the Senate Watergate committee alleging the attempt to blame the CIA: "I can only hazard the quess that it is the result of Mr. McCord's faulty recollection." *(p. 57)*

Rep. Mills' Death

Rep. William O. Mills (R Md.) was found dead May 24 at his home in Easton, Md., in what authorities described as an apparent suicide. The week before his death, Mills had become embroiled in a controversy over funds used in his 1971 campaign for the House seat vacated by Interior Secretary Rogers C. B. Morton.

A General Accounting Office (GAO) report issued May 19 showed that Mills had received $25,000 in cash from the Finance Committee to Re-elect the President before April 7, 1972, when reporting of such contributions became mandatory. Hugh Sloan, former treasurer of the finance committee, told the GAO he gave the money to Morton's executive assistant, Robert J. Hitt, sometime in 1971. The report quoted Hitt as saying that the $25,000 was "all used in the 1971 campaign to select (Morton's) successor as a Maryland congressman."

Mills issued a statement May 22 denying any improper behavior. "I personally did not receive or disburse any money during my campaign.... My campaign manager advised me that the (Nixon) administration had arranged for funds to be made available. I had no access to the money, nor did I direct or authorize expenditure of any of the money," he said. According to press reports, the contribution was not reported by Mills or any of his campaign committees to the Maryland State Board of Elections, as required by state law.

Mills was the 14th member of Congress to meet a violent death since Jan. 1, 1946, and the third to commit suicide in that period. (Rep. Joseph Wilson Ervin (D N.C. Jan. 3-Dec. 25, 1945), brother of Sen. Sam J. Ervin Jr. (D N.C.), committed suicide Dec. 25, 1945). Three members of the House, Reps. Hale Boggs (D La.), Nick Begich (D Alaska) and George W. Collins (D Ill.) died in plane crashes in 1972.

Witnesses May 24

The question of who was lying, McCord or Alch, and who was telling the truth reached an apparent impasse on May 24 as the committee interrogated Alch. The Boston attorney concluded his testimony that morning with a suggestion that he, McCord and McCord's lawyer submit to lie detector tests. The suggestion met with cool responses.

Two men involved in the break-in and bugging of Democratic national headquarters testified in the afternoon. The first was Bernard L. Barker, one of the five men arrested in the burglary and later convicted. The second was Alfred C. Baldwin III, the man who tapped Democratic phones from a motel room across the street from the Watergate building and traded his cooperation with investigators for immunity from prosecution.

Alch Testimony. Before Alch resumed testifying, Committee Chairman Sam J. Ervin Jr. (D N.C.) announced that the committee had requested McCord and Fensterwald to submit written statements of rebuttal to the charges Alch made against them on May 23. Ervin said

Television, Radio Coverage

Both commercial and non-commercial radio and television networks scheduled heavy coverage of the Senate Watergate hearings. All three privately owned television networks—the American Broadcasting Company, Columbia Broadcasting System and National Broadcasting Company—had complete "live" coverage, starting on opening day and continuing through the second week.

But the networks kept their options open for later coverage. Spokesmen for all three said they planned to devote extensive time to the hearings, both in their regular newscasts and in special reports on highlights. And they might return to "live" coverage of important developments or interesting witnesses. "It depends on events," said a CBS official. "We'll use our editorial discretion," said an ABC spokesman. The only complete coverage was promised in advance by the non-commercial network, the Public Broadcasting Service. A PBS spokesman said the hearings would be taped and made available for showing in full during the evening by affiliated stations.

Radio. Only the National Public Radio network scheduled complete "live" broadcasts of the hearings. The commercial radio networks—ABC, CBS, NBC and Mutual—all planned some special broadcasts to cover highlights of the hearings. Periodic interruptions of regular programs were anticipated to bring listeners on-the-scene coverage of significant developments.

the two would meet with the committee staff, but he indicated reluctance to have them appear before the committee again at the public hearings. "The committee does not intend to become bogged down in controversy between lawyers," he said.

Vice Chairman Baker noted the dilemma the committee faced in trying to reconcile the differences between Alch's and McCord's testimony. He asked Alch for suggestions on how to reconcile the differences.

Alch offered two solutions: obtaining testimony from other persons present at the contested meetings or having closely supervised lie detector tests administered to him and McCord. He later extended the lie detector (polygraph) suggestion to Fensterwald.

At the close of the morning session, Fensterwald, who was present with McCord for the Alch testimony, said he and McCord would agree to the tests if Ervin announced that they would be given, as a matter of committee policy, to all witnesses.

Sen. Herman E. Talmadge (D Ga.) put witnesses on notice that if perjury was indicated in their testimony, a transcript would be given to legal authorities for possible prosecution.

Inouye said that any Democrat involved in illegal political activity should be indicted. He recommended that the investigating committee request the Justice Department's internal security division to provide the committee with any evidence it had collected pertaining to criminal conspiracies involving Democrats. Ervin directed the committee staff to make the request.

Barker Testimony. Barker, a former CIA employee, explained how he had participated in trying to locate documents at Democratic headquarters and, the year before, in the office of Pentagon Papers defendant Daniel Ellsberg's former psychiatrist. He said he found none in either place.

He denied McCord's assertion that he had applied pressure on McCord to plead guilty and receive executive clemency during the Watergate trial in January. He said he had been recruited for the operations by fellow conspirator E. Howard Hunt, his boss in the 1962 Bay of Pigs invasion of Cuba, because of his interest in protecting national security.

In the break-ins in which he participated, said Barker, he and his colleagues sought records of contributions to the Democrats—at the psychiatrist's office, at Democratic headquarters and at presidential candidate George McGovern's headquarters, which were not entered—by Castro's Cuba. "I am a bilingual American who is dedicated to the liberation of Cuba," said the Cuban-born Barker, now a Miami, Fla., realtor.

Baldwin Testimony. Baldwin, a former FBI agent from Hamden, Conn., denied that he had been a "double agent" for the Nixon re-election committee and the Democrats. He recounted how he had served briefly in 1972 as a bodyguard for Martha Mitchell, wife of the former attorney general. He described how McCord, who recruited him, had given him a .38-caliber pistol. He told the senators how he had observed antiwar members of Congress and antiwar demonstrations in the capital. And he repeated much of what he had said for the record earlier about his electronic eavesdropping on Democratic officials across the street from his motel room.

Additional Hearings. The first round of Senate committee hearings had been scheduled to recess until June 12. But Ervin announced at the start of the May 24 hearings that three extra days of testimony had been scheduled for June 5, 6 and 7.

Daily Chronology

Following is a day-to-day chronology of the week's events:

MAY 17

(Earlier May 17 events, p. 69)

CIA Hearings. After a third day of Senate Armed Services Committee hearings on CIA involvement in domestic activities, Sen. Stuart Symington (D Mo.) said it was hard for him to "visualize" that Nixon was unaware of attempts by White House officials to enlist the CIA in a Watergate coverup, although there had been no direct testimony to that effect. Testifying at the closed session were former CIA Director Richard Helms, former CIA Deputy Director Gen. Robert Cushman and Lt. Gen. Vernon A. Walters, current CIA deputy director.

A sworn statement Walters had submitted to various congressional committees during the week, which the

'President's Wish' of CIA Aid: Stated or Inferred?

Chapter two in the story of alleged White House pressure on the Central Intelligence Agency (CIA) to help coverup the Watergate case unfolded May 21 with a statement that former Nixon chief of staff H. R. Haldeman told the deputy director of the CIA that "it is the President's wish" that the CIA assist in one area of the coverup attempt.

Haldeman's remark reportedly was made in July 1972 at a meeting with Gen. Vernon A. Walters and contained in a memorandum of the conversation Walters wrote after the meeting.

The memorandum was referred to during a hearing before the Senate Foreign Relations Committee by Sen. Stuart Symington (D Mo.). The committee had invited the former director of the CIA, Richard Helms, to answer questions concerning a report that the White House had pressured the CIA to assist in a coverup in the Watergate case. *(p. 66)*

According to Symington, the memorandum recorded Haldeman as telling Walters: "It is the President's wish that you go to see Mr. Gray."

Walters testified May 14 at a Senate Armed Services Committee hearing that White House aides had asked that he convince the former acting director of the FBI, L. Patrick Gray III, that an investigation of Nixon campaign funds in Mexico would impair CIA operations there. The campaign funds from Mexico had turned up in the bank account of one of the men arrested during the Watergate break-in June 17, 1972.

Walters later was said to have told a House Armed Services subcommittee that he might have made a mistake in attributing the phrase about "the President's wish" to Haldeman.

According to subcommittee chairman Lucien N. Nedzi (D Mich.), Walters testified May 21 that he may have incorrectly inferred that the President "wished" the CIA to help in blocking the Mexican investigation. Nedzi said Walters might have inserted the remark in his memorandum because he thought the remark "was implicit" in the conversation with Haldeman.

Although Helms' appearance before the committee was intended to discuss the CIA's assistance to one of the Watergate defendants prior to the break-in at the Watergate, the committee's interest in the alleged coverup operation dominated the hearing.

Helms testified that he could not remember Haldeman referring to the President in asking Walters to meet with Gray, but did not discredit the Walters memorandum. Asked why he had not reported attempts to involve the CIA to the President personally, Helms answered: "My interest was to keep the CIA out of this (Watergate). Frankly, I wanted to stay as head of the agency and keep it out of all of this. It is always a question of moral judgments, and I was doing the best I could."

Committee member Charles H. Percy (R Ill.) asked Helms if the former director thought his removal as head of the CIA following the November elections could be construed as a reprisal for the CIA's refusal to assist the White House.

"I don't know," Helms answered. "I talked to the President, and I think our conversation is privileged."

Helms had met with Nixon to discuss his direction of the CIA. *The Washington Post* quoted sources close to the former agency director as saying that Helms was fired during the meeting. He later accepted the President's appointment to be ambassador to Iran.

Armed Services Committee had released in summary form, was made public in its entirety. According to the document, Walters stated that L. Patrick Gray III, former acting FBI director, said he was prepared to resign over alleged White House pressure on the CIA and FBI to cover up the Watergate scandal.

Special Prosecutor Guidelines. Elliot L. Richardson issued a proposed eight-point charter defining the authority of the special Watergate prosecutor. Richardson promised not to "countermand or interfere with" the prosecutor's decisions or to remove him from office "except for extraordinary improprieties."

Senate Judiciary Committee members, still considering Richardson's nomination as attorney general, continued to express dissatisfaction with his insistence that the prosecutor's independence would have to be "consistent with the attorney general's statutory accountability for all matters falling within the Department of Justice." *(Hearings, p. 96)*

Casey Denial. Former SEC Chairman William J. Casey issued a statement denying that he had agreed to delete a controversial item from the agency's complaint against financier Robert L. Vesco. Casey, under secretary of state for economic affairs, said the decision not to mention a $200,000 Vesco contribution to the Nixon campaign was made by G. Bradford Cook, who resigned as SEC chairman May 16. In his resignation statement, Cook said that Casey had "concurred" in the decision. *(Cook resignation, p. 67)*

Ziegler Comments. Presidential Press Secretary Ronald L. Ziegler said at a White House briefing that the President was aware of critical statements such as the one made May 16 by Sen. Barry Goldwater (R Ariz.) on the Watergate issue, and that he was continuing to work on foreign and domestic matters. Ziegler denied any knowledge of a *Washington Post* report that former presidential assistant John D. Ehrlichman had possession of the medical records of Sen. Thomas F. Eagleton (D Mo.) before the news of Eagleton's psychiatric treatment broke in July 1972 after he was picked as the Democratic vice presidential nominee. In response to a question, Ziegler said he had no intention of resigning as press secretary. *(Goldwater statement p. 69)*

Pressure Continues. Speaking before the National Press Club in Washington, D.C., Sen. Charles H. Percy (R Ill.) warned that "for practical purposes there will be no real government...until Watergate has been put behind us." Percy called upon the White House to disclose voluntarily all facts related to the case.

In separate speeches, Sargent Shriver, who replaced Eagleton as 1972 Democratic vice presidential candidate, and Joseph A. Califano Jr., a top White House aide in the Johnson administration, suggested that the President consider resigning because of the Watergate scandal.

Houston Jury. A federal grand jury in Houston, Texas, ordered Arthur M. Urech, vice president and treasurer of Gulf Resources and Chemical Corporation, to testify in its investigation of a $100,000 contribution the company made to the 1972 Nixon campaign. The grand jury was investigating reports that part of the contribution went into the Miami bank account of convicted Watergate conspirator Bernard L. Barker and was used to help finance the Watergate bugging. Urech appeared before the grand jury on May 18. *(Presidential adviser John Connally's law firm connection, p. 65)*

MAY 18

Cox Named. Attorney General-designate Elliot L. Richardson said he would appoint former Solicitor General Archibald Cox as the special prosecutor for the Watergate case. *(Details, p. 96)*

McCord Testimony. Testifying before the Senate investigating committee, convicted Watergate conspirator James W. McCord Jr. said that John J. Caulfield, then a White House aide, offered him executive clemency in the President's name. *(Details, p. 63)*

White House Denial. Presidential Press Secretary Ronald L. Ziegler responded to McCord's assertions by repeating an earlier White House denial. "The President did not participate in any way, or have any knowledge regarding the coverup and at no time authorized anyone to represent him in offering executive clemency," he said.

Mitchell As 'Fall Guy.' In a late evening telephone interview with United Press International, former Attorney General John N. Mitchell said of the Watergate scandal: "Somebody has tried to make me the fall guy, but it isn't going to work.... I've never stolen any money. The only thing I did was to try to get the President re-elected. I never did anything mentally or morally wrong."

CIA Hearings. After more testimony by CIA Deputy Director Lt. Gen. Vernon A. Walters before the Senate Armed Services Committee, Sen. Stuart Symington (D Mo.) announced that additional information supplied by Walters made it "even more difficult for me to visualize that the President" knew nothing about White House attempts to involve the agency in a Watergate coverup. *(Hearings, p. 79)*

Fielding Deposition. In a pretrial deposition released to the press, Fred F. Fielding, who was an assistant to John W. Dean III at the White House, made wide-ranging allegations about the involvement of White House aides in the alleged Watergate coverup. The testimony was prepared for a number of civil suits connected with the case.

California Suit. The California Committee for Eugene McCarthy filed suit in San Francisco Superior Court against officials of the Nixon campaign and others, charging that a bogus letter was sent out under the Committee's letterhead during the 1972 California primary campaign. Named in the suit were Donald H. Segretti, Herbert W. Kalmbach, Maurice Stans, John Mitchell, the Committee for the Re-election of the President and 15 others.

Kissinger Leaks. Citing former National Security Council staff members as sources, *The Washington Post* reported that Henry A. Kissinger, White House national security adviser, was himself a "prime source" of information leaks the government tried to plug by wiretapping officials and newsmen between 1969 and 1971. *(Earlier charges, p. 69)*

MAY 19

GAO Report. The federal elections division of the General Accounting Office (GAO) released a report charging that Nixon's former personal lawyer, Herbert W. Kalmbach, raised at least $210,000 for distribution to "the Watergate defendants or their attorneys" through unidentified intermediaries. The report also said that former White House aide Gordon Strachan received $350,000 in cash from the Finance Committee to Re-elect the President immediately before the new campaign finance law took effect April 7, 1972, in "an obvious attempt to evade" the law.

IRS Request. John J. Caulfield, then a White House aide, tried unsuccessfully in 1970 to get investigative data of the Internal Revenue Service on C. Arnholdt Smith, a Nixon associate, *The New York Times* reported. According to the Times sources, Caulfield asked an IRS agent to give the information to John D. Ehrlichman, then serving as presidential counsel. Caufield had been named by James W. McCord Jr. as the person who offered him executive clemency in exchange for silence on the Watergate bugging.

Casey-Dean Contact. *The Washington Post* quoted former SEC Chairman William J. Casey as saying he rejected a November 1972 request by John W. Dean III to help block an SEC investigation of a secret contribution to the Nixon campaign made by financier Robert L. Vesco. *(Vesco indictment, p. 46)*

Bush On Money. At a meeting of Republican state chairmen in Chicago, the party's national chairman, George Bush, said the Republican National Committee would like to take over all funds remaining in the hands of the Nixon re-election committee. It is normal practice for the national committee to assume the debts of a presidential candidate after an election, Bush explained.

ADA Asks Resignation. The liberal Americans for Democratic Action (ADA) voted at its national convention in Washington, D.C. to call for Nixon's resignation and for Congress to censure him for "the worst political scandal in American history."

MAY 20

Ervin Barb. Sen. Sam J. Ervin Jr. (D N.C.), chairman of the Senate Watergate committee, criticized the Justice Department for waiting until after the 1972 election to try the "five men caught red-handed in actual burglary" at the Watergate. Ervin, speaking on ABC-TV's "Issues and Answers," also emphasized that

(Continued on p. 89)

Excerpts From White House Aides on Nixon Statement

Following are excerpts from a White House briefing May 22 on the President's Watergate statement. Participants were Leonard Garment, the President's counsel; J. Fred Buzhardt, special counsel, and Ronald L. Ziegler, presidential press secretary:

Q: This statement says on page 5 that "Within a few days, however, I was advised that there was a possibility of CIA involvement in some way." Just who advised the President of this? The statement doesn't say.

GARMENT: There are some transactions that can be stated with certainty. There are others that must be stated with a certain degree of generality. The question of who, out of a possible number of persons, whether it be two, three or four, who might have drawn particular information to his attention, or the totality of circumstances from which that suspicion or knowledge of supposed fact came, is something that really cannot be stated with certainty at this time.

* * * *

Q: Can I ask why Mr. Hoover objected to the plan which was formed and why he broke off relations with the rest of the intelligence community, and why the President didn't order him to restore them?

BUZHARDT: The details of why liaison was broken off between the FBI and the CIA in May, I believe it was, 1970, are not a matter of record. They appear to have been matters that arose in private discussions. I gather from the record that there was some dispute as to whose job was what. But that is not specified in the records, so we don't know.

I think that as to the others, it was partly a question of manpower, partly a question of organization with the Bureau. That is my understanding.

Q: Does that mean Mr. Hoover had a veto over the President of the United States?

BUZHARDT: No.

* * * *

Q: Mr. Garment, I would like to get a reconciliation of two statements, one in today's release in which Mr. Gray suggested to the President that the matter of Watergate might lead higher, and the President told him to press ahead with an investigation.

Now, in the April 30th speech, the President says, "As the investigation went forward, I repeatedly asked those conducting the investigation whether there was any reason to believe that members of my Administration were in any way involved. I received repeated assurances that there were not." Could you reconcile those two statements for us?

GARMENT: I think the reconciliation has to be furnished by the fact that this matter has been under very extensive and extremely intensive study over the past weeks since the April 30th statement. There is much more that is known now. Recollection is clear here. The documents have been examined. There has been some, although limited, access to persons who have recollections of transactions, and we are at a point where we can make certain statements with a reasonable degree of certainty with respect to transactions some time back.

Q: Is the President's April 30th statement wrong in that regard, Len?

GARMENT: No. I think the April 30th statement represented the President's knowledge and recollection at that point stated to the finest state of certainty, and that process of investigation and examination has continued since then, and this statement is a more complete statement.

* * * *

Q: At the bottom of page 2, the President speaks of a security problem that arose in 1970, and this security problem deals with the campus unrest, some bombings, campus demonstrations, mostly—as a matter of fact, all that I can see here—domestic situations. Then the President approved a plan—I understand it never went into effect, but he approved it—which included authorization for surreptitious entry, breaking and entering in effect, on specific categories of targets and specified situations relating to national security.

Now, I have several questions about it. One, what is the jump that the President was making from domestic security here in speaking at the bottom of page 2 about entirely domestic situations, to justifying breaking and entering in cases relating to national security?

BUZHARDT: The plan—which, incidentally, is still classified—was not confined to domestic matters. There were also, as is evident from the fact that some agencies which were concerned exclusively with foreign intelligence were also participating, so it was not a matter that was exclusively domestic.

Q: Was the breaking and entering justified entirely on the basis of national security, or did it relate to internal security as well?

BUZHARDT: I don't think I could specify more specifically, except to say that the type of intelligence operations which were considered were ones that had been conducted prior to 1966, and the question was whether to resume them.

Q: Well, could you declassify the paragraphs that relate to breaking and entering so we can see what the President—

BUZHARDT: No, I could not.

Q: Len, sticking to the report, I would like to put the specific question, whether this plan that the President approved on July 28th—five days before that, in July of 1970—whether this plan authorized breaking and entering in so-called domestic security cases.

GARMENT: I really don't know. Basically, what I know about the document is that it was signed by the officers of the major intelligence agencies of the government, including Mr. Helms, Admiral (Noel) Gayler, General (Donald V.) Bennett, and J. Edgar Hoover.

Q: Did it authorize breaking and entering into domestic security cases? That is a simple question.

BUZHARDT: I would not address it further for the simple reason it is a classified document. I have no authority to declassify the document.

Q: Classified or otherwise, do you realize you are leaving unanswered the question whether or not the President of the United States approved felonies? Do you understand that?

Q: You certainly know enough about law to know that, Fred.

BUZHARDT: I know quite well what the law is.

Q: Ron, based on this briefing alone, I come away with the impression that the President engaged in a conspiracy to commit an illegal act; that is, the evidence is here on the top of page 3 that the President approved an illegal act.

Now, there has not been any statement from Mr. Garment or Mr. Buzhardt or anyone else to counter that suspicion and I am wondering if you can clear it up?

ZIEGLER: First of all, there was no act. Second of all, the President did not engage in a conspiracy, as he clearly states in both statements, and there you have a specific comment in relation to that assertion.

(Continued from p. 87)
the committee had "received no competent evidence to connect the President" with the Watergate scandal.

MAY 21

Haldeman Request. Lt. Gen. Vernon A. Walters, CIA deputy director, said that former White House chief of staff H. R. Haldeman told him "it is the President's wish" that the CIA help block an FBI investigation of Nixon campaign money that was reportedly "laundered" in a Mexican bank, Sen. Stuart Symington (D Mo.) revealed. (Haldeman later told *The New York Times* the President was not "at any time" involved in a coverup attempt.) The Walters disclosure was contained in a memorandum he wrote after a White House meeting June 23, 1972, which he said was also attended by former CIA Director Richard M. Helms.

Meanwhile, Walters discussed the memorandum and 10 others he wrote during the summer of 1972 at a closed hearing of the House Armed Services Intelligence Subcommittee.

Helms Testimony. Former CIA Director Richard M. Helms, appearing before the Senate Foreign Relations Committee to explain the agency's involvement in the Pentagon Papers case, was asked about the June 23 meeting. Helms said he assumed Haldeman's request had "authority," but that he could not recall the phrase "it is the President's wish."

Asked why he never informed the President of White House efforts to enlist the CIA in a Watergate coverup, Helms replied, "Frankly, I wanted to stay as head of the agency and to keep it out of all this." Helms was replaced as CIA director by James R. Schlesinger on Dec. 21, 1972.

Intelligence Plan. Late in the day, former White House aide Tom Charles Huston testified at a closed hearing of the Senate Armed Services Committee about an aborted plan for domestic espionage by the FBI, CIA and other agencies. Symington announced after the hearing that Huston had drafted such a plan, which allegedly included proposals for breaking into foreign embassies, in 1970—but that it was rejected by the late FBI Director J. Edgar Hoover. *(Hearings, p. 79)*

Mitchell, Stans Plea. Former Nixon cabinet officers John N. Mitchell and Maurice H. Stans and New Jersey Republican politician Harry L. Sears pleaded not guilty to charges of conspiracy to defraud the United States and obstruct justice before a federal judge in New York. The charges were connected with an alleged attempt to intervene with the SEC in behalf of financier Robert L. Vesco. A bench warrant was issued for the arrest of Vesco, who was believed to be out of the country. *(Indictments, p. 46)*

Mystery Caller. *Newsweek* magazine reported in its May 28 issue that Senate investigators had identified the caller who relayed an offer of executive clemency to Watergate conspirator James W. McCord Jr. as Anthony T. Ulasewicz. The magazine said that Ulasewicz, a former New York City policeman, was hired in 1969 by former White House aide John D. Ehrlichman to do political investigating. Ulasewicz later acknowledged making the calls to McCord. *(McCord testimony, p. 94)*

Cox Assurance. Archibald Cox, Elliot L. Richardson's nominee for special Watergate prosecutor, assured the Senate Judiciary Committee that he would pursue his investigation of the case independently and without sparing the President if evidence implicated him. Cox spoke during continuing hearings on Richardson's nomination for attorney general. *(Hearings, p. 96)*

MAY 22

Nixon Statement. President Nixon released to the press a 4,000-word statement on the Watergate case, in which he conceded for the first time that there had been "wide-ranging efforts" in the White House to cover up aspects of the Watergate case—but denied that they took place with his approval or knowledge. The White House coverup efforts, Nixon asserted, were linked to his desire to protect national security by preventing disclosure of intelligence operations. *(Text of statement, p. 90)*

Presidential counsels Leonard Garment and J. Fred Buzhardt briefed reporters on the statement, which was Nixon's first comment on the Watergate case since his May 9 speech to a Republican fund-raising dinner in Washington. *(May 9 speech, p. 48)*

McCord-Caulfield Testimony. Convicted Watergate conspirator James W. McCord Jr. returned for a second day of testimony before the Senate investigating committee. He was followed by John J. Caulfield, a former White House aide then on leave from the Treasury Department, who told the committee that John W. Dean III ordered him to offer McCord executive clemency. Caulfield said he had "no knowledge of my own" that Nixon had approved the offer, as McCord had testified he was led to believe.

Richardson Recalled. Attorney General-designate Elliot L. Richardson was unexpectedly recalled by the Senate Judiciary Committee for testimony on his contacts with Egil Krogh Jr., a former White House aide who assumed responsibility for the break-in at the office of Daniel Ellsberg's psychiatrist. The committee had been expected to approve Richardson's nomination without further delay, but was reportedly warned by Ellsberg that Richardson was not telling all he knew about the Krogh affair.

Prosecutors to Resign. *The New York Times* reported that, according to Justice Department sources, the three federal prosecutors in the Watergate case were "on the verge" of resigning from the case, because they resented the appointment of a special prosecutor. The three—Assistant United States Attorneys Earl J. Silbert, Seymour Glanzer and Donald E. Campbell—reportedly delayed their decision until after meeting the next day with the designated special prosecutor, Archibald Cox.

CIA Documents. Sen. Stuart Symington (D Mo.) announced that "high level representatives" of the CIA had delivered to the Senate Armed Services Committee copies of letters received by the CIA between July 1972 and January 1973, warning of attempts to blame the CIA for the Watergate bugging. Most of the letters were anonymous, Symington said, but there was "some reason to believe" they were written by James W. McCord Jr., the former CIA employee convicted in the bugging case.

The senator said he was forwarding copies of the letters to the Senate investigating committee and to the U.S. attorney's office. He listed two other sets of documents the committee had passed on to those bodies:

- Eleven memorandums of conversations, written by CIA Deputy Director Lt. Gen. Vernon A. Walters and dealing with events in late 1972 and early 1973.

• Two documents, dated during the summer of 1970 and dealing with potential illegal domestic intelligence operations.

Colson SEC Case. *The Washington Post* printed a memo allegedly written April 19 to former special presidential counsel Charles W. Colson by one of his law partners. The memo asked for White House pressure to appoint King Mallory, SEC acting director, as SEC general counsel. A note written across the top of the memo said, "I'll call Cook if necessary, but I think Jerry Jones could lock this one up for us."

The Post said Colson acknowledged writing the note on the memo, but denied that he ever acted on the recommendation it contained. G. Bradford Cook, the former SEC chairman mentioned in Colson's note, told the paper he had resented the pressure tactics of the Colson law firm. Mallory said he had never heard of the pressure in his behalf, but was "outraged" by the memo.

MAY 23

McCord-Alch Clash. Gerald Alch, the Boston attorney who defended James W. McCord Jr. in the Watergate criminal trial, read a statement to the Senate investigating committee disputing charges McCord made against him in previous testimony. Alch denied that he suggested portraying the burglary as a CIA operation or that he had participated in an offer of executive clemency for McCord. Alch said that McCord and his new lawyer, Bernard Fensterwald of Washington, D.C., were engaged in a "vendetta" against Nixon.

John J. Caulfield, the former White House aide and McCord associate, preceded Alch in the witness chair. Caulfield said he believed Nixon had known of his offer to McCord of executive clemency, although he had no concrete proof.

Richardson Confirmed. After long, close scrutiny by the Senate Judiciary Committee, the Senate quickly confirmed Elliot L. Richardson as Attorney General by a vote of 82 to 3.

CIA Involvement. Lt. Gen. Vernon A. Walters, deputy director of the CIA, testified at a Senate Appropriations subcommittee investigating White House efforts to involve the agency in a Watergate coverup. Walters said Nixon had never asked him about CIA involvement in the case, subcommittee Chairman John L. McClellan (D Ark.) disclosed after the closed session.

After appearing at a closed Senate Armed Services Committee hearing, CIA Director James R. Schlesinger said White House aides were "at least overzealous" in carrying out Nixon's instructions to protect the secrecy of CIA operations throughout the Watergate investigation.

In his May 22 statement, Nixon said he was "advised that there was a possibility of CIA involvement in some way" shortly after the June 17 break-in.

Nixon and Congress. Demonstrating his new policy of receptiveness to Congress, the President met at the White House with 22 Republican senators and representatives to discuss legislation. Sen. Hugh Scott (R Pa.), minority leader, said after the meeting: "I have full confidence in the President." In a floor speech, Senate Democratic Whip Robert C. Byrd (D W.Va.) termed the idea of impeaching Nixon "at best premature and at worst reckless."

Vesco Surfaces. Robert L. Vesco, the financier indicted in connection with a secret contribution to the Nixon campaign, said in a television interview in Costa Rica that he would not return to the U.S. until he was assured of "absolute impartiality" by Watergate special prosecutor Archibald Cox.

MAY 24

Watergate Hearings. Attorney Gerald Alch returned for a second day of testimony before the Senate investigating committee. He volunteered to undergo a lie detector test to verify his account of his defense of James W. McCord Jr. in the Watergate criminal trial, which differed from McCord's version.

Convicted Watergate conspirator Bernard L. Barker appeared before the committee in the afternoon to answer questions about his role in the break-in.

Alfred C. Baldwin II, the former FBI agent who monitored the wiretaps on the Democratic National Committee from a motel across the street, also testified.

Dean Appearance. John W. Dean III, former presidential counsel, testified under oath at a closed hearing of a House investigating subcommittee about the removal of some files on the International Telephone and Telegraph Corporation (ITT) from the SEC to the Justice Department.

NIXON ON WATERGATE

Following are White House texts of two statements issued by the President May 22 on the Watergate affair —an "accompanying statement" summarizing the President's views and his decision not to resign, and a longer background statement giving the President's knowledge of facts surrounding the Watergate affair and related activities:

Accompanying Statement

Recent news accounts growing out of testimony in the Watergate investigations have given grossly misleading impressions of many of the facts, as they relate both to my own role and to certain unrelated activities involving national security.

Already, on the basis of second and third-hand hearsay testimony by persons either convicted or themselves under investigation in the case, I have found myself accused of involvement in activities I never heard of until I read about them in news accounts.

These impressions could also lead to a serious misunderstanding of those national security activities which, though totally unrelated to Watergate, have become entangled in the case. They could lead to further compromise of sensitive national security information.

I will not abandon my responsibilities. I will continue to do the job I was elected to do. In the accompanying statement, I have set forth the facts as I know them as they relate to my own role.

With regard to the specific allegations that have been made, I can and do state categorically:

1) I had no prior knowledge of the Watergate operation.

2) I took no part in, nor was I aware of, any subsequent efforts that may have been made to cover up Watergate.

3) At no time did I authorize any offer of Executive clemency for the Watergate defendants, nor did I know of any such offer.

4) I did not know, until the time of my own investigation, of any effort to provide the Watergate defendants with funds.

5) At no time did I attempt, or did I authorize others to attempt, to implicate the CIA in the Watergate matter.

6) It was not until the time of my own investigation that I learned of the break-in at the office of Mr. Ellsberg's psychiatrist, and I specifically authorized the furnishing of this information to Judge Byrne.

7) I neither authorized nor encouraged subordinates to engage in illegal or improper campaign tactics.

In the accompanying statement, I have sought to provide the background that may place recent allegations in perspective. I have specifically stated that Executive privilege will not be invoked as to any testimony concerning possible criminal conduct or discussions of possible criminal conduct, in the matters under investigation. I want the public to learn the truth about Watergate, and those guilty of any illegal actions brought to justice.

Statement by the President

Allegations surrounding the Watergate affair have so escalated that I feel a further statement from the President is required at this time. A climate of sensationalism has developed in which even second- or third-hand hearsay charges are headlined as fact and repeated as fact.

Important national security operations which themselves had no connection with Watergate have become entangled in the case.

As a result, some national security information has already been made public through court orders, through the subpoenaing of documents and through testimony witnesses have given in judicial and Congressional proceedings. Other sensitive documents are now threatened with disclosure. Continued silence about those operations would compromise rather than protect them, and would also serve to perpetuate a grossly distorted view—which recent partial disclosures have given—of the nature and purpose of those operations.

Purpose of Statement

The purpose of this statement is threefold:

- First, to set forth the facts about my own relationship to the Watergate matter.
- Second, to place in some perspective some of the more sensational—and inaccurate—of the charges that have filled the headlines in recent days, and also some of the matters that are currently being discussed in Senate testimony and elsewhere.
- Third, to draw the distinction between national security operations and the Watergate case. To put the other matters in perspective, it will be necessary to describe the national security operations first.

In citing these national security matters, it is not my intention to place a national security "cover" on Watergate, but rather to separate them out from Watergate—and at the same time to explain the context in which certain actions took place that were later misconstrued or misused.

Long before the Watergate break-in, three important national security operations took place which have subsequently become entangled in the Watergate case.

- The first operation, begun in 1969, was a program of wiretaps. All were legal, under the authorities then existing. They were undertaken to find and stop serious national security leaks.
- The second operation was a reassessment, which I ordered in 1970, of the adequacy of internal security measures. This resulted in a plan and a directive to strengthen our intelligence operations. They were protested by Mr. Hoover, and as a result of his protest they were not put into effect.
- The third operation was the establishment, in 1971, of a Special Investigations Unit in the White House. Its primary mission was to plug leaks of vital security information. I also directed this group to prepare an accurate history of certain crucial national security matters which occurred under prior administrations, on which the Government's records were incomplete.

Here is the background of these three security operations initiated in my Administration.

1969 Wiretaps

By mid-1969, my Administration had begun a number of highly sensitive foreign policy initiatives. They were aimed at ending the war in Vietnam, achieving a settlement in the Middle East, limiting nuclear arms, and establishing new relationships among the great powers. These involved highly secret diplomacy. They were closely interrelated. Leaks of secret information about any one could endanger all.

Exactly that happened. News accounts appeared in 1969, which were obviously based on leaks—some of them extensive and detailed—by people having access to the most highly classified security materials.

There was no way to carry forward these diplomatic initiatives unless further leaks could be prevented. This required finding the source of the leaks.

In order to do this, a special program of wiretaps was instituted in mid-1969 and terminated in February, 1971. Fewer than 20 taps, of varying duration, were involved. They produced important leads that made it possible to tighten the security of highly sensitive materials. I authorized this entire program. Each individual tap was undertaken in accordance with procedures legal at the time and in accord with long-standing precedent.

The persons who were subject to these wiretaps were determined through coordination among the Director of the FBI, my Assistant for National Security Affairs, and the Attorney General. Those wiretapped were selected on the basis of access to the information leaked, material in security files, and evidence that developed as the inquiry proceeded.

Information thus obtained was made available to senior officials responsible for national security matters in order to curtail further leaks.

The 1970 Intelligence Plan

In the spring and summer of 1970, another security problem reached critical proportions. In March a wave of bombings and explosions struck college campuses and cities. There were 400 bomb threats in one 24-hour period in New York City. Rioting and violence on college campuses reached a new peak after the Cambodian operation and the tragedies at Kent State and Jackson State. The 1969-70 school year brought nearly 1800 campus demonstrations, and nearly 250 cases of arson on campus. Many colleges closed. Gun battles between guerrilla-style groups and police were taking place. Some of the disruptive activities were receiving foreign support.

Complicating the task of maintaining security was the fact that, in 1966, certain types of undercover FBI operations that had been conducted for many years had been suspended. This also had substantially impaired our ability to collect foreign intelligence information. At the same time, the relationships between the FBI and other intelligence agencies had been deteriorating. By May, 1970, FBI Director Hoover shut off his agency's liaison with the CIA altogether.

On June 5, 1970, I met with the Director of the FBI (Mr. Hoover), the Director of the Central Intelligence Agency (Mr. Richard Helms), the Director of the Defense Intelligence Agency

(General Donald V. Bennett) and the Director of the National Security Agency (Admiral Noel Gayler). We discussed the urgent need for better intelligence operations. I appointed Director Hoover as chairman of an interagency committee to prepare recommendations.

On June 25, the committee submitted a report which included specific options for expanded intelligence operations, and on July 23 the agencies were notified by memorandum of the options approved. After reconsideration, however, prompted by the opposition of Director Hoover, the agencies were notified five days later, on July 28, that the approval had been rescinded. The options initially approved had included resumption of certain intelligence operations which had been suspended in 1966. These in turn had included authorization for surreptitious entry —breaking and entering, in effect—on specified categories of targets in specified situations related to national security.

Because the approval was withdrawn before it had been implemented, the net result was that the plan for expanded intelligence activities never went into effect.

The documents spelling out this 1970 plan are extremely sensitive. They include—and are based upon—assessments of certain foreign intelligence capabilities and procedures, which of course must remain secret. It was this unused plan and related documents that John Dean removed from the White House and placed in a safe deposit box, giving the keys to Judge Sirica. The same plan, still unused, is being headlined today.

Coordination among our intelligence agencies continued to fall short of our national security needs. In July, 1970, having earlier discontinued the FBI's liaison with the CIA, Director Hoover ended the FBI's normal liaison with all other agencies except the White House. To help remedy this, an Intelligence Evaluation Committee was created in December, 1970. Its members included representatives of the White House, CIA, FBI, NSA, the Departments of Justice, Treasury, and Defense, and the Secret Service.

The Intelligence Evaluation Committee and its staff were instructed to improve coordination among the intelligence community and to prepare evaluations and estimates of domestic intelligence. I understand that its activities are now under investigation. I did not authorize nor do I have any knowledge of any illegal activity by this Committee. If it went beyond its charter and did engage in any illegal activities, it was totally without my knowledge or authority.

The Special Investigations Unit

On Sunday, June 13, 1971, *The New York Times* published the first installment of what came to be known as "The Pentagon Papers." Not until a few hours before publication did any responsible Government official know that they had been stolen. Most officials did not know they existed. No senior official of the Government had read them or knew with certainty what they contained.

All the Government knew, at first, was that the papers comprised 47 volumes and some 7,000 pages, which had been taken from the most sensitive files of the Departments of State and Defense and the CIA, covering military and diplomatic moves in a war that was still going on.

Moreover, a majority of the documents published with the first three installments in *The Times* had not been included in the 47-volume study—raising serious questions about what and how much else might have been taken. There was every reason to believe this was a security leak of unprecedented proportions.

It created a situation in which the ability of the Government to carry on foreign relations even in the best of circumstances could have been severely compromised. Other governments no longer knew whether they could deal with the United States in confidence. Against the background of the delicate negotiations the United States was then involved in on a number of fronts—with regard to Vietnam, China, the Middle East, nuclear arms limitations, U.S.-Soviet relations, and others—in which the utmost degree of confidentiality was vital, it posed a threat so grave as to require extraordinary actions.

Therefore during the week following the Pentagon Papers publication, I approved the creation of a Special Investigations Unit within the White House—which later came to be known as the "plumbers." This was a small group at the White House whose principal purpose was to stop security leaks and to investigate other sensitive security matters. I looked to John Ehrlichman for the supervision of this group.

Egil Krogh, Mr. Ehrlichman's assistant, was put in charge. David Young was added to this unit, as were E. Howard Hunt and G. Gordon Liddy. The unit operated under extremely tight security rules. Its existence and functions were known only to a very few persons at the White House. These included Messrs. Haldeman, Ehrlichman and Dean.

At about the time the unit was created, Daniel Ellsberg was identified as the person who had given the Pentagon Papers to *The New York Times*. I told Mr. Krogh that as a matter of first priority, the unit should find out all it could about Mr. Ellsberg's associates and his motives. Because of the extreme gravity of the situation, and not then knowing what additional national secrets Mr. Ellsberg might disclose, I did impress upon Mr. Krogh the vital importance to the national security of his assignment. I did not authorize and had no knowledge of any illegal means to be used to achieve this goal.

However, because of the emphasis I put on the crucial importance of protecting the national security, I can understand how highly motivated individuals could have felt justified in engaging in specific activities that I would have disapproved had they been brought to my attention.

Consequently, as President, I must and do assume responsibility for such actions despite the fact that I, at no time approved or had knowledge of them.

I also assigned the unit a number of other investigatory matters, dealing in part with compiling an accurate record of events related to the Vietnam War, on which the Government's records were inadequate (many previous records having been removed with the change of Administration) and which bore directly on the negotiations then in progress. Additional assignments included tracing down other national security leaks, including one that seriously compromised the U.S. negotiating position in the SALT talks.

The work of the unit tapered off around the end of 1971. The nature of its work was such that it involved matters that, from a national security standpoint, were highly sensitive then and remain so today.

These intelligence activities had no connection with the break-in of the Democratic headquarters, or the aftermath.

I considered it my responsibility to see that the Watergate investigation did not impinge adversely upon the nation security area. For example, on April 18th, 1973, when I learned that Mr. Hunt, a former member of the Special Investigations Unit at the White House, was to be questioned by the U.S. Attorney, I directed Assistant Attorney General Petersen to pursue every issue involving Watergate but to confine his investigation to Watergate and related matters and to stay out of national security matters.

Subsequently, on April 25, 1973, Attorney General Kleindienst informed me that because the Government had clear evidence that Mr. Hunt was involved in the break-in of the office of the psychiatrist who had treated Mr. Ellsberg, he, the Attorney General, believed that despite the fact that no evidence had been obtained from Hunt's acts, a report should nevertheless be made to the court trying the Ellsberg case. I concurred, and directed that the information be transmitted to Judge Byrne immediately.

Watergate

The burglary and bugging of the Democratic National Committee headquarters came as a complete surprise to me. I had no inkling that any such illegal activities had been planned by persons associated with my campaign; if I had known, I would not have permitted it. My immediate reaction was that those guilty should be brought to justice and, with the five burglars themselves already in custody, I assumed that they would be.

Within a few days, however, I was advised that there was a possibility of CIA involvement in some way. It did seem to me possible that, because of the involvement of former CIA personnel, and because of some of their apparent associations, the investigation could lead to the uncovering of covert CIA operations totally unrelated to the Watergate break-in.

In addition, by this time, the name of Mr. Hunt had surfaced in connection with Watergate, and I was alerted to the fact that he had previously been a member of the Special Investigations Unit in the White House. Therefore, I was also concerned that the Watergate investigation might well lead to an inquiry into the activities of the Special Investigations Unit itself.

In this area, I felt it was important to avoid disclosure of the details of the national security matters with which the group was concerned. I knew that once the existence of the group became known, it would lead inexorably to a discussion of these matters, some of which remain, even today, highly sensitive.

I wanted justice done with regard to Watergate; but in the scale of national priorities with which I had to deal—and not at that time having any idea of the extent of political abuse which Watergate reflected—I also had to be deeply concerned with ensuring that neither the covert operations of the CIA nor the operations of the Special Investigations Unit should be compromised.

Therefore, I instructed Mr. Haldeman and Mr. Ehrlichman to ensure that the investigation of the break-in not expose either an unrelated covert operation of the CIA or the activities of the White House investigations unit—and to see that this was personally coordinated between General Walters, the Deputy Director of the CIA, and Mr. Gray of the FBI. It was certainly not my intent, nor my wish, that the investigation of the Watergate break-in or of related acts be impeded in any way.

On July 6, 1972, I telephoned the Acting Director of the FBI, L. Patrick Gray, to congratulate him on his successful handling of the hijacking of Pacific Southwest Airlines plane the previous day. During the conversation Mr. Gray discussed with me the progress of the Watergate investigation, and I asked him whether he had talked with General Walters. Mr. Gray said that he had, and that General Walters had assured him that the CIA was not involved. In the discussion, Mr. Gray suggested that the matter of Watergate might lead higher. I told him to press ahead with his investigation.

It now seems that later, through whatever complex of individual motives and possible misunderstandings, there were apparently wide-ranging efforts to limit the investigation or to conceal the possible involvement of members of the Administration and the campaign committee.

I was not aware of any such efforts at the time. Neither, until after I began my own investigation, was I aware of any fund raising for defendants convicted of the break-in at Democratic headquarters, much less authorize any such fund raising. Nor did I authorize any offer of Executive clemency for any of the defendants.

In the weeks and months that followed Watergate, I asked for, and received, repeated assurances that Mr. Dean's own investigation (which included reviewing files and sitting in on FBI interviews with White House personnel) had cleared everyone then employed by the White House of involvement.

Summarizing

In summary, then:

(1) I had no prior knowledge of the Watergate bugging operation, or of any illegal surveillance activities for political purposes.

(2) Long prior to the 1972 campaign, I did set in motion certain internal security measures, including legal wiretaps, which I felt were necessary from a national security standpoint and, in the climate then prevailing, also necessary from a domestic security standpoint.

(3) People who had been involved in the national security operations later, without my knowledge or approval, undertook illegal activities in the political campaign of 1972.

(4) Elements of the early post-Watergate reports led me to suspect, incorrectly, that the CIA had been in some way involved. They also led me to surmise, correctly, that since persons originally recruited for covert national security activities had participated in Watergate, an unrestricted investigation of Watergate might lead to and expose those covert national security operations.

(5) I sought to prevent the exposure of these covert national security activities, while encouraging those conducting the investigation to pursue their inquiry into the Watergate itself. I so instructed my staff, the Attorney General and the Acting Director of the FBI.

(6) I also specifically instructed Mr. Haldeman and Mr. Ehrlichman to ensure that the FBI would not carry its investigation into areas that might compromise these covert national security activities, or those of the CIA.

(7) At no time did I authorize or know about any offer of Executive clemency for the Watergate defendants. Neither did I know until the time of my own investigation, of any efforts to provide them with funds.

Conclusion

With hindsight, it is apparent that I should have given more heed to the warning signals I received along the way about a Watergate cover-up and less to the reassurances. With hindsight, several other things also become clear:

• With respect to campaign practices, and also with respect to campaign finances, it should now be obvious that no campaign in history has ever been subjected to the kind of intensive and searching inquiry that has been focused on the campaign waged in my behalf in 1972.

It is clear that unethical, as well as illegal, activities took place in the course of that campaign.

None of these took place with my specific approval or knowledge. To the extent that I may in any way have contributed to the climate in which they took place, I did not intend to; to the extent that I failed to prevent them, I should have been more vigilant.

It was to help ensure against any repetition of this in the future that last week I proposed the establishment of a top-level, bipartisan, independent commission to recommend a comprehensive reform of campaign laws and practices. Given the priority I believe it deserves, such reform should be possible before the next Congressional elections in 1974.

• It now appears that there were persons who may have gone beyond my directives, and sought to expand on my efforts to protect the national security operations in order to cover up any involvement they or certain others might have had in Watergate. The extent to which this is true, and who may have participated and to what degree, are questions that it would not be proper to address here. The proper forum for settling these matters is in the courts.

• To the extent that I have been able to determine what probably happened in the tangled course of this affair, on the basis of my own recollections and of the conflicting accounts and evidence that I have seen, it would appear that one factor at work was that at critical points various people, each with his own perspective and his own responsibilities, saw the same situation with different eyes and heard the same words with different ears. What might have seemed insignificant to one seemed significant to another; what one saw in terms of public responsibility, another saw in terms of political opportunity; and mixed through it all, I am sure, was a concern on the part of many that the Watergate scandal should not be allowed to get in the way of what the Administration sought to achieve.

The truth about Watergate should be brought out—in an orderly way, recognizing that the safeguards of judicial procedure are designed to find the truth, not to hide the truth.

With his selection of Archibald Cox—who served both President Kennedy and President Johnson as Solicitor General—as the special supervisory prosecutor for matters related to the case, Attorney General-designate Richardson has demonstrated his own determination to see the truth brought out. In this effort he has my full support.

Executive Privilege

Considering the number of persons involved in this case whose testimony might be subject to a claim of Executive privilege, I recognize that a clear definition of that claim has become central to the effort to arrive at the truth.

Accordingly, Executive privilege will not be invoked as to any testimony concerning possible criminal conduct or discussions of possible criminal conduct, in the matters presently under investigation, including the Watergate affair and the alleged cover-up.

I want to emphasize that this statement is limited to my own recollections of what I said and did relating to security and to the Watergate. I have specifically avoided any attempt to explain what other parties may have said and done. My own information on those other matters is fragmentary, and to some extent contradictory. Additional information may be forthcoming of which I am unaware. It is also my understanding that the information which has been conveyed to me has also become available to those prosecuting these matters. Under such circumstances, it would be prejudicial and unfair of me to render my opinions on the activities of others; those judgments must be left to the judicial process, our best hope for achieving the just result that we all seek.

As more information is developed, I have no doubt that more questions will be raised. To the extent that I am able, I shall also seek to set forth the facts as known to me with respect to those questions.

McCORD STATEMENT

Following is the text of a statement read May 18 at the Senate Watergate hearing by James W. McCord Jr., former security coordinator for the Committee for the Re-election of the President and one of the conspirators in the break-in. (p. 63)

SUBJECT: POLITICAL PRESSURE ON THE WRITER TO ACCEPT EXECUTIVE CLEMENCY AND REMAIN SILENT

Political pressure from the White House was conveyed to me in January 1973 by John Caulfield to remain silent, take executive clemency by going off to prison quietly, and I was told that while there I would receive financial aid and later rehabilitation and a job. I was further told in a January meeting in 1973 with Caulfield that the President of the United States was aware of our meeting, that the results of the meeting would be conveyed to the President and that at a future meeting there would likely be a personal message from the President himself. The dates of the telephone calls set forth below are the current dates to the best of my recollection.

On the afternoon of Jan. 8, 1973, the first day of the Watergate trial, Gerald Alch, my attorney, told me that William O. Bittman, attorney for E. Howard Hunt, wanted to meet with me at Bittman's office that afternoon. When I asked why Alch said that Bittman wanted to talk with me about "whose word I would trust regarding a White House offer of executive clemency." Alch added that Bittman wanted to talk with both Bernard Barker and me that afternoon.

I had no intention of accepting executive clemency, but I did want to find out what was going on, and by whom, and exactly what the White House was doing now. A few days before, the White House had tried to lay the Watergate operation off on CIA, and now it was clear that I was going to have to find out what was up now. To do so involved some risks. To fail to do so was in my opinion to work in a vacuum regarding White House intentions and plans, which involved even greater risks, I felt.

Around 4:30 p.m. that afternoon, Jan. 8, while waiting for a taxi after the court session, Bernard Barker asked my attorneys and me if he could ride in the cab with us to Bittman's office, which we agreed to. There he got out of the cab and went up towards Bittman's office. I had been under the impression during the cab ride that Bittman was going to talk to both Barker and me jointly, and became angered at what seemed to me to be the arrogance and audacity of another man's lawyer calling in two other lawyers' clients and pitching them for the White House. Alch saw my anger and took me aside for about a half hour after the cab arrived in front of Bittman's office, and let Barker go up alone. About 5 p.m. we went up to Bittman's office. There Alch disappeared with Bittman, and I sat alone in Bittman's office for a period of time, became irritated and went next door where Bernard Shankman and Austin Mittler, attorneys for me and Hunt respectively, were talking about legitimate legal matters. Alch finally came back, took me aside and said that Bittman told him I would be called that same night by a friend I had known from the White House. I assumed this would be John Caulfield who had originally recruited me for the Committee for the Re-election of the President position.

UNIDENTIFIED CALLER

About 12:30 p.m. that same evening, I received a call from an unidentified individual who said that Caulfield was out of town and asked me to go to a pay phone booth near the Blue Fountain Inn on Route 355 near my residence, where he had a message for me from Caulfield. There the same individual called and read the following message:

"Plead guilty. One year is a long time. You will get executive clemency. Your family will be taken care of and when you get out, you will be rehabilitated and a job will be found for you. Don't take immunity when called before the grand jury."

The same message was once again repeated, obviously read. I told the caller I would not discuss such matters over the phone. He said that Caulfield was out of town.

On Wednesday evening, Jan. 10, the same party called and told me by phone that Jack would want to talk with me by phone on Thursday night, Jan. 11, when he got back into town, and requested that I go to the same phone booth on Route 355 near the Blue Fountain Inn. He also conveyed instructions regarding meeting Caulfield on Friday night, Jan. 12.

On Thursday evening, Jan. 11, the same party called me at home and told me that Caulfield's plane was late and that he wanted to meet with me personally the same evening after arrival. I told him that I would not do so but would meet with him Friday night if he desired. Later that evening, about 9:30 p.m., Caulfield called me on my home phone and insisted on talking with me, but my family refused to let him do so, since I was asleep.

MEETINGS WITH CAULFIELD

On Friday night, Jan. 12, from about 7 p.m. to 7:30 p.m., I met with Caulfield at the second overlook on George Washington Parkway in Virginia and talked with him in his car. Caulfield advised that he had been attending a law enforcement meeting in San Clemente, Calif., and had just returned. I advised him that I had no objection to meeting with him to tell him my frame of mind but that I had no intention of talking executive clemency or pleading guilty: that I had come to the meeting at his request and not of my own, and was glad to tell him my views.

He said that the offer of executive clemency which he was passing along and of support while in prison and rehabilitation and help toward a job later "was a sincere offer." He explained that he had been asked to convey this message to me and was only doing what he was told to do. He repeated the last statement several times.

My response was that I would not even discuss executive clemency or pleading guilty and remaining silent, but I was glad to talk with him, so that there was no misunderstanding on anyone's part about it.

Caulfield stated that he was carrying the message of executive clemency to me "from the very highest levels of the White House." He stated that the President of the United States was in Key Biscayne, Fla., that weekend, had been told of the forthcoming meeting with me and would be immediately told of the results of the meeting." He further stated that "I may have a message to you at our next meeting from the President himself."

I advised Caulfield that I had seen the list of witnesses for the trial and had seen Jeb Magruder's name, appearing as a government witness. I advised him that it was clear then that Magruder was going to perjure himself and that we were not going to get a fair trial. Further I told him that it was clear that some of those involved in the Watergate case were going to trial, and others were going to be covered for (I was referring to John Mitchell, John Dean and Magruder) and that was not my idea of American justice. I further advised Caulfield that I believed that the government had lied in denying electronic interception of my phone calls from my residence since June 17, 1972, and that I believed that the administration had also tapped the phones of the other defendants during that time. I mentioned two specific calls of mine which I had made during September and early October 1972, which I was certain had been intercepted by the government, and yet the government had blithely denied any such tapping. I compared this denial to the denial the government had made in the Ellsberg case, in which for months the government had denied any such impermissible interception of the calls, and yet in the summer of 1972 had finally been forced to admit them when the judge ordered, by court order, a search of about a dozen government agencies, and calls intercepted were then disclosed. I stated that if we were going to get a fiction of a fair trial, through perjured testimony to begin with, and then for the government to lie about illegal telephone interceptions, that the trial ought to be kicked out and we start all over again, this time with all of those involved as defendants. At least in this was, "some would not be more equal than others" before the bar of justice and we would get a fair trial.

The executive clemency offer was made two or three times during this meeting, as I recall, and I repeated each time that (I) would not even discuss it, nor discuss pleading guilty, which I had been asked to do in the first telephone call received on the night of Jan. 8, from Caulfield's friend, whose identity I do not know. I told him that I was going to renew the motion on disclosure of government wiretapping of our telephones.

Caulfield ended the conversation by stating that he would call me the next day about a meeting that same afternoon, Saturday, Jan. 13, and that if I did not hear from him, he would want to talk with me by telephone on the evening of Monday, Jan. 15, 1973.

'THE GOVERNMENT MAY FALL'

I did not hear from Caulfield on Saturday, but on Sunday afternoon he called and asked me to meet me that afternoon about an hour later at the same location on George Washington Parkway. He stated that there was no objection to renewing the motion on discovery of government wiretapping, and that if that failed, that I would receive executive clemency after 10 to 11 months. I told him I had not asked anyone's permission to file the motion.

He went on to say that "the President's ability to govern is at stake. Another Teapot Dome scandal is possible, and the government may fall. Everybody else is on track but you. You are not following the game plan. Get closer to your attorney. You seem to be pursuing your own course of action. Don't talk if called before the grand jury, keep silent, and do the same if called before a congressional committee."

"MASSIVE INJUSTICE"

My response was that I felt a massive injustice was being done, that I was different than the others, that I was going to fight the fixed case and had no intention of either pleading guilty, taking executive clemency or agreeing to remain silent. He repeated the statement that the government would have difficulty in continuing to be able to stand. I responded that they do have a problem, but that I had a problem with the massive injustice of the whole trial being a sham, and that I would fight it every way I knew how. He asked for a commitment that I would remain silent, and I responded that I would make none. I gave him a memorandum on the dates of the two calls of mine in September 1972 and October 1972 that I was sure had been intercepted, and said that I believed the government had lied about them. He said that he would check and see if in fact the government had done so.

On Monday night, Jan. 15, 1973, Caulfield called me again at the phone booth on Route 355 near my residence. I informed him that I had no desire to talk further, that if the White House had any intention of playing the game straight and giving us the semblance of a fair trial, they would check into the perjury charge of mine against Magruder and into the existence of the two intercepted calls previously referred to, and hung up.

On Tuesday morning, about 7:30 a.m., Caulfield called my residence, but I had already left for court.

On Tuesday evening, Caulfield called and asked me again to meet with him, and I said not until they had something to talk about on the perjured testimony and the intercepted calls. He said words to the effect "give us a week," and a meeting was subsequently arranged on January 25, 1973 when he said he would have something to talk about.

About 10 a.m. on Thursday, Jan. 25, 1973, in a meeting lasting until about 12:30 a.m., we drove in his card toward Warrenton, Va., and returned, and a conversation ensued which repeated the offers of executive clemency and financial support while in prison, and rehabilitation later. I refused to discuss it. He stated that I was "fouling up the game plan." I made a few comments about the "game plan." He said that "they" had found no record of the interception of the two calls I referred to, and said that perhaps it could wait until the appeals. He asked what my plans were regarding talking publicly, and I said that I planned to do so when I was ready; that I had discussed it with my wife and she said that I should do what I felt I must and not to worry about the family. I advised Jack that my children were now grown and could understand what I had to do, when the disclosures came out. He responded by saying that "You know that if the Administration gets its back to the wall, it will have to take steps to defend itself." I took that as a personal threat and I told him in response that I had had a good life, that my will was made out and that I had thought through the risks and would take them when I was ready. He said that if I had to go off to jail that the administration would help with the bail premiums. I advised him that it was not a bail premium, but $100,000 straight cash and that that was a problem I would have to worry about, through family and friends. On the night before sentencing, Jack called me and said that the administration would provide the $100,000 in cash if I could tell him how to get it funded through an intermediary. I said that if we ever needed it I would let him know. I never contacted him thereafter; neither have I heard from him. ✓

RICHARDSON, COX WIN JUDICIARY COMMITTEE APPROVAL

Action—Senate Judiciary Committee May 23 unanimously reported favorably the nomination of Secretary of Defense Elliot L. Richardson as attorney general.

After two more days of questioning, the Senate Judiciary Committee May 23 voted unanimously to approve the move of Elliot L. Richardson, currently serving as secretary of defense, from the Pentagon to the Justice Department, where he would serve as attorney general. Within two hours, the Senate had voted to confirm Richardson as well. *(Box, p. 98)*

The vote of approval from the Senate committee also endorsed Richardson's selection of Harvard Law Professor and former Solicitor General Archibald Cox as the special prosecutor for the executive branch investigation of the charges arising from the Watergate affair and the 1972 presidential campaign. *(Watergage hearing, p. 79)*

Cox did not have to be confirmed by the Senate, but Richardson had earlier agreed that he would withdraw any nomination for that post which the committee failed to approve.

After questioning both men May 21 concerning the guidelines under which Cox would operate, the committee seemed satisfied that Richardson had met their demands for true independence for the special prosecutor, a major point of disagreement between the committee and the nominee during the first days of the confirmation hearings. An executive session was set for the morning of May 22 to vote on the Richardson nomination.

But after telephone calls from former Pentagon Papers defendant Daniel Ellsberg to certain committee members, the executive session became another public hearing. Summoned on short notice from the Pentagon, Richardson was subjected to another lengthy interrogation session by committee members concerned by Ellsberg's claim that Richardson had encouraged the concealment of the role of the CIA in the break-in into the office of Ellsberg's psychiatrist. *(p. 52)*

Cox: Even to the Oval Office

"The only authority he's retained is the authority to give me hell if I don't do the job," Cox stated to the committee May 21, dealing with the touchy question of Richardson's ultimate responsibility—as attorney general—for the special prosecutor. Cox, who had served as solicitor general in the Kennedy and Johnson administrations, expressed his full satisfaction with the guidelines drawn up by Richardson for the work of the special prosecutor. *(Cox biography, box this page)*

The guidelines, which were made public in final form May 21, gave him "the best of both worlds," said Cox—independence from, but strong support by, Richardson and the Justice Department. "I'll have the whip hand,"

Prosecutor Archibald Cox

Harvard Law Professor Archibald Cox received an important telephone call on his 61st birthday. Calling May 17 was a former student, Attorney General-designate Elliot L. Richardson. He asked Cox—who had served three Democratic Presidents—to come back to Washington to head the government's investigation of the spreading scandals surrounding the Watergate break-in and the 1972 presidential election.

The next day Cox agreed. On May 21, he and Richardson faced the Senate Judiciary Committee, which was considering Richardson's nomination and had been given a virtual veto over the selection of the special prosecutor. There was little doubt that Cox would win their approval.

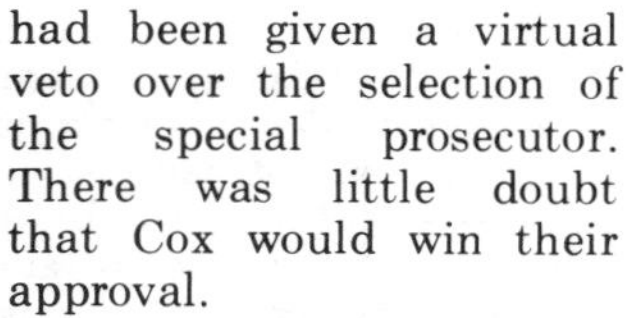

Born in New Jersey in 1912, Cox has spent all of his adult life either in Richardson's own home-state of Massachusetts or in Washington. A graduate of Harvard College and Harvard Law School, Cox began teaching law there in 1945 after serving for two years in the office of the solicitor general and then for two more years as associate solicitor for the Labor Department.

Only a year after he began his teaching career, Cox was named a full professor at Harvard. Serving for a year as co-chairman of the Construction Industry Stabilization Commission in 1951-1952, he then accepted the post of chairman of the Truman administration's Wage Stabilization Board. Demonstrating his strong-minded independence, he resigned that post after only four months, when Truman overruled one of the board's decisions. Cox returned to teaching labor law at Harvard.

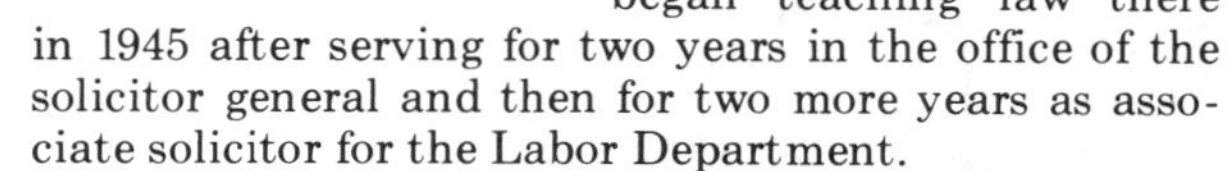

In 1961, Cox was again summoned to Washington. This time he served President Kennedy as solicitor general. After Kennedy's death, Cox served President Johnson in that same post until the summer of 1965 when he again returned to Cambridge.

In 1968, he headed a commission which inquired into the causes of student disorders at Columbia University. In 1972, he was counsel to a committee of the Massachusetts legislature which studied charges of wrongdoing against two state judges.

Duties and Responsibilities of the Special Prosecutor

Following are guidelines relating to the special Watergate prosecutor issued by Attorney General-designate Elliot L. Richardson May 19:

THE SPECIAL PROSECUTOR

There will be appointed by the attorney general, within the Department of Justice, a special prosecutor to whom the attorney general shall delegate the authorities and provide the staff and other resources described below.

The special prosecutor shall have full authority for investigating and prosecuting offenses against the United States arising out of the unauthorized entry into Democratic National Committee headquarters at the Watergate, all offenses arising out of the 1972 presidential election for which the special prosecutor deems it necessary and appropriate to assume responsibility, allegations involving the President, members of the White House staff, or presidential appointees, and any other matters which he consents to have assigned to him by the attorney general.

In particular, the special prosecutor shall have full authority with respect to the above matters for:

- Conducting proceedings before grand juries and any other investigations he deems necessary.
- Reviewing all documentary evidence available from any source, as to which he shall have full access.
- Determining whether or not to contest the assertion of "executive privilege" or any other testimonial privilege.
- Determining whether or not application should be made to any federal court for a grant of immunity to any witness, consistently with applicable statutory requirements, or for warrants, subpoenas, or other court orders.
- Deciding whether or not to prosecute any individual, firm, corporation or group of individuals.
- Initiating and conducting prosecutions, framing indictments, filing informations, and handling all aspects of any cases within his jurisdiction (whether initiated before or after his assumption of duties), including any appeals.
- Coordinating and directing the activities of all Department of Justice personnel, including United States attorneys.
- Dealing with and appearing before congressional committees having jurisdiction over any aspect of the above matters and determining what documents, information, and assistance shall be provided to such committees.

In exercising this authority, the special prosecutor will have the greatest degree of independence that is consistent with the attorney general's statutory accountability for all matters falling within the jurisdiction of the Department of Justice. The attorney general will not countermand or interfere with the special prosecutor's decisions or actions. The special prosecutor will determine whether and to what extent he will inform or consult with the attorney general about the conduct of his duties and responsibilities. The special prosecutor will not be removed from his duties except for extraordinary improprieties on his part.

STAFF AND RESOURCE SUPPORT

Selection of Staff. The special prosecutor shall have full authority to organize, select, and hire his own staff of attorneys, investigators, and supporting personnel, on a full or part-time basis, in such numbers and with such qualifications as he may reasonably require. He may request the assistant attorneys general and other officers of the Department of Justice to assign such personnel and to provide such other assistance as he may reasonably require. All personnel in the Department of Justice, including United States attorneys, shall cooperate to the fullest extent possible with the special prosecutor.

Budget. The special prosecutor will be provided with such funds and facilities to carry out his responsibilities as he may reasonably require. He shall have the right to submit budget requests for funds, positions, and other assistance, and such requests shall receive the highest priority.

Designation and Responsibility. The personnel acting as the staff and assistants of the special prosecutor shall be known as the Watergate special prosecution force and shall be responsible only to the special prosecutor.

Continued Responsibilities of Assistant Attorney General, Criminal Division. Except for the specific investigative and prosecutorial duties assigned to the special prosecutor, the assistant attorney general in charge of the criminal division will continue to exercise all of the duties currently assigned to him.

Applicable Departmental Policies. Except as otherwise herein specified or as mutually agreed between the special prosecutor and the attorney general, the Watergate special prosecution force will be subject to the administrative regulations and policies of the Department of Justice.

Public Reports. The special prosecutor may from time to time make public such statements or reports as he deems appropriate and shall upon completion of his assignment submit a final report to the appropriate persons or entities of the Congress.

Duration of Assignment. The special prosecutor will carry out these responsibilities, with the full support of the Department of Justice, until such time as, in his judgment, he has completed them or until a date mutually agreed upon between the attorney general and himself.

said Cox. "And you won't hesitate to use it?" asked Assistant Senate Majority Leader Robert C. Byrd (D W.Va.). "No, sir," replied Cox. *(Guidelines, p. 97)*

Declaring that he felt no obligation to inform or consult with the attorney general on matters arising during the investigation, Cox said that should Richardson demand information he would revert to his professional role and say to his former student: "Look, Elliot, that isn't the way we understood it." If the disagreement continued, he said, the only alternative for Richardson would be to fire him.

Promising the committee that he would have no compunctions in pursuing the trail of any federal crime involved in the Watergate-presidential campaign scandal, Cox agreed that he would follow all leads to their conclusion. "Even if that trail should lead...to the Oval Office of the White House itself ?" pressed Byrd. "Whereever that trail may lead," responded Cox.

And what if the President should ask for a report on the work of the special prosecutor, continued Byrd. Richardson replied that such a request would be referred to the special prosecutor. Cox said that he would feel no obligation to respond affirmatively and would simply exercise his own judgment in responding to such an "extraordinary request."

Noting his own lack of prosecutorial experience, Cox said he would select as his chief deputy someone with such a background. Asked when he would name this assistant, Cox replied that he would look for one as soon as the committee advised him that "it's safe to begin...I wish I could have done it two months ago."

Richardson described to the committee the elements of the statutory authority he would retain over the special prosecutor as attorney general. He would retain this responsibility, he said, in order to avoid having to amend the law spelling out the duties and functions of the attorney general. His residual authority as attorney general in regard to the special prosecutor would consist, he said, of the power to appoint the special prosecutor, to delegate full authority to him, to provide him with full back-up and all possible staff support, and the power to remove the special prosecutor. He noted that the exercise of this last power was limited by the language of the guidelines which said that the special prosecutor could only be removed for "extraordinary improprieties." It was "inconceivable" to him, said Richardson, that his former professor, Cox, would ever be guilty of such misdeeds.

Richardson: Maximum Disclosure

The committee probed Richardson's memory further about recent contacts with figures implicated in the Watergate case. Again Richardson related the fact of his luncheon meeting on May 1 with Egil Krogh Jr., at the latter's request, to discuss the course of action Krogh should take with his knowledge of the break-in at the office of Ellsberg's psychiatrist. As he had previously testified, Richardson said that he counseled Krogh to make the information available to the judge in the Pentagon Papers case. Krogh, who had received contrary counsel from his own attorney, said Richardson, did so.

Richardson said that his only other recent contact with persons named in the spreading allegations was a telephone conversation on April 30 with former White House aide John D. Ehrlichman. Ehrlichman had called, said Richardson, only to say that Krogh wanted to talk with Richardson. Ehrlichman did not say what Krogh wanted to talk about, Richardson said.

Called unexpectedly from the Pentagon May 22 to appear again before the judiciary panel, Richardson was questioned about Ellsberg's claim that Richardson knew of—and condoned concealment of—CIA involvement in the break-in at the office of Ellsberg's psychiatrist. With some vehemence, Richardson replied that he had participated in no cover-up, that on the contrary, he had advised "maximum disclosure" by Krogh.

Krogh's statement to the Pentagon Papers judge did not mention CIA involvement in the break-in, but Richardson's own notes of their earlier conversation revealed that Krogh had mentioned to him the use of CIA documents and disguises by some of the White House "plumbing" crew whose work it was to find and stop security leaks.

Krogh's omission of this information left the impression, John V. Tunney (D Calif.) said, that he was covering up CIA involvement. Richardson protested this interpretation of the omission: he said his own reading of the statement found it quite in keeping with what Krogh had told him at their meeting.

Nixon had indicated concern, Richardson said, at their April 29 meeting that disclosure of the Ellsberg break-in not bring full disclosure of the work of the "plumbers," a disclosure which the President felt would endanger national security. But on May 2 Krogh told Richardson that he had received a message from Nixon through Ehrlichman, whose resignation had been announced by Nixon two days earlier, that this national security concern had been resolved and that no claim of executive privilege would be made in regard to information concerning the "plumbers' " break-in. ✓

Richardson Confirmed

Elliot L. Richardson was confirmed by the Senate as attorney general May 23 by a vote of 82-3. The roll-call vote came only hours after the Senate Judiciary Committee had unanimously approved the nomination. *(p. 96)*

Richardson, who at the time of the nomination was serving as secretary of defense, had previously served in the Nixon administration as undersecretary of state and secretary of health, education and welfare (HEW).

Explaining the committee's views on the nomination and the reason for its three-week delay in approving it, Senate Assistant Majority Leader Robert C. Byrd (D W.Va.), a member of the committee, indicated that the delay did not involve any questions concerning Richardson's personal integrity. Instead, he said, it was the committee's concern that the administration was choosing one of its own men to hold final responsibility for the Watergate investigation.

Voting against the nomination were Joe Biden (D Del.), Mike Gravel (D Alaska) and Harold E. Hughes (D Iowa). ✓

WATERGATE: DISAGREEMENT BETWEEN SENATE, PROSECUTOR

As the Senate Watergate committee prepared to resume hearings on June 5, controversy flared up between the committee and the government's special prosecutor over the proper course of action.

It was reported in the June 1 *Washington Post* that Archibald Cox, the special prosecutor, had asked the Senate select committee to drop the hearings completely. The story, quoting Senate sources, went on to say that Cox had told Samuel Dash, chief counsel to the committee, that he would consider court action to stop the hearings if the committee did not agree to do so. Dash reportedly told Cox that suspension of the hearings, which began on May 17, "would be impossible."

The only part of the Post story that was denied unequivocally by either Cox or Dash later that day was the reported threat of court action by Cox, who denied it. Both men issued statements acknowledging that they had met on May 30. Included in the meeting was James Vorenberg, an assistant to Cox.

Cox Statement. The "long and informal talk," according to Cox's statement, was held "for the purpose of exploring in preliminary fashion relationships between the select committee and the investigations in my charge. Among the topics discussed were the risk of serious damage to the investigations and any resulting prosecution, and the various possible ways of reducing the harm. Questions of immunity also were discussed, but there was no mention whatsoever, and I have never considered for a moment, 'court action to have them (the hearings) stopped.' "

When he had important requests to make, Cox continued, he would make them to the Senate committee chairman, Sam J. Ervin (D N.C.). Cox, like Dash, said that he understood the May 30 meeting was to be confidential.

Dash Statement. Dash's statement went farther than Cox's on the confidentiality question. "The news story in *The Washington Post* this morning...did not result from any statement made by me, or to my knowledge by any staff or committee member of the select committee," he said. "The only comment I will make at this time is that the quoted portions of the news story do not accurately report what was stated by either Prof. Cox or me at the meeting."

The meeting, of which Ervin was informed, "involved an exploratory discussion concerning the relationship between the special prosecutor and our select committee," said Dash. He and Cox agreed, he added, to make no public comment on the substance of the discussion, because it was preparatory to a meeting planned between Cox and Ervin. "No decisions were made or related at this meeting," Dash said.

Continuing Friction. The dispute between committee investigators and government prosecutors had been simmering for weeks. It was the belief of the prosecutors, even before Cox's appointment by Attorney General Elliot L. Richardson on May 18, that the televised Senate hearings would interfere severely with grand jury investigations.

Ervin told reporters in Winston-Salem, N.C., May 31 concerning possible court action to stop the Senate hearings: "The committee has the same powers under the Constitution to conduct the hearings that the courts have to institute prosecution. The courts cannot force the U.S. Senate to halt the hearings."

The latest hearings before the seven-member committee were held on May 24. The committee then took a one-week Memorial Day recess.

New Developments. But even with the committee in recess, other facets of the scandal and related events continued to develop during the week ended June 2. These were some of the latest ones:

- John D. Ehrlichman, former domestic adviser to President Nixon, and H.R. Haldeman, the President's former chief of staff, testified before a Senate Appropriations subcommittee May 30 and 31 about their roles and the role of the Central Intelligence Agency (CIA) in the Watergate case. Their testimony conflicted sharply with that of CIA officials. *(Details below)*
- In his May 31 conversation with reporters in Winston-Salem, Ervin discussed the secret papers that had been prepared by John W. Dean III, former counsel to the President. Dean, who was fired along with Haldeman and Ehrlichman on April 30, had locked up the papers. On May 4, he had turned them over to Chief Judge John J. Sirica of U.S. District Court in Washington, D.C. Sirica gave copies to government prosecutors and the Senate committee.

"I interpret the papers as being an effort or a plan to set up an operation to spy on the American people in general or at least on those who didn't agree with the administration," said Ervin. "The result of the operation would be carried in a pipeline to the White House."

Ervin said that "those making this plan had the same mentality employed by the Gestapo in Nazi Germany." But he replied, in answer to a reporter's question, that nothing in the documents appeared to implicate Nixon. The President, in a May 22 statement, had referred to the Dean documents as part of an unused 1970 intelligence plan. *(p. 79)*

- One of the select committee members, Sen. Edward J. Gurney (R Fla.), wrote in a letter to Ervin May 31 that the committee should act "faster and more decisively" on the question of whether or not Nixon had a part in the scandal. With the testimony of what he described as "minor witnesses" in their first days, Gurney wrote, the hearings "could be likened to a preliminary impeachment proceeding based on hearsay evidence of the rankest kind, embellished by opinions and innuendo."

Testimony on CIA

Two former top-level Nixon aides testified May 30 and 31 that the White House had not attempted to enlist the assistance of the Central Intelligence Agency (CIA) in blocking an investigation of Watergate-related activities. The testimony of both Nixon aides appeared to directly contradict the statements of present and former CIA officials before congressional committees during the past three weeks.

Ehrlichman and Hunt. John D. Ehrlichman, Nixon's former domestic affairs adviser, told the Intelligence Operations Subcommittee of the Senate Appropriations Committee May 30 that he did not "have even the faintest recollection" of having called the CIA during July 1971 to request assistance for E. Howard Hunt Jr., later convicted in the Watergate break-in.

Ehrlichman testified that the first time he was informed of Hunt's activities came during a telephone conversation in August 1971. The call, Ehrlichman said, came from the deputy director of the CIA, Gen. Robert Cushman. According to Ehrlichman, Cushman said that Hunt's requests for assistance from the CIA were becoming excessive and that the CIA wished to "terminate its assistance to Hunt."

During the conversation, Ehrlichman said he asked Cushman whom Hunt was working for and what his assignment was. The conversation with Cushman in August 1971 was the first time he had spoken to Cushman about Hunt, Ehrlichman told the Senate subcommittee.

Cushman Statement. However, Cushman testified before a House Armed Services subcommittee May 11 that Ehrlichman called him "about July 7, 1971," to request that the CIA provide assistance to Hunt. Cushman said in an affidavit to the House subcommittee that Ehrlichman's call informed the CIA that "Hunt was a bona fide employee, a consultant on security matters" for the White House.

Calling the apparent contradiction "most troubling," Ehrlichman contended that he objected to Cushman's use of his name in reference to the July 7 call. Ehrlichman suggested that someone might have mentioned his name during the call to Cushman on that date, and that Cushman mistakenly remembered Ehrlichman as the caller.

Records Check. Yet at a May 31 news conference, Cushman disclosed that a check of CIA records substantiated his earlier testimony that the caller had indeed been Ehrlichman. Cushman told reporters that the minutes of a CIA meeting of top agency executives on July 8—the day after the disputed call from the White House—revealed that he had specifically identified Ehrlichman as having called to request CIA assistance for Hunt.

Ehrlichman testified that he first met Hunt on July 7, 1971, again the day of the disputed call to the CIA, during a "brief introductory meeting" in his office. The meeting between Hunt and Ehrlichman had been arranged by Charles Colson, a former White House aide responsible for hiring Hunt to work on certain aspects of the Pentagon Papers case. On that same day, Ehrlichman said, he later left for the western White House at San Clemente, Calif.

"As of then," Ehrlichman told the Appropriations subcommittee, "I knew of no reason for Hunt to have CIA aid." Hunt, the alleged leader of the Watergate break-in, reportedly used CIA equipment also to break into the office of Daniel Ellsberg's psychiatrist in September 1971. The Senate subcommittee has been trying to find out if the CIA acted illegally in providing assistance to Hunt.

White House Meeting. Concerning the Watergate case, Ehrlichman later told the subcommittee that he remembered attending a White House meeting on June 23, 1972, six days after the break-in at the Watergate. During the meeting, a discussion took place concerning the FBI investigation of Nixon campaign funds that passed through a Mexican bank and ended up in the Miami bank account of one of the Watergate burglars. But, said Ehrlichman, the meeting was not scheduled to pressure the CIA into blocking an FBI investigation of the "Mexican connection."

According to Ehrlichman, President Nixon "was concerned" that an FBI investigation of the Mexican funds "might lead to agency (CIA) people or activities either in this country or abroad." For that reason, Nixon requested that a meeting be arranged between White House aides and CIA officials to discuss the Mexican investigation, Ehrlichman testified.

Coverup Denied. However, the former Nixon aide disputed the previous testimony of the deputy director of the CIA that the meeting was called by the White House to seek CIA assistance in blocking the investigation by the FBI. The CIA deputy, Gen. Vernon Walters, told the Senate Armed Services Committee May 14 that he had been instructed during the White House meeting to inform the acting director of the FBI, L. Patrick Gray III, that an investigation by the bureau would jeopardize CIA operations in Mexico. Walters met with Gray following the meeting, but later informed the FBI director that the investigation would in no way affect the CIA.

In his testimony May 30, Ehrlichman suggested that White House aides were not convinced—on the basis of what Walters told them during the meeting—that the FBI investigation would not jeopardize the agency's activities. In fact, Ehrlichman said, Walters "would not say that the CIA had no concern on the question of Mexican operations.

"As a result of this equivocal response by General Walters respecting Mexican operations, he was asked to make contact with Acting FBI Director Gray and give him all the facts," Ehrlichman told the subcommittee. He said that it was only through John Dean, the former White House counsel, that he later learned of Walters telling Gray that the CIA would not be harmed by the investigation.

Haldeman Statement. In a prepared statement that was markedly shorter, and far less precise, former Nixon chief of staff H.R. Haldeman told the Appropriations subcommittee the following day, May 31, that he did not "specifically recall" the question of "Mexican aspects being discussed at this meeting." But Haldeman said that he did not "question" Walters' statement that the Mexican investigation was covered during the June 23 meeting.

According to Haldeman, the meeting was called to discuss in general terms whether the CIA had any in-

(Continued on p. 102)

Ehrlichman on the CIA: No Recollection of a Call

Following are excerpts from the testimony of John D. Ehrlichman before the Intelligence Operations Subcommittee of the Senate Appropriations Committee May 30:

HOW DID HUNT SECURE CIA AID?

I received a phone call from Gen. Robert Cushman, deputy director of the CIA, in late August 1971 (he says it was August 27), saying that Hunt (E. Howard Hunt Jr.) was receiving aid from the agency which was becoming potentially awkward. I asked him whether Hunt was acting for the agency or the White House. He said the White House. I asked him what his assignment was from the White House. He said he did not know.

In response to his request, I told the general I would take responsibility for the agency terminating its assistance to Hunt and, if there were any squawks or kickbacks from anyone in the White House, to simply refer them to me.

I can say flatly that I do not have the faintest recollection of having (called the CIA to request assistance for Hunt). I can say with assurance that any call to the CIA is the kind of call that I usually have little or no difficulty remembering.... I do not recall phoning to ask for help for Mr. Hunt in July 1972...(CIA) Director Helms and Mr. Colby came to see me in December 1972. At that time they suggested that I might have initiated the aid to Hunt. I told them that I did not recall doing so. Apparently the CIA memorandum of that meeting reflects my reaction as "genuinely perplexed...." One does not invoke CIA aid lightly, at least I never did. I only did so a total of three times that I can recall, each time at the specific instruction of the President.

I am certain that the President did not instruct me to secure CIA aid for Hunt.

THE CIA AND THE PLUMBERS

The press has pyramided a number of inferences to make it appear that I asked for CIA help so that Hunt could break into (Ellsberg's psychiatrist's) office in aid of the White House unit which was trying to plug government leaks of secret documents....the chronological timing is such as to reduce the probabilities of such speculation to an inadmissible minimum....

The general and I discussed cutting off Hunt's CIA support on Aug. 27, 1971, according to his records. The break-in in California did not occur until either Friday, Sept. 3, or Monday, Sept. 6. Either seven or 10 days had passed since the general and I agreed Hunt should be cut off.

...If, in fact, Hunt used CIA equipment or other support in the break-in, it is not clear to me why he still had it then. I do not suggest that the general or anyone at the agency knew in advance of Hunt's intent to commit the California break-in. Nor did I.... The general did not tell me what aid Hunt had requested nor did he ask me to cause any equipment to be returned.

Some senators on other committees have told the press that the CIA felt intimidated by the White House and therefore extended aid to Mr. Hunt. In my few contacts with the CIA, I did not detect any such symptoms of intimidation.... In retrospect, one must ask why Hunt would be extended *carte blanche* at the agency for nearly a month without asking what he was doing. Especially since CIA management has shown no reticence in the past in describing the legal limits of the agency's ability to help.... In my personal experience, the White House has never insisted that the CIA do something which the director has firmly objected to or, for that matter, anything which the deputy director has objected to.... The committee will be slow, I am sure, to accept the suggestion that Gen. Cushman was in any way coerced or forced into extending aid to Hunt. There is not a scintilla of evidence in your record to support such a story.

THE CIA AND THE WATERGATE—JUNE 1972

Mr. Haldeman said the President was concerned about the effect of the FBI investigation upon the agency. The President intended to require a full, vigorous FBI investigation with no strings but believed that the trail might lead to agency people or activities either in this country or abroad. The President was especially concerned about agency activities in Mexico which might be disclosed.... Mr. Helms and Gen. Walters were asked first, if the CIA had a part in the Watergate break-in. They replied that it did not.

...Helms and Walters were told that John Dean was following the Watergate matter closely for the President and any future White House contact could be with him.... Later Dean told me he had been in touch with Walters and that the CIA did not believe an investigation would harm their operations.

...During the first week of July 1972, the President told me Pat Gray told him on the telephone that Gen. Walters had told Gray there was no CIA objection to a full FBI investigation of the Mexican aspects of the Watergate case. The President said he then instructed Gray to conduct a full investigation.

The President told me then that he still personally believed and feared that the FBI investigation might harm the agency.... The President said substantially: A man makes a grave mistake in covering up for subordinates....

Some questions have arisen because I advised Mr. Gray not to hold a meeting he proposed to have on this CIA question. First, I did not "cancel" Mr. Gray's meeting. I did object to the idea of the staffs of the bureau and agency meeting with Gray and Helms and Walters on this, because we strongly suspected that *Time* magazine had a freely running leak source at the top level of Gray's staff. I urged that Gray meet with Walters on a one-to-one basis, without including staff, until the matter was resolved.

SUMMARY

No one person can provide all the answers to all the questions that can be asked about White House conduct relating to the CIA over the 1969-1972 term....I, for one, treated such contacts (with the CIA) with as much delicacy and care as possible. My business with the CIA was almost invariably at the President's direction but, even so, I consistently deferred to agency executives' views of the propriety of the requests I transmitted.

...However begun, the Hunt aid was cut off in time to have avoided CIA involvement in the break-in. I concurred totally in the cut-off, consistent with my practice of deferring to agency views concerning legal limitation on CIA activities .... The press has said that we attempted to coerce the CIA into accepting blame for the Watergate break-in at the meeting. We did not.

As the President has said, to the extent that the CIA had a stake in the outcome of the Mexican investigation (as Gen. Walters indicated the CIA might), we were concerned that this information be given to Director Gray at the FBI. I consider my participation in the meeting to have been entirely proper.

Haldeman on the CIA: National Security, not Coverup

Following is the text of a statement read by H. R. Haldeman to the Intelligence Operations Subcommittee of the Senate Appropriations Committee May 31:

Mr. Chairman: I believe that the only area in which I can be helpful to you in your current investigation is with respect to the reported meeting of White House and CIA officials last June.

On June 23, 1972, John Ehrlichman and I were requested by the President to meet with Director Richard Helms and Deputy Director Vernon Walters of the CIA. John Dean had reported to me that the FBI had requested guidance regarding some aspects of the Watergate investigation, and I advised the President of Mr. Dean's report. He in turn asked me to meet with Ehrlichman, Helms and Walters.

To the best of my recollection, the purpose of this meeting was five-fold:

1—To ascertain whether there had been any CIA involvement in the Watergate affair;

2—To ascertain whether the relation between some of the Watergate participants and the Bay of Pigs was a matter of concern to the CIA;

3—To inform the CIA of an FBI request for guidance regarding some aspects of the Watergate investigation because of the possibility of CIA involvement, directly or indirectly;

4—To discuss White House concern regarding possible disclosure of non-Watergate-related covert CIA operations or other national security activities that had been undertaken previously by some of the Watergate principals;

5—To request Walters to meet with Acting Director Gray of the FBI to express these concerns and to coordinate with the FBI so that the FBI's area of investigation of the suspects not be expanded into unrelated matters which could lead to disclosure of their earlier national security and CIA activities.

The meeting was held in Mr. Ehrlichman's office on the afternoon of June 23 and, to the best of my recollection, all of the above points were covered.

As I recall, Director Helms assured us that there was no CIA involvement in the Watergate and also that he had no concern from the CIA's viewpoint regarding any possible connections of the Watergate personnel with the Bay of Pigs. Helms told us he had given this assurance to Gray directly.

Walters agreed to meet with Gray as requested. I do not recall having any further communication or meeting with Walters, Helms or Gray on this subject.

I do not specifically recall the question of "Mexican aspects" being discussed at this meeting, although I do not question General Walters' report that this was covered. We did discuss the concern that, in the interest of national security and the former relationships of some of the principals with CIA, the FBI investigation be limited to the Watergate case specifically and not expanded into prior activities of the individuals involved. We did this in the full belief that we were acting in the national interest and with no intent or desire to impede or "cover up" any aspect of the Watergate investigation itself.

I do not recall any subsequent discussion with John Dean regarding this meeting. I do not recall any discussion at any time of a suggestion to involve the CIA in the Watergate matter except as described above. Specifically, I do not recall hearing of any idea of having CIA furnish bail or pay suspects' salaries while in jail, using covert action funds.

It must be understood that, at the time of our meeting with the CIA, we had only very sketchy knowledge of what and who were involved in the Watergate affair. We had no reason to believe that anyone in the White House was involved and no reason, therefore, to seek any coverup of the Watergate investigation from the White House. On the contrary, everyone in the White House was instructed to cooperate fully with the Watergate investigation—and, so far as I knew at the time, was doing so.

At the same time, there was concern at the White House that activities which had been in no way related to Watergate or to the 1972 political campaign—and which were in the area of national security—would be compromised in the process of the Watergate investigation and the attendant publicity and political furor. Recent events have fully justified that concern—with the disclosure of the FBI wiretaps on press and NSC personnel, the details of the "plumbers' operation," etc.

In summary, the meeting of June 23 with the CIA was held at the President's request in the interest of national security. I do not believe there was any intention to "cover up" the Watergate. I do not believe there was any direct connection between this meeting and Gen. Walters' subsequent meetings with John Dean. I believe I acted properly, in accord with the President's instructions, and in the national interest.

Mr. Chairman, in reviewing the transcript of the testimony before this committee by Ambassador Helms on May 16, I find some areas that require clarification.

First—it should be emphasized that there was only one meeting in which Helms, Ehrlichman and I participated—the one on June 23—at which Gen. Walters was also present. The other meetings to which Gen. Walters refers in his affidavit and memoranda were between him and John Dean—and, as I stated above, I do not believe there was any direct connection between the June 23 meeting and the subsequent meetings.

Second—at the June 23 meeting there was no discussion, intimation, or feeler about the CIA taking any responsibility for the Watergate operation.

(Continued from p. 100)
volvement in the Watergate break-in. In his statement, Haldeman referred to White House concerns that a Watergate investigation might lead to disclosure "of non-Watergate-related covert CIA operations or other national security activities." These same concerns for national security were the primary reasons he ordered Haldeman and Ehrlichman to meet with CIA officials, President Nixon said in his May 22 speech.

Apparent Contradictions. The Haldeman-Ehrlichman statements in many respects contradicted the CIA's official recollection of what took place during the June 23 meeting.

Both Walters and former CIA Director Richard Helms have testified that Nixon aides knew the CIA was not involved in the Watergate break-in prior to their request that Walters meet with Gray to discuss the FBI investigation. Helms reportedly has testified that he informed Gray on the day before the White House meeting that the FBI investigation would not injure CIA operations. He subsequently informed Haldeman and Ehrlichman during the meeting of his conversation with Gray, but the Nixon aides still requested that Walters meet with Gray.

During hearings before the Senate Foreign Relations Committee May 21, former CIA Director Richard Helms said he assumed the White House aides who requested aid from the CIA were doing so on orders from Nixon. Asked why he did not consult the President when the requests proved questionable, Helms answered:

"My interest was to keep the CIA out of this (Watergate). Frankly, I wanted to stay as head of the agency and keep it out of all this. I felt I'd be more successful than someone who might come afterward." Helms was replaced as head of the CIA after the 1972 elections in what some of his supporters said was punishment for his reluctance to honor all White House requests of the CIA.

Helms declined to speculate on why Nixon replaced him as head of the CIA in December 1972. He told Sen. Charles H. Percy (R Ill.) during his appearance before the Foreign Relations Committee that his discussion with the President was "privileged." But he said the President did not mention Watergate during their conversation.

Helms was quick to defend the CIA's assistance to the White House during the period under investigation. "Giving assistance to the presidency," he told the Senate investigators, "has not been a crime until recently."

FBI Memo. In a related development, the Justice Department May 31 released the summary of a memorandum from FBI files which revealed that the CIA had requested that two of its agents not be interviewed during the FBI's investigation of the Watergate. According to the Justice Department, the two CIA agents were to have been interviewed in a matter totally unrelated to the "Mexican aspects" of the Watergate case.

The disclosure further complicated the elements of the Watergate investigation, because the CIA has steadfastly contended before congressional investigators that the agency played no part in any of the Watergate-related scandals. The FBI memo said the CIA feared the agents might be in danger should their "covers" be destroyed by the FBI interviews.

The National Security Act of 1947 prohibits the CIA from engaging in domestic surveillance not related to matters of national security. The act specifically prohibits the agency from taking on the powers of "police, subpoena, law enforcement...or internal security function."

Presidential Subpoena: Violation of Constitution?

Continuing concern and uncertainty about the President's role in the Watergate scandal appeared to be moving the concept of separated powers to one of its most severe tests.

The White House made its position clear May 29. President Nixon said he would not provide information through oral or written testimony to the Watergate grand jury or to the Senate select committee. For him to do so, he said through press secretary Ronald L. Ziegler, would be "constitutionally inappropriate" and a violation of the separation of powers.

Thus the limits of inquiry were apparently set, both for the co-equal judicial branch within which the grand jury investigation was continuing and for the co-equal legislative branch within which the select committee was working. The White House statement followed reports that the prosecutors working with the grand jury had informed the Justice Department that they had sufficient evidence to call Nixon to appear. The Justice Department was said to support the White House position that the only way in which the President could be compelled to answer questions was by a summons from the House of Representatives as part of impeachment proceedings.

Ervin Position. The Supreme Court, said Sen. Sam J. Ervin Jr. (D N.C.), has ruled that Congress can issue a subpoena to a witness, but it has not ruled that Congress can subpoena anyone except White House aides—the decision does not exempt anyone. White House officials, said Ervin—chairman of the Senate investigating committee and of the Senate Judiciary Subcommittee on Separation of Powers—are not royalty; they retain the obligations of other citizens. And one of those obligations—as the administration pointed out to Ervin's subcommittee earlier in 1973 when the subcommittee was considering bills to protect newsmen from grand jury demands for testimony—is to provide information concerning possible crimes to grand juries.

During one of the first days of the Watergate hearings, Ervin directed attention on this question back to 1807, when former Vice President Aaron Burr was on trial for treason. Burr asked Chief Justice John Marshall, who was presiding over the trial at the circuit level, to subpoena President Thomas Jefferson. Burr contended that Jefferson had a letter which would contradict testimony that had been given against Burr.

Ervin related that Marshall found that without doubt the court could issue a subpoena to the President. The only question was, he said, whether or not the subpoena could require the President to produce the letter referred to. The uncertainty lay, Ervin said, not in the character of the witness but in the testimony he was being asked to give. Eventually, Marshall ruled that the subpoena requiring the letter from the President could be issued.

'Magnificent Example.' Setting a "magnificent example which has been honored as much in the breach as in the observance," noted Ervin, Jefferson said he would produce the letter without the compulsion of a subpoena. In a footnote to the 1972 Supreme Court ruling that newsmen had to answer grand jury subpoenas, Justice Byron R. White noted that the Burr case resolved the point concerning the President: "Chief Justice Marshall, sitting on circuit, opined that in proper circumstances, a subpoena could be issued to the President of the United States."

The question of proper circumstances may have been what Jefferson was concerned about when he wrote to the prosecutor in the Burr case, explaining why he himself would not bring the letter to the trial at Richmond, Va. For him to do so, he wrote, "would leave the nation without an executive branch...the sole branch which the Constitution requires to be always in function. It could not then intend that it should be withdrawn from its station by any coordinate authority."

Poll Report

Watergate and other issues have driven President Nixon's popularity to its lowest point. For the first time since the early 1950s, large numbers of Americans are concerned with corruption in government—and specifically with Watergate. And the scandal is having an adverse effect on Republican prospects for the 1974 congressional elections. These are the findings of the latest nationwide polls. *(Earlier poll report, p. 50)*

Nixon Popularity. The Gallup Poll, in interviews of 1,531 adults May 4-6—just after the President's April 30 television speech—found that his popularity had sunk more than 20 percentage points from its high mark in January.

	Latest	April 27-30
Approve	45%	48%
Disapprove	42	40
No opinion	13	12

Corruption Issue. Gallup asked the same persons for their assessment of the most important problems facing the country. Corruption in government (and Watergate), with 16 per cent, tied with drugs for third. Only living costs and crime ranked higher.

House Races. In a Harris Survey, "Recently, a cross-section of the country was asked: 'Suppose the 1974 election for Congress were being held today and you had to decide right now, in this congressional district, would you vote for the Republican or Democratic candidate for Congress?' "

	1974	1972
Democratic	48%	53%
Republican	35	47
Not sure	17	—

"If this lead were to hold up through November 1974, the Democrats could dominate the next Congress by majorities they have not held since the 1930s," said Harris.

Daily Chronology

Following is the day-to-day chronology of the week's events:

MAY 24

(Earlier May 24 events, p. 90)

Indictments Expected. U.S. Attorney Harold H. Titus Jr. of Washington, D.C., announced that further indictments in the Watergate case were expected within 60 to 90 days and that a key figure would plead guilty and serve as a prosecution witness at the trial. *The New York Times* identified that person as Jeb Stuart Magruder, deputy director of the Nixon re-election committee and a former White House aide.

Titus also said that the three prosecutors who had been handling the investigation from its beginning—Earl J. Silbert, Seymour Glanzer and Donald E. Campbell—would stay on the job. They had threatened to resign in protest against the take-over of the investigation by special prosecutor Archibald Cox, who reportedly was still considering whether or not to retain the three prosecutors permanently. *(Resignation threat, p. 89)*

Gray Testimony. Former acting FBI Director L. Patrick Gray III told a Senate Appropriations subcommittee of warning Nixon in a July 6, 1972, telephone conversation that "people on your staff are trying to mortally wound you" by hampering the FBI's investigation of the Watergate affair. Gray's testimony, in closed hearings, was recounted by Subcommittee Chairman John L. McClellan (D Ark.).

Nixon had acknowledged Gray's admonition in his May 22 statement on the Watergate case, saying: "Mr. Gray suggested that the matter of Watergate might lead higher. I told him to press ahead with his investigation." *(Statement text, p. 90)*

Nixon POW Speech. Addressing a large, friendly crowd of former Vietnam prisoners of war at the State Department auditorium, the President declared, "It is time in this country to quit making national heroes out of those who steal secrets and publish them in the newspapers."

Caulfield Resignation. John J. Caulfield, the former White House aide who testified that he offered executive clemency to Watergate conspirator James W. McCord Jr., resigned from the Treasury Department, where he had been assistant director of criminal enforcement in the Bureau of Alcohol, Tobacco and Firearms. Caulfield had gone on administrative leave from the department May 18. *(Caulfield testimony, p. 82)*

MAY 25

Richardson Statement. In a White House ceremony, Elliot L. Richardson was sworn in as attorney general, his third cabinet post in the Nixon administration. During a farewell news conference at the Pentagon the previous day, former Defense Secretary Richardson said he thought the Watergate scandal had created "a kind of sleaziness that has infected" government. *(Senate Judiciary Committee hearings, p. 96)*

CIA vs. Administration. *The New York Times,* citing White House and intelligence sources, reported that in 1969 and 1970, Central Intelligence Agency (CIA) studies found "no substantial evidence to support the Nixon administration's view that foreign governments were supplying undercover agents and funds to radicals and Black Panther groups in the U.S." Nixon's May 22 statement mentioned a rejected 1970 "intelligence plan" he had put forward to protect national security.

Talmadge Restlessness. Sen. Herman E. Talmadge (D Ga.), a member of the Senate Watergate investigating committee, told reporters that the committee should focus on the question of Nixon's involvement in the Watergate affair. "I think it's important that we get the principals in the matter before our committee at the earliest possible date and remove the cloud of uncertainty that hangs over the country," he said. Committee Chairman Sam J. Ervin Jr. (D N.C.) reportedly continued to favor a more gradual, circumspect development of the evidence.

Magruder Job. *The Washington Post* revealed that Jeb Magruder, former deputy director of the President's re-election committee, had been rehired by the Nixon Inaugural Committee, on which he had served as executive director. The Post quoted the committee's chairman, J. Willard Marriott Sr., as saying Magruder's job would include "overseeing financial records" and would last for an indefinite period. Magruder resigned from a Commerce Department post April 26, after being implicated in the Watergate case. *(Magruder profile, p. 40)*

White House Employment. Deputy press secretary Gerald L. Warren said that in spite of the Watergate affair, the White House was "having no trouble whatsoever" filling high-level government positions. The vacancy rate for non-career, executive-level administration positions was less than 10 per cent, "about standard," he said.

Chicago Plane Crash. The National Transportation Safety Board announced it would look into allegations made by a Chicago legal researcher that the crash of a United Airlines jet at Chicago's Midway Airport in December 1972 was related to a Watergate coverup. The wife of Watergate conspirator E. Howard Hunt Jr. was found to have been carrying $10,000 in $100 bills—the denomination reportedly used in many Watergate transactions. Mrs. Hunt was killed in the crash.

Prisoners Transferred. Five convicted Watergate conspirators—E. Howard Hunt Jr., Bernard L. Barker, Virgilio R. Gonzalez, Eugenio R. Martinez and Frank A. Sturgis—were transferred from the District of Columbia jail to the medium-security federal prison at Danbury, Conn.

MAY 26

Symington Protest. Sen. Stuart Symington (D Mo.), acting chairman of the Senate Armed Services Committee, made public a letter he had written to former Secretary of Defense Richardson questioning the legality of Gen. Alexander M. Haig Jr.'s serving as White House chief of staff while he was still serving as Army vice chief of staff.

Clemency Offer. *The Washington Post* identified former White House counsel John W. Dean III as the source of a message that Watergate conspirator McCord would receive a phone call from "a friend"—a call that turned out to be an offer of executive clemency. *(Testimony, p. 84)*

Martinez Plan. Conspirator Martinez tried to recruit anti-Castro Cubans for activities aimed at disrupting anti-war demonstrations during the 1972 campaign, according to Pablo Fernandez, a Miami Cuban quoted in *The Washington Post.*

MAY 27

Campaign Practices. The Fair Campaign Practices Committee released its report on the 1972 campaign, which called the Watergate affair the worst scandal since the committee began monitoring political campaigns nearly 20 years ago. *(Box, above)*

Haldeman, Ehrlichman. *The New York Times* reported that, according to its sources, federal prosecutors had evidence directly linking former presidential aides H. R. Haldeman and John D. Ehrlichman to illegal activities against Daniel Ellsberg in 1971, including the break-in at Ellsberg's psychiatrist's office. The Times said prosecutors had concluded those activities were a major factor in the White House decision to limit the Watergate investigation. Spokesmen for the two men denied that they had "participated in or covered up any criminal activities while serving in the White House."

The Times' sources said that the evidence against Haldeman and Ehrlichman had been provided to the federal grand jury by David R. Young Jr., a former National Security Council aide who served as codirector of the White House "plumbers" group organized to stop information leaks in 1971. Young was granted partial immunity from prosecution May 16, the story said.

Ehrlichman Denial. In an interview on ABC-TV, Ehrlichman said there was "no functional relationship" between the White House "plumbers" group set up to plug national security leaks and the men involved in the Watergate break-in. Ehrlichman added that he was surprised when he heard of the Ellsberg psychiatrist break-in about a week after it happened.

Fair Campaign Practices Report

The Fair Campaign Practices Committee, in a report issued May 27, described the Watergate scandal as "a conscious conspiracy to violate laws, to manipulate voters and to make a mockery of the democratic system of self-government." The committee is a private, nonpartisan organization with headquarters in Washington, D.C.

Disagreeing with an April 30 statement by President Nixon that both political parties had engaged in similar campaign excesses in the past, the report said: "In nearly 20 years of studying the political process, (the committee) has uncovered no campaign tactics comparable in extent or in potential damage to a free, self-governing society."

Among the unethical or illegal practices associated with Watergate, according to the report, were theft of campaign documents, electronic eavesdropping, personal vilification, falsification of letters and advertisements, stacking of polls, illegal financial reporting, spying on opponents and attempts to cover up apparent crimes. Such tactics, the committee said, are neither "symptoms of a cancer permeating the entire body politic" nor the tactics of professional politicians.

In 1972, the report stated, 80 complaints were filed with the committee in presidential, gubernatorial and congressional campaigns—a 19 per cent increase over the average of 67 complaints in recent election years. But the Watergate affair did not account for much of the increase. Only two complaints were filed in that category before the election, the report said.

Strauss Counterattack. Democratic Chairman Robert S. Strauss attacked Nixon's May 22 statement that the Watergate investigation was limited by national security requirements. "I think the public will understand the difference between national security and Nixon security," he said on NBC-TV's "Meet the Press."

Symington Interview. In an interview on CBS-TV's "Face the Nation," Sen. Symington of Missouri mentioned that some of the secret documents he had seen were marked "copy to the President." That fact, Symington said, made it "hard to believe" Nixon knew nothing about the attempted coverup of the Watergate burglary.

LeBlanc Offer. Norman P. LeBlanc, a Canadian businessman and associate of indicted financier Robert L. Vesco, announced in San Jose, Costa Rica, that he and Vesco possessed a "missing link" in the Watergate case. Le Blanc invited special prosecutor Archibald Cox to meet with them to see their documents.

MAY 28

Dean Developments. CBS News reported that the Watergate prosecutors had offered former presidential counsel John W. Dean III the opportunity to plead guilty to one count of obstruction of justice, a felony, in exchange for his testimony. In an interview printed in the June 4 *Time* magazine, Dean warned that, "if indicted, I'll probably never testify," and predicted that "when all the facts are known, there will be several additional federal grand juries in this country...."

Indictments Expected. *Newsweek* magazine reported June 4 that the Watergate grand jury had agreed to indict former administration officials Haldeman, Ehrlichman, Mitchell and Magruder.

Fensterwald Performance. *The New York Times* reported that Bernard Fensterwald Jr., the lawyer for conspirator James W. McCord Jr., made "false statements and false implications" while serving as counsel to a Senate subcommittee investigating electronic snooping

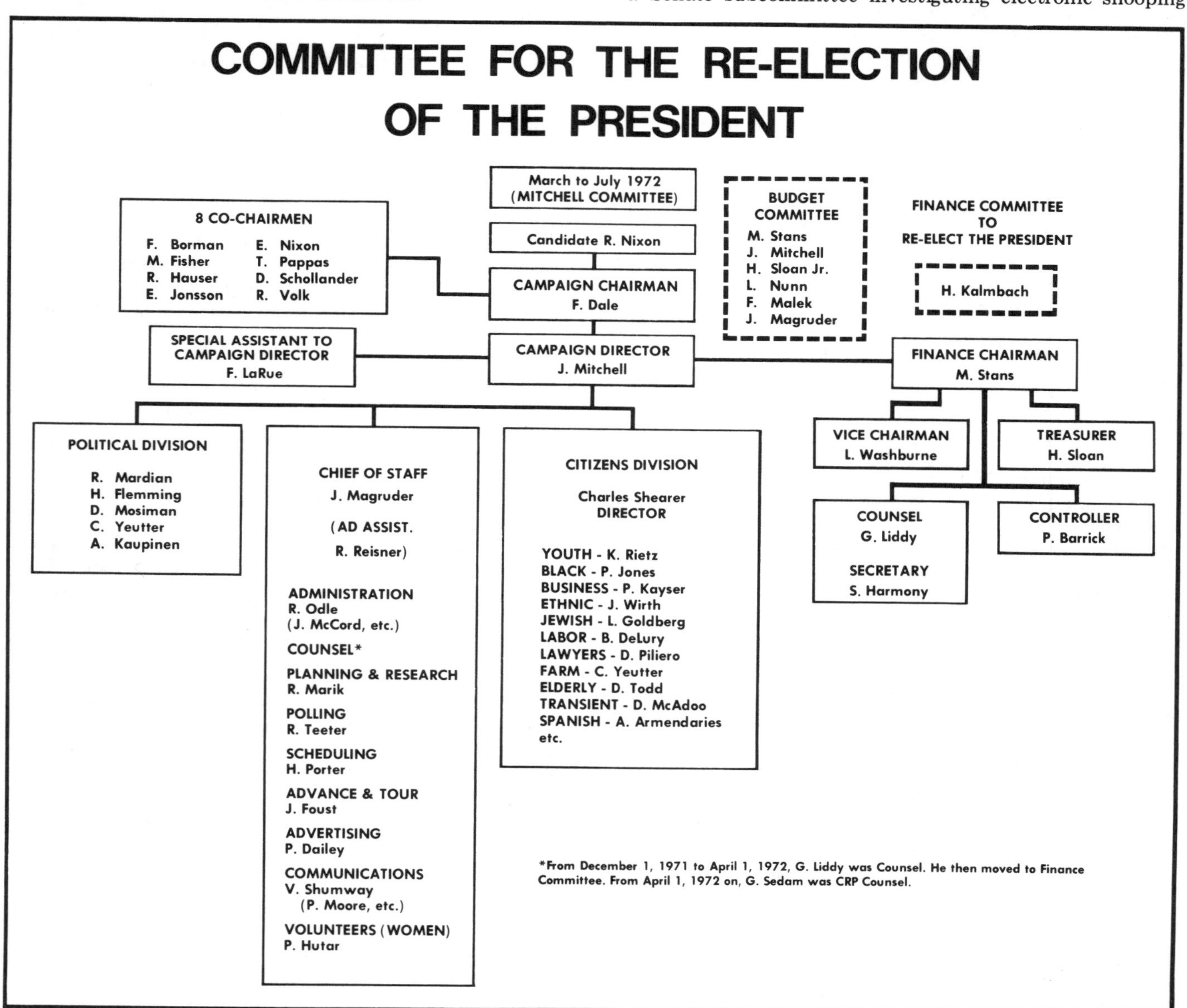

in 1965, according to sources close to the investigation. Fensterwald had "no clear recollection" of the matter, the Times said. *(Senate testimony, p. 83)*

MAY 29

Nixon Questioning. *The Washington Post* reported that federal prosecutors had told the Justice Department that there was "justification" for calling Nixon to answer questions before the federal grand jury investigating the Watergate case. Citing government sources, the Post said that Nixon's role was "the one key question" remaining in the grand jury's investigation and that prosecutors were debating the constitutional issue of whether and how the President could be questioned.

Presidential press secretary Ziegler said that Nixon would not testify orally or in writing before the grand jury or the Senate investigating committee, because "it would be constitutionally inappropriate" and "would do violence to the separation of powers."

Ziegler had issued a statement the night before, saying the Post story reflected "a shocking and irresponsible abuse of authority on the part of federal prosecutors. Grand jury proceedings are by law secret." He said the White House would ask Attorney General Richardson and special prosecutor Cox to investigate immediately the circumstances of the charges.

Cox Statements. Cox issued a statement saying, in part, "All decisions about theories of investigation or prosecution, the grant of immunity, the acceptance of pleas in return for testimony, and the conduct of the investigation will be made by me. I have made no such decisions and authorized none." He did not specifically mention Ziegler's request for an investigation of leaks.

Cox also announced that James F. Neal, a Nashville, Tenn., lawyer and former aide to Attorney General Robert F. Kennedy, would serve "for two weeks or longer" as a special assistant to the prosecution. Two Harvard Law School professors—Philip E. Heymann and James Vorenberg—also were sworn in as special assistants.

Kissinger Denial. Henry A. Kissinger, Nixon's national security adviser, told reporters he did not specifically request the use of wiretaps in 1969 to plug newsleaks, but acknowledged that he gave the FBI the names of White House staff members who had access to classified information. Kissinger—who had been accused in press reports of requesting wiretaps on some of his aides and had denied those reports—labeled wiretapping a distasteful practice.

Cushman Testimony. Marine Gen. Robert E. Cushman Jr., former CIA deputy director, was the first witness to testify before a Los Angeles grand jury investigating the break-in at the office of Daniel Ellsberg's psychiatrist. At a news conference later, Cushman said he had called former White House aide John D. Ehrlichman to inform him that Watergate conspirator E. Howard Hunt Jr. had "questionable judgment" and that the CIA could not assist Hunt, as Ehrlichman reportedly had requested. *(Story, p. 99)*

MAY 30

Ehrlichman Testimony. Ehrlichman testified at a closed session of the Senate Appropriations Subcommittee on Intelligence Operations, which was investigating alleged CIA involvement in Watergate. In a statement to the committee and in comments to reporters, Ehrlichman gave his version of a June 23, 1972, meeting he attended with H.R. Haldeman, former CIA director Richard Helms, and Army Gen. Vernon A. Walters, Helms' deputy.

Mail Tampering. Rep. Charles H. Wilson (D Calif.), a member of the House Post Office Committee, asked the postmaster general to investigate allegations that first-class mail had been opened and turned over to Nixon campaign officials in 1972.

LaRue Testimony. Frederick C. LaRue, a campaign aide to former Attorney General Mitchell, told the Watergate grand jury he paid about $250,000 in cash to the Watergate conspirators in exchange for their silence, *The Washington Post* reported.

Immunity Delayed. Chief U.S. District Judge John J. Sirica signed an order for a 20-day delay in granting immunity from prosecution for Dean and Magruder. The delay, which was requested by the Justice Department, prevented Magruder from testifying before the Senate investigating committee before June 8 and Dean, before June 12. Sirica also asked the committee and the Justice Department for opinions on whether he could legally deny the immunity request.

Mitchell, Stans Trial. A federal judge in New York City set a tentative date of Sept. 11 for the trial of John N. Mitchell, Maurice H. Stans and Harry L. Sears on charges that they illegally aided financier Robert L. Vesco in his dealings with the government. *(Indictments, p. 46)*

Trial Delayed. U.S. District Judge Charles R. Richey delayed for 90 days the trial of the Democrats' $6.4-million civil suit against the Republicans over the Watergate affair.

MAY 31

Haldeman Testimony. Haldeman appeared at a closed session of the Senate Appropriations Subcommittee on Intelligence Operations to discuss his involvement in the Watergate coverup. *(p. 102)*

Urge for Speed. In a letter to other members of the Senate investigating committee, Sen. Edward J. Gurney (R Fla.) urged that the committee "get to the heart of Watergate with a few witnesses" who could clarify Nixon's role in the affair. Vice President Agnew expressed similar sentiments in an interview with *The New York Times.*

Intelligence Committee. According to news reports, the Justice Department was preparing to abolish the Intelligence Evaluation Committee, a secret domestic intelligence unit set up in December 1970. The Senate investigating committee reportedly was investigating the group, which Nixon mentioned in his May 22 statement on the Watergate case. *(Text, p. 91)*

1969 Break-In. *The New York Times,* quoting two former Army intelligence operatives, reported that FBI agents broke into the office of a Washington, D.C., radical newspaper shortly before Nixon's 1969 inauguration, in an attempt to find evidence of foreign communist influence. ✓

A WATERGATE VACUUM: 60 TOP JOBS STILL NOT FILLED

More than four months into President Nixon's second term, the White House was still searching for an under secretary of the treasury and a deputy secretary of defense.

A Congressional Quarterly study shows these were but two of 60 high-level presidential appointments requiring Senate confirmation that were unfilled by May 31.

Whether the slow pace of filling those vacancies was attributable directly to the Watergate scandal was difficult to determine.

"The White House is having no trouble recruiting people," said deputy press secretary Gerald L. Warren on May 24. "None whatsoever." But a White House source told Congressional Quarterly that Watergate is having an effect, especially when coupled with the President's request for formal resignations from executive branch staff members in late 1972.

On Nov. 8, 1972, the day after Nixon's landslide re-election victory, the White House publicly informed some 2,000 presidential appointees that they were to submit their resignations to the President.

Many officeholders did not learn for several weeks whether the President intended to fire them, switch them to a different job, or keep them on as before. This procedure, attributed to the President's former chief of staff, H. R. Haldeman, put many administration officials in limbo for long periods, angered others and undoubtedly affected outsiders being considered for government jobs, the source said.

In April, the Watergate scandal began making headlines and at the end of the month Haldeman and John D. Ehrlichman, the top presidential aides, had signed. Haldeman and Ehrlichman had considered all appointments before passing them on to Nixon. Just before their resignations, as charges of complicity in Watergate and other campaign excesses became almost daily occurences, Haldeman and Ehrlichman were unable to devote much time to processing appointments. As a result, little has been done for weeks.

In order to overcome the backlog of appointments, Roy L. Ash, director of the Office of Management and Budget, and Gen. Alexander M. Haig, Haldeman's temporary replacement, have been providing final staff clearances for high-level posts.

Congressional Quarterly's study of high-level vacancies was limited to departmental jobs—those which are filled at the President's pleasure and generally are considered "administration" positions. The figures came from the White House and department officials.

The study showed that the State Department had the greatest number of vacancies—24—including 17 ambassadorial posts. Among countries lacking U.S. ambassadors were the Soviet Union, Sweden and Brazil. In addition, the State Department post of Inspector General-Foreign Assistance has been vacant since Feb. 26, 1971, longer than any other administration post.

The White House's most recent figures, issued May 24 by the deputy press secretary, Gerald L. Warren, showed vacancies for 65 out of 520 executive level jobs. He also said there were only 13 ambassadorial posts vacant out of 115 slots, but did not name them.

Warren's figure of 65 openings included 48 posts where the occupant left before his replacement came aboard, and 17 where the occupant was still serving although he had announced his resignation. That meant a vacancy rate of 12.5 per cent. Warren said a 10 per cent vacancy rate "is about standard."

SAN CLEMENTE HOME

The White House disclosed May 25 that Robert Abplanalp, millionaire manufacturer and friend of the President, has owned most of the Nixon property at San Clemente, Calif., for the past two years.

Abplanalp, inventor of the spray valve used on aerosol cans, is the owner of a New York firm, Precision Valve Corporation. His own home on Grand Cay in the Bahamas is a frequent vacation spot for the Nixon family.

A White House statement said Abplanalp in 1969 loaned Nixon $625,000 at 8 per cent interest to help the President acquire 26 acres at San Clemente. The Nixons put up $400,000 of their own money toward the $1.4-million purchase price. *(Text below)*

The statement said the Nixons initially wanted only 5.9 acres for their home, but purchased the larger tract in order to provide for greater security and privacy.

On Dec. 15, 1970, the Nixons sold all but the first 5.9 acres for $1,249,000 to an investment company set up by Abplanalp, who canceled the original loan. The White House refused to reveal the name of the investment company. The President's net investment in the San Clemente property, which includes a 10-room house, was put at $374,514. Deputy press secretary Gerald L. Warren told reporters May 26 that the Nixons still owed $300,000 on the property and were paying off the mortgage at 7½ per cent interest.

Improvements. Warren also said the government had spent $39,525 for improvements on the property, most of them to satisfy security requirements. These included $13,500 for a glass screen between the beach and a pool, $12,964 for a fence between nearby railroad tracks and the home and $1,500 for asphalt paving, all for security reasons.

The Associated Press reported May 28, however, that an examination of San Clemente building permit records showed the government had spent more than $100,000 on the property since the Nixons acquired it, and that the improvements enhanced its value.

The White House said it was issuing a statement on the San Clemente house to counter a "totally unfounded" story which had appeared in the press. The reference was to a May 13 article in the Santa Ana, Calif., *Register*, quoting an unnamed source on the Senate select committee investigating the Watergate scandal as saying that money for the property came from leftover 1968 presidential campaign funds. Members and staff of the Watergate committee denied the story.

White House press spokesmen refused to elaborate on the information provided in the statement.

Related Development. The Associated Press reported May 31 that a Yonkers, N.Y., bank in which Abplanalp is a principal stockholder received a charter in 1971 following Abplanalp's purchase of much of the San Clemente land. A presidential spokesman said that no one on the White House staff was aware of or involved in the charter application.

Text of Statement

Following is the White House text of a May 25 statement explaining President Nixon's purchase of his San Clemente, Calif., home:

A newspaper on the West Coast recently published a totally unfounded news account concerning the funds with which the President's home in San Clemente was purchased.

The Nixons' purchase of their San Clemente home was financed by a combination of proceeds from the sale of their New York apartment, a mortgage executed by the Title Insurance and Trust Company, and loans from a personal friend. There were absolutely no other outside sources of funds involved in the purchase of the home.

The attached statement is a chronological summary of the transactions involved.

San Clemente Property

In July, 1969, having sold their New York City apartment, the Nixons bought their present home in San Clemente. The 5.9 acre homesite that the Nixons wished to buy was part of a larger (26 acre) tract which the sellers insisted be sold as a single unit. It was the Nixons' intention to seek a compatible buyer for all but the 5.9 acres on which the residence they wished to buy was located, and this was announced at the time.

The recognized need for privacy and security for a President's home necessitated the search for a compatible buyer. It was thought that at some future date the Richard Nixon Foundation might be a compatible buyer of the property if it met the needs of the Foundation as a possible site for a Presidential library.

Prior to the closing of the sale in July 1969, no compatible buyer had been found and, therefore, it was necessary for the Nixons to acquire, temporarily, the entire tract. To meet the larger down payment which this required, the Nixons received a loan from a personal friend, Mr. Robert Abplanalp. This loan, and a subsequent loan from Mr. Abplanalp in 1970, were the only outside financing used in the purchase of the property.

The Title Insurance and Trust Company was appointed as the trustee to buy the property and to hold formal title to it in order to facilitate the disposal of the portion of the property the Nixons did not plan on keeping for their own use. Under this arrangement the portion of the surrounding property which the Nixons did not intend to keep could later be sold to a compatible buyer without renegotiating the mortgage.

On July 15, 1969, the trustee completed the purchase of the property for a total of $1,400,000. The trustee paid $400,000 in cash, furnished by the Nixons, and executed a mortgage to the sellers for the balance. Under California law, the mortgage was secured only by the property and involved no further personal liability.

In September 1969, the Nixons directed the Title Insurance and Trust Company—acting as their trustee—to acquire from S. H. Elmore for $100,000 an additional 2.9 acres immediately adjacent to the Cotton property to provide better access and privacy. The trustee acquired this property by paying $20,000 in cash, furnished by the Nixons, and by executing a purchase money mortgage to the seller for the remaining $80,000. This mortgage and the mortgage on the Cotton property are recorded in Orange County, California.

Thus, the total price of the entire property, consisting of the Cotton and Elmore tracts, was $1,500,000. In addition, the Nixons have spent, to date, $123,514 for improvements to the house and the 5.9 acre homesite.

In order to provide temporary financing to meet the objective of the purchases as previously explained, the Nixons borrowed a total of $625,000 from Mr. Abplanalp, and gave Mr. Abplanalp their personal promissory notes bearing interest at 8 percent.

On December 15, 1970, the Nixons carried out their plan to sell the property they did not want. It was purchased by an investment company set up by Mr. Abplanalp for the purpose of acquiring and holding this land. The price was $1,249,000 which was paid as follows: The cancellation of the outstanding loans from Mr. Abplanalp (with the exception of accrued interest) totalling $625,000; the assumption of the mortgage on the Elmore property, which at that time amounted to $64,000; and the assumption of $560,000 of the $900,000 remaining mortgage on the Cotton property. This left the Nixons responsible for only that portion of the mortgage covering their 5.9 acres in accordance with their original intent. This sale was accomplished by executing an assignment of an interest in the trust and delivering it to the trustee, the Title Insurance and Trust Company.

Therefore, the total cost of the San Clemente property, and the investment of the Nixons is as follows:

Cotton property	$1,400,000
Elmore property	100,000
Improvements to date by the Nixons	123,514
TOTAL COST	$1,623,514
Less; Purchase price of surrounding land as described above	$1,249,000
Net investment by the President (5.9 acre home-site area)	$ 374,514

Key Biscayne (Fla.) Property

As previously announced, the Nixons own the houses at 516 and 500 Bay Lane in Key Biscayne. Mr. C. G. Rebozo has owned and occupied the residence at 490 Bay Lane for many years.

In order to provide Presidential support such as office space, communications and security, the Government Services Administration leases the two other houses in the compound, the house at 478 Bay Lane which is owned by Mr. and Mrs. Robert H. Abplanalp and the house at 468 Bay Lane which is owned by Mr. Edwin H. Underwood. Mr. Underwood is trustee for the Indiana National Bank of Indianapolis which in turn is trustee for the family of A. Edward Campbell, the former owner.

The ownership of these properties and the mortgages on them are a matter of public record. √

WATERGATE: NIXON REPORTED EAGER TO 'CLEAR IT UP'

President Nixon was portrayed by one of his former top aides as being anxious to make public the full story on Watergate. Whenever a new development was reported, said H. R. Haldeman, the former White House chief of staff, "there was a concern expressed on the President's part, usually to me, that we try to get the facts in this matter determined and made known."

Haldeman's comments were contained in a deposition he made May 22 and 24 in connection with a $6.4-million civil suit filed by the Democrats against the Republicans after the Watergate bugging and break-in on June 17, 1972. The deposition was made public on June 7. *(Excerpts, p. 113)*

Two days earlier, a deposition by John D. Ehrlichman, Nixon's former adviser on domestic affairs, was made public. Ehrlichman told attorneys for the Democratic Party that former Attorney General John N. Mitchell had approved the bugging plans. *(Excerpts, p. 125)*

Release of the Haldeman and Ehrlichman depositions were only two events among many during the week ended June 9 as revelations in the Watergate affair accumulated daily. Among them:

• Fired presidential Counsel John W. Dean III and White House spokesmen engaged in a battle for veracity. Dean said that he and Nixon had met some 35 times between January and April to discuss Watergate. At first the White House denounced this report as part of a strategy to "prosecute a case against the President in the press." A few days later, however, the White House acknowledged that meetings had been held.

• A credibility conflict also opened up between the White House and the Senate Select Committee on Presidential Campaign Activities, the Watergate investigating committee. At first the White House did not want to provide the committee with its logs of the Dean-Nixon meetings. Later a White House press spokesman made a "speech of contrition" and agreed to supply the logs to the committee.

Before the agreement was reached, Samuel Dash, the committee's chief counsel, was reported to have said he planned to issue a subpoena for the logs. He denied the report the day it was published.

• A third area of friction was between the Senate committee and Archibald Cox, the special prosecutor named by Attorney General Elliot L. Richardson to investigate the case. Cox's request for a 90-day delay in committee hearings, on grounds that testimony from some witnesses might interfere with their later prosecution, was rejected unanimously by the committee. Then Cox sought a court order to force the committee to hear some of its witnesses in private in order to prevent prejudicial publicity. The committee opposed that idea, too. *(Box, next page)*

• A Republican representative, Paul N. McCloskey of California, attempted to hold a one-hour discussion on the House floor on the subject of presidential impeachment. Parliamentary maneuvering by conservatives in his party prevented him from doing so. *(Box, p. p. 115)*

• Nixon, as part of his effort to put his own shattered house back in order, appointed former Defense Secretary Melvin R. Laird as his domestic affairs counsel, replacing the deposed Ehrlichman. Gen. Alexander M. Haig Jr., under fire for doubling as White House chief of staff, said he would resign from active duty in the Army on Aug. 1 so that he could devote full time to the presidential appointment. *(p. 130)*

• A batch of theretofore secret memos found their way into the newspapers. One series of Central Intelligence Agency (CIA) memos further implicated White House officials in trying to involve the CIA and the FBI in a Watergate coverup. Another document contained recommendations made to the President in 1970 for tightening domestic security rules. *(Excerpts, p. 126)*

• The Senate Watergate committee, after a one-week Memorial Day layoff, spent its third week listening to testimony. The two principal witnesses were Hugh W. Sloan Jr., former treasurer of the Nixon re-election campaign, and Herbert L. Porter, the former scheduling director of the re-election committee. Sloan described how he had resisted attempts to make him perjure himself. Porter, on nationwide television, confessed to perjury.

Late Developments

Haldeman Deposition. In his deposition made public June 7, Haldeman told Democratic Party lawyers of the President's "natural concern," in the summer and fall of 1972, that Watergate might damage his re-election chances. Nixon feared, Haldeman said, "that the insinuations and appearances and allegations that were arising would be detrimental to that campaign effort," and "there was a desire that the facts be known, cleared up and established in the public mind as well as legally, so that those doubts would not persist."

Both Haldeman and Ehrlichman, in their depositions, placed much of the blame for Republican involvement in Watergate on former counsel Dean and on Jeb Stuart Magruder, former deputy director of the Committee for the Re-election of the President. But Haldeman and Ehrlichman differed on Mitchell's role. Ehrlichman's statement implicated the former attorney general, while Haldeman's reinforced Mitchell's denials.

Haldeman explained, in greater detail than before, the circumstances surrounding his control of a $350,000 cash fund during the campaign. The money, he said, actually went to his assistant, Gordon Strachan, about April 6, 1972, the day before a new law required contributions to be made public.

(Continued on p. 112)

Cox's Efforts to Delay, Limit Senate Investigation

In one of his first moves as Watergate special prosecutor, Archibald Cox June 4 urged the Senate committee investigating the case to call off its public hearings for one to three months. "The continuation of hearings at this time would create grave danger that the full facts about the Watergate case and related matters will never come to light and that many of those who are guilty of serious wrong-doing will never be brought to justice," Cox said in a letter to Committee Chairman Sam J. Ervin Jr. (D N.C.).

Elaborating on his reasons for requesting a delay, Cox told reporters that "public hearings prior to the investigation will increase the risk that major guilty parties will go unpunished.... Quite possibly all would go free." Other reasons he offered were:

- "Immediate public hearings would impede the investigation" and "make it impossible to get at the truth from bottom to top."
- All the facts about Nixon's involvement should be brought out "at one time and in a comprehensive presentation...."
- A grant of partial immunity for certain witnesses before the committee might prevent them from being convicted later.
- Witnesses might be less likely to make full disclosures before television cameras than privately to prosecutors.
- The committee lacks some powers held by the prosecution, such as a promise of access to all documents and files in the executive branch.
- Persons inclined to fabricate explanations might be aided by premature disclosure of testimony by other witnesses.

Ervin responded promptly with a 300-page rebuttal to Cox's argument, and the committee resumed televised hearings the following day. Its members met behind closed doors June 5 to consider Cox's recommendation and voted unanimously to reject it.

When the hearings convened later that day, Ervin listed these reasons for pressing ahead without delay:

- The committee had been authorized by the Senate to conduct the investigation and had no authority to postpone it.
- The committee did not agree with Cox's contention that the courts will permit guilty parties to escape justice because of the hearings.
- There was a greater chance for indicted persons to get a fair trial "in an atmosphere of judicial calm after rather than before" the hearings.

Pretrial Publicity. Undaunted, Cox moved June 6 to require that the committee take testimony from two key witnesses—Jeb Stuart Magruder and John W. Dean III—in closed session, or at least without live media coverage. In a motion submitted to U.S. District Judge John J. Sirica, Cox asked for the restriction because "widespread pretrial publicity...might prevent bringing to justice those guilty of serious offenses in high government offices."

Magruder and Dean, who were scheduled to appear before the committee the following week, were known to be under consideration for indictment in connection with the Watergate scandal. They reportedly were prepared to offer evidence of the involvement of top White House officials, including the President.

Senate Response. The Senate committee's lawyers went to work immediately preparing a 15-page legal brief opposing Cox's request. Filed with the court June 7, it argued that under the doctrine of separation of powers the court had no jurisdiction over the committee's actions.

It also countered Cox's contention that the televised hearings would create damaging pretrial publicity, saying that such a threat was minimized by the fact that "indictments in the Watergate case are not expected for three months and...consequently, trial must be six months to a year away...."

"It is our view that we would be unpardonably remiss if, in this time of national emergency, we did not push forward to full revelation of the facts," the brief stated.

This second assault on their proceedings enflamed members of the Senate investigating committee. "To try to get the jucidial branch of the government to enjoin the legislative from functioning is without precedent in the history of the republic," said Sen. Herman E. Talmadge (D Ga.), who earlier had publicly urged the committee to call key witnesses promptly.

Chairman Ervin, always mindful of the constitution, declared that "no agency of the government has the power to dictate...how (the committee) should exercise the constitutional powers of the Senate."

Immunity Hearing. Judge Sirica heard arguments June 8 on his power to deny the Senate committee's request for immunity for Dean and Magruder, and on Cox's request for limited coverage of their testimony. In his June 6 motion, Cox acknowledged that there was no legal way to prevent the immunity grants, which the committee unanimously voted in May.

The Justice Department, however, had exercised its power to delay the grants for the legal limit of 30 days. The waiting period expired June 8 in Magruder's case, and was due to expire June 12 in Dean's case. Under the law, the two men could still be prosecuted if the evidence against them was gathered independently of their Senate testimony. *(Delay, p. 107)*

The question of whether the court had the power to block immunity grants of the Senate committee was closely connected to the question of whether it could modify the committee's procedures. The committee's position was that since even Cox agreed there were no grounds for denying the grants, there was no basis for any other sort of court interference in its operations. Sirica said he would announce his decision June 12.

Poll Report

President Nixon's popularity sank one percentage point in the latest Gallup Poll. It was the lowest point of his presidency. *(Earlier poll, p. 104)*

The poll was published June 7. Interviewers asked 1,548 adults May 11-14: "Do you approve or disapprove of the way Nixon is handling his job as President?"

	Latest	May 4-7
Approve	44%	45%
Disapprove	45	42
No opinion	11	13

(Continued from p. 112)

The money was to be used for private polling, Haldeman said. The only expenditure from the fund that he recalled in his deposition was $22,000 "for some advertising that was not directly related to the campaign" in April or May 1972.

Committee Appearance. Haldeman testified on June 7 before a closed meeting of the House Armed Services subcommittee that is investigating alleged attempts by the White House to involve the CIA in a Watergate coverup. His only statement to the press was a brief one saying that he had cooperated with the subcommittee.

But the subcommittee chairman, Rep. Lucien N. Nedzi (D Mich.), quoted Haldeman as saying he was just a conduit between Nixon and the drafters of the intelligence plans in 1970. Nedzi said Haldeman told the subcommittee he was not "directly involved in preparation of those plans nor in recommending their approval by the President."

Dean and Hunt. Charles W. Colson, former special counsel to the President, was reported in the June 8 *New York Times* to have told investigators that Dean was one of the first participants in a White House effort to cover up Watergate. Colson quoted Dean as saying he had acted on orders from Ehrlichman.

Attributing its story to "three sources close to the case," the Times reported that Colson had said that Dean had ordered conspirator E. Howard Hunt Jr. to flee the country two days after the break-in. The order was later rescinded, according to the testimony quoted.

"I recall losing my temper and reacting very angrily," the Times quoted Colson as telling investigators. "I said something to the effect of 'that is the dumbest thing I have ever heard. You will have the White House party to a fugitive from justice charge.' "

Election Law. In a development related to the Senate Committee's mandate to recommend reforms in election laws, the Senate Rules Committee June 7 turned down a Justice Department appeal for delay on a reform bill. "I can assure you that members of Congress are not in a mood to delay action," Sen. Howard W. Cannon (D Nev.) told Assistant Attorney General Robert G. Dixon Jr.

Stans Testimony. Testimony before the Senate Watergate committee by Maurice H. Stans, finance director of the Nixon campaign, would not violate Federal Judge Lee P. Gagliardi's order against pretrial publicity, the judge ruled June 8 in New York City.

Stans had pleaded innocent to charges of conspiring to defraud the government, obstructing justice and perjury in connection with a $200,000 secret contribution to the Nixon campaign by financier Robert L. Vesco. Mitchell also was indicted.

Witnesses June 5

As the Senate committee hearings resumed on June 5, Robert Reisner, a former aide to Jeb Stuart Magruder, former deputy director of the Nixon campaign, described how "sensitive material" was sent to former Attorney General John N. Mitchell by the re-election committee. Reisner and Sally J. Harmony, former secretary to G. Gordon Liddy, a convicted conspirator who was once counsel to the re-election committee and the finance committee, were the day's two witnesses.

Harmony Testimony. When she went to work for Liddy in March 1972, Harmony told the senators, he mentioned to her that he might be involved in some clandestine activities. She did not equate such activities with anything illegal, she added, and "I can keep a secret."

Harmony said that she typed intelligence memorandums and, unknown to her at the time, summaries of wiretapped telephone conversations dictated to her by Liddy. These files were prepared, she said, on stationery with a "Gemstone" letterhead. Gemstone was the code word for the re-election committee's intelligence-collecting operation, which included the Watergate bugging and break-in on June 17, 1972.

Among the code names used in the intelligence memos, said Harmony, were "Ruby 1," "Ruby 2" and "Crystal." She said she did not know who these persons were.

One stack of documents she remembered included 20 or 25 photographs from the Democratic National Committee, some with fingers holding them. "I guess at this point they were fingers with rubber gloves," she recalled in reference to the surgical gloves the burglars wore the night of the burglary.

The day before the break-in, said Harmony, she Xeroxed a sheet of stationery from the headquarters of George McGovern, the Democratic presidential candidate. On Liddy's instructions, she said, she typed a letter on the sheet, authorizing the bearer to enter McGovern headquarters, and signed Gary Hart's name to the letter. Hart was McGovern's campaign director.

After he was fired from the committee for refusing to answer the FBI's questions about his role in the bugging, Liddy asked Harmony to check his files and shred any papers with his handwriting on them, his former secretary told the committee.

(Continued on p. 114)

Excerpts from Haldeman's Testimony in Civil Suit

Following are excerpts, as published by The New York Times, *from testimony by former presidential assistant H.R. Haldeman given in May in a civil suit by the Democratic National Committee. The deposition was made public June 7.*

Q. Prior to June 17, 1972, did you have any conversations with Jeb Magruder relative to facts involving the Watergate operation?

A. No.

Q. Did you have any further conversations with him up to the present time in which he made any statements to you indicating that he did have knowledge of the Watergate matter prior to June 17, 1972?

A. Yes, he did. I think that would have been the conversation that I had with him with John Mitchell present in late March of 1973. I had a meeting at Mitchell's request, as I recall, first with Mitchell alone and then joined by Magruder with Mitchell remaining.

Q. Will you tell us, please, what was said by the various parties to that meeting?

A. To the best of my recollection there was a discussion of the question which Mr. Mitchell had raised and which Mr. Magruder also wanted to discuss and which the two of them wanted subsequently to discuss with John Dean. That was the question of the number and content of meetings that had been held the early part of 1972, possibly the end of '71, but either the end of '71 or early '72, regarding so-called intelligence operations.

There was a feeling on Mr. Mitchell's part that there was a disagreement as to how many such meetings had been held and as to what the content of those meetings was. I am not exactly sure the reason for this question being raised in a meeting with me except that as I understood it Mr. Mitchell wanted subsequently to meet with Mr. Dean on this subject. I was brought into the question in terms of whether Mr. Dean had said anything to me about any such meetings.

Because I tried to reconstruct a conversation from a long time ago and it is difficult for me to do in view of all the intervening events and things I have read. But I will try to put it in what I believe was the content of that conversation at that time. To do that, however, I have to refer to an earlier conversation with John Dean in which he reminded me or said he was reminding me that he told me that there had been two such meetings regarding intelligence planning attended by John Mitchell, Jeb Magruder, Gordon Liddy and himself; that those meetings were held in John Mitchell's office and were for the purpose of Gordon Liddy presenting to them plans and recommendations for intelligence activity.

Dean told me that after the second of those two meetings he reported to me that he had attended these two meetings or at least had attended the second one; that at the second meeting there had been a plan discussed by Mr. Liddy which he found to be totally unacceptable and I believe his word was incredible; that it was a plan so out of the question that he says he told me at the time that he had said that it should not even be discussed in the Attorney General's office and he made very strongly at the meeting the point that there should be no further such discussion of such kinds of things, and that the reason that he was reporting this to me was to tell me that he intended not to involve himself in any further meetings if there should be any regarding intelligence planning with Mr. Liddy; that he felt this was not a productive thing for him to do and he intended not to do so, and he says I agreed with him. I have strayed off this earlier conversation, but I need this point as a base for the purpose of the conversation with Magruder and Mitchell.

During that period of time, the July, August, and I would add September and October period, in others words, from the time of the Watergate break-in to the election, really, there were periodic new developments with regard to Watergate that would appear in the press or that would come forth as a part of the investigation or the various actions that were being taken by the prosecutors, court and so on. Whenever there was such a development, there was a concern expressed on the President's part, usually to me, that we try to get the facts in this matter determined and made known.

There was a natural concern on his part being at that time up for re-election and conducting a campaign for re-election that the insinuations and appearances and allegations that were arising would be detrimental to that campaign effort and that there was a desire that the facts be known, cleared up and established in the public mind as well as legally so that those doubts would not persist. Those questions from the President or urgings from the President would give rise to my inquiry of Dean again.

"Can't we get the full story out?"

As I recall it, and I, again, can't give you specific time points, during the course of that time there were varying reasons why a full story wasn't available. They related to the lack of knowledge of what really did happen and of who really was involved at some points, at least, of conflicting statements of testimony of various individuals who would be presumed to have knowledge of what was involved; and then other factors were also brought in—the questions of rights of defendants, the questions of the ongoing legal process as contrasted to the ongoing political process.

Q. Then after the election and until the meeting you have told us about in March did you have any further conversations with Dean relative to the Watergate break-in?

A. I am sure there were some; I don't think there were very many. They would have been of the same nature. In the period from the election through the end of the year, once the election was over, there was a new concern on the President's part, having just been reelected, that this matter, any questions pending on the Watergate and so on, be cleared up not for the reason of the effect on the election but for the effect on the start of the new term and the desire that before the Congress returned and before the President was inaugurated that the whole matter be cleared up and made known so that it wouldn't be hanging over into the second term.

As a result of that concern (and I think during that period there were probably some developments in the case—I am not sure what the chronology is there but we are leading up to the time of the trial, I guess, at that point) he would have raised again questions as to why this couldn't now be cleared up. Basically, the answers continued to be the same. There was still a very real question as to what the facts were; the same negative answer that there was still in his, in Dean's, view no involvement of White House personnel was sustained very strongly. It basically continued in that same pattern.

Q. In other words, would it be fair to say, Mr. Haldeman, that from July until the early meeting which you had with Dean there was essentially no change in what he told you so far as pre-June 17th events were concerned and that the essence of what he kept telling you was that there was no involvement by White House personnel? Is that a fair statement?

A. Yes, I think it is with the modification that I wouldn't necessarily put the fix on early March as the time of an expansion of that. It could have been mid-until late-February.

(Continued from p. 112)

Harmony, who said she was still on the Republican payroll as a secretary at the President's inaugural committee, denied a newspaper report that she had said she perjured herself by trying to protect Liddy in her appearances before a federal grand jury in 1972. She appeared before the grand jury four times and met with the Senate committee staff three times, she said.

When Liddy was fired, according to Harmony, she removed from his office two cartons of his personal belongings, including a "voluminous gun-control file," and took them home with her.

Later, she said, she received a $57 invoice for the Gemstone stationery. Magruder instructed her to destroy the bill after paying it, she said.

Liddy Refusal. At the close of the morning's testimony by Harmony, Sen. Sam J. Ervin Jr. (D N.C.), the committee chairman, announced that Liddy had met privately with the committee and had refused to testify, citing his rights under the Fifth and Sixth Amendments to the Constitution. He repeated his refusal when offered immunity from further prosecution, Ervin said. Because Liddy's appeal from his conspiracy conviction was pending in U.S. District Court, Ervin said the committee had decided not to insist on his testifying as scheduled at that time.

Reisner Testimony. The baby-faced, 26-year-old Reisner, a $23,000-a-year employee of the Office of Management and Budget, told of a meeting in February 1972 of Liddy, Magruder and Mitchell, while Mitchell was still attorney general. (He became Nixon's campaign director on March 1.) Reisner recollected that Liddy wanted an easel for the meeting, and he remembered seeing a package that he said might have contained posters for the easel.

Reisner told the committee that at least once he had sent Gemstone documents to Mitchell. Magruder had handed some documents to him "in such a way that it was clearly not for me to observe, that it was clearly not for my consumption," he said. Copies of all the memos that went to Mitchell also went to H. R. Haldeman, then White House chief of staff, said Reisner.

The afternoon after the break-in, Reisner testified, Magruder told him by phone from California that "there are sensitive things in the office...take them out and keep them over the weekend." Magruder spoke of some Gemstone papers in a blue folder, Reisner said, and this folder was taken home by Robert Odle, then office manager for the re-election committee. *(Odle testimony, Weekly Report p. 63)*

Also removed from Magruder's files, said Reisner, were analyses of polls, campaign plans for key states and other strategic materials on presidential contenders. In testimony at the Watergate trial in January, Magruder said he had no knowledge of the bugging operations.

Questioned by Fred D. Thompson, the committee's minority counsel, Reisner said Liddy might have been a capable legal counsel, "but he occasionally did some rather bizarre things." On one occasion, Reisner recalled, Liddy gave his secretary a 6-by-4-foot poster of himself standing beside a police car and holding a bullhorn. Reisner discussed, as had previous witnesses, the unfriendly relationship between Magruder and Liddy. The trouble may have been, he surmised, that Liddy resented working for a younger man.

Reisner said that Herbert L. Porter, director of scheduling for the re-election committee, kept several thousand dollars in petty cash in his safe, perhaps totaling $40,000 to $50,000 over a period of time. He said an unknown person called "Sedan Chair" was paid $1,000 a month for six to nine months from the fund and Liddy was paid between $5,000 and $8,000 a month. "Sedan Chair," Reisner speculated, might have been a disgruntled worker for Sen. Hubert H. Humphrey (Minn.), a candidate for the Democratic presidential nomination. He did not elaborate.

After the June 17 break-in, said Reisner, he asked Magruder about Gemstone, and Magruder replied that he did not know what it meant. Magruder also indicated that he had not been involved in the break-in, Reisner added.

On June 16, the day before the break-in, Liddy gave him some papers labeled "sensitive material," Reisner testified. Reisner, who did not read the file, said he later destroyed it rather than turning it over to Magruder.

Clark MacGregor, Nixon's director of congressional relations, replaced Mitchell as campaign director on July 1 and thereafter received copies of all memos, Reisner said. There was no doubt in his mind, said Reisner, that MacGregor had questioned other campaign officials about the Watergate affair. Reisner said he felt MacGregor might have been misled by some of the others.

Witnesses June 6

The single important witness to come before the Senate committee on June 6 was Hugh W. Sloan Jr., former treasurer of the Nixon re-election campaign. Sloan gave the senators a detailed accounting of nearly $1.8-million in cash disbursements by the President's finance committee before a tighter reporting law took effect on June 7, 1972.

The slender 32-year-old, who has taken a job with a manufacturing firm in Troy, Mich., also described in some detail the efforts of campaign officials to force him to perjure himself. Rather than do so, he explained, he resigned from the campaign in July 1972.

Chairman Ervin, never one to miss a chance to inject an appropriate quotation or a folksy epigram into the proceedings, had the kindest observation yet made about any witness at the end of his interrogation of Sloan. "An honest man is the noblest work of God," he drawled.

Finances. Sloan told a story or raising so much money that his boss, campaign finance director Maurice H. Stans, felt that he had lost control over what Sloan called a "runaway situation." Before April 7, the date on which campaign contributors lost their anonymity, the Nixon committee had received about $20-million, he said, including $1.7-million to $1.8-million in cash. About $6-million poured in during the two days before the deadline, said Sloan. The money was kept in bank safety deposit boxes at first and later was transferred to two safes in the finance committee offices.

Sloan used a chart to show the committee how some $1,777,000 was disbursed. Among the items he discussed were:

- $250,000 to Herbert W. Kalmbach, Nixon's former personal attorney and Stans' predecessor as campaign finance director.

McCloskey's Impeachment Debate Dies in House Snarl

Rep. Paul N. McCloskey Jr. (R Calif.) gave his House colleagues a week's notice that they were invited to join him June 6 to discuss what he termed "the special constitutional responsibilities of the House with respect to investigation of the matters revealed in President Nixon's public statement of May 22."

What he meant was that he thought the President's statement about a special White House investigations unit came close enough to cause for impeachment for impeachment to be discussed. To many representatives, Democrats and Republicans alike, this bordered on the unspeakable.

So, when the appointed hour arrived just before 9 p.m., McCloskey found himself effectively barred from giving his speech, which, he had hoped, would be followed by debate on the subject of impeachment.

Tactics

Only a few members were on hand when McCloskey rose to begin what he said would be a "tempered discussion." But, just minutes into his speech, he was interrupted on a point of order that a quorum was not present by Rep. Earl F. Landgrebe (R Ind.). Landgrebe often votes as a Nixon administration loyalist, and McCloskey opposed Nixon in early presidential primaries in 1972.

A call for a quorum is not debatable and takes precedence over other business. Thus, McCloskey was halted for a roll call. The House was far short of the 217 it needed to constitute a quorum or majority. Then Rep. H. R. Gross (R Iowa) invoked a rule providing that at least 15 minutes be allowed for members to answer the roll.

Next followed a motion by Rep. Joe D. Waggonner Jr. (D La.) for the House to adjourn. That motion—also privileged and non-debatable—was defeated on a 9-143 roll call.

As the parliamentary maneuvering took up the better part of an hour, McCloskey himself then moved to adjourn. The motion carried on a voice vote.

McCloskey said he wanted a reasonable debate, which would have been impossible if members had to be summoned back to the floor from their homes or wherever they had gone. Nevertheless, the debate will go on "across the country and in the Congress until this is resolved," he said.

The Speech

Although he did not get to give his speech, McCloskey had it printed in the *Congressional Record.* In it, he listed seven points which "bear on the question as to whether impeachment proceedings should be brought against President Nixon." They were:

- Nixon admitted the establishment, at his order, of a special investigations unit in the White House.
- Members of that unit broke into the office of Daniel Ellsberg's psychiatrist in California.
- Members of that unit broke into Democratic National Committee headquarters in the Watergate office building.
- Nixon instructed his top aides to be sure that the Watergate investigation did not expose secret operations of the CIA or the activities of the White House group.
- Nixon had said in August 1972 that investigations of the Watergate burglary by various government units had the "total cooperation of not only the White House but also of all agencies of the government." This, McCloskey said, was a misrepresentation. "He had expressly ordered a coverup...."
- In April 1973, after those arrested in the Democratic National Committee offices had been tried and one had been instrumental in getting the case reopened, Nixon instructed the Justice Department to confine the new inquiry to Watergate and "to stay out of national security matters."
- "It was not until May 22, 1973, that the President finally admitted to the actions taken to cover up any criminal activities which might have been conducted by White House personnel.

McCloskey said that, "without drawing conclusions at this point...it is pertinent to list several federal criminal statutes which a U.S. attorney might consider relevant to such facts." He then cited portions of the U.S. criminal code dealing with obstruction of justice and other offenses.

- $350,000 to Gordon Strachan, assistant to former White House Chief of Staff Haldeman and liaison with the reelection committee. The money went to the Nixon media committee.
- $199,000 to G. Gordon Liddy, then counsel to the finance committee. Sloan testified that he became concerned with the initial disbursement of some $83,000 to Liddy and questioned Stans about the sum. "I do not want to know and you don't want to know," he said Stans told him.
- $20,000 to Magruder, the deputy campaign director. This money was paid to Victor Lasky, an author and freelance writer, to assist Martha Mitchell, John Mitchell's wife, with speeches and magazine articles.
- $50,000 to Alexander (Sandy) Lankler, a Maryland Republican official, for a fund-raising dinner for Vice President Agnew. The money later was repaid to the committee.
- $25,000 to Robert J. Hitt, administrative assistant to Interior Secretary Rogers C. B. Morton, for the special election campaign to elect Republican William O. Mills as Morton's successor in the House from Maryland's first district. Mills committed suicide after the contribution was revealed. *(p. 84)*
- $10,000 to Lyn Nofziger, director of Nixon's campaign in California. *The Washington Post* June 7 reported

Sloan on Campaign Reform

During the June 6 appearance of Hugh W. Sloan Jr., former Nixon campaign treasurer, before the Senate select committee, Vice Chairman Howard H. Baker Jr. (R Tenn.) sought Sloan's opinions on prospective changes in campaign laws. The committee is charged with making recommendations for reform before its mandate expires on Feb. 28, 1974.

Baker began with the wry observation that Sloan probably enjoys the unwelcome distinction of being the nation's leading authority on secret funding of political campaigns. Then he asked Sloan how he felt about an absolute ban against cash contributions to and disbursements by campaign committees. The 1971 law prohibits neither.

Such a ban would be of great assistance to campaign accountants, Sloan replied. He said he saw "no problem whatsoever" in the suggestion.

Referring to the customary flood of last-minute campaign contributions, Baker asked Sloan his opinion of a statutory moratorium on contributions two weeks before elections.

Although he admitted that he was not a qualified judge, Sloan said that he did not think a moratorium would jeopardize a campaign.

Sloan said he thought one of the most effective curbs on abuses might be a time limit on election campaigns. Placing a spending ceiling on campaigns might lead to the point where public funding might be the only way to pay for them, he said.

Baker disagreed. He said he feared abuses of that kind of money. And he expressed "great fear of the federal bureaucracy taking over the electoral system."

One of the "great tragedies" of the 1972 presidential campaign, said Sloan, was having old and new laws overlapping each other. The public disclosure provisions of the 1971 law, which took effect on April 7, 1972—after the early phase of the campaign was well under way—were welcomed by everyone, he said. He would like to see the law as it stands "given a fair chance" in another presidential election, he continued, because "I think it's a workable law."

that the money was used in an elaborate but unsuccessful scheme to block George C. Wallace's presidential campaign in California in 1972.

- $3,000 to Sen. Robert Dole (Kan.), former Republican national chairman, for a trip to Vietnam.

Magruder. Sloan described his role as chiefly that of a conduit for funds. He said he seldom questioned what the money would be used for. "My curiosity had really run out by that point in time," he said. "So much money had been distributed in a similar way without my knowing why. I was beyond the point of really asking."

A few days after the June 17 break-in, however, Sloan said he asked Magruder about the cash that Magruder had authorized him to give Liddy. Magruder suggested a figure of about $75,000 to $85,000, said Sloan.

Although he did not have the correct figure at that time, Sloan said, he told Magruder that his figure was too low, adding, "I have no intention of perjuring myself."

"You may have to," Sloan quoted Magruder as replying.

In July, Sloan testified, Magruder proposed telling the U.S. attorney investigating the Watergate case that the amount was $40,000 or $50,000. "I was a little flabbergasted," said Sloan, and he refused.

Mitchell Advice. The same day he talked with Magruder, Sloan said, he sought guidance from John Mitchell, then Nixon's campaign director, before he conferred with FBI agents.

Mitchell advised him, he said: "When the going gets tough, the tough get going." The crowd in the hearing room roared with laughter. Sloan did not. "I understood that I wasn't getting any particularly helpful guidance," he said.

Meetings with Aides. After his conversation with Mitchell, Sloan said, he talked with Frederick C. LaRue, one of Mitchell's assistants, about the conversation. LaRue mentioned the "politically sensitive" money given to Liddy and suggested that a lower figure would have to be used, said Sloan.

The next day he met with several top aides at the White House, telling them of the "tremendous problem" at the finance committee. Dwight Chapin, then the President's appointments secretary, "suggested that the important thing is that the President be protected," according to Sloan.

Ehrlichman, Nixon's domestic affairs adviser, said he would help Sloan get a lawyer. Sloan said Ehrlichman told him he did not want to hear details. "My position would have to be until after the election that I would have to take executive privilege," Sloan quoted him as saying.

Angry Reactions. A week after the break-in, Sloan said, he mentioned the $199,000 Liddy payment to Robert Mardian, then the political coordinator for the re-election committee. Mardian "blew up, staggered by the amount," Sloan testified. "He said, 'Goddamn, Magruder lied to John Mitchell. He told him it was only $40,000.' "

On July 6, Sloan met with attorneys for the re-election committee and told them of Magruder's proposals to lower the amount of money given to Liddy. They reacted angrily and said, "We've been lied to by the people here," according to Sloan.

Stans, the finance director, became "extremely defensive" about the money spent for Watergate, Sloan said. "I think he was angry. I think he was upset with the political side of the campaign."

Unwilling to perjure himself or to take the Fifth Amendment, Sloan said, he resigned from the committee on July 14.

Dean Suggestion. Sloan testified in the fall of 1972 at the trial in Florida of Bernard L. Barker, one of the Watergate conspirators, who was accused of falsely notarizing a check to the Nixon campaign.

James T. Treese, Sloan's attorney, told the Senate committee June 6 that he had received a call from John Dean, then the White House counsel, on Oct. 31, 1972, asking if Sloan would take the Fifth Amendment at the Florida trial. Treese said that Dean told him Sloan "would be a real hero around here if he took the Fifth."

Treese refused on behalf of his client. "I laughed," he said.

CIA Memos Raise Question of Bugging Motives

A series of memorandums describing discussions of the Watergate investigation by top White House aides and officials of the FBI and CIA beginning shortly after the 1972 break-in were published June 4 in *The New York Times.* The documents, nine of them written by CIA Deputy Director Gen. Vernon A. Walters and one by CIA Director James R. Schlesinger, had been the source of press reports and speculation by members of Congress on White House involvement in the Watergate coverup. *(Texts of memos, p. 126)*

The Times interpreted the memos to imply that, from the beginning, White House officials saw the investigation of the bugging not as a possible threat to national security—as Nixon argued in his May 22 statement—but as "a potential political bombshell." Walters submitted the memos to the Intelligence Operations Subcommittee of the Senate Appropriations Committee, one of several congressional panels that held hearings during May on possible CIA involvement in the cover-up. *(Previous hearings, p. 86)*

Walters reportedly told the Senate Armed Services Committee May 14 that White House aides pressured the CIA to assist in a coverup of the scandal. Central to his allegation was a White House meeting attended by former Nixon aides John D. Ehrlichman and H. R. Haldeman, Walters and former CIA Director Richard Helms on June 23, 1972—one week after the break-in.

According to Walters' record of the session, Haldeman said the FBI's investigation of the bugging "was leading to a lot of important people" and that "the whole affair was getting embarrassing." Walters said Haldeman asked him to contact acting FBI Director L. Patrick Gray III to warn against pushing the investigation into areas that could jeopardize CIA operations —even after repeated assurances by Helms that Gray had already been informed that the CIA was not involved.

Haldeman and Ehrlichman presented different versions of the meeting during testimony before the intelligence subcommittee. Haldeman May 31 said it was "held at the President's request in the interest of national security," and that he didn't believe there was an attempt to hide anything. Ehrlichman's statement of May 30 denied any attempt during the meeting to "coerce the CIA into accepting blame for the Watergate break-in." *(Details and text of testimony, p. 100)*

Walters told of going to see Gray immediately after the meeting to ask that the FBI "taper off" its investigation "south of the border" because it might endanger covert CIA projects in that area. Haldeman later said he did not specifically recall discussing "Mexican aspects" of the case on June 23, but Ehrlichman testified that they were of special concern to Nixon at that time.

Walters' memo on his meeting June 23 with Gray indicated that Gray mentioned "a check on a Mexican bank for $89,000." The same day, Watergate prosecutor Earl J. Silbert disclosed that one of the arrested buggers, Bernard L. Barker, had cashed $89,000 in checks payable to a Mexico City attorney. The money was later reported by investigators to be a contribution by a Houston firm, Gulf Resources and Chemical Corp., which was "laundered" in Mexico and then passed on to Barker. *(Grand jury investigation, p. 88)*

Walters' memo described three meetings he had with former presidential counsel John W. Dean III in the week after June 23, at which Dean pressed him to arrange for the CIA to pay bail for the Watergate conspirators and otherwise involve the agency in a coverup. Both he and Gray decided they would rather resign than discredit their agencies by complying with these requests, Walters related.

The documents also included these disclosures:

- Dean told Walters June 26 that Barker had been involved in "a clandestine entry into the Chilean Embassy."
- Officials urged Gray to block attempts by U.S. Attorney Harold H. Titus to subpoena financial records of the Nixon re-election committee.
- Dean told former CIA Director Schlesinger on Feb. 9, 1973, that a Senate Foreign Relations Committee investigation into the International Telephone and Telegraph Company's operations in Chile "could be rather explosive" and asked his advice on the subject.

Witnesses June 7

Herbert L. Porter, a former Nixon campaign aide, admitted during Senate hearings June 7 that he gave false testimony to a grand jury and in the Watergate trial as part of a coverup effort.

The young Californian told the committee that Jeb Magruder, former deputy director of the Nixon campaign, asked him to tell a fabricated story about what happened to $100,000 in cash given to convicted Watergate conspirator G. Gordon Liddy.

Assistant committee counsel David M. Dorsen asked Porter if he had related the false account of how the funds were used to the FBI, to the Watergate federal grand jury and in response to questions at the Watergate trial in January. Porter answered "yes" to each question.

No Deals. Although Porter was clearly leaving himself open to the possibility of perjury charges, he began his testimony before the Senate committee with a prepared statement saying that he was "voluntarily cooperating" with the committee and federal prosecutors in the case.

Neither he nor his attorney had sought immunity before his appearance, Porter stated. He became the first witness from the original Watergate trial to admit publicly that he had perjured himself.

Porter joined the Committee for the Re-election of the President in May 1971 and was director of scheduling in charge of surrogate candidates, high-ranking elected or appointed officials who spoke on the campaign trail on Nixon's behalf.

The Coverup. Porter said that about 10 days after the 1972 break-in at Democratic Party headquarters, Magruder called him into a meeting and stated Porter's name had been mentioned "as someone who could be... counted on in a pinch, a team player." Magruder then added, according to Porter, that there was a problem because "Gordon (Liddy) was authorized some money for dirty tricks, nothing illegal," but nevertheless things that "could be very embarrassing to the President of the United States...."

Porter said Magruder then asked: "Can you corroborate a story that the money was for something a bit more legal-sounding than dirty tricks...." And the deputy campaign director suggested, according to Porter: "You were concerned about radical elements disrupting the campaign. How about if we said Liddy had been authorized to infiltrate those groups. How could that cost $100,000?"

"I said, 'Jeb, very easy, you could get 10 college people over 10 months and pay them $1,000 a month. That's $100,000.' "

"He said, 'That's right. Would you be willing if I made that statement to the FBI, would you be willing to corroborate?' "

"I said, 'Yes, I guess I'd do that.' "

Perjury Refused. Despite agreeing to the false story about the $100,000 for "dirty tricks," Porter told the Senate committee that he absolutely refused to perjure himself a second time when Magruder asked that he tell prosecutors and the Watergate trial jury that he had given Liddy $75,000 when the amount was actually only $30,000 to $35,000.

In the case of the $100,000 lie, Porter related, he was influenced by a strong feeling that radical groups were a real danger to the Nixon campaign. At the time of his requests for fake stories, Magruder denied that he or anyone higher up in the campaign organization had prior knowledge of Liddy's illegal activities, Porter testified.

Referring to the break-in at Democratic headquarters, Porter said that Magruder commented: "Doesn't that sound like something stupid that Gordon would do?"

"I agreed with that," Porter recalled, causing the audience at the hearing to break into laughter.

Morality Questioned. Sen. Howard H. Baker Jr. (R Tenn.) pressed in on the soft-spoken, mild-mannered Porter, questioning him closely on why he failed to protest the "dirty tricks" and fabricated stories.

"My loyalty to this man Richard Nixon goes back longer than any person you will see sitting at this witness table during any of these hearings," the 33-year-old Porter said. "I first met Mr. Nixon when I was 8 years old in 1946 when he ran for Congress in my home district. I wore Nixon buttons when I was 8, when I was 10 and when I was 12, and when I was 16. My family worked for him. My father worked for him in campaigns. My mother worked for his campaigns. I felt I had known this man all my life. I felt a deep sense of loyalty to him."

But Baker commented dryly: "I really suspect that the greatest disservice a man could do to a President of the United States would be to abdicate his conscience."

Sloan Testimony. During the morning session June 7, former Nixon campaign treasurer Sloan continued his testimony from the preceding day. He said he had talked with former White House Chief of Staff H.R. Haldeman in January after testifying as a government witness at the Watergate trial.

Sloan recalled that he told Haldeman there had been attempts made to get him to commit perjury and that Haldeman had acknowledged some "mistakes" being made early in the case.

According to Sloan, he did not identify Magruder as the person who had urged him to commit perjury. A few days later, Sloan read that Magruder had been appointed to a policy post in the Commerce Department. "At that time I just threw up my hands," he said.

Daily Chronology

Following is the day-to-day chronology of the week's events:

MAY 31

(Earlier May 31 events, p. 107)

Ervin on Dean Papers. Sen. Sam J. Ervin Jr. (D N.C.), chairman of the Senate Watergate investigating committee, told reporters in Winston-Salem, N. C., that documents former presidential counsel John W. Dean III took from the White House "would be a great shock to the American people if they were released." The papers, which Nixon described in his May 22 statement as containing plans for an aborted domestic intelligence operation, were given to the Senate committee by U.S. District Judge John J. Sirica, who received them from Dean. *(Details, p. 99)*

Gurney Letter. Another member of the investigating committee, Sen. Edward J. Gurney (R Fla.), wrote to Ervin urging that the committee act quickly to call "key witnesses" in order to clarify Nixon's role in the scandal. *(Details, p. 99)*

Special Prosecutor. Attorney General Elliot L. Richardson ordered that all Justice Department reports on possible administration offenses be turned over to special prosecutor Archibald Cox and his investigators. Meanwhile, Cox's office announced the appointment of another staff assistant, Thomas F. McBride, a former Justice Department prosecutor.

JUNE 1

Cox, Dash on Hearings. *The Washington Post* reported that, according to Senate sources, special prosecutor Archibald Cox met with the Senate investigating committee's chief counsel Samuel Dash on May 30 and asked that the committee halt its hearings because they were jeopardizing future trials. Cox threatened court action if it became necessary in order to stop the hearings, the newspaper said.

Later in the day, both Cox and Dash confirmed that they had met to discuss ways to avoid prejudicing criminal trials, but both men disputed the Post report that Cox had threatened court action. *(Details, p. 99)*

California Grand Jury. Cox issued a statement promising his "full cooperation" with the Los Angeles grand jury investigating the break-in at the office of Daniel Ellsberg's psychiatrist. The assurance came after *The Los Angeles Times* had reported that Cox wanted to delay the proceedings, which were scheduled to begin June 5.

Cox also authorized the appearance of Watergate conspirators E. Howard Hunt Jr., Bernard L. Barker and Eugenio R. Martinez before the California panel.

Dairy Funds. The FBI was investigating a $50,000 contribution to the Nixon re-election campaign from a Pennsylvania dairy group, Lehigh Valley Cooperative Farmers, according to *The Washington Post.* The cash donation, reportedly listed anonymously in violation of the law, went into a secret campaign fund, the paper said.

Smith Donation. *The Washington Star-News* reported that a pretrial deposition made by Eveline M. Hyde, assistant to former Nixon campaign treasurer Hugh W. Sloan, revealed that C. Arnholdt Smith donated $350,000 to the Nixon campaign before April 7, 1972, when the reporting of contributions became mandatory. According to the deposition, made public May 31, Smith's contribution was returned to him. Smith, a San Diego businessman and Nixon associate, was sued May 31 by the Securities and Exchange Commission for fraud and misappropriation of funds in connection with his business dealings. *(Previous allegation, p. 87)*

Covert Activities. *The Washington Post* published a report that Charles W. Colson, former special adviser to the President, or an aide, W. Richard Howard, were responsible for disruptive counter-demonstrations at an anti-war rally at the Capitol on May 4, 1972. Both denied the allegations.

Watergate Television Coverage

The third week of Senate Watergate hearings brought curtailed coverage by the three commercial television networks. Starting June 5, the American Broadcasting Company, Columbia Broadcasting System and National Broadcasting Company began rotating their coverage, with one network broadcasting the proceedings "live" each day.

All three networks had broadcast the first five days of hearings, starting May 17. Despite large audiences, complaints poured in from viewers who were deprived of their regular daytime shows. *(Earlier story, p. 85)*

The non-commercial Public Broadcasting Service continued to tape the complete hearings for showing during prime evening hours.

JUNE 2

Intelligence Plan. *The New York Times* reported that the FBI was investigating the possibility that parts of a domestic intelligence plan drawn up by the Nixon administration in 1970 were put into effect. Nixon said in his May 22 statement that the proposal "never went into effect" because it was rejected by FBI Director J. Edgar Hoover. The agency—like the Senate investigating committee—had been studying documents on the plan, which were taken from the White House by former counsel Dean.

The Times reported that the FBI's investigation focused on the break-in at the office of Daniel Ellsberg's psychiatrist and on a series of four break-ins in 1971 and 1972 at the offices and residences of Chilean diplomats in Washington, D.C., and New York City.

Harmony Challenged. *The Washington Post* reported that two employees of the Nixon re-election committee—in pre-trial depositions given May 23 in connection with Watergate civil suits—alleged that Sally J. Harmony, secretary to conspirator G. Gordon Liddy, had admitted committing perjury in her testimony before the federal grand jury investigating the case. The depositions of the two accusers, Eveline M. Hyde and Arden Chambers, were made public May 31.

FBI Break-In. *The New York Times* reported that the FBI had denied an earlier allegation the paper printed that agents illegally broke into the office of a Washington, D.C., radical newspaper in 1969. A bureau spokesman said the search was carried out at the invitation of the building manager. *(Previous story, p. 107)*

JUNE 3

Dean vs. Nixon. *The Washington Post* reported that, according to "reliable sources," former presidential counsel Dean was planning to tell the Senate investigating committee that Nixon was "deeply involved" in the Watergate coverup, and that Dean would testify with or without immunity. The paper said Dean had told Senate investigators that he discussed aspects of the coverup with Nixon or in Nixon's presence at least 35 times between January and April of 1973, and also that Nixon had prior knowledge of payments and offers of executive clemency aimed at silencing the Watergate conspirators. The Post said Dean would rely on his own recollection of events, because he had "little or no" documentary evidence to support his charges.

Accompanying the story was a denial by deputy White House press secretary Gerald Warren, charging that the report was "part of a careful, coordinated strategy by an individual or individuals determined to prosecute a case against the President in the press using innuendo, distortion of fact and outright falsehood.... We categorically deny the assertions and implications of the story."

McCloskey Move. Rep. Paul N. McCloskey Jr. (R Calif.) announced that he planned to raise the possibility of impeaching Nixon during a speech on the House floor June 6. McCloskey urged his colleagues to join in a "full discussion" of the grounds for impeachment, arguing that while Nixon was "entitled to the presumption of innocence," the facts called for "a careful and impartial inquiry" by the House. *(Impeachment background, p. 55)*

Huston Interview. In an interview published in *The Washington Post,* former presidential aide Tom Charles Huston described the administration's 1970 domestic intelligence plan, which he helped draw up. Huston said the plan did not include specific "widespread uses of illegal acts" and was to be aimed almost entirely at the Black Panthers and the militant Weathermen.

If Nixon had not yielded to FBI Director Hoover's objections to the plan, Huston told the Post, "there never would have been a Watergate." He described the "plumbers," a group subsequently organized to plug White House information leaks, as "an ad hoc vigilante group of clowns." *(Earlier reference, p. 89)*

Pentagon Papers and Soviets. Reports in *The New York Times* and *The Washington Post* said that the Russian embassy in Washington, D.C., received copies of the Pentagon Papers after the Times began printing the documents in June of 1971. Former White House aide Egil Krogh Jr., who took responsibility for the Ellsberg break-in, said in a sworn statement made public at the Ellsberg trial May 7 that FBI officials told him the Soviets had received the documents before they were published in the Times.

Ervin vs. Cox. Sen. Sam J. Ervin Jr. (D N.C.), chairman of the Senate investigating committee, revealed at a Boston news conference that he had rejected a request of special prosecutor Archibald Cox that the committee postpone its hearings until indictments had been returned in the case. "If the prosecution doesn't have enough after a year to convict, I do not think they should ask someone else to delay," Ervin said.

Strauss Break-In. Democratic National Chairman Robert S. Strauss revealed that his Dallas, Texas, home was broken into and his papers rifled the weekend of July 7-8, 1972, when he was serving as treasurer of the Democratic National Committee. Speaking at Lake Tahoe, Nev., where he was attending the National Governors' Conference, Strauss speculated that "the same crowd" that participated in the June 17 break-in were responsible.

McCord Interview. Convicted conspirator James W. McCord Jr., appearing on CBS-TV's "Face the Nation," said he believed Nixon "set in motion the Watergate operation, approved it and followed through on it."

JUNE 4

Cox Asks Delay. In a letter to Sen. Ervin, special prosecutor Cox asked the Senate investigating committee to delay its Watergate hearings for one to three months. In a 300-word rebuttal statement, Committee Chairman Ervin refused the request. *(Box, p. 111)*

In a related development, *Newsweek* magazine reported that Cox was planning to remove the three assistant U.S. attorneys—Earl Silbert, Seymour Glanzer and Donald Campbell—who had been handling the Watergate case, after "a respectable grace period." *(Earlier developments, p. 104)*

Walters Memos. *The New York Times* published a series of memos on the Watergate investigation written by CIA Deputy Director Gen. Vernon A. Walters and CIA Director James R. Schlesinger. The documents, which described efforts of top White House officials to enlist the FBI and CIA in a coverup of the scandal, were originally submitted by Walters to a Senate Appropriations subcommittee investigating the matter. *(Box, p. 117)*

More Break-Ins and Revelations. The June 11 issue of *Newsweek* magazine reported that Senate investigators had learned from "high administration officials" that techniques such as burglary and unauthorized wiretaps had been widely used to try to "stop sensitive leaks, to monitor the domestic left and gather information for the prosecution of cases against radicals." Burglaries occurred in connection with the Seattle Seven, Chicago Weathermen, Detroit Thirteen and Berrigan cases, and possibly at the Brookings Institution, according to the report.

Liddy, Mardian Leaks. *Newsweek* also attributed these revelations to Senate investigators:

- Conspirator G. Gordon Liddy told former Assistant Attorney General Robert C. Mardian that the break-in at the office of Daniel Ellsberg's psychiatrist had Nixon's "express approval," according to Mardian.
- Mardian told investigators that Liddy said he "whisked ITT lobbyist Dita Beard out of Washington to a Denver hospital" during the 1972 controversy over an incriminating memo she allegedly wrote. *(ITT case, 1972 Almanac p. 207)*
- Mardian said Nixon personally ordered him to take charge of the logs of 17 wiretaps that had been authorized by Nixon and cleared in part by national security adviser Henry A. Kissinger between 1969 and 1971.

Nixon-Dean Meetings. White House Deputy Press Secretary Gerald Warren acknowledged at a news briefing that Nixon conferred frequently in 1973 with his former counsel Dean about the Watergate affair. Nixon had logs of the times and places of these meetings, Warren said, but it would be "constitutionally inappropriate" to release them.

Lucey Calls for Resignation. Gov. Patrick J. Lucey (D) of Wisconsin called upon Nixon to resign in a statement issued from the National Governors' Conference at Lake Tahoe, Nev. The previous day, Gov. Linwood Holton (R) of Virginia, chairman of the Republican Governers' Association, had asked Nixon to hold a series press conferences to answer questions about the Watergate case.

Richardson. Attorney General Elliot L. Richardson told reporters that if the White House and special prosecutor Cox clashed over the Watergate case, the Justice Department would side with Cox, leaving Nixon to be represented by his own counsel. Richardson described the national security rationale used by White House officials to justify creation of the plumbers group to plug information leaks as "not convincing."

JUNE 5

Watergate Hearings. The Senate investigating committee met in executive session and voted unanimously to reject the request of special prosecutor Cox that the hearings be postponed. The committee decided to take no immediate action on the refusal of convicted conspirator G. Gordon Liddy to testify. *(Box, p. 114)*

Sally J. Harmony, Liddy's former secretary, and Robert A. Reisner, who was assistant to Jeb Stuart Magruder, former deputy director of the Nixon re-election committee, testified before the committee. Reisner indicated that Mitchell and Haldeman may have seen reports on wiretaps placed on the phones of Democrats during the 1972 campaign.

White House Retraction. Deputy White House press secretary Gerald L. Warren said at a news briefing that he had a "speech of contrition" to make on the subject of logs of 1973 meetings Nixon and Dean had on the Watergate case. Warren said his previous statement that it would be "constitutionally inappropriate" to release the records did not necessarily mean they would not be given to prosecutors, but added that the logs were "considered to be presidential papers, and, as such, their production cannot be required under subpoena."

Shortly after the briefing, the Senate investigating committee's chief counsel, Samuel Dash, announced that the committee would subpoena the records within one day, according to newspaper accounts.

Ehrlichman Deposition. A 187-page deposition given May 22 and 23 by former presidential aide John D. Ehrlichman in the Democrats' $6.4-million civil suit against the Republicans was made public. Ehrlichman stated that former Attorney General John N. Mitchell personally chose three sites—the Watergate, McGovern's Washington headquarters and the Democratic National Committee headquarters at the Miami convention—for electronic bugging in 1972.

California Grand Jury. A Los Angeles, Calif., grand jury officially opened its investigation of the Sept. 3, 1971, break-in at the office of Daniel Ellsberg's psychiatrist, taking testimony from Ellsberg. *(Hunt testimony on break-in, p. 50)*

Detroit Order. A federal judge in Detroit, Mich., ordered the government to disclose by June 18 whether "representatives of the White House" had used illegal espionage and sabotage techniques against Weatherman militants. He was presiding over a criminal case involving the group.

Soviets and Pentagon Papers. The Soviet Embassy denied news reports that it had received copies of the Pentagon Papers after *The New York Times* began publishing them in June 1971.

JUNE 6

Watergate Hearings. Hugh W. Sloan Jr., who resigned as treasurer of the Finance Committee to Re-elect the President shortly after the June 17, 1972, break-in, was the Senate committee's only witness. He told of Dean's efforts to persuade him to plead the Fifth Amendment at the Miami trial of conspirator Bernard L. Barker and of attempts by Nixon campaign officials Magruder and Frederick C. LaRue to get him to falsify financial transactions between campaign officials and the bugging team.

Executive Appointments and Changes. Acting to rebuild a staff decimated by the Watergate scandal, Nixon named former Secretary of Defense Melvin R. Laird as his chief domestic adviser to replace Ehrlichman. At a news conference in Washington, Laird said he had taken on the job reluctantly but with the sense that government "in some quarters is at a standstill." He expressed confidence in Nixon's "non-involvement" in the Watergate case.

Nixon also announced that Gen. Alexander M. Haig Jr. would retire from active duty in the Army on Aug. 1 and continue on a regular basis as White House chief of staff, a post previously held by H. R. Haldeman. Haig had been accused of a conflict of interest for serving at the White House at the same time he was Army vice chief of staff. *(p. 105)*

In a third change, the duties of press secretary Ronald L. Ziegler were expanded to include those of former Communications Director Herbert Klein, who resigned June 5.

Cox on Immunity. In a motion submitted to U.S. District Judge John J. Sirica, special prosecutor Cox urged that the court order any testimony before the Senate committee by Dean or Magruder be conducted in closed session or at least without live radio and television coverage. But Cox noted that the court had no legal grounds for denying congressional grants of immunity. The Justice Department had used its authority to delay immunity grants the committee requested for Dean and Magruder. The two men, who were expected to appear before the committee the following week, were reportedly planning to testify on Nixon's role in the case. *(Previous development, p. 107)*

Impeachment Talk Stifled. A late-evening attempt by Rep. Paul N. McCloskey Jr. (R Calif.) to open "a tempered discussion" of the possibility of impeaching Nixon on the House floor was blocked by the parliamentary maneuvers of conservative members.

Ellsberg Prosecution Dropped. The Justice Department announced that it would not appeal the May 11 decision of Federal District Judge William Matthew Byrne Jr. dismissing all charges against Daniel Ellsberg and Anthony J. Russo in the Pentagon Papers case. *(Previous story, p. 46)*

Ehrlichman Missions. *The New York Times* reported that Ehrlichman authorized a series of espionage missions and illegal wiretaps beginning in 1969.

Nixon Logs. The White House agreed to turn over to the Senate investigating committee logs of Nixon's conversations with his former counsel Dean relating to Watergate. The committee had threatened to subpoena the documents.

JUNE 7

Intelligence Plan Revealed. *The New York Times* published three memorandums relating to a 1970 White House plan for domestic intelligence-gathering operations that Nixon had approved. The memos contained warnings that parts of the plan were "clearly illegal" and involved "serious risks" to the administration. The Times quoted Tom Charles Huston, a former White House aide and author of the documents, as saying: "We don't want the President linked to this thing with his signature on paper ...all hell would break loose if this thing leaks out."

In his May 22 statement on the Watergate case, Nixon said he ordered the plan put into operation, but then rescinded the order several days later because of the objections of FBI Director J. Edgar Hoover. Nixon said the plan contained proposals for "surreptitious entry" by federal agents in the course of national security investigations. *(Text of Nixon statement, p. 91)*

The Huston memos mentioned proposals for illegal entry, electronic surveillance, the opening of mail and stepped up use of undercover agents on college campuses. *(Text of memos, p. 122)*

Watergate Hearings. Former Nixon campaign treasurer Hugh W. Sloan Jr. testified for a second day before the Senate investigating committee. He was followed by Herbert L. Porter, a former Nixon re-election committee official.

New FBI Nominee. Nixon announced that his new nominee for FBI director was Clarence M. Kelley, police chief of Kansas City, Mo. His first choice for the post, L. Patrick Gray III, resigned as acting director after being implicated in the Watergate coverup.

Maryland Funds. *The Washington Post* reported that Alexander Lankler, chairman of the Maryland Republican Party, had admitted he used $50,000 in undisclosed funds from the Nixon re-election committee to rig a May 1972 testimonial for Vice President Agnew.

California Funds. The Post also reported that the Nixon committee spent $10,000 on "an elaborate plan" to deter a possible third-party presidential drive in California by George C. Wallace in 1971. Jeb Magruder, former committee deputy director, reportedly authorized payments for the operation. The Post pieced together its story from the testimony of Hugh W. Sloan Jr. and reports of Nixon campaign workers in California.

1970 SECURITY RECOMMENDATIONS

Following are texts of recommendations for domestic security operations made to President Nixon in July 1970 and accompanying documents. The texts were published June 7 by The New York Times *without attribution as to source.*

Sen. Sam J. Ervin Jr. (D N.C.), chairman of the Senate select Watergate committee, and Sen. Howard H. Baker Jr. (Tenn.); ranking minority member of the committee, said their copies of documents on the security recommendations, given to the committee and to federal prosecutors by U.S. District Judge John J. Sirica, were safely locked away. A Senate source confirmed, however, that the texts were authentic versions of documents carried from the White House by former presidential counsel John W. Dean III and accepted from Dean's bank safety deposit box by Judge Sirica.

Abbreviations used here include: B.N.D.D. (Bureau of Narcotics and Dangerous Drugs); C.I.A. (Central Intelligence Agency); C.P.U.S.A. (Communist Party U.S.A.); D.I.A. (Defense Intelligence Agency); F.B.I. (Federal Bureau of Investigation; I. & R. (Intelligence and Research); I.R.S. (Internal Revenue Service); N.S.A. (National Security Agency).

RECOMMENDATIONS

TOP SECRET

Handle via Comint Channels Only

Operational Restraints on Intelligence Collection

A. Interpretive Restraints on Communications Intelligence. RECOMMENDATION: Present interpretation should be broadened to permit and program for coverage by N.S.A. of the communications of U.S. citizens using international facilities.

RATIONALE: The F.B.I. does not have the capability to monitor international communications. N.S.A. is currently doing so on a restricted basis, and the information is particularly useful to the White House and it would be to our disadvantage to allow the F.B.I. to determine what N.S.A. should do in this area without regard to our own requirements. No appreciable risk is involved in this course of action.

B. Electronic Surveillance and Penetrations. RECOMMENDATION: Present procedures should be changed to permit intensification of coverage of individuals and groups in the United States who pose a major threat to the internal security.

Also, present procedures should be changed to permit intensification of coverage of foreign nationals and diplomatic establishments in the United States of interest to the intelligence community.

At the present time, less than (unclear) electronic penetrations are operative. This includes coverage of the C.P.U.S.A. and organized crime targets, with only a few authorized against subject of pressing internal security interest.

Mr. Hoover's statement that the F.B.I. would not oppose other agencies seeking approval for the operating electronic surveillances is gratuitous since no other agencies have the capability.

Everyone knowledgeable in the field, with the exception of Mr. Hoover concurs that existing coverage is grossly inadequate. C.I.A. and N.S.A. note that this is particularly true of diplomatic establishments, and we have learned at the White House that it is also true of new Left groups.

C. Mail Coverage. RECOMMENDATION: Restrictions on legal coverage should be removed.

Also, present restrictions on covert coverage should be relaxed on selected targets of priority foreign intelligence and internal security interest.

RATIONALE: There is no valid argument against use of legal mail covers except Mr. Hoover's concern that the civil liberties people may become upset. This risk is surely an acceptable one and hardly serious enough to justify denying ourselves a valuable and legal intelligence tool.

Covert coverage is illegal and there are serious risks involved. However, the advantages to be derived from its use outweight the risks. This technique is particularly valuable in identifying espionage agents and other contacts of foreign intelligence services.

D. Surreptitious Entry. RECOMMENDATION: Present restrictions should be modified to permit procurement of vitally needed foreign cryptographic material.

Also, present restrictions should be modified to permit selective use of this technique against other urgent security targets.

RATIONALE: Use of this technique is clearly illegal: it amounts to burglary. It is also highly risky and could result in great embarrassment if exposed. However, it is also the most fruitful tool and can produce the type of intelligence which cannot be obtained in any other fashion.

The F.B.I., in Mr. Hoover's younger days, used to conduct such operations with great success and with no exposure. The information secured was invaluable.

N.S.A. has a particular interest since it is possible by this technique to secure material with which N.S.A. can break foreign cryptographic codes. We spend millions of dollars attempting to break these codes by machine. One successful surreptitious entry can do the job successfully at no dollar cost.

Surreptitious entry of facilities occupied by subversive elements can turn up information about identities, methods of operation, and other invaluable investigative information which is not otherwise obtainable. This technique would be particularly helpful if used against the Weathermen and Black Panthers.

The deployment of the executive protector force has increased the risk of surreptitious entry of diplomatic establishments. However, it is the belief of all except Mr. Hoover that the technique can still be successfully used on a selective basis.

E. Development of Campus Sources. RECOMMENDATION: Present restrictions should be relaxed to permit expanded coverage of violence-prone campus and student-related groups.

Also, C.I.A. coverage of American students (and others) traveling or living abroad should be increased.

RATIONALE: The F.B.I. does not currently recruit any campus sources among individuals below 21 years of age. This dramatically reduces the pool from which sources may be drawn. Mr. Hoover is afraid of a young student surfacing in the press as an F.B.I. source, although the reaction in the past to such events has been minimal. After all, everyone assumes the F.B.I. has such sources.

The campus is the battleground of the revolutionary protest movement. It is impossible to gather effective intelligence about the movement unless we have campus sources. The risk of exposure is minimal, and where exposure occurs the adverse publicity is moderate and short-lived. It is a price we must be willing to pay for effective coverage of the campus scene. The intelligence community, with the exception of Mr. Hoover, feels strongly that it is imperative the (was unclear) increase the number of campus sources this fall in order to forestall widespread violence.

C.I.A. claims there are not existing restraints on its coverage of over-seas activities of U.S. nationals. However, this coverage has been grossly inadequate since 1965 and an explicit directive to increase coverage is required.

F. Use of Military Undercover Agents. RECOMMENDATION: Present restrictions should be retained.

RATIONALE: The intelligence community is agreed that the risks of lifting these restraints are greater than the value of any possible intelligence which would be acquired by doing so.

Budget and Manpower Restrictions

RECOMMENDATION: Each agency should submit a detailed estimate as to projected manpower needs and other costs in the event the various investigative restraints herein are lifted.

RATIONALE: In the event that the above recommendations are concurred in, it will be necessary to modify existing budgets to provide the money and manpower necessary for their implementation. The intelligence community has been badly hit in the budget squeeze. (I suspect the foreign intelligence operations are in the same shape) and it may be will be necessary to make some modifications. The projected figures should be reasonable, but will be subject to individual review if this recommendation is accepted.

Measures to Improve Domestic Intelligence Operations

RECOMMENDATION: A permanent committee consisting of the F.B.I., C.I.A., N.S.A. D.I.A. and the military counterintelligence agencies should be appointed to provide evaluations of domestic intelligence estimates, and carry out the other objectives specified in the report.

RATIONALE: The need for increased coordination, joint estimates, and responsiveness to the White House is obvious to the intelligence community. There are a number of operational problems which need to be worked out since Mr. Hoover is fearful of any mechanism which might jeopardize his autonomy. C.I.A. would prefer an ad hoc committee to see how the system works, but other members believe that this would merely delay the establishment of effective coordination and joint operations. The value of lifting intelligence collection restraints is proportional to the availability of joint operations and evaluation, and the establishment of this interagency group is considered imperative.

Top Secret
Analysis and Strategy

Memorandum for: H.R. Haldeman
From: Tom Charles Huston
Subject: Domestic intelligence review

1. Background. A working group consisting of the top domestic intelligence officials of the FBI, CIA, DIA, NSA and each of the military services met regularly throughout June to discuss the problems outlined by the President and to draft the attached report. The discussions were frank and the quality of work first-rate. Cooperation was excellent, and all were delighted that an opportunity was finally at hand to address themselves jointly to the serious internal security threat which exists.

I participated in all meetings, but restricted my involvement to keeping the committee on the target the President established. My impression that the report would be more accurate and the recommendations more helpful if the agencies were allowed wide latitude in expressing their opinions and working out arrangements which they felt met the President's requirements consistent with the resources and missions of the member agencies.

2. Mr. Hoover. I went into this exercise fearful that C.I.A. would refuse to cooperate. In fact, Dick Helms (Director of Central Intelligence) was most cooperative and helpful, and the only stumbling block was Mr. Hoover. He attempted at the first meeting to divert the committee from operational problems and redirect its mandate to the preparation of another analysis of existing intelliegence. I declined to acquiesce in this approach, and succeeded in getting the committee back on target.

When the working group completed its report, Mr. Hoover refused to go along with a single conclusion drawn or support a single recommendation made. His position was twofold:

(1) Current operations are perfectly satisfactory and (2) No one has any business commenting on procedures he has established for the collection of intelligence by the F.B.I. He attempted to modify the body of the report, but I successfully opposed it on the grounds that the report was the conclusion of all the agencies, not merely the F.B.I. Mr. Hoover then entered his objections as footnotes to the report. Cumulatively, his footnotes suggest that he is perfectly satisfied with current procedures and is opposed to any changes whatsoever. As you will note from the report, his objections are generally inconsistent and frivolous—most express concern about possible embarrassment to the intelligence community (i.e., Hoover) from public disclosure of clandestine operations.

Admiral Gayler and General Bennett were greatly displeased by Mr. Hoover's attitude and his insistence on footnoting objections. They wished to raise a formal protest and sign the report only with the understanding that they opposed the footnotes. I prevailed upon them not to do so since it would only aggravate Mr. Hoover and further complicate our efforts. They graciously agreed to go along with my suggestion in order to avoid a nasty scene and jeopardize the possibility of positive action resulting from the report, I assured them that their opinion would be brought to the attention of the President.

3. Threat Assessment. The first 23 pages of the report constitute an assessment of the existing internal security threat, our current intelligence coverage of this threat, and areas where our coverage is inadequate. All agencies concurred in this assessment, and it serves to explain the importance of expanded intelligence collection efforts.

4. Restraints on Intelligence Collection. Part Two of the report discusses specific operational restraints which currently restrict the capability of the intelligence community to collect the types of information necessary to deal effectively with the internal security threat. The report explains the nature of the restraints and sets the arguments for and against modifying them. My concern was to afford the President the strongest arguments on both sides of the question so that he could make an informed decision as to the future course of action to be followed by the intelligence community.

I might point out that of all the individuals involved in the preparation and consideration of this report, only Mr. Hoover is satisfied with existing procedures.

Those individuals within the F.B.I. who have day-to-day responsibilities for domestic intelligence operations privately disagree with Mr. Hoover and believe that it is imperative that changes in operating procedures be initiated at once.

I am attaching to this memorandum my recommendations on the decision the President should make with regard to these operational restraints. Although the report sets forth the pros and cons on each issue, it may be helpful to add my specific recommendations and the reasons therefore in the event the President has some doubts on a specific course of action.

5. Improvement in Inter-Agency Coordination. All members of the committee and its working group, with the exception of Mr. (Hoover agree it is) imperative that a continuing mechanism be established to effectuate the coordination of domestic intelligence efforts and the evaluation of domestic intelligence data. In the past there has been no systematic effort to mobilize the full resources of the intelligence community in the internal security area and there has been no mechanism for preparing community-wide domestic intelligence estimates such as is done in the foreign intelligence area by the United States Intelligence Board. Domestic intelligence information coming into the White House has been fragmentary and unevaluated. We have not had, for example, a community-wide estimate of what we might expect short or long—term in the cities or on the campuses or within the military establishment.

Unlike most of the bureaucracy, the intelligence community welcomes direction and leadership from the White House. There appears to be agreement, with the exception of Mr. Hoover, that effective coordination within the community is possible only if there is direction from the White House. Moreover, the community is pleased that the White House is finally showing interest in their activities and an awareness of the threat which'they so acutely recognize.

I believe that we will be making a major contribution to the security of the country if we can work out an arrangement which provides for institutionalized coordination within the intelligence community and effective leadership from the White House.

6. Implementation of the President's decisions. If the President should decide to lift some of the current restrictions and if he should decide to authorize a formalized domestic intelligence struction, I would recommend the following steps:

(A) Mr. Hoover should be called in privately for a stroking session at which the President explains the decision he has made, thanks Mr. Hoover for his candid advice and past cooperation, and indicates he is counting on Edgar's cooperation in implementing the new de-report, announce his decisions.

(B) Following this Hoover session, the same individuals who were present at the initial session in the Oval Office should be invited back to meet with the President. At that time, the President should thank them for the report, announce his decisions, indicate his desires for future activity, and present each with an autographed copy of the photo of the first meeting which Ollie took.

(C) An official memorandum setting forth the precise decisions of the President should be prepared so that there can be no misunderstanding. We should also incorporate a review procedure which will enable us to ensure that the decisions are fully implemented.

I hate to suggest a further imposition on the President's time, but think these steps will be necessary to pave over some of the obvious problems which may arise if the President decides, as I hope he will, to over-rule Mr. Hoover's objections to many of the proposals made in this report. Having seen the President in action with Mr. Hoover, I am confident that he can handle this situation in such a way that we can get what we want without putting Edgar's nose out of joint. At the same time, we can capitalize on the good will the President has built up with the other principals and minimize the risk that they may feel they are being forced to take a back seat to Mr. Hoover.

7. Conclusion. I am delighted with the substance of this report and believe it is a first-rate job. I have great respect for the integrity, loyalty, and competence of the men who are operationally responsible for internal security matters and believe that we are on the threshold of an unexcelled opportunity to cope with a very serious problem in its germinal stages when we can avoid the necessity for harsh measures by acting swift, discreetly, and decisively to deflect the threat before it reaches alarming proportions.

I might add, in conclusion, that it is my personal opinion that Mr. Hoover will not hesitate to accede to any decision which the President makes, and the President should not, therefore, be reluctant to overrule Mr. Hoover's objections. Mr. Hoover is set in his ways and can be bull-headed as hell, but he is a loyal trooper. Twenty years ago he would never have raised the type of objections he has here, but he's getting old and worried about his legend. He makes life tough in this area, but not impossible —for he'll respond to direction by the President and that is all we need to set the domestic intelligence house in order.

TOP SECRET

Decision Memorandum

The White House
Washington
July 15, 1970

TOP SECRET

Handle via Comint Channels only

Subject: Domestic Intelligence

The President has carefully studied the special report of the Interagency Committee on Intelligence (ad hoc) and made the following decisions:

1. Interpretive Restraint on Communications Intelligence. National Security Council Intelligence Directive Number 6 (NSCID-6) is to be interpreted to permit N.S.A. to program for coverage the communications of U.S. citizens using international facilities.

2. Electronic Surveillances and Penetrations. The intelligence community is directed to intensify coverage of individuals and groups in the United States who pose a major threat to the internal security. Also, coverage of foreign nationals and diplomatic establishments in the United States of interest to the intelligence community is to be intensified.

3. Mail Coverage. Restrictions on legal coverage are to be removed, restrictions on covert coverage are to be relaxed to permit use of this technique on selected targets of priority foreign intelligence and internal security interest.

4. Surreptitious Entry. Restraints on the use of surreptitious entry are to be removed. The technique is to be used to permit procurement of vitally needed foreign cryptographic material and against other urgent and high priority internal security targets.

5. Development of Campus Sources. Coverage of violence-prone campus and student-related groups is to be increased. All restraints which limit this coverage are to be removed. Also, C.I.A. coverage of American students (and others) traveling or living abroad is to be increased.

6. Use of Military Undercover Agents. Present restrictions are to be retained.

7. Budget and Manpower. Each agency is to submit a detailed estimate as to projected manpower needs and other costs required to implement the above decisions.

8. Domestic Intelligence Operations. A committee consisting of the directors or other appropriate representatives appointed by the directors, of the F.B.I., C.I.A., N.S.A., D.I.A., and the military counterintelligence agencies is to be constituted effective August 1, 1970, to provide evaluations of domestic intelligence, prepared periodic domestic intelligence estimates, carry out the other objectives specified in the report, and perform such other duties as the President shall, from time to time, assign. The director of the F.B.I. shall serve as chairman of the committee. Further details on the organization and operations of this committee are set forth in an attached memorandum.

The President has directed that each addressee submit a detailed report, due on September 1, 1970, on the steps taken to implement these decisions. Further such periodic reports will be requested as circumstances merit.

The President is aware that procedural problems may arise in the course of implementing these decisions. However, he is anxious that such problems be resolved with maximum speed and minimum misunderstanding. Any difficulties which may arise should be brought to my immediate attention in order that an appropriate solution may be found and the President's directives implemented in a manner consistent with his objectives.

Tom Charles
Huston.

TOP SECRET

Handle via Comint Channels Only

Organization and Operations of the Interagency Group on Domestic Intelligence and Internal Security (IAG)

1. Membership. The membership shall consist of representatives of the F.B.I., C.I.A., D.I.A., N.S.A., and the counterintelligence agencies of the Departments of the Army, Navy, and Air Force. To insure the high level consideration of issues and problems which the President expects to be before the group, the directors of the respective agencies should serve personally. However, if necessary and appropriate, the director of a member agency may designate another individual to serve in his place.

2. Chairman. The director of the FBI shall serve as chairman. He may designate another individual from his agency to serve as the FBI representative on the group.

3. Observers. The purpose of the group is to effecutate community-wide coordination and secure the benefits of community-wide analysis and estimating. When problems arise which involve areas of interest to agencies or departments not members of the group, they shall be invited, at the discretion of the group, to join the group as observers and participants in those discussions of interest to them. Such agencies and departments include the Departments of State (I & R, Passport); Treasury (IRS, Customs); Justice (BNDD, Community Relations Service); and such other agencies which may have investigative or law enforcement responsibilities touching on domestic intelligence or internal security matters.

4. White House Liaison. The President has assigned to Tom Charles Huston staff responsibility for domestic intelligence and internal security affairs. He will participate in all activities of the group as the personal representative of the President.

5. Staffing. The group will establish such sub-committees or working groups as it deems appropriate. It will also determine and implement such staffing requirements as it may deem necessary to enable it to carry out its responsibilities, subject to the approval of the President.

6. Duties. The group will have the following duties:

(A) Define the specific requirements of member agencies of the intelligence community.

(B) Effect close, direct coordination between member agencies.

(C) Provide regular evaluations of domestic intelligence.

(D) Review policies governing operations in the field of domestic intelligence and develop recommendations.

(E) Prepare periodic domestic intelligence estimates which incorporate the results of the combined efforts of the intelligence community.

(F) Perform such other duties as the President may from time to time assign.

7. Meetings. The group shall meet at the call of the chairman, a member agency, or the White House representative.

8. Security. Knowledge of the existence and purposes of the group shall be limited on a strict "need to know" basis. Operations of, and papers originating with, the group shall be classified "top secret handle via Comint channels only."

9. Other Procedures. The group shall establish such other procedures as it believes appropriate to the implementation of the duties set forth above.

(TOP SECRET)

EXCERPTS OF EHRLICHMAN STATEMENT

Following are excerpts from a deposition given in May by John D. Ehrlichman, former domestic affairs adviser to President Nixon, in a civil suit by the Democratic National Committee. The deposition was made public June 5.

Q. Mr. Ehrlichman, will you tell us, please, the contents of the conversation which you had with Mr. Magruder on or about April 14, 1972, relative to the Watergate affair?

A. A number of proposals were made for the establishment of an information- and intelligence-gathering facility in the months of, I believe, January and February of 1972.

There were meetings between Gordon Liddy and John Dean and Jeb Magruder and John Mitchell at which Gordon Liddy presented a proposal for the creation of a very elaborate intelligence-gathering organization—at the first meeting.

This was so grandiose and so extreme in its concept that it was rejected by the other three gentlemen out of hand.

There was a modified proposal at the second meeting by Liddy which was also rejected. It was understood that Liddy and Magruder would then try and work out a realistic proposal for resubmission and this effort resulted in Mr. Magruder going to Florida to meet with John Mitchell and, I believe, Fred LaRue was also present at that meeting to discuss a considerably modified and curtailed proposal.

The proposal which was presented at that Florida meeting specifically contemplated and proposed electronic surveillance of the Watergate Democratic National Committee headquarters, the Fontainebleau Hotel during the Democratic convention, and one other place which I can't recall but which my notes, I think, have noted.

Q. Would that have been McGovern or Muskie headquarters?

A. One or the other, yes, and I don't recall which.

On one occasion John Dean told me that he had been told by Magruder that John Mitchell had literally signed off, that is in writing, on a proposal for three electronic surveillance sites.

Magruder told me that prior to the Florida meeting he and Liddy had not arrived at a meeting of the minds on what the proposal should be and during that period of indecision he received a telephone call from Mr. Colson urging him to go forward with intelligence-gathering operations.

I asked him whether Mr. Colson had in any way indictated the nature of the intelligence-gathering which he urged.

He said that in that conversation and, in fact, in all conversations that he had ever had with Mr. Colson there were no suggestions that illegal or electronic or bugging or tapping or other such activities should be conducted.

He said that the thrust of Mr. Colson's conversation with him on the occasion of this call was that there was no information-gathering capability in general but he did not in that conversation make any specific proposal as to means or method.

He was urging a quick resolution of the indecision. That was the essence of it as I got it.

It was after that phone call, not necessarily as a result of it—although I had invited Mr. Magruder's attention to any contact he had had from the White House because that was one of the things the President asked me particularly to look into—it was in response to that inquiry on my part that he mentioned this call from Mr. Colson. I believe there was only one, at least at this juncture.

After the Florida meeting—and my impression is that that is in March of 1972—and I gather late in March. It could have been April. I am not sure. I don't recall.

There were actually two entries into the Democratic headquarters. The first one was for the purpose of installing electronic devices and apparently examining whatever was on the premises.

He said that the results of the surveillance were very poor. There was Mr. Oliver whose telephone was bugged. They learned a great deal more about Mr. Oliver than anybody really wanted to know.

The attempt to monitor Mr. O'Brien's conversations was apparently mechanically a failure.

Mr. Mitchell was made aware of the—was given the results of the surveillance. I don't know whether it was logs or in what form, but he was aware of the unsatisfactory results.

Mr. Magruder told me that Mr. Mitchell very vigorously criticized Mr. Liddy to his face, so to speak, and that the second entry was not by reason or any prior planning on the part of either Mr. Mitchell or Mr. Magruder or others responsible but was a reaction by Mr. Liddy to the heavy criticism that he received for the inadequate results of the first entry.

Q. In other words, he was a self starter.

A. Mr. Magruder said that in the couple of days prior to the second break-in he was out of the city, I think, out on the West Coast, and that the second break-in was as much of a surprise to him as it was to most people.

He said that his relations with Liddy had been steadily deteriorating over the months of early 1972 and that around the middle of March of that year Liddy had actually threatened his life.

He said that Liddy had been known to carry a gun, that he considered him to be a rather unstable character and he wanted to fire him, that instead he transferred him to the finance committee, or talked the finance people into taking him, something of that kind, and that this transfer contributed to the delay in the final decision on whether or not there would be an intelligence-gathering activity; that he was approached by Fred Larue and also by Gordon Strachan to urge him to take Mr. Liddy back in order that his intelligence-gathering activities could go on.

I would want to footnote and refer back at that point.

Mr. Strachan was asked about this and it was stated to me that that conversation never took place but that Mr. Magruder had approached him at a later time and urged him to corroborate his, Mr. Magruder's testimony in that regard. There is a conflict in the testimony there.

Q. Did you get the understanding from Mr. Magruder that the final proposal was the result of a step-by-step reduction of the original grandiose proposal?

A. Yes, he referred to them by dollar amounts.

The first one was the $1-million proposal which he said was a figure which had been suggested by John Dean, or at least that's what Liddy had told him.

The second was the half-million-dollar proposal and the final one, as I recall, was in the neighborhood of $200,000 or $250,000.

****

Q. Will you give us whatever details you can recall, sir, concernings the threat which Liddy made upon Magruder?

A. Magruder put his hand on Liddy's shoulder or touched him in some way and Liddy reacted very violently.

Q. Did he strike Mr. Magruder?

A. He did not. He just threatened to kill him. And what the conversation was that was the context for that I don't know and nobody said.

Q. You did not ask Mr. Magruder?

A. I didn't.

Q. And he did not volunteer it?

A. No.

EXCERPTS OF CIA MEMOS

Following are excerpts from nine memorandums and a note of transmittal by Army Lt. Gen. Vernon A. Walters, deputy director of the Central Intelligence Agency (CIA), and a memorandum by James R. Schlesinger, CIA director. The excerpts were published in The New York Times *June 4. The documents were provided in May to a Senate Appropriations subcommittee in connection with its investigation of the Watergate affair.* *(Earlier CIA story, p. 100)*

COVERING NOTE DATED MAY 18, 1973

The attached memoranda were never intended to be a full or verbatim account of the meetings they covered. These were notes to refresh my memory if I should need it. Originally, the only copy was held in my personal files.

Apparent inconsistency between my testimony that the President's name was not used by (H.R.) Haldeman (former White House chief of staff) in our June 23 conversation and a note that he had said that "It was the President's wish"—I wrote this note five days after the talk. When I showed it to Mr. (Richard) Helms, (director of central intelligence at the time), he pointed out that Haldeman had not actually used the expression, "It was the President's wish." Obviously the thought was implicit in my mind. I did not, however, correct the memo since it was for my own use only. The fact that I agreed with Helms is shown by my saying to (L. Patrick) Gray (acting director of the FBI) on 5 July that it was "implicit." And in several other talks, both with Gray and (John W.) Dean (President Nixon's counsel), showing clearly that I did not believe the President knew.

In my talk with Dean on 26 June, I said, "those who were not touched by the matter would be so" if I were to do what Dean wanted.

The fifth paragraph of my memo on my talk with him on 28 June covers this also.

My whole talk with Gray on 6 July also makes this view clear.

Paragraph 5 of my memo of July 28 conversation with Gray also reflects this view.

With regard to the reference to the Cubans in my notes on my talks with Dean on 28 June, he had expressed the view that there were three hypotheses on the bugging: 1) The Committee to Re-elect the President; 2) The CIA; 3) Some other group. He never admitted any participation by the first group. I told Dean CIA was not involved. He was casting about desperately for someone and pressed me for ideas. My remarks were intended only as a hypothetical assumption.

VERNON A. WALTERS

MEMO DATED JUNE 28, 1972

On June 23 at 1300 (1 p.m.) on request I called with director Helms on John Ehrlichman (former presidential adviser on domestic affairs) and Robert Haldeman at Ehrlichman's office at the White House. Haldeman said that the "bugging" affair at the Democratic National Committee headquarters at the Watergate apartments had made a lot of noise and that the Democrats are trying to maximize it.

The FBI had been called in and was investigating the matter. The investigation was leading to a lot of important people and this could get worse. He asked what the connection with the agency was and the director repeated that there was none.

Haldeman said the whole affair was getting embarrassing and it was the President's wish that Walters call on Acting Director L. Patrick Gray and suggest to him that, since the five suspects had been arrested, this should be sufficient and that it was not advantageous to have the inquiry pushed, especially in Mexico, etc.

Director Helms said he had talked to Gray on the previous day and made plain to him that the agency was not behind this matter and that it was not connected with it. None of the suspects was working for it nor had worked for the agency in the last two years. He had told Gray that none of his investigators was touching any covert projects of the agency, current or ongoing.

Haldeman then stated that I could tell Gray that I had talked to the White House and suggested that the investigation not be pushed further. Gray (was) receptive as he was looking for guidance in the matter.

The director repeated that the agency was not connected with the matter. I then agreed to talk to Gray, as directed. Ehrlichman implied that I should do this soon and I said that I would try to do it today.

Upon leaving the White House, I discussed the matter briefly with the director. Upon returning to the office, I called Gray (and) indicated that this was a matter of some urgency, and he agreed to see me at 1430 (2:30 p.m.) that day.

VERNON A. WALTERS
Lieutenant General
U.S.A.

MEMO DATED JUNE 28, 1972

At 1430 on 23 June I called on the acting director of the FBI, L. Patrick Gray, at his office in the FBI building and saw him alone. I said that I had come to see him after talking to the "White House." I cited no names and he asked for none.

I added that I was aware of the director's conversation with him the previous day and while the further investigation of the Watergate affair had not touched any current or ongoing covert projects of the agency, its continuation might lead to some projects.

I recalled that the FBI and the agency had an agreement in this respect and that the bureau had always scrupulously respected it. Gray said that he was aware of this and understood what it was conveying. His problem was how to low-key the matter now that it was launched.

He said that a lot of money was apparently involved and that it was a matter of a check on a Mexican bank for $89,000. He asked if the name "Dahlberg" meant anything to me and I said it did not. But that was not really significant as I had only been with the agency for a few months.

Gray then said that this was a most awkward matter to come up during an election year and he would see what he could do. I repeated that if the investigations were pushed "south of the border" it would trespass on some of our covert projects and, in view of the fact that the five men involved were under arrest, it would be best to taper off the matter there.

He replied that he understood and would have to study the matter to see how it could best be done. He would have to talk to John Dean about it. Gray said he looked forward to cooperating closely with the agency.

After some pleasantries about J. Edgar Hoover and our past military careers, I left saying that my job had been an awkward one but he had been helpful and I was grateful.

VERNON A. WALTERS

MEMO DATED JUNE 28, 1972

June 26 at about 10 a.m. I received a phone call from Mr. Dean at the White House. He said he wished to see me about the matter that John Ehrlichman and Bob Haldeman had discussed with me on the 23d of June. I could check this out with them if I wished.

I agreed to call on him at his office in Room 106 (of the) Executive Office Building at 1145 that morning. Immediately after hanging up, I called Ehrlichman to find out if this was all right and after some difficulty I reached him and he said I could talk freely to Dean.

At 11:45 I called at Dean's office and saw him alone. He said that the investigation of the Watergate "bugging" case was extremely awkward and that there were a lot of leads to important people and that the FBI, which was investigating the matter, was working on three theories: 1) It was organized by the Republican National Committee; 2) It was organized by the CIA; 3) It was organized by some other party.

I said that I had discussed this with Director Helms and I was quite sure that the agency was not in any way involved and I knew that the director wished to distant himself and the agency from the matter.

Dean then asked whether I was sure the agency was not involved. He believed that Barker had been involved in a clandestine entry into the Chilean Embassy. I said that I was sure none of the suspects had been on the payroll for the past two years.

Dean then said that some of the accused were getting scared and "wobbling." I said that even so, they could not implicate the agency. Dean then asked whether there was not some way that the agency could pay bail for them (they'd been unable to raise bail), added that it was not just bail, but that if these men went to prison could we (the CIA) find some way to pay their salaries while they were serving out their convictions?

I said that I must be quite clear. I was a deputy director and as such had only authority specifically delegated to me by the director and was not in the chain of command but that the great strength of the agency and its value to the President of the United States lay in the fact that it was apolitical and had never gotten itself involved in political disputes. Despite the fact that I had only been with the agency a short time, I knew that the director felt strongly about this.

I then said that as big as the troubles might be with the Watergate affair, if the agency were to provide bail and pay salaries, this would become known sooner or later in the current "leaking" atmosphere of Washington and that at that point, the scandal would be 10 times greater, as such action could only be done upon direction at "the highest level" and that those who were not touched by the matter now certainly would be so.

Dean seemed at first taken aback and then very much impressed by this argument and said that it was certainly a very great risk that would have to be weighed. I repeated that the present affair would be small potatoes compared to what would happen if we did what he wanted and it leaked. He nodded gravely.

I said that, in addition, the agency would be completely discredited with the public and the Congress and would lose all value to the President and the Administration. Again he nodded gravely.

He then asked if I could think of any way we could help. I said that I could not think of any but I would discuss the matter with the director and would be in touch with him. However, I felt that I was fully cognizant of the director's feelings in the matter. He thanked me and I left.

VERNON A. WALTERS

MEMO DATED JUNE 29, 1972

On 28 June, at 1130, John Dean asked me to see him at his office in the Executive Office Building. I found him alone.

He said that the director's meeting with L. Patrick Gray, FBI director, was canceled and that John Ehrlichman had suggested that Gray deal with me instead.

The problem was how to stop the FBI investigation beyond the five suspects. Leads led to two other people—Ken Dahlberg, and a Mexican named Guena. Dean said that the $89,000 was only related to the bugging case and that Dahlberg was refusing to answer questions. Dean then asked hopefully whether I could do anything or had any suggestions.

I repeated that as the deputy director, I had no independent authority. I was not in the chain of command and had no authority other than that given me by the director. The idea that I act independently had no basis in fact.

Dean then asked what might be done and I said that I realized he had a tough problem, but if there were agency involvement, it could only be at Presidential directive and that the political risks that were concomitant appeared to me to be unacceptable.

At present it was a high-explosive bomb but intervention such as he suggested could transform it into a megaton hydrogen bomb. The present caper was awkward and unpleasant. Direct intervention by the agency would be electorally mortal if it became known and the chances of keeping it secret to the election were almost nil.

I noted that scandals had a short life in Washington and that other newer, spicier ones soon replaced them. I urged him to not become unduly agitated by this one.

He then asked if I had any ideas and I said that this affair already had a strong Cuban flavor and that everyone knew that the Cubans were conspiratorial and anxious to know what the policies of both parties would be toward Castro. They, therefore, had a plausible motive for attempting this amateurish job which any skilled technician would deplore. This might be costly but it would be plausible.

Dean said he agreed that this was the best tack to take, but it might cost a half million dollars. He also agreed (for the second time) that the risks of agency involvement were unacceptable.

After a moment's thought, he said that he felt that Gray's cancellation of the appointment with Director Helms might well be reversed within the next few hours.

Dean thanked me and I left.

VERNON A. WALTERS

MEMO DATED JULY 5, 1972

MEMO FOR THE RECORD

On July 5, '72 at 5:50 P.M., I received a phone call from the acting director of the FBI, L. Patrick Gray. He said that the pressures on him to continue the investigation were great. Unless he had documents from me to the effect that their (FBI) investigation was endangering national security, he would have to go ahead with the investigation of Dahlberg and Daguerre. He had talked to John Dean. I said I could not give him an immediate answer but would give him one by 10:00 on 6 July. He said that would be agreeable.

VERNON A. WALTERS

MEMO DATED JULY 6, 1972

At 10:05 on 6 July I saw acting director L. Patrick Gray at his office. We were alone during our conversation. I handed him the memorandum which is attached and said that it covered the entire relationship between the Watergate suspects and the agency.

In all honesty I could not tell him to cease future investigations on the grounds that it would compromise the security interests of the United States. Even less so could I write him a letter to this effect. He said that he fully understood this. He himself had told Ehrlichman and Haldeman that he could not possibly suppress the investigation of this matter.

Even within the FBI there were leaks. He had called in the components of his field office in Washington and chewed them out on this case because information had leaked to the press concerning the Watergate case which only they had.

I said that the only basis on which he and I could deal was absolute frankness and I wished to recount my involvement in this case. I said that I had been called to the White House with Director Helms and had seen two senior staff assistants (I specifically did not name Haldeman and Ehrlichman).

I said that we had been told that if this case were investigated further, it would lead to some awkward places, and I had been directed (the implication being that the President directed this although it was not specifically said) to go to acting director Gray and tell him that if this investigation were pursued further, it could uncover some ongoing covert operatons of the agency. I had done this.

Subsequently, I had seen Mr. Dean, the White House counsel, and told him that whatever the current and present implications of the Watergate case were, that to implicate the agency would not serve the President but would enormously increase the risks to the President.

I had a long association with the President and was as desirous as anyone of protecting him. I did not believe that a letter from the agency asking the FBI to lay off this investigation on spurious grounds that it would uncover covert operations would serve the President.

Such a letter in the current atmosphere in Washington would become known prior to election. What was now a minor wound would become a mortal wound. I said quite frankly that I wouldn't write such a letter.

Gray thanked me for my frankness and said that this opened the way for fruitful cooperation between us. He would be frank with me, too. He could not suppress this investigation with the FBI. He had told Kleindienst this. He told Ehrlich- and Haldeman that he would prefer to resign, but his resignation would raise many questions that would be detrimental to the President's interest.

He did not see why he or I should jeopardize the integrity of our organizations to protect some mid-level White House figures who had acted imprudently. He was prepared to let this go to Ehrlichman, to Haldeman, or to Mitchell, for that matter. He felt it important that the President should be protected from his would-be protectors. He had explained this to Dean as well as to Ehrlichman and to Haldeman.

He said he was anxious not to talk to Mitchell because he was afraid that at his confirmation hearings he would be asked whether he had talked to Mitchell about the Watergate case and he wished to be in a position to reply negatively. He said that he would like to talk to the President about it but he feared that a request from him to see the President would be misinterpreted by the media.

I said that if I were directed to write a letter to him saying that the future investigation of this case would jeopardize the security of the United States and covert operations of the agency, I would ask to see the President and explain to him the disservice I thought this would do to his interest.

The potential danger to the President of such a course far outweighed any protective aspects it might have for any other figures in the White House and I was quite prepared to resign myself on this issue. Gray said he understood this fully and hoped I would stick to my guns. I assured him I would.

Gray then said though this was an awkward position, our mutual frankness had created the basis for a new and happy relationship between the two agencies. I said the memorandum I had given him described in detail the exact measure of agency involvement and noninvolvement in this case, including information on Dahlberg and Daguerre. He thanked me again for my frankness and confidence and repeated that he did not believe that he could sit on this matter and that the facts would come out eventually. He walked me to the door.

VERNON A. WALTERS

MEMO DATED JULY 13, 1972

On 12 July at 1450 I called on acting director L. Patrick Gray at his office and saw him alone.

I told him that shortly after I had seen him the last time and given him the memorandum concerning former CIA association of the suspects in the Watergate case, I had since discovered one additional item concerning Howard Hunt. I gave him that memorandum concerning the assistance given to Hunt, which terminated in August, 1971, when his demands escalated to an inappropriate level. We had assisted him following a request from the White House and it was our understanding that it was for the purpose of tracking down security leaks in the Government.

He thanked me and said that this case could not be snuffed out and it would lead quite high politically. Dahlberg was in the clear. He had gotten the check from Maurice Stans and deposited it in the Mexican bank. It was undoubtedly political money.

Last Friday, the President called (Gray) to congratulate him on the FBI action which had frustrated the aircraft hijacking in San Francisco. The President asked him if he had talked to me about the case. Gray replied that he had.

The President then asked him what his recommendation was on the matter. Gray had replied that the case could not be covered up and would lead quite high and he felt that the President should get rid of the people that were involved. Any attempt to involve the FBI or the CIA in this case would only prove a mortal wound (he used my words) and would achieve nothing.

The President then said, "Then I should get rid of whoever is involved no matter how high?" Gray replied that was his recommendation.

The President then asked what I thought and Gray said my views were the same as his. The President took it well and thanked Gray. Later that day, Gray had talked to Dean and repeated the conversation to him. Dean had said, "O.K."

Gray had heard no more on the subject. He asked whether the President had spoken to me and I said he had on another matter but had not brought up this matter with me.

Gray then said that the U.S. Attorney had subpoenaed the financial records of the Committee to Re-elect the President. It had been suggested to him that he stop this. He had replied that he could not. Whoever wanted this done should talk to the Attorney General and see if there was any legal way to do this. He could not.

He said that he had told the President in 1968 that he should beware of his subordinates who try to wear his Commander in Chief stripes. I agreed, saying that in my view the President should be protected from the self-appointed protectors who would harm him while trying to cover their own mistakes.

Gray said that our views coincided on this matter. He would resign on this issue if necessary and I said that in maintaining the integrity of our agencies we were rendering the President the best possible service. I too, was quite prepared to resign on this issue.

He thanked me for my frankness and said that we had established a warm, personal, frank relationship at outset of our tenure in our respective jobs.

VERNON A. WALTERS

MEMO DATED JULY 28, 1972

(1)

On Friday, July 28, 1972, at 11 A.M. I called on the acting director of the FBI, L. Patrick Gray, at his office in the FBI building. He saw me alone. I said I had come to clarify the last memorandum I had given him in reply to inquiries from Mr. Pirham "Cleo."

(2)

I said that "Cleo" was Mr. Cleo (blank), an electronics engineer who was in contact with Mr. Hunt during August of 1971. Mr. (blank) supplied a recorder pursuant to Mr. Hunt's request and had assisted him to get it in shape for use in overt, not clandestine, recordings of meetings with agents. There was no attempt to make the recorder useful for clandestine activities.

Mr. (blank) had two additional meetings, generated by a phone call to the above number (a sterile telephone in one of our offices), to straighten out some difficulties that had arisen with respect to the microphones. We never recovered the recorder.

Aside from the above contact with respect to the recorder, there were contacts with Mr. Hunt with respect to false docucuments and disguises for himself and an associate. He was also loaned a clandestine camera, which he returned. We developed one roll of film for Mr. Hunt, of which we have copies showing some unidentified place, possibly the Rand Corporation. We had no contact whatsoever with Mr. Hunt subsequent to 31 August 1971.

He thanked me for this information. I added that when Hunt's request had escalated, we terminated our assistance to him and had no further contact with him subsequent to 31 August 1971. He was grateful for this information.

Gray asked me if the President had called me on this matter and I replied that he had not. Gray then said a lot of pressure had been brought on him on this matter but he had not yielded.

I told him that we intended to terminate the 965-9598 number (the CIA's sterile phone) and he nodded. Then he said, "This is a hell of a thing to happen to us at the outset of our tenure with our respective offices." I agreed heartily.

(7)

He thanked me for coming to see him and for maintaining such a frank and forward relationship with him. I left him a short, unsigned memo embodying what I had told him.

VERNON A. WALTERS

SCHLESINGER LETTER DATED FEB. 9, 1973

SUBJECT: TELEPHONE CALL FROM JOHN DEAN.

This evening at 6:10 I received a telephone call from John Dean at the White House. Dean indicated that he wanted to discuss two topics.

First, he (referred) to a packet of material that had been sent to the Department of Justice in connection with the Watergate investigation. He suggested that Justice be required to return this package to the agency (the CIA).

The only item that would be left at Justice would be a card in the files indicating that a package had been returned to the agency, since the material in the package was no longer needed for the purposes of the investigation. He indicated that the agency had originally provided these materials to the Department of Justice at the request of the (assistant) Attorney General, Mr. (Henry E.) Petersen.

The second subject that he raised was the pending investigation by the Senate on the I.T.T. affair in relation to the Chilean problem. He felt that this investigation could be rather explosive. He also indicated that there might be some sensitive cables at the agency that might be requested by the Senate investigators.

I indicated to him that while I had not seen any cables, I had been briefed on the subject, and that the role of the Government appeared to be clean. He expressed his delight at hearing this assessment. I indicated that I would look into the cables for that period.

In this connection, he mentioned that there is a hot story being passed about in the press, primarily instigated by Seymour Hersh of The New York Times. The story suggests that (Frank) Sturgis, who sometimes went by the code name Federini, was the individual responsible for the burglarizing of the Chilean Embassy in Washington.

He also indicated that he expected Senator (J.W.) Fulbright to request the Justice Department to produce Sturgis for the Senate hearings.

I indicated that I would look further into the matter. He then made some rather jovial remarks about not always being the bearer of bad tidings and I inquired what the good news might be. Further references were made to a pending appointment at the A.E.C.

Shortly thereafter, I discussed those matters with Bill Colby (then a high-ranking CIA official), who indicated that Sturgis had not been on the payroll for a number of years and that whatever the allegations about the Chilean Embassy, the agency had no connection at all.

We also agreed that he would discuss the question of the package relative to the Watergate investigation with General Walters and a discussion would be made with regard to the appropriate action.

J.R.S.

CC: General Walters
(James R. Schlesinger)

MEMO DATED MAY 11, 1973

MEMORANDUM OF CONVERSATION OF FEB. 21, 1973

At the request of the director, Dr. Schlesinger, I called on Mr. John Dean in his office at the White House at 4:30.

I explained to him that, in connection with his request that the agency ask the Department of Justice to return a package of material that had been sent to them in connection with the Watergate investigation, it was quite impossible for us to request the return of this, as this would simply mean that a note would be left in the Department of Justice files that the material in any way related to the case.

I again told him that there was no agency involvement in this case, and that any attempt to involve the agency could only be harmful to the United States. He seemed disappointed. I then left.

VERNON A. WALTERS ✓

IN THE WAKE OF WATERGATE, A NEW WHITE HOUSE STAFF

For the third time in only five months, President Nixon June 6 reshuffled his top staff. Although the structure of the White House organization was not radically changed, new individuals were chosen to replace the staff that had been decimated in recent weeks by the Watergate scandal.

There were these major changes June 6:

- Melvin R. Laird, former secretary of defense, was named counsellor to the President for domestic affairs.
- Gen. Alexander M. Haig Jr., the President's acting chief of staff, will retire from the Army August 1 and be appointed as an assistant to the President.
- Ronald L. Ziegler, the President's press secretary, was named an assistant to the President and will assume the duties of Herbert B. Klein, director of communications for the executive branch, whose resignation was announced June 5.
- Professor Charles A. Wright of the University of Texas law school will become a part-time legal consultant to the President, assisting presidential counsel Leonard Garment and special counsel J. Fred Buzhardt on Watergate matters. Wright helped formulate the Nixon administration's anti-busing legislative proposals of 1971.

Laird. The politically astute former Republican representative from Wisconsin (1953-69) enters the White House at a time of great difficulty for the President. Apart from the Watergate affair, the President has been criticized—even among Republicans—over his positions on impoundment of appropriated funds, executive privilege and war policy.

Laird's job description as announced by the White House—"he will be responsible for the over-all formulation and coordination of domestic policy"—is similar to that of former presidential aide John D. Ehrlichman. Ehrlichman and H. R. Haldeman, another presidential assistant, resigned April 30 in the wake of the Watergate scandal.

But it was understood that Laird will assume greater responsibilities than those held by Ehrlichman. Laird will hold cabinet rank, have a seat on the National Security Council and advise the President on economic matters.

In what was seen as tacit acknowledgment of the friction that had existed between Ehrlichman and Congress, Laird stressed in a briefing for reporters that he would be in direct contact with Congress and its leaders.

Laird said he already had met with House Speaker Carl Albert (Okla.) and Senate Majority Leader Mike Mansfield (Mont.) about his new position and had promised "open and complete communication" with Congress.

On more than one occasion during the briefing, Laird stressed his "love for Congress," where he served 16 years before becoming defense secretary from 1969 to 1973. He said he would attend caucuses of both parties on invitation and always be ready to answer questions from congressmen and the press.

Laird stressed that William E. Timmons, assistant to the President for congressional relations, and Kenneth R. Cole Jr., executive director of the domestic council, would retain their posts and duties.

Congressional Reaction. Laird's appointment drew uniform praise from congressmen of both parties. "It's about time they got a professional politician down there" at the White House, said Senate Majority Leader Mike Mansfield. "It can't help but improve White House relations with Congress, said Sen. Thomas J. McIntyre (D N.H.).

Rep. Paul N. McCloskey Jr. (R Calif.), a persistent critic of President Nixon, called Laird "a very competent guy." Sen. Ted Stevens (R Alaska) said Laird "had the finest congressional relations in the history of the Defense Department. He reached out to people in Congress. Unfortunately, an adversary relationship had developed between some of the President's staff and the Hill."

A 'Standstill.' In answer to a question about why he was rejoining the government after earlier announcing he would not, Laird said the "government in some quarters is at a standstill" because of Watergate and he felt he had to help.

Laird also credited Vice President Agnew with persuading him to accept the counsellor's job.

Laird was reminded of a statement he had made May 1, that if the President was involved in Watergate "I wouldn't want to know about it." Laird said he made the comment as a private citizen, but now was a member of the government.

"I have great confidence in the President," Laird said. "I have been assured of his non-involvement" in Watergate.

He said he had set no time limit for himself, but promised that he would remain on the job for "at least a year." He insisted that his appointment was not a "cosmetic" one and that he would have "regular...24-hour a day access to the President."

Haig. Haig's decision to leave the Army came after complaints from Congress and elsewhere that the White House had violated the law in using his services while he remained on active duty. In calling for Haig's resignation, Sen. Stuart Symington (D Mo.), acting chairman of the Armed Services Committee, Sen. William Proxmire (D Wis.) and consumer advocate Ralph Nader contended it was illegal for a military officer on active duty to serve in a civil position either by appointment or election. The Pentagon insisted in a letter to Nader May 23 that the appointment was legal.

There was no official explanation of Haig's decision to retire from active Army duty. It was known he had great respect for the President and owed his rapid rise through Army ranks to Nixon. Haig was a colonel when he first came to the White House in 1969 as Henry Kissinger's military adviser. He left four years later as a four-star general and Army vice chief of staff. *(Biography, p. 53)*

Haig's duties will not change, the White House said. Since taking over for Haldeman May 4, he has been responsible for administration of the White House and the President's appointments. Deputy presidential press secretary Gerald Warren refused to equate Haig's responsibilities with Haldeman's and Laird's with Ehrlichman's. It was generally believed that Haldeman wielded more power than Haig. "The man makes the job," Warren remarked.

Ziegler. Klein's resignation and Ziegler's assumption of his duties came as no surprise. Klein reportedly submitted his resignation months ago, but Nixon's acceptance of it was held up because of the Watergate affair.

Klein, 55, had accepted a position as vice president for corporate relations with Metromedia, a Los Angeles communications empire. He is a former newspaper editor and long-time friend of Nixon.

The White House said Klein's job title would not be filled, although Ziegler will take over his duties. These were largely liaison with editors and publishers.

Ziegler was to continue briefing the press, the White House said, although there were indications most of that task would be shifted to Warren. As Warren made the announcements, Ziegler was with Kissinger in Paris for what was described as an effort to familiarize the press secretary with the peace negotiations.

As a presidential assistant, the White House said, Ziegler also will be involved "in policy meetings both with the President and other senior staff members."

Ziegler has been criticized severly by the press in recent weeks because of misleading remarks about White House innocence in the Watergate affair. But Warren said the President has "utmost faith in and respect for Ron Ziegler." ✓

A NEW OPENNESS

With many of his most trusted and influential aides washed away in the wake of the Watergate scandal, President Nixon in recent weeks has been relying increasingly on congressional leaders and his cabinet officers.

Figures provided Congressional Quarterly by the White House show the President's meetings this year with the cabinet and congressional leaders of both parties either exceed those for previous years or are occuring at a rate that probably will top earlier years. *(Box, this page)*

As of June 7, for example, the figures show the President had held 11 cabinet meetings, equaling the number he held in all of 1972.

The nine meetings between Nixon and bipartisan congressional leaders exceed the totals of five for 1972 and eight for 1971. Republican leaders have been in to see the President six times in 1973, more than half the total of 11 for 1972, the figures show.

The announcement June 6 that former Defense Secretary Melvin R. Laird will become an assistant to the President for domestic affairs, coupled with his stated eagerness to cooperate with Congress, lent credence to the view of a more open administration. *(Story, p. 130)*

Scott and Ford. In addition, House Minority Leader Gerald R. Ford (Mich.) and Senate Minority Leader Hugh Scott (Pa.) emerged from a White House meeting with the President June 5 to tell reporters that henceforth the two leaders will be included in all cabinet meetings and that Nixon was going along with their request for closer contacts with them on legislative matters.

Ford said that day's meeting with the President was the first at which the two leaders had set the agenda, that it was successful and that the President had agreed that every third meeting with them would be one where they set the agenda for discussion.

Ford said the aim of such meetings was an "earlier input to proposed legislation" and "closer cooperation... as the legislation progresses" through Congress.

Scott added that Nixon told them he had requested all cabinet members and agency heads to cooperate fully with them on legislative and other matters.

Ford denied that the increased cooperation between the President and his congressional leaders was linked to the departures of former presidential aides H.R. Haldeman and John D. Ehrlichman.

Ford said the increased cooperation between himself, Scott and the White House was an outgrowth of his and Scott's request in January 1973. He said they felt that, based on their experience in the first Nixon term, it was necessary to have closer liaison in order to get the President's program through Congress.

Expanding Contacts. A White House aide who attends many cabinet meetings told Congressional Quarterly he was sure the resignations had the effect of expanding contacts between Nixon and cabinet members. He explained that without Haldeman and Ehrlichman to intercede for him, the President was forced to establish more direct relationships with his cabinet.

The aide said the cabinet was "enjoying the direct access now—it's been a problem in the past." Walter J. Hickel, Nixon's first interior secretary, was fired in 1970 after he publicly complained about the lack of accessibility to the President for cabinet members.

Ehrlichman, when he briefed reporters Jan. 5, 1973, on an executive reorganization plan that became known as the "super cabinet" idea, referred to cabinet meetings as "show and tell" sessions and said Nixon preferred working with groups like the Domestic and National Security Councils. But the "super cabinet" fell apart when Ehrlichman and Haldeman resigned.

Presidential Meetings

Following are White House figures on the numbers of meetings between President Nixon and his cabinet, Republican congressional leaders and bipartisan congressional leaders through June 7, 1973:

	Cabinet	GOP Leaders	Bi-partisan Leaders
1971	21	8	8
1972	11	11	5
6/7/73	11	6	9

WATERGATE: MAGRUDER IMPLICATES TOP OFFICIALS

The most detailed account so far of high-level Nixon administration involvement in the Watergate affair and its coverup emerged from testimony before a Senate investigating committee during the week ended June 16. The most damaging statements came from Jeb Stuart Magruder, the former deputy director of the Committee for the Re-election of the President.

Magruder, now a private consultant in Washington, related to the seven-member committee his version of the events leading up to the June 17, 1972, break-in and bugging and the calculated planning to keep the facts from coming out.

He named names. Implicated most strongly in Magruder's testimony, both in the planning and coverup, was John N. Mitchell, Nixon's former attorney general and law partner who later became his campaign director.

John W. Dean III, the former White House counsel who has become a vital figure in the various investigations of the scandal, received prominent mention in Magruder's statements. Magruder testified under a grant of partial immunity from further prosecution. Dean, with a similar grant, was expected to follow Magruder in appearing before the committee when it reconvened.

In a full day of testimony June 14, Magruder freely admitted his own complicity in the well-financed scheme to spy on the Democrats. His implications reached as high in the White House hierarchy as H. R. Haldeman, the President's former chief of staff. But they stopped at the door of the oval office. Magruder stated repeatedly that, to his knowledge, Nixon was unaware of the crimes or their coverup.

Magruder was preceded in the witness chair June 12 and 13 by Maurice H. Stans, Nixon's former commerce secretary and later his campaign finance director. Stans denied any advance knowledge of the Watergate, describing himself as only a fund-raiser and a conduit for money that went to the political side of the operation.

But Stans was contradicted by Magruder. June 24, 1972, became a date of contention, because Magruder claimed Stans had been briefed by Mitchell that day on the burglary at Democratic national headquarters. Stans could recall no such briefing.

Other Developments. These were among the week's other highlights in the Watergate case.

- A federal judge refused to bar television and radio coverage of the Senate hearings. Special prosecutor Archibald Cox had asked that they be removed.

- Convicted conspirator James W. McCord Jr. asked for a new trial. His sentencing, scheduled for June 15, was postponed indefinitely.

- Nine representatives took the House floor to discuss presidential impeachment proceedings.

- Morton Halperin, a former consultant to the National Security Council, sued Henry Kissinger and other officials for wiretapping.
- Vice President Agnew and Interior Secretary Rogers C. B. Morton criticized the Senate Watergate hearings. Republican National Chairman George Bush defended them.
- Convicted Watergate conspirator E. Howard Hunt Jr. was paid more than $200,000 after blackmailing the White House with threats to expose administration officials for involvement in illegal activities, *The Washington Post* reported.
- David Young, a former member of the White House investigations unit, or "plumbers," refused to testify before a Los Angeles County grand jury June 14 in connection with the 1971 burglary of the office of Daniel Ellsberg's former psychiatrist. Egil Krogh Jr., former head of the "plumbers," was ordered to appear before the grand jury on July 5.
- Financier Robert L. Vesco, already under criminal indictment for donating an unreported $200,000 to the Nixon campaign, was charged with illegal use of a telegram to order the transfer of $250,000 from the Bahamas to New York City. The United States is trying to extradite Vesco from Costa Rica. Vesco reportedly left Costa Rica for the Bahamas.

Witnesses June 12

Maurice H. Stans, President Nixon's chief fundraiser for the 1972 re-election campaign, disclaimed all knowledge of the Watergate affair and its coverup, saying his job was only to raise money. "The finance committee played no part in the strategy or tactics of the campaign," said Stans, the committee chairman, in his statement to the Senate Watergate investigating committee June 12. "If they (the tactics) went wrong, it was the fault of the campaign committee." *(Text, p. 141)*

Thus Stans was attempting to absolve himself and his committee from all blame in the scandal and to place it instead on the Committee for the Re-election of the President, headed for four months in 1972 by John N. Mitchell, the former attorney general. Stans and Mitchell are under indictment in New York City for obstructing justice by interfering with a federal investigation and lying to a grand jury about a $200,000 cash contribution to the Nixon campaign by financier Robert L. Vesco. *(p. 46)*

Maurice H. Stans

Stans at first tried to get the Senate committee to delay his appearance until the Vesco case indictment was disposed of. When this was denied, he agreed to testify, provided he was not questioned about the Vesco case. His appearance followed that of Herbert L. Porter, director of scheduling for the President's "surrogate" candidates in 1972. At the committee's morning session, Porter completed the testimony he had started the week before. *(p. 117)*

Stans Testimony. Questioning by the committee during Stans' testimony concerned the flow of cash into and out of the finance committee from the time Stans joined the committee on Feb. 15, 1972, after resigning as secretary of commerce. Stans denied any knowledge of a July 28, 1971, memorandum saying he had set aside $1-million in Commerce Department funds for pre-campaign activities. The memo was from Jeb Stuart Magruder to Mitchell. Magruder is a former White House aide who later became deputy director of the Nixon campaign. Stans said the memo "must have been based on some misunderstanding."

Stans explained how he raised $75,000 for Herbert W. Kalmbach, the President's former private attorney, who used the money for payments to Watergate defendants. Stans said he met Kalmbach June 29, 1972, 12 days after the Watergate break-in, in a Washington hotel. Kalmbach said he was on a "special mission" for the White House, Stans related, and that he needed all the money he could get in cash. Stans said Kalmbach told him he was asking for the money on "high authority," but did not give any names.

Stans said he learned from Kalmbach only six weeks before his testimony that the request for the money had come from former White House counsel John W. Dean III. Kalmbach had been assured by Dean and former presidential assistant John D. Ehrlichman that it was a legal transaction, Stans told the committee. Dean and Ehrlichman resigned from the White House under pressure April 30. Stans said that Kalmbach was a man of "highest integrity" whom he had known for several years and that he therefore did not question the request, even though Kalmbach told him the money was not for campaign use.

Stans said $30,000 of the $75,000 came from three Filipino businessmen. The committee later decided it would be illegal to accept the foreign money, and it was returned. *(p. 139)*

The other $45,000 given Kalmbach was the remainder of $50,000 in cash that Kalmbach had given Stans when Stans became finance chairman. At that time, Stans explained, he was not on salary and had many expenses, but he spent only about $5,000 of the $50,000 and kept the remainder in his safe deposit box. "When Kalmbach said he had an urgent need for that money, I went to the safe deposit box and gave it to him," Stans said. "It was not money belonging to the finance committee."

At one point, after explaining many financial transactions, Stans said he had been disturbed at the large amounts of money being spent by the re-election committee. He referred to it as "overkill."

He said he had believed Nixon could be re-elected for $30-million, but the re-election committee was budgeting more than $40-million. Stans said he tried to get H. R. Haldeman, then Nixon's chief of staff, to intercede with the President to hold down spending, but that he "didn't see any significant consequences" of his meetings with Haldeman.

In his prepared testimony, Stans said the actual spending for the re-election might, when finally audited, top $50-million. He said that at one time, during a meeting of officials of the finance and re-election committees, he walked out because he could not get the re-election committee to hold down spending. Stans explained that the role of the finance committee was only to raise money and that the re-election committee directed how it would be spent. "In effect, their decisions fixed the amount the campaign would cost," he said.

There were no intentional violations of the campaign spending laws, Stans said, but he conceded that "some unintended technical violations" may have been made by the committee because of unfamiliarity with the new law and the large amount of work to be done. Concerning his own role in the campaign, Stans said he had "no responsibility in connection with the internal handling of funds, banking, recording, accounting and reporting. I did not sign checks. I did not expend from the treasurer's cash fund."

Stans said he believed the $350,000 secret cash fund supplied to an aide of Haldeman, Gordon Strachan, was a legitimate arrangement. Reports of the deal said the money went to Watergate defendants. Stans said he had been told the money was for polling.

Stans also said the $114,000 in contributions that wound up in the Miami bank account of convicted Watergate burglar Bernard L. Barker could only have gotten there "through the hands of G. Gordon Liddy." Liddy, former counsel to the re-election finance committee, also is a convicted conspirator. The money in Barker's account was from four checks totaling $89,000 that came via Mexico and a check for $25,000 from Minnesota businessman Dwayne Andreas.

Stans defended the donations as legal and proper. The Mexican donation came from U.S. citizens, whom he did not name, who lived in Texas but who had U.S. money in Mexican banks. The money from Andreas was promised in March 1972, but was not received until April 11, four days after a new law went into effect requiring names of donors to be made public. Stans said Andreas' name was not reported because the money was considered contributed before April 7.

Barker Arguments. Before Stans testified, his attorney, Robert W. Barker, pleaded that his client's committee appearance be put off until his role in the Vesco case was disposed of. Barker said that "directly or indirectly, this hearing will jeopardize" Stans' right to a fair trial because of the effect of publicity from the hearings on prospective Vesco case jurors.

He said Stans was in "an impossible situation." If he testified, he might lose his due process rights. If he did not answer the committee's questions, he could be cited for contempt of Congress, Barker said. Stans could invoke the Fifth Amendment against self-incrimination, his attorney continued, but that too could prejudice jurors. Stans is left no "reasonable choice or fair opportunity," Barker said.

Committee Chairman Sam J. Ervin Jr. (D N.C.) replied that the committee already had considered Barker's arguments in a morning session and had decided unanimously that no questions would be asked concerning Stans' role in the Vesco matter. Ervin added that if Stans refused to testify about non-Vesco matters, he might be cited for contempt. Americans have a "paramount interest" in the roles of high officials, Ervin said, and the hearings should not be put off until the courts make their determinations. "The courts have had approximately a year to deal with it," he added.

Sen. Lowell P. Weicker Jr. (R Conn.), a committee member, said he would not question Stans because it might appear he was taking vengeance for remarks Stans made against him in a 1970 Senate primary campaign. "I don't want it said by anyone that I'm trying to get even," Weicker said. "Therefore, I'll refrain from questioning Mr. Stans now or at any time in the future."

Porter Testimony. Porter, the former scheduling director, said he disbursed $69,000 during the campaign, most of it for small, miscellaneous travel expenses, but $31,000 of which went to Liddy for what Porter said were purposes unknown to him. Some of the $69,000 went to persons who were assigned to wave pro-Nixon placards at opposing candidates, Porter said, adding that an unexplained $300 was donated to the New Hampshire primary campaigns of two Nixon rivals, Sen. George McGovern (D S.D.) and Rep. Paul N. McCloskey Jr. (R Calif.).

Porter also testified that in late 1971 he had seen a photograph of an internal memorandum from Sen. Edmund S. Muskie's (D Maine) staff suggesting that the senator's subcommittee hold tax hearings in California for campaign publicity purposes. Porter said Magruder told him to copy the memo and give it anonymously to columnists Rowland Evans and Robert Novak. They printed the story, and the hearings never were held, Porter said.

Magruder had given him 35-millimeter film strips of other Muskie interoffice memos, Porter testified, but later took them back, explaining that he wanted to show them to Mitchell. Porter said he did not know if Mitchell ever saw them. He also said he may have sent copies of some of the Muskie documents to Strachan at the White House, but he was not sure.

Porter said he did not think it was illegal to photograph the Muskie documents. "I put the photographing of documents in the same category as Xeroxing," he said. "I knew it was surreptitious, but I didn't think it was illegal."

Porter was not asked how the photos of the documents were obtained. *The New York Times* reported June 12 that Porter had told Senate investigators in April that the photos came from a taxi driver who worked as a courier for Muskie's campaign headquarters. The taxi driver photographed the documents and gave them to Kenneth Rietz, the Nixon campaign youth director, who paid the driver from funds given Rietz by Porter, the Times reported. Porter testified that he gave Rietz $3,000 of the $69,000 he spent during the campaign, but he did not state the purpose of the disbursement.

Porter also described events at a June 17, 1972, California breakfast of Republican campaign officials when it was learned there had been a break-in at Democratic headquarters. He said he and his wife were seated with Magruder, Mitchell, Robert Mardian and Frederick LaRue and their wives when he overheard Magruder ask, "Does anyone know where I can find a secure phone?"

"He asked me personally, saying, 'Liddy wants to talk to me,' " Porter related. "I told him to use the pay phone." Porter said he did not know if Magruder took his suggestion or not, because Magruder did not leave the room at that time. He said his wife told him that Mrs. Magruder had told her that Magruder had been up early that morning on the phone to Key Biscayne, Fla.

Later, said Porter, Magruder, Mitchell, LaRue and Mardian huddled in the corner of a hotel ballroom for three or four serious discussions. "I was asked to stand some 50 feet away" and guard the door, Porter said.

Magruder Statement

Following is the formal statement made by Jeb Stuart Magruder before the Senate Watergate committee on June 14:

I did help organize the Committee for the Re-election of the President beginning in May of 1971, and I remained there throughout the entire campaign. Unfortunately, we made some mistakes in the campaign which have led to a major national concern.

For those errors in judgment that I made, I take full responsibility. I am, after all, a mature man and I am willing to face the consequences of my own acts. These mistakes were made by only a few participants in the campaign. Thousands of persons assisted in the campaign to re-elect the President and they did nothing illegal or unethical.

As far as I know, at no point during this entire period, from the time of planning the Watergate to the time of trying to keep it from public view, did the President have any knowledge of our errors in this matter. He had confidence in his aides, and I must confess that some of us failed him.

I regret that I must today name others who participated with me in the Watergate affair. This is not through any desire to implicate others, but simply to give you the facts to the best of my recollection.

Witness June 13

Stans, the Senate committee's only witness June 13, testified that campaign contribution records for the pre-April 7, 1972, period were destroyed after the Watergate break-in on the advice of G. Gordon Liddy, who was later convicted for his part in the Watergate burglary.

Stans insisted under heated questioning by Chairman Ervin that it was "pure and innocent coincidence" that the destruction of the records took place after the June 17 break-in. He said Liddy advised him that there was no legal requirement to keep them and that counsel John Dean concurred with Liddy on the legal requirements.

"In retrospect, we'd have saved an awful lot of questions if we hadn't destroyed them," Stans conceded. But he added that Liddy and Dean "were in good standing" at that time.

"It's a rather suspicious coincidence that records showing these matters were destroyed six days after the break-in at the Watergate," Ervin persisted.

"The adjectives are yours," replied Stans, who said his committee kept 99 per cent of its records.

Ervin, at times almost shouting at the witness, insisted that Stans owed it to the American public to have maintained the records rather than destroying them just because the law did not require his committee to keep them. Stans answered that he had to balance one ethical principle against another. Making the names of the contributors public would have violated the trust of those who asked anonymity, he explained.

Stans said the finance committee did not care one way or another if the contributors wanted to publicize their donations, but it was up to them individually. Congress, in passing the 1925 law that operated until April 7, 1972, gave contributors the option to remain anonymous, he noted.

Gurney vs. Ervin. Ervin's continued pressure on the witness about alleged "laundered checks" from Mexico led to the first open disagreement among the committee members. Sen. Edward J. Gurney (R Fla.), regarded as the administration's staunchest defender on the committee, charged Ervin with harassing Stans. "I, for one, have not appreciated the harassment of this witness by the chairman in the questioning that is just finished," said Gurney. "I think the Senate committee ought to act in fairness."

"Well, I'm sorry my distinguished friend from Florida does not approve of my method of questioning the witness," Ervin said in his folksy manner. "I'm just an old country lawyer and I don't know the finer ways to do it. I just have to do it my way." The audience applauded.

Sen. Howard H. Baker Jr. (R Tenn.), the committee vice chairman, suggested—and the committee agreed—that the committee subpoena the records and officials of the Democratic National Committee and representatives of all major presidential candidates in the period before April 7, 1972, in order to study how they handled contributions and records.

'Laundered' Checks. Stans denied that four checks that found their way to the finance committee through the Miami bank account of Bernard Barker, or the $25,000 check from Dwayne Andreas, were "laundered." He said campaign treasurer Hugh Sloan had accepted Liddy's recommendation that the checks be converted to cash through Barker's account.

"Don't you call that laundered checks?" asked Ervin.

"I call that stupidity on the part of our general counsel (Liddy)," Stans responded.

In the main, Stans' testimony was the same as the previous day's, except to fill in holes here and there. Time and again, he insisted that he had no control over campaign spending—he just raised the money—and his attempts to urge others to hold down expenditures were failures.

Pre-deadline Spending. Stans' lack of knowledge about the committee's expenditure of $1,777,000 in cash before April 7, 1972, kept recurring through the day. Sen. Herman E. Talmadge (D Ga.) persistently questioned the witness about why the finance committee kept detailed records of expenditures for such things as bumper stickers, souvenir jewelry and other small items, but apparently was unconcerned about the nearly $2-million in cash outlays.

Stans said that most of the cash outlay was made before April 7, when it did not have to be reported, but after that date the new law required detailed accounting for all spending. That was when the committee began buying up the bumper stickers and other items, he said.

"That strikes me as inconceivable," said Talmadge. He asked Stans why he apparently was not curious about how much money Liddy was getting. "Liddy was accountable in money terms to the treasurer (Sloan), not to me," Stans replied.

New Law. Stans said the committee never solicited cash donations and the cash it received amounted to about 2 to 3 per cent of its total income. Asked if he would recommend a new law against cash contributions to political campaigns, Stans replied that he was "ambivalent on that."

He said it would cut down on some public suspicions, but cash would be needed quickly for small expenditures, as from a petty cash fund. "A carefully drafted law" on the subject might work, he said.

At one point, Stans agreed that a $50,000 cash transfer to a 1972 fund-raising party in Maryland honoring Vice President Agnew amounted to deception. "If you want to indict me for that, all right," said Stans in his only show of exasperation during six hours of testimony. *(List of expenditures, p. 114)*

First Word. Stans said that the first time he learned the finance committee might be linked to the Watergate break-in was June 23, 1972, when Frederick LaRue called him and asked if he knew someone named Dahlberg, because Dahlberg's contribution was in Barker's account.

Stans said he had lunch with Mitchell that day and that they might have discussed Watergate, but he could not recall if they did. He added that neither Mitchell nor any other persons linked to the break-in or the coverup ever tried to tell him what actually happened concerning Watergate.

In an impromptu closing statement, Stans said he and men like Dahlberg, Andreas and Sloan had been "dragged through unrelenting publicity" because of their work or contributions and that it had damaging effects on their lives and businesses. "All I ask, Mr. Chairman, is that when you write your report you give me back my good name," he said.

Witness June 14

Jeb Stuart Magruder, the former deputy director of the President's re-election campaign, testified before the Senate Watergate committee June 14 that former Attorney General John N. Mitchell had approved plans for the break-in at the Democrats' Watergate headquarters and later had participated in a coverup of the incident.

Magruder, the first high-level figure involved in the Watergate scandal to detail the events that led up to and followed the break-in, told the committee, "I must today name others who participated with me in the Watergate affair...not through any desire to implicate others but simply to give you the facts to the best of my **recollection."** *(Box, p. 134)*

At the outset of the day's five-hour hearing, the handsome, 38-year-old former campaign deputy said that as far as he knew, President Nixon did not have any knowledge of the events surrounding the break-in.

Poll Report

If congressional elections were being held now, "Republican loss of House seats would go far beyond the normal loss that an administration suffers in off-year elections," according to the latest Gallup Poll The poll was published June 10. It was based on interviews of 2,356 registered voters April 6-9 and May 4-7.

Allocating the undecided vote equally between Democrats and Republicans, this is what Gallup found:

	1972 Election	Today	Change
Republicans	47%	40%	—7%
Democrats	53	60	+7

Although, Gallup wrote, percentages of the popular vote cannot be translated directly into House seats, the outlook for 1974 resembles that of 1964, when the percentage of the popular vote was 57-43 in favor of the Democrats. The breakdown in House seats that year was 295 Democrats and 140 Republicans. The lineup in 1973 is 243 Democrats and 192 Republicans. *(Earlier report, p. 112)*

Besides naming Mitchell as the official who authorized espionage activities against the Democrats, Magruder revealed that Gordon Strachan, an aide to former White House chief of staff H.R. Haldeman, had advance knowledge of the Watergate plan and reviewed transcripts of taped phone conversations of Democratic officials. Although Magruder, under intense and repeated questioning, stopped short of saying that Haldeman knew about the Watergate operation in advance, he told Sen. Lowell P. Weicker Jr. (R Conn.): "I had to assume, since I communicated with Strachan on these matters, that Mr. Haldeman had to know about them to a certain extent." Later, however, Magruder told the committee that "it's unfair to say Haldeman know about (the Watergate) in advance."

Jeb S. Magruder

Magruder also contradicted the June 13 testimony of former campaign finance director Maurice H. Stans, who claimed that his knowledge of the Watergate affair had come only from press accounts. According to Magruder, he and Mitchell met with Stans on June 24, 1972, and told him some of the details about the break-in.

"Do you basically feel Stans knew (about the Watergate)?" asked majority counsel Samuel Dash.

"Yes, that's correct," Magruder replied. As for himself, he said he would take "full responsibility" for the "errors in judgment" he made during the campaign.

Plans. During a lengthy question-and-answer session between Dash and Magruder, the steps that led up to Mitchell's alleged approval of the Watergate break-in were disclosed. On Jan. 27, 1972, Magruder said, he met with Mitchell, John Dean and G. Gordon Liddy, then counsel to the Nixon campaign committee, and discussed a $1-million Liddy proposal that included the use of call girls on a "wired" yacht in Miami to gather information from Democratic officials. The plan also called for the "abduction of radical leaders" who might cause trouble at the Republican national convention. Magruder said that "they would be detained in a place like Mexico and returned to this country at the end of the convention."

But "Mitchell, in his understated way," Magruder said, rejected the idea as an "unacceptable project." On Feb. 4, the four met again in Mitchell's office at the Justice Department, where Liddy presented a $500,000 project. That, too, was rejected, Magruder said.

Following the second meeting, Charles W. Colson, then special counsel to the President, called Magruder and told him "to get off the stick and get the budget approved for Liddy's plan to get information on Democratic Chairman Lawrence O'Brien," Magruder said.

Approval. At a third meeting, held in Key Biscayne, Fla., March 30, 1972, Mitchell "agreed to approve (the Watergate) project," Magruder told the committee. According to Magruder, Mitchell said, "O.K., let's give him (Liddy) $250,000."

"What was the project, specifically?" asked Dash.

"It involved approval for initial entry into the Democratic National Committee headquarters in Washington and, if needed, entry into Democratic presidential contenders' offices," replied Magruder.

"Did Mr. Mitchell's approval include electronic surveillance?" Dash asked.

"Yes," Magruder answered.

Later in the hearing, Sen. Howard H. Baker Jr. (R Conn.) asked Magruder if there was "any doubt" Mitchell had approved the break-in.

"No, sir," Magruder said, adding that it was a "reluctant decision."

"Why reluctant?" Baker probed.

Magruder: "We knew it was illegal and nothing might come of it."

Motivation. Baker pressed Magruder on his own reaction to the espionage plan. "I was not overwhelmed with the program. I had personal problems with Liddy," Magruder replied in his composed manner.

"If you doubted the success, what on earth would it have taken you to decide against the plan?" Baker asked.

"Not much," Magruder said.

Baker then asked Magruder to explain what had motivated him to go along with the proposal. "In the White House, we saw continual violations of the law by anti-war, radical groups," Magruder explained. "There was a feeling of resentment and frustration in trying to deal with these matters on a legal basis." Later, during questioning by Chairman Ervin, Magruder said that activities by the anti-war demonstrators "had caused us to become more callous about our procedures" and that "this atmosphere" pervaded the White House.

"Were you distrubed by the demonstrators?" Ervin asked.

"Yes, we were," Magruder stated.

Coverup. In early June 1972, Magruder said, he received from Liddy two sets of transcripts (on Gemstone stationery) of telephone conversations overheard on the wiretaps installed during the Memorial Day weekend Watergate break-in, a few weeks before the June 17 break-in during which five men were arrested.

"I brought them into Mr. Mitchell's office at the re-election headquarters. He reviewed the documents and agreed with me there was no substance," Magruder said. "Mitchell indicated he was dissatisfied because the materials were worthless for what we paid for."

Magruder also revealed that he told Haldeman's assistant, Strachan, the reports were available but said that when Strachan came to the re-election headquarters to look at them, he too agreed there was little substance in the transcripts.

After the arrests of the Watergate burglars June 17, Magruder said a series of meetings took place in Mitchell's apartment and office to devise a cover-up. "One solution recommended was to destroy the Gemstone file," Magruder said, adding that he later did that. Gemstone was the code word for the surveillance operation.

Magruder said that at one point he volunteered to take the blame for the Watergate entry ("there were some takers on that") but the idea was cast aside, because "if it got to me it would go higher." It was agreed that a believable story was that Liddy had come up with the plan on his own and acted on his own.

"We told that to everyone who was not directly connected with the coverup," Magruder explained. Campaign officials, such as Clark MacGregor, "were completely in the dark," Magruder said. "He was probably glad he was."

In January 1973, when it became obvious the "story would not hold up I went to Haldeman," Magruder said. "It had become scapegoat time, and I thought I'd be the scapegoat," Magruder continued, referring to John Dean, who, he said, "had expressed a lack of memory over the meetings where the (Watergate) plans were discussed."

Daily Chronology

Following is the day-to-day chronology of the week's events:

JUNE 7

(Earlier June 7 events, p. 121)

Haldeman Deposition. A 287-page deposition given by former presidential aide H.R. Haldeman in connection with the Democrats' $6.4-million civil suit against the Nixon re-election committee was made public. The testimony blamed former presidential counsel John W. Dean III for keeping the truth about the Watergate scandal from Nixon, Haldeman and John D. Ehrlichman, the President's chief domestic affairs adviser.

Haldeman Testimony. Haldeman appeared before a House Armed Services subcommittee investigating alleged White House attempts to involve the Central Intelligence Agency (CIA) in a Watergate coverup. Subcommittee Chairman Lucien N. Nedzi (D Mich.) told reporters after the private hearing that Haldeman denied any direct involvement in the 1970 domestic intelligence plan approved and later canceled by the President. *(p. 117)*

Secret Memos. The White House confirmed the authenticity of secret memos on the 1970 domestic intelligence plan of the Nixon administration, published June 7 in *The New York Times.* But deputy press secretary Gerald L. Warren deplored "the seeming impossibility of maintaining the confidentiality of sensitive government documents." Meanwhile, the Senate investigating committee, which had its own copies of the documents, denied leaking them. *(Texts, p. 122)*

Cox vs. Committee. The Senate investigating committee filed a brief in U.S. District Court in Washington, D.C., opposing special prosecutor Archibald Cox's request that the testimony of several key witnesses be taken in closed session or at least without live television and radio coverage.

Krogh Refusal. Egil Krogh Jr., who resigned a White House staff position because of his involvement in the break-in at the office of Daniel Ellsberg's psychiatrist, refused to appear before a Los Angeles grand jury investigating the incident. *(Krogh role, p. 52)*

Humphrey Donor. John L. Loeb, a Wall Street investment banker, was fined $3,000 in federal court in New York City for illegally disguising a $48,000 contribution to the 1972 presidential primary campaign of Sen. Hubert H. Humphrey (D Minn.). Loeb pleaded no contest to charges that he violated the Federal Election Campaign Act of 1971.

JUNE 8

Cox vs. Committee. U.S. District Judge John J. Sirica heard testimony on whether the court should ban all radio and television coverage of the testimony of John W. Dean III and Jeb Stuart Magruder before the Senate investigating committee. Special prosecutor Cox sought the ban, which the committee opposed. *(Box, p. 111)*

ITT Investigation. Attorney General Elliot L. Richardson announced that he was giving special prosecutor Cox authority to investigate the circumstances surrounding the merger of the International Telephone and Telegraph Corporation (ITT) with the Hartford Fire Insurance Company, because "the ITT inquiry has begun to overlap with the Watergate investigation." *(ITT case, 1972 Almanac p. 207)*

Stans Ruling. Judge Lee Gagliardi of U.S. District Court in New York City ruled that former Commerce Secretary Maurice H. Stans could testify before the Senate investigating committee. Stans, who was under indictment in the Vesco case, asked for exemption from testifying on grounds that the publicity would be prejudicial to his case. *(p. 112)*

McCord Trial. Convicted Watergate conspirator James W. McCord Jr. appeared before Judge Sirica to ask for a new trial, arguing that at least one witness at the original trial had committed perjury and that the government had withheld pertinent evidence. Sirica delayed McCord's sentencing, previously set for June 15, indefinitely.

Ehrlichman, Colson Testimony. Former Nixon aides Ehrlichman and Charles W. Colson testified before the Los Angeles grand jury investigating the Ellsberg break-in. Ehrlichman told reporters that until February 1973, he and Haldeman had trusted Dean's information on the Watergate case.

Colson Order. *The New York Times* reported that Charles W. Colson, former special counsel to the President, told federal prosecutors that John Dean ordered Watergate conspirator E. Howard Hunt Jr. to leave the country two days after the June 17, 1972, break-in. Colson reportedly said he strongly criticized the plan, which never was carried out. The Times also said Colson told investigators that Dean said he acted under orders from Ehrlichman.

Anderson Phone. Rep. John B. Anderson (Ill.), chairman of the House Republican Conference, told reporters he suspected that his phone was tapped in April 1969, when he was speaking in the House for an extension of the Voting Rights Act, which then Attorney General John N. Mitchell opposed. "In view of the type of mentality which apparently existed in the Justice Department at that time...it does not seem implausible it happened," Anderson said.

Stans on Payroll. The Finance Committee to Re-elect the President released a summary of a report on its financial transactions, which included the information that former campaign finance director Maurice H. Stans, under indictment in the Vesco case, was drawing a salary from the committee's $4.8-million leftover treasury. The report, submitted to the General Accounting Office (GAO), detailed the committee's expenditures for legal fees for some of its members.

Judge's Ruling, Cox's Response

Chief Judge John J. Sirica of U.S. District Court in Washington, D.C., June 12 denied special prosecutor Archibald Cox's request that the Senate Watergate hearings either be delayed or, if continued, be held without radio and television coverage. The judge granted limited immunity to John W. Dean III and Jeb Stuart Magruder, thus clearing them to appear before the committee.

In the case, Sirica wrote in his 18-page opinion, the court's duties are "purely ministerial, and...any attempted exercise of discretion on its part, either to deny the requests or to grant immunity with conditions, would be an assumption of power not possessed by the court." Later in the opinion, he wrote that "the court lacks completely any power of intervention."

Cox had argued that both Dean and Magruder probably would be indicted by a grand jury and that nationwide television and radio coverage would endanger their right to a fair trial, the validity of future indictments and the ability of the government to prosecute them.

Sirica noted that "there are no indictments, no defendants and no trials. However much the court may sympathize with the Special Prosecutor's wish to avoid serious potential dangers to his mission, it cannot act on suppositions, and the Special Prosecutor himself has been unable to show where any court has so acted. The matter is simply not ripe for judicial action." Because of the court's lack of discretion, wrote Sirica, "to comment would be not only gratuitous but graceless."

Cox Response. The special prosecutor issued a statement in which he said he had decided not to appeal Sirica's order. "Both points have now been fairly heard," he wrote. "I regret the outcome, but to press the legal argument further would risk unduly delaying proceedings and divert attention from our essential tasks."

Noting the common goals of his investigation and the Senate hearings, Cox wrote that he was anxious for cooperation between the two. He suggested that he and Committee Chairman Sam J. Ervin Jr. (D N.C.) or his counsel might meet from time to time to discuss adjustments in the hearings schedule "or other arrangements that might seem necessary in order to minimize any possible danger to holding fair trials."

JUNE 9

Kalmbach Testimony. Nixon's former personal lawyer, Herbert W. Kalmbach, agreed to testify for the prosecution against Haldeman, Ehrlichman and other former White House officials in any criminal trials, *The New York Times* reported. Kalmbach was said to be prepared to state that Ehrlichman officially authorized him to collect cash to be used to pay the Watergate defendants and their attorneys. A May 19 GAO report accused Kalmbach of raising at least $210,000 in cash after the June 17 break-in for distribution to the defendants and their attorneys. *(p. 87)*

Ellsberg Break-in. The Times quoted Chairman Sam J. Ervin Jr. (D N.C.) as saying the Senate Watergate committee would expand its investigation to include the 1971 Ellsberg break-in, the administration's 1970 domestic intelligence plan and its involvement in the ITT case—but only as those incidents related to the June 17 break-in or the 1972 presidential campaign. Ervin's plan reportedly was supported by Democratic members of the committee and by ranking Republican Howard H. Baker Jr. (Tenn.). But Sen. Edward J. Gurney (R Fla.) was said to oppose such an expansion of the committee's investigation.

Democrats Warned. According to a report in *The Washington Post,* a New York private investigator warned Democratic National Chairman Lawrence F. O'Brien before the Watergate break-in that the Nixon campaign was forming a political espionage unit to bug the Democrats.

JUNE 10

Weicker Charge. Sen. Lowell P. Weicker Jr. (R Conn.), a member of the Senate Watergate committee, charged during a television interview in New York that at least one phase of a White House domestic intelligence plan went into effect despite President Nixon's contention that it had been withdrawn because of objections from the late FBI Director J. Edgar Hoover in 1970. *(Background, p. 119)*

Weicker said an internal FBI memorandum showed that Hoover had approved the hiring by the FBI of "student informers" and "potential student informers" to report on certain student activities. The memo was dated Sept. 16, 1970. In his May 22 statement on Watergate, President Nixon contended that the July 1970 proposal "never went into effect" because of Hoover's objections. *(p. 79)*

"It is clear that at least this aspect (of the proposal) was put into effect," Weicker said. He called on Nixon to "stand before the American people and tell them every single fact" about Watergate.

Newsweek Report. *Newsweek* magazine reported that John Dean told unidentified Senate investigators he had "supporting documents and memorandums, no one of which 'convicts' the President, but which taken together suggest a damning pattern." The report also stated that Dean "is said also to have some embarrassing tapes of senior White House officials, though none of Mr. Nixon himself."

Newsweek also reported that Dean made the following allegations:

- Nixon was "personally aware" of campaign gifts of more than $300,000 contributed to his 1972 campaign by the dairy industry, and knew that the funds were "intended to influence the government."
- Some "low-level" White House officials considered a plan to assassinate Panama's military ruler, Gen. Omar Torrijos, because they felt the Panamanian government had been uncooperative in renegotiating the Panama Canal treaty and because they suspected that a number of important Panamanian officials had been involved in illicit heroin trafficking. One of the conspirators convicted in the Watergate case, E. Howard Hunt Jr., had a team operating in Mexico "before the mission was aborted," Newsweek reported.
- In an effort "to justify its own misuse of the FBI," the White House ordered a secret report prepared on similar activity in past administrations.

Morton and Bush. Interior Secretary Rogers C.B. Morton, interviewed on CBS News' "Face the Nation," said he opposed continuation of the Senate Watergate hearings "because I think there's too big a tendency there to try people in a forum which is not designed for that." But Republican National Committee Chairman George Bush, interviewed on NBC's "Meet the Press," disagreed; "the more information out on this," he said, "the better."

JUNE 11

Agnew Speech. Vice President Agnew, addressing the National Association of Attorneys General at St. Louis, Mo., criticized the Senate Watergate hearings as a "beauty contest" with "Perry Masonish impact." The select committee, he said, "can hardly hope to find the truth and can hardly fail to muddy the waters of justice beyond redemption." *(Box, p. 140)*

Philippine Money. In its June quarterly report filed with the GAO, the finance committee of the Nixon re-election campaign disclosed a payment of $30,000 in cash from the Philippine sugar industry to help pay for the Watergate coverup. According to *The Washington Star-News,* the money was sought by Herbert W. Kalmbach, Nixon's former personal attorney and campaign fund-raiser, for an "urgent White House project."

The money later was returned when the recipients came to believe it had been contributed illegally. Payments to Watergate defendants and their attorneys began 12 days after the burglary in June 1972. The report did not indicate when the Philippine money was returned to its donor. The Star-News identified the apparent donor as Ramon Nolan, a Philippine sugar planter and lobbyist for his country's sugar industry.

Ellsberg Burglary. John Ehrlichman reportedly knew of in advance, and approved, the September 1971 break-in at the office of Pentagon Papers defendant Daniel Ellsberg's former psychiatrist. The report appeared in the Star-News; it was attributed to informed sources quoting from grand jury testimony by a White House aide.

The aide was David Young, a former member of the White House "plumbers," or special investigations unit, that was responsible for the burglary. His statements contradicted those of Ehrlichman, who had told the FBI he did not know about the burglary until after it had taken place.

"I don't know that he testified that way," Ehrlichman was quoted as telling the Star-News when he was informed of the reported testimony. He declined further comment.

Gray Testimony. L. Patrick Gray III, former acting director of the FBI, agreed to testify without immunity in any Watergate criminal trials about his dealings with administration officials after the break-in at Democratic headquarters, *The New York Times* reported.

Dean Testimony. Attorneys for John Dean, the former White House counsel, filed a motion in U.S. District Court in Washington to quash a subpoena requiring Dean to testify before the Watergate grand jury. At a hearing on the motion, federal prosecutors in the case made public a letter they had written to Dean on May 22.

In the letter, the government lawyers offered Dean the opportunity to plead guilty to one count of conspiracy if he would tell the grand jury everything he knew about Watergate. Evidence established, the letter said, "that you were at the center of a very profound kind of corruption. Involved was your exploitation of a position of trust in order to foster a pervasive scheme to obstruct justice."

A lawyer for Dean, Charles N. Shaffer, called the letter "the most self-serving I have ever read. That letter was written by three people who hear the Senate clamoring for a new prosecution team.... It's a letter to clean skirts. I laughed when I read it."

Ziegler Reversal. Presidential press secretary Ronald L. Ziegler admitted that he had erred in telling reporters that Nixon had phoned White House counsel Dean on March 26 to discuss a newspaper report that Dean had prior knowledge of the Watergate break-in. At a briefing that day, Ziegler denied the allegations about Dean and said the President had "absolute, total confidence in Mr. Dean in this regard."

Ziegler, responding to a *Newsweek* magazine report that Dean had labeled Ziegler's report of the phone call a "flat-out lie," admitted that staff chief Haldeman, not Nixon, had called Dean on March 26. The mistake was his own and not the President's, Ziegler said.

JUNE 12

Senate Hearings. Maurice H. Stans, former secretary of commerce and chief Nixon fund-raiser in 1972, testified before the Senate Watergate committee that he had nothing to do with the scandal. Any blame, he said, should be placed on the re-election committee and not on his finance committee. *(Details, p. 132; text of Stans statement, p. 141)*

Court Rulings. Judge Sirica of U.S. District Court in Washington granted the Senate committee's request for partial immunity for Dean and for Jeb Magruder. The immunity, known as "use immunity," meant that nothing they said in testimony before the committee could be used against them in a criminal prosecution. Sirica ruled that he had no discretion to do anything else. *(Box, p. 138)*

The judge denied Dean's motion to quash a subpoena requiring him to testify before a grand jury. Dean subsequently made a brief appearance before the jury, reportedly invoking the Fifth Amendment to protect him from self-incrimination.

Sirica also denied the motion of special prosecutor Archibald Cox to prevent television and radio coverage of key witnesses testifying at the Senate hearings. Cox had argued that the publicity would interfere with judicial proceedings. *(p. 111)*

Memo on Break-in. *The Washington Post* reported that a memo had notified former White House aide John D. Ehrlichman of plans to burglarize the office of Pentagon Papers defendant Daniel Ellsberg's psychiatrist before the burglary occurred in September 1971. Ehrlichman had told the FBI on April 27 that he had no advance knowledge of the burglary.

Quoting government sources, the Post reported that the memo was sent to Ehrlichman by two former White House aides, David Young and Egil (Bud) Krogh Jr. Young reportedly was prepared to testify that Ehrlichman had approved the burglary.

Vesco Indictment. The Post reported that financier Robert L. Vesco had been indicted secretly by a federal grand jury in New York City the previous week on charges of illegal use of the telegraph in connection with his $250,000 contribution to the Nixon campaign in 1972. Vesco and others had been indicted on other charges May 10. *(p. 56)*

Impeachment Discussion. Several representatives took the floor of the House for a 90-minute discussion of whether there were grounds to impeach Nixon. *(Earlier discussion attempt, p. 115)*

JUNE 13

Senate Hearings. Stans testified for a full day before the Senate select committee, continuing to proclaim his innocence of involvement in the Watergate scandal. He told the committee that financial records had been destroyed on orders from G. Gordon Liddy. Stans was subjected to some of the roughest questioning of the hearings to date, leading to a sharp exchange between Chairman Ervin and Sen. Edward J. Gurney (R Fla.). *(Details, p. 135)*

GAO Disagreement. In an interview with *The Washington Post,* Philip S. Hughes, director of the GAO Office of Federal Elections, disagreed with some of the June 12 Senate testimony of Stans. He questioned the legality of the Nixon finance committee's accounting for its funds. In response to Stans' contention that the finance committee had filed all its reports in compliance with the new law, Hughes said: "All the reports weren't complete or accurate."

Vesco Contribution. In a related development, the Justice Department filed a brief in U.S. District Court in Washington urging conviction of the Nixon re-election committee for concealing a $200,000 contribution from financier Robert L. Vesco. The brief was filed in response to one filed by the committee two weeks earlier, pleading not guilty.

"To this first challenge to the 1971 Federal Election Campaign Act, this court should respond with vigor and firmness...that Congress in enacting it intended that the era of reporting loopholes be finally and forever put to rest," the Justice Department brief said.

Maryland Indictment. A grand jury in Anne Arundel County, Maryland, indicted a Maryland Republican on four counts of violating a state election law by manipulating $50,000 in Nixon re-election funds in connection with a May 1972 dinner honoring Vice President Agnew. The person indicted was not named.

Ellsberg Break-in. John Ehrlichman, appearing in closed session before the House Armed Services sub-

Agnew's Watergate Speech

Before a friendly audience of lawyers, Vice President Agnew June 11 attacked the Senate Watergate hearings as lacking a "rigorous set of procedural safeguards" such as would be provided in a judicial proceeding. "Lacking such safeguards," said Agnew, "the committee, I am sad to say, can hardly hope to find the truth and can hardly fail to muddy the waters of justice beyond redemption." He spoke to the National Association of Attorneys General at St. Louis, Mo.

Agnew was especially critical of the effects of television on the hearings. "There is no escaping the fact that the hearings have a Perry Masonish impact," he said. "The indefatigable camera will paint both heroes and villains in lurid and indelible colors before the public's very eyes in the course of these proceedings. This is essentially what is known in politics as a 'beauty contest,' and the attractiveness and presence of the participants may be more important than the content of the testimony."

Agnew's gloomy conclusion: "There is no question whatever that some men, despite their innocence, will be ruined by all this, even though I am sure that the Senate intended nothing of the kind when it commissioned this investigation." Guilty persons, on the other hand, may go free in court trials as a result of prejudicial publicity in the hearings, he said. He listed "seven missing safeguards" of legal rules of fair play that he claimed are missing from the committee's procedures:

- Cross-examination.
- Representation by legal counsel. (Witnesses have lawyers beside them but answer committee members' question themselves.)
- Rebuttal of testimony.
- Introduction of evidence to impeach an accuser's credibility.
- Prohibition of the introduction of hearsay evidence.
- Prohibition of testimony that includes inferences, impressions and speculations.
- Prohibition against cameras.

committee, said he did not remember authorizing the burglary of the office of Daniel Ellsberg's former psychiatrist in September 1971. "He could not categorically state his recollections," said Subcommittee Chairman Lucien N. Nedzi (D Mich.) after the meeting. Ehrlichman declined comment.

JUNE 14

Senate Hearings. Jeb Magruder, testifying before the Senate investigating committee, directly contradicted the testimony of Stans on the preceding two days. Magruder, a Washington consultant since leaving his job with the Commerce Department, said the former commerce secretary had been fully briefed on the Watergate burglary by John Mitchell, then the campaign director, a week after the break-in. Magruder admitted his complicity but denied that Nixon was involved. *(Details, p. 132)*

More Wiretaps. Another Post story reported that, for at least several months in 1971, the White House special investigations unit, known as the "plumbers," received information from previously undisclosed wiretaps on the phones of Daniel Ellsberg and two former *New York Times* reporters, Neil Sheehan and Tad Szulc.

Publicity Opposition. A Gallup Poll published June 4 (and conducted among 1,552 adults June 1-4) found that 44 per cent of those interviewed felt there had been too much media coverage of the Watergate affair. Another 38 per cent said the coverage had been about right, and 11 per cent said it had been too little. Seven per cent had no opinion. *(Other poll results, box, p. 136)*

Agnew Loyalty. In an interview published in *The Washington Star-News,* Vice President Agnew said he had "undiminished confidence" that Nixon had not been involved either in the Watergate bugging or in its coverup. His confidence, he admitted, was based on faith, not on firm knowledge.

"If I'm proven wrong, I'm going to admit I'm wrong," Agnew told the newspaper. "I'm not going to fly in the face of evidence. But if I'm right, I'd like to have the chance to be right, too."

Halperin Suit. Morton H. Halperin, a former consultant to the National Security Council, filed suit in U.S. District Court in Washington for the bugging of his telephone from 1969 to 1971 for as long as 25 months. Halperin, a senior fellow at the Brookings Institution, asked $100 a day in damages for each day of the tap, the amount specified as the fine for illegal wiretapping in the 1968 Omnibus Crime Control and Safe Streets Act.

Named as defendants in the suit were Henry A. Kissinger, the President's national security adviser; former White House aides H.R. Haldeman and John D. Ehrlichman; Alexander Haig, former Kissinger deputy and now White House chief of staff; John Mitchell; William C. Sullivan, former assistant to the late FBI Director J. Edgar Hoover; William D. Ruckelshaus, acting FBI director; the Chesapeake and Potomac Telephone Company, and unnamed agents of the FBI and other government agencies.

U.S. District Judge W. Matthew Byrne Jr. of Los Angeles revealed the tap on May 10 as a result of a memo he had received from Ruckelshaus. The acting FBI director discussed it further at a news conference May 14. *(Text of statement, p. 69)*

STANS STATEMENT

Following is the opening statement made by Maurice H. Stans, chairman of the Finance Committee to Re-elect the President, at hearings of the Senate Watergate committee June 12:

Mr. Chairman and members of the committee:

At the outset, may I state that I am very sorry that the circumstances of my appearance have made it necessary for my counsel to raise legal points in order to protect my right of fair trial in New York. I personally would have much preferred it if I had been able to testify without any need to protect myself in the pending criminal action, in which I feel that in the setting of a fair and impartial trial I would be exonerated.

However, I want to assure you now that I will do my very best to be helpful to the committee in my testimony.

Less than two years ago, one of the proudest moments of my experience occurred here on the Senate side of the Capitol, as I approached the end of my service as secretary of commerce.

Some of you and many of your colleagues on the Senate Commerce Committee were extremely generous in a public hearing in praise of my efforts over a three-year period as head of the Department of Commerce—and some of the Democratic senators even wished me success in my new undertaking as fund-raiser—but not too much success!

All of those comments remain highly valued to me now, as much as any reward of the many years I spent in public service in two administrations.

I would like my appearance here today to be another service in the public interest. The circumstances that bring us together are extremely regrettable, but I still share a strong mutual concern with you—in this case establishing the facts and the truth of these matters of national interest.

For that reason, as you know, I have cooperated with your staff prior to my appearance here today, just as I intend to do fully with the committee here now. My sense of integrity compels me to do so.

In the past, I have refrained from answering in a piecemeal fashion various questions which have been raised by the media concerning the presidential campaign and other related matters. For that I have been highly criticized. But I felt that it was better if I could answer these questions before an appropriate forum in the setting and perspective of the over-all situation. This would enable me to give a complete picture rather than a piecemeal response, and this is what I hope to do today, to the extent I am able. This may help resolve some questions as to which there has been a minimum of understanding and much erroneous public information.

COOPERATION

Next, let me say that I have cooperated fully with every official agency that has sought information from me. I have met twice with the staff of this committee, once with the staff of the House Banking and Currency Committee, have had three meetings with the FBI and at least six with the General Accounting Office, have given a deposition to the assistant United States attorney in Washington and have met with the assistant United States attorney in New York and twice testified before a New York grand jury. All of this has been voluntary. I have also testified several times by deposition in civil suits and once in a Florida criminal case.

Also, during all the investigations which have commenced since June 17, 1972, I have instructed all finance committee personnel to cooperate fully and candidly. The reported testimony of Hugh Sloan Jr., Paul Barrick, Judy Hoback, Evelyn Hyde and Arden Chambers is evidence that this is being done. I am convinced that none of these persons had a part in Watergate or subsequent events. However, as will come out, Mr. Sloan's recollections and mine may differ in a few respects. This is obviously attributable to the passage of time, the pressures of events at the time and subjective recall. Just as he has given you his best recollection, I will give you mine on the various financial matters. On the major issue, that of involvement in the Watergate matter, I am satisfied that he is completely innocent.

It is my understanding that the committee is probing three matters on which it might assume that I have some knowledge—the espionage charges, including the Watergate bugging, and the coverup that allegedly followed; the sabotage charges, including the Segretti operation; and the handling of campaign finances. On these three matters I would like to state:

(1) I had no knowledge of the Watergate break-in or any other espionage efforts before I read about them in the press, or of the efforts to cover up after the event.

(2) I had no knowledge of any sabotage program to disrupt the campaign by Segretti or anyone else.

(3) To the best of my knowledge, there were no intentional violations of the laws relating to campaign financing by the finance committees for which I had responsibility. Because of the complexity of the new law that became effective in the course of the campaign, and the vast amount of work that had to be done, there may have been some unintended technical violations by the committee.

FOUR DISTINCTIONS

What I want particularly to stress in this opening statement is the fact that this committee cannot effectively evaluate the work of the finance committee or my own activities without having in mind four fundamental distinctions:

(1) The distinction between the functions and activities of the campaign committee and the functions and activities of the finance committee.

(2) The distinction between the election financing law which expired on April 6, 1972, and the new election financing law which was effective on April 7, 1972.

(3) Within the finance committee, the distinction between the functions and activities of the chairman and the functions and activities of the treasurer.

(4) The activities of the finance committee before I joined it on Feb. 15, 1972, and the activities of that committee after Feb. 15, 1972.

By the campaign committee I mean, of course, the Committee for the Re-election of the President. **By the finance committee I mean the Finance Committee for the Re-election of the President and its predecessors up to April 6, 1972, and the Finance Committee to Re-elect the President beginning April** 7, 1972 (together with their associated committees in each time frame).

During the time of my affiliation with the finance committee as its chairman, the treasurer was Hugh Sloan Jr., until July 15, 1972, and thereafter the treasurer was Paul E. Barrick. I shall refer to the treasurer as though it were the same individual, letting the time period identify which of these persons it relates to.

CAMPAIGN COMMITTEE AND FINANCE COMMITTEE

The campaign committee had all of the responsibility for the planning of the campaign, the development of its strategy and the execution of its tactics. The questions of how many people to employ, the efforts to be expended in each state, the determination of the relative use of direct mail, personal solicitation and media advertising, the kinds of appeals to voters, and the entire gamut of the political effort was developed, organized, managed and conducted by the campaign committee. In effect, their decisions fixed the amount the campaign would cost.

The finance committee had no part in any of these basic decisions. The role of the finance committee was directed toward a single objective—to raise enough money to pay the bills. The finance committee had nothing to say about which bills to incur. Under the arrangements in effect, the finance committee paid any bill or made any payment which bore the approval of an appropriate official of the campaign committee.

The campaign committee was supposed to see that the amounts it okayed were within the limits of an approved budget. It turned out that the controls did not work as they were intended, and spending overran the budget by more than $8-million. Perhaps, more likely, $10-million.

In practical terms, the two committees operated in watertight compartments. They were physically separated on different floors. The campaign committee ran the campaign and created the debts; the finance committee raised the money and paid the bills.

There was only one forum for the exchange of opinions with respect to campaign spending, and that was the budget committee. The budget committee consisted of three officials of the campaign committee and three officials of the finance committee. Formal meetings of the budget committee with recorded minutes did not take place until after Labor Day, 1972. A number of informal meetings on budget matters were held before that, but most of those centered on the over-all amount of funding at the national and state levels.

The meetings of the budget committee were not in my opinion very effective. Each one opened by me with a general statement of the current cash position and the expectations of future contributions, which until the last few days of the campaign never equaled the expended spending. I pressed continuously for reductions in over-all spending, but the actual trend was constantly upward. At times the meetings became bitter, and I walked out of one meeting at which I thought there was no understanding of the difficulties of fund-raising on the part of those who were doing the spending. The budget grew to $40-million, then $43-million, and ended up in excess of $48-million. Our latest accounting, which is not completed, shows it could be in excess of $50-million. A late surge of contributions, as a result of the effective organization we had built across the country, made it possible for us to end up with a surplus.

OLD LAW AND NEW LAW

Prior to April 7, 1972, the controlling law on candidates for federal office was the Corrupt Practices Act enacted in 1925. This act made a major distinction between fund-raising for a candidate to secure a *nomination* (through primaries or conventions) and fund-raising in a general *election.* There was no reporting required of any kind on contributions and expenditures to secure a nomination. There was a requirement that contributions and expenditures in a general election be reported to the clerk of the House.

The Federal Election Campaign Act of 1971, which became effective April 7, 1972, changed that by eliminating entirely the distinction between a campaign for nomination and a campaign for election. It required that all contributions and expenditures in any political campaign be reported. Although the bill was signed by the President on Feb. 7, it did not become effective until April 7, because the Congress specifically allowed 60 extra days for operation under the old law.

The distinction between election financing and nomination financing had existed for almost 50 years, and countless candidates for the presidency, the Senate and the House of Representatives had observed the requirements of the one and the exemption of the other.

In 1972, candidates for such offices in both political parties formed finance committees that did not have to publish or file their transactions prior to April 7, and organized new reporting committees after that date. In the President's campaign, a **Finance Committee for the Re-election of the President had been** created solely to raise funds for the *renomination,* and this committee terminated its activities on April 6; it was not under the law required to file reports. A new Finance Committee to Re-elect the President was created to operate beginning April 7, and it has filed all public reports required by the new law.

We readily acknowledge that our fund-raising operated under the old law until April 7, 1972. We used the 60-day period allowed by Congress. Under this law, the fact that contributions need not be reported gave the committee and its contributors a right of confidentiality.

The issue of confidentiality versus disclosure of such information has never been fairly presented to the public. It has been made to appear that the committee engaged in secret, thereby concealed and suspect, transactions which would not have occurred had they been required to be disclosed. That is not true. The transactions were valid and proper, and the question of whether they were to be reported was a question of law that involved important rights of individuals.

The committee's position all along has been that non-disclosure created no advantage to it, but that privacy was a right of the contributor which the committee could not properly waive. The right to live without undue intrusion is a long-respected benefit of the American system. Therefore, the committee did not release the names of contributors before April 7. It has never objected to any contributor disclosing his contribution. And on one occasion, just before the election, the committee released a list of such contributors (up to March 9, 1972) only after consulting with those making the larger gifts.

Much has been made of the fact that a few records of the committee before April 7 were destroyed. The fact is that the very large part of such records has been preserved, and the committee believes that the others can be reconstructed if needed. But the important point is that there was no illegal act in throwing away any of these records, and even those that were retained could have been disposed of. Not only was there no statutory requirement that records of transactions before April 7 be preserved; it was not even necessary that any recordings be made at all. At least, that's what our lawyers told us at the time, and that corresponded with what we had been told in the 1968 campaign.

The Finance Committee to Re-elect the President undertook to observe strictly all the provisions of the new law, beginning April 7, and also urged its state committees to do likewise. Systems and controls were developed to insure that would be the case. Notwithstanding this, there have been a few instances in which the committee has been cited by the General Accounting Office and the Department of Justice for failure to report transactions which occurred after April 7. The committee believes that it has valid explanations for this small number of technical violations—and in at least one case, the Department of Justice has ruled in favor of the committee—and that considering the hundreds of thousands of contributions received and bills paid, its record of operation under a new and highly complex law should be commended rather than criticized.

CHAIRMAN AND TREASURER

As chairman of the committee, I had a personal responsibility for over-all coordination of its activities. The principal vehicle in this respect was a daily staff meeting attended by the treasurer, the controller, the general counsel and several vice chairmen working in Washington.

But without doubt, my prime personal responsibility was to raise the money required to finance the campaign, and that occupied almost all of my time and attention. Between Feb. 15 and Nov. 7, 1972, I visited approximately 45 cities in 32 states to meet with fund-raising committees, groups of potential contributors, and individual potential contributors. I also met with individuals and groups in Washington and made many hundreds of phone calls to fund-raisers and contributors. And this was not a campaign financed by a few large contributors. To insure participation by hundreds of thousands of individuals, I directed a direct mail program that reached 30 million homes and a group fund-raising plan to reach people at their places of employment. These took a great deal of time.

As chairman of the committee, I had no responsibility in connection with the internal handling of funds, banking, recording, accounting and reporting. I did not sign checks. I did not expend cash from the treasurer's cash fund. It was my regular practice when I accepted contributions for the committee to turn them over to the treasurer promptly. I did not have relationships with the banks. I did not make entries in the books or even see the books. And I did not prepare the public reports and did not review them except to scan their summary pages.

These were all the responsibility of the treasurer, not only within the working format of our committee, but also under the provisions of the Federal Election Campaign Act. His was the responsibility for all day-to-day internal operations, and generally I consulted with him only when he came to me for guidance on a specific problem, which was on a limited number of occasions.

PRE-FEB. 15 AND POST-FEB. 15

When I joined the committee on Feb. 15, a considerable number of activities were under way, and a number of people were in place. Fund-raising and campaign activities had been engaged in for almost a year. Programs had been planned or committed by the campaign people, funds had been collected and disbursed, committees had been formed and terminated and some well-publicized transactions had already occurred.

Patterns of payment to Herbert Porter and Gordon Liddy were a practice. Magruder had blanket authority to direct payments. Kalmbach had turned over to the committee the funds in his possession. But no steps had been taken to comply with the new law, and the procedures generally were inadequate to cope with the volume of work sure to come.

When I joined the committee, the bank balance was $3-million, and there was still $30-million or $40-million or more to be raised. I did not review what had happened before, but began to work with the problem at hand. I did not learn about many of the earlier transactions until a much later time. From Feb. 15 to April 7, I had 45 working days, and 13 of these were spent outside Washington. It was not a period in which I could spend time on detail. I trusted the people already in the committee organization and relied heavily on the treasurer, because of his previous experience in 1968 and 1971. I was after contributions.

CONCLUSION

What I would like to emerge from all of this information are a few simple conclusions:

(1) The finance committee played no part in the strategy or the tactics of the campaign. If they went wrong, it was the fault of the campaign committee. Its only responsibility was to raise enough money to pay the costs that were incurred by the campaign committee.

(2) The finance committees in existence prior to April 7, 1972, operated under legal advice that their transactions need not be recorded or reported, as a matter of law.

(3) Within the finance committee, the chairman's basic job was to raise the money, and the treasurer's basic job was to account for it and disburse it.

(4) The responsibility of raising the largest amount ever spent in a political campaign obviously put massive pressure on the finance committee, particularly those engaged in fund-raising. In my own case, too, the stress was multiplied manyfold by the serious illness of my wife, beginning Aug. 9 and continuing into early 1973.

I repeat to you that I had no advance knowledge of the Watergate affair and no knowledge of any efforts that may have been made to cover it up, nor do I know about any other espionage or sabotage activities on the part of the campaign committee. I can assure the committee that I have made an honest and careful effort to abide by the spirit and intent of the election laws. √

COLSON DISCLAIMS EFFORT TO INFLUENCE SEC APPOINTMENT

Hearings—House Interstate and Foreign Commerce subcommittee June 14 investigating independence of the Securities and Exchange Commission.

Charles W. Colson, former special counsel to the President now in private law practice, told a House investigations subcommittee June 14 that he had never acted on a memo urging his firm to try to influence the appointment of a new general counsel of the Securities and Exchange Commission (SEC).

Colson also told the House Interstate and Foreign Commerce Special Subcommittee on Investigations that he had not been directly involved in negotiations between International Telephone and Telegraph Corp. (ITT) and the Justice Department over settlement of an antitrust suit. *(1972 Almanac p. 207)*

However, Colson did acknowledge that he had sent E. Howard Hunt, one of the men convicted for the burglary of the Democratic National Committee Watergate headquarters, to Denver in March 1972 to interview ITT lobbyist Dita Beard about the authenticity of the memo she allegedly wrote linking promises of ITT financial aid for the 1972 Republican National Convention to a favorable settlement of the ITT antitrust case.

Internal Memo. The hearing was called to investigate whether Colson and two law partners, Charles H. Morin and Henry C. Cashen, improperly tried to influence the selection of an SEC general counsel. In an internal memo written April 19, 1973, by Morin to Colson and Cashen, Morin suggested that the firm "lean on" then SEC Chairman G. Bradford Cook to appoint King Mallory, acting SEC executive director, as general counsel.

In his memo, Morin said Cook "ought to be reminded of how he got the job and how he almost did not get the job. This is one of the chips we really should pick up, because it is a key job in the commission and one of extreme importance to us in representing our clients."

Morin suggested that John D. Ehrlichman, then White House domestic affairs adviser; his assistant, Kenneth Cole, or Jerry Jones, a White House aide responsible for recruiting personnel, might be contacted in order to put White House influence behind the Mallory suggestion.

Morin, who appeared with Colson before the subcommittee, said that the memorandum was "a silly document" dictated "off the top of my head." Admitting that the choice of language was unfortunate, Morin said he had no intention of placing a general counsel at SEC "who would do my bidding," but rather sought to recommend a man who he thought was highly qualified to fill the post. (Mallory was not appointed to the position.)

Colson said that neither he nor Cashen took any action on the memo. Colson did admit writing a note to Cashen on the top of his copy of the memo which read: "HCC, Can you handle this—I'll call Cook if necessary but I think Jerry Jones can lock this one for us. CWC."

ITT Settlement. Colson was questioned extensively about several interoffice memos and letters written by ITT officials to administration figures concerning the antitrust suit. Any mention of his name in those memos, Colson said, stemmed from a meeting he had attended with Ehrlichman, ITT President Harold S. Geneen and William R. Merriam, ITT vice president in charge of the Washington office on Aug. 4, 1970.

Colson maintained that the meeting was simply a discussion of administration policy on antitrust cases, not dealing with specific points in the ITT case. Harley O. Staggers (D W.Va.), chairman of the subcommittee and the full committee, called the repeated references to Colson in the memos "damaging."

Beard Visit. The Beard memo, supposedly written in June 1971, and released by columnist Jack Anderson Feb. 29, 1972, led to the reopening of 1972 hearings on the confirmation of Richard G. Kleindienst as attorney general.

Colson said that during the Kleindienst hearings he had agreed that Hunt should go to Denver where Beard was reportedly recuperating from a heart attack to determine "whether it was an authentic memo. The case against Kleindienst turned on the language in the memo," Colson said. "It became critical for the administration to know whether it was Beard's memo or a forger." *The Washington Post* June 15 reported that sources said Colson had received at least five messages from Hunt between June 1972 and March 1973 demanding money and clemency for his role in the Watergate affair. Colson, according to the Post sources, taped one of the conversations with Hunt, apparently in order to protect his own interests, and later supplied the tape to investigators. ✓

CAMPAIGN REFORM

The tocsin of Watergate sounded throughout two days of hearings on two bills that would study and strengthen the campaign reforms instituted by the 1971 Federal Election Campaign Act, which took effect May 7, 1972.

"These hearings are not due to the Watergate affair, as I'm sure this committee is aware, but to the failure to enact sufficient legislation to police campaign spending practices," Sen. Hugh Scott (R Pa.) told the Senate Subcommittee on Privileges and Elections during the first day of hearings, June 5.

Subcommittee Chairman Claiborne Pell (D R.I.), however, said he was following the Senate Watergate hearings closely "for any helpful suggestions and recommendations that might emerge on improvement of our election laws."

On the second day of hearings he angrily accused the administration of such pre-occupation with the Watergate affair that it was failing to respond to congressional inquiries on legislative matters.

On the first day of hearings, Sen. Edward M. Kennedy (D Mass.) told the subcommittee he saw Watergate "as more an opportunity than a challenge for the country."

"If we learn the lessons that are already beginning to emerge, we can use this present crisis as an unprecedented opportunity to repair the machinery of all our institutions of government," he said.

WATERGATE: ENTER BREZHNEV, EXIT SENATE HEARINGS

Soviet Communist Leader Leonid I. Brezhnev spent the week ended June 23 in summit conferences with President Nixon. His visit led to the postponement of televised hearings before the Senate Select Committee on Presidential Campaign Activities.

The committee had been scheduled to hear testimony from John W. Dean III, the former White House counsel, starting on June 19. But the majority and minority leaders of the Senate wrote a letter June 18 to Committee Chairman Sam J. Ervin Jr. (D N.C.), suggesting the postponement. *(Box, this page)*

With only one dissenting vote, that of Sen. Lowell P. Weicker Jr. (R Conn.), the committee agreed to delay Dean's appearance for a week. He was scheduled to begin testifying on June 25.

Leaks on Leaks. The absence of committee hearings seemed to have little influence on damming the flood of information that gushed from anonymous sources onto newspapers and television screens. Dean was expected to be one of the witnesses most damaging to the Nixon administration because of his charges of White House involvement in the Watergate and its coverup.

The administration was interested in destroying Dean's credibility as a witness. The result of the clash was the release to the press, by both sides, of secret documents intended to buttress one side or the other.

Dean met privately with the committee on June 16 as a preliminary to his public testimony. Within a few days, unnamed sources had released not only a summary of Dean's statements to the committee, but a White House log of his conversations with the President early in the year. "This is not just a bit of a leak," the release of the committee summary prompted one senator to say. "This is a hemorrhage."

All the leakage threatened to interfere with committee procedures. On June 19, one of Dean's lawyers refused to allow his client to make any more statements at closed sessions of the committee. On June 21, lawyers for former Attorney General John N. Mitchell reported they had temporarily prevented the committee from hearing Mitchell's testimony in private. Mitchell had asked to be excused from testifying at the public hearings; he asked that he not be required to appear privately until the committee had decided on his initial request.

"I know of no way to stop men from talking," said Chairman Ervin. "The only way men who have responsibility for keeping secrets can do so is by exercising will power, and if they refrain from using will power, then no one can force them to do so."

Summary Contents. According to the summary of Dean's closed-door testimony, he implicated Nixon and his top aides in the Watergate coverup. He charged Nixon with trying to stop tax audits on his friends and with scheming for post-election retribution against unfriendly reporters. He talked about a blackmail threat by conspirator E. Howard Hunt against the White House as a payoff for Hunt's silence.

Mansfield-Scott Letter

Following is the text of a letter written June 18 by Senate Democratic Leader Mike Mansfield (Mont.) and Senate Republican Leader Hugh Scott (Pa.) to Sam J. Ervin Jr., chairman of the Senate select committee investigating the Watergate:

We have been discussing the fact that the hearings of the Select Committee on Presidential Campaign Activities and the official visit of Secretary General Leonid I. Brezhnev are both occurring during the same week.

After giving consideration to this duality of events, recognizing the importance of each, we have come to the conclusion that it is a part of our responsibility as the joint leaders of the United States Senate to request, most regretfully, that the Select Committee postpone its hearings until the conclusion of the state visit to this country by Secretary General Leonid Brezhnev.

It is not an easy decision for us to make because both the hearings and the visit are being conducted with the best interests of the country in mind, but it is our considered judgment that a delay of one week would not jeopardize the hearings and that one week might give President Nixon and Mr. Brezhnev the opportunity to reconcile differences, arrive at mutual agreements, and in the field of foreign policy, be able to achieve results which would be beneficial not only to our two countries but, hopefully, to all mankind.

We would appreciate your consideration of this request and as early a response as possible.

Dean's statements were in conflict with the White House log. According to the log made public June 21, Dean did not tell Nixon his theory of what had happened in the Watergate affair until March 21. Dean had said the President knew about the matter earlier.

It was disclosed June 19 that Dean had borrowed $4,850—later repaid—from campaign funds to pay for his wedding and honeymoon in 1972. And, it was reported, he kept another $14,000 in leftover campaign money, which he put in a special trust fund after Nixon fired him on April 30.

Hunt Payoff. Sources close to the Watergate case were quoted as telling *The New York Times* June 21 that a final cash payment of $72,000 had been made in mid-March to E. Howard Hunt Jr. after he had threatened to tell all he knew about White House operations against Daniel Ellsberg in 1971.

The threat reportedly was made to John D. Ehrlichman, then the President's chief domestic affairs adviser. Hunt and another Watergate conspirator, G. Gordon Liddy, were involved in a burglary of the office of Ellsberg's former psychiatrist in September 1971.

Daily Chronology

Following is a day-to-day chronology of the week's events:

JUNE 14

(Earlier June 14 events, p. 141)

Finance Records. Senate Watergate Committee Chairman Sam J. Ervin Jr. (D N.C.) signed a subpoena requesting the campaign finance records of five 1972 Democratic presidential candidates—George McGovern, Edmund S. Muskie, Hubert H. Humphrey, Henry M. Jackson and George C. Wallace. Ervin's action came in response to a suggestion by Sen. Howard H. Baker (R Tenn.), vice chairman of the committee, that the panel investigate Democratic as well as Republican finances to get an over-all view of 1972 campaign spending. *(p. 135)*

JUNE 15

Haldeman Denial. John J. Wilson, lawyer for former White House aide H. R. Haldeman, denied that Haldeman had learned of the Watergate coverup in January 1973, as Jeb Stuart Magruder had testified the previous day. Magruder, former deputy director of the Nixon re-election committee, told the Senate Watergate committee June 14 that he went to Haldeman in January, before testifying at the Watergate trial, and "went through a monologue on what had occurred," out of fear that he would become a "scapegoat" in the affair. *(p. 136)*

According to Wilson, an appointment log kept by Haldeman's secretary showed that the two men did not meet in 1973 until Feb. 14, when their discussion was limited to the possibility of a government job for Magruder. Magruder also told the committee he assumed Haldeman knew of the planned bugging operation before June 17, 1972, because he had sent reports on the plan to one of Haldeman's assistants, Gordon C. Strachan.

In a sworn deposition taken in a Watergate civil suit, Haldeman had denied any prior knowledge of the break-in. *(p. 113)*

Cox Inquiry. Special prosecutor Archibald Cox's Watergate investigating team was planning to "look into everything" connected with the scandal—including aspects of the case not yet mentioned—according to James Vorenberg, one of the top prosecutors under Cox. "There are possible lines of inquiry other than those which are being explored," he told newsmen.

Vorenberg listed a number of related incidents the prosecution was preparing to investigate, including the Watergate burglary, ITT influence on the campaign, the Vesco case, the Ellsberg burglary, the alleged campaign sabotage efforts of Donald H. Segretti and the general subject of campaign contributions. On June 9, Sen. Ervin had been quoted as saying the Watergate committee would broaden its investigation to include some of those incidents. *(p. 138)*

'Sedan Chair' Uncovered

One of the more colorful but obscure figures of the Senate Watergate hearings, a person known only as "Sedan Chair 2," was identified June 21 by *The St. Louis Post-Dispatch.*

At the June 5 hearing, Robert Reisner, a former employee of the Committee for the Re-election of the President, described "Sedan Chair" as a Republican undercover agent working in the campaign of Sen. Hubert H. Humphrey (Minn.), a candidate for the Democratic presidential nomination. Reisner told the Senate investigating committee that "Sedan Chair" had been paid $1,000 a month for six to nine months out of a petty cash fund. *(p. 114)*

The Post-Dispatch said that "Sedan Chair" was Michael W. McMinoway, a 26-year-old private detective from Louisville, Ky. The newspaper quoted McMinoway as saying that he had been unaware of his code name.

Senate sources told the Post-Dispatch that McMinoway was hired by the re-election committee to work in Pennsylvania, California and possibly other states. The sources said he was known to have worked in those states in Humphrey's presidential primary campaigns.

Martha Mitchell's Call

Martha Mitchell, wife of former Attorney General John N. Mitchell, said June 20, "I don't like Vice President Agnew, but, by God, I think he's better than Nixon." Mrs. Mitchell made the observation in a telephone call from New York City to White House correspondent Helen Thomas of United Press International. Thomas has been a regular recipient of Mrs. Mitchell's calls since the 1972 campaign.

Mrs. Mitchell told Thomas she was urging her husband to disclose whatever he knew about White House involvement in the Watergate scandal, no matter whom it concerned. She repeated her earlier statement that the President should resign.

Mitchell left the cabinet on March 1, 1972, to become Nixon's campaign director. He served in that position until July 1, when he resigned, purportedly to spend more time with his family. Mrs. Mitchell had threatened publicly to leave him if he did not resign.

In her latest call to UPI, Mrs. Mitchell said, "I've told him repeatedly that I may not be here many years, but Marty will be, and his grandchildren." Marty is the Mitchells' daughter.

Mrs. Mitchell, who grew up in Pine Bluff, Ark., told Thomas she was going south for the summer with Marty because "all I want is peace of mind." Mitchell, she said, would join them later. He has been indicted by a federal grand jury in New York City in connection with the $200,000 campaign contribution of financier Robert L. Vesco, and he is expected to be a witness before the Senate Watergate committee.

Vorenberg also told reporters that the special prosecutor had not yet received a response from the White House to a request for several documents, including logs of Nixon's acknowledged meetings with his former counsel, John W. Dean III, in early 1973.

Common Cause Suit. White House counsel Leonard Garment accepted a subpoena on behalf of Rose Mary Woods, Nixon's longtime personal secretary and newly named "executive assistant." Woods was ordered to produce all records and "writings" on pre-April-7 Nixon contributions, in connection with a suit filed by Common Cause, a so-called citizen's lobby, seeking to compel the Finance Committee to Re-elect the President to make a full disclosure of its income and expenditures before April 7, 1972, the date such disclosure became mandatory.

Maurice H. Stans, chairman of the finance committee, had told the Senate Watergate committee that all such records had been destroyed.

But Common Cause reportedly learned from Hugh W. Sloan Jr., former treasurer of the finance committee, that the records remained in the White House. *(Stans testimony, p. 134)*

Common Cause had received a partial list of early Nixon donors, showing a total of over $19-million, from Garment on June 6. A copy of the list was later given to the Senate Watergate committee.

Oliver Suit. Democratic Party official R. Spencer Oliver, whose phone at the Democratic National Committee headquarters was tapped, filed a $5-million lawsuit against Nixon campaign officials and others alledgedly involved in the Watergate break-in.

Hearing Sentencing. George Hearing, who was indicted by a Tampa, Fla., grand jury along with Donald H. Segretti on charges of printing and conspiring to distribute a bogus letter during the 1972 presidential campaign, was sentenced to a maximum of one year in prison. Hearing had pleaded guilty to one count of the two-count indictment. Segretti pleaded not guilty.

Nixon Speech. Nixon, speaking to a friendly audience at ceremonies opening the Everett McKinley Dirksen Congressional Leadership Center in Pekin, Ill., referred obliquely to the Watergate scandal. "It would be a tragedy if we allowed the mistakes of a few to obscure the virtues of most who are in the profession of politics or if we let our disappointments with some aspects of a system turn into despair with the system as a whole," he said.

McGovern on Watergate

Some good news is coming out of the Watergate affair, said Sen. George McGovern, paraphrasing historian Charles Beard's statement that "it gets darkest just before the stars come out." The South Dakota Democrat, who lost to President Nixon in 1972, spoke June 15 at a high school commencement in Gaithersburg, Md.

He called Watergate "the most serious scandal in the 200-year life of our nation. It symbolized a rapid and dangerous drift toward an official secrecy and intrigue that would spell certain death for freedom and representative government."

But he found hope in some developments. It is good news, he said, that:

- The political system "is demonstrating a capacity to identify and correct its own evil."
- "Persistent, courageous journalists have exposed the crimes that powerful men attempted to hide."
- "A clear-headed, responsible judge has insisted that justice be done."
- The Senate investigating committee is "moving with dignity and fairness to develop the essential facts and to clarify the central issues."
- Indictment, interrogation and possible conviction of high government officials demonstrates that the rule of law includes "the mighty as well as the small."
- Congress has been challenged "to insist on its rightful check on the executive.... Hopefully, we will never again accept the notion that the President has either a divine or a man-made mandate to rule behind closed doors without reference to the Congress, the press and the people."

JUNE 16

Seattle Judge. A report published in the *Seattle Post-Intelligencer* revealed that former White House adviser John D. Ehrlichman had asked a Seattle federal judge to head a White House committee on domestic intelligence. The judge, Morell E. Sharp, said he turned down the 1970 offer after learning that the committee would operate secretly. At the time of the offer, Sharp was a Washington state supreme court judge; Nixon later appointed him to the federal bench. Sharp and Ehrlichman had known each other when Ehrlichman practiced law in Seattle as a young man.

House Investigation. In an interview published in *The New York Times,* Rep. Peter W. Rodino (D N.J.), chairman of the House Judiciary Committee, said the committee was planning a broad investigation into Justice Department and FBI operations, to culminate in open hearings in late 1973 or early 1974. "As a result of Watergate, I have seen the obvious need for the examination of the Justice Department, which in my opinion has been politicized," Rodino said. He added that legislative oversight of the FBI "is not sufficient today and needs to be strengthened."

JUNE 17

Ellsberg Burglary. Quoting sources close to the Watergate case, *The New York Times* reported that John Dean had told government investigators, and was planning to tell the Senate Watergate committee, that former White House aide Egil Krogh Jr. had told him early in 1973 that Nixon ordered the 1971 burglary of the offices of Daniel Ellsberg's psychiatrist. Krogh, who resigned when the break-in became known in May 1973, was the leader of the White House "plumbers" team assigned by Nixon to investigate Ellsberg after publication of the Pentagon Papers in June 1971.

The Times also said that Dean would tell the Senate committee he had one explicit discussion with Nixon about the coverup shortly before the March 23, 1973, publication of a letter written by conspirator James W. McCord Jr. to the Watergate judge that revealed details of the coverup for the first time.

A White House statement issued in response to the report declined to comment on "this type of 'John Dean source' story." An attorney for Krogh also refused to comment.

Strachan Testimony. Gordon C. Strachan, a former aide to H. R. Haldeman, would tell the Senate committee he briefed Haldeman on plans for the bugging of the Democratic National Committee, *The Washington Post* said. Jeb Stuart Magruder, testifying June 14 before the Senate investigating committee, said he had relayed details of plans for the bugging to Strachan—and that he assumed, but did not know, that Haldeman was aware of them. *(p. 136)*

Haldeman's lawyer, John J. Wilson, said June 16 that "if Strachan had knowledge, he did not transmit it to Haldeman." *The New York Times* reported June 18 that Senate Watergate committee lawyers had confirmed that Strachan planned to implicate Haldeman.

The Senate committee had voted June 15 to grant Strachan immunity to testify, but the Justice Department invoked its authority to delay the grant for 30 days.

Baker Interview. In an interview on ABC-TV's "Issues and Answers," Sen. Baker, the vice chairman of the Senate Watergate committee, said he had been approached earlier in the year by Wallace H. Johnson Jr., a White House aide, who asked for "some say" in the committee's choice of counsel. Baker said he rejected the overture. The only other contact he had with the White House on Watergate, Baker said, came in February 1973, when he urged Nixon "not to invoke the doctrine of executive privilege" to limit the testimony of past and present White House staff members on the Watergate scandal.

Alioto Criticism. San Francisco, Calif., Mayor Joseph L. Alioto, appearing with other mayors on NBC-TV's "Meet the Press," charged that his 1969 indictment on fee-splitting charges was engineered by a secret "political sabotage" organization headed by former Attorney General John N. Mitchell. Alioto later was acquitted of the charges, which were brought at the time he was planning to challenge the re-election of California Gov. Ronald Reagan (R).

JUNE 18

Hearings Postponed. The Senate Watergate committee suspended its hearings for one week in deference to the state visit of Soviet Communist Party Leader Leonid I. Brezhnev. Committee Chairman Ervin said the action was taken at the request of Senate Leaders Mike Mansfield (D Mont.) and Hugh Scott (R Pa.), who had written the committee asking for the delay so that Nixon's talks with the Soviet leader would not be jeopardized.

Ervin said he agreed to the request "with some degree of reluctance." The only committee member to vote against the postponement, Sen. Lowell P. Weicker (R Conn.), argued that "whereas the Brezhnev visit is important, this particular exercise in democracy is important also. I don't know why the two can't move along together. They might give an idea to Brezhnev of the strength of our kind of government."

New Nixon Strategy. A "major shift" in Nixon's Watergate strategy was in the works, *The Washington Post* reported. In order to combat Dean's expected testimony on the involvement of White House aides in the coverup effort, the President reportedly was planning to claim he had been misled by Haldeman and Ehrlichman. Such a move would have been in direct contradication to Nixon's April 30 television speech, when he announced their resignations and described them as "two of the finest public servants" he had ever known.

The Post quoted a high-level White House official as saying, "The charges and the evidence are too much (against Haldeman and Ehrlichman). They've been cut down to nothing and the President can't stand with them." Nixon was said to be retreating from his claim of complete ignorance of all aspects of the case, adopting instead a narrower defense based on the argument that he had committed no crimes.

Gerald L. Warren, deputy White House press secretary, denied the accuracy and authority of the Post's story and deplored "the extreme unfairness to all parties, of such 'source' stories."

Presidential Subpoena. In response to reporters' questions, special prosecutor Archibald Cox acknowledged that his office was studying the question of whether a President could be subpoenaed in a criminal case and whether a President could be indicted before impeachment.

Cox also announced that the White House had forwarded at least some of the papers his office had requested June 7 and 8. Among the documents requested were logs of meetings Nixon held with Dean in early 1973. *(p. 120)*

More Dean Leaks. The June 25 *Time* magazine reported that Dean would tell the Senate committee that Haldeman ordered the tap on the phone of Lawrence F. O'Brien, former chairman of the Democratic National Committee. Dean also would say that Charles W. Colson, former special counsel to the President, had prior knowledge of the bugging, the magazine said. Colson had repeatedly denied such knowledge.

Gray-Dean Meeting. Former acting FBI Director L. Patrick Gray III would tell the Senate Watergate committee that he had "a secret park-bench meeting" with Dean three weeks after the Watergate arrests and was convinced by Dean to hand over FBI interrogation reports on the case, according to *Newsweek* magazine June 25. Gray said he cooperated because Dean assured him he was "reporting directly to the President." Gray was also said to be prepared to testify about two previously undisclosed meetings he had with Nixon during his confirmation hearings in April 1973.

Mitchell Defense. Lawyers for Mitchell acknowledged they were planning to cite the publicity generated by Mitchell's planned appearance before the Senate Watergate committee as an argument in his defense if he was indicted in connection with the bugging, *The New York Times* reported. But one of the attorneys added that Mitchell would not invoke the Fifth Amendment in his testimony before the committee.

Poll Report

High percentages of the American public are skeptical about the degree of President Nixon's involvement in the Watergate scandal, according to the latest public-opinion polls. *(Earlier poll report, p. 136)*

Gallup. The Gallup Poll, in interviews of 1,546 adults June 1-4—published June 17—asked which one of these statements came closest to their own point of view:

Nixon planned the Watergate "bugging" from the beginning.	8%
Nixon did not plan the "bugging" but knew about it before it took place.	28
Nixon found out about the "bugging" after it occurred, but tried to cover it up.	31
Nixon had no knowledge of the "bugging" and spoke up as soon as he learned about it.	19
No opinion/Not heard or read.	14

A growing number of Americans take Watergate seriously, Gallup found. Persons interviewed were asked, as they had been in April, if they thought Watergate was a very serious matter, revealing corruption in the administration, or it was "just politics—the kind of thing that both parties engage in."

	Latest	April 6-9
Serious matter	47%	31%
Just politics	46	53
No opinion/not heard or read	7	16

The survey found that 97 per cent of the adult public had heard or read about Watergate, a figure that has risen steadily in 1973.

CBS. Opinion Research Corporation of Princeton, N.J., interviewed 711 adults who voted in 1972, in a telephone survey taken for CBS News June 8-10. The results were broadcast June 17. The principal findings:

- While 48 per cent said they believed the President knew of the Watergate coverup, only 29 per cent thought he knew in advance about the break-in.
- Fifty per cent said they would favor impeachment proceedings if evidence disclosed that Nixon had prior knowledge of both the break-in and the coverup. But if he knew only about the coverup, 41 per cent said they would support impeachment proceedings.
- Pluralities said they still would vote for Nixon over his 1972 Democratic opponent, Sen. George McGovern (S.D.), or two other Democrats, Senators Hubert H. Humphrey (Minn.) and Edmund S. Muskie (Maine). Not counting those who said they would not vote or were undecided, the survey found Nixon beating McGovern, 43 to 30 per cent; Humphrey, 41 to 37 per cent, and Muskie, 41 to 35 per cent.

JUNE 19

Dean Evidence. Acting to protect possible future criminal cases against former presidential counsel John Dean, the special prosecutor's office presented a sealed folder of evidence it had gathered against Dean to U.S. District Judge John J. Sirica. Under the limited immunity granted Dean by the Senate Watergate committee, prosecutors were required to show they had gathered evidence for prosecution independently of any testimony Dean gave the committee. Dean was scheduled to testify June 25.

Judge Sirica ordered that the documents be opened only if, in the course of any criminal proceeding, Dean challenged evidence brought against him on grounds that it was derived from his Senate testimony.

Dean Fund. Dean told federal investigators that he kept $14,000 in 1972 Republican campaign funds, putting it in a special trust fund after his April 30 dismissal from the White House, *The New York Times* reported. Dean reportedly said he had borrowed $4,850 from the fund to finance his wedding and honeymoon in 1972, but later returned the money. The $14,000 was the remainder of a special $22,000 fund set up to buy newspaper ads in support of Nixon's war policies in May 1972, according to the Times' sources.

The same day, one of Dean's lawyers, Charles N. Shaffer, met with Senate committee leaders Ervin and Baker. According to Baker, he expressed concern about leaks to the press of statements Dean made during an executive session with the committee on June 16.

Maryland Indictment. Blagden H. Wharton, a Maryland banker and 1972 Republican campaign official, was served with an indictment on charges that he violated state elections laws by falsifying campaign contribution reports on a dinner held for Vice President Agnew in May 1972. Wharton and Alexander M. Lankler, chairman of the state Republican Party, admitted that they had listed a $49,500 loan from the Nixon re-election committee as 32 nonexistent contributions.

Colson Testimony. Former White House aide Charles W. Colson, testifying at a closed hearing of the Senate Appropriations Subcommittee on Intelligence Operations, said he personally had asked Ehrlichman to help E. Howard Hunt Jr. establish "liaison with the CIA" in July 1971. Hunt, a convicted Watergate conspirator, had been working in the White House then as a member of the "plumbers" group set up to plug information leaks.

Colson's version of Ehrlichman's role was revealed after the hearing by Sen. John L. McClellan (D Ark.), chairman of the subcommittee, which was investigating CIA involvement in the Watergate. Ehrlichman had told the subcommittee on May 30 that he had no recollection of contacting the CIA about Hunt in the summer of 1971. *(p. 100)*

Executive Privilege. John Wilson, attorney for former White House aides Haldeman and Ehrlichman, told reporters he interpreted Nixon's May 22 revision of the executive privilege doctrine to apply only to oral testimony and not to documents. Nixon said May 22 that he would not invoke executive privilege in relation to criminal aspects of the Watergate case.

JUNE 20

Dean Leaks. *The Washington Post* quoted parts of a summary of Dean's testimony at a closed meeting of the Senate Watergate committee June 16. According to the summary, Dean alleged that:

- He had documents showing that Nixon requested that tax audits of his friends be stopped.
- Nixon told him to keep a list of reporters who were giving the White House trouble, so that they could be punished after the election.
- The White House thought Sen. Howard H. Baker Jr. (R Tenn.), vice chairman of the Senate Watergate committee, was going to assist the administration during the hearings—an assertion Baker denied.
- At a Feb. 10, 1973, meeting in La Costa, Calif., Dean, Haldeman, Ehrlichman and special presidential counsel Richard A. Moore discussed paying off the Watergate defendants.
- Dean received a threat from convicted conspirator E. Howard Hunt Jr. that he would talk if the White House did not come across with $72,000 for living expenses and $50,000 for attorneys' fees. Dean then learned that Mitchell had "taken care of" Hunt.
- Charles W. Colson told Dean that Nixon had approved an offer of executive clemency for Hunt. Colson got the information from Ehrlichman, who had discussed the matter with Nixon.

A White House statement on the Post article said, "Fragmentary leaks of charges attributed to John Dean have been appearing over the past several weeks. He will be testifying in public under oath next week. We will have no comment on that testimony before it is given."

Dean Fund. Charles N. Shaffer, one of Dean's lawyers, told the Senate committee staff that Dean would make no further statements to the committee before the public hearings resumed, because the news leaks were jeopardizing his client's testimony and reputation. Dean and his lawyers were especially upset by the report that he borrowed $4,850 in campaign funds to finance his wedding and honeymoon in October 1972.

Scott Attack. Sen. Hugh Scott (R Pa.), referring to Dean during his daily news briefing, said, "Nothing is so incredible that this turncoat will not be willing to testify to it in exchange for a reward...a man who can embezzle can easily tell lies."

Finance Probe. *The New York Times* reported that the Senate Watergate committee had been "quietly subpoenaing personal bank records and other data" in order to determine whether anyone connected with the Nixon campaign misused funds.

Committee Fine. The Finance Committee to Re-elect the President was found guilty and fined the maximum penalty of $3,000 in Federal District Court in Washington, D.C., for concealing a $200,000 cash contribution from indicted financier Robert L. Vesco. The committee argued that the money was not reportable under the new election finance law, because it was verbally pledged before the April 7, 1972, deadline. But Judge George L. Hart ruled that, because the money was delivered on April 10, it should have been reported.

The misdemeanor conviction was the second under the Federal Election Campaign Act of 1971 and the second for the Nixon re-election committee. The committee pleaded no contest and was fined $8,000 in January 1973 for failing to report cash payments to G. Gordon Liddy, one of the convicted Watergate conspirators.

ACLU Report. The American Civil Liberties Union (ACLU) released a 106-page report on the January Watergate trial, concluding that it had been tainted by perjury and a "sham prosecution." The report called for a new trial "under a properly drawn indictment which charges all of those responsible for the Watergate conspiracy regardless of their station in life." The ACLU had submitted its report to special prosecutor Cox on June 18.

In addition, the group presented a motion to Chief U.S. District Judge John J. Sirica calling for a new trial. Formal filing of the motion was postponed until Sirica determined whether the ACLU could intervene as a friend of the court in the motion of conspirator James W. McCord Jr. for a new trial. *(McCord motion, p. 125)*

JUNE 21

Dean Leaks. The flood of leaks from the planned testimony of former presidential counsel Dean before the Senate Watergate committee continued unabated, as *The New York Times* printed excerpts from a summary of Dean's June 16 private interview with the committee. *The Washington Post* also quoted extensively from the summary, which was prepared by the committee staff.

Dean's account, as documented in the summary, included allegations that former Nixon aides Haldeman and Ehrlichman were deeply involved in the Watergate coverup, contrary to their own sworn testimony and statements to the press. *(Haldeman, Ehrlichman depositions, Weekly Report p. 113, 125)*

White House Logs. The Times also printed excerpts from a five-page White House analysis of 18 conversations between Nixon and Dean during the early months of 1973. The Times said it obtained the document from a person with access to Senate committee records. The analysis stated that Dean "gave the President his theory of what happened" in the Watergate affair for the first time on March 21. Dean's version, as portrayed in the Senate summary, indicated Nixon knew of the coverup earlier.

Senate Reaction. Senate Democratic Leader Mike Mansfield (Mont.) said he hoped the Senate committee would adopt "stricter procedures" to prevent future leaks to the news media, while Senate Republican Leader Hugh Scott (R Pa.) charged that the leaks were "organized and manipulated" by "all sides in the controversy." Scott added that Dean's credibility as a witness had been "considerably shaken."

Bremer Break-In. Watergate conspirator E. Howard Hunt Jr. told Senate committee investigators that he was ordered by Charles W. Colson, former special presidential counsel, to break into the Milwaukee apartment of Arthur H. Bremer shortly after Bremer attempted to assassinate Alabama Gov. George Wallace on May 15, 1972, according to a report in *The Washington Post.* Hunt said Colson wanted him to look for evidence that Bremer was connected with left-wing political causes, but that he refused the mission because it was too risky. Colson denied the report. ✓

WATERGATE: MOST DAMAGING CHARGES YET BY DEAN

John W. Dean III was the star of the Watergate show for a whole week, and the customers got their money's worth. From Monday through Friday, June 25-29, the former White House counsel made statements and answered questions before the televised hearings of the Senate Select Committee on Presidential Campaign Activities.

He began with a 245-page statement that took him six hours to read. It contained the most comprehensive indictment yet heard against the men who had been closest to President Nixon, and Dean accused the President himself of having known since September 1972 about attempts to suppress the scandal. *(p. 163, 154)*

Much of the cross-examination by committee lawyers and senators the rest of the week was devoted to trying to break down Dean's testimony. But the 34-year-old attorney, fired by Nixon on April 30, stood by his original statement. He remained unflustered in the face of sometimes open hostility from the senators, often appearing to control the situation with his somber composure.

Accompanying Dean's testimony were dozens of documents, some 50 altogether, that he turned over to the committee as supporting evidence. One set of papers opened up a new area of alleged administration political pressure: the use of tax audits to harass its opponents. Lists of political enemies, persons singled out for retribution because of their opposition to the administration, were revealed. *(p. 153)*

The White House began the week with a terse statement that it would have nothing to say about Dean's testimony. But a few days later, a memorandum from J. Fred Buzhardt, special counsel to the President, was given to the committee, rebutting some of Dean's statements and accusing him and his "patron," former Attorney General John N. Mitchell, of being the chief culprits in the scandal. A day after releasing the memo, Buzhardt issued a statement describing it as "an hypothesis prepared as a basis for cross-examination" but not a "White House position."

Presidential Testimony. The clear conflict between Dean and the White House prompted both the Democratic chairman and the Republican vice chairman of the Senate investigating committee to raise the question of seeking presidential testimony. Neither suggested specifically that Nixon should appear before the committee in person.

Chairman Sam J. Ervin Jr. (D N.C.) asked Dean on June 28, "Is there any way whatsoever to test the credibility of anybody when the credibility has to be judged merely on the basis of a written statement?" Dean said there was not.

Vice Chairman Howard H. Baker Jr. (R Tenn.) made reference to an important meeting of Dean, the President and others on Sept. 15, 1972. "I'm not prepared to say at this point how we may be able to gain access to the President's knowledge of that meeting," said Baker. He expressed hope that, at a later hearing, the committee could obtain "statements from the President—in whatever manner can be arranged."

The White House continued its resistance to direct presidential testimony. Deputy press secretary Gerald L. Warren said in San Clemente, Calif., June 28 that Nixon would not testify voluntarily and that it would be "constitutionally inappropriate" for him to respond to a subpoena.

Weicker Charge. The most emotional episode of the hearings so far was provided by a committee member, Sen. Lowell P. Weicker (R Conn.), who accused the White House of trying to smear him. Weicker has been a leading Republican critic of administration handling of the scandal. He asked special prosecutor Archibald Cox to investigate the alleged smear.

To enthusiastic applause from spectators in the hearing room, Weicker said heatedly on June 28: "Let me make it clear, because I've got to have my partisan moment. Republicans do not cover up, Republicans do not go ahead and threaten, Republicans do not go ahead and commit illegal acts, and God knows Republicans don't view their fellow Americans as enemies to be harassed; but rather I can assure you that Republicans and those that I serve with look upon every American as a human being to be loved and won."

Dean's Inaccessible Files

When John W. Dean III was fired as White House counsel on April 30, the files from his White House office were locked up in a room in the basement of the adjacent Executive Office Building.

Since then, Dean told the Senate select Watergate committee June 29, he has had access to the documents, but he has been denied the right to make photocopies of them or to remove them from the storage room. To copy the information in the papers, he said, he has had to write it in longhand on top of a safe in the room.

Dean said he had written President Nixon requesting permission to make photocopies of the documents. His request was denied by the White House, he said, and J. Fred Buzhardt, special counsel to the President, informed him that he could do nothing more to help him.

The matter came up when several members of the committee said they would like to have documents to support some of the statements Dean made. Chairman Sam J. Ervin (D N.C.) said he would ask the committee staff to write the White House to seek access to a copying machine for the files.

Witness June 25

Former White House counsel John W. Dean III testified that he believed President Nixon was aware of the Watergate coverup as early as September 1972.

This was the first testimony at the Senate Watergate hearings to point directly to presidential involvement in the coverup of the break-in June 17, 1972, at Democratic national headquarters.

The 34-year-old lawyer testified that on Sept. 15, 1972, the day seven men were indicted for the break-in, he received congratulations from the President that the case had reached no higher than G. Gordon Liddy, the former legal counsel to Nixon's re-election and finance committees. Liddy was one of the seven men tried and convicted.

John W. Dean III

Dean said he told Nixon "that all I had been able to do was contain the case and assist in keeping it out of the White House.... I left the meeting with the impression that the President was well aware of what had been going on regarding the success of keeping the White House out of the Watergate scandal, and I also had expressed to him my concern that I was not confident that the coverup could be maintained indefinitely."

Dean made his statements during six hours it took him on June 25 to read the 245 pages of his prepared testimony. No questions were asked by members of the Senate select committee conducting the hearings. *(Text excerpts, p. 133)*

Dean began his sworn testimony with a brief preface admitting his role in obstructing justice, assisting in the commission of perjury and making unauthorized use of funds in his possession. "It is my honest belief," he said, "that while the President was involved, that he did not realize or appreciate at any time the implications of his involvement, and I think that when the facts come out, I hope the President is forgiven."

Principal Points. Dean also made these points during his testimony, for which he had been granted partial immunity from prosecution:

- He did not know of the break-in in advance.
- Nixon discussed executive clemency for E. Howard Hunt Jr., one of the convicted Watergate burglars, with former aides John D. Ehrlichman and Charles W. Colson.
- Dean never made a report to the President absolving persons then in the White House from a role in the break-in.
- The order to break into Daniel Ellsberg's psychiatrist's office came directly from the "oval office."
- Nixon did not begin an investigation of the Watergate affair on March 21, 1973, as he stated April 17. *(Text of statement, p. 18)*

Dean said the Watergate affair "was an inevitable outgrowth of a climate of excessive concern over the political impact of demonstrations, excessive concern over leaks, an insatiable appetite for political intelligence, all coupled with a do-it-yourself White House staff, regardless of the law." *(Other Dean disclosures, p. 145)*

Coverup Warning. Dean discussed a series of meetings he had with the President in February, March and April 1973. On Feb. 27, he said, they had their first meeting since Sept. 15, 1972, that related to Watergate. Dean testified that Nixon directed him to report directly to him regarding all Watergate matters, because presidential aides Ehrlichman and H. R. Haldeman were spending too much time on the case.

Dean testified that on their way out of Nixon's office that day, he repeated what he had told the President Sept. 15, that he was not sure the coverup would be maintained indefinitely. "He told me that we would have to fight back and he was confident that I could do the job," Dean quoted the President as saying.

On Feb. 28, Dean said, he told the President that he had been involved in the coverup and a possible obstruction of justice, but that Nixon "reassured me not to worry, that I had no legal problems."

Money Demands. At a March 13 meeting, Dean said, he told Nixon that the seven Watergate defendants were making money demands and the President asked how much it would cost. Dean testified that he estimated $1-million, and that the President "told me that was no problem, and he also looked over at Haldeman and repeated the same statement."

Dean said that on March 21 he met with the President to give him a full report on what he knew about Watergate, because "the President did not seem to understand the full implications of what was going on."

Dean testified that he began by telling Nixon "there was a cancer growing on the presidency" and that if it was not removed "the President himself would be killed by it." He testified that he told Nixon how the planning began in January and February 1972; that former Nixon lawyer Herbert W. Kalmbach had raised money to buy the seven defendants' silence; that he had assisted Jeb Stuart Magruder in committing perjury before the grand jury, and that Ehrlichman, Haldeman and former Attorney General John N. Mitchell had been involved in the coverup.

"After I finished," Dean related, "I realized that I had not really made the President understand" because "he did not seem particularly concerned with their (the revelations') implications."

Dean said that after a meeting with the President, Haldeman and Ehrlichman, "it was quite clear that the coverup as far as the White House was going to continue." Subsequent conversations among himself, Haldeman and Ehrlichman made clear that the White House wanted Mitchell to take the blame for all that had transpired after the 1972 break-in, he said.

Written Report. Dean said the President called him on March 23, the day a letter from Watergate defendant James W. McCord Jr. to the judge in the Watergate trial was made public indicating that perjury had been committed during the criminal trial in January. Dean said Nixon told him to go to Camp David, the presidential retreat in Maryland, and "analyze the situation." Nixon did not order him to write a report, as had been reported, he added.

It was Haldeman, he said, who asked him to write a report on what he knew about Watergate. At Camp David, he continued, he began to think he should step forward,

(Continued on p. 154)

Plans for 'Political Enemies'—and Mills' Response

One of the documents given to the Senate Watergate committee by former White House counsel John W. Dean III was a copy of a confidential memorandum written by Dean on "dealing with our political enemies." Another of the documents was a copy of a memo to Dean from former special White House counsel Charles Colson containing the names of 20 persons to be given priority in that "dealing."

Dean said in his memo and in testimony to the committee that "available federal machinery" was to be used against persons opposed to the Nixon administration. Techniques such as audits by the Internal Revenue Service (IRS), denial of federal grants, prosecution and litigation were included.

The disclosure of the scheme June 27 brought an immediate threat of a congressional investigation of IRS activities by Rep. Wilbur D. Mills (D Ark.). He is chairman of the House Ways and Means Committee and the Joint Committee on Internal Revenue Taxation.

Mills said June 27 he had directed the staff of the joint committee to begin preliminary checks into the charges that the IRS was used for political purposes. If evidence indicated that the charges might be true, Mills said, he would give priority to that investigation and set aside work on trade and tax reform bills which are important to the administration. "I want to know more before we decide" whether to go ahead with a full-scale inquiry, Mills said.

Following are excerpts from the memos. The one by Dean was to John D. Ehrlichman, former White House domestic affairs adviser, and was dated Aug. 16, 1971. Colson's was written Sept. 9, 1971.

'Dealing With...Enemies'

This memorandum addresses the matter of how we can maximize the fact of our incumbency in dealing with persons known to be active in their opposition to our Administration. Stated a bit more bluntly—how we can use the available federal machinery to screw our political enemies.

After reviewing this matter with a number of persons possessed of expertise in the field, I have concluded that we *do not* need an elaborate mechanism or game plan, rather we need a good project coordinator and full support for the project. In brief, the system would work as follows:

- Key members of the staff [e.g., Colson, (Harry) Dent, (Peter) Flanigan, (Patrick) Buchanan] should be requested to inform us as to who they feel we should be giving a hard time.
- The project coordinator should then determine what sorts of dealings these individuals have with the federal government and how we can best screw them (e.g., grant availability, federal contracts, litigation, prosecution, etc.).
- The project coordinator then should have access to and the full support of the top officials of the agency or department in proceeding to deal with the individual.

I have learned that there have been many efforts in the past to take such actions, but they have ultimately failed—in most cases—because of lack of support at the top. Of all those I have discussed this matter with, Lyn Nofziger appears the most knowledgeable and most interested. If Lyn had support he would enjoy undertaking this activity as the project coordinator. You are aware of some of Lyn's successes in the field, but he feels that he can only employ limited efforts because there is a lack of support.

The Priority List

1. **Picker, Arnold M.,** United Artists Corporation: Top Muskie fundraiser. Success here could be both debilitating and very embarrassing to the Muskie machine. If effort looks promising, both Ruth and David Picker should be programmed and then a follow-through with United Artists.
2. **Barkan, Alexander E.,** National Director of AFL-CIO's Committee on Political Education: Without a doubt the most powerful political force programmed against us in 1968. ($10 million dollars, 4.6 million votes, 115 million pamphlets, 176,000 workers—all programmed by Barkan's C.O.P.E.—So says Teddy White in The Making of the President '68). We can expect the same effort this time.
3. **Guthman, Ed,** Managing Editor L.A. Times: Guthman, former Kennedy aide, was a highly sophisticated hatchetman against us in '68. It is obvious he is the prime mover behind the current Key Biscayne effort. It is time to give him the message.
4. **Dane, Maxwell,** Doyle, Dane and Bernbach: The top Democratic advertising firm—They destroyed Goldwater in '64. They should be hit hard starting with Dane.
5. **Dyson, Charles,** Dyson-Kissner Corporation: Dyson and Larry O'Brien were close business associates after '68. Dyson has huge business holdings and is presently deeply involved in the Businessmen's Educational Fund which bankrolls a national radio network of 5 minute programs—Anti-Nixon in character.
6. **Stein, Howard,** Dreyfus Corporation: Heaviest contributor to McCarthy in '68. If McCarthy goes, will do the same in '72. If not, Lindsay or McGovern will receive the funds.
7. **Lowenstein, Allard:** Guiding force behind the 18 year old "dump Nixon" vote drive.
8. **Halperin, Morton,** leading executive at Common Cause: A scandal would be most helpful here.
9. **Woodcock, Leonard,** UAW: No comments necessary.
10. **S. Sterling Munro, Jr.,** Senator Jackson's AA: We should give him a try. Positive results would stick a pin in Jackson's white hat.
11. **Feld, Bernard T.,** President, Council for Livable World: Heavy far left funding. They will program an "all court press" against us in '72.
12. **Davidoff, Sidney:** (Mayor) Lindsay's top personal aide: A first class S.O.B., wheeler-dealer and suspected bagman. Positive results would really shake the Lindsay camp and Lindsay's plans to capture youth vote. Davidoff in charge.
13. **Conyers, John,** Congressman, Detroit: Coming on fast. Emerging as a leading black anti-Nixon spokesman. Has known weakness for white females.
14. **Lambert, Samuel M.,** President, National Education Association: Has taken us on vis a vis federal aid to parochial schools—a '72 issue.
15. **Mott, Stewart Rawlings:** Nothing but big money for radic-lib candidates.
16. **Dellums, Ronald,** Congressman, California: Had extensive EMK-Tunney support in his election bid. Success might help in California next year.
17. **Schorr, Daniel,** Columbia Broadcasting System: A real media enemy.
18. **S. Harrison Dogole:** President of Globe Security Systems: Fourth largest private detective agency in U.S. Heavy Humphrey contributor. Could program his agency against us.
19. **Paul Newman:** Radic-Lib causes. Heavy McCarthy involvement '68. Used effectively in nationwide T.V. commercials. '72 involvement certain.
20. **McGrory, Mary,** Columnist: Daily hate Nixon articles.

(Continued from p. 152)
"because there was no way the situation was going to get better—rather it would only get worse." Dean said he never gave the full report to Haldeman, but provided the Senate committee with a copy of it. The report was one of 47 documents he gave the committee.

Dean said he met privately with the President on April 15 in the Executive Office Building and told Nixon that he had been telling his story to federal prosecutors in what he saw as an "act of loyalty" to Nixon. Nixon, he continued, then began asking him "leading questions, which made me think that the conversation was being taped." Dean said they discussed the Watergate affair, and during the conversation Nixon told him he had been joking when he made the comment about how easy it would be to get the $1-million for Watergate hush money.

Later in the conversation, Dean said, "the most interesting thing happened." Nixon, he testified, got out of his chair and walked to the corner of his office and, "in a barely audible tone," admitted he had been foolish to have discussed Hunt's clemency with Colson.

Dean said Nixon called him into a private meeting in his oval office the next day—April 16—and asked him to sign a prepared letter of resignation. Dean, describing the conversation as "tense," said he told the President he would not resign unless Haldeman and Ehrlichman did also. "I told him that I was not willing to be the White House scapegoat for the Watergate," Dean testified.

Taped Conversation. That evening Dean learned from his attorney that the President "had informed the government that he allegedly had taped a conversation in which I had told him I was seeking immunity from the government in exchange for testimony on Haldeman and Ehrlichman," according to the former counsel. Dean testified that he had no recollection of ever telling Nixon he was negotiating for immunity, "and the President told me very specifically that he did not want to do anything to interfere with any negotiations I was having with the government."

Dean said he believed the tape was of his April 15 meeting with Nixon. "I do not know if such a tape exists," he testified, "but if it does and has not been tampered with and is a complete transcript of the entire conversation that took place in the President's office, I think that this committee should have that tape because I believe that it would corroborate many of the things that this committee has asked me to testify about."

Regarding the President's April 17 statement to the press about Watergate, Dean questioned one remark. He said Nixon did not begin an investigation on March 21, as the President had said, but "rather, the President, Haldeman and Ehrlichman commenced to protect themselves against the unraveling of the coverup."

No Immunity. Dean also said a paragraph had been put into the statement, possibly by Ehrlichman, that there would be no immunity for administration figures. It was "very evident to me what the President was saying: Dean will not be a witness against anyone so the government might as well stop dealing with him," he said.

Dean testified that the no-immunity paragraph "quite obviously" meant Nixon was trying to affect discussions Dean was having with government prosecutors. That, plus the request from Nixon that he sign "a virtual confession" in his resignation statement, meant that "I was being set up and that it was time that I let the word out that I would not be a scapegoat."

Dean issued his "scapegoat" statement April 19 and since then has had little contact with the White House staff. He said the President called him April 22 to wish him a happy Easter and that on April 30, while he was out of Washington, his secretary informed him that his "resignation had been requested and accepted" and that Haldeman and Ehrlichman had resigned.

First Knowledge. Dean testified that he first learned of the Watergate break-in on June 18 while stopping in San Francisco, Calif., on his return from the Far East. The information came from his aide, Fred Fielding, he said.

The sequence of events that led to the break-in began with the hiring of Liddy as general counsel to the reelection committee, according to Dean. Liddy not only was to give legal advice, Dean testified, but was ordered by Mitchell to draw up an intelligence plan to counter expected demonstrators at the Republican national convention.

Liddy Proposals. Dean said he attended a meeting in Mitchell's office with Magruder on Jan. 27, 1972, at which Liddy presented his intelligence plan. "Some of the concepts were mind-boggling," Dean said, explaining that they included mugging squads, kidnapping teams, prostitutes and electronic surveillance. Potential targets suggested by Liddy for the surveillance, Dean, said, were Lawrence F. O'Brien, the Democratic national chairman, the Democratic headquarters at the Watergate, and the Fontainebleau Hotel in Miami Beach, Fla., during the Democratic convention. Liddy said the plan would cost about $1-million, Dean said.

Mitchell told Liddy to revise the plan, being too polite to throw Liddy out of his office "or tell him he was out of his mind," Dean told the committee. He said at that point, "I thought the plan was dead, because I doubted if Mitchell would reconsider the matter."

Dean said the next discussion of the plan of which he was aware took place Feb. 4, 1972, again in Mitchell's office. He arrived late, he related, and when he came in Liddy was presenting a scaled-down version of the first plan. Dean said he listened for a few minutes and then interjected that such discussions should not go on in the office of the attorney general. He interrupted, he added, because he felt Mitchell was being put on the spot. The meeting ended after Dean's remarks.

After the second meeting, Dean testified, he told Haldeman about Liddy's presentation, and Haldeman agreed that the plan would be unwise. Dean said he had no knowledge of what became of Liddy's proposal after the meeting. Dean said he talked to Liddy June 19, two days after the break-in, and Liddy told him "Magruder had pushed him into doing it."

'Dean Report.' The first time he heard of the so-called "Dean report" absolving persons then in the White House from complicity in the Watergate affair was on a television news broadcast after the President mentioned it on Aug. 29, 1972, he said. He had "no advance knowledge the President was going to indicate that I had investigated the matter" and if he had, he would have advised against it, he added.

Dean testified that his reasons for giving such advice, if he had been asked, were that he knew that Gordon C. Strachan, a Haldeman aide, had carried information about wiretapped conversations to the White House from the re-election committee and later had destroyed incriminating materials at Haldeman's direction; that he did not know for sure if Haldeman had advance knowledge; that he always suspected Colson knew more than he professed to know, and that Haldeman and Ehrlichman knew he had attended the two meetings in Mitchell's office.

But, Dean said, it was his belief that no one at the White House knew there was going to be a break-in on June 17, "because I don't believe that anybody other than those directly involved knew that that was going to happen. I don't know if the President's statement was meant to be a very literal play on carefully chosen words or whether he intended to give it the broad-brush interpretation that it later received. However, I would have certainly counseled the President against issuing the statement. And I was very unhappy to have my name associated with the statement without being consulted whatsoever, and put out in front on the issue."

Dean said the incident caused him to think for the first time that "I might be set up in case the whole thing crumbled at a later time." The White House had maintained until May 16 that the President's remarks were based on an investigation by Dean. But on that date, it confirmed a newspaper story that Nixon based his statement on information supplied him by Ehrlichman.

Ellsberg Burglary. Dean's information about the origin of the order to break into the office of Daniel Ellsberg's psychiatrist came from Egil Krogh Jr., the head of the White House "plumbers," a group ordered organized by Nixon to stop information leaks, Dean testified. Ehrlichman was in over-all charge of the group's activities.

Information about the burglary eventually forced the judge at Ellsberg's espionage trial to drop all charges May 11. *(p. 46)*

Dean said the subject came up during a conversation with Krogh on March 28 or 29, 1973. He said he told Krogh that the Justice Department had documents that included a photograph of Liddy in front of the psychiatrist's office and that the photo came from film in Hunt's camera. Hunt and Liddy worked for a time with the "plumbers."

Dean asked Krogh, he said, whether Ehrlichman had ordered the burglary, and Krogh answered no. "He did not believe that Ehrlichman had been aware of the incident until after it happened," Dean testified. "Rather, he had received his orders right out of the 'oval office.' I was so surprised to hear this that I said, 'You must be kidding.' And he repeated again that he had received his instructions out of the oval office."

Dean's testimony did not link the President by name to the order for the burglary of Ellsberg's psychiatrist. It did confirm Ehrlichman's public contention that he (Ehrlichman) learned of the burglary only after it happened.

Committee Influence. Dean also discussed White House efforts to influence the Senate committee and its investigation into the Watergate scandal. He testified that White House efforts to have the Senate Judiciary Committee handle the probe were unsuccessful, as were attempts to alter the Senate resolution outlining the select committee's mandate. Dean testified that the Judiciary Committee had many administration friends on it.

After the Senate passed the resolution creating the investigating committee, said Dean, he, Haldeman, Ehrlichman and others met on the weekend of Feb. 9 in a resort hotel near San Clemente, Calif., to outline their strategy. He testified that Haldeman and Ehrlichman concluded that the committee would be dealt with in this way: "The White House will take a public posture of full cooperation, but privately will attempt to restrain the investigation and make it as difficult as possible to get information and witnesses. A behind-the-scenes media effort would be made to make the Senate inquiry appear very partisan. The ultimate goal would be to discredit the hearings and reduce their impact by attempting to show that the Democrats have engaged in the same type of activities."

Shielding Nixon. In other testimony, Dean painted a picture of broad White House efforts to shield the President from demonstrators and at the same time to try to learn all it could, by legal or illegal means, about what the demonstrators and political opponents were up to.

At one point in 1971, Dean told the committee, Nixon was angered about a lone demonstrator with a 10-foot sign in front of Lafayette Park, across from the White House. Dean said Dwight Chapin, Nixon's appointments secretary, told him he was going to get some "thugs" to remove the man, but that Dean managed to have the man moved before Chapin could act.

On another occasion in 1971, said Dean, the President was angered by demonstrators outside his motel in Akron, Ohio. He told the secret service agent beside him "in some rather blunt synonyms, to get the demonstrators out of there," Dean said, but nothing could be done.

Information Leaks. Concern about leaks of information was also high in the White House staff's minds, and Dean told the committee how White House aide John Caulfield had described to him the tapping of columnist Joseph Kraft's telephone. *(Caulfield testimony, p. 82)*

The publication of the Pentagon Papers in June 1971 caused "a quantum jump" in White House concern over leaks, Dean said. Sometime later, Dean said, Caulfield told him that Colson, acting on instructions from Ehrlichman, had ordered him to burglarize the Brookings Institution in Washington to learn if it contained certain leaked documents.

Dean said Caulfield came to him because he thought the assignment was unwise and that Colson's instructions—to plant a firebomb in the Brookings building to retrieve the documents during the commotion—"were insane." Dean later had the burglary called off, he said.

The persons most interested in political intelligence, Dean testified, were Haldeman, Ehrlichman and Colson. There were frequent attempts to get politically embarrassing information, he added, on Democratic Chairman Lawrence F. O'Brien, Sen. Edmund S. Muskie (D Maine) and Sen. George McGovern (D S.D.).

Dean testified that in the fall of 1971, Larry Higby, a Haldeman aide, called him to say that Haldeman wanted 24-hour surveillance of Sen. Edward M. Kennedy (D Mass.) and regular reports on his activities. Dean said he discussed this with Caulfield, and they agreed it would be unwise. Instead, Caulfield was to keep a "general overview" of Kennedy's activities, Dean related.

Another White House aide, Anthony Ulasewicz, who handled several investigatory matters, was sent in July 1969 to Chappaquiddick, Mass., to probe Kennedy's auto accident, in which a secretary, Mary Jo Kopechne, was drowned, Dean said. This occurred while Dean was working in the Justice Department. Dean related that then Deputy Attorney General Richard G. Kleindienst called him into his office in the summer of 1969 and instructed him to call Cartha DeLoach, an assistant FBI director, to get information regarding the foreign travels of Kopechne. Dean did not say whether he got the information.

Witness June 26

In his second full day of testimony, Dean said the President was not being truthful when Nixon said April 17 that he condemned "any attempts to cover up in this case, no matter who is involved." *(Text of statement, p. 18)*

Asked by Sen. Joseph M. Montoya (D N.M.) whether he believed Nixon was telling the truth in his remark about condemning coverups, Dean replied after a brief pause: "No, sir." Dean went on to explain that by April 17, Nixon "knew the full implications of the case" because of Dean's discussions with the President and possibly from others.

Asked further by Montoya whether Nixon was telling the truth in his May 22 statement, in which he said he was innocent of any knowledge of the Watergate burglary or its coverup, Dean replied that he did not know if the President had prior knowledge of Watergate, but he said Nixon was aware of efforts to cover it up at least by Sept. 15, 1972. *(Text of statement, p. 90)*

Unshaken Story. Dean's testimony June 26 essentially covered the same ground as that of the previous day, particularly on the issue of Nixon's knowledge of the coverup. Committee counsel Samuel Dash questioned Dean repeatedly about the President's alleged involvement in the coverup, but was not able to shake the witness' story.

Advance Knowledge. Dean also linked the President to advance knowledge of the Watergate break-in itself by testifying that he believed Haldeman, who allegedly was aware of the surveillance plans, probably reported them to the President. Dean said Gordon C. Strachan, Haldeman's aide, was the liaison between the White House and the re-election committee and had "frequent contact" with Jeb Stuart Magruder, the deputy campaign director. Magruder earlier testified that Strachan had advance knowledge of the break-in plans and reviewed transcripts of bugged conversations of Democratic officials. *(Magruder testimony, p. 135)*

Dean testified that, in his opinion, "he (Strachan) would report everything he knew in some form to Haldeman," and "I believe he (Haldeman) probably would have reported it" to Nixon.

Motivation. The second day of testimony provided Dean with his first opportunity to discuss his motivation for participating in the coverup. He said the coverup already had begun when he returned to Washington June 19, 1972, two days after the break-in, and that he "inherited a situation" which became an "instant way of life," with little or no thought given to it by him.

Dean told the committee he never worried about possible criminal charges against himself, because the "stakes were too high for any personal problems I had"—an apparent reference to Nixon's re-election campaign. "I found myself helping out others; I was in the process before I began thinking about the process," Dean said.

Asked why he did not go to Nixon with the story of Watergate soon after the break-in, Dean replied that he did not have access to the President and that it would have been "presumptuous" of him to try to see Nixon, because his reporting channel to the oval office was through Haldeman and Ehrlichman. Then he added, almost as an afterthought, "I was part of the coverup at that time."

Dean earlier had explained his role of White House counsel as little more than a message carrier for Haldeman, Ehrlichman, Mitchell and Nixon. "The title was the best part of the job," he said.

He denied that his motive in testifying was to gain immunity from prosecution, and that he came to the Senate committee with his information after first failing to get immunity from federal prosecutors. He pointed out that he was testifying in the Senate under a judicial order.

Petersen, Ziegler. Dean also countered reports, based on his testimony of June 25, that Henry E. Petersen, the assistant attorney general who was in charge of the Justice Department's Watergate investigation, and Ronald L. Ziegler, the President's press secretary, participated in the coverup. "I know of no impropriety" regarding Petersen's investigation, Dean testified. He said Petersen tried to be fair to the White House, and that the opportunity for private grand jury testimony which Petersen arranged for White House personnel was merely an attempt to avoid embarrassment for them. Dean said his impression, after talking with Petersen a few days after the break-in, that Petersen "would handle the matter fairly" meant only that he would not attempt to investigate everything about the White House for the previous four years.

Dean testified that Ziegler, who has been criticized by the press for misleading them on Watergate, was duped by himself and others. Dean said Ziegler never knew the truth about Watergate, because Haldeman had instructed Dean not to brief Ziegler on the subject.

Instead, Dean said, he instructed Ziegler on how to "hedge, bob and weave" on press questions about Watergate and to take the offensive at some points. As an example, Dean said that when Ziegler would ask him about reports of a "secret" White House fund, Dean told him it was no secret to some people in the White House, so therefore it was not a "secret" fund.

Dean said the same tactics were used by him and others to put off Clark MacGregor, who succeeded Mitchell as re-election campaign director, when MacGregor had questions about Watergate.

Asked to characterize the Watergate burglary, Dean called it "the opening act of one of America's great tragedies."

Discreditation Attempts. Dean testified that many efforts had been made to discredit him since he decided to tell his story. "Every conceivable inch of my life has been gone over," he said, explaining that private investigators had questioned his grocer, banker, friends and neighbors.

Conspiracy, Obstruction Laws

Following are some of the sections of the United States Code pertaining to conspiracy and obstruction of justice. All are part of Title 18, "Crimes and Criminal Procedure."

Section 201 (h): "Whoever, directly or indirectly, gives, offers, or promises anything of value to any person, for or because of the testimony under oath or affirmation given or to be given by such person as a witness upon a trial, hearing, or other proceeding, before any court, any committee of either House or both Houses of Congress, or any agency, commission, or officer authorized by the laws of the United States to hear evidence or take testimony, or for or because of his absence therefrom....Shall be fined not more than $10,000 or imprisoned for not more than two years, or both."

Section 371: "If two or more persons conspire either to commit any offense against the United States, or to defraud the United States, or any agency thereof in any manner or for any purpose, and one or more of such persons do any act to effect the object of the conspiracy, each shall be fined not more than $10,000 or imprisoned not more than five years, or both...If, however, the offense, the commission of which is the object of the conspiracy, is a misdemeanor only, the punishment for such conspiracy shall not exceed the maximum punishment provided for such misdemeanor."

Section 1503: "Whoever corruptly, or by threats or force, or by any threatening letter of communication, endeavors to influence, intimidate, or impede any witness, in any court of the United States or before any United States magistrate or other committing magistrate, or any grand or petit juror, or officer in or of any court of the United States, or officer who may be serving at any examination or other proceeding before any United States magistrate or other committing magistrate, in the discharge of his duty, or injures any party or witness in his person or property on account of his attending or having attended such court or examination before such officer, magistrate, or other committing magistrate, or on account of his testifying or having testified to any matter pending therein, or injures any such grand or petit juror in his person or property on account of any verdict or indictment assented to by him, or on account of his being or having been such juror, or injures any such officer, magistrate, or other committing magistrate in his person or property on account of the performance of his official duties, or corruptly or by threats or force, or by any threatening letter of communication, influences, obstructs, or impedes, or endeavors to influence, obstruct, or impede, the due administration of justice, shall be fined not more than $5,000 or imprisoned not more than five years, or both."

He said false reports had been circulated that he feared homosexual attacks if sent to prison and that he had been running around with a "beautiful foreign woman" while his wife was vacationing in Florida. He did not indicate the source of the reports or who was reportedly probing his background.

Classified Documents. Committee Chairman Sam J. Ervin Jr. (D N.C.) announced midway through the day that the White House had agreed to a committee request to disclose certain classified domestic intelligence reports. White House counsel Leonard Garment wrote in a letter to Ervin that the committee should "use its discretion" concerning documents relating to 1970 administration plans for gathering domestic intelligence. Ervin had requested that the documents be introduced as evidence in a letter to Garment June 25. *(Texts of other documents, p. 122)*

The documents, Ervin said, were those that Dean had removed from the White House and placed in a safe, giving the key to U.S. District Court Judge John J. Sirica, who conducted the trial of the Watergate defendants. Sirica subsequently gave the papers to the committee. Ervin said one of the documents, concerning foreign intelligence operations, would not be made public.

Dean read one of the declassified documents, a top secret memo he had sent to Mitchell Sept. 18, 1970, regarding creation of a secret interdepartmental intelligence evaluation committee. Dean had mentioned the memo in his testimony June 25.

Government Activities. Dean also enlarged on earlier testimony that various government agencies helped the White House with extra-legal activities. He related how, after two reporters for the Long Island, N.Y., newspaper, *Newsday*, had written a story on the financial dealings of Bebe Rebozo, the President's friend, that "I got instructions that one of the authors should have some problems."

He did not say who gave him the instructions. Dean took the matter up with White House aide John J. Caulfield, who had contacts in the Internal Revenue Service. An extensive audit was performed on the reporter, Dean said, but he did not know the outcome of the audit.

An FBI probe of CBS newsman Daniel Schorr was initiated by Haldeman, Dean said. "But to the dismay of the White House," he went on, the FBI did a full field investigation on Schorr, requiring the White House to put out a false story that he was being considered for a high administration job. *(Schorr statement, 1972 Almanac p. 975)*

Witness June 27

Toward the end of Dean's third day in the witness chair, he was confronted with a memorandum accusing him and his "patron," former Attorney General Mitchell, of being chiefly responsible for the planning and coverup of the Watergate affair. It was read by Sen. Daniel K. Inouye (D Hawaii), who said he wanted to give the President "his day in court." *(Text, p. 162)*

The memo, drafted by J. Fred Buzhardt, special White House counsel, said there was no reason to doubt that Dean was "the principal actor in the Watergate coverup, and that while other motivations may have played a part, he had a great interest in covering up for himself."

Dean was described later in the memorandum, which quoted and paraphrased statements of several officials in sworn depositions and committee testimony, as "not merely one of the architects of the coverup plan," but "also its most active participant."

Moreover, the document continued, Dean became "the principal author of the political and constitutional crisis that Watergate now epitomizes." Disclosure of the facts immediately after the 1972 break-in would have been "the kind of embarrassment that an immensely popular President could easily have weathered," the memo stated. "The political problem has been magnified 1,000-fold because the truth is coming to light so belatedly, because of insinuations that the White House was a party to the coverup, and, above all, because the White House was led to say things about Watergate that have since been found to have been untrue. These added consequences were John Dean's doing."

Inouye offered Dean the chance to interject his own views about statements in the memo. Dean's responses reaffirmed the positions he had taken in his opening statement. At one point, he interjected that the memo appeared to have been prepared by someone unfamiliar with White House operations who "put it together from newspaper accounts."

Gurney Questioning. Despite 3½ hours of close questioning by Sen. Edward J. Gurney (R Fla.), earlier in the day, Dean could not be budged from his story that the President was aware of the coverup by Sept. 15, 1972. Gurney led Dean through practically all the events he had mentioned in his statement June 25. Dean could not be shaken from his previous testimony.

Gurney gave Dean the toughest going-over on the subject of the September meeting with Nixon, about which Dean testified he believed the President was aware of efforts to cover up White House involvement in the Watergate scandal. Dean told Gurney that the meeting lasted about 30 to 40 minutes and included discussions of pending suits by the Democratic National Committee and Common Cause, in addition to the upcoming Watergate trial. The coverup was not specifically mentioned, Dean said, nor were the FBI interviews of White House personnel, which Dean sat in on, or the destruction of some of Howard Hunt's papers.

Gurney asked Dean if at the meeting he discussed Haldeman's instructions to Gordon Strachan to destroy transcripts of the initial Watergate bugging of Democratic Party headquarters, in May 1972; the plan to involve the CIA in the coverup, and Dean's coaching of Jeb Magruder for his Watergate grand jury testimony. Dean said no to all three matters.

Gurney: "Well, now, how can you say that the President knew all about these things from a simple observation by him that 'Bob tells me you are doing a good job?' "

Dean: "Well, Senator, I assume you know how your staff operates. I assume members of your staff understand how you operate, how reporting requirements proceed. I was aware of the fact that Mr. Haldeman often made notes. Mr. Haldeman has a good memory. Mr. Haldeman does not leave details aside. This was the hottest issue that was going in the campaign. I can't believe that the fact that we were going to contain this matter would totally escape the President's attention, and it was to me a confirmation and a compliment to me that I had done this."

Gurney: "Don't you think the President might have been complimenting you on the—I will use the word investigation even if you don't desire that word—of the involvement of the people in the White House, the FBI interviews, all of that business; don't you think he might have been discussing that?"

Dean: "I would think he would say something to the effect that, 'Well, your investigation has been very accurate' rather than 'Bob's been telling me everything you have been doing and you have been doing a good job.' "

Gurney: "We are talking about something very important, whether the President of the United States knew on Sept. 15 about the Watergate and the coverup."

Dean: "I am totally aware. My mind is not a tape recorder. It does recall impressions of conversations very well, and the impression I had was that he had told me that Bob had reported to him what I had been doing."

Gurney: "In other words, your whole thesis on saying that the President of the United States knew about Watergate on Sept. 15 is purely an impression; there isn't a shred of evidence that came out of this meeting."

Dean: "Senator, I don't have a thesis. I am reporting the facts as I am able to recall them thoroughly to the committee."

Gurney insisted, however, that Dean had misinterpreted the President's remarks at the Sept. 15 meeting and that the President "didn't know about all this business" until a series of meetings with Dean that began in late February 1973. Gurney also questioned Dean about an earlier statement by Magruder that in January 1973 or December 1972 Dean "expressed a lack of memory" about meetings both had attended at which Liddy presented his intelligence plans that ultimately resulted in the Watergate break-in. *(Magruder testimony, p. 135)*

Dean said he thought Magruder had his meetings confused and that he really was "referring to the fact that on March 28, when I came back from Camp David, that I was playing very dumb, and I was. I did not want to engage in a discussion of my recollections of those meetings because we had gone over that before, and I had made my decision by that time as to what I was going to do, and I did not want to get into a debate on it."

Documents. During the morning session, Dean gave the committee a series of documents dealing with a so-called "political enemies" project in the White House. The documents contained a list of about 200 important people in politics, business, the arts, labor and journalism, and a strategy outlining how the Nixon administration could "use the available federal machinery to screw our political enemies." One of the documents contained the names and brief background descriptions of 20 persons in various fields marked for "priority activity" in the enemies project. *(Box, p. 153)*

Secret reprisals apparently were to be taken against those on the list of 20, while those on the larger list were to be excluded from government jobs, appointments, White House invitations and other administration courtesies.

As the afternoon session began, Dean handed over to the committee other documents apparently related to political activities by the FBI under previous administrations. Most of the documents were memorandums from William Sullivan, a former top FBI official, to the late FBI director, J. Edgar Hoover. Ervin accepted the documents but said he would not release them immediately, because he was not sure the select committee's mandate authorized it to investigate such matters.

Witness June 28

Sen. Lowell P. Weicker Jr. (R Conn.) startled the Watergate hearings June 28 by charging that attempts had been made by the White House to smear him in order to influence his work on the committee. Weicker said he had asked special Watergate prosecutor Archibald Cox to investigate whether the actions amounted to an illegal "obstruction of proceedings before special committees." *(Conspiracy, obstruction statutes, box, p. 157)*

Weicker said he was informed April 10 that persons in the White House had approached someone he did not name and asked if there was anything illegal about contributions to Weicker's 1970 campaign. The senator also said that in "the last several days" another individual he did not name was told by former White House aide Charles W. Colson that Colson had given money to Weicker's campaign.

According to Weicker, Colson told the person "the money was not properly handled" and that "I (Weicker) was being a disloyal Republican and the time had come to swing around."

Heated Statement. Weicker then asked Dean whether attempts had been made to influence his testimony, and when Dean answered yes, Weicker went into a long, heated statement addressed as much to White House personnel as to the hearing room and television audience:

"Whether it's you in that witness chair or whether it's me in this committee chair or any man in back of this committee, there is (sic) going to be no more threats, intimidation, no innuendo, no working through the press to go ahead and destroy the credibility of individuals. If the executive branch of government wants to meet the standards that the American people set for it in their minds, then the time has come to stop reacting and stop playing this type of a game and either disavow it completely or make the very specific charges that apparently are being leaked out....

"Let me make it clear, because I've got to have my partisan moment, Republicans do not cover up, Republicans do not go ahead and threaten, Republicans do not go ahead and commit illegal acts, and God knows Republicans don't view their fellow Americans as enemies to be harassed; but rather I can assure you that Republicans and those that I serve with look upon every American as a human being to be loved and won."

The audience applauded Weicker's remarks. Committee Vice Chairman Howard H. Baker Jr. (R Tenn.) said the committee would investigate the attempts to influence Weicker as well as any other attempts to influence witnesses of committee members.

Further Dean Testimony. Meanwhile, Dean emerged unscathed from his fourth full day of testimony, despite close questioning by Baker and Daniel K. Inouye (D Hawaii), who asked Dean a series of questions propounded by White House special counsel J. Fred Buzhardt. Buzhardt denied, however, that the questions Inouye asked and a Buzhardt statement Inouye read the day before concerning Dean were White House documents.

Baker and Committee Chairman Sam J. Ervin Jr. (D N.C.) indicated they wanted to hear from the President about Dean's testimony. Ervin indicated a preference for direct presidential testimony, and Baker said information would be sought from Nixon "in whatever manner can be arranged."

"You can't cross-examine a written statement," Ervin said.

Baker led Dean through a series of questions concentrating on his Sept. 15, 1972, meeting with the President, about which Dean had testified he realized Nixon was aware of the Watergate coverup.

"This is really a terribly important meeting in history, you know," Baker said.

Dean said he told the President, "It (Watergate) has been contained." Then he went on to say, "I don't believe it can continue to be contained," Dean related. "Those are my exact words."

Baker asked if the President appeared puzzled or startled and how H. R. Haldeman, also present at the meeting, reacted. Dean said he had not been studying their faces. But Dean was forced to concede to Baker that the President did not make a direct statement at the meeting mentioning the coverup. "In effect, you drew inferences from the President's remarks," said Baker.

"That's correct," Dean replied.

Several questions Inouye asked Dean—questions that had been submitted by Buzhardt—concerned whether or not the witness deliberately leaked his impending testimony to the press in an effort to get federal prosecutors to give him immunity in exchange for his cooperation.

Dean answered that his dealings with the press always were "on the record" and that he had no leak strategy. "I dealt directly with the appropriate investigative forums," he said.

Dean was pressed on the Sept. 15 meeting. He said he could not recall the exact words the President used, but that "my mind received a clear message" that the President knew of the coverup.

Inouye asked Dean if he took notes on the meeting. Dean said no, "I didn't want to make a record of it." Why? asked Inouye. Because it was "very incriminating to the President of the United States," Dean answered.

Another Buzhardt question relayed by Inouye asked whether Dean in March 1972 interceded on Liddy's behalf when Liddy and Jeb Magruder had a serious argument. The point of the question appeared to be that Dean knew of the break-in plan and wanted to make sure Magruder did not fire Liddy. Dean denied any intercession for Liddy.

Ervin, with obvious relish, led the witness through a series of questions tending to show that constitutional guarantees had been violated by Watergate and White House intelligence-gathering plans. Ervin asked if Dean knew anything that the President did between the date of the break-in and June 28, 1973, to see that "the laws be faithfully executed," as Article 2 of the Constitution requires him to do. Dean asked to be excused from drawing a conclusion on that.

Ervin also drew from Dean the admission that First and Fourth Amendment guarantees had been breached in a 1970 domestic intelligence plan drawn up by former White House aide Tom Charles Huston. The plan, which the White House said was rescinded after five days, included breaking and entering and electronic surveillance of domestic radicals. *(p. 122)*

Dean testified that he never saw a document showing revocation of the plan and that two months after it was approved he was asked to get it started.

Daily Chronology

Following is a day-to-day chronology of the week's events:

JUNE 21

(Earlier June 21 events, p. 150)

Strauss Break-In. In a deposition released to the press on the Democrats' $6.4-million damage suit against the Nixon re-election committee, Democratic National Chairman Robert S. Strauss gave details of a break-in at his Dallas, Texas, home in July 1972, when he was treasurer of the Democratic National Committee. Strauss said his files had been rifled but no valuables had been taken, and that he later came to suspect it had been done by "people who did the Watergate or people with the same motives." The testimony was taken May 29. *(Earlier statement, p. 120)*

Strauss also said that former Democratic Chairman Lawrence F. O'Brien feared for his life after the June 17 Watergate break-in.

JUNE 22

McCord Testimony. Convicted conspirator James W. McCord Jr. testified at a closed hearing of the House Armed Services Subcommittee on Intelligence, which was investigating Central Intelligence Agency (CIA) involvement in the Watergate case. He told reporters after the session that he had written a number of letters to CIA officials in 1972, warning them of efforts to blame the agency for the Watergate bugging.

Hunt Payment. *The New York Times* reported that convicted conspirator E. Howard Hunt Jr. was paid $72,000 in March, after threatening to "tell all" about White House operations against Daniel Ellsberg in 1971. The threat came in a letter to Dean that was to be relayed to former White House aide Ehrlichman. The money reportedly was delivered by Frederick C. LaRue, a former aide to John N. Mitchell.

The same day, a *Washington Post* article cited a memorandum on the Hunt bribery incident obtained by the Senate Watergate committee from the White House. The memo quoted Nixon as saying March 21 that a Hunt request for $1-million to maintain silence on White House intelligence operations was "wrong, that it would not work (and) that the truth would come out anyway." *(p. 150)*

Baker Statement. Sen. Howard H. Baker Jr. (R Tenn.), vice chairman of the Senate Watergate investigating committee, repeated an earlier denial for reporters: "I have made it a point not to talk to the President or the cabinet about the substance of Watergate.... I have never asked the White House for guidance. I have never sought it." Baker was responding to news leaks implying that he or his staff had consulted with the White House on Watergate matters. *(Earlier statement, p. 148)*

White House Questions. The White House had submitted a list of questions to Watergate committee minority counsel Fred D. Thompson to be asked of Dean when he appeared before the committee, *The Washington Star-News* reported. Thompson was said to have passed the questions along to Democrats on the committee.

Richardson Statement. Attorney General Elliot L. Richardson told newsmen in Chicago he wished the Senate investigating committee would suspend its hearings until after the Justice Department had finished its investigation of former White House officials. Continuation of the hearings inevitably would influence future criminal cases, he said.

McGovern Charge. Sen. George McGovern (D S.D.) said in an interview with Associated Press that he was planning to "seek an appropriate forum to make clear the integrity" of his 1972 presidential campaign—and was thinking of speaking at the Senate Watergate hearings if Chairman Ervin approved. McGovern said he was upset that so many people thought dirty campaign tactics were used by both political parties. *(Earlier statement, p. 147)*

JUNE 23

Petersen Warning. Assistant Attorney General Henry E. Petersen met with Nixon and then Attorney General Richard G. Kleindienst on April 15 and urged the President to suspend aides John D. Ehrlichman and H. R. Haldeman immediately because of their involvement in the Watergate coverup, according to sources quoted by *The New York Times.* In his April 30 television address, Nixon announced the resignations of his aides and said that the action should not be "seen by anyone as evidence of any wrongdoing by either one." *(p. 148)*

JUNE 24

Final Leak. The Times came out with one final leaked item in advance of Dean's June 25 appearance before the Senate Watergate committee. The report said Dean would tell the committee that Nixon told him in mid-March of a discussion Nixon had with Charles W. Colson on executive clemency for conspirator Hunt. Colson, a former special counsel to the President, had denied earlier press reports that he relayed a Hunt request for clemency to Dean and Ehrlichman.

Klein Comment. Nixon's outgoing director of communications, Herbert G. Klein, said on NBC-TV's "Meet the Press" he thought some people entrusted with power in the White House had "misused" or "misinterpreted" that power. He predicted that Nixon would hold a news conference soon but would not fully answer all questions on the Watergate case because of ongoing investigations. Nixon's last press conference had been on March 15.

Sedan Chair. *The St. Louis Post-Dispatch,* which had identified a Republican undercover agent mentioned in Senate testimony as "Sedan Chair," reported that the agent, Michael W. McMinoway, infiltrated the 1972 campaigns of both Hubert H. Humphrey and McGovern. McMinoway reportedly posed as a volunteer security guard at the Democratic national convention in Miami Beach, Fla., and overheard McGovern campaign director Frank Mankiewicz discussing the health of Sen. Thomas

F. Eagleton (D Mo.) before Eagleton was chosen as the vice presidential nominee. *(Earlier story, p. 146)*

JUNE 25

Dean Testimony. John W. Dean III, fired as presidential counsel on April 30, made his long-awaited public appearance before the Senate investigating committee and became the first person to implicate the President directly in a White House conspiracy to cover up the Watergate scandal. Testifying under a grant of limited immunity, Dean said the President was aware of the coverup as early as September 1972. *(Testimony, p. 154, excerpts of statement, p. 163)*

Percy Speech. Sen. Charles H. Percy (R Ill.), principal sponsor of a resolution calling for an independent Watergate prosecutor, attacked suggestions that Nixon should be subpoenaed or should resign over Watergate as attempts to "distort constitutional principles to fit the needs of the moment." Percy said that "though the President was not intended to be the equivalent of a monarch, he was also not intended to become the stepchild of Congress." *(Resolution, p. 28)*

McCloskey Charge. Rep. Paul N. McCloskey Jr. (R Calif.) charged that Nixon had violated his oath of office by ordering the creation of an extra-legal intelligence unit directed by the White House. He said all the information gathered by the Senate investigating committee should be turned over to the House Judiciary Committee so the House could begin its own inquiry into the grounds for impeachment. *(Earlier statement, p. 115)*

JUNE 26

Dean Testimony. In his second day of testimony before the Senate investigating committee, Dean stuck to the allegations he had made the previous day. In response to a series of questions by Sen. Joseph M. Montoya (D N.M.), Dean asserted that Nixon's public statements on the Watergate case had been misleading, unfounded or overly broad. *(Testimony, p. 156)*

White House Reaction. Deputy White House press secretary Gerald L. Warren asserted that Nixon would continue to stand behind his May 22 statement, which Dean's testimony challenged.

Colson Counterattack. Former Nixon aide Charles W. Colson, speaking on NBC-TV's "Today" show, denied a series of allegations Dean made against him in testimony the previous day, and charged that the former counsel was the leader of a "conspiracy" aimed at keeping the truth from Nixon. Colson said he had never discussed executive clemency with convicted conspirator Hunt, never knew "hush money" was being paid to the defendants and did not remember proposing a burglary at the Brookings Institution—all charges made by Dean.

Nixon Subpoena. Testifying at a joint Senate committee hearing on executive privilege and government secrecy, Attorney General Elliot L. Richardson said he thought it was "very doubtful" that a congressional committee could compel the President to appear before it.

JUNE 27

Dean Testimony. In his third day before the Senate Watergate committee, Dean faced three hours of close, often hostile questioning by Sen. Edward J. Gurney (R Fla.) on aspects of his testimony, including his personal use of Republican funds. In the afternoon, Sen. Daniel K. Inouye (D Hawaii) read into the record a White House summary attacking Dean's testimony and portraying him as the "mastermind" of the cover-up attempt. Dean interrupted Inouye frequently to dispute the charges. *(Testimony, p. 157)*

LaRue Plea. Frederick C. LaRue, former aide to Attorney General John N. Mitchell, pleaded guilty in U.S. District Court in Washington, D.C., to charges of conspiracy to obstruct justice. "I joined in (the Watergate) coverup, at least by acquiescence," he admitted as he waived his right to go before a grand jury. Judge John J. Sirica postponed sentencing until further indictments in the Watergate case were handed down.

LaRue's plea was the result of an agreement reached with special prosecutor Archibald Cox that he would cooperate with the government by testifying at criminal trials connected with the case and by telling the prosecutors all he knew.

Kleindienst Denials. Former Attorney General Richard G. Kleindienst disputed several points of Dean's Senate testimony in an interview in *The Washington Post.* Dean had consistantly misled him and Assistant Attorney General Henry E. Petersen on Watergate, Kleindienst said, and had led them to believe he communicated directly with Nixon on the case and had warned the President of its seriousness immediately after the 1972 break-in. Kleindienst said that in his own occasional personal contacts with Nixon, "the President never suggested anything to me but a full investigation, with the chips falling where they may."

JUNE 28

Dean Testimony. Dean spent a fourth day being questioned by members of the Senate investigating committee. *(p. 159)*

Hunt Testimony. Convicted Watergate conspirator E. Howard Hunt Jr. testified privately before the House Armed Services Subcommittee on Intelligence about an alleged plot by defendants to blame the CIA for the Watergate break-in. The charge was made by another defendant, James W. McCord Jr., in his testimony before the Senate investigating committee. *(p. 80)*

Montoya Funds. *The Wall Street Journal* carried an article charging that Sen. Joseph M. Montoya (D N.M.), a member of the Senate Watergate committee, had concealed the sources of "as much as $100,000" in contributions to his 1970 re-election campaign. The story said Montoya funneled the money, which came from labor unions, construction contracts and other special interest groups, through "phony committees." After the election, he reportedly filed a sworn financial statement that did not mention the contributions, but they showed up later in reports filed with the House clerk by the original donors. An aide to the senator was quoted as saying that Montoya had complied with "all laws governing senatorial campaign contributions at the time."

TEXT OF WHITE HOUSE MEMO

Following is the edited text of a White House memorandum prepared by the office of J. Fred Buzhardt, special counsel to the President, and used by the Senate select Watergate committee in its questioning of John W. Dean III on June 27. Sources of the quotations and many paraphrased statements are sworn depositions and previous Senate testimony of other Watergate figures.

It is a matter of record that John Dean knew of and participated in the planning that went into the break-in at Watergate, though the extent of his knowledge of that specific operation or of his approval of the plan ultimately adopted have not yet been established. There is no reason to doubt, however, that John Dean was the principal actor in the Watergate coverup, and that while other motivations may have played a part, he had a great interest in covering up for himself.

PRE-JUNE 17

Dean came to the White House from Justice from a background of working on problems of demonstrations and intelligence. Among those working under him at the White House were Tom Huston and John Caulfield. Dean was involved in discussions in 1971 about the Sandwedge plan Caulfield proposed. Ehrlichman was told that the original authors of the $1,000,000 plan were Dean and Liddy. Whatever the fact about this, it is clear that Dean attended the meetings that led up to adoption of the Watergate plan. Dean introduced Mitchell (who had sponsored Dean for his White House position) to Liddy on November 24, 1971. Dean introduced Magruder to Liddy in December, 1971, and suggested Liddy for the combined position of general counsel and chief of intelligence gathering for CRP. He told Magruder that Mitchell had hired Liddy.

Dean, Liddy, Mitchell, and Magruder met to discuss intelligence plans of this kind on January 27, 1972, and on February 4th. Dean was not present at the final meeting on March 30 when the $250,000 plan was approved. It is not clear whether he was not there because he disapproved or simply because he was not in Key Biscayne or because he wanted to try to keep his own record clean. He is reported as having said that he "didn't think it was appropriate for him to be in on these conversations." He is also reported to have said, at a meeting in Mitchell's office, that "We shouldn't discuss this in front of Mitchell or in the Attorney General's office." At some point during the spring Magruder phoned Dean and asked him to talk to Liddy to try and calm him down. At another point Dean, knowing that a bugging operation was under serious consideration, called Magruder and referred to the importance of Liddy's intelligence activities. This arose after an argument between Magruder and Liddy; Dean urged Magruder not to let personal animosity "get in the way of the project." Also in March, 1973, Dean claimed to Haldeman that, in the spring of 1972, he had told Haldeman that he had been to two meetings at which unacceptable and outlandish ideas for intelligence gathering had been rejected by himself and by Mitchell and that he, Dean, proposed not to attend any more such meetings. Haldeman has no personal recollection of Dean telling him about the meetings at the time but is "willing to accept that as a possibility."

POST-JUNE 17

Whatever the facts may be on the matters that are uncertain in the spring of 1972 about Dean's knowledge of specific approval of the breakin, it must have been clear to Dean, as a lawyer, when he heard on June 17th of Watergate, that he was in personal difficulty. The Watergate affair was so clearly the outgrowth of the discussions and plans he had been in on that he might well be regarded as a conspirator with regard to them. He must immediately have realized that his patron, Mitchell, would also be involved.

It appears that Ehrlichman called Dean on June 17th to advise him of the problem and to direct him to take charge of it for the White House. Even without an instruction, this would have been his responsibility, as Counsel for the President, from the time of the occurrence and he was active in that role from the moment of his return to the city a day or two after the breakin.

On June 19th Dean met with Liddy, Mitchell, Strachan, Magruder, and Sloan. Dean, Mitchell and Magruder also met with LaRue and Mardian that evening in Mitchell's apartment. At these meetings the coverup plan was hatched. A series of meetings followed throughout the summer. Dean and Mitchell were Magruder's principal contacts on the coverup.

Dean was not merely one of the architects of the coverup plan. He was also its most active participant. Magruder correctly concluded that Dean "was involved in all aspects of this coverup."

- It was Dean who suggested to Haldeman that the FBI was concerned that it might run into a CIA operation.
- It was Dean who suggested to General Walters on January 26th that CIA pay the Watergate defendants while in jail.
- It was Dean, purportedly acting on behalf of Mitchell, who came to Ehrlichman several weeks after the break-in to obtain approval for fundraising by Kalmbach for the arrested persons.
- It was Dean who reviewed the papers found in Hunt's safe and declared that they were "politically sensitive" and should be given special treatment.
- It was Dean who sought unsuccessfully to have the others omit his name from the list of those who attended meetings on the Liddy plans.
- It was Dean who urged Hunt to flee the country two days after the burglary.
- It was Dean and Mitchell who prepared Magruder for his perjurious grand jury testimony.
- It was Dean who said of a memorandum Colson had prepared on August 29th stating the facts as he knew them: "For God's sake destroy the memo, it impeaches Magruder."
- It was Dean who suggested that Sloan take the Fifth Amendment, though Sloan was innocent.
- It was Dean who was the agent in some of the money dealings with arrested persons.
- It was Dean who told Colson not to make a transcript of Colson's taped conversation with Hunt and said that he, Dean, would handle the matter.

Throughout all of this Dean was perfectly situated to mastermind and to carry out a coverup since, as Counsel to the President and the man in charge for the White House, he had full access to what was happening in the investigation. He sat in on FBI interviews with White House witnesses and received investigative reports. Dean and Ehrlichman met with Attorney General Kleindienst late in July. The Attorney General described the investigation and said that "it did not appear that any White House people or any high-ranking Committee people were involved in the preparation or planning or execution of the breakin." History fails to record that at that moment Dean corrected the Attorney General's erroneous impression by pointing out that Mitchell, Magruder, and Dean had all been involved in planning of operations of which Watergate was an obvious derivative, or that Strachan had knowledge of the fruits of this kind of operation, or that all of them were suborning perjury and otherwise seeking to conceal the facts.

Dean's activity in the coverup also made him, perhaps unwittingly, the principal author of the political and constitutional crisis that Watergate now epitomizes. It would have been embarrassing to the President if the true facts had become known shortly after June 17th, but it is the kind of embarrassment that an immensely popular President could easily have weathered. The political problem has been magnified 1,000-fold because the truth is coming to light so belatedly, because of insinuations that the White House was a party to the coverup, and, above all, because the White House was led to say things about Watergate that have since been found to have been untrue. These added consequences were John Dean's doing.

Dean was responsible within the White House for becoming apprised of what had happened. From June 17th on, Dean had periodic coversations with Ehrlichman "about virtually every aspect of this case." Dean reported also to Haldeman and to Ziegler, to whom he gave repeated assurances that he had made an "intensive investigation" and had found no White House involvement. Dean was "the foundation of the proposition that the White House was not involved."

SPRING 1973

With the election past and public interest in Watergate on the wane, Dean may have thought that this coverup had been a success, although he purported to continue an ongoing investigation. At the same time Dean was affecting a failing memory and talking to Magruder as if Dean did not recall the pre-Watergate planning meetings in which he had participated. In February, however, with the Ervin Committee beginning its work, the President was again concerned that all of the available facts be made known. In the middle of February, 1973, Dean and Richard Moore met with Ehrlichman and Haldeman at San Clemente. Dean was assigned to reduce "to written form all of the detailed facts as they related both to the Committee to Re-elect and the White House." Dean was pressed continually for that statement, particularly by Haldeman, but never produced it.

At this point the Gray confirmation hearings were imminent and the Ervin hearings were on the horizon. The President, who had barely known Dean, determined that Counsel to the President was the appropriate person with whom to work in formulating the President's position on executive privilege and similar legal issues that these hearings—and news conferences on March 2nd and 15th at which they would arise—would present. Between February 27th and April 16th the President met with Dean (and usually others) 21 or 22 times and there were 14 telephone conversations between March 10th and April 22nd. It is probable that Dean helped induce the views on attorney-client privilege and on separation of powers that would have immunized Dean himself from having to testify under oath. During this period Dean was developing other problems. On March 10th there were press reports that it was Dean who had recommended Liddy to CREP. On March 22nd Pat Gray testified that Dean had lied to him during the course of the FBI investigation of Watergate. On March 23rd McCord's letter to Judge Sirica was made public. The coverup coming uncovered.

During this period the point was frequently raised by various people, including primarily the President, that the whole story of Watergate should be made public. "Dean's answer always was we can't do it while the investigation is continuing, there are conflicting versions of events and the rights of defendants might be prejudiced by a statement."

On March 20th the President indicated that he still did not have all the facts. In the preceding week Dean had begun to express to to Richard Moore concern about Dean's own involvement, referring to the meetings in Mitchell's office, the plumbers' operation and the Ellsberg break-in, and the demand by Hunt, possibly on March 16th, for more money. After the two of them met with the President on March 20th, Moore told Dean: "I don't think the President has any idea of the kinds of things that you've told me about." When Dean agreed that the President did not, Moore told Dean that it was his obligation to advise the President and lectured Dean on this subject. On March 21st Dean gave the President a more complete, but still laundered, version of the facts, and so surprised the President that, according to press accounts of what Dean is saying: "The President came out of his chair." At this meeting Dean indicated that Magruder was involved but that he did not know about Mitchell. He mentioned the Ellsberg break-in and possibly a second story job at the Brookings Institution. He told about the attempt by Hunt to blackmail Ehrlichman over the Ellsberg break-in. He suggested that Haldeman, Ehrlichman, and Dean might all have some problem about the financial transactions with the defendants but that he thought they were more technical and political than legal. He gave no hint, however, of his own orchestration of perjured testimony by Magruder and others.

Ehrlichman suggested that everyone be made to appear before the grand jury and waive executive privilege. Dean thought this would be a good idea but only if the persons who appeared before the grand jury were given immunity. At another meeting that day Ehrlichman strongly opposed immunity. On March 23rd Dean was sent to Camp David in order to complete the long-promised report. Dean was at Camp David for six days but came down on the night of the 28th and "delivered nothing."

The failure of Dean's Muse while he was on the mountain is understandable, since by this time it would have been impossible to write a believable report that would not have been self-indicting. While he was at Camp David, Dean told Ehrlichman's assistant that he was "not getting the statement done but was planning his own defense." Haldeman talked with him several times and felt that "Dean was not having much progress in writing his report but it became clear that he was worrying more about himself." On the 25th the President suggested it be announced that Dean would appear before the grand jury. On the 26th Dean agreed but said that he would do so only if given immunity.

On March 30th the President relieved Dean of any further responsibility for the Watergate investigation. He called Ehrlichman in, told him that it was evident to the President that "Dean was in the thing up to his eyebrows," and assigned Ehrlichman to look into Watergate. The President indicated to Ehrlichman that his conversations with Dean throughout the preceding month had given him "a growing awareness of Dean's personal involvement in this...."

Relieved of his Watergate duties by the President and aware that his own complicity had become obvious, Dean decided to strike out on his own to hunt for immunity for the long list of wrongs he had committed. According to the press, it was April 2nd when he first established contact with the prosecutors and attempted to bargain for immunity. While he carried on these negotiations, Ehrlichman completed his report and advised the President on April 14th that Mitchell, Magruder, and Dean were all involved. On the 16th Dean was asked by the President to resign but refused to do so. On the 30th he was dismissed. His increasingly shrill efforts since that date to save himself by striking out recklessly at others are too familiar and too painful to require mention.

EXCERPTS FROM DEAN STATEMENT

Following are excerpts from the text of a statement made by John W. Dean III, former White House counsel, before the Senate Watergate investigating committee on June 25. All the testimony below is related to Dean's meetings with President Nixon in 1972 and 1973.

MEETING WITH THE PRESIDENT SEPT. 15, 1972

On Sept. 15 the Justice Department announced the handing down of the seven indictments by the federal grand jury. Late that afternoon I received a call requesting me to come to the President's oval office. When I arrived at the oval office I found Haldeman (H.R. Haldeman, then White House chief of staff) and the President. The President asked me to sit down. Both men appeared to be in very good spirits and my reception was very warm and cordial. The President then told me that Bob (Haldeman) had kept him posted on my handling of the Watergate case. The President told me I had done a good job and he appreciated how difficult a task it had been and the President was pleased that the case had stopped with Liddy (conspirator G. Gordon Liddy). I responded that I could not take credit because others had done much more difficult things than I had done. As the President discussed the present status of the situation I told him that all that I had been able to do was to contain the case and assist in keeping it out of the White House. I also told him that I thought that there was a long way to go before this matter would end and that I certainly could make no assurances that the day would not come when this matter would start to unravel.

Early in our conversation the President said to me that former FBI Director Hoover had told him shortly after he had assumed office in 1969 that his campaign had been bugged in 1968. The President said that at some point we should get the facts out on this and use this to counter the problems that we were encountering.

The President asked me when the criminal case would come to trial and would it start before the election. I told the President that I did not know. I said that the Justice Department had held off as long as possible the return of the indictments, but much would depend on which judge got the case. The President said that he certainly hoped that the case would not come to trial before the election.

The President then asked me about the civil cases that had been filed by the Democratic National Committee and Common Cause and about the counter-suits that we had filed. I told him that the lawyers at the re-election committee were handling these cases and that they did not see the Common Cause suit as any real problem before the election because they thought they could keep it tied up in discovery. I then told the President that the lawyers at the re-election committee were very hopeful of slowing down the civil suit filed by the Democratic National Committee because they had been making *ex parte* contacts with the judge handling the case and the judge was very understanding and trying to accommodate their problems. The President was pleased to hear this and responded to the effect that "well, that's helpful." I also recall explaining to the President about the suits that the re-election lawyers had filed against the Democrats as part of their counter offensive.

There was a brief discussion about the potential hearings before the Patman committee (the House Banking and Currency Committee). The President asked me what we were doing to deal with the hearings and I reported that Dick Cook, who had once worked on Patman's committee's staff, was working on the problem. The President indicated that Bill Timmons (White House congressional liaison chief) should stay on top of the hearings, that we did not need the hearings before the election.

The conversation then moved to the press coverage of the Watergate incident and how the press was really trying to make this into a major campaign issue. At one point in this conversation I recall the President telling me to keep a good list of the press people giving us trouble, because we will make life difficult for them after the election. The conversation then turned to the use of the Internal Revenue Service to attack our enemies. I recall telling the President that we had not made much use of this because the White House didn't have the clout to have it done, that the Internal Revenue Service was a rather Democratically oriented bureaucracy and it would be very dangerous to try any such activities. The President seemed somewhat annoyed and said that the Democratic administrations had used this tool well and after the election we would get people in these agencies who would be responsive to the White House requirements....

I left the meeting with the impression that the President was well aware of what had been going on regarding the success of keeping the White House out of the Watergate scandal, and I also had expressed to him my concern that I was not confident that the coverup could be maintained indefinitely.

MEETING OF FEB. 27, 1973

This was the first meeting I had had with the President since my Sept. 15, 1972, meeting which related to the Watergate. It was at this meeting that the President directed that I report directly to him regarding all Watergate matters. He told me that this matter was taking too much time from Haldeman's and Ehrlichman's (John D. Ehrlichman, then chief adviser on domestic affairs) normal duties, and he also told me that they were principals in the matter, and I, therefore, could be more objective than they. The President then told me of his meetings with Sen. Baker (Howard H. Baker (R Tenn.)) and the attorney general (Richard G. Kleindienst). He told me that Sen. Baker had requested that the attorney general be his contact point and that I should keep in contact with the attorney general to make sure that the attorney general and Sen. Baker were working together.

He asked me to follow up immediately to determine if the attorney general and Baker had met. I informed him that I had earlier discussed this with the attorney general and the attorney general was planning to meet with Sen. Baker and Sen. Ervin (Sen. Sam J. Ervin Jr., chairman of the investigating committee) to discuss turning over FBI data regarding the Watergate investigation. A brief discussion followed in which the President recounted what had already been reported to me by Haldeman, that he had told Sen. Baker that he would not permit White House staff to appear before the select committee, rather he would only permit the taking of written interrogatories. He asked me if I agreed with this and I said that written interrogatories were something that could be handled, whereas appearances might create serious problems. He told me he would never let Haldeman and Ehrlichman go to the Hill.

He also told me that Sen. Gurney (Edward J. Gurney (R Fla.), a member of the select committee) would be very friendly to the White House and that it would not be necessary to contact him, because the President said Sen. Gurney would know what to do on his own. On the way out of his office, he told me I had done an excellent job of dealing with this matter during the campaign; that it had been the only issue that (George) McGovern had had and the Democrats had tried to make something out of it but to no avail. I told him as we were walking together out of the office that I had only managed to contain the matter during the campaign, but I was not sure it could be contained indefinitely. He told me that we would have to fight back and he was confident that I could do the job.

MEETING OF FEB. 28

I had received word before I arrived at my office that the President wanted to see me. He asked me if I had talked to the attorney general regarding Sen. Baker. I told him that the attorney general was seeking to meet with both Sen. Ervin and Sen. Baker. but that a meeting date had not yet been firmed up. I told him that I knew it was the attorney general's wish to turn over the FBI investigation, and the President said that he didn't think we should, but asked me what I thought of the idea. I told him that I did not think that there was much damaging information in the FBI investigation although there could be some bad public relations from it. He told me to think about this matter.

He also said that he had read in the morning paper about the Vesco case and asked me what part if any his brother Ed had had in the matter. I told him what I knew of his brother's involvement, which was that he was an innocent agent in the contribution transaction. We then discussed the leak to *Time* magazine of the fact that the White House had placed wiretaps on newsmen and White House staff people. The President asked me if I knew how this had leaked. I told him that I did not; that I knew several people were aware of it. But I didn't know any who had leaked it....

We...talked about the executive privilege statement, and the President expressed his desire to get the statement out well in advance of the Watergate hearings so that it did not appear to be in response to the Watergate hearings.... I told him that I thought he should know that I was also involved in the post-

June-17 activities regarding Watergate. I briefly described to him why I thought I had legal problems, in that I had been a conduit for many of the decisions that were made and therefore could be involved in an obstruction of justice. He would not accept my analysis and did not want me to get into it in any detail other than what I had just related. He reassured me not to worry, that I had no legal problems. (Note: I raised this on another occasion with the President, when Dick Moore (a White House aide) was present.)

MEETING OF MARCH 1

The first meeting on this date and the afternoon meeting which occurred on March 1 related to preparing the President for his forthcoming press conference. The President asked me a number of questions about the Gray (L. Patrick Gray III, nominee for FBI director) nomination hearings and facts that had come out during these hearings. In particular I can recall him stating that there should be no problem with the fact that I had received the FBI reports. He said that I was conducting an investigation for him and that it would be perfectly proper for the counsel to the President to have looked at these reports. I did not tell the President that I had not conducted an investigation for him, because I assumed he was well aware of this fact and that the so-called Dean investigation was a public relations matter, and that frequently the President made reference in press conferences to things that never had, in fact, occurred.

I was also aware that often in answering Watergate questions that he had made reference to my report and I did not feel that I could tell the President that he could not use my name. There had been considerable adverse publicity stemming from the Gray hearings and the fact that Gray was turning over FBI information to the Senate Judiciary Committee which caused the President to tell me at this morning meeting that Gray must be "pulled up short"....

He...told me the FBI Watergate materials should not be turned over by Gray. I informed him that I had had a meeting several days prior with Mr. Sullivan (William C. Sullivan, former assistant FBI director), who had been at the FBI for many years, and Sullivan had alluded to the fact that the FBI had been used for political purposes by past administrations. I cited a few examples that Mr. Sullivan had given me. The President told me to get this information from Sullivan.... He also told me that I should gather any material I could gather regarding the uses and abuses of the FBI by past administrations so that we could show that we had not abused the FBI for political purposes. The President told me that he was convinced that he had been wiretapped in 1968 and the fact that DeLoach (Cartha DeLoach, assistant FBI director) had not been forthcoming indicated to the President that DeLoach was probably lying. He told me that I should call Don Kendall, DeLoach's employer, and tell him that DeLoach had better start telling the truth because "the boys are coming out of the woodwork." He said this ploy may smoke DeLoach out. He also asked me who else might know about the bugging of his 1968 campaign, and I suggested that Mr. (Clyde) Tolson, Hoover's former assistant, might have some knowledge of it. He told me that he probably ought to call Mr. Tolson and wish him happy birthday or good health and possibly get some information from him when he talked to him.

MEETING OF MARCH 7

The President was very unhappy with Gray's performance before the Senate Judiciary Committee. In my meeting with him on this date, he made a reference to the fact that Gray's comment regarding my sitting in on the investigations by the FBI was absurd. He felt it was perfectly proper that I was present at those interviews and said that Gray's attitude that he "jolly well" went forward because he had no alternative was absurd.... At the end of the meeting, the President instructed me to tell the attorney general to cut off Gray from turning over any further Watergate reports to the Senate Judiciary Committee. He said this just had to cease.

MEETING OF MARCH 13

This was a rather lengthy meeting, the bulk of which was taken up by a discussion about the Gray hearings and the fact that the Senate Judiciary Committee had voted to invite me to appear in connection with Gray's nomination. It was at this time we discussed the potential of litigating the matter of executive privilege and thereby preventing anybody from going before any Senate committee until that matter was resolved. The President liked the idea very much, particularly when I mentioned to him that it might be possible that he could also claim attorney/client privilege on me so that the strongest potential case on executive privilege would probably rest on the counsel to the President. I told him that obviously this area would have to be researched. He told me that he did not want Haldeman and Ehrlichman to go before the Ervin hearings and that if we were litigating the matter on Dean, that no one would have to appear.

Toward the end of the conversation, we got into a discussion of Watergate matters specifically. I told the President about the fact that there were money demands being made by the seven convicted defendants, and that the sentencing of these individuals was not far off. It was during this conversation that Haldeman came into the office. After this brief interruption by Haldeman's coming in, but while he was still there, I told the President about the fact that there was no money to pay these individuals to meet their demands. He asked me how much it would cost. I told him that I could only make an estimate that it might be as high as a million dollars or more. He told me that that was no problem, and he also looked over at Haldeman and repeated the same statement. He then asked me who was demanding this money and I told him it was principally coming from Hunt (defendant E. Howard Hunt Jr.) through his attorney.

The President then referred to the fact that Hunt had been promised executive clemency. He said that he had discussed this matter with Ehrlichman, and contrary to instructions that Ehrlichman had given Colson (Charles W. Colson, then a special counsel to the President) not to talk to the President about it, that Colson had also discussed it with him later. He expressed some annoyance at the fact that Colson had also discussed this matter with him. The conversation then turned back to a question from the President regarding the money that was paid to the defendants. He asked me how this was done. I told him I didn't know much about it other than the fact that the money was laundered so it could not be traced and then there were secret deliveries. I told him I was learning about things I had never known before, but the next time I would certainly be more knowledgeable. This comment got a laugh out of Haldeman....

MEETINGS OF MARCH 14

The meetings which occurred on this day principally involved preparing the President for a forthcoming press conference. I recall talking about executive privilege and making Dean a test case in the courts on executive privilege. The President said that he would like very much to do this and if the opportunity came up in the press conference, he would probably so respond.

I also recall that during the meetings which occurred on this day that the President was going to try to find an answer that would get Ziegler (Ronald L. Ziegler, presidential press secretary) off the hook of the frequent questions he was asked regarding the Watergate. He said that he was going to say that he would take no further questions on the Watergate until the completion of the Ervin hearings and that Ziegler could in turn repeat the same statement and avoid future interrogation by the press on the subject.

MEETING OF MARCH 15

It was late in the afternoon after the President's press conference that he asked Dick Moore and I to come over to visit with him. He was in a very relaxed mood and entered into a general discussion about the press conference. The President was amazed and distressed that the press had paid so little attention to the fact that he made an historic announcement about Ambassador (David K. E.) Bruce opening up the liaison office in Peking. He said he was amazed when the first question following that announcement was regarding whether or not Dean would appear before the Senate Judiciary Committee in connection with the Gray hearings....

MEETING OF MARCH 17

This was St. Patrick's Day, and the President was in a very good mood and very relaxed, and we engaged in a rambling conversation with only some brief reference to the Gray hearings and the problems that were then confronting the White House regarding the President's statements on executive privilege and his willingness to go to court on the matter. He opined that he did not think that the Senate would be dumb enough to go for the bait he had given them but he was hopeful that they might.

MEETING OF MARCH 20

It was during the afternoon of March 20 that I talked again with Dick Moore about this entire coverup matter. I told Moore that there were new and more threatening demands for support money. I told him that Hunt had sent a message to me—through Paul O'Brien (an attorney for the President's re-election committee)—that he wanted $72,000 for living expenses and $50,000 for attorney's fees, and if he did not receive it that week, he would reconsider his options and have a lot to say about the seamy things he had done for Ehrlichman while at the White House.

I told Moore that I had about reached the end of the line, and was now in a position to deal with the President to end the coverup. I did not discuss with Moore the fact that I had discussed money and clemency with the President earlier, but I told him that I really didn't think the President understood all of the facts involved in the Watergate and particularly the implications of those facts. I told him that the matter was continually compounding itself, and I felt that I had to lay the facts out for the President as well as the implication of those facts. Moore encouraged me to do so.

MEETINGS OF MARCH 21

As I have indicated, my purpose in requesting this meeting particularly with the President was that I felt it necessary that I give him a full report of all the facts that I knew and explain to him what I believed to be the implication of those facts. It was my particular concern with the fact that the President did not seem to understand the implications of what was going on. For example, when I had earlier told him that I thought I was involved in an obstruction of justice situation he had argued with me to the contrary after I had explained it to him.

Also, when the matter of money demands had come up previously, he had very nonchalantly told me that that was no problem, and I did not know if he realized that he himself could be getting involved in an obstruction of justice situation by having promised clemency to Hunt. What I had hoped to do in this conversation was to have the President tell me that we had to end the matter—now. Accordingly, I gave considerable thought to how I would present this situation to the President and try to make as dramatic a presentation as I could to tell him how serious I thought the situation was that the coverup continue.

I began by telling the President that there was a cancer growing on the Presidency and that if the cancer was not removed that the President himself would be killed by it. I also told him that it was important that this cancer be removed immediately because it was growing more deadly every day. I then gave him what I told him would be a broad overview of the situation and I would come back and fill in the details and answer any questions he might have about the matter.

I proceeded to tell him how the matter had commenced in late January and early February, but that I did not know how the plans had finally been approved. I told him I had informed Haldeman what was occurring, and Haldeman told me I should have nothing to do with it. I told him that I had learned that there had been pressure from Colson on Magruder, but I did not have all the facts as to the degree of pressure. I told him I did not know if Mitchell had approved the plans, but I had been told that Mitchell had been a recipient of the wiretap information and that Haldeman had also received such information through Strachan (Gordon C. Strachan, a Haldeman aide).

I then proceeded to tell him some of the highlights that had occurred during the coverup. I told him that Kalmbach (Herbert W. Kalmbach, then Nixon's personal attorney) had been used to raise funds to pay these seven individuals for their silence at the instructions of Ehrlichman, Haldeman and Mitchell and I had been the conveyors of this instruction to Kalmbach. I told him that after the decision had been made that Magruder (Jeb Stuart Magruder, deputy campaign director) was to remain at the re-election committee, I had assisted Magruder in preparing his false story for presentation to the Grand Jury. I told him that cash that had been at the White House had been funneled back to the re-election committee for the purpose of paying the seven individuals to remain silent.

I then proceeded to tell him that perjury had been committed, and for this coverup to continue it would require more perjury and more money. I told him that the demands of the convicted individuals were continually increasing and that with sentencing imminent, the demands had become specific. I told him that on Monday the 19th, I had received a message from one of the re-election committee lawyers who had spoken directly with Hunt and that Hunt had sent a message to me demanding money. I then explained to him the message that Hunt had told Paul O'Brien the proceding Friday to be passed on to me. I told the President I'd asked O'Brien why to Dean and O'Brien had asked Hunt the same question. But Hunt had merely said you just pass this message on to Dean.

The message was that Hunt wanted $72,000 for living expenses and $50,000 for attorneys' fees, and if he did not get the money and get it quickly that he would have a lot of seamy things to say about what he had done for John Ehrlichman while he was at the White House. If he did not receive the money, he would have to reconsider his options. I informed the President that I had passed this message on to both Haldeman and Ehrlichman. Ehrlichman asked me if I had discussed the matter with Mitchell. I had told Ehrlichman that I had not done so, and Ehrlichman asked me to do so. I told the President I had called Mitchell pursuant to Ehrlichman's request but I had no idea of what was happening with regard to the request.

I then told the President that this was just typical of the type of blackmail that the White House would continue to be subjected to and that I didn't know how to deal with it. I also told the President that I thought that I would, as a result of my name coming out during the Gray hearings, be called before the grand jury and that if I was called to testify before the grand jury or the Senate committee, I would have to tell the facts the way I know them. I said I did not know if executive privilege would be applicable to any appearance I might have before the grand jury. I concluded by saying that it is going to take continued perjury and continued support of these individuals to perpetuate the cover-up and that I did not believe it was possible to so continue it; rather I thought it was time for surgery on the cancer itself and that all those involved must stand up and account for themselves and that the President himself get out in front of this matter. I told the President that I did not believe that all of the seven defendants would maintain their silence forever. In fact, I thought that one or more would very likely break rank.

After I finished, I realized that I had not really made the President understand, because after he asked a few questions, he suggested that it would be an excellent idea if I gave some sort of briefing to the cabinet and that he was very impressed with my knowledge of the circumstances but he did not seem particularly concerned with their implications. It was after my presentation to the President and during our subsequent conversation the President called Haldeman into the office and the President suggested that we have a meeting with Mitchell, Haldeman and Ehrlichman to discuss how to deal with this situation. What emerged from that discussion after Haldeman came into the office was that John Mitchell should account for himself for the pre-June-17 activities, and the President did not seem concerned about the activities which had occurred after June 17.

In the late afternoon of March 21, Haldeman and Ehrlichman and I had a second meeting with the President. Before entering this meeting I had a brief discussion in the President's outer office of the executive office building suite with Haldeman in which I told him that we had two options: One is that this thing goes all the way and deals with both the pre-activities and the post-activities; or the second alternative, if the cover-up was to proceed, we would have to draw the wagons in a circle around the White House and that the White House protect only itself. I told Haldeman that it had been the White House's assistance to the re-election committee that had gotten us into much of this problem and now the only hope would be to protect ourselves from further involvement.

The meeting with the President that afternoon with Haldeman, Ehrlichman and myself was a tremendous disappointment to me, because it was quite clear that the coverup as far as the White House was going to continue. I recall that while Haldeman, Ehrlichman and I were sitting at a small table in front of the President in his Executive Office Building, that I for the first time said in front of the President that I thought that Haldeman, Ehrlichman and Dean were all indictable for obstruction of justice and that was the reason I disagreed with all that was being discussed at that point in time.

I could tell that both Haldeman, and particularly Ehrlichman, were very unhappy with my comments. I had let them very clearly know that I was not going to participate in the matter any further and that I thought it was time that everybody start thinking about telling the truth. I again repeated to them I did not think it was possible to perpetuate further the coverup, and the important thing now was to get the President out in front of it.

MEETING OF MARCH 22

The meeting with the President, Ehrlichman, Haldeman, Mitchell and me was again a general discussion of the Senate Watergate hearings situation and did not accomplish anything. Rather it was a further indication that there would be no effort to stop the coverup from continuing. I recall that Mitchell told the President that he felt that the only problem that he now had was the fact that he was taking a public beating on his posture on executive privilege; that the statement on executive privilege was too broad and that probably something should be done to change his posture on this matter. Mitchell was not suggesting that members of the White House go to the Hill to testify, rather that some more cooperative position be developed to avoid the adverse publicity.

It was at this time that the President said that Kleindienst (then Attorney General Richard G. Kleindienst) was supposed to be working these things out with Sen. Baker, and he apparently had not been doing so. The President said that Timmons had told him that a member of Sen. Baker's staff was very desirous of a meeting to get guidance. It was at this point that the President called the attorney general and told him that he should get up to meet with Baker as soon as possible and get some of these problems regarding executive privilege and the turning of documents over resolved with the committee immediately....

The President told me that the White House should start directly dealing with the committee and that I should go up and commence discussions with Sen. Ervin as to the perameters of executive privilege. I told the President that I did not think this would be wise, because I was very much the party in issue with regard to the Judiciary Committee hearings and that it would be unwise for me to go to the Hill and negotiate my own situation. The President agreed and Ehrlichman said that he would commence discussions.

The meeting was almost exclusively on the subject of how the White House should posture itself vis-a-vis the Ervin committee hearings. There was absolutely no indication of any changed attitude, and it was like one of many meetings I had been in before, in which the talk was of strategies for dealing with the hearings rather than any effort to get the truth out as to what had happened both before June 17 and after June 17.

Following this meeting with the President, it was apparent to me that I had failed in turning the President around on this subject, but Ehrlichman and Haldeman began taking over with regard to dealing with a new problem, which had become John Dean, as they were aware that I was very unhappy about the situation.

MEETING OF APRIL 15

The President was very cordial when we met. I was somewhat shaken when I went in to meet him, because I knew I had taken it upon myself to end the coverup, and what I had started was going to cause serious problems for the President. I shall attempt to recall the highlights of the conversation that transpired on the meeting which occurred about 9 p.m. on April 15.

I told the President that I had gone to the prosecutors,and that I did not believe that this was an act of disloyalty but rather, in the end, it would be an act of loyalty. I told him I felt this matter had to end. I informed the President that I told the prosecutors of my own involvement and the involvement of others. At one point in the conversation, I recall the President asking me about Haldeman's knowledge of the Liddy plans. He asked me if I had told him earlier about the fact that I had met with Haldeman after the second meeting in Mitchell's office and told Haldeman what was going on and my reaction to what was going on. I told the President that I had reported this fact to him earlier.

The President then made some reference to Henry Petersen (assistant attorney general in charge of the Watergate investigation) asking about why Haldeman had not turned it off at that point and told me to testify that I had told Haldeman about the meeting in Mitchell's office. The President almost from the outset began asking me a number of leading questions, which made me think that the conversation was being taped and that a record was being made to protect himself. Although I became aware of this because of the nature of the conversation, I decided that I did not know it for a fact and that I had to believe that the President would not tape such a conversation. Some question came up, by the President, as to whether I had immunity. As best as I can recall, I told him my lawyers had discussed this with the prosecutors, but certainly I had no deal with the government. He told me that he did not want to do anything to hurt my negotiations with the government. I do not recall commenting on his remark.

I also recall that the conversation turned to the matter of Liddy not talking. He said something about Liddy was waiting for a signal and I told him that possibly he was waiting for a signal from the President. I discussed with him the fact that maybe if Liddy's lawyer met with him that Liddy would begin to open up, because I said that I thought that that would be very helpful if Liddy did talk. It was during this part of the conversation that the President picked up the telephone and called

Henry Petersen and pretended with Petersen that I was not in the room but that the matter of Liddy's coming forward and talking had arisen during our conversation. The President relayed to Petersen that if Liddy's lawyer wanted to see him to get a signal that the President was willing to do this. The President also asked me about Petersen, and I told him if anyone could give him good advice, Henry Petersen could.

The President also asked me if I remembered what day it was in March that I had reported to him on some of the details of the Watergate matter. He said that he thought it was the 21st but wasn't certain. I said that I could not recall for certain without checking. At another point in the conversation the matter of the degree of discussions that I had had with the prosecutors came up, and I informed the President that I had had no discussions with the prosecutors relating to conversations I had had with him or in anything in the area of national security. The President told me that I could not talk about national security areas and that I should not talk about conversations I had had with him, because they were privileged conversations.

Toward the end of the conversation, the President recalled the fact that at one point we had discussed the difficulty in raising money and that he had said that one million dollars was nothing to raise to pay to maintain the silence of the defendants. He said that he had, of course, only been joking when he made that comment.

As the conversation went on, and it is impossible for me to recall anything other than the high points of it, I became more convinced that the President was seeking to elicit testimony from me and put his perspective on the record and get me to agree to it. The most interesting thing that happened during the conversation was, very near the end, he got up out of his chair, went behind his chair to the corner of the Executive Office Building office and in a barely audible tone said to me, he was probably foolish to have discussed Hunt's clemency with Colson. I do not recall that I responded. The conversation ended shortly thereafter.

As I was on my way out of the office after exchanging parting pleasantries, I told the President that I hoped that my going to the prosecutors and telling the truth would not result in the impeachment of the President. He jokingly said, "I certainly hope so also," and he said that it would be handled properly.

MEETING OF APRIL 16

I arrived at (Nixon's) office about 9:45, and rather than going to the reception entrance normally used by other members of the staff and me, I went into Mr. Steve Bull's office. Mr. Bull is the one who had informed me that the President wanted to see me, so I went to his office. Mr. Bull told me I would have to wait a few minutes, because the President was in another meeting. A few minutes later, Haldeman and Ehrlichman emerged laughing from the President's office, and when they saw me in Mr. Bull's office, their faces dropped. They said hello, put on a serious look and departed. I went into the President's office.

The President told me that he had been thinking about this entire matter and thought it might be a good idea if he had in his drawer a letter from me requesting that he accept my resignation or in the alternative an indefinite leave of absence. He said that he had prepared two letters for my signature and he would not do anything with them at this time but thought it would be good if he had them. He then passed me a Manila file folder with two letters in it. The President said that he had prepared the letters himself and that no one would know I had signed them. I read the letters and was amazed at what I was being asked to sign. I have submitted to the committee copies of the letters, but since they are very brief I will read them.

- The first letter, dated April 16 1973, read:
  Dear Mr. President:

  In view of my increasing involvement in the Watergate matter, my impending appearance before the grand jury and the probability of its action, I request an immediate and indefinite leave of absence from my position on your staff.

- The second letter, which was even more incriminating, read:
  Dear Mr. President:

  As a result of my involvement in the Watergate matter, which we discussed last night and today, I tender you my resignation effective at once.

After reading the letters, I looked the President squarely in the eyes and told him that I could not sign the letters. He was annoyed with me, and somewhat at a loss for words. He said that maybe I would like to draft my own letter. I told him that the letters that he had asked me to sign were virtual confessions of anything regarding the Watergate.

I also asked him if Ehrlichman and Haldeman had signed letters of resignation. I recall that he was somewhat surprised at my asking this and he said no, they had not, but they had given him a verbal assurance to the same effect. He then elaborated that Haldeman and Ehrlichman had said that if they were called before the grand jury they would seek an indefinite leave of absence. They had given him their verbal assurances. I then told him that he had my verbal assurance to the same effect.

It was a tense conversation, but I was not going to sign the letters under any circumstances. As I sat there talking with the President, I had very much on my mind the laughter in Ehrlichman's and Haldeman's voices when they walked out of the office before they realized that I was waiting outside to see the President. To break the impasse, the President said that he would like me to draft my own letter and report back to him later. He said that he was working on a statement regarding the Watergate and the recent developments that had come to his attention as a result of his meetings with Kleindienst and Petersen and would appreciate my thoughts. He said that he would also like a suggested draft letter for Haldeman and Ehrlichman or maybe a form letter that everyone could sign. I told him I would draft a letter and would report back to him.

The President called me to come to his EOB office about 4 that afternoon. He asked me if I had drafted a letter. I said that I had as well as I had prepared some thoughts for his statement. He asked to see the letter, a copy of which I have submitted to the committee, but again shall read it because it is very brief:

> Dear Mr. President:
>
> You have informed me that Bob Haldeman and John Ehrlichman have verbally tendered their requests to be given an immediate and indefinite leave of absence from your staff. By this letter I also wish to confirm my request that I be given such a leave of absence from your staff.

After the President read the letter, he handed it back to me and said it isn't what he wanted. I then told him that I would not resign unless Haldeman and Ehrlichman resigned. I told him that I was not willing to be the White House scapegoat for the Watergate. He said that he understood my position and he wasn't asking me to be a scapegoat. I then gave him my recommendations of the draft statement. Before he read the draft statement, he said that he had checked his records and it had been on March 21 that I had met with him and given him the report on the problems of the Watergate and its coverup.

I have submitted to the committee a copy of the draft statement I prepared for the President. The gist of the statement was two-fold: First, the President had learned of new facts in the case over the weekend, and as a result of this information had directed Henry Petersen to take charge and leave no stone unturned; secondly, that he had accepted requests from Haldeman, Ehrlichman and Dean to be placed on leave of absence. The President said virtually nothing about the statement, and after reading it told me to talk with Len Garment (a Nixon adviser), who he said was also preparing a draft. ✓

HISTORIAN DECRIES WATERGATE AS 'CULT OF PERSONALITY'

Historian Daniel J. Boorstin sees the Watergate scandal as different—and more dangerous—than other typically American political misconduct because it suggests a rise in "the cult of personality." Boorstin, whose generally conservative views once found favor with Nixon administration officials, made this and other provocative statements about Watergate in an exclusive interview with Congressional Quarterly.

Although taking issue with those who see Watergate as the obituary of American civilization, Dr. Boorstin warned of the growth of presidential power and of executive branch power in general.

"In a practical way," he told CQ Editor William B. Dickinson Jr., "one of the questions which should arise immediately is the question of the nature of the Executive Office of the President. I think that should be subject to investigation and scrutiny.... The Executive Office of the President has expanded beyond all bounds and has tended to supersede the executive branch of the government."

Dr. Boorstin, who presently is director of the Smithsonian Institution's National Museum of History and Technology and will become its senior historian this fall, said he could not believe that the responsibility of the office of the President is served by its proliferation.

"How many of these people and how many of these White House positions were simply superfluous?" Boorstin asked. "As I watched some of the Watergate hearings I kept asking myself what all these people—Dean and others—were doing there in the first place. Was there really an honest job there that needed doing?"

The interview follows:

Democracy and Discontents

CQ: Dr. Boorstin, your newly published book bears the title, *The Americans: The Democratic Experience.* Knowing what you now know about the Watergate scandal, would you describe Watergate as typical or atypical of the American experience?

Boorstin: Well, I would rather say that it's a parable of "Democracy and its Discontents." With apologies to Sigmund Freud, I think the Watergate drama really is a symbol of many of the problems of democracy in a country like ours where we have the technology and the power to give everything to nearly everybody. What I mean by that is that democracy, like civilization itself, depends on the repression of many things. That is, it depends on self-denying ordinances, on people who have the power to do something refusing to do that thing. And I think there has not been another example, in recent history at least, of so vivid a drama of this aspect of the problem of democracy.

There's something to be noted, however, in view of all the self-flagellation and crying of woe of those who say that this is the obituary of American civilization, which, of course, it is not. We have to recognize that one

"The separation of powers is proving itself in some interesting new ways."

of the distinctions between democracy and other forms of government is that while democracy is messy on the surface, other forms of government are messy underneath. In fact, in most countries in the world (I have recently visited Greece, for example) the sorts of things that are reported with such horror in the Watergate episode wouldn't even make the newspapers.

Now this, of course, is not to justify them at all. But it is simply to remind us that one of the characteristics of our society and one of the things in which we can take satisfaction is that violations of the rights of individuals, when they come to public attention, reach the whole community.

CQ: Many Americans seem to feel that Watergate is just politics as usual. Others see the series of scandals as unprecedented in American political history, profoundly different and more serious than previous misconduct. What do you think?

Misuse of Power

Boorstin: Well, if we consider the problem of democracy to be essentially that of people in power refusing to use the power in ways that are not authorized and not decent and not constitutional, I would say that what makes this different from earlier problems in our society is that today the opportunities for the misuse of power are greater. Just stop to think for a moment about some of the central implements in the Watergate scandal. The most conspicuous was the Executive Office of the President. Why there are hundreds of people who write on White House stationery. This is a new phenomenon. In fact, it's a phenomenon which has astonished, and properly astonished, some senators who asked the counsellor of the President if he ever saw the President and he said he didn't. And I think there are something like 40 persons who bear some title such as counsellor to the President or assistant to the President or something of that sort, Now this is a relatively new phenomenon: the opportunity for the President to get out of touch with the people who speak in his name.

The growth of presidential power, and of executive power in general, is symbolized in welfare legislation and

"The respect of the American people for the Congress has been increased. They can see the Congress as a vigilant Congress."

in the increased activities of the federal government. Just think of some of the peripheral questions that have been raised. The SEC (Securities and Exchange Commission), for example, is an institution of recent creation. And, in fact, look at two of the main organizations that have figured so largely in the problem of the cover up. The Federal Bureau of Investigation, for example, didn't begin to come into existence until 1908. It was then reformed under Attorney General Harlan Stone in 1924 and didn't get its present title until 1935, I believe. The Central Intelligence Agency—the CIA—is another example of an organization that didn't come into being really until 1947 under the National Security Act.

And then, the techniques of electronic bugging. And here there is a rather interesting irony in that the crime and the punishment use the same technology. The crime of bugging is punished by a universal diffusion of the information about the people to everybody in the United States—also by electronic techniques. The opportunities to misuse power have increased. That means that for a functioning democracy the demand for self-control is greater than ever. Yet in Watergate we see the failure to repress primitive desires—the desire to kill off the enemy, the desire to follow the leader wherever he leads, the refusal to compromise with others, the lack of liberal charity toward your electoral opponent. All these things are dramatized. But it takes more self-control now because the opportunities to misuse power are greater and the opportunity for the leader to be separate from those who exercise it—from those who can speak in his name.

Conscience of Democracy

CQ: The public seems to express its cynicism about the question of self-control with the phrase "everybody is doing it in politics." Is that a dangerous state of public mind?

Boorstin: Well, of course. This again is one of the curious problems of democracy. And it is the result of the development of the electronic media to a large extent. We used to think of the conscience as being a private, intimate, still, small voice within. Now the conscience of democracy becomes the whole community sitting in the living room watching what has been done. Now I think it is very important when we think of this as the conscience of democracy, which indeed it is, that we separate two things which can easily be confused. On the one hand there is what could be called the *conscience of the marketplace*—the people's feeling of outrage at the violation of common decency, of legal and constitutional rules.

And on the other hand, what might be called *the judgment of the marketplace.* The judgment of the marketplace is lynch law, and that is something we must beware of. So that while it is wholesome that the community should have an opportunity to be outraged at the spectacle of certain facts, and of certain crimes that have been committed, the judgment of the community and the force of law must still be scrupulously hedged around by technicality. And that's why the Founding Fathers, the people who wrote the Constitution, were so circumspect, for example, in describing the process of impeachment. They thought that it was not to be undertaken lightly.

CQ: A number of past historical incidents are cited as resembling Watergate: The Hayes election of 1868, the Teapot Dome are examples. What's the closest parallel you see between Watergate and other typically American political scandals?

'Lawless Sheriffs'

Boorstin: Well, I don't think there is really a specific parallel. I think that there has been a continuing tendency in American life, which I describe in *The Americans: The Democratic Experience* in a chapter entitled "Lawless Sheriffs and Honest Desperadoes." The circumstances of the United States being so vast a country with so many diffused agencies of law enforcement has tended to confuse the law enforcer with the violator of the law. It is an old American tradition (and *not* a good one!) for the sheriff to shoot first and investigate afterwards, on the assumption that if the man he shot was a suspicious character and not liked in the community he probably deserved it anyway. This is an ancient and traditional American procedure in the West, in old mining camps and frontier communities.

CQ: Now transferred to the White House?

Boorstin: Well, I think the earlier scandals have been distinct in at least one way—in that they tended to be connected with greed and with the desire of people to make something out of it—the Teapot Dome, something of that sort. But one of the frightening aspects of this is that so far, at least, none of those high in the government stood to make any substantial sums of money out of what was done.

This suggests the danger of what, in the Soviet Union, they call the cult of personality, which I think is not too far from one of the problems we've been discerning. Where loyalty to the leader seemed to override everything else. And it should be recalled that the committee that was involved was not the Republican National Committee but the Committee to Re-elect the President. And it was focused on the particular man, and this is one of the most disturbing aspects of it.

Separation of Powers

CQ: One of the obvious effects of Watergate has been to undermine the effectiveness of the President very early in his second term. Are there any historical precedents for this and, if so, what are the implications for the balance of power between the Congress and the President?

Boorstin: One of the things that we've witnessed which has not been sufficiently pointed out is the great advantage that the nation has at the moment in having a fixed-term election. If this had been a parliamentary system the government would have fallen, there would have been, perhaps, another party put in power and then there would have been criminal prosecutions. The problem would not have been dramatized as a political problem. The members of Congress or Parliament as it might have been, who were in the party of the President, would have been interested to minimize the episode so that it wouldn't affect their re-election. They would have to go to the people to be re-elected. It would be in their interest to minimize.

Now, in the present situation, where we see such an even-handed concern among Republicans and Democrats over this problem, this is to no small extent due to the fact that they're in there and that they are re-elected for a fixed term, especially the Senators—for a senatorial term—and that when they expose the misdeeds of the leader of their party in the White House, they are not thereby requiring themselves to go to the people and stand for election. So that there's a kind of antisepsis.

The separation of powers is proving itself in some interesting new ways, and I would say that one of the consequences of this, in public opinion, has been that whatever effect this may have had on the prestige of the presidency, the respect of the American people for the Congress has been increased. They can see the Congress as a vigilant Congress. The virtue of vigilance is certainly dramatized and the integrity of the courts is dramatized so that in quite a new way we have seen the wisdom—in almost an unsuspected way—the wisdom of the writers of the Constitution in separating the powers this way.

Another interesting point also which comes up, which is something the political scientists always debate about, is the special problem in our kind of government where you can have a President of one party and a majority in both houses of Congress of another party. Recent American history should at least give political scientists some pause in this regard and, in this case, we see certain advantages in having this disparity without a paralysis of government. I think in several recent administrations we've seen that it is possible to get legislation. Under President Eisenhower we had a similar situation—with a President of one party and majorities of the other party in the Congress. There are even some advantages in having that division. In that way you have some scrutiny of the executive power and yet it remains possible for the executive to do some fairly dramatic and important things in foreign policy.

CQ: On the other hand, under the parliamentary system, the President or party leader would have been removed. And we may face the possibility of living with a President, who the public may decide has been discredited, for more than three years before a change. Does this bother you in any way? Is it fatal to our system of government to live with a President as powerful as he is in this kind of condition if it lasts for three more years?

Boorstin: Well, it certainly doesn't cheer me up. It's a discouraging thought, but in our society it is not disastrous. One of the great things about our form of government is that the nation doesn't stand or fall with the President. It was remarked during one presidential election that Divine Providence must watch over the United States, attested by the fact that we have survived the Presidents that we have had. That was said at the time of the election of President Lincoln. But this nation can survive all sorts of Presidents and its existence, fortunately, does not depend on the President.

22nd Amendment

CQ: Watergate, then, to you, doesn't reveal any fundamental weaknesses in the present system that require change by Constitution or by law?

Boorstin: I think the passage of the 22nd Amendment in the Constitution (limiting Presidents to two terms) was a mistake. I think that the proposal for a six-year term for the President is also misguided. I think one of the points in having a representative government is to have the elected person in power always subject to the possibility of being re-elected or not being re-elected. It's just conceivable that the President might have been more vigilant if he had known that he was going to be a candidate in another election or at least might be a candidate in another election.

That was a very shortsighted and, I think, malicious constitutional amendment. It doesn't belong in the Constitution. And I think that the notion that it is desirable to have a President who can give his full attention to the "presidency" and not worry about re-election is quite a mistake. What we want is a President who will be thinking about the prospects of re-election and will wonder what reaction the public will have to what he's doing as President. That's what we mean by representative government.

CQ: David Broder of the *Washington Post* has raised the same point in several of his columns. But it's not likely, is it, that this amendment will be repealed during the presidency of Richard Nixon or, at least, in a way that would enable him to seek re-election?

Boorstin: It's very unlikely that it will be repealed. The important thing is to realize that the President must consider himself to be subject to the public approval or disapproval. If he's a lame duck President and not subject to re-election, and also if there is as little concern for the party as a whole as there seems to have been recently, then that removes one of the main incentives of the President to keep in touch with the public will.

CQ: There seems to be an impression that the quality of the men and women going into politics for elective office and into places like the White House or the Cabinet is lower today than in our past history. Is this a valid belief?

Quality of Politicians

Boorstin: No. The quality of people in politics today is as high as it ever was. You know the old quip that a statesman is a dead politician. It's our tendency to think that way but we have as high a quality of intelligence and integrity in the Congress, in the judiciary and in the executive branch, on the whole, as we've ever had. The demands are greater and many of the tasks are almost undo-able. And obviously, the needs for people with a broad vision of the economic problems and the other problems are so much greater with the increase of the powers of government.

"One of the distinctions between democracy and other forms of government is that while democracy is messy on the surface, other forms of government are messy underneath."

"The notion that it is desirable to have a President who can give his full attention to the 'presidency' and not worry about re-election is quite a mistake."

CQ: Are people getting the kind of government they deserve? In other words, to what extent do the people themselves bear responsibility for a Watergate and its off-shoots?

Boorstin: There are two questions here. One is the question of public morals in general, and I don't think there's any dividing line. If we condone the violation of the rules of confidence—of confidentiality—and the laws by newspapermen condone it and recognize it and admire it—then we are on the way to condoning similar acts among others, including government officials.

Credibility vs. Truth

CQ: We've seen over recent years a breakdown of credibility of almost all institutions—the church, the press, the military, the educational system—and even now the spectre of the final collapse of faith in government. How do we restore that faith in government, particularly among the young people whose cynicism and distrust of government may already be near a breakdown?

Boorstin: Well, may I suggest that part of the problem is contained in the way we are now accustomed to put the question. We talk about "credibility" and the "credibility" gap. From ancient times, the critics of democracy beginning with Plato have always said that democracy was apt to be too much concerned with appearances—the way things looked to people. Part of our problem is that we've become concerned with credibility rather than truth. People talk about the credibility gap. They should talk about the truth gap. And I think that the development of the public media, the development of the public relations profession and of advertising, and of all the things that we like to look at, enjoy looking at or can't help looking at, tends to put a premium on the believable rather than the true.

This is something that we must remind ourselves of, and I think that Watergate serves as an example of this too, in the sense that the concern of the coverup was to produce a credible story. The impact of the hearings will depend on the credibility of the witnesses. But that's a different question. We will eventually reach the point—I hope—it's important to be sure that the government agencies do reach the point—not of talking about credibility but talking about truth. What were the facts of the case? Not what sounds good, or looks good enough for people to believe if they don't know any more than they do.

CQ: And you see that then as the key to restoration of the public faith in government is the return to truth?

Boorstin: Oh, I believe in truth and motherhood and all that. Don't quote me. But, seriously, what I'm trying to describe as an historian is the large developments in our society that have led us to put a premium on what's credible rather than on what's true, and what looks good rather than what are the facts of the case.

The rise of advertising is a very good example of this, which I would call the rhetoric of democracy. If we define democracy as the effort to give everything to everybody, then in order to get things to people you have to persuade them that the things are worth having. You have to put the best light on things that you want to sell them. You then become preoccupied with appearances—with what looks good, with what sounds good. And you're going down that road of credibility. We have been led almost to assume by implication that it's good to be concerned with credibility—that it's good to be credible. That's the wrong way to put it. It's good to state the truth, but the ability to be credible is a dangerous ability—not a virtue.

Ervin Hearings

CQ: In your new book, you use the phrase "mass producing the moment." Looking at the Ervin hearings in the Senate, how much of this is mass production of the moment? How much is image and how much is reality?

Boorstin: Well, I don't know. There are really two opposite problems. One is the problem of a flood of miscellaneous sensations brought to us day after day with the Ervin hearings. And, on the other hand, the power of the reporter to select—which is the case at a national convention when we have a reporter who can direct the camera to certain objects and ignore others. All this is bewildering to the citizen who doesn't know what to make out of it.

"It's that bewilderment which is probably the curse of our situation, the fact that the citizen receives a flood of sensations which are "undeniable facts." This, of course, is something new. The assumption seems to be—which is, of course, an old American assumption—that if *some* of a thing is good then more of it is always better. If it's good for people to have some information about Watergate, then the more they have the better. But the question, of course, is what we mean by information. Information is not knowledge. Information is a flood of miscellaneous facts which reach a person before he or anybody else has had a chance to know what they might mean.

In the past, the great problems of political theory were the nature of sovereignty, the nature of property, the nature of equality and similar related questions. But, it seems to me, the essential problem of modern political theory is knowledge. Who knows what and why—and that has been dramatized in the Watergate. The crimes were committed to gain information and the additional crimes were committed to prevent information about the information-getting people. And finally, public conscience will be aroused by the exposure to information, by people seeing what's what. Although we take all this for granted, this is new. In the past, the question was who commanded the Army or what kind of property ownership there was or something of this sort. But now the overriding question is: who knows what and who can get that information and when?

CQ: How long will it take the public to assimilate and sort out all this information and come to some kind of conclusion in its own mind about what is involved?

Boorstin: Well, I don't know. You personify the public. I don't think there is any answer to your question. I can't think of the public as being a single entity as you describe it.

Electronic Media

CQ: Would you try to report the Watergate story in a different fashion than you now see?

Boorstin: I have thought that the basic problem that electronic media have brought to news reporting is: "Too much too soon." We are flooded with stuff before we know what it's about. And to expect a citizen to sort all this out is to expect the impossible. But it would be a public service if, as a self-denying ordinance, the networks would agree not to publish news until a week after it is reported. Give them a chance to sort it out, and the citizen too. There are not very many cases where the public interest requires that everybody in the nation should know something this week or today or this morning. The information gets to us because the networks are there. They have to fill up their time. And, of course, Watergate has been a godsend to the networks.

CQ: In a sense, Watergate did come to public attention somewhat through the mechanism you're describing. Certain events occurred a year or more ago and yet it took a lot of piecemeal reporting and assimilation before the whole scandal burst into public consciousness.

Boorstin: That's right. And that would be a confirmation of the special usefulness of what I would call the "*delayed* media." By contrast with the electronic media, the print media are delayed. That is, they don't reach everybody instantaneously, simply because it takes time to set up the type. It has to be edited and delivered to each person and so on. So that I would say that one of the many things about the Watergate episode is that it reveals a special role for the press in American life—especially after the coming of TV. This is an investigative role. And it is interesting to note how this came about. TV has actually increased the responsibility of the press in this direction. For the press can print information without having to show the picture of the person who gave the information and without our having to hear his voice. It's possible for them to go out and investigate it and present the thing at length with a lot of background.

Of course, there's another aspect to the hearings. While they are, on the whole in the public interest, they somehow exemplify one of the very problems which they are investigating. The cry of public interest—that the "national interest" (sometimes loosely called "national security") overrides the rights of individuals—is exactly the cry that was raised by those people in and around the White House. In trying to justify what they did in committing their crimes, they have talked about their worry over the public interest. But one of the things we mean by a constitutional government is a government in which the public interest is always subordinated to the private interests—the rights of individuals. And there is the danger in our enthusiasm, our eagerness, to uncover these particular criminal acts—that we may be tempted into the same vice ourselves. Although the hearings have been conducted with remarkable restraint, admirable nonpartisanship, there's no way of conducting public hearings of the kind that the Ervin committee has been holding without infringing upon the privacy of individuals. I think that we must just watch our step. We must not let ourselves be led into the belief that the "public interest" always overrides. In that direction lies totalitarian disregard of the citizen. The so-called "public interest" is what was used to defend concentration camps and lynchings.

"As I watched some of the Watergate hearings I kept asking myself what all those people—Dean and others—were doing there in the first place. Was there really an honest job there that needed doing?"

Institutional Continuity

CQ: A final question. What do you see as the ultimate result of Watergate? Will it change our political institutions in any profound manner? Where is this episode going to lead us as a nation or as a people?

Boorstin: As a historian I am inclined to be impressed by the continuity of our institutions, and I am extremely skeptical when I read the obituaries for our nation. There has probably never been a scandal in American history which was not decried as the end of American civilization and the destruction of all public and private morality. I think this episode has probably had the effect abroad of dramatizing our concern with certain standards of public morality. And in that sense it's probably been a good thing. And it has dramatized the power of Congress. It has dramatized the integrity of our courts and it will probably have the effect of making anybody who sits in the presidential chair be more scrupulous of his use of the government—of the powers of the presidency.

In a practical way, one of the questions which should arise immediately is the question of the nature of the Executive Office of the President. I think that should be subject to investigation and scrutiny. Perhaps there should be some committee investigating that. The Executive Office of the President has expanded beyond all bounds and has tended to supersede the executive branch of the government. Some drastic reconsideration of that is in order. American citizens in general do not realize the extent of the Executive Office.

The dangers of that growth have been dramatized in Watergate, and in several ways. First, by making it possible for people to use or seem to use the authority of the President without his knowledge. And, then, by making it possible for a President to say (with some credibility) that he didn't know what was going on. That is an equally disastrous fact and one which should give us pause. The Executive Office of the President ought to be scrutinized. I cannot believe that the responsibility of the office is served by its proliferation. How many of these people and how many of these White House "positions" were simply superfluous? As I watched some of the Watergate hearings I kept asking myself what all those people—Dean and others—were doing there in the first place. Was there really an honest job there that needed doing? √

WATERGATE HEARINGS: PERHAPS LONGER THAN EXPECTED

Watergate dropped out of the banner headlines for the first time in months during the week ended July 7, as Congress recessed for a short holiday and the President remained in seclusion at his San Clemente, Calif., home.

But the lull was short. The Senate Select Committee on Presidential Campaign Activities was to resume its hearings on July 10, and its first witness was scheduled to be one of the most important of the whole investigation: John N. Mitchell, former attorney general and former director of the President Nixon's 1972 re-election campaign.

Moreover, the committee indicated it might extend its hearings through most of the summer. The hearings, it was reported, would be held each weekday and might continue into August, after Congress had adjourned for its annual month off.

Even without the televised Senate hearings, Watergate attracted its share of attention. These were some of the late developments:

- Egil Krogh Jr., former chief of the White House special investigations unit, or "plumbers," pleaded the Fifth Amendment against self-incrimination and refused to answer questions in a July 5 appearance before the Los Angeles grand jury investigating the 1971 break-in at the office of Daniel Ellsberg's psychiatrist. Ellsberg was a defendant in the Pentagon Papers trial.

GAO: More Campaign Violations

The General Accounting Office (GAO) issued a report July 5 charging eight "apparent violations" of federal election and perjury laws in connection with $50,000 spent on a fund-raising dinner honoring Vice President Agnew in May 1972.

Named in the report were the Maryland Salute to Ted Agnew Night Committee and the Finance Committee to Re-elect the President. Implicated were Alexander Lankler, former Maryland Republican state chairman, and Blagden H. Wharton, a Baltimore banker and treasurer of the Agnew testimonial committee.

The $50,000 was loaned by the re-election finance committee to the Agnew dinner committee in an attempt to make the proceeds look larger than they were. The money was returned later, and what appeared to be false reports were filed with federal and state authorities.

Wharton, the only dinner committee member named in the GAO report, was said to have lied by supporting the committee's claim that 31 persons had contributed the $50,000 when, in fact, they had not. Wharton lied again, according to the report, during a GAO audit of dinner committee funds.

The GAO report was expected to be turned over to Archibald Cox, the special prosecutor in the Watergate case. The $50,000 loan from the finance committee to Lankler became public with the testimony of Hugh W. Sloan Jr., former campaign treasurer, before the Senate Watergate investigating committee on June 6. *(p. 114)*

After Krogh's appearance, the Los Angeles district attorney said he would seek indictments in September against White House aides for conspiring to break into the psychiatrist's office. He did not name the aides.

- *The New York Times* disclosed July 5 that the disciplinary counsel for the California State Bar Association had written a letter to Sen. Sam J. Ervin (D N.C.), chairman of the Senate investigating committee, asking for information that could lead to disbarment proceedings against five persons implicated in the Watergate scandal.

Those named in the request were John D. Ehrlichman, Nixon's former domestic affairs adviser; Herbert W. Kalmbach, the President's former personal lawyer; Gordon C. Strachan, a former aide to H.R. Haldeman, former White House chief of staff; Robert C. Mardian, a former political consultant to the Nixon re-election committee, and Donald H. Segretti, alleged director of a Republican sabotage campaign in 1972. All five are members of the California bar.

- In a July 5 interview with the Times, Walter J. Hickel, former Alaska governor and former Nixon secretary of the interior, said the President had "created the atmosphere and the attitude for it (Watergate) to happen." Hickel, fired by Nixon in 1970 for his criticism of the Cambodia bombing, said, "I don't think that I know of a presidency in history that quite operated the way the Nixon administration did, one that was isolated from the reality of the American public."
- Nixon's new domestic affairs adviser, former Defense Secretary Melvin R. Laird, said June 28 that the President would answer "all questions" after key witnesses had testified before the Senate investigating committee.
- Julie Nixon Eisenhower, the President's younger daughter, said July 4 that her father, playing "devil's advocate," had asked his family whether he should resign because of Watergate. His family told him that he should not, she added.

The next day, deputy White House press secretary Gerald L. Warren reaffirmed earlier statements of press secretary Ronald L. Ziegler that Nixon had never given serious thought to resigning.

Witness June 29

John W. Dean III ended his testimony before the Senate select Watergate committee after five days—the longest appearance of any witness—still unshaken in his conviction that the President knew of the Watergate coverup as early as September 1972. *(Earlier Dean testimony, p. 152)*

Knowing that other witnesses were expected to contradict his version of events, notably former presidential aides H. R. Haldeman and John D. Ehrlichman, who were to testify later, the former presidential counsel asserted on June 29, near the end of his 25 hours of testimony: "I am quite aware of the fact that in some circumstances it is going to be my word against one man's word, it is going to be my word against two men, it is going to be my word against three men, and probably in some cases it is going to be my word against four men. But I am pre-

Presidential Resignation: No Historic Precedents

Debate over whether President Nixon should resign because of the Watergate affair has sent participants on both sides back to the text of the Constitution to bolster their arguments. *(Impeachment background, p. 55)*

No President has ever resigned—and only one Vice President, John C. Calhoun, stepped down voluntarily. He left Andrew Jackson's administration in 1832 to become a senator. Article II of the Constitution addresses the possibility of presidential resignation:

"In Case of the Removal of the President from Office, or at his Death, Resignation, or Inability to discharge the Powers and Duties of the said Office, the Same shall devolve on the Vice President, and the Congress may by Law provide for the Case of Removal, Death, Resignation or Inability, both of the President and Vice President, declaring what Officer shall then act as President, and such Officer shall act accordingly, until the Disability be removed, or a President shall be elected." (Section I, Clause 6)

25th Amendment. The ambiguity of that language—particularly the term "disability"—had provoked occasional debate ever since the Constitutional Convention of 1787. Prompted by President Eisenhower's 1955 heart attack and the Kennedy assassination, Congress in 1965 proposed the 25th Amendment to the Constitution, which prescribed a method for determing presidential disability and a procedure to follow in such cases. The amendment was ratified Feb. 10, 1967.

The 25th Amendment also remedies the constitutional silence on the question of a vacant vice presidency. The first two sections deal with that possibility and with presidential resignation.

"Section 1. In case of the removal of the President from office or his death or resignation, the Vice President shall become President.

"Section 2. Whenever there is a vacancy in the office of the Vice President, the President shall nominate a Vice President who shall take office upon confirmation by a majority vote of both houses of Congress."

Clifford Plan. Clark Clifford, who served as presidential counsel in the Truman administration and as secretary of defense in the Johnson administration, based an argument for the resignation of both Nixon and Agnew on those sections of the amendment.

In an article in *The New York Times* June 4, Clifford proposed the following chain of events: Agnew would resign; Nixon would ask Congress for a list of three qualified individuals to replace him; Nixon would name one of the three as the replacement; Congress would confirm the new Vice President; Nixon would resign, and the newly confirmed Vice President would become President.

"Although we do not have the parliamentary system, there is more flexibility in our Constitution than first meets the eye," Clifford argued. He added that Congress should insist that the person chosen to succeed Nixon promise not to try for a second term in 1976.

In a speech on the Senate floor June 25, Charles H. Percy (R Ill.) disputed the Clifford plan, saying, "Any suggestion that President Nixon resign in favor of a coalition-caretaker government uses obtuse reasoning to support a preposterous mechanism to achieve what the Democratic Party failed to achieve in the last election." Percy, himself a vocal administration critic on the Watergate issue, warned that such proposals "distort constitutional principles to fit the needs of the moment."

Truman. Historical examples of proposals such as Clifford's—for presidential resignation because of political, rather than physical, disability—are rare. One example occurred after the mid-term congressional election of 1946, when a Democratic President faced Republican majorities in both houses of Congress.

Sen. J. W. Fulbright (D Ark.) suggested that President Truman appoint Sen. Arthur Vandenberg (R Mich.) to be secretary of state and then step down. In the absence of a Vice President and under the existing order of succession, Vandenberg then would have become President, and the Republicans would have controlled both the legislative and executive branches of government.

pared to stand on my word and the truth and the knowledge and the facts I have. I know the truth is my ally in this, and I think, ultimately, the truth is going to come out."

Tempering Influence. During his last day in the witness chair, Dean, as he had in previous days, pictured himself as attempting to limit some of the more bizarre White House activities, such as reprisals against persons deemed enemies of the administration.

Sen. Daniel K. Inouye (D Hawaii) asked Dean how he could consider himself a restraining influence when he wrote the memo outlining how the administration could "screw" its enemies through governmental action. *(Excerpts of Dean memo and enemies list, p. 153)*

Dean said he never had a political enemies project that was operational. He explained that whenever he received "enemies" memos from other White House aides, he merely filed them away, taking no action on them. He said he never did try to find an enemies project coordinator, as he called for in his memo. He added that he stalled for a long time before even writing the memo, calling it "a wild and crazy scheme."

Under further questioning by Inouye, Dean revealed that the White House had refused his request that he be allowed to photocopy his documents that were locked in the Executive Office Building after he was fired April 30. Committee Chairman Sam J. Ervin Jr. (D N.C.) said he would ask the White House to allow Dean to photocopy papers the committee wanted to examine. *(Box, p. 151)*

Apparent Slip. The only time Dean appeared to have tripped up on a question of fact during his lengthy testimony occurred in the morning session, but it was quickly explained by the witness. Dean had insisted throughout his appearance that a meeting he had with attorney Herbert W. Kalmbach to discuss silence money for the seven Watergate defendants took place June 29, 1972, in the Mayflower hotel in Washington. Dean said repeatedly that the two first met in the hotel's coffee shop, but quickly moved to Kalmbach's room in the hotel when it became obvious that the public coffee shop was not conducive to their discussions.

Sen. Edward J. Gurney (R Fla.) said he had subpoenaed the Mayflower hotel's records for that date and that no one named Kalmbach was registered at the hotel. Gurney said he also subpoenaed the records of the Statler-Hilton hotel and that a Herbert Kalmbach was registered there on June 29 and 30, 1972.

Asked to explain the contradiction, Dean said he often confused the two hotels, but the one he had in mind was on 16th St., a few blocks from the White House. (He was referring to the Statler-Hilton; the Mayflower hotel, also near the White House, is on Connecticut Ave.)

Moments later, after Gurney had moved on to other questions, Dean interjected that his lawyer had informed him that the name of the coffee shop in the Statler-Hilton was the Mayflower. The audience, obviously sympathetic to the 34-year-old Dean, burst into sustained applause.

Report to Cabinet. In further answers to Gurney questions, Dean said he could not explain why the President suggested, during a March 21, 1973, meeting, that Dean report to the cabinet on his role. Dean had testified that at that meeting he first explained to the President his role in the coverup.

"It doesn't make any sense to me at all," Gurney said. Dean said that he was surprised by the President's response and told him it would not be a good subject for a cabinet meeting. Dean said he did not think the President intended him to report it in full to the cabinet.

Gurney suggested that possibly the President was not fully aware of what was going on, despite Dean's explanation.

Money, Perjury. Later, in answer to questions by Committee Vice Chairman Howard H. Baker Jr. (R Tenn.), Dean said he told the President at the March 21 meeting that "continued support money would be necessary" (for the Watergate defendants) and "continued perjury would be necessary."

"Did you use those terms?" asked Sen. Baker. "Yes," Dean replied.

Presidential Testimony. Baker, Ervin and Lowell P. Weicker Jr. (R Conn.) continued their efforts to get presidential testimony in some form by citing historical precedents for the appearance of Presidents before Congress.

Weicker said President Lincoln appeared before a Senate committee to deny that his wife was a spy for the Confederacy. Ervin said Lincoln also offered to appear before the House Judiciary Committee.

Baker related how President Wilson once invited the Senate Foreign Relations Committee to meet with him. "So, as we say in Tennessee," Baker went on, "there are lots of ways to skin a cat, and I wouldn't presume to say how we go about it. But I do hope that there is some way to supply additional information on these crucial and important points."

Poll Report

The abrupt decline in President Nixon's popularity has halted, at least temporarily. A majority of the American people does not think he should resign at this time, but a plurality thinks he should if it is proven that he ordered the Watergate coverup. And a plurality looks upon Watergate as a serious issue.

These were the findings of the three latest public opinion polls. *(Earlier poll report, p. 149)*

Popularity. A Gallup Poll published June 24 found that Nixon's popularity remained at the low point of his administration, but it had not changed in a month. The percentages were the same in interviews conducted June 1-4 and May 11-14:

Approve	44%
Disapprove	45
No opinion	11

Resignation. These were the responses to a Harris Survey, conducted among 1,509 adults June 14-18 and published June 25:

"Do you feel that President Nixon personally knew about the attempt to wiretap Democratic headquarters before it happened, or don't you feel he knew about that?"

	Latest	May
Knew	40%	34%
Did not know	36	45
Not sure	24	21

"Do you feel President Nixon personally ordered the attempted coverup of White House involvement in Watergate, or do you feel he did not order it?"

Ordered	30%
Did not order	40
Not sure	30

"If it is proven that President Nixon ordered the coverup of White House involvement in Watergate, after Republican agents were caught there, do you think he should resign or not?"

Should resign	46%
Not resign	40
Not sure	14

Integrity. Harris interviewers asked the same sample of adults for a poll published June 26: "Do you think the Watergate episode is a very serious question involving the honesty of the White House, or do you think it is mostly politics?"

	June	May	April	October 1972
Serious question	47%	40%	36%	26%
Mostly politics	43	52	48	62
Not sure	10	8	16	12

Daily Chronology

Following is a day-to-day chronology of the week's events:

JUNE 28

(Earlier June 28 events, p. 161)

Tax Study. The Joint Committee on Internal Revenue Taxation, chaired by Rep. Wilbur D. Mills (D Ark.), directed its staff to investigate allegations that the Nixon administration had used tax audits to punish its enemies and help its friends. Former Nixon counsel John W. Dean III mentioned the scheme in his testimony before the Senate investigating committee June 27. *(p. 153)*

Casey Testimony. Former Securities and Exchange Commission (SEC) Chairman William J. Casey told the House Interstate and Foreign Commerce Investigations Subcommittee of direct pressures put on him by former Attorney General John N. Mitchell and Dean in 1971 and 1972 to tone down an SEC investigation of financier Robert L. Vesco. Mitchell and Vesco were indicted May 10 for attempting to obstruct the investigation. *(p. 46)*

Laird Interview. In an interview with *The Washington Post*, Nixon's new domestic adviser, Melvin R. Laird, said the President intended to answer "all questions" about his role in the Watergate affair at a press conference after the major witnesses had testified before the Senate investigating committee. Laird also hinted that press secretary Ronald L. Ziegler, who had been portrayed in Dean's testimony as ignorant of coverup activities in the White House at the time he was answering questions on that subject, would be replaced as Nixon's principal spokesman by deputy press secretary Gerald L. Warren. *(Dean testimony, p. 156)*

JUNE 29

Prosecutors' Withdrawal. The three original Watergate prosecutors—Earl J. Silbert, Seymour Glanzer and Donald E. Campbell—withdrew from the case, saying their investigation had been conducted "forthrightly, vigorously and professionally." The prosecutors offered to resign when special prosecutor Archibald Cox took over the case May 25, but Cox had asked them to stay on to make a smooth transition.

In a letter to Cox, the prosecutors said they thought it would be appropriate for them to resign, because they might be called as witnesses before the Senate Watergate committee or a grand jury. *(Earlier development, p. 89)*

IRS Pressure. News reports quoted Randolph W. Thrower, former commissioner of the Internal Revenue Service (IRS), as saying he was told in mid-1970 that Nixon wanted John J. Caulfield appointed to head the agency's alcohol, tobacco and firearms division. (Dean named Caulfield June 26 as the person who gave the IRS his order to audit the tax return of a reporter.) Thrower said he rejected Caulfield as too inexperienced for the post. Caulfield was appointed assistant director for enforcement in the Treasury Department's Bureau of Alcohol, Tobacco and Firearms July 1, 1972. *(Dean testimony, p. 157; Caulfield testimony, p. 82)*

Ehrlichman Interview. In an interview on CBS-TV, Nixon's former chief domestic adviser, John D. Ehrlichman, repeated earlier statements that he had no role in the Watergate bugging or coverup, and also told of a Santa Monica, Calif., meeting he had with W. Matthew Byrne Jr., presiding judge in the Pentagon Papers trial. Ehrlichman said Byrne requested the meeting to discuss his possible appointment as FBI director. The former aide denied that pressure was brought on the judge in connection with the Ellsberg trial, which was still in progress at the time. *(p. 32, 24)*

Mitchell Testimony. Former Attorney General Mitchell "definitely has no information implicating the President in the Watergate bugging or the coverup," Mitchell's attorney, William G. Hundley, told *The Washington Post.* Hundley refused to provide further details of his client's testimony before the Senate investigating committee, scheduled to begin July 10. But the Post quoted sources as saying Mitchell would testify that he had been aware of the coverup but had no direct knowledge of the involvement of former White House aides H. R. Haldeman or John D. Ehrlichman.

Montoya Funds. Responding to a news report that his 1970 campaign funds had not been properly reported, Sen. Joseph M. Montoya (D N.M.) said he hoped "this matter is not just a political move to try to damage me because of my position on the Watergate investigating committee." Montoya said he had just discovered that the signatures on his 1970 campaign spending report, filed with the New Mexico secretary of state, were forgeries—but said the report itself was in order and he was "shocked" by the forgeries. *(p. 161)*

Colson Testimony. Former Nixon special counsel Charles W. Colson testified for five hours before the House Armed Services Subcommittee on Intelligence, and confirmed reports that he had authorized a 1971 probe into the life of Sen. Edward M. Kennedy (D Mass.). Colson admitted dispatching Watergate conspirator E. Howard Hunt Jr. to seek scandalous information about Kennedy. But he said he did not know Hunt was using CIA equipment—something Hunt told the subcommittee in testimony the previous day.

The same day, a deposition given by Colson May 28 in connection with a Watergate civil suit was released to the press. In it, the former counsel admitted ordering Hunt to allow a newsman to read a number of classified State Department cables.

JUNE 30

Weicker Smear. *The Washington Post* reported that Jack Gleason, a former Nixon staff assistant, had admitted he was asked to provide the White House with information that could be used to discredit Sen. Lowell P. Weicker Jr. (R Conn.), a member of the Senate investigating committee. Gleason reportedly said requests for information on possible financing irregularities in Weicker's 1970 Senate campaign were conveyed to him by Harry Dent, a former Nixon political strategist—but that both he and Dent rejected the requests as "asinine."

In an emotional speech during the hearings the day before, Weicker had accused the administration of trying to smear him. *(p. 151)*

JULY 1

Colson Charge. Continuing his one-man Watergate counter attack, Charles W. Colson said that Nixon phoned him on the evening of March 21 to say "he (Nixon) knew at that point he was not being told the truth, that he was being given confusing information" on the matter. That was the same date Dean had testified he told the President all he knew about the case. Colson made the charge on CBS-TV's "Face the Nation." *(Dean testimony, p. 152)*

Colson also denied reports in that day's *New York Times* that government sources had accused him of puting "improper" pressure on the Labor Department in an effort to influence Nixon's 1972 campaign. He did not try to influence a Teamsters Union case before the National Labor Relations Board or a construction union case in the Pennsylvania Supreme Court, Colson said.

Teamster Funds. The July 9 *Time* magazine reported that special prosecutor Archibald Cox was looking into allegations that the Teamsters Union used its influence to collect as much as $600,000 for the Nixon campaign "from individuals in the Las Vegas area who had received loans from the union's welfare plan." Union officials quoted in the magazine said Colson promised that in exchange for the financial support, he would have the legal restrictions on union activity by former Teamsters president James R. Hoffa lifted.

JULY 2

Nixon Promise. Press secretary Ronald L. Ziegler told reporters in San Clemente, Calif., that Nixon would "address" the Watergate issue in an "appropriate" manner, but not until the Senate investigating committee had completed its first series of hearings, including the planned appearances of former top administration figures such as Mitchell, Haldeman and Ehrlichman. But Ziegler added that the President would not appear before the committee or submit a written rebuttal to charges made the previous week by Dean.

Gurney Funds. *The Miami Herald* reported that Sen. Edward J. Gurney (R Fla.) received $100 donations to his 1974 re-election campaign treasury from Nixon friends Murray Chotiner and Bebe Robozo during a fund-raising party in Washington, D.C., May 23, after Gurney was assigned to the Senate Watergate committee. Gurney issued a statement denying any impropriety or conflict of interest in his acceptance of the money.

JULY 3

Strachan Plea. Citing informed sources, *The New York Daily News* reported that former White House aides Gordon C. Strachan and Herbert L. Porter planned to plead guilty, for their involvement in the Watergate cover-up, to one count of conspiracy to obstruct justice. Strachan, who served as liaison between the White House and the Nixon re-election committee and reported directly to former White House staff chief H.R. Haldeman, reportedly would tell the Senate investigating committee that Haldeman knew of the coverup "from the beginning." Strachan was granted immunity for his planned testimony before the committee.

Testifying at the Senate hearings June 7, Porter admitted that he gave false testimony to a grand jury and in the Watergate trial as part of the coverup effort. *(p. 117)*

JULY 4

Indictment Report. CBS-TV revealed the highlights of a "status report" on the Watergate investigation, submitted to the special prosecutor by outgoing prosecutors Silbert, Glanzer and Campbell. The report, which called the investigation "85 per cent complete," recommended the indictment of former administration officials Haldeman, John D. Ehrlichman, John N. Mitchell and John W. Dean III. Evidence against these men, CBS said, was described in the report as "documentary as well as verbal."

The prosecutors also reportedly suggested that guilty pleas in exchange for reduced charges be sought from former acting FBI Director L. Patrick Gray III, former White House aide Strachan and former deputy campaign director Jeb Stuart Magruder. Nixon's former personal attorney, Herbert W. Kalmbach, was said to be recommended for complete immunity in exchange for his testimony. *(Earlier reports, p. 104)*

Richardson Prohibition. In a related development, *The Washington Star-News* reported that Attorney General Elliot L. Richardson had ordered the three former prosecutors to cancel a scheduled appearance on CBS-TV's July 7 "Face the Nation" interview program, because of the possibility of damaging publicity about the Watergate case. The network confirmed that they would not appear.

Julie Eisenhower Remarks. Julie Nixon Eisenhower, the President's younger daughter, told wire service interviewers that Nixon had considered resigning over Watergate as an act of patriotism, but his family dissuaded him, because it would look like an "admission of wrongdoing." *(Presidential resignation background, box, p. 175)*

Dean Recall. Samuel Dash, chief counsel of the Senate investigating committee, said he was planning to recall John Dean in the fall to testify about Nixon's personal finances. Dash was quoted as saying Dean would be asked if Republican campaign funds were used in the purchase of Nixon's $1.5-million estate in San Clemente, Calif. *(p. 109)*

According to the report, Dash said the committee would decide within a few weeks whether to focus its second phase of hearings—expected to begin in late September—on political sabotage or on campaign financing.

JULY 5

Cox Response. Special prosecutor Archibald Cox issued a statement in response to the CBS report on indictments, saying the grand jury investigation of the Watergate affair "is not nearly complete." He said "it would be grossly premature for us or anyone else to reach even tentative conclusions as to who should or should not be prosecuted."

Young Immunity. U.S. District Judge John J. Sirica approved the Senate committee's request for limited immunity from prosecution for former White House aide David Young, who was codirector of the "plumbers unit" set up in 1971 to plug news leaks. ✓

WATERGATE: TESTIMONY FROM TACITURN JOHN MITCHELL

John N. Mitchell told his side of the story to the Senate select Watergate committee during the week ended July 14. His story conflicted repeatedly with the accounts of previous witnesses at the televised hearings, especially those of John W. Dean III and Jeb Stuart Magruder, his former close associates.

The former attorney general and campaign director spent 2½ days on the witness stand. Appearing under a subpoena from the committee, he made no opening statement. He volunteered little information, and most of his answers were terse.

Sometimes Mitchell's testimony appeared to contradict the record of his responses to earlier interrogations. This obviously strained the credulity of some committee members and counsel, reflected in a new testiness between the questioned and the questioner.

Mitchell, who is under indictment by a federal grand jury in New York City for obstruction of justice involving an illegal campaign contribution, denied prior knowledge of the break-in and bugging of Democratic national headquarters on June 17, 1972. He admitted he had a hand in the subsequent coverup, (although he refused to label it thus) and that he had not informed Nixon of his knowledge. He defended his decision not to tell the President what he knew on grounds that to do so would have hampered Nixon's re-election chances.

As Mitchell neared the conclusion of his testimony on July 12, Samuel Dash, chief counsel for the committee, asked in some exasperation: "What I have to say on that (the conflicting statements), Mr. Mitchell, is that since you may have given false testimony under oath on prior occasions, is there really any reason for this committee to believe your testimony before this committee?"

Presidential Testimony. Outside the hearings themselves, a conflict was building between the committee and the White House. In a letter to Committee Chairman Sam J. Ervin Jr. (D N.C.) July 6 (made public July 7), the President refused to appear before the committee in person or to make presidential files available to it. Nixon cited the constitutional doctrine of separation of powers as his reason for refusing.

Ervin disagreed. He said the committee had the authority to subpoena Nixon and his papers, but he opposed using that authority. The committee went into executive session July 12 and adopted a resolution supporting Ervin's position. The same day, Ervin wrote Nixon a letter warning of "the very grave possibility of a fundamental constitutional confrontation between the Congress and the presidency."

Both the resolution and the letter urged a meeting between the two sides. Nixon and Ervin conferred briefly by telephone and agreed to meet. No date was set, but Nixon's illness would be a delaying factor.

The prospective value of the meeting also remained uncertain because of White House intransigence on the documents issue. Gerald L. Warren, deputy White House press secretary, told reporters the meeting would cover procedural matters and that "there will be no change" in the President's position. The meeting, said Warren, would be "a matter of courtesy."

Nixon Illness

President Nixon was taken to Bethesda Naval Hospital on July 12 for treatment of viral pneumonia. His physician, Major Gen. Walter R. Tkach, told reporters at a White House press conference that the President's condition was without complications. He added that Nixon would remain in the hospital at least a week for "rest and recuperation."

News of the President's sudden illness came as a surprise to newsmen. This is the first time Nixon has been hospitalized during his presidency.

Presidential Press Secretary Ronald L. Ziegler told reporters that Nixon would be able to carry on "necessary work" while at the hospital.

Moore Testimony. The next witness after Mitchell was Richard A. Moore, special counsel to Nixon, a 59-year-old former West Coast broadcasting executive. Moore, too, disagreed with Dean's testimony. He was convinced, he said, that the President had no knowledge of Watergate or its coverup until March 21.

In his second day on the stand, July 13, Moore told the committee that he did not tell Nixon what he had learned from former White House counsel Dean about Watergate because he felt that the Dean account lacked credibility. Dean, Moore said, "never told me of an actual criminal situation" until March 20, when, according to Moore, Dean informed him of E. Howard Hunt Jr.'s money requests. Hunt at that time had been convicted in the break-in and was awaiting sentencing. On March 20, Dean told Moore he was going to tell everything he knew to the President, and did so the next day.

Moore said he suggested that Nixon move quickly on the scandal, particularly urging him to get legal advice from outside the White House. Moore quoted the President as responding: "I understand, thank you."

Nixon did meet with an outside counsel in Key Biscayne, Fla., on April 20, according to a White House announcement, but the name of the adviser has never been revealed. Moore said that at a May 8 meeting, the President told him he had racked his mind over the scandal and asked, "Were there any clues I should have seen?" Moore said he reassured him that there had been none.

Other Developments. These were among the other highlights of the week's Watergate news:

- John D. Ehrlichman, Nixon's former domestic affairs adviser, said Dean's statement that Nixon had agreed to offer E. Howard Hunt executive clemency was "180 degrees" from the truth.

- *The New York Times* published two articles describing the 1972 sabotage against the Democrats as "a two-pronged operation approved by some of President Nixon's most influential aides, directed in part by White House officials, and financed with more than $100,000 in unreported contributions to the Nixon campaign."

- Impeachment action against Nixon, warned Senate Majority Mike Mansfield (D Mont.), would "bring the whole government to a halt. We have to differentiate between the man and the office—the institution is what counts."

- Ten Senate conservatives had cocktails with the President and assured him of their continuing support despite Watergate. But the American Civil Liberties Union attacked the President for showing "a contemptuous disregard for human freedoms."

Witness July 10

John N. Mitchell denied sworn testimony that he approved the Watergate break-in and wiretapping of Democratic national headquarters, but acknowledged that he played a role in covering up the affair. Mitchell told the Senate select Watergate committee July 10 that he did not tell President Nixon about Watergate cover-up actions by himself and other White House officials for fear of crippling Nixon's 1972 re-election chances.

The former attorney general and director of the Committee for the Re-election of the President said that to his knowledge, the President was unaware of the true story of the break-in and coverup until long after his re-election. Mitchell's testimony was in direct contradiction on key points to that of Jeb Stuart Magruder, his former deputy campaign director, concerning two meetings where plans were discussed for the bugging of Democratic headquarters. Mitchell also contradicted testimony by former White House counsel John W. Dean III on the extent of Mitchell's knowledge and participation in the cover-up. *(Magruder testimony, p. 135; Dean testimony, p. 152)*

John N. Mitchell

Testifying without a prepared statement, Mitchell said that on three occasions, he rejected electronic surveillance plans proposed by G. Gordon Liddy, the re-election committee's general counsel, who later was convicted along with six others for the break-in. Mitchell said the June 17, 1972, break-in at the Watergate office building came as a surprise to him, because he thought the plan had been canceled at his orders. Nevertheless, Mitchell said that to reveal all he knew about the break-in plans and the subsequent coverup to the President would have "scarred the presidency" and might have ruined Nixon's re-election chances. "To my mind," Mitchell testified, "his re-election, compared to what was available on the other side," made it imperative to keep the President in the dark about what really was going on. *(Box, p. 183)*

According to Mitchell, the President, if informed of the coverup, would have "lowered the boom" on his aides, and a whole catalog of White House "horror stories" would have been revealed. Mitchell said that by "horror stories" he meant the break-in at the office of Daniel Ellsberg's psychiatrist by Liddy; the removal from Washington by Liddy of Dita Beard, an International Telephone and Telegraph Corporation (ITT) lobbyist who was a central figure in an alleged ITT scheme to influence the Justice Department to stop antitrust proceedings; the forging of State Department cables by former White House aide E. Howard Hunt Jr. to make it appear the late President Kennedy wanted the late South Vietnamese President Ngo Dinh Diem murdered, and a scheme to firebomb the Brookings Institution.

"The best thing to do was to keep the lid on," said the 59-year-old New York City lawyer.

Mitchell was Nixon's first attorney general, serving from January 1969 to March 1972. He become campaign director in April 1972. He resigned from the re-election committee on July 1, 1972, two weeks after the Watergate break-in, explaining that he wanted to spend more time with his family. As Mitchell's testimony revealed, however, he maintained an active role in election-year politics, even though he had returned to New York City.

Surveillance Plans. Mitchell's testimony about a meeting in his office Jan. 27, 1972, at which Liddy first discussed his surveillance plans, coincided with that of Magruder and Dean. Liddy had been directed to develop a plan for countering expected demonstrations at the Republican national convention; what he came up with, according to Mitchell, was "a complete horror story. It was a mish-mash of code names, lines of authority... the call-girl bit and all the rest of it," Mitchell told the committee. "As I recall, I told him (Liddy) to go burn the charts, that what we were interested in was protection and information on demonstrators."

Committee counsel Samuel Dash, pointing out that Mitchell was attorney general at the time, asked why he did not throw Liddy out of his office for suggesting an illegal scheme. Mitchell replied that he believed Liddy would go back to his original assignment. "In hindsight, I not only should have thrown him out of the office, I should have thrown him out of the window," Mitchell said.

The next meeting with Liddy took place on Feb. 4, 1972, when he presented a scaled-down version of his first plan, this one costing $500,000 instead of the original $1-million. Here Mitchell departed from Magruder's testimony. Magruder told the committee June 14 that at the Feb. 4 meeting, Liddy specifically mentioned electronic surveillance of the Democratic headquarters and possible photographing of Democratic Party documents. Mitchell said, "I violently disagree" with Magruder that bugging the Democratic headquarters was discussed. "To the best of my recollection, no discussion of targets took place," Mitchell testified.

Asked by Dash why he did not fire Liddy after the Feb. 4 meeting, Mitchell replied again that he presumed Liddy would return to his original assignment.

Again contradicting Magruder's testimony, Mitchell said that at a March 30, 1972, meeting in Key Biscayne,

Poll Report

Seven of 10 Americans think President Nixon was involved in the planning or coverup of the Watergate scandal, but fewer than one in five believe he should be impeached. These were the findings in a Gallup Poll published July 8. *(Earlier poll report, p. 176)*

Interviewers asked 1,451 adults June 22-25: "Here are four statements concerning President Nixon's connection with the Watergate affair. Will you please tell me which one comes closest to your own point of view?"

	June 1-4	June 22-25
Nixon planned the Watergate "bugging" from the beginning.	8%	8%
Nixon did not plan the "bugging" but knew about it before it took place.	28	27
Nixon found out about the "bugging" after it occurred but tried to cover it up.	31	36
Nixon had no knowledge of the "bugging" and spoke up as soon as he learned about it.	19	17
No opinion/not heard or read about Watergate.	14	12

The sample interviewed was also asked: "Should Nixon be compelled to leave office?"

Yes	18%
No	71
No opinion	11

The poll found that 98 per cent of the persons questioned had heard or read about Watergate.

Fla., he did not approve a third plan by Liddy, costing $250,000 and also calling for electronic surveillance of the Democratic headquarters in the Watergate. Mitchell testified he told Magruder, "We do not need this (the Liddy plan). Let's not discuss it any further."

Mitchell said his former re-election committee aide, Frederick C. LaRue, who attended the meeting, would back him up. LaRue has pleaded guilty to one count of obstructing justice in the Watergate affair and has agreed to cooperate with prosecutors in the case. *(p. 161)*

Asked by Dash what might have given Magruder the idea the second scaled-down Liddy plan would be approved, Mitchell said, "I assume others were interested in implementing the plan." Mitchell declined, however, to speculate on who the others were.

Could Magruder have been misled? Dash asked. "I would hope not," replied Mitchell. Dash then asked how Mitchell could explain Magruder's testimony that Mitchell approved the Liddy plan. "I can't explain anyone's testimony except my own," Mitchell responded.

Dash also asked Mitchell why, if he rejected the plan, Magruder would have told another campaign aide, Robert Reisner, to tell Liddy it had been approved, and why he would have told campaign treasurer Hugh W. Sloan that a budget of $250,000 had been approved for espionage. Mitchell again said he could not account for the activities of other people, but added that it was either "a misunderstanding or a contravention of my orders." Asked further by Dash if Magruder would have taken it upon himself to order Liddy's plan into operation, Mitchell said many "dirty tricks" were carried out without his knowledge. He did not elaborate.

'Palpable Lie.' Mitchell also described as "a palpable, damnable lie" Magruder's testimony that he showed Mitchell wiretap logs resulting from the first Watergate break-in on May 28, 1972. Magruder told the committee that Mitchell was dissatisfied with the results of the initial wiretaps, and that this led to the second break-in June 17 to install another tap.

Mitchell said he first learned of the June 17 break-in while on a trip to California. He said he did not imediately connect it to the Liddy plans because "the players were different," a reference to the fact that none of those arrested in the Watergate building had been mentioned by Liddy at the planning meetings.

He contradicted Magruder's testimony that the idea to destroy wiretap and other files on illegal activities originated at a meeting in Mitchell's Washington apartment June 19. Mitchell said the meeting was merely a general discussion of the Watergate break-in.

Mitchell said he received a complete briefing on the break-in and the White House "horror stories" on June 21 or 22 from LaRue and Robert Mardian, another campaign aide, who had talked to Liddy. Mitchell indicated the coverup was under way by that time. "We sure as hell weren't volunteering anything," he said. Mitchell testified that he, Dean and former top presidential aides H. R. Haldeman and John D. Ehrlichman primarily were concerned that information given to prosecutors did not touch on the so-called White House "horror stories." He said he knew in advance that Magruder would perjure himself before the Watergate grand jury.

Dean Testimony. The former attorney general's testimony generally coincided with that of Dean concerning the pre-June 17 events, but diverged on the coverup activities. He denied Dean's testimony that he suggested Dean get former Nixon lawyer Herbert W. Kalmbach to raise "silence money" for the Watergate defendants; that Dean was merely a message-carrier in the coverup between Mitchell and Haldeman and Ehrlichman; that Mitchell discussed silence money for Hunt; that Mitchell told Dean that Dean's theory of how the break-in came about was "not far wrong," and that the White House in 1972 wanted Mitchell to take the blame for the whole affair.

Mitchell said he was in New York June 28, 1972, the day Dean claims the two spoke about enlisting Kalmbach's efforts in raising money for the Watergate defendants, and that, in any case, he never discussed silence money for the defendants with anyone. He said he "refused at all times" to raise money himself for the defendants. Asked if he thought Dean made up his testimony about the discussions, Mitchell said, "I think it's a matter of confusion of people."

'Fall Guy.' Mitchell said he was not sure he would not be the "fall guy" for the Watergate affair after reading the memo from White House counsel J. Fred Buzhardt concerning Mitchell's and Dean's role in

Contradictory Mitchell Testimony?

John N. Mitchell and Sen. Herman E. Talmadge (D Ga.) engaged in a short debate July 10 over Mitchell's role in President Nixon's campaign while Mitchell was still attorney general.

"Did you play an active supervisory role in the campaign before you resigned as attorney general?" asked Talmadge.

"What I did," answered Mitchell, "was succumb to the President's request to keep an eye on what was going on over there, and I had frequent meetings with individuals dealing with matters of policy...."

Talmadge: "You would consider, then, that you did play an active supervisory role before you resigned as attorney general?"

Mitchell: "If you would change 'supervisory' to 'consulting,' I think I would be much happier."

The former attorney general had an answer ready when Talmadge asked him if he had not testified to the contrary on March 14, 1972, at confirmation hearings on former Attorney General Richard G. Kleindienst before the Senate Judiciary Committee. He quoted from a segment of dialogue between himself and Sen. Edward M. Kennedy (D Mass.) at those hearings.

Kennedy: "Do you remember what party responsibilities you had prior to March 1?"

Mitchell: "Party responsibilities?"

Kennedy: "Yes. Republican Party."

Mitchell: "I do not have and did not have any responsibilities. I have no party responsibilities now, Senator."

Talmadge read further from the Mitchell-Kennedy exchange:

Kennedy: "No re-election campaign responsibilities?"

Mitchell: "Not as yet. I hope to. I am going to make the application to the chairman of the committee if I ever get through these hearings."

After some more give and take, Talmadge told Mitchell that "you testified under oath in response to a question of mine a moment ago that at the request of the White House, you were actively involved in the campaign. If I can read the English language correctly, on March 14 of last year, you testified to the opposite before the Judiciary Committee. One or the other of your statements is in error...."

Mitchell: "I dispute your statement with respect to the discussion before the Judiciary Committee, and I would like to go back to my statement and stand on that answer."

The inconclusive debate ended when the Watergate committee chairman, Sen. Sam J. Ervin Jr. (D N.C.), asked Mitchell: "It is your position that working for a Republican candidate for President gave you no responsibilities in respect to the Republican Party?"

Mitchell answered: "That is it entirely, Mr. Chairman. That is the question that I asked of Sen. Kennedy."

the break-in and coverup. Buzhardt's memo, implicating Dean and Mitchell in both actions, was read to the committee during Dean's testimony. Mitchell referred to Buzhardt as the "misguided White House counsel." *(Buzhardt memo, p. 162)*

Mitchell also denied that he told Magruder at a March 21, 1973, meeting in New York that he would help get him executive clemency if he told the truth to federal prosecutors, as Magruder testified. Mitchell said he offered to help Magruder as best he could but did not promise executive clemency.

Apparent Conflict. Sen. Herman E. Talmadge (D Ga.) questioned the witness about statements he made in March 14, 1972, testimony before the Senate Judiciary Committee on the ITT antitrust case. At that time, Mitchell testified he had no active role at the re-election committee while attorney general. But that appeared to conflict with his statements before the Watergate committee that he made many decisions concerning the re-election committee while in the Justice Department, including budget approval, primary election efforts and direct mail activities.

Mitchell said he was only keeping an eye on things at the re-election committee at the President's request, and suggested he acted only in a consulting role at the committee.

He insisted that there was no conflict between the separate testimony, saying what he did in a consulting role for the re-election committee was Republican Party responsibility, not re-election campaign responsibility. *(Box, this page)*

Witness July 11

John N. Mitchell remained firm in his statements that President Nixon's re-election chances would have been badly damaged if he had informed the President of all he knew about the Watergate break-in and coverup. Mitchell told the Senate select Watergate committee July 11 that he still believed "the most important thing" to the country at the time was Nixon's re-election, and that he "was not about to countenance anything that would stand in the way of that goal."

He admitted, when grilled by Sen. Lowell P. Weicker Jr. (R Conn.), that he probably had not done "the right thing" when he did not reveal to prosecutors or the courts his knowledge of the coverup and other illegal activities.

He also maintained, as he had the previous day, that his motive for silence had more to do with the so-called White House "horror stories" than with the Watergate break-in itself, which he characterized as having been blown up out of proportion by the press.

Mitchell conceded, however, that in the long run it might have been better for the President and the country if he had revealed to Nixon what he knew, at least after the election was over. He said the President never asked him about Watergate.

The former attorney general and re-election campaign director continued to play down his own role in the Watergate coverup, refusing even to use the word "coverup" to describe his actions. "I certainly was not about to do anything" that would disclose what had happened, he said in describing his activities after the break-in June 17, 1972.

Eavesdropping Contradiction. Mitchell continued to maintain that he had no advance knowledge of the break-in and that three times he had rejected electronic eavesdropping plans put forward by the re-election committee's general counsel, G. Gordon Liddy.

Even when read the testimony given to the committee in private by his former aide, Frederick C. LaRue, that Liddy's last plan was not rejected, Mitchell did not appear shaken. He had testified repeatedly he had rejected Liddy's third eavesdropping plan, presented to him at Key Biscayne, Fla., March 30, 1972.

This contradicted sworn testimony by Mitchell's deputy at the re-election committee, Jeb Stuart Magruder, who said that Mitchell approved the plan at the Key Biscayne meeting. Mitchell testified July 10 that LaRue was at the meeting and would back up his version of the event. But Weicker, reading from a digest of LaRue's private testimony, quoted LaRue as saying Mitchell said the matter did not have to be decided at that time.

"My recollection is very distinct," Mitchell told Weicker. "The matter was rejected, and it was rejected on the basis that I was tired of hearing these things and I didn't want to hear about them again." Despite the contradictions between Mitchell and Magruder and LaRue, and at other times between Mitchell and former White House counsel John W. Dean III, Mitchell refused to say the others perjured themselves.

Presidential Information. Howard H. Baker (R Tenn.), the committee vice chairman, repeatedly questioned Mitchell about how he could have taken it upon himself not to inform the President about Watergate soon after the break-in. "Is the presidency so shrouded in mystique...is the splendor of isolation so great that the President must be protected and, if so, in what cases?" asked Baker.

Mitchell answered that Nixon should not have been involved in the matter because it would have affected his re-election chances. But why, Baker asked, should not the President himself make that decision?

Because, answered Mitchell, Nixon then either would have become involved in the coverup or would have had to make disclosures that might have destroyed his re-election chances. "Knowing the current President and his respect for the presidency, that would have been no option," Mitchell said.

Baker persisted. Doesn't that imply a distrust of the President? he asked. Mitchell answered no, repeating that Nixon might have taken actions "deleterious to his campaign," such as firing his top aides.

Baker: "What is the constitutional basis for arrogating unto yourself a decision of this kind?"

Mitchell: "I haven't found one."

Baker: By what authority did you act?

Mitchell: It was "a matter of judgment."

Baker: Doesn't this theory have a significantly diminishing effect on the powers of the President?

Mitchell: Yes. "If I'd been assured at that time (June, 1972) that the President would have been re-elected, I'd agree with you wholeheartedly."

Baker: Wouldn't that have saved the present suspicion and hostility toward the President?

Mitchell: "I don't believe the nation feels that way."

A moment later, in a remark that drew gasps from the audience, Mitchell said that in hindsight, "It'd have been simpler to take them (those involved in the break-in and coverup) out on the White House lawn and shot (sic) them all."

Asked by Weicker how far he was willing to go now to protect the President, and whether he would be willing to lie for him, Mitchell said he did not have to lie for Nixon, because the facts about Watergate are public. But he added that "I would not lie here under oath."

Executive Privilege. Mitchell also was questioned extensively about the doctrine of executive privilege.

Mitchell's Reasons for Silence

In his testimony before the Senate Watergate committee on July 10, former Attorney General John N. Mitchell explained his reasons for not informing President Nixon of details of the Watergate affair. The exchange below, excerpted from the transcript of the hearings, occurred between Mitchell and Sen. Herman E. Talmadge (D Ga.), a committee member.

Talmadge: One thing I can't understand, Mr. Mitchell. As I understand it, you have been probably closer associated with the President than probably any man. You were his law partner, probably his most trusted confidant and adviser. You had immediate access to the White House at any time, to the President's office, including a direct line. Is that a fair statement?

Mitchell: It is extremely complimentary.

Talmadge: Now, you have been in public office, in positions of high responsibility in government. I have had that privilege also as governor of my state and now for 16½ years in the United States Senate. To my mind, the first requirement of a subordinate and adviser and confidant in any capacity is absolute and implicit trust. If they see anything going wrong involving their superior that needs immediate corrective action, they report it instantly. When you found out all these crimes and conspiracies and cover-ups were being committed, why on earth didn't you walk into the President's office and tell him the truth?

Mitchell: It wasn't a question of telling him the truth. It was a question of not involving him at all so that he could go through his campaign without being involved in this type of activity, and I am talking about the White House horrors particularly. As I have testified this morning, I was sure that, knowing Richard Nixon, the President, as I do, he would just lower the boom on all of this matter and it would come back to hurt him and it would affect him in his re-election. And that is the basis upon which I made the decision. And apparently others concurred with it.

Now, I am not speaking for them. It may very well be that I was wrong, that it was a bad matter of judgment.

Talmadge: Am I to understand from your response that you placed the expediency of the next election above your responsibilities as an intimate to advise the President of the peril that surrounded him? Here was the deputy campaign director involved, here were his two closest associates in his office involved, all around him were people involved in crime, perjury, accessory after the fact, and you deliberately refused to tell him that.

Would you state that the expediency of the election was more important than that?

Mitchell: Senator, I think you have put it exactly correct. In my mind, the re-election of Richard Nixon, compared with what was available on the other side, was so much more important that I put it in just that context.

Nixon invoked the doctrine in refusing to appear before the committee or give it certain White House papers.

Mitchell said he thought the President was "ill served" with the thought that he should invoke executive privilege before the committee, even though he said Nixon had that right under the Constitution. Asked about documents, Mitchell said he did not think the doctrine applied to political papers, such as those concerning Watergate, unless national security interests were involved.

Committee Chairman Sam J. Ervin Jr. (D N.C.) asked whether Nixon's silence on Watergate indicated that he had something to hide. Mitchell replied that some people might believe that, but that it was not so simple a matter.

Mitchell told Baker that it would be "brash" on his part to say how the President should respond on the question of separation of powers inherent in executive privilege. He said he thought the President eventually would respond to charges against him, but repeatedly refused to say whether he thought Nixon should appear before the committee.

At one point, just as Baker asked the witness how the committee could learn Nixon's version of his Sept. 15, 1972, conversation with Dean, the television lights failed, darkening the hearing room. Quipped Baker: "I hope its not significant that at that point the lights went out."

Liddy Plan. Mitchell also said that when he told Liddy after their Jan. 27, 1972, meeting, to burn the charts Liddy had presented to explain the surveillance scheme, he meant that Liddy should "abandon the concept of any such activity." Nevertheless, on two subsequent occasions, scaled-down versions of Liddy's plan were presented to Mitchell.

He said he could not understand why the plan kept coming back, except that someone unknown to him must have been pushing it. Mitchell disagreed that the fact the plan kept coming back meant his rejections were not strong enough.

Witnesses July 12

Richard A. Moore, a special counsel to President Nixon since 1971, testified July 12 that it was his "deep conviction" that the President knew nothing about Watergate or its coverup until he met with John W. Dean III March 21, 1973. This was one of several contradictions between Moore and Dean, the White House counsel, who had testified earlier that he believed Nixon knew about Watergate at least as early as September 1972.

Moore was not a major figure in the Watergate scandal. His name had hardly surfaced at all until Dean mentioned that on several occasions he had confided to Moore his concerns regarding the coverup.

Moore, 59, was an associate of Dean in the White House and worked for former Attorney General John N. Mitchell in the Justice Department from 1970 to 1971. Moore described his White House duties as assisting the President and his staff in "communicating their positions in the most convincing manner to the general public."

Reading from a prepared statement before the Senate select Watergate committee, the tall, crew-cut Moore said that he did not dispute Dean's account of their meetings and that he had no knowledge of Dean's meetings with the President after March 21. "But nothing said in my meetings with the President suggests in any way that before March 21 the President had known—or that Mr. Dean believed he had known—of any involvement of White House personnel in the bugging or coverup," Moore said.

"It is my deep conviction—as one who has known the President over the years and has had many private conversations with him—that the critical facts about the Watergate did not reach the President until the events that began when John Dean met with him on March 21, 1973." *(Moore statement, text, p. 205)*

Dean had testified that he told the President all he knew about the Watergate break-in and the coverup on March 21, but believed that the President was aware of the coverup on Sept. 15, 1972.

Documents. The day also saw the end of Mitchell's testimony—after 2½ days in the witness chair and much skeptical questioning by committee members and counsel—and the committee's decision that it is entitled to see all executive branch documents relating to Watergate, despite the President's announced determination to bar their release by invoking executive privilege.

Committee Chairman Ervin announced he had sent the President a letter July 12, based on a unanimous committee resolution the same day, stating that Nixon's position represented "a very grave possibility of a fundamental constitutional confrontation." *(Texts of letter and resolution, box p. 186)*

The resolution, Ervin announced, noted that the committee was entitled to all White House or executive branch documents relevant to its investigation and that it was anxious for the chairman to meet with the President to avoid an impasse. Ervin said he talked with the President by telephone at midday and that Nixon promised to meet privately with him after certain "pressing matters" had been disposed of.

Nixon's willingness to meet with Ervin put off for the time being a confrontation that might have to be settled in court. Committee sources said that if Nixon turned down the committee's request for certain documents, the committee would subpoena them.

Meetings with Dean. Moore said he had several meetings early in 1973 with Dean and Nixon to discuss various matters, including the upcoming Senate Watergate hearings. The President, he added, urged that his two aides be forthcoming with information and advice concerning all Watergate-related matters. Moore said Dean had confided to him on March 19 or 20 that E. Howard Hunt Jr., a convicted Watergate burglar, was demanding a large sum of money before his sentencing on March 23. Moore said he told Dean that amounted to blackmail and that Dean should have nothing to do with it. Dean agreed, he said.

Moore said this was the "culmination of several other guarded comments" by Dean. These included remarks about Dean's presence at two meetings at which G. Gordon Liddy proposed his surveillance schemes, and what Moore described as "earlier activities of Hunt and Liddy, not directly related to Watergate." This was an apparent reference to the break-in at the office of Daniel Ellsberg's psychiatrist.

Moore related his impression of a March 20 meeting with Dean and Nixon in the President's oval office. "As I sat through the meeting," Moore said, "...I came to the conclusion in my own mind that the President could not be aware of the things that Dean was worried about or had been hinting at to me, let alone Howard Hunt's blackmail demand. Indeed, as the President talked about getting the whole story out—as he had done repeatedly in the recent meetings—it seemed crystal clear to me that he knew of nothing that was inconsistent with the previously stated conclusion that the White House was uninvolved in the Watergate affair, before or after the event."

After the meetings, Moore said that he raised the matter directly with Dean and that Dean said he had never told the President what he knew. Moore said he recommended that Dean tell everything to the President and that Dean did so the next day.

One of the contradictions between Dean's testimony and that of Moore occurred when Moore described Dean's comment on the result of his talk with Nixon March 21. Dean had testified that after talking to Nixon "I realized that I had not really made the President understand," because "he did not seem particularly concerned" and suggested Dean tell his story at a cabinet meeting. According to Moore, however, "I asked (Dean) if the President had been surprised and he said yes."

Moore's testimony also conflicted with Dean's on two other points. Moore told the committee that at a meeting near San Clemente, Calif., in February 1973, former White House aide John D. Ehrlichman told the gathering that the President wanted the White House position on the Senate hearings "to be one of full cooperation, subject only to the doctrine of separation of powers."

According to Dean's testimony, however, it was decided that the White House's public posture would be one of cooperation, but privately the administration would try to impede the committee's investigation.

Another conflict stemmed from the two witnesses' testimony concerning their conversation when the meeting ended. Dean testified that Moore was told in the San Clemente meeting to go to New York City to meet with Mitchell to try to get him to raise money for the Watergate defendants. Dean said he warned Moore against asking Mitchell to raise money, but Moore said he had "absolutely no recollection of any such conversation, and I am convinced it never took place."

Despite the apparent contradictions, Moore said he did "not dispute Mr. Dean's account of the meetings between us as to any substantive point." He said he believed Dean "had no advance knowledge of the Watergate bugging or break-in."

Moore's meeting with Mitchell, at which he asked him to raise money for the defendants, took place Feb. 15. Moore's and Mitchell's testimony on the meeting coincided, both agreeing that Mitchell quickly turned down the idea of being a fund-raiser. According to Mitchell, Moore put the question in the context of "support money" rather than silence money, the latter being illegal. Moore's recollection was that the money would go to re-election committee lawyers.

Mitchell Testimony. In earlier testimony July 12, Mitchell disputed a suggestion by committee counsel Samuel Dash that he might have lied in sworn testimony prior to the Senate hearings. "Since you may have given false testimony under oath on prior occasions, is there any reason you didn't give it here?" Dash asked.

Mitchell replied that the committee could judge for itself. "Anything I would say would be self-serving," he said.

Dash replied that to believe Mitchell's testimony, he would have to discount the earlier testimony of five or six witnesses. "I disagree violently," said Mitchell, suggesting that future witnesses would back him up.

Dash made his remarks after he led Mitchell through a series of apparent contradictions between his committee testimony and depositions Mitchell gave in FBI interviews on July 5 and Oct. 5, 1972, and on Sept. 5 in a civil suit filed by the Democratic National Committee.

For example, Mitchell testified that his former aides, Frederick C. LaRue and Robert Mardian, told him all about Watergate and so-called White House "horror stories" on June 21 or 22, 1972, after interviewing Liddy. But in his deposition Sept. 5, 1972, Mitchell said neither Mardian nor LaRue talked to him about their conversation with Liddy, except about his being fired from the re-election committee, where Liddy was general counsel.

Mitchell maintained that there were two separate questions at the deposition, and that he answered negatively regarding Liddy's firing but was equivocal on the subject of his conversations with LaRue and Mardian. In other testimony, Mitchell repeated previous assertions that Nixon never had asked him about Watergate, but insisted that he "would have laid out chapter and verse" on the subject if the President had.

Mitchell also implicated Ehrlichman and former White House aide H.R. Haldeman in the coverup. Asked if the two men had taken an active role in the coverup, Mitchell responded: "I would say they had a very active

Mitchell's Retrospect on Ellsberg

The Senate Watergate hearings July 11 concluded with this acrimonious exchange between Sen. Lowell P. Weicker Jr. (R Conn.) and John N. Mitchell:

Weicker: Is there anything in this country, aside from the President of the United States, that puts you in awe, Mr. Mitchell?"

Mitchell: To put me where?

Weicker: That puts you in awe.

Mitchell: There are very, very many things.

Weicker: Do the courts put you in awe?

Mitchell: Very much so.

Weicker: Do you feel as an officer of the court you did the right thing?

Mitchell: In connection with the Ellsberg matter (the White House-inspired burglary of the office of the former psychiatrist of Daniel Ellsberg, a defendant in the Pentagon Papers trial, in 1971)?

Weicker: When you did not notify the prosecution or you did not notify rather Judge Byrne (U.S. District Judge W. Matthew Byrne Jr. of Los Angeles) of the information you had in your possession?

Mitchell: I think, in retrospect, it probably would have been the right thing to do.

Weicker: I have no further questions at this time.

Mitchell: It is a great trial being conducted up here, isn't it?

concern, just as I had." He referred to his own role as being part of a "consensus."

Mitchell also denied Dean's testimony that Mitchell suggested the CIA as a good source of coverup money for the Watergate defendants and that H. Roemer McPhee, a Republican Party attorney, had interceded with Judge Charles R. Richey to delay the Democrats' civil suit until after the 1972 election.

Daily Chronology

Following is a day-to-day chronology of the week's events:

JULY 5

(Earlier July 5 events, p. 178)

Krogh Plea. Egil Krogh Jr., former chief of the White House special investigations unit, or "plumbers," pleaded the Fifth Amendment against self-incrimination and refused to answer questions in an appearance before the Los Angeles grand jury investigating the 1971 break-in at the office of Daniel Ellsberg's psychiatrist.

GAO Report. The General Accounting Office issued a report charging eight apparent violations of federal election and perjury laws in connection with $50,000 spent on a fund-raising dinner honoring Vice President Agnew in May 1972. *(p. 174)*

Tax Investigation. U.S. District Judge Charles R. Richey ordered the Justice Department to conduct an "emergency" investigation to discover whether the White House had blocked the granting of tax-exempt status to the Center on Corporate Responsibility Inc., a nonprofit Washington public interest group. The organization filed suit against the Internal Revenue Service in May, charging that a 2½-year delay in ruling on its application had caused contributions to dry up.

In his appearance before the Senate investigating committee June 27, former Nixon counsel John W. Dean III released a memo he had written on how the White House could use the IRS for political purposes. The Center on Corporate Responsibility charged in its suit that it had been singled out by the administration for discriminatory treatment. *(Dean memo, p. 153)*

JULY 6

Airline Contributions. George A. Spater, chairman of American Airlines, issued a statement admitting that his company illegally contributed $55,000 to Nixon's 1972 campaign. He said the airline had given a total of $75,000 to the campaign, of which all but $20,000 came from corporate sources in violation of federal law prohibiting corporate political contributions. *(Box, p. 187)*

JULY 7

Nixon Refusal. In a July 6 letter to Sen. Sam J. Ervin Jr., chairman of the Watergate committee, President Nixon said he would neither appear in person before the committee nor open presidential files to the committee. Nixon based his refusal on his concern for the constitutional doctrine of the separation of powers and cited a similar refusal by President Truman in 1953. He promised to address the Watergate issue publicly "at an appropriate time" during the hearings. *(Texts of Nixon, Truman letters, p. 189)*

Ervin Response. "If a President wants to withhold information from the committee and the American people, I would just let him take the consequences of that," Ervin retorted. Ervin said he thought the committee had the power to subpoena Nixon and his papers, but added that he would oppose such a course. An "unfavorable inference" can be drawn against anyone who refuses to give evidence he has to an investigative body, the senator concluded. Ervin's remarks were quoted in *The Washington Post* July 8. *(Presidential subpoena, p. 103)*

Committee Resolution, Ervin Letter

Meeting in executive session July 12, the Senate Watergate committee took steps to avoid a confrontation with the Nixon administration over the availability to the committee of White House documents. This is the text of a resolution adopted by the committee:

Resolved by the Senate Select Committee on Presidential Campaign Activities:

1. That the Committee is of the unanimous opinion that the Committee is entitled to have access to every document in the possession of the White House or any Department or agency of the Executive Branch of the Federal Government, which is relevant to prove or disprove any of the matters the Committee is authorized by Senate Resolution 60 to investigate.

2. That the Committee is anxious to avoid any confrontation with the White House in respect to this matter and for this reason authorizes the Chairman to meet with the President to ascertain whether there is any reasonable possibility of working out any reconciliation between the position of the Committee in this respect and that announced by the President in his letter to the Chairman bearing date July 6, 1973, which will enable the Committee to gain access to documents necessary to enable it to make the inquiry which it is authorized by Senate Resolution 60 to make.

Following is the text of a letter written by Sen. Sam J. Ervin Jr. (D N.C.), the committee chairman, to Nixon July 12. *(Nixon letter to Ervin, p. 189)*

Dear Mr. President:

I acknowledge receipt of your letter of July 6, addressed to me with a copy to Senator Baker.

The Committee feels that your position as stated in the letter, measured against the Committee's responsibility to ascertain the facts related to the matters set out in Senate Resolution 60, present (sic) the very grave possibility of a fundamental constitutional confrontation between the Congress and the Presidency. We wish to avoid that, if possible. Consequently, we request an opportunity for representatives of this Committee and its staff to meet with you and your staff to try to find ways to avoid such a confrontation.

We stand ready to discuss the matter with you at your convenience. We would point out that the hearings are ongoing and that time is of the essence. We trust that this may be done very promptly.

Airline's Admission of an Illegal Campaign Donation

George A. Spater, board chairman of American Airlines, announced July 6 that his company had made illegal contributions to President Nixon's 1972 campaign. In a statement issued in New York City, Spater said the airline gave a total of $75,000 in cash, of which all but $20,000 came from "corporate sources," in violation of federal law.

Spater said the money was solicited by Nixon's former personal attorney, Herbert W. Kalmbach, whom he knew to be counsel for his company's major competitor, United Airlines. "I concluded that a substantial response was called for," Spater said.

The money was delivered in five installments from November 1971 through March 1972, a period when American was seeking White House and Civil Aeronautics Board (CAB) approval of a merger with Western Airlines—a request opposed by United. The CAB rejected the proposed merger in July 1972.

"Under the existing laws," Spater said, "a large part of the money raised from the business community for political purposes is given in fear of what would happen if it were not given." But he portrayed all parties involved in the transactions as victims of a bad campaign financing system.

Cox Appeal. The illegal contribution was first announced July 6 by special Watergate prosecutor Archibald Cox, who added that he hoped other corporate executives would follow suit "in an effort to put an end to such practices." Cox said voluntary disclosures would be considered in deciding what charges to bring against violators, but an aide emphasized that the prosecutor's office had made no special deal with American's attorneys.

Spater said he volunteered the information on American's contributions "before any knowledge of these facts had reached the government from other sources." But the possibility that undisclosed contributions to the Nixon campaign would be revealed was raised in June, when Common Cause, a "citizens' lobby," announced it had obtained a list of early Nixon contributors. The list reportedly accounted for more than $19-million. Common Cause was seeking a court order requiring full disclosure of all 1972 Nixon re-election funds.

Campaign Law. Under the Corrupt Practices Act of 1925, which governed campaign contributions when American Airlines made its illegal contributions, it was a criminal offense to give or receive political contributions from corporate funds. The new campaign law that took effect April 7, 1972, retained that prohibition and defined more strictly the roles corporations could play in political campaigns.

In his statement, Spater condemned the new law as "hypocritical and unconstitutionally vague" because it permits political contributions from salaried officers, corporate employees and substantial stockholders, while outlawing direct corporate donations. "The corporation, however, is usually the target of the solicitation and usually receives the political credit for the contributions that are made. The corporation with independently wealthy officers or stockholders is thus placed in a preferred position in comparison with a corporation whose officers or stockholders are less fortunately endowed."

Spater did not specify how the $55,000 was raised, but informed sources quoted in *The Washington Post* said it was collected through the use of phony invoices for which payments were listed on the airline's books.

Reaction. Kalmbach's attorney issued a statement in Phoenix, Ariz., acknowledging that his client had solicited funds from Spater in 1972 and had received a pledge of $100,000, but adding that Kalmbach had "no involvement in the form or nature" of the contribution.

The Finance Committee to Re-elect the President responded to the revelation with an indignant denial: "At no time did the committee authorize anyone to solicit or knowingly accept contributions from corporations." The committee announced July 11 it had returned the $55,000 to American.

Other Airlines. Inquiring reporters could find no other airline willing to admit to a contribution similar to the ones made by American. But Jonathan Rinehart, an Eastern Airlines senior vice president, said his company had rejected an appeal by an unidentified person for a corporate contribution to the Nixon campaign. United Airlines released a statement saying it was "unaware of any corporate contributions to any federal political organization or campaign fund."

Kopechne Tap. An illegal wiretap was placed on the phone in the Washington, D.C., home of Mary Jo Kopechne shortly after she died July 18, 1969, in a car accident that involved Sen. Edward M. Kennedy (D Mass.), *The New York Times* reported. Citing a source close to the Senate investigating committee, the account said the tap was installed by John J. Caulfield and Anthony T. Ulasewicz, two former New York policemen who went to work at the White House in early 1969. Both men had testified at the Senate hearings. *(Testimony, p. 80, 82-83)*

JULY 8

Gurney, Talmadge Remarks. Senators Edward J. Gurney (R Fla.) and Herman E. Talmadge (D Ga.) of the Senate Watergate committee, interviewed on ABC-TV's "Issues and Answers," criticized Nixon's refusal to turn over to the committee presidential papers bearing on its investigation. They agreed that the committee did not have authority to subpoena the President to appear, but Talmadge wondered: "If he had nothing to hide, why does he refuse to appear?" Gurney said he thought the best way for Nixon to answer charges against him would be in a "free-swinging press conference."

Campaign Funding. *The Washington Post* reported that special prosecutor Archibald Cox was considering impaneling a special federal grand jury to investigate the financing of 1972 presidential campaigns, with emphasis on Nixon's.

Kalmbach Testimony. Nixon's former personal attorney, Herbert W. Kalmbach, was planning to tell the Senate investigating committee that former White House aide John D. Ehrlichman approved secret cash payments to the Watergate defendants, *The Washington Star-News* reported. The paper printed a chronology, obtained from Senate sources, describing 1972 meetings the lawyer had with administration officials to arrange the payments.

JULY 9

Ehrlichman Remarks. Ehrlichman challenged Dean's Senate testimony in an interview published in *The Seattle Post-Intelligencer.* He and Nixon had discussed the subject of executive clemency for the Watergate defendants once in July 1972, Ehrlichman said, but concluded that it would be "an extremely dangerous subject" for the President to get into. Ehrlichman quoted Nixon as saying at that time, "Let's agree now this is a subject we'll never discuss." Dean's allegation that the President agreed to an offer of executive clemency for conspirator E. Howard Hunt Jr. was "180 degrees" from the truth, he asserted. *(Dean testimony, p. 152)*

Vesco Case. Defense attorneys for Mitchell, former Commerce Secretary Maurice H. Stans and New Jersey Republican leader Harry L. Sears filed motions in U.S. District Court in New York asking dismissal of federal indictments charging the three with conspiracy to influence a fraud investigation of financier Robert L. Vesco in exchange for Vesco's $200,000 campaign contribution. The attorneys accused government prosecutors of improperly injecting the Watergate case into the grand jury investigation of the Vesco contribution. *(Indictments, p. 46)*

Huston Testimony. Tom Charles Huston, a former White House aide who helped draft the administration's 1970 intelligence-gathering plan, told the House Armed Services Intelligence Subcommittee that the plan was never formally canceled, as Nixon said in his May 22 statement. Huston's claim was repeated by Subcommittee Chairman Lucien N. Nedzi (D Mich.) after the closed hearing. *(p. 121)*

Sabotage Report. In an extensive report on attempts to sabotage Democratic presidential candidates in 1972, *The New York Times* described the efforts as "a two-pronged operation approved by some of President Nixon's most influential aides, directed in part by White House officials, and financed with more than $100,000 in unreported contributions to the Nixon campaign."

One aspect of the program, carried out by California lawyer Donald H. Segretti, was conceived by former presidential aides Dwight L. Chapin and Gordon C. Strachan and approved in advance by former Nixon staff chief H. R. Haldeman, the article said. A second sabotage campaign reportedly was managed by Jeb Stuart Magruder, a former official of the Nixon re-election committee, with "some direction" from Charles W. Colson, former special counsel to the President.

Support Payments. The Times also reported that a Cuban exile leader from Miami, Fla., had admitted to the Dade County state's attorney that he delivered $21,000 in "support" money to four Watergate conspirators from Miami. The cash was said to have come from another member of the bugging team, E. Howard Hunt Jr.

Ziegler Subpoena. Attorneys for the Democratic National Committee filed a subpoena in U.S. District Court in Washington, demanding that White House press secretary Ronald L. Ziegler produce all written or electronic materials he might have related to the Watergate affair. The action was taken in connection with the Democrats' civil suit against the Nixon re-election committee. One of the attorneys said Ziegler's information was of particular interest in light of Dean's Senate testimony, which implied that the press secretary never was briefed on White House involvement in the scandal but was coached by other officials on how to respond to press queries. *(Dean testimony, p. 156)*

JULY 10

Mitchell Testimony. Former Attorney General John N. Mitchell, once Nixon's most trusted political adviser, appeared before the Senate investigating committee and admitted that he never had warned the President of the Watergate scandal because he wanted to "keep the lid on through the election," and later because the knowledge "would affect his (Nixon's) presidency." Contradicting the sworn testimony of other former White House and campaign officials, Mitchell denied he approved in advance the 1972 bugging operation against the Democrats. *(Mitchell testimony, p. 1866)*

Mansfield Remarks. Senate Majority Leader Mike Mansfield (D Mont.) told reporters it was "debatable" whether Nixon could be impeached for not knowing of his staff's involvement in the Watergate affair. He cautioned that an impeachment trial should be a last resort, a cataclysmic action that would "bring the whole government to a halt. We have to differentiate between the man and the office—the institution is what counts." Mansfield also suggested that Nixon meet informally with the Senate investigating committee after the initial phase of the hearings was complete. *(Impeachment background, p. 55)*

White House Documents. Samuel Dash, chief counsel of the Senate investigating committee, accused the White House of refusing to cooperate with the committee's request for certain documents pertaining to the Watergate case. His remarks to newsmen came amid reports that the committee would move to subpoena the documents.

Reuss Move. Rep. Henry S. Reuss (D Wis.) called on the Internal Revenue Service to seize the assets of the Finance Committee to Re-elect the President for taxes before the committee "dissipates" them. "Like any other taxpayer," he said, the committee "ought to pay taxes on gains realized on the sale of contributed appreciated property and on other income as defined in the income and gift tax laws." Reuss estimated the committee's assets at between $4-million and $5-million and its possible liability for income and gift taxes at more than $5-million.

JULY 11

Mitchell Testimony. In his second day before the Senate investigating committee, Mitchell defended his failure to inform Nixon of the Watergate scandal. "To this day I believe that I was right in not involving the President," he told his skeptical interrogators. *(p. 182)*

Ehrlichman Interview. News reports quoted from a 33-page summary prepared by the Senate investigating committee staff on an interview with John D. Ehrlichman four days after he resigned as Nixon's chief domestic adviser. Accounts of the May 4 interview said Ehrlichman's disclosures included:

• He approved payments to Watergate defendants in July 1972 but did not know that the payments were to be used to buy silence or that they came from campaign funds.

• He was not involved in planning the bugging operation or its coverup, but he tried to learn as little as possible about it because he knew he would have to testify in civil proceedings related to the case.

• Herbert W. Kalmbach had given him a personal loan of $20,000 sometime in the past year.

• The Justice Department knew of White House involvement in the 1971 burglary of Daniel Ellsberg's psychiatrist almost a year before April 15, 1973, the date the department said it learned of the incident.

Ehrlichman told the interviewers he came to believe shortly after the June 17, 1972, burglary that high officials of the Nixon campaign had been involved, but, pleading the doctrine of executive privilege, refused to say whether he had told Nixon of his belief. In a statement May 22, Nixon changed his position on executive privilege, saying his current and former aides should tell investigators all they knew. *(p. 94)*

White House Documents. Deputy press secretary Gerald L. Warren told reporters that since May 23, former White House aides involved in the Watergate investigations had been prohibited from copying documents they worked on at the White House. They could only look at such papers, he said. Former Nixon counsel John W. Dean III had asked the Senate investigating committee to intercede with the White House to let him copy some documents he had left in the Executive Office Building. *(p. 151)*

Senate Delegation. Ten conservative Republican senators, led by Carl T. Curtis (Neb.), met with Nixon for cocktails at the White House and told him of their continuing support in the face of Watergate. Absent from the group were Barry Goldwater (Ariz.), an early administration critic on Watergate, and Edward J. Gurney (Fla.) of the Senate investigating committee.

ACLU Position. In a position paper on civil liberties issues raised by the Watergate case, the American Civil Liberties Union said Nixon's temporary approval of a 1970 plan for domestic intelligence-gathering showed "a contemptuous disregard for constitutional freedoms." The organization also said it might feel compelled to intervene on behalf of some defendants in Watergate-related cases because of prejudicial pretrial publicity.

JULY 12

Mitchell Testimony. Former Attorney General Mitchell returned for a third day of questioning by the Senate investigating committee. His chief attorney, William Hundley, told reporters that the hearings had destroyed his client's chances of getting a fair trial in any future legal action connected with the Watergate affair. Mitchell was followed in the afternoon by Richard A. Moore, a special counsel to the President. *(Testimony, p. 184)*

White House Documents. The committee met in executive session in the morning and during the lunch break to discuss whether or not to subpoena White House papers Nixon had refused to hand over. The result was a letter to the President requesting a meeting between committee and White House spokesmen to discuss the matter. Chairman Sam J. Ervin Jr. warned that the meeting was necessary to stave off "the very grave possibility of a fundamental constitutional confrontation between the Congress and the presidency." *(p. 186)*

Committee member Joseph M. Montoya (D N.M.) told newsmen after the noon meeting that Ervin had just talked to Nixon on the phone and accepted an invitation to meet with the President to discuss the documents. Montoya said no date had been set for the meeting.

Bush Comment. National Republican Chairman George Bush urged rapid completion of the Senate Watergate hearings in order to "end the speculation" about Nixon's involvement in the scandal. "Let's get all the facts out, let's get the whole thing over with," he said at a press conference in Atlanta, Ga., where he was attending a convention of Young Republicans.

NIXON LETTER TO ERVIN

Following is a letter written July 6 by President Nixon to Sam J. Ervin Jr. (D N.C.), chairman of the Senate Watergate investigating committee, in response to the committee's request for presidential testimony and access to presidential papers:

Dear Mr. Chairman:

I am advised that members of the Senate Select Committee have raised the desirability of my testifying before the Committee. I am further advised that the Committee has requested access to Presidential papers prepared or received by former members of my staff.

In this letter I shall state the reasons why I shall not testify before the Committee or permit access to Presidential papers.

I want to strongly emphasize that my decision, in both cases, is based on my Constitutional obligation to preserve intact the powers and prerogatives of the Presidency and not upon any desire to withhold information relevant to your inquiry.

My staff is under instructions to cooperate fully with yours in furnishing information pertinent to your inquiry. On 22 May 1973, I directed that the right of executive privilege, "as to any testimony concerning possible criminal conduct or discussions of possible criminal conduct, in the matters presently under investigation," no longer be invoked for present or former members of the White House staff. In the case of my former Counsel, I waived in addition the attorney-client privilege.

These acts of cooperation with the Committee have been genuine, extensive and, in the history of such matters, extraordinary.

The pending requests, however, would move us from proper Presidential cooperation with a Senate Committee to jeopardizing the fundamental Constitutional role of the Presidency.

This I must and shall resist.

No President could function if the private papers of his office, prepared by his personal staff, were open to public scrutiny. Formulation of sound public policy requires that the President and his personal staff be able to communicate among themselves in complete candor, and that their tentative judgments, their exploration of alternatives, and their frank comments on issues and personalities at home and abroad remain confidential. I recognize that in your investigation as in others of previous years, arguments can be and have been made for the identification and perusal by the President or his Counsel of selected documents for possible release to the Committees or their staffs. But such a course, I have concluded, would inevitably result in the attrition, and the eventual destruction, of the indispensable principle of confidentiality of Presidential papers.

The question of testimony by members of the White House staff presents a difficult but different problem. While notes and papers often involve a wide-ranging variety and intermingling of confidential matters, testimony can, at least, be limited to matters within the scope of the investigation. For this reason, and because of the special nature of this particular investigation, I have agreed to permit the unrestricted testimony of present and former White House staff members before your Committee.

The question of my own testimony, however, is another matter. I have concluded that if I were to testify before the Committee irreparable damage would be done to the Constitutional principle of separation of powers. My position in this regard is supported by ample precedents with which you are familiar and which need not be recited here. It is appropriate, however, to refer to one particular occasion on which this issue was raised.

In 1953 a Committee of the House of Representatives sought to subpoena former President Truman to inquire about matters of which he had personal knowledge while he had served as President. As you may recall, President Truman declined to comply with the subpoena on the ground that the separation of powers forbade his appearance. This position was not challenged by the Congress.

It is difficult to improve upon President Truman's discussion of this matter. Therefore, I request that his letter, which is enclosed for the Committee's convenience, be made part of the Committee's record.

The Constitutional doctrine of separation of powers is fundamental to our structure of government. In my view, as in the view of previous Presidents, its preservation is vital. In this respect, the duty of every President to protect and defend the Constitutional rights and powers of his Office is an obligation that runs directly to the people of this country.

The White House staff will continue to cooperate fully with the Committee in furnishing information relevant to its investigation except in those instances where I determine that meeting the Committee's demands would violate my Constitutional responsibility to defend the Office of the Presidency against encroachment by other Branches.

At an appropriate time during your hearings, I intend to address publicly the subjects you are considering. In the meantime, in the context of Senate Resolution 60, I consider it my Constitutional responsibility to decline to appear personally under any circumstances before your Committee or to grant access to Presidential files.

I respect the responsibilities placed upon you and your colleagues by Senate Resolution 60. I believe you and your Committee colleagues equally respect the responsibility placed upon me to protect the rights and powers of the Presidency under the Constitution.

TRUMAN LETTER TO VELDE

Following is the text of the letter written Nov. 12, 1953, by President Truman to Harold H. Velde (R Ill. 1949-57), chairman of the House Un-American Activities Committee, that was referred to in the Nixon letter to Ervin:

Dear Sir:

I have your subpoena dated November 9, 1953, directing my appearance before your committee on Friday, November 13, in Washington. The subpoena does not state the matters upon which you seek my testimony, but I assume from the press stories that you seek to examine me with respect to matters which occurred during my tenure of the Presidency of the United States.

In spite of my personal willingness to cooperate with your committee, I feel constrained by my duty to the people of the United States to decline to comply with the subpoena.

In doing so, I am carrying out the provisions of the Constitution of the United States; and am following a long line of precedents, commencing with George Washington himself in 1796. Since his day, Presidents Jefferson, Monroe, Jackson, Tyler, Polk, Fillmore, Buchanan, Lincoln, Grant, Hayes, Cleveland, Theodore Roosevelt, Coolidge, Hoover and Franklin D. Roosevelt have declined to respond to subpoenas or demand for information of various kinds by Congress.

The underlying reason for this clearly established and universally recognized constitutional doctrine has been succinctly set forth by Charles Warren, one of our leading constitutional authorities, as follows:

"In this long series of contests by the Executive to maintain his constitutional integrity, one sees a legitimate conclusion from our theory of government. ***Under our Constitution, each branch of the Government is designed to be a coordinate representative of the will of the people. ***Defense by the Executive of his constitutional powers becomes in very truth, therefore, defense of popular rights—defense of power which the people granted to him.

"It was in that sense that President Cleveland spoke of his duty to the people not to relinquish any of the powers of his great office. It was in that sense that President Buchanan stated the people have rights and prerogatives in the execution of his office by the President which every President is under a duty to see 'shall never be violated in his person' but 'passed to his successors unimpaired by the adoption of a dangerous precedent.' In maintaining his rights against a trespassing Congress, the President defends not himself, but popular government; he represents not himself but the people."

President Jackson repelled an attempt by the Congress to break down the separation of powers in these words:

"For myself I shall repel all such attempts as an invasion of the principles of justice as well as of the Constitution, and I shall esteem it my sacred duty to the people of the United States to resist them as I would the establishment of a Spanish Inquisition."

I might commend to your reading the opinion of one of the committees of the House of Representatives in 1879, House Report 141, March 3, 1879, Forty-fifth Congress, Third Session, in which the House Judiciary Committee said the following:

"The Executive is as independent of either house of Congress as either house of Congress is independent of him, and they cannot call for the records of his actions, or the action of his officers against his consent, any more than he can call for any of the journals or records of the House or Senate."

It must be obvious to you that if the doctrine of separation of powers and the independence of the Presidency is to have any validity at all, it must be equally applicable to a President after his term of office has expired when he is sought to be examined with respect to any acts occurring while he is President.

The doctrine would be shattered, and the President, contrary to our fundamental theory of constitutional government, would become a mere arm of the Legislative Branch of the Government if he would feel during his term of office that his every act might be subject to official inquiry and possible distortion for political purposes.

If your intention, however, is to inquire into any acts as a private individual either before or after my Presidency and unrelated to any acts as President, I shall be happy to appear. ✓

WATERGATE: NEAR SHOWDOWN ON WHITE HOUSE RECORDS

Despite a prank that offered temporary hope for reconciliation, the Senate Select Committee on Presidential Campaign Activities seemed to be headed toward a showdown with the Nixon administration over the release of presidential tapes and records.

The conflict intensified during the week ended July 21 with the unexpected testimony of Alexander P. Butterfield, head of the Federal Aviation Administration and former White House aide. Butterfield revealed, and the White House confirmed, that President Nixon's private conversations had been taped since the spring of 1971.

Sources on Capitol Hill reported that the revelation, more than any other development in the Watergate scandal, eroded support for Nixon in Congress. Even among some conservatives who had been his strongest supporters, according to the sources, feelings of betrayal ran strong over the realization that conversations presumed to be private had been secretly recorded.

The immediate concern of the Watergate investigating committee was obtaining tapes of Nixon's personal and telephone conversations with key witnesses who had appeared before the committee. The chief interest was in John W. Dean III, the former White House counsel who had put his word against Nixon's by linking the President directly to the Watergate coverup.

Disclosure of the presidentially ordered bugging, for historical purposes, intensified the dilemma of a Chief Executive already weakened by Watergate. Either he could turn the tapes over to the Senate committee or he could refuse to do so. If he turned them over, he could be absolved or implicated. If he did not, he would be suspected of having something to hide.

All indicators pointed toward refusal. White House sources told reporters July 19 that Nixon would stand by his position, expressed in a letter to Watergate Committee Chairman Sam J. Ervin Jr. (D N.C.) July 6, that White House documents are protected by the doctrine of separation of powers.

Nixon spent the week in the hospital, recuperating from viral pneumonia. After Butterfield's disclosure July 16, he ordered the Secret Service, which has custody of the tapes, to withhold all information from the committee. The date of a previously scheduled meeting with Ervin was in doubt. An official White House statement on the tapes was expected to be made public on July 23.

Meanwhile, the pressure on Nixon continued to build. After his release from Bethesda Naval Hospital July 20, he spoke briefly and informally to members of the White House staff in the rose garden. Talk of his resigning before the end of his term, he told them, was "just plain poppycock." He promised to "work right up to the hilt" and suggested: "Let others wallow in Watergate. We're going to do our job."

Committee Hearings. Chairman Ervin's job was made embarrassing by a prankster who, representing himself as Treasury Secretary George P. Shultz, phoned Ervin July 19 to say that Nixon was ready to release the tapes. Ervin happily announced the news to the nationally televised hearings.

A few minutes later, after a call from the White House, he announced, with reddened face, that he had been taken in. The Bible-quoting, 76-year-old southerner denounced the telephone as an "instrument of the devil." The FBI started an investigation of who made the call.

Testifying before the committee July 19 and 20 was Robert C. Mardian, a former assistant attorney general and political coordinator of the 1972 Nixon re-election campaign. Mardian told the committee July 20 that Nixon authorized the removal of wiretap materials from the office of an FBI official that ultimately resulted in the mistrial of Daniel Ellsberg on espionage charges in the Pentagon Papers case.

The logs, summaries and correspondence making up the wiretap materials stemmed from national security taps placed on 17 National Security Council officials and newsmen in 1970 and 1971. One of those tapped was Morton S. Halperin, a member of the National Security Council at that time. Ellsberg, a friend of Halperin, was overheard on Halperin's telephone.

The revelation in April at Ellsberg's trial that he had been overheard, plus the government's inability to quickly locate the logs of the Ellsberg conversation, resulted in a mistrial and dismissal of all charges against Ellsberg and a codefendant, Anthony Russo. The wiretap materials eventually were located in the office of John D. Ehrlichman, a former presidential aide, who resigned April 30. *(p. 66, 46)*

Mardian said he first learned of the existence of the wiretaps in June or July 1971 from a friend, William C. Sullivan, then an associate director of the FBI. Mardian said Sullivan told him he had "very sensitive" national security logs, which he had removed from bureau files, in his safe in his FBI office.

Mardian, who was an assistant attorney general at the time, said Sullivan was concerned that if he were fired—he later was—the materials would be found in his safe, and he wanted to know what to do with them. Mardian told Sullivan he would report the conversation to then Attorney General John N. Mitchell.

Mardian said that he told Mitchell what he had learned, but that the attorney general gave him no instructions about what to do with the materials. Sometime in July 1971, Mardian said, he got a call from either Ehrlichman or another former presidential aide, H. R. Haldeman. The caller told him to go to San Clemente, Calif., immediately to tell the President what he knew of the materials. Mardian said he did this, and the President ordered him to get the materials from Sullivan and give them to Ehrlichman. Mardian said the materials concerned electronic surveillance authorized by the President and undertaken at the direction of the National Security Council.

Witness July 13

White House special counsel Richard A. Moore maintained his "firm conviction" that President Nixon was unaware of efforts to cover up the Watergate scandal until March 21, 1973. This was in direct contradiction to the thrust of testimony by former presidential counsel John W. Dean III, who earlier told the Senate select Watergate committee that he believed Nixon knew of the coverup as early as September 1972. *(Earlier Moore testimony, p. 184, 179; Dean testimony, p. 152)*

One of the rare instances of open partisanship on the committee occurred as Edward J. Gurney (R Fla.) was questioning Moore on July 13 about an apparent contradiction between his and Dean's testimony concerning demands for "silence money" and executive clemency for Watergate defendants.

Dean had testified that he discussed this with the President March 13, 1973, but Moore said Dean told him on March 20 that he (Dean) had not told the President anything about the coverup. Gurney asked Moore whether Dean would have told him if he had discussed silence money and executive clemency with the President.

At this point, Committee Chairman Sam J. Ervin Jr. (D N.C.) interrupted, claiming the question was improper. Gurney angrily replied, "Well, I must say, Mr. Chairman, that I think that question is less free-wheeling than about a million I have heard in this committee room today." Ervin allowed the question, and Moore said, "I kind of go along with the notion that if that had happened, he might have told me."

Gurney earlier showed his sympathy to Moore by remarking that "you don't really impress me from your background as being any kind of a Watergate rascal." He apparently was trying to counter a tough grilling of Moore the day before by deputy majority counsel Terry Lenzner, who left the witness confused and stammering about meetings and other events he was unable to recall. Lenzner at one point charged Moore with saying one thing in private before the committee and another thing in public. Moore replied: "I'll let my answer stand—whatever it was."

Later Ervin asked a long series of leading questions seeking to show that the President should have known about the attempts to cover up the Watergate simply from reading the newspapers. Ervin's questions stemmed from a statement by Moore that the President had asked Moore on May 8 whether he should have known about the coverup before March 21. Moore quoted the President as saying, "I have racked my brain. I have searched my mind. Were there any clues I should have seen that should have tipped me off?"

Ervin read Moore a list of newspaper headlines beginning with the arrest of five of the seven Watergate defendants on June 17, 1972, detailing the involvement of White House and re-election committee personnel in the scandal. Moore said he had read the stories.

"Now, I have recounted a great many things," Ervin said, "all of which except one I think you admit were made known by the news media within two months after the Watergate burglaries were discovered. Can you imagine any better way in which a person interested in the President's campaign and people who read the Washington papers and *The New York Times* and watched the radio and listened to television could have had more reason to suspect that something was rotten in the committees to re-elect the President than were divulged in these news media?"

Moore replied: "The question was, Mr. Chairman, whether that offense went beyond the seven...and I think that most evidence you cited there all is consistent with the President's view, which was...what the President said on Aug. 29 (1972), that this could and probably was an unauthorized action (that) I have described as kind of a James Bond group...."

Witnesses July 16

A surprise witness told the Senate select Watergate committee July 16 that all of President Nixon's conversations in his White House and Executive Office Building offices were bugged and his telephones in each office were tapped beginning in the spring of 1971. This meant that tape recordings of Nixon conversations with John Dean were a matter of record and could be used to prove or disprove Dean's contention that Nixon knew of efforts to cover up the Watergate break-in.

The revelation was given the committee by Alexander P. Butterfield, administrator of the Federal Aviation Administration and a former White House aide. Butterfield said the listening devices were installed under Nixon's authority for posterity's sake. The White House confirmed his statements.

After Butterfield's 30-minute appearance at the witness table, the committee heard from one of Nixon's personal lawyers, Herbert W. Kalmbach, whose name had been mentioned in connection with the raising of silence money for the seven men convicted of breaking into the Watergate building headquarters of the Democratic National Committee June 17, 1972. Kalmbach denied any knowledge of the alleged coverup, saying the $150,000 he raised was understood by him to be for support of the defendants' families and their lawyers' fees. *(Opening statement, p. 204)*

During the morning session, the committee completed its questioning of Richard A. Moore, the White House aide who began his testimony July 12. *(Opening statement, p. 205)*

Butterfield Testimony. Butterfield was questioned primarily by minority counsel Fred D. Thompson, but also briefly by the entire committee and by majority counsel Samuel Dash. He said the eavesdropping devices were installed in the summer or fall of 1970 and were still in place when he left the White House March 14, 1973.

Alexander P. Butterfield

However, a letter to the committee from J. Fred Buzhardt, a White House special counsel handling the Watergate affair for the President, was read into the record indicating the devices were installed in the spring of 1971. Butterfield said he would not dispute the date of the installation or Buzhardt's claim that the practice was used by the Johnson administration. Butterfield testified that he had "heard rumors" while in the White House that other administrations had done similar things. Buzhardt's letter to the committee was dated July 16, indicating he had been informed in advance of Butterfield's testimony.

Butterfield told the committee that the bugs in the President's two offices were triggered automatically by Nixon's presence in either room and that there also was a device in the cabinet room that was activated manually. There were no bugs or taps in the President's Key Biscayne, Fla., or San Clemente, Calif., homes, he said. *(Transcript excerpts, box, p. 194)*

The bugs, Butterfield said, would pick up any sound or conversation in the room, including the lowest tones. This was of some significance, because Dean, the President's former counsel, indicated in his testimony that during a conversation with Nixon in his Executive Office Building office April 15, the President mentioned "in a barely audible tone" that he had discussed executive clemency for one of the Watergate defendants. If Nixon did say that, presumably the bug would have picked it up. *(Dean statement text, p. 163)*

Butterfield said he did not know if any of the tapes had been transcribed. He said he once suggested that some secretaries get busy on the effort, but nothing was done.

Asked by Dash whether the tapes were stored by date, Butterfield replied they were. Were, therefore, the President's talks with Dean recorded and available? Dash asked. Yes, Butterfield replied.

Dean had testified that several conversations he had with the President, beginning Sept. 15, 1972, and extending through mid-April 1973, led him to the conclusion that Nixon was aware of Watergate coverup efforts, including offers of executive clemency and silence money to the seven defendants. The President has denied ever offering money or executive clemency to the defendants and has said he was not aware of the coverup until March 21, 1973, when "major new developments in the case" came to his attention. *(p. 18, 17)*

Kalmbach Testimony. Reading from a prepared statement, the 52-year-old Kalmbach denied "any prior knowledge of the Watergate break-in or participation in the formulation of any planned conspiracy to cover up that incident or acts of campaign sabotage or unethical activity.

"My actions in the period immediately following the break-in which involved the raising of funds to provide for the legal defense of the Watergate defendants and for the support of their families were prompted in the belief that it was proper and necessary to discharge what I assumed to be a moral obligation that had arisen in some manner unknown to me by reason of earlier events.

"The fact that I had been directed to undertake these actions by the number two and number three men on the White House staff (Ehrlichman and Dean) made it absolutely incomprehensible to me that my actions in this regard could have been regarded in any way as improper or unethical."

Kalmbach's testimony differed from Dean's concerning their meetings in June after the break-in to discuss money for the defendants. Dean testified that he met with Kalmbach June 29, 1972, that he told Kalmbach everything he knew about the case at that time and that Haldeman, Ehrlichman and John N. Mitchell, the former campaign director and former attorney general, wanted him to raise the money. Later, Dean testified, Kalmbach said he wanted former New York City policeman Anthony Ulasewicz to handle the deliveries of the money, explaining he was the only man Kalmbach trusted. *(Ulasewicz testimony, p. 83, 82)*

Dean also testified that about a week later he and Kalmbach met in Lafayette Park, across from the White House, where Kalmbach reported that he had raised the money and was on his way to give it to Ulasewicz. Dean said that several days later he met in his office with Kalmbach and Frederick LaRue, a Mitchell aide, to discuss how the money should be split up among the defendants.

In answer to questions by Dash, Kalmbach testified that Lafayette Park was the site of his first meeting with Dean, that he was not told who wanted the money raised and that it was Dean who recommended Ulasewicz for the deliveries. Kalmbach said he did not recall Dean's telling him what he knew about the Watergate break-in. Their second meeting, according to Kalmbach, was June 30.

Kalmbach testified that he accepted the assignment to raise the money because it came from the President's counsel (Dean). Ehrlichman later confirmed to him, he said, that Dean was exercising proper authority in requesting his help. He said he made no independent attempt to ascertain the propriety of what he was doing, even though he knew persons charged with crimes were receiving the money he raised.

Kalmbach said his fund-raising efforts continued until middle or late August 1972, when he began to worry about his role and when Ehrlichman's assurances "were no longer enduring." It was at that point that he withdrew from the activity, he testified. Kalmbach said another attempt was made on Jan. 19, 1973, to get him to raise money for the defendants, but he refused.

The fund-raising work began after a telephone call from Dean on June 28, 1972, Kalmbach testified. He said Dean told him there was "a matter of extreme importance" he wanted to discuss with him and asked him to fly to Washington from his California home on the first available plane.

Kalmbach said Dean explained to him in Washington the next day that the reason for wanting to see him was that "we" (Dean never mentioned any names, Kalmbach said) wanted him to raise money for Watergate defendants' legal affairs and their families. Kalmbach said he asked if it was not preferable for a public committee to raise the money. Dean replied, he testified, that there was not enough time and that a public committee might be misinterpreted by the press and public.

Kalmbach testified that Dean told him $50,000 to $100,000 would be required and that he made "the very strong point" that secrecy was important. Dean further said that LaRue would provide directions for how much money should go to each defendant and that Ulasewicz would be a good man to handle the distribution, Kalmbach stated.

He said he immediately returned to his hotel and called Maurice H. Stans, the head of the finance committee for the re-election campaign, and asked him for $50,000 to $100,000. Stans later gave him $75,000 in

(Continued on p. 195)

Butterfield's Explanation of Presidential Wiretaps

Following are excerpts from the transcript of an exchange between Fred D. Thompson, minority counsel of the Senate Watergate committee, and Alexander P. Butterfield, administrator of the Federal Aviation Administration and former deputy assistant to President Nixon. Thompson was questioning Butterfield about the taping of presidential conversations. The exchange occurred at committee hearings July 16.

Thompson: Mr. Butterfield, are you aware of the installation of any listening devices in the oval office of the President?

Butterfield: I was aware of listening devices, yes, sir.

Thompson: When were those devices placed in the oval office?

Butterfield: Approximately the summer of 1970. I cannot begin to recall the precise date. My guess, Mr. Thompson, is that the installation was made between—and this is a very rough guess—April or May of 1970 and perhaps the end of the summer or early fall 1970.

Thompson: Are you aware of any devices that were installed in the Executive Office Building office of the President?

Butterfield:... They were installed at the same time.

Thompson: Would you tell us a little bit about how those devices worked, how they were activated, for example?

Butterfield: I don't have the technical knowledge, but I will tell you what I know about how those devices were triggered. They were installed, of course, for historical purposes, to record the President's business, and they were installed in his two offices, the oval office and the EOB (Executive Office Building) office....

Butterfield:.... In that the oval office and the Executive Office Building office were indicated on this locator box, the installation was installed in such a way that when the light was on "oval office," the taping device was at least triggered. It was not operating, but it was triggered—it was spring-loaded, if you will, then it was voice-actuated.

So when the light was on "oval office," in the oval office and in the oval office only, the taping device was spring-loaded to a voice-actuating situation. When the President went to the EOB office, the EOB light was on. In the EOB office, there was the same arrangement.

Thompson:....What about the cabinet room? Was there a taping device in the cabinet room?

Butterfield: Yes, sir, there was.

Thompson: Was it activated in the same way?

Butterfield: No, sir, it was not, and my guess is, and it is only my guess, is because there was no cabinet room location per se on the locator box.

To ensure the recording of business conversations in the cabinet room, a manual installation was made....

Thompson: There were buttons on the desk in the cabinet room there that activated that device?

Butterfield: There were two buttons... There was an off-on button, one said "Haldeman" and one that said "Butterfield" that was on and off respectively, and one on my telephone.

Thompson: So far as the oval office and the EOB office is concerned, would it be your testimony that the device would pick up any and all conversations no matter where the conversations took place in the room and no matter how soft the conversations might have been?

Butterfield: Yes, sir....

Thompson: Was it a little more difficult to pick up in the cabinet room?

Butterfield: Yes, sir, it was a great deal more difficult to pick up in the cabinet room.

Thompson: All right. We talked about the rooms now, and if we could move on to telephones, are you aware of the installation of any devices on any of the telephones, first of all, the oval office?

Butterfield: Yes, sir.

Thompson: What about the Executive Office Building office of the President?

Butterfield: Yes, sir. The President's business telephone at his desk in the Executive Office Building.

Thompson: What about the Lincoln Room?

Butterfield: Yes, sir, the telephone in the Lincoln sitting room in the residence.

Thompson: What about Aspen cabin at Camp David?

Butterfield: Only in, on the telephone at the President's desk in his study in the Aspen cabin, his personal cabin.

Thompson: It is my understanding this cabin was sometimes used by foreign dignitaries. Was the device still present during those periods of time?

Butterfield: No, sir, the device was removed prior to occupancy by chiefs of state, heads of government and other foreign dignitaries.

Thompson: All right. Would you state who installed these devices, all of these devices, so far as you know?

Butterfield:... The Secret Service. The technical security division of the Secret Service.

Thompson: Would you state why, as far as your understanding is concerned, these devices were installed in these rooms?

Butterfield: There was no doubt in my mind they were installed to record things for posterity, for the Nixon library. The President was very conscious of that kind of thing. We had quite an elaborate setup at the White House for the collection and preservation of documents, and of things which transpired in the way of business of state.

Thompson: On whose authority were they installed, Mr. Butterfield?

Butterfield: On the President's authority by way of Mr. Haldeman and Mr. Higby. (H. R. Haldeman, then White House chief of staff, and Lawrence M. Higby, deputy assistant to the President)....

Thompson: Where were the tapes of those conversations kept, maintained?

Butterfield: I cannot say where. I am quite sure in the Executive Office Building in some closets or cupboards or files which are maintained by the technical security division of the U.S. Secret Service.

Thompson: Were these tapes checked periodically?

Butterfield: Yes, they were checked at least daily...I think some were used more frequently than others. The Secret Service knew this; they made sure that they were checked periodically and sufficiently....

Thompson: Were any of these tapes ever transcribed, reduced to writing or typewritten paper, so far as you know?

Butterfield: To my recollection, no.

Thompson: Mr. Butterfield, as far as you know from your own personal knowledge, from 1970 then until the present time all of the President's conversations in the offices mentioned...were recorded as far as you know?

Butterfield: That is correct, until I left. Someone could have taken the equipment out, but until the day I left I am sure I would have been notified.

Thompson: And as far as you know, those tapes are still available?

Butterfield: As far as I know, but I have been away for four months, sir....

(Continued from p. 193)
$100 bills, Kalmbach said. The witness stated that $45,000 of that money was left over from $50,000 he had given Stans when the former commerce secretary took over the finance committee. This conformed with Stans' testimony before the committee July 12. *(p. 132)*

Kalmbach said he gave Ulasewicz the money the next day, explained that it was for the defendants and urged him not to tell anyone about it. Ulasewicz returned to New York with the money to await instructions, Kalmbach said.

Kalmbach described the cloak-and-dagger manner in which he was instructed to contact Ulasewicz with instructions for distributing the money. He said code names were used, such as "Mr. Rivers" for Ulasewicz, "the writer" for E. Howard Hunt Jr., a defendant in the criminal case, and "the writer's wife" for Mrs. Hunt.

According to Kalmbach, he always would call Ulasewicz from a pay telephone after receiving directions from Dean or LaRue as to which defendant or defendant's attorney should be given a certain amount of money. Ulasewicz then would give Kalmbach the number of a pay phone near Ulasewicz's home, and Kalmbach would call him there 15 minutes later with his instructions.

Kalmbach said his first order was to give $25,000 to C. Douglas Caddy, a defense lawyer. But Caddy refused to accept it, Kalmbach testified, so he was told to give the sum to Paul O'Brien, a re-election committee attorney. O'Brien turned it down, too, Kalmbach said. Finally, William O. Bittman, another defense lawyer, accepted the $25,000 during the second week of July, Kalmbach testified. According to Kalmbach, most of the remaining money went to Mrs. Hunt, who distributed it among various defense attorneys. (Mrs. Hunt was killed in a plane crash in December 1972. At the time of her death, she was carrying $10,000 in cash.)

Kalmbach said he was given $40,000 by LaRue in a meeting in Dean's office July 19 and gave the money to Ulasewicz in New York City. Kalmbach did not mention the source of the funds.

About a week later, after Dean and LaRue asked him to raise some more money, Kalmbach said, he "began to have a degree of concern" about the assignments. He explained that the secrecy and the "James Bond scenario" bothered him. It was "very distasteful to me," he said.

Kalmbach told the senators he asked for a meeting with Ehrlichman to confirm Dean's authority and receive assurances of the propriety of the assignments. The meeting took place in Ehrlichman's office July 26, he said.

Kalmbach said he told Ehrlichman that the secrecy of the operation bothered him and that press accounts of the connections of the Watergate defendants to the re-election committee concerned him. "John, I'm looking right into your eyes," Kalmbach said he told Ehrlichman as he asked if Dean had the authority to have him raise money, if what he was doing was proper and if he should continue.

Ehrlichman answered yes to all three questions, Kalmbach told the committee, and urged him to maintain secrecy. Kalmbach quoted Ehrlichman as saying "they would have our heads in their laps" if the story ever got out. Kalmbach said he took that remark to mean disclosure would affect Nixon's re-election chances. That "washed out" his concern, Kalmbach said.

Returning to California, Kalmbach said he was able to get $75,000 in $100 bills on Aug. 1 from Thomas V. Jones, chairman of the Northrop Corporation. Jones, Kalmbach related, had informed him earlier that he was willing to contribute to the re-election campaign. Kalmbach said he never told Jones where the money would go except that it was for a "special assignment." This money, too, was turned over to Ulasewicz, Kalmbach said.

This was the last money he raised for the defendants, Kalmbach said, because in middle to late August he decided he could no longer rely on Ehrlichman's assurances.

Witness July 17

The seven-member Senate Watergate committee voted unanimously July 17 to ask President Nixon to release the tape recordings of his conversations relating to the Watergate affair. The request was based on the previous day's revelations by Alexander P. Butterfield. The tapes presumably would confirm or refute John Dean's contention that the President was aware of efforts to cover up the break-in at Democratic national headquarters in the Watergate building June 17, 1972.

The committee's action came after Nixon refused to allow Secret Service agents to testify before the committee concerning their White House duties. Butterfield said the Secret Service was in charge of installing listening devices in the White House and Executive Office Building and storing the tapes of recorded conversations.

Meanwhile, Herbert W. Kalmbach, the President's former personal attorney and a fund-raiser for the seven Watergate defendants, completed his testimony after a day and a half at the witness table.

Two Letters. The President's refusal to allow testimony by Secret Service agents was revealed in a letter from Nixon to Treasury Secretary George P. Shultz. The letter was read by Committee Chairman Sam J. Ervin Jr. (D N.C.). The letter, dated July 16, directed that no Secret Service officer or agent testify before the committee "concerning matters observed or learned while performing protective functions for the President or in their duties at the White House." The Secret Service is part of the Treasury Department.

The letter did not refer to the tape recordings. It ended by telling Shultz to inform Ervin "that requests for information on procedures in the White House will be given prompt consideration when received by me."

Ervin explained that the committee had subpoenaed Alfred C. Wong, deputy assistant director of the Secret Service, who was believed responsible for the tapes, for a private session July 17 with Ervin and Committee Vice Chairman Howard H. Baker Jr. (R Tenn.). Wong appeared in answer to the subpoena, Ervin said, but the general counsel of the Treasury Department, who accompanied him, invoked executive privilege to prevent Wong from testifying.

The chairman announced that, as a consequence, he and Baker called the committee into executive session. It was decided it was "not worthwhile" to engage in a "controversy" with the President over Secret Service testimony, Ervin said.

Seizing on the last sentence of the President's letter, Ervin said he hoped Nixon meant that all records and

Nixon, Ervin Letters on Tapes

Following is the letter written July 16 by President Nixon to Treasury Secretary George P. Shultz:

Dear Secretary Shultz:

I hereby direct that no officer or agent of the Secret Service shall give testimony to Congressional committees concerning matters observed or learned while performing protective functions for the President or in their duties at the White House.

This applies to the Senate Select Committee which is investigating matters relating to the Watergate break-in and the current efforts which I am informed are being made to subpoena present or former members of the White House detail of the Secret Service.

You will please communicate this information to the Director of the Secret Service promptly and either you or he should then personally notify the Chairman of the Senate Select Committee. You should further advise the Chairman that requests for information on procedures in the White House will be given prompt consideration when received by me.

Following is the letter written July 17 by Sam J. Ervin Jr. (D N.C.), chairman of the Senate Watergate investigating committee, to Nixon:

Dear Mr. President:

Today the Select Committee on Presidential Campaign Activities met and unanimously voted that I request that you provide the Committee with all relevant documents and tapes under control of the White House that relate to the matters the Select Committee is authorized to investigate under S. Res. 60. I refer to the documents mentioned in my letter to Mr. Leonard Garment of June 21, 1973, and the relevant portions of the tapes alluded to by Mr. Alexander Butterfield before the Committee on July 16, 1973.

If your illness prevents our meeting to discuss these issues in the next day or two, I should like to suggest that you designate members of your staff to meet with members of the Select Committee to make arrangements for our access to White House documents and tapes pertinent to the Committee's investigation.

I should like respectfully to relate that the Committee's investigation is on-going and that access to relevant documents should not be delayed if the Committee is to perform its mission. May we hear from you at your earliest convenience?

The Committee deeply regrets your illness and hopes for you a speedy recovery.

tapes in the White House would be turned over to the committee. Ervin said he had just sent a letter to Nixon, based on the committee's vote, asking for the tapes and "all relevant documents." Ervin's letter also said that the committee and White House staffs could meet to discuss arrangements if Nixon himself was too ill to meet with him. *(Texts of Nixon, Ervin letters, box, this page)*

"I sincerely hope this course of action will bear fruit," Ervin said. Baker said the letter was sent to Nixon "in a spirit of conciliation" and that the committee wanted answers to three questions: Who has custody of the tapes? Who had access to them? How can the committee obtain the tapes?

Nixon on July 6 refused to give up White House documents requested by the committee, saying such an action would violate the constitutional doctrine of separation of powers. Ervin at that time noted his belief that the President could not withhold documents relating to a criminal activity. *(Text of Nixon letter to Ervin, p. 189)*

Ehrlichman Tape. Kalmbach reacted with surprise and bitterness when Ervin read him portions of a transcript of a taped telephone conversation between Kalmbach and John D. Ehrlichman, Nixon's former domestic affairs adviser. The conversation took place April 19, an hour before Kalmbach was due to appear before federal prosecutors investigating the Watergate affair.

Kalmbach described the transcript as self-serving for Ehrlichman, insisting that he did not know the conversation was being taped. In the transcript, Ehrlichman appeared to be suggesting to Kalmbach that he tell the prosecutors that Dean was the mastermind of the fund-raising scheme. Ehrlichman also asked Kalmbach to tell the Watergate grand jury the next day (April 20) that the two had discussed Kalmbach's testimony in California, when Ehrlichman was investigating Watergate for the President, rather than on the phone that day.

Kalmbach maintained throughout his testimony before the committee, however, that while Dean was the first person to approach him regarding the fund-raising effort, it was Ehrlichman who had assured him of the propriety of what he was doing. "I didn't understand that he (Dean) was the button pusher" in the scheme, Kalmbach said. "I think he had received the assignment to approach me knowing whoever gave the directions, that I trusted Mr. Dean."

Later, under questioning by Lowell P. Weicker Jr. (R Conn.), Kalmbach said he had been "used" by persons who knew the true purpose of his assignment. He acknowledged that former White House aides H. R. Haldeman, Ehrlichman, Dean and former re-election campaign director John N. Mitchell were among those who used him "if they had knowledge and did not inform me."

'Absolute Trust.' In earlier testimony, Kalmbach said over and over that it was inconceivable to him that Dean and Ehrlichman would involve him in any wrongdoing. He used phrases such as "complete and implicit trust" and "absolute trust" in reference to his feelings toward the two men and why he agreed on June 29, 1972, to raise money for the Watergate defendants.

Kalmbach said he never told the President what he had been doing, even after he decided in August 1972 to stop raising funds for the defendants. "Did it never flicker a light that there might be trouble for the President?" asked Baker. "It didn't flicker that there was trouble," Kalmbach replied. "It bothered me; the secrecy was distasteful to me. But it never reached the point in my mind that I felt I should go to the President." Kalmbach said he never felt that the President himself approved payments to the defendants.

Fund-Raising. While Kalmbach testified to raising $150,000 for the defendants and their attorneys, he said he was responsible for passing about $220,000 to Anthony Ulasewicz, a retired New York City policeman who actually did the disbursing.

In answer to questions from Sen. Edward J. Gurney (R Fla.), Kalmbach accounted for $215,000 of the money. He said $150,000 went to the late wife of E. Howard

Hunt Jr.; $30,000 to Frederick LaRue, a re-election committee aide; $25,000 to William O. Bittman, an attorney for the defendants; $8,000 to G. Gordon Liddy, the ringleader of the Watergate burglars; $1,000 to Ulasewicz for his expenses, and $1,000 to Gordon Strachan, a White House aide who acted as a go-between for H. R. Haldeman with the re-election committee.

Kalmbach said he did not know what Strachan did with the funds. The money for Mrs. Hunt went to various attorneys and defendants, he said.

Kalmbach explained that he would be given demands for money from Ulasewicz, who had received them from Mrs. Hunt or others. Kalmbach said he would pass the demands to Dean and LaRue, who would tell him how much to give each defendant or attorney. Kalmbach then relayed the orders to Ulasewicz, he testified.

In addition to Bittman, Kalmbach also named Henry Rothblatt, F. Lee Bailey and Peter Maroulis as attorneys who were paid through Ulasewicz.

Kalmbach said he understood the money was for legitimate, humanitarian purposes, but Dean testified that it went to buy the silence of the defendants. The witness stuck to his testimony of July 16 that Thomas V. Jones, a California business executive, gave him $75,000 in cash that, unknown to Jones, went to the defendants. Jones had contradicted Kalmbach's testimony, saying he gave the lawyer only $50,000.

Expanding on why he decided to stop raising money for the defendants, Kalmbach said that Ulasewicz had given him some "cautionary words." Asked what those words were, Kalmbach said he could not recall them exactly, but that they were "so unusual" that it led him to believe he should stop the activity. He said Ulasewicz never told him the money was for silencing the defendants.

Disbursements. In answer to questions from Herman E. Talmadge (D Ga.), Kalmbach also explained his disbursement of $400,000 during the 1970 election campaign. There were reports that some or all of that money went to an unsuccessful attempt to defeat George C. Wallace's try for re-election to the governorship of Alabama, but Kalmbach said he did not know what was done with the funds. He said he knew only that they went to unspecified political campaigns.

The funds were disbursed in three lots, Kalmbach testified, each time at the direction of Lawrence M. Higby, a Haldeman aide. The source of the money was left-over 1968 presidential primary funds in Kalmbach's control, the witness said.

The first disbursement amounted to $100,000 and was delivered by Kalmbach to someone he said he did not know. Kalmbach related that after getting Higby's order, he went to a safe deposit box in New York City's Chase Manhattan Bank, took out the money and delivered it to a man who approached him in a New York hotel. To skeptical questioning by Talmadge, Kalmbach said he did not recall how he recognized the man, but that no signal was used.

Kalmbach said the second disbursement, for $200,000, was given by one of the signatories on the safe deposit box to a man Kalmbach told him to meet in the same hotel. The third payment, for $100,000, Kalmbach said he personally delivered in Los Angeles, again to a recipient unknown to him.

Kalmbach was questioned closely by Weicker on how he could believe that his fund-raising and disbursement orders in the summer of 1972 could be legal and proper if he constantly was using code names and contacting Ulasewicz from public telephone booths. He answered that he was told there was a need for an "abundance of caution in carrying out the assignment."

The witness also was questioned about his financing of alleged campaign sabotage activities by California attorney Donald Segretti in 1972. Kalmbach said he did not know what Segretti was to use the money for, but he assumed it was proper, because the man who requested the money for Segretti, Dwight L. Chapin, was working for Haldeman. He conceded that he never talked to Haldeman about the funds for Segretti and could not recall whether Chapin used Haldeman's name in requesting the funds.

Asked how he felt in retrospect about his activities, Kalmbach admitted he was involved in something illegal. "It's like a kick in the stomach," he remarked.

Witnesses July 18

Fred C. LaRue, a former assistant to John N. Mitchell at the Nixon re-election committee, said Mitchell neither approved nor disapproved an electronic surveillance plan at a March 30, 1972, meeting in Key Biscayne, Fla. LaRue's testimony thus presented a third version of events at the meeting which was a prelude to the break-in at Democratic Party headquarters in the Watergate building June 17, 1972.

One of the subjects for discussion at the March 30 meeting of LaRue, Mitchell, the re-election committee director, and Jeb Stuart Magruder, Mitchell's deputy, was the surveillance plan of G. Gordon Liddy. Liddy has been convicted of conspiracy in the break-in.

Magruder testified that Mitchell approved Liddy's plan and a budget of $250,000 for the operation. Mitchell testified that he disapproved of the plan. *(Magruder, Mitchell testimony, p. 180, 135)*

LaRue, however, quoted Mitchell as saying the plan was "not something that will have to be decided at this meeting." LaRue agreed with committee majority counsel Samuel Dash, that Mitchell "did not reject it out of hand."

LaRue also conceded it was possible that Mitchell and Magruder could have discussed the plan outside his presence, because he was not in the room with them at all times. Both Mitchell and Magruder testified, however, that Mitchell's decision was reached in LaRue's presence.

LaRue, a Jackson, Miss., businessman, has spent most of his time in Washington since 1969 working for the President and the re-election committee. He has pleaded guilty to one count of conspiracy to obstruct justice in the Watergate affair.

In his prepared statement before the Senate select Watergate committee July 18, LaRue admitted that he participated in the Watergate coverup, including helping to deliver cash intended for the seven defendants in the criminal trial. He said he recommended against Liddy's plan when it was discussed at the Key Biscayne meeting and that he first learned of the break-in after it occurred.

He told the committtee that he was "fully aware" that what he had done was wrong, "both ethically and legally.... I really had no intent to violate the law," he

(Continued on p. 199)

Prosecution Force: Young Men, Impressive Credentials

Young, bright and heavily Democratic: that was the image of the Watergate special prosecution force that emerged from a 67-page compendium of staff biographies released July 14.

Two days earlier, special prosecutor Archibald Cox asked a Senate Appropriations subcommittee for $2.8-million to support a staff of 90 for fiscal year 1974. The existing staff numbers 59, 25 of whom are secretarial and clerical help. Cox is aiming for a lineup of about 60 plus 30 clerical workers, public affairs assistant James S. Doyle told Congressional Quarterly.

Calling the work of the team "a task of the highest national priority," Cox in his budget testimony staked out a broad territory for investigations and prosecutions, including the Watergate break-in itself and "all offenses arising out of the 1972 presidential election for which the special prosecutor deems it necessary and appropriate to assume responsibility (including) allegations involving the President, members of the White House staff, or presidential appointees, and any other matters which (Cox) consents to have assigned to him by the attorney general (Elliot L. Richardson)."

Tight Security. Working behind doors protected by elaborate electronic security devices and a general mood of secrecy—one wall poster in the downtown Washington office suite occupied by the team reads: "Loose Talk Is Explosive Anytime"—the staff is already "deep into the investigation," Cox said.

The average of the 32-member legal force to date is 32. Except for the two non-lawyers on the team, all have impressive records in the legal academic world, in government or private practice—in many cases in all three areas.

The lawyers are all graduates of prestigious eastern law schools. Harvard, with 17, contributed more than half, including Cox.

The Democratic cast of the staff was not surprising, since Cox himself served as solicitor general under Presidents Kennedy and Johnson. Seven of the eight lawyers comprising his senior staff also held important jobs in the Kennedy or Johnson administration, or both. Many of Cox's appointments, particularly the early ones, included people he had known in government. *(Earlier story on Cox, p. 96)*

The Senior Staff. The prosecution force was divided into five task forces, each investigating a major aspect of Watergate.

- James F. Neal, 43, special assistant, is handling the main Watergate case and its subsequent coverup. He is aided by assistant special prosecutor Richard Ben-Veniste, 30. Neal at one time was a special assistant to Attorney General Robert F. Kennedy. He practices law in Nashville, Tenn.
- William Merrill, 50, associate special prosecutor, heads the team investigating the "plumbers"—the group of men hired by the White House in 1971 to trace security leaks—and the related burglary of the office of Pentagon Papers figure Daniel Ellsberg's former psychiatrist. Merrill was chief assistant U.S. attorney of the eastern district of Michigan during the Kennedy administration and part of the Johnson administration. He has been in private practice in Detroit.
- Thomas McBride, 44, associate special prosecutor, is investigating campaign contributions. A former assistant district attorney in New York City, McBride was a member of the Kennedy Justice Department's organized crime section and later served as Peace Corps director in Latin America. He is on a leave of absence from his job as staff director of the Police Foundation, a private organization that funds programs to improve law enforcement.
- Richard J. Davis, 27, assistant special prosecutor, was named to head the team investigating political espionage ("dirty tricks"). Davis was an assistant U.S. attorney for the southern district of New York for three years before joining the team. He specialized in corruption investigations.
- Joseph J. Connolly, 32, assistant special prosecutor, is acting chief of the force investigating the alleged involvement of the International Telephone and Telegraph Corporation with the 1972 Republican national convention. Connolly is one of the few members of the team who served in the Nixon administration; he was an assistant to the solicitor general from 1968 to 1970. He is on a leave of absence from a private Philadelphia law firm.

Other senior members of the prosecution team:

- Henry S. Ruth Jr., 42, deputy special prosecutor, who held a variety of high-level jobs under the Kennedy and Johnson Justice Departments and served as director of the department's National Institute of Law Enforcement and Criminal Justice in 1969 and 1970. Before joing the Cox staff, he was director of New York City Mayor John V. Lindsay's Criminal Justice Coordinating Council.
- James Vorenberg, 45, special assistant, who served in the Justice Department under Kennedy and Johnson. He is director of the Center for Criminal Justice at Harvard.
- Philip B. Heymann, 40, special assistant, who held various positions in the Justice and State Departments under Kennedy and Johnson. He is a law professor at Harvard.
- Philip A. Lacovara, 29, counsel, who also served under Nixon before joining the force; he was deputy solicitor general. Lacovara graduated first in his 1966 law class at Columbia University.
- Peter M. Kreindler, 28, executive assistant, who was a law clerk to Supreme Court Justice William O. Douglas.
- The two non-lawyers: special assistant Doyle, 38, formerly a national reporter for *The Washington Star-News,* and Harry M. Bratt, 45, chief of the information system section. Bratt will coordinate the investigatory material the team is developing.

(Continued from p. 197)
said. "I was motivated solely by my concern for the presidential campaign in which we were engaging." *(Text, p. 204)*

In other testimony, LaRue charged Mitchell with suggesting to Magruder after the break-in that Magruder destroy electronic surveillance files. He also said that although he concluded that the break-in was approved at a high level in the White House or the re-election committee, he never reported this to the President. LaRue said he felt he was not concealing anything from Nixon, just from the public, which he believed might have turned against the President during the campaign.

In other testimony July 18, Anthony L. Ulasewicz, a former New York City policeman who was a money courier between Kalmbach and the defendants and their attorneys, returned to the witness table to explain his activities. Ulasewicz regaled the committee and audience with tales of money drops and code names, embellished by humorous asides.

March 30 Meeting. LaRue said the Liddy plan was one of a large number of items on the agenda for Mitchell's decision March 30, 1972. LaRue was responsible for drawing up the meeting agenda, and he said he put the plan last, because he felt it was not a priority item and because he thought it should be something only he, Mitchell and Magruder should discuss. There were other campaign aides in the meeting from time to time, he explained.

When the time came to discuss the plan, he said, he gave a paper to Mitchell outlining it. Mitchell read it, LaRue testified, and asked what LaRue thought of it. LaRue said he told Mitchell it was not worth the risk. He then quoted Mitchell as deferring a decision on the plan.

Post-Break-in Activities. LaRue said he first heard of the break-in while at a campaign meeting with other re-election committee officials in Beverly Hills, Calif. LaRue said that when he told Mitchell about the break-in and the arrest of five men, "he was very surprised." LaRue quoted Mitchell as saying, "That's incredible."

LaRue said he returned to Washington that night (June 18, 1972) and the next evening attended a meeting in Mitchell's Watergate apartment with Mitchell, Dean, Magruder and Robert Mardian, another re-election committee official.

He told the committee that the men discussed the Watergate break-in and that he specifically recalled Magruder's mentioning some "sensitive files" and asking for advice about what to do with them. LaRue quoted Mitchell as answering that it "might be a good idea if Mr. Magruder had a fire." LaRue testified that he could not recall whether the name "Gemstone" was used in reference to the files, but that he recalled the files were on the subject of electronic surveillance.

Prior testimony had revealed that Gemstone was the code word for the surveillance operation. Magruder testified that he had the file destroyed. Mitchell testified that he had no knowledge of such a file and denied any recollection of the meeting.

LaRue next testified about a meeting in his apartment June 20 with Mardian and Liddy, at which Liddy explained the entire Watergate scheme. Liddy also mentioned his part in the break-in at the office of Daniel Ellsberg's psychiatrist and an unsuccessful break-in at the headquarters of Sen. George McGovern (S.D.), the Democratic presidential nominee.

LaRue said Liddy assured them that he would never reveal anything to anyone about his role and added that if they were not satisfied with his assurances, "he'd be on any street corner at any time and we could have him assassinated."

LaRue also testified that he attended a meeting where Magruder's Watergate grand jury testimony scheduled for Aug. 16, 1972, was discussed by Mitchell, Mardian, Dean, Magruder and himself. LaRue said he knew Magruder was to give false testimony.

Money Distribution. The witness then discussed his role in distributing money to Watergate defendants and their lawyers. He said he met with Kalmbach on June 28 or 29, 1972, to talk over preliminary arrangements. Kalmbach and he both used the code name, "Mr. Bradford," LaRue stated.

LaRue's testimony largely conformed to that of Kalmbach concerning the disbursements. He said the $40,000 he gave Kalmbach at a July meeting in Dean's office came from $81,000 he had been given by Mardian and Hugh Sloan Jr., the treasurer of the re-election finance committee.

But after about two months, Kalmbach wanted out of his fund-raising role. LaRue described a Sept. 19, 1972, meeting in Dean's office at which Kalmbach said he wanted to stop the activity. LaRue said Kalmbach returned about $30,000 he had not disbursed, plus the records of his disbursements, and that the records were burned.

LaRue said he then took it upon himself to distribute the money, and ultimately transferred a total of $210,000 to William O. Bittman, the lawyer for E. Howard Hunt Jr., one of the seven defendants. He said it was his understanding that Bittman would disburse the money to the various defendants and their lawyers.

LaRue said most of the money he gave to Bittman was distributed according to directions he received from Dean, based on Dean's talks with Kenneth L. Parkinson and Paul O'Brien, re-election committee lawyers. It was his understanding then, said LaRue, that the money was for legal fees and that the commitment to pay it was made by someone who knew that if the funds were not paid the re-election committee might be "embarrassed." He did not elaborate.

LaRue said he paid Bittman $25,000 in late September or early October 1972, $50,000 in December 1972, $25,000 and $35,000 in January and $75,000 in March 1973. All the payments but the last were ordered by Dean, LaRue testified.

Dean refused, LaRue said, to involve himself further in the payments by March, so he had to go to Mitchell for approval. LaRue said he told Mitchell the money was for lawyers' fees and Mitchell advised him to go ahead.

LaRue did not specify where the money he was disbursing came from, but he did say he received $280,000 at one point from Gordon Strachan, an aide to former White House chief of staff H. R. Haldeman. He said he believed the Strachan money came from a secret $350,000 fund kept by Haldeman. LaRue said another of his payments, for $20,000, went to Peter Maroulis, Liddy's lawyer.

The witness said press publicity and other factors caused him to decide in mid-April to tell his story to federal prosecutors. He said that he talked over the move with Dean beforehand and that Dean said he was going to do the same thing and advised him to hire a lawyer.

At that time, LaRue said, he had $113,000 stuffed in his filing cabinet at home, and his lawyer advised him to put it in a bank. He did this, later returning the money to the re-election committee, he said.

Ulasewicz Testimony. Ulasewicz made his second appearance before the committee to tell how he distributed money given him by Kalmbach. *(Prior Ulasewicz testimony, p. 83)*

Ulasewicz said that he met Kalmbach June 30, 1972, in a Washington hotel to discuss the payment plan and that Kalmbach appeared ill at ease. Kalmbach finally said the money was for the Watergate defendants, but insisted it was legal, the former policeman testified. They agreed on code names, "Novak" for Kalmbach and "Miller" for Ulasewicz, he said.

Ulasewicz said Kalmbach eventually gave him $219,000 over four meetings, mostly in $100 bills. About a week after their first meeting, he said, Kalmbach instructed him to contact various lawyers for the defendants, but none would accept the $25,000 he had been told to hand over.

Ulasewicz said he was shuttling back and forth between New York and Washington at one point with $75,100 in a paper bundle under his arm. "Running around with $75,100 trying to get rid of it was becoming a problem," he said. Finally, he was able to give $25,000 to attorney William O. Bittman. He said he put it in an envelope, left it on the ledge of a telephone booth in Bittman's office building and watched as the lawyer picked it up.

Each of his deliveries was ordered by Kalmbach, he related, and their conversations always took place in public telephone booths.

Ulasewicz said he disbursed a total of $154,500 to Hunt's wife on four occasions, $8,000 to Liddy and $29,000 to LaRue, all under similar circumstances. He explained that his method was to put the drop money in a locker at National Airport in Washington, tape the key to the bottom of a pay phone and inform the person picking up the money where to find the key. Ulasewicz said he watched to make sure the right person picked up the key.

Ulasewicz said he and Kalmbach grew concerned in August, particularly about Mrs. Hunt's growing demands for money, which at one point reached $450,000. "Something here is not kosher," he said he told Kalmbach, who agreed it was time to stop what they were doing. Nevertheless, Ulasewicz said he made two more payments on Sept. 19, on Kalmbach's orders, one to Mrs. Hunt and one to LaRue.

Late in his testimony, Ulasewicz admitted that some of his responsibilities at the White House included investigating people's drinking and sexual habits, domestic problems and social activities, and that many of those people were political opponents of the Nixon administration.

"It's fair to say that you dealt in dirt, isn't it?" asked Sen. Lowell P. Weicker Jr. (R Conn.).

"Allegations of it, yes," Ulasewicz replied.

Weicker said, "What we see here is not a joke, but a very great tragedy."

'A Right Dirty Trick'

For a few brief moments, it appeared that a potential legal confrontation between President Nixon and the Senate Watergate investigating committee had been averted.

After the luncheon break on July 19, Chairman Sam J. Ervin Jr. (D N.C.) announced to the packed hearing room that the President had decided to provide the committee with tape recordings of White House conversations with witnesses who had testified. The source of his information, said Ervin, was a telephone conversation with Treasury Secretary George P. Shultz. Ervin said he would meet with Nixon the next week to work out procedures for obtaining the tapes.

Minutes later, the chairman had to announce that what he had called "a very wise decision on the part of the President" was, instead, a hoax. He had learned from the White House and from Shultz that no such call had been made.

"I think it's the unanimous opinion of this committee that this was a right dirty trick," Ervin said.

Witnesses July 19

Robert C. Mardian, a former top official in the Nixon re-election committee whose name had been heavily implicated in the Watergate coverup by previous witnesses, denied any role in trying to hide the events connected with the 1972 break-in at Democratic national headquarters. In denying any coverup role, Mardian contradicted the sworn testimony of John W. Dean III, former counsel to the President; John N. Mitchell, former director of the re-election committee, and Jeb Stuart Magruder, Mitchell's former deputy. *(Previous witnesses' testimony, p. 135, 152, 180)*

Mardian, now in the construction business in Phoenix, Ariz., was a political coordinator for the re-election committee and one of its chief troubleshooters. Before working at the committee, he was an assistant attorney general in charge of the Justice Department's internal security division. He was a close friend of Mitchell.

In explaining how his name had been linked to the coverup, Mardian said in his prepared statement before the Senate select Watergate committee July 19 that on the day of the break-in he was relieved of his political responsibilities at the committee and charged with acting as counsel to the committee for Watergate matters. *(Text p. 226)*

In other testimony July 19, Frederick C. LaRue, a key aide of Mitchell at the re-election committee, acknowledged that he, Dean and Mitchell took part in a "grand coverup scheme" regarding the Watergate affair. Meanwhile, in a bizarre twist of events, Committee Chairman Ervin admitted he was the victim of a hoax when he announced that the White House had agreed to release tape recordings of presidential discussions bearing on the committee's investigation. *(Box above)*

Conflicting Testimony. In order to substantiate his non-involvement in the coverup, Mardian denied testimony by Magruder, Dean and Mitchell that he was one of the people who knew Magruder would perjure himself before the grand jury investigating the Watergate affair in the summer of 1972. Mardian conceded he was present at the meeting where Magruder discussed his upcoming testimony, but he insisted that Magruder did not say he was about to commit perjury and that he did not know even the substance of Magruder's testimony.

He denied Magruder's testimony that Mardian suggested he erase a reference in his diary to a Feb. 4, 1972, meeting where G. Gordon Liddy's plans for electronic surveillance of Democratic headquarters were discussed. "That discussion never took place in my presence," Mardian testified.

"That statement is not true," he said when read Magruder's testimony that Mitchell had ordered Mardian to call Liddy after the break-in to have Liddy contact then Attorney General Richard G. Kleindienst about getting the five Watergate burglars out of jail.

Mardian also rejected as untrue Dean's testimony that Mardian suggested soon after the break-in that the Central Intelligence Agency (CIA) could help with the coverup and that the FBI was being too aggressive in its investigation of the break-in. Mardian said he believed then that the CIA was involved, and "I may have said it's a CIA problem." Regarding the FBI probe, Mardian said of Dean, "On that score, he's dead wrong."

Break-in. In other testimony, Mardian said Liddy, the break-in planner, told him he sometimes acted on orders from the President and that the budget for the Watergate operation was approved by Mitchell and the White House.

Mitchell testified that he rejected the break-in scheme at a meeting in Key Biscayne, Fla., March 30, 1972. Magruder and LaRue disputed this. Mardian testified that during a discussion of the break-in with Mitchell after it took place, Mitchell did not deny he had approved the budget.

Mardian also testified that he had no recollection that Mitchell suggested destroying Watergate papers at a meeting two days after the break-in. Magruder and LaRue have testified to the contrary, with Dean agreeing with Mitchell and Mardian that no destruction was ordered. All five men attended the meeting.

Mardian said that by July 13, 1972, he had removed himself from Watergate-related activities. He said he subsequently had talks about Watergate with two lawyers for the re-election committee, Paul O'Brien and Kenneth L. Parkinson, but only in his capacity as a committee counsel.

Liddy Meeting. Mardian gave a broad description of a meeting he and LaRue had with Liddy after the break-in. Mardian said the meeting took place on June 21, contrary to the testimony of LaRue, who said it had been June 20.

Liddy entered the meeting in LaRue's apartment, Mardian related, and first went to a radio, turned in on and asked the two men to sit in chairs beside it. "It's not that I don't trust you," Mardian quoted Liddy, "but this conversation can't be recorded."

Mardian said Liddy told him all about the break-in and that he had nothing to fear, because the five men arrested were professionals and would disclose nothing. Mardian said he urged Liddy to give himself up, but that Liddy rejected that idea. Liddy also told the two men of his role in the break-in at the office of Daniel Ellsberg's psychiatrist and the spiriting of Dita Beard, a Washington lobbyist, to a Denver hospital, Mardian testified.

Mardian said he asked Liddy under whose authority he was acting in those two activities. The words Liddy used, he continued, "were clearly meant to imply he was acting on the express orders of the President of the United States with the assistance of the Central Intelligence Agency."

Liddy told him, Mardian said, that his budget for the Watergate break-in had been approved by Mitchell and someone in the White House. Liddy said, however, that he had shredded all the serialized money he had received for the operation, Mardian told the committee.

When Mitchell was told of the meeting with Liddy, Mardian said, he appeared "sincerely shocked" and ordered that no re-election committee money be given Liddy, as had been requested.

California Meetings. Mardian also described in detail the meetings in California among high committee officials the day after the break-in. He said he first learned of the crime when Magruder told him he had a "slight PR problem he wished to discuss with me." Magruder, Mardian said, told him what he had learned from Liddy, including the fact that all five persons arrested had fake identification cards supplied by the CIA and that Liddy himself "was some kind of a nut."

Mardian said Magruder told him Mitchell had approved the Liddy budget, which included dirty tricks and "black advance." This was the first time the term "black advance" had been connected with Watergate. Mardian said he interpreted it to mean countermeasures to political opponents' advance scheduling.

Asked if Mitchell, who was meeting periodically with Mardian the same day, ever said he had approved the budget, Mardian replied: "The subject was discussed, and he didn't deny it."

LaRue Testimony. LaRue completed his testimony during the morning session. Asked by Sen. Daniel K. Inouye (D Hawaii) whether he considered the payments he made to lawyers for the defendants to be "a part of a grand coverup scheme," LaRue replied, "Yes, sir."

In answer to other questions, LaRue provided an accounting of the money he handled. He accounted for $455,000 in receipts and $240,000 in disbursements.

LaRue said receipts were $81,000 in early July 1972 from the re-election finance committee; $30,000 in September from Anthony T. Ulasewicz, a money courier; $50,000 in December from Gordon Strachan, an aide to former White House chief of staff H.R. Haldeman; $14,000 in January from Tim Babcock, former governor of Montana, and $280,000 in January from Strachan. LaRue said the total of $330,000 from Strachan was from a secret White House fund of $350,000.

Of the $240,000 in disbursements, $210,000 went to William O. Bittman and $20,000 to Peter Maroulis, both lawyers for Watergate defendants, LaRue said. The $230,000 in LaRue disbursements, added to the $219,000 Ulasewicz testified he paid out, make a total of $449,000 for Watergate defendants and lawyers.

Daily Chronology

Following is a day-to-day chronology of the week's events:

JULY 12

(Earlier July 12 events, p. 189)

Campaign Contributions. In the aftermath of a disclosure by American Airlines that it made illegal corporate contributions to Nixon's 1972 campaign, *The Detroit Free Press* reported that Chrysler Corporation also had made such contributions. A company spokesman denied the report but acknowledged that Nixon's former personal attorney, Herbert W. Kalmbach, had solicited a contribution from Chrysler's board chairman, Lynn A. Townsend, in August 1971. Kalmbach did not ask for a corporate contribution, which is illegal under federal campaign finance law, nor did he promise special favors for the firm, the spokesman said.

American Motors Corporation announced that its Washington representative had been asked in March 1972 for a $100,000 contribution to the Nixon campaign, but rejected the request even when the amount was reduced to $50,000. *(Illegal airline gift, p. 187)*

JULY 13

Moore Testimony. Richard A. Moore, a White House special adviser on media affairs, returned to the Senate investigating committee witness chair for a second day. He said Nixon was deeply troubled about not recognizing earlier the coverup going on at the White House—an assertion that contradicted earlier testimony by former presidential counsel John W. Dean III that the President was aware of the coverup as early as the previous September. *(Moore testimony, p. 192)*

Haldeman Interview. *The New York Times* published excerpts from a May 4 interview of H. R. Haldeman conducted by the Senate Watergate investigating committee. The former Nixon chief of staff denied any involvement in the planning or coverup of the Watergate burglary. He said he first learned of the coverup attempts in March. Haldeman's story, as recounted in the report, contradicted the sworn testimony of other witnesses, including Dean, deputy campaign director Jeb Stuart Magruder and former Attorney General John N. Mitchell.

Quoting from the May 4 interview summary, *The Washington Post* reported July 14 that Haldeman admitted to Senate investigators that he approved the hiring of alleged political saboteur Donald H. Segretti. *(Haldeman civil suit deposition, p. 113)*

Clemency Offer. The Times also reported that Henry B. Rothblatt, former attorney for four of the convicted Watergate conspirators, had told the special federal prosecutor that the men pleaded guilty at their trial in January because they had been promised support payments and executive clemency by another defendant, E. Howard Hunt Jr. The men—Bernard L. Barker, Frank A. Sturgis, Eugenio R. Martinez and Virgilio R. Gonzalez—said in court that they had not been pressured into changing their original pleas of not guilty.

Cox Appointments. Special Watergate prosecutor Archibald Cox announced four new appointments to his permanent staff of investigators, which he said had been divided into five separate task forces. *(Box, p. 198)*

JULY 14

Stone Contributions. Chicago insurance multimillionaire W. Clement Stone revealed that he contributed $2.8-million to Nixon's 1968 presidential campaign and more than $2-million to his 1972 campaign. While insisting that his gifts had not been used for Watergate-related activities, Stone said he was investigating the use of his $2-million contribution to the 1972 Nixon re-election effort because of the possibility that some of the funds were "misused."

White House Files. In an interview published in *The Washington Star-News*, Sam J. Ervin Jr. (D N.C.), chairman of the Senate Watergate investigating committee, said the committee would not go to court to enforce a subpoena of White House files on the Watergate scandal, because the process would take too long. The committee would just have to allow the public to make the "adverse inference" that Nixon had something to hide in refusing to reveal the documents, Ervin said. *(Files controversy, p. 189)*

JULY 15

White House Files. Sen. Daniel K. Inouye (D Hawaii) of the Watergate committee said on CBS-TV's "Face the Nation" that he would vote to subpoena White House papers "that are useful to the committee." In a separate television interview in New York, Sen. Lowell P. Weicker Jr. (R Conn.), another committee member, said he thought such a subpoena would violate the doctrine of separation of powers. But both members urged Nixon to meet privately with the committee to discuss allegations that he and some of his top aides had been involved in a coverup.

Campaign Contributions. *The New York Times* concluded from a telephone survey of numerous large corporations that 1972 Nixon fund-raisers Maurice H. Stans and Herbert W. Kalmbach made "standard" requests for $100,000 contributions from business executives. Such individual donations are legal. Most of the major defense contractors and many firms in trouble with or awaiting rulings from federal agencies were reportedly asked for donations. *(Illegal campaign contributions, p. 187)*

JULY 16

Butterfield Testimony. Surprise witness Alexander P. Butterfield, head of the Federal Aviation Administration and former White House aide, told the Senate investigating committee Nixon would have automatically tape-recorded his conversations with Dean and other key figures in the Watergate case. He said the tapes had been stored in the Executive Office Building by the Secret Service.

Late in the afternoon, the White House acknowledged that all of Nixon's conversations since early 1971 had been recorded. In a letter to Committee Chairman Ervin, Nixon counsel J. Fred Buzhardt said the automatically triggered recording of Nixon's conversations was a practice "similar to that employed by the last administration and which had been discontinued from 1969 until the spring of 1971." *(Butterfield testimony, p. 192)*

Moore, Kalmbach Testimony. Before Butterfield appeared, special White House consultant Richard A. Moore and former Nixon personal attorney Kalmbach testified before the committee. Kalmbach told of raising $220,000 for the seven Watergate defendants, with the express approval of former Nixon aide John D. Ehrlichman. Kalmbach said he did not know the money was being given to keep the defendants from talking, as Dean had testified. *(Kalmbach testimony, p. 193)*

Vesco Case. Attorneys for Mitchell, former Commerce Secretary Stans and New Jersey Republican leader Harry L. Sears filed a second series of motions in U.S. District Court in New York, asking dismissal of federal indictments charging the three with conspiracy to influence a fraud investigation of financier Robert L. Vesco in exchange for Vesco's $200,000 campaign contribution. The attorneys argued that "massive, pervasive and prejudicial publicity" made fair trials impossible. *(Earlier motion, p. 188)*

McCord Plea. The special Watergate prosecution filed papers in U.S. District Court in Washington, D.C., opposing a motion by convicted Watergate conspirator James W. McCord Jr. asking that his conviction be thrown out or that he be granted a new trial. McCord contended that he had been led to believe the Watergate bugging operation was necessary for national security.

JULY 17

White House Tapes. Claiming executive privilege, Nixon ordered the Secret Service to withhold from the Senate investigating committee all information about secretly made recordings of the President's White House conversations. In response, the committee sent a letter to Nixon asking his "cooperation in making available to the committee records and tapes which are relevant" to its investigation. Sen. Howard H. Baker Jr. (R Tenn.), ranking minority member of the committee, said obtaining the tapes was "a matter of monumental importance" to the committee. *(Details, p. 195)*

Dean Response. Dean's attorney, Robert McCandless, said his client would welcome the release of the White House tapes and predicted they would corroborate Dean's assertions about Nixon's awareness of the coverup.

JFK Tapes. A spokesman for the John F. Kennedy library in Cambridge, Mass., said a search of the library's archives had turned up tapes of telephone conversations and staff meetings from the Kennedy administration, almost all of them dealing with "highly sensitive foreign policy and defense matters."

Kalmbach Testimony. Nixon's former personal attorney and fund-raiser, Herbert W. Kalmbach, completed his testimony before the Senate committee. He admitted that in hindsight, his payments to the Watergate defendants constituted "an improper, illegal act," and speculated that he may have been "used" by former Nixon advisers Haldeman, Ehrlichman, Dean and Mitchell. *(Kalmbach testimony, p. 196)*

Krogh Appearance. Former White House aide Egil Krogh Jr., who headed the White House "plumbers" group that burglarized the office of Daniel Ellsberg's psychiatrist, appeared before the House Armed Services Intelligence Subcommittee and invoked the Fifth Amendment on all questions about the Watergate affair. He refused June 7 to appear before a Los Angeles grand jury investigating the burglary.

JULY 18

Ulasewicz, LaRue Testimony. Anthony T. Ulasewicz, a retired New York policeman who worked as a private investigator for the White House, told the Senate Watergate committee how he channeled $220,000 to the Watergate defendants or their lawyers between June and September 1972. His testimony was followed by that of Frederick C. LaRue, a former Nixon re-election committee official who voluntarily pleaded guilty June 27 to a charge of conspiracy to obstruct justice for his part in the Watergate coverup. LaRue said he assumed Ulasewicz' task in September and distributed $230,000 in hush money to the defendants or their lawyers. *(Testimony, p. 197; LaRue plea, p. 161)*

White House Tapes. The White House continued to stall on the question of whether it would release to the committee tape recordings of Nixon's conversations with aides—items the committee deemed essential to its investigation. Press secretary Ronald L. Ziegler would say only that the White House would have "something further to say in the future" on the subject. Special prosecutor Archibald Cox reportedly was preparing to make his own request for the recordings.

Phone Company Inquiry. A spokesman for the Chesapeake & Potomac Telephone Company said the firm had contacted the White House to find out if regulations on the use of recording devices on telephones had been followed. He said the Federal Communications Commission had requested the American Telephone and Telegraph Company, the parent corporation, to investigate the matter.

Jackson Investigation. Sen. Henry M. Jackson (D Wash.) announced that his Permanent Investigations Subcommittee would begin public hearings in September on government and industry wiretapping practices. "The civil liberties of all our citizens are at stake," Jackson said.

Tax Suit. U.S. District Judge Charles R. Richey called on the White House to release "documents, memoranda, notes, and other writings" pertaining to "activist organizations," including the Center on Corporate Responsibility. The organization was suing the federal government to obtain tax-exempt status, which it claimed was denied because of White House political pressure on the Internal Revenue Service.

The government's attorney in the case told Richey the White House would invoke executive privilege to prevent the court from seeing the documents. Richey responded by giving the Justice Department 10 days to answer his request and threatened to formally order the White House to produce the documents. He said he had communicated with special prosecutor Cox on possible criminal violations in connection with the alleged pressure. *(Earlier development, p. 186)*

Young Testimony. Former White House aide David R. Young Jr. appeared before the House Armed Services Intelligence Subcommittee and repeatedly invoked the Fifth Amendment when asked about activities of the White House "plumbers" group, including the 1971 burglary of the office of Daniel Ellsberg's psychiatrist. Young, along with Egil Krogh Jr., supervised the "plumbers' " intelligence-gathering operations. Subcommittee officials said after the closed hearing that Young refused to say whether John Ehrlichman had approved the Ellsberg burglary in advance.

Civil Suit. Special prosecutor Cox filed a memorandum in U.S. District Court, suggesting that it might be necessary to postpone hearing the Democrats' $6.4-million civil suit against the Nixon re-election committee in order to ensure fairness in forthcoming criminal trials. Cox said a deposition sought by the Democrats from John Dean "might jeopardize the rights of both potential defendants and the public to a fair trial."

Socialist Workers' Suit. The Socialist Workers Party, joined by the Young Socialist Alliance and several individual members, filed suit in federal court in New York City seeking more than $27-million in damages from Nixon and other government officials on charges of violating the party's constitutional rights. The suit contended that the government had engaged in a "systematic campaign of excessive interrogation, employment discrimination and other harassment" that impaired the party's effectiveness in federal, state and local elections.

Johnson Tapes. United Press International reported that two former Johnson administration officials had given the White House affidavits saying that Johnson had the conference table in the White House cabinet room bugged at least since early 1965, and that he had taped certain phone conversations. White House counsel J. Fred Buzhardt said in announcing Nixon's taping of White House conversations that the same practice had been followed by the Johnson administration.

JULY 19

LaRue, Mardian Testimony. LaRue completed his Senate committee testimony. He acknowledged that he, Mitchell and Dean were aware of a "grand coverup scheme" to hide the facts of the Watergate bugging. LaRue was followed by Robert C. Mardian, former assistant attorney general and former official of the Nixon re-election committee. *(Testimony, p. 200)*

Grand Jury. U.S. District Judge John J. Sirica empaneled a second Washington, D.C., federal grand jury to investigate possible violations of several federal laws, including campaign contribution violations, conspiracy to defraud the United States and obstruction of justice. Special Watergate prosecutor Cox had requested the second grand jury because of the volume of Watergate-related material to be investigated.

LARUE STATEMENT TEXT

Following is the opening statement of Fred C. LaRue, former special consultant to the President, before the Senate Watergate committee on July 18:

My home is in Jackson, Miss. Since 1969, however, I have spent a substantial part of my time in Washington, D. C., first working on the transition of administrations, then as a special consultant to the President, and since January 1972 I have served as a special assistant on the Committee to Re-elect the President.

I learned that the Democratic National Committee headquarters had been broken into on June 17, 1972, shortly after the occurrence.

Prior to that time, I did know of the existence of a proposal to conduct political espionage by electronic surveillance. I learned of this plan at a meeting I attended in late March 1972; and this is the only time I heard it discussed. At that meeting I recommended against the plan. It was not approved in my presence, and I have no personal knowledge of its approval by anyone.

After the Watergate arrests and subsequent to June 17, 1972, my knowledge and involvement increased. I learned from Mr. Gordon Liddy on June 20 that he, an official of the committee, had in fact been involved in this fiasco.

I later sat in on meetings with Mr. Magruder and others at which the protective story he had evolved was discussed, and I joined in that coverup, at least by acquiescence.

Then I was the recipient of several deliveries of cash which, at various times, I was called upon to distribute to a number of persons in satisfaction of commitments made by others to the defendants in the Watergate trial.

I am fully aware now that what I did then was wrong, both ethically and legally, and I have faced up to that fact and I am prepared to accept the consequences. It is difficult to recreate a mood and even one's own attitudes in a time of stress; but when this was transpiring, I really had no intent to violate the law. I was motivated solely by my concern for the presidential campaign in which we were engaging.

I have given my full cooperation, to the best of my ability and recollection, to the staff of this committee in preparation for these hearings. Furthermore, I have and will continue to fully cooperate with the Watergate prosecutors and the federal grand jury inquiring into these matters. I am prepared to try to answer any questions you may have for me.

KALMBACH STATEMENT TEXT

Following are excerpts from the opening statement of Herbert W. Kalmbach, President Nixon's former personal attorney, before the Senate Watergate committee on July 16:

Prior to the time this Committee began to take testimony in this matter and before the issuance of a subpoena, I voluntarily appeared and offered to testify to whatever knowledge I had that would be helpful to the Committee in its investigation. My decision to do so was prompted by the Chairman's remarks to the Senate on February 6, 1973, and by my desire to clear my name of any suggestion of improper activity with respect to events leading up to or following the so-called Watergate break-in on June 17, 1972. Also, for the record, I wish to state that I have never asked for immunity nor have I indicated that I would exercise my Fifth Amendment rights before this Committee or any other investigative body relative to the subject of this inquiry....

Since graduating from law school, I have been active in the practice of law and in corporate management work in Southern California and in Arizona.... Also, for more than twenty years, I have been active in political work—particularly in recent years in the area of campaign finance.

Since early 1969, I have been engaged in activities on the President's behalf in three major areas:

- First, it has been the source of great pride and personal satisfaction to me and to my partners to have had the responsibility for handling personal legal matters for President Nixon and members of his immediate family for the past four years. During this period, practically all of the contacts that I had relative to these matters were handled through either John Ehrlichman or John Dean.

• Second, I acted as trustee during the period from January of 1969 to early February of 1972 for certain surplus funds which had accrued principally from the primary period of the 1968 campaign. While Maurice H. Stans was the individual with whom I dealt at the time I accepted such trusteeship, I disbursed from such funds only at the express direction of H.R. Haldeman or others clearly having the authority to direct such disbursements.

• Third, I agreed to solicit early pledges of financial support for the President's 1972 campaign beginning in November of 1970. This assignment was completed in the Spring of 1972. The original records of this activity were turned over to the Finance Committee after Mr. Stans had assumed the post of finance chairman on Feb. 15, 1972. I thereupon directed my secretary to destroy my files, which were wholly personal and supportive of the original files earlier transferred to the Finance Committee. This action on my part was intended to insure the continued confidentiality of the contacts that I had had with various contributors with whom I had dealt during this period. Copies of what remaining records I have and such bank records as I have been able to retrieve have been supplied to the Committee's staff prior to my appearance here today.

Finally I want to take this opportunity to deny any prior knowledge of the Watergate break-in or participation in the formulation of any planned conspiracy to cover up that incident or acts of campaign sabotage or unethical activity. My actions in the period immediately following the break-in which involved the raising of funds to provide for the legal defense of the Watergate defendants and for the support of their families were prompted in the belief that it was proper and necessary to discharge what I assumed to be a moral obligation that had arisen in some manner unknown to me by reason of earlier events. The fact that I had been directed to undertake these actions by the number two and number three men on the White House staff made it absolutely incomprehensible to me that my actions in this regard could have been regarded in any way as improper or unethical.

I'm here before you today to tell the truth about my activities during the period in question. It is not my purpose to testify for or against any individual. I wish to cooperate fully with the Committee, and in that spirit, I am now ready to answer your questions to the very best of my ability.

MOORE STATEMENT TEXT

Following are excerpts from the opening statement of Richard A. Moore, special counsel to the President, before the Senate Watergate investigating committee July 12:

....For a year beginning in April 1970, I served as a special assistant to Attorney General Mitchell. I assisted him primarily in the preparation of speeches, statements and position papers on current public issues within the department's responsibilities. In April 1971 I was appointed a special counsel to the President. My principal role has been to assist the President and his staff in communicating their positions in the most convincing manner to the general public. Since convincing communications depend on having a convincing position to communicate, my job necessarily involves me in the substance of particular issues in the public eye. But I do not have a line responsibility either on the communications or on the substantive side. I serve primarily as an extra hand—as a source of white-haired advice and experience—whenever the President or the younger men with line responsibility seek my help.

I shall be glad, of course, to answer any questions concerning any aspect of these hearings, but I believe that the most significant testimony I can give to this committee relates to a limited time frame—that is basically the period from February 6, 1973, the day Senator Ervin introduced his resolution creating this select committee, to March 21, 1973. March 21 is the date when President Nixon, as he later announced to the nation, learned of "serious charges" which caused him to begin "intensive new inquiries into this whole matter." This was the day when Mr. Dean, at my urging, went into the President's office and, as he has testified, told him "everything."

Much of my testimony will involve my recollections about conversations with the President and John Dean. The good faith recollections of one party to a conversation often differ from those of the other....

In latter December 1972 and January 1973, I was primarily involved with inaugural matters and can recall no particular meetings or consultations with regard to the Watergate or related matters until February 6. On that day I attended a meeting in Mr. Ehrlichman's office to discuss our legislative position with respect to the proposed resolution creating this select committee. Except for the discussion at this meeting, I knew of no other planning or preparation that had been going on with regard to these hearings. Within the White House, I was a critic of this lack of preparation.

CALIFORNIA MEETINGS

This may explain why I was called to the meetings in California on February 10-11.... Late on the afternoon of February 9, Mr. Dean called me at home to say that we were both asked by Mr. Ehrlichman to meet with Mr. Haldeman and himself in San Clemente on February 10 to discuss the forthcoming Senate hearings....

Mr. Dean and I met on Saturday, February 10, 1973, at San Clemente with Messrs. Haldeman and Ehrlichman in Ehrlichman's office from 10:30 or 11:00 in the morning until 3:00 or 4:00 in the afternoon. On Sunday, we went to Mr. Haldeman's cottage at La Costa.

All four of us were present for the majority of the time. One or more of us would leave the group on occasion to make or take a telephone call or to perform some other function. Summarizing these meetings is difficult because they involved about eight hours of conversation, with none of the participants adhering to any strict agenda. In addition, the many things that were said during these sessions were heard by anywhere from two to four people (depending on who was absent at the moment), each with a different background or degree of knowledge or point of view.... Let me now give you my best recollection of what transpired while I was present.

At the outset Mr. Ehrlichman or Mr. Haldeman asked Mr. Dean and me what we had been doing to prepare for the hearings. The answer was nothing. The focus of these hearings, they said, would be the activities of the Committee to Re-elect the President, and it would be the committee that would have to take the primary responsibility for the defense. Had we had any discussions or, as they put it, any input, from John Mitchell? The answer was no. Either Mr. Haldeman or Mr. Ehrlichman then said that in that case, Dick Moore ought to sit down with John Mitchell as soon as he could and fill him in on the things that we discuss here and get Mr. Mitchell actively interested—he is the only one who could give real leadership to the people at the committee.

Either Haldeman or Ehrlichman then suggested that Mr. Dean be the White House coordinator for the hearing, and that I hold myself available to advise him. I suggested that the White House have a writer-spokesman who could issue statements or go on television, if necessary, to reply quickly to testimony or commentary that was wrong or slanted. Mr. Dean, I believe, suggested that Pat Buchanan be this spokesman.

The meeting then turned to a discussion of our relationship with the minority members of the committee. It was pointed out that in an ordinary hearing there is an open relationship between the White House and the committee leadership of the same party, and the White House has a perfectly proper role in presenting its views to the members affiliated with its party on the particular committee. No one in the group had any firm view as to what was appropriate here, but the general feeling was that since this was in effect an investigation of the administration, the normal relationship might not apply and we probably should maintain an arm's length approach even to the Republican members. In any event, it was agreed that Wally Johnson, then of the White House congressional relations staff, would be made available for whatever liaison with the committee might be appropriate.

Early in the discussions, Mr. Ehrlichman made it clear that the President wanted our position in the hearings to be one of full cooperation, subject only to the doctrine of separation of powers. It was agreed it would be important to work out a statement on executive privilege (the President had recently promised the press he would do so) that would enable us to cooperate and supply the information that the committee wanted. It is my recollection that at this time the question whether presidential advisors would be permitted to appear was still unresolved, although the consensus was that appearances should be permitted where the subject matter did not relate to their official duties for the President.

There was, as I have said, no prepared sequence to our discussions, and I cannot recall all the other subjects we discussed. I do recall a discussion about putting out a White House statement in advance of the hearings setting forth all the known facts about the Watergate episode. It was also agreed that more manpower would be needed by the Committee to Re-elect the President—possibly in the form of young lawyers and researchers to review each day's testimony and prepare rebuttals. This was among the items I agreed to discuss with Mr. Mitchell.

Mr. Dean, of course, has testified about a discussion of money. His recollection differs from mine.... The brief mention of money made at this meeting may have had a very different significance to a person with Mr. Dean's knowledge of the circumstances than it had to a person with my lack of knowledge. My recollection on that subject is as follows: The subject came up, I believe, on the second day at the hotel. In the context of a discussion of the litigation in which the committee was then involved, John Dean, in a sort of by-the-way reference, said he had been told by the lawyers that they may be needing some more money, and did we have any ideas? Someone said, isn't that something that John Mitchell might handle with his rich New York friends. It was suggested that since I would be meeting with Mr. Mitchell, I should mention this when I saw him and I said I would.

As I look back now, of course, with the knowledge I subsequently began acquiring in the latter part of March, Mr. Dean's reference to a need for money might well have stimulated some further inquiries on my part at La Costa. But I did not have that knowledge on February 11—at that point I knew nothing about any prior payments to any defendants or their counsel—and no one else at the meeting went into any details. Moreover, I had served for a year as special assistant to Mr. Mitchell at the Department of Justice, and I know him well. I was certain that he wasn't about to be programmed into becoming a fund raiser by Mr. Haldeman and Mr. Ehrlichman, and I anticipated that Mitchell's answer would be no, as it turned out to be.

We discussed several other matters and the meeting ended, as I recall, with Ehrlichman asking me about my draft of the statement on executive privilege. He indicated that he would like a revised draft to be prepared and cleared for review by the President on the flight east the next day. At some time during or just after the Sunday meeting, I called my secretary in Washington and dictated some changes in the statement to be cleared among those in Washington who were working on the draft.

Mr. Dean has testified that we left the meeting together and that he had a conversation with me at which time he cautioned me against conveying this fund-raising request when I saw Mr. Mitchell. I have absolutely no recollection of of any such conversation and I am convinced it never took place.

MEETING WITH MITCHELL

I returned to my office in Washington on February 13, and telephoned Mr. Mitchell to inquire whether he had any immediate plans to be in Washington. He said he did not, and I said I needed two or three hours with him to tell him about the meetings in California. He suggested that I come to New York and we could take as much time as we needed. On February 15, I took a morning shuttle to New York, went to Mr. Mitchell's office, visited briefly before lunch, and after lunch we had a discussion about the California meetings and the upcoming hearings.

Knowing Mr. Mitchell as I do, I felt there were several points where he would resist being "programmed" by the White House staff, as I mentioned earlier, and I elected to get those out of the way at the start. At the beginning of our discussion I said something like this: "Well, you will be glad to know that the group in San Clemente thinks you should be taking a more active interest in the Ervin hearings." I had a somewhat blunt reply, such as, thank them very much, I am indeed interested and, as you know, I may be a star witness. I told him it was suggested that it would be most helpful if he could spend part of each week in his law firm's Washington office. He made a chilly reply that he would come to Washington whenever he felt it necessary. Then I said to him that I didn't know what it was all about but that it had been suggested that the committee lawyers might be needing more money and that his White House friends had nominated him for the honor of being a fund raiser. I don't remember his exact words, but I believe he said something like "tell them to get lost."

Thereafter I began my report of the meetings. We had a wide-ranging discussion and a pleasant visit that lasted most of the afternoon. I left his office at about 4 or 5 o'clock and took the shuttle home.

MEETINGS WITH NIXON

From mid-February to early March, I was not asked to participate in any follow-up to the La Costa-San Clemente discussions about preparing for these hearings, except for my continuing participation in the preparation of the statement on executive privilege. By the beginning of March, the Gray nomination hearings had become a major preoccupation for me and for Mr. Dean. During those hearings, Mr. Dean's role in the Watergate investigation became a subject of headline news. The Judiciary Committee's invitation to Mr. Dean to testify before it brought the question of executive privilege into critical focus. A presidential press conference was scheduled for March 15, and Mr. Dean and I prepared, for the President's "briefing book," a list of more than twenty possible questions on the subject. Although it was not the President's usual practice to hold face-to-face briefing sessions before a press conference, he chose to do so on this occasion. And so began a series of meetings about which Mr. Dean has testified and which marked the first occasion I had to discuss with the President any subject related to Watergate.

The first meeting on March 14 was in progress when I was called to the President's office. Messrs. Ziegler and Dean were already there. We went over the questions and answers with considerable discussion on each. The meeting recessed temporarily while the President kept another appointment and had lunch. It reconvened after lunch for several hours.

At no time during this meeting, or during succeeding meetings on March 15, 19 and 20—all of which were attended only by the President, Mr. Dean and myself—did anyone say anything in my presence which related to or suggested the existence of any coverup, or any knowledge or involvement by anyone in the White House, then or now, in the Watergate affair, including the coverup.

Late on the afternoon of March 15, after the President concluded his press conference, Mr. Dean and I were called to the oval office. We had a relaxed and informal session in which we discussed the press conference and the President's view of the doctrine of separation of powers.

The topic to which the President devoted most attention and emphasis was the separation of powers. He made the point that the term "executive privilege" doesn't properly express the principle. He asked Mr. Dean and me to advise others who were dealing with the subject to use the term "separation of powers." He emphasized several times that the President has the constitutional responsibility to preserve the separation of powers, a responsibility he cannot disregard.

The President made the point that he cannot command any member of Congress to come to see him at the White House, but they usually come when invited, just as our people go up to the Hill when invited. He said our Cabinet people seem to be up there testifying voluntarily practically every day. But the point is, he said, that one branch cannot, as a matter of right, command the other to appear; that, he said, would destroy the separation of powers.

On March 19, I was called to meet with the President and Mr. Dean in the President's Executive Office Building office. The President reiterated his desire to get out a general statement in advance of the hearings. He asked us to be thinking about ways that this could be done. This would include issuing a full statement or "white paper"; he was also interested in our thoughts about ways to present our story to the Senate in terms of possible depositions, affidavits, or possible conferences or meetings which would give the Senate all the information it wished but which would not cut across the separation of powers. He asked Dean and me to consider ways to do this.

On March 19 or possibly on March 20—before we met later that day with the President—Mr. Dean told me that Howard Hunt was demanding that a large sum of money be given to him before his sentencing on March 23, and that he wanted the money by the 21st. If the payment were not made, Dean said, Hunt had threatened to say things that would be very serious for the White House. I replied that this was pure blackmail, and that Dean should turn it off and have nothing to do with it. I could not imagine, I said, that anything that Hunt could say would be as bad as paying blackmail. I don't recall Mr. Dean's exact words, but he expressed agreement.

This revelation was the culmination of several other guarded comments Mr. Dean had made to me in the immediately preceding days. He had said that he had been present at two meetings attended by Messrs. Mitchell, Magruder and Liddy before the bugging arrests, during which Liddy had proposed wild schemes that had been turned down—specifically espionage, electronics surveillance and even kidnapping. He said that the Watergate location had not been mentioned, and that he had "turned off the wild schemes." I believed then and believe today that Mr. Dean had no advance knowledge of the Watergate bugging and breakin. In addition, he had said that if he ever had to testify before the grand jury, his testimony would conflict with Mr. Magruder's, and that he had heard that if Magruder faced a perjury charge, he would take others with him.

Mr. Dean had also mentioned to me that earlier activities of Messrs. Hunt and Liddy—not directly related to Watergate—could be seriously embarrassing to the administration if they ever came to light. He had also implied to me that he knew of payments being made to the defendants for litigation expenses, and Hunt's explicit blackmail demand raised serious questions in my mind as to the purpose of these payments.

This brings me to the afternoon of March 20, when Mr. Dean and I met with the President in the oval office. The meeting lasted about half an hour. The President again stated his hope that we could put out a full statement in advance of the hearings, and again he expressed his desire that we be forthcoming, as he put it. He made some comparisons as to our attitude and the attitude of previous administrations, and he wanted us to make sure that we were the most forthcoming of all.

As I sat through the meeting of March 20 with the President and Mr. Dean in the oval office, I came to the conclusion in my own mind that the President could not be aware of the things that Dean was worried about or had been hinting at to me, let alone Howard Hunt's blackmail demand. Indeed, as the President talked about getting the whole story out—as he had done repeatedly in the recent meetings—it seemed crystal clear to me that he knew of nothing that was inconsistent with the previously stated conclusion that the White House was uninvolved in the Watergate affair, before or after the event.

DEAN'S REVELATIONS

As we closed the door of the oval office and turned into the hall, I decided to raise the issue directly with Mr. Dean. I said that I had the feeling that the President had no knowledge of the things that were worrying Dean. I asked Dean whether he had ever told the President about them. Dean replied that he had not, and I asked whether anyone else had. Dean said he didn't think so. I said, "Then the President isn't being served, he is reaching a point where he is going to have to make critical decisions, and he simply has to know all the facts. I think you should go in and tell him what you know. You will feel better, it will be right for him and it will be good for the country."

I do not recall whether he told me he would take action or not, but I certainly have the impression that he was receptive. In any event, the question was resolved that very evening when I received a call at home sometime after dinner and it was Mr. Dean, who said that the President had just phoned him and that he had decided that this was the moment to speak up. He said that he told the President that things had been going on that the President should know about and it was important that Dean see him alone and tell him. Dean said that the President readily agreed and told Dean to come in the following morning. I congratulated Mr. Dean and wished him well.

The next day, March 21, Mr. Dean told me that he had indeed met with the President at 10 o'clock and had talked with him for two hours and had "let it all out." I said, "Did you tell him about the Howard Hunt business?" Dean replied that he had told the President everything. I asked if the President had been surprised and he said yes.

Following this critical meeting on March 21, I had several subsequent meetings and telephone conversations with Mr. Dean alone, as well as several meetings with the President which Mr. Dean did not attend. I do not dispute Mr. Dean's account of the meetings between us as to any substantive point, and I have no direct knowledge of what transpired in Mr. Dean's subsequent meetings with the President. But nothing said in my meetings with Mr. Dean or my meetings with the President suggests in any way that before March 21 the President had known—or that Mr. Dean believed he had known—of any involvement of White House personnel in the bugging or the coverup. Indeed, Mr. Dean's own account that he and I agreed on the importance of persuading the President to make a prompt disclosure of all that the President had just learned is hardly compatible with a belief on Mr. Dean's part that the President himself had known the critical facts all along. In one of my talks with the President, the President kept asking himself whether there had been any sign or clue which should have led him to discover the true facts earlier. I told him that I wished that I had been more skeptical and inquisitive so that I could have served the presidency better.

I have given you the most complete account I can as to my knowledge of the events being examined by this committee. It is my deep convicton—as one who has known the President over the years and has had many private conversations with him—that the critical facts about the Watergate did not reach the President until the events that began when John Dean met with him on March 21, 1973. √

WATERGATE: A HISTORIC CONSTITUTIONAL CONFRONTATION

Sen. Sam J. Ervin Jr., the bushy-browed old North Carolinian who heads the Senate select committee that is investigating the Watergate affair, called it "the greatest tragedy this country has ever suffered." The committee vice chairman, Howard H. Baker Jr. of Tennessee, described it as a "historic conflict" between the legislative and executive branches of government.

With the five other members of the committee, Ervin and Baker concluded on July 26 that the best way to break the deadlock with President Nixon over his refusal to grant the committee access to certain records would be to take him to court. The committee was expected to seek a declaratory judgment ordering the President to turn over the tapes and documents.

The constitutional confrontation was arrived at when Nixon refused to hand over the tapes and papers sought in two subpoenas from the committee on July 23. Arguing the doctrines of executive privilege and separation of powers, he replied: "I cannot and will not consent to giving any investigatory body private presidential papers."

The same day the committee was moving toward court action, a U.S. District Court judge in Washington, D.C., signed an order directing Nixon's lawyers to "show cause why there should not be full and prompt compliance" with another subpoena. That subpoena, also seeking tapes and documents related to Watergate, was served on White House lawyers by attorneys working with Archibald Cox, the government's special prosecutor of the case.

In a letter to the judge explaining his reasons for resisting the third subpoena, Nixon wrote that he was following "the example of a long line of my predecessors as President of the United States who have consistently adhered to the position that the President is not subject to compulsory process from the courts."

And so the issue edged toward eventual solution by the Supreme Court, with both sides claiming faith in their legal and ethical positions. Nixon became the second President in U.S. history to be served with a subpoena. The first was Thomas Jefferson, in 1807.

The next step in the litigation probably would be the filing of a petition by the Senate committee in U.S. District Court. Attorneys for the President had until Aug. 7 to reply to the "show cause" order.

A final decision by the Supreme Court, after the appeals processes had been exhausted, was expected within a few months. "The President, just as in other matters, would abide by a definitive decision of the highest court," said a White House spokesman.

As the dispute over records raged on, the Watergate committee hearings continued. The week ended July 28 started with testimony from Gordon C. Strachan, assistant to former White House chief of staff H. R. Haldeman, and continued through four days of testimony by John D. Ehrlichman, Nixon's former domestic affairs adviser. Ehrlichman claimed innocence of wrongdoing in the Watergate scandal and defended an administration-sponsored burglary as legal and justified on national security grounds.

In his opening statement July 24, Ehrlichman spoke of the tumultuous events that led to White House emphasis on security. "Some of these events in 1969 and 1970 included hundreds of bombings of public buildings, a highly organized attempt to shut down the federal government, intensive harassment of political candidates and violent street demonstrations which endangered life and property," he testified.

He defended his old boss, the President: "From close observation I can testify that he is not paranoid, weird, psychotic on the subject of demonstrators or hypersensitive to criticism. He is an able, tough international politician, practical, complex, able to integrate many diverse elements and to see the interrelationships of minute and apparently disassociated particles of information and events."

Part of Ehrlichman's testimony was devoted to refuting claims made earlier before the committee by former White House counsel John W. Dean III. Ehrlichman charged that Dean's statement that Watergate was the "major thing" occurring in the White House from June 17 to Sept. 15, 1972, was "falser than all the other falsehoods" in his testimony.

Witnesses July 20

Robert C. Mardian, political coordinator of the 1972 Nixon re-election campaign and a former assistant attorney general, finished his testimony before the Senate Watergate committee on July 20. He was followed to the witness chair by Gordon C. Strachan, a former White House aide who was liaison between former chief of staff H. R. Haldeman and the re-election committee. *(Mardian opening statement, p. 226; testimony, p. 200, 191)*

Before the committee adjourned for the weekend, Strachan, a young alumnus of Nixon's New York law firm, read a 15-page statement. Cross-examination was put over until the next week. *(Statement text, p. 226)*

Intelligence-Gathering. One of his functions, Strachan told the senators, was the periodic preparation of "political matters" memos for Haldeman. He said he wrote one of those memos in early April 1972, reporting on a March 30 meeting in Key Biscayne, Fla., that he had been told about by Jeb Stuart Magruder, the deputy campaign director.

In the memo, Strachan recalled, he stated: "Magruder reports that 1701 (1701 Pennsylvania Ave. in Washington, the address of re-election committee

(Continued on p. 210)

Conflict Issue is Joined: On to the Supreme Court

For the first time in 166 years, on July 23 an American President was subpoenaed. Richard M. Nixon and Thomas Jefferson are the only two Presidents to share the distinction.

Jefferson was subpoenaed by Chief Justice John Marshall in the treason trial of Aaron Burr in 1807. He was ordered to testify at the trial in Richmond, Va., and to provide certain correspondence. He did not testify, but said he would if the trial were in Washington. And he gave Marshall a letter that the chief justice sought.

Nixon has outdone Jefferson. He was served with three subpoenas from two sources. Two of the subpoenas, one for tape-recorded conversations and the other for written records, came from the Senate Select Committee on Presidential Campaign Activities. The third, for both tapes and papers, came from Archibald Cox, the government's special prosecutor in the Watergate case.

Court Action. White House lawyers were ordered to respond to the subpoenas by 10 a.m. July 26. That morning, Douglas M. Parker of the White House counsel's staff delivered a letter from Nixon to Chief Judge John J. Sirica of U.S. District Court in Washington. The letter was in response to the Cox subpoena.

"I must decline to obey the command of that subpoena," Nixon wrote. "In doing so I follow the example of a long line of my predecessors as President of the United States who have consistently adhered to the position that the President is not subject to compulsory process from the courts.

"The independence of the three branches of our government is at the very heart of our constitutional system. It would be wholly inadmissible for the President to seek to compel some particular action by the courts. It is equally inadmissible for the courts to seek to compel some particular action from the President."

Besides the separation of powers doctrine, the letter declined the command of the subpoena on the basis of executive privilege. Nixon quoted from an 1865 attorney general's opinion to support his position.

He noted that he was voluntarily giving the federal grand jury in Washington a memorandum from W. Richard Howard to Bruce Kehrli, two White House aides, which the jury wanted, and several political memos from former aide Gordon C. Strachan to his boss, former White House chief of staff H.R. Haldeman. But Nixon refused to turn over the requested tapes. "Like all of my predecessors," he wrote, "I have always made relevant material available to the courts except in those rare instances when to do so would be inconsistent with the public interest."

After reading Nixon's letter to the court, Judge Sirica was asked by Cox to sign an order directing the President to "show cause why there should not be full and prompt compliance" with the subpoena. Sirica polled the 20 members of the grand jury who were present, and they unanimously approved the order. Nixon's lawyers were given until Aug. 7 to reply.

Committee Action. At the same time the letter was being delivered to the court, a similar letter was in the hands of Sam J. Ervin Jr. (D N.C.), chairman of the Senate Watergate committee. "I cannot and will not consent to giving any investigatory body private presidential papers," the letter concluded, reaffirming what Nixon had written in letters July 6 and July 23. *(Text, p. 220)*

As in his letter to Sirica, Nixon left open the possibility that he would provide other specific materials upon request of the committee.

On a motion from Vice Chairman Howard H. Baker Jr. (R Tenn.), the committee voted unanimously to authorize its lawyers to go to court. Sometime in the next week, the committee was expected to seek a declaratory judgment in U.S. District Court that would order Nixon to comply with its subpoenas.

"The chair recognizes that there is no precedent for litigation of this nature, but there originally was no precedent for any litigation," said Ervin. "And I think this litigation is essential if we are to determine whether the President is above the law and whether the President is immune from all of the duties and responsibilities in matters of this kind which devolve upon all the other mortals who dwell in this land."

Baker held out hope that "there is some way to ameliorate the situation." He suggested again that a small panel of persons outside government be formed for the purpose of going over tapes and documents and deciding which ones could be given to the committee. This suggestion had been rejected by the committee previously.

The committee action deliberately avoided another course that could have been followed: asking the full Senate to cite Nixon for contempt. Seeking a declaratory judgment would, Baker explained, be quicker and cleaner and "gets away from the emotional issue" of a contempt proceeding.

Supreme Court. The conflict between the administration and its investigators would be resolved eventually by the Supreme Court, weeks or months later. Deputy White House press secretary Gerald L. Warren said July 26 that Nixon would abide by a "definitive" decision of the court. But Charles A. Wright, a White House consultant and University of Texas law professor who was expected to argue the case before the court, said that Supreme Court rulings are not always definitive. Failure of the court to treat the separation of powers issue fully could lead to Nixon's continued refusal to release tapes and documents, he suggested.

Wright said he would like to see the case concluded as quickly as possible. "The sooner we can get to the bottom of Watergate," he said, "the better off the country will be."

"The President is very confident of his constitutional position as outlined in the letters," said deputy press secretary Warren. And, Warren added, he "fully expects his position to be upheld in the courts."

Cox, quoting from an 1803 Supreme Court decision *(Marbury v. Madison)*, differed. Nixon's position "is not legally sound," he said. "Separation of powers from the beginning of history has not disabled a court from issuing orders to the executive branch."

(Continued from p. 208)
headquarters) now has a sophisticated political intelligence-gathering system with a budget of 300."

Enclosed with the memo, said Strachan, was a sample intelligence report entitled "Sedan Chair II." At first, he said, he thought this might have been a code name for a wiretap summary. Not until the Senate hearings in June 1973 did he discover that Sedan Chair was a Republican informer in the campaign of Democratic presidential aspirant Hubert H. Humphrey, he said.

Attending the Key Biscayne meeting were Magruder; John N. Mitchell, then attorney general, and Fred C. LaRue, a campaign aide. Magruder reported to him on about 30 major campaign decisions, said Strachan. His report included few details on intelligence-gathering, and Strachan's subsequent memo to Haldeman contained only one paragraph on the subject, he said.

Destruction of Files. But Strachan said he started to become suspicious after the Watergate break-in June 17, 1972. "I certainly began to wonder who else but people from 1701 could have been involved," he testified. "I suspected that maybe the Watergate break-in was part of the 'sophisticated political intelligence operation' Mr. Magruder had mentioned to me on the phone in early April."

When he phoned Magruder in California, to obtain information for a report to Haldeman, Strachan said, Magruder told him he had been on the phone with Haldeman "and the matter was being taken care of."

Strachan testified that he met with Haldeman June 19 or 20 and showed him the early-April "political matters" memo. After the meeting, according to his opening statement, he destroyed that memo and several other documents, including the "Sedan Chair" report, a $300,000 intelligence budget and three confidential memos that he suspected of being wiretap reports.

Returned Money. After the November election, said Strachan, he returned about $350,000 in cash to Fred LaRue. The cash had been controlled by Haldeman. "I was not told by anyone, nor did I know what use was being made of this money," he said. Others have testified that it was given to defendants in the Watergate criminal trial and to their attorneys.

Originally, Strachan testified, the money had been intended for public-opinion polling in 1972. But, he said, it had not been used for that purpose.

He said he returned the cash to LaRue in two parts in December 1972 and January 1973. The first part, he said, was about $40,000 in two envelopes. Both deliveries were made to LaRue's apartment in the Watergate complex, said Strachan.

On the second delivery, Strachan recalled, LaRue donned a pair of gloves before accepting the bills and said, "I never saw you." And when, on the instructions of White House counsel John W. Dean III, Strachan asked LaRue for a receipt for the money, LaRue refused, according to Strachan. "I don't know if he (Dean) ever got the receipt," said Strachan, "but I imagine he tried to follow up on it, because I have since learned from Mr. Dean's testimony that it was Mr. Haldeman who asked that a receipt be given."

At no time, said Strachan, did Dean or LaRue tell him "what was being done with the money or that payments were being made to the defendants. Neither of them ever asked me to do or say anything that I can interpret as being part of a coverup."

Magruder Relationship. Strachan's testimony conflicted with Magruder's assertions that he had been informed of or involved in the intelligence plans of the Nixon re-election committee. A hostile attitude toward Magruder was evident throughout Strachan's testimony. *(Magruder testimony, p. 135)*

For example, he said in his opening statement: "Had anyone ever heard the details of prostitution, goon squads, kidnapping and wiretaps, he would be unlikely to forget it. I certainly would not forget it. Mr. Magruder never gave me that information and certainly not those details, because if he had, I would immediately have passed it on to Mr. Haldeman, I would remember it and I would be here today testifying about it."

Strachan described the meetings at which the intelligence-gathering proposals of G. Gordon Liddy were discussed "classic examples of poor staff work by the committee and a waste of time." If the meetings had been routinely reported to Haldeman, "as evidence of Mr. Magruder's administrative ability and judgment," he said, "the January and February meetings would not very likely inspire the confidence of Mr. Haldeman or the President."

Witness July 23

Most of the June 23 session of the Senate Watergate hearings was devoted to questioning Gordon Strachan. But the day's highest drama resulted from President Nixon's refusal to give the committee access to his tape-recorded conversations and from the committee's response to that refusal.

Meeting in executive session from the luncheon break until nearly 3:30 p.m., the seven members of the committee unanimously approved a brief resolution to subpoena presidential tapes and other records. *(Text, p. 225)*

In his letter to Chairman Ervin, the President reaffirmed the position he had taken in his July 6 letter denying the committee access to White House records. "Indeed," he wrote, "the special nature of tape recordings of private conversations is such that these principles apply with even greater force to tapes of private presidential conversations than to presidential papers." *(Text, p. 225; text of July 6 letter, p. 189)*

Ervin Comments. When the committee returned to the Senate caucus room after its closed meeting, Ervin announced the subpoena decision and said he deeply regretted it. He took issue with Nixon's interpretation of the doctrines of separation of powers and executive privilege.

In an emotional statement, Ervin said he thought that "high moral leadership demands that the President make available to this committee any information in the form of tapes or records which will shed some light on that crucial question: How did it happen that burglars were caught in the headquarters of the opposition party with the President's campaign funds in their pockets and in their hotel bedrooms at the time? And I don't think the people of the United States are interested so much in abstruse arguments about the separation of powers or executive privileges as they are in finding the answer to that question."

Ervin called the Watergate "the greatest tragedy this country has ever suffered," even greater than the

(Continued on p. 212)

Ervin, Baker Responses to Nixon Denial of Records

Sam J. Ervin Jr. (D N.C.), chairman of the Senate select Watergate committee, and Howard H. Baker Jr. (R Tenn.), the vice chairman, made these comments at the public hearings July 23 after receiving Nixon's letter rejecting the committee's request for access to White House records and tapes:

ERVIN

....This is a rather remarkable letter about the tapes. If you will notice, the President says he has heard the tapes, or some of them, and they sustain his position. But he says he's not going to let anybody else hear them for fear they might draw a different conclusion. *(Letter text, p. 225)*

In other words, the President says that they are suscepible of, the way I construe it, two different interpretations, one favorable to his aides and one not favorable to his aides.

I deeply regret this action of the committee (voting to issue subpoenas of the tapes and records). I have very different ideas of separation of powers from those expressed by the President. If such a thing as executive privilege is created by the doctrine of separation of powers, it has these attributes. First, if it exists at all, it only exists in connection with official duties.

Second, under no circumstances can it be involved in either alleged illegal activities or political campaign activities.

I am certain that the doctrine of separation of powers does not impose upon any President either the duty or the power to undertake to separate a congressional committee from access to the truth concerning alleged criminal activities.

I was in hopes that the President would accede to the request of this committee for these tapes and these papers.

I love my country. I venerate the office of the President, and I have the best wishes for the success of the...present incumbent of that office, because he is the only President this country has at this time.

A President not only has constitutional powers which require him to see to it or to take care that the law be faithfully executed, and I think it's his duty under those circumstances to produce information which would either tend to prove or disprove that criminal activities have occurred. But beyond that, the President of the United States, by reason of the fact that he holds the highest office in the gift of the American people, owes an obligation to furnish a high standard of moral leadership to this nation and his constitutional duties, in my opinion, and undoubtedly his duty of affording moral leadership of the country place upon him some obligation under these circumstances.

We have evidence here that during the time the President was running for re-election to the highest office in the gift of the people of this nation that some of his campaign funds were found in the possession of burglars in the headquarters of the opposition political party. And I think that high moral leadership demands that the President make available to this committee any information in the form of tapes or records which will shed some light on that crucial question: How did it happen that burglars were caught in the headquarters of the opposition party with the President's campaign funds in their pockets and in their hotel bedrooms at the time? And I don't think the people of the United States are interested so much in abstruse arguments about the separation of powers or executive privilege as they are in finding the answer to that question.

I deeply regret that this situation has arisen, because I think that the Watergate tragedy is the greatest tragedy this country has ever suffered. I used to think that the Civil War was our country's greatest tragedy, but I do remember that there were some redeeming features in the Civil War in that there was some spirit of sacrifice and heroism displayed on both sides. I see no redeeming features in Watergate.

BAKER

Mr. Chairman, it is difficult for me to express my disappointment that we arrive at the place where at least the leading edge of a confrontation on the question of separation of powers between the Congress and the White House is before us. You have pointed out, I am sure, that this committee has authorized by unanimous vote the issuance of a subpoena *duces tecum* for certain documents and certain portions of the so-called Butterfield tapes relevant to the inquiry of this committee.

As my colleagues on the committee know, I have tried as hard as I know how to find a way around this confrontation. I have suggested various and several alternative possibilities. Even now, I don't despair of hope that we can find a way to reconcile our differences in the conflict that impends between the Congress and the executive department. But I concur with my colleagues on the committee in the evaluation that there was no other practical course of action except to authorize the action which has now been described, and I voted for it and I support it.

I think the material sought by the subpoena *duces tecum* or, more accurately, by the subpoenas *duces tecum,* are essential, if not vital, to the full, thorough inquiry mandated and required of this committee.

I shall refrain from expressing my evaluation of the entire situation, that is, the totality of the testimony and the inferences to be drawn from it, until we have heard all of the information, all the witnesses, all of the testimony, and examined all of the documents that are made available to us. On Feb. 24, 1974, or prior thereto, if the committee files its report at an earlier date, I will express my conclusions, but not before.

It is my fond hope, however, that when we do finally get to the business of writing a report, that we have all of the available information and that we can in fact write a definitive statement on Watergate—not trying to indict or persecute anyone nor to protect anyone.

The committee has been criticized from time to time for its absence of rules of evidence, the right of confrontation, of cross-examination by counsel, and a number of other legal concepts that we do not have. But we do not have defendants, either, and we are not trying to create defendants. We are trying to find fact, to establish circumstances, to divine the causes, to ascertain the relationships that make up in toto the so-called Watergate affair.

I am unhappy that it is necessary for us to come to the brink of a constitutional confrontation, and although that is a hackneyed phrase, it is an accurate phrase, a constitutional confrontation between the Congress and the White House, a confrontation that has never been resolved in its totality by the courts, a principle and doctrine that has never been fully elaborated and spelled out, in order to fully discharge our obligation as a committee. But I think that is precisely where we are.

I have no criticism of any person. I will not sit in judgment of any person or the conduct of any person until all of the evidence is taken, but I can do no less than try to gain all of the information available on which to base such a conclusion later.

(Continued from p. 210)
Civil War. The war, he said, had some redeeming features such as the spirit of sacrifice and heroism. But, he concluded, "I see no redeeming features in Watergate."

Baker Comments. (Howard H. Baker Jr. (R Tenn.), the committee vice chairman, said the committee had come to "the brink of a constitutional confrontation between the Congress and the White House, a confrontation that has never been resolved in its totality by the courts." While concurring with the committee's demand for the tapes and documents, he said: "Even now, I don't despair of hope that we can find a way to reconcile our differences in the conflict that impends between the Congress and the executive department." *(Ervin, Baker remarks, p. 211)*

Nixon-Ervin Meeting. Nixon and Ervin had agreed by telephone July 12 to meet personally to discuss the availability of White House documents. The meeting was described coolly as a "matter of courtesy" by a White House spokesman, and its date remained indefinite because of the President's hospitalization for pneumonia. *(Earlier story, p. 179)*

The meeting was called off on July 23. "I know of no useful purpose that would be served by our having a meeting at this time," Nixon wrote Ervin that day.

"Well, at long last I have got something I agree with the President on in connection with this matter," Ervin said at the hearings. "If the President does not think there is any useful purpose that can be obtained by our meeting together, I will not dissent from that view, so I will not ask for the privilege of visiting the White House."

Subpoena Delivery. At the end of the day, two lawyers for the Senate select committee delivered the two subpoenas—one for tapes, the other for documents—to the White House. The subpoenas were accepted by presidential counsel Leonard Garment and special counsel J. Fred Buzhardt, who was handling the Watergate case for the administration.

Also served the same day was a third subpoena, from Archibald Cox, the special prosecutor in the Watergate case. Cox's request for tapes had been turned down in a letter sent to him earlier that day by Charles Alan Wright, a consultant to Buzhardt. *(Texts of Cox request, Wright letter, p. 224)*

Haldeman Orders. In his second day of committee testimony, Strachan said in response to questions that he had destroyed intelligence files on Haldeman's instructions. "He told me, 'Well, make sure our files are clean,' " Strachan answered majority counsel Samuel Dash.

"What did that mean to you?" Dash asked.

"Well," Strachan answered, "I went down and shredded that document and others related." After shredding the documents on June 20, he said, he "went over to John Dean's office and give him a list orally of the documents that I had shredded and told him that those had been Mr. Haldeman's instructions."

Intelligence Interest. Strachan described his former boss as being interested in political intelligence, especially regarding Sen. Edward M. Kennedy (D Mass.). In 1971, Strachan said, Haldeman had proposed putting a "24-hour tail" on Kennedy. Strachan said he later was told by Dean that the "tail" had been reduced to "periodic."

By April 1972, according to Strachan, Haldeman's interest in candidates had shifted. At that time, Strachan said, Haldeman ordered him to contact G. Gordon Liddy "and tell him to transfer whatever capability he had from Muskie to McGovern with particular interest in discovering what the connection between McGovern and Sen. Kennedy was."

The only "capabilities" he knew about, Strachan testified, were "plants" in the presidential campaign organization of Sen. Edmund S. Muskie (D Maine). "It was fairly common knowledge that Muskie's driver was either in the pay of the CRP (Committee for the Reelection of the President) or supplying information to us. I presumed that these employees would be transferred over to Sen. McGovern."

Magruder, Dean. Several times as he testified, Strachan contradicted statements made by Magruder. He denied, for example, Magruder's testimony that he had been shown "Gemstone" files. Gemstone was the code word for certain wiretap materials.

Strachan said Magruder, then under investigation for perjury by a federal grand jury, asked him in March to testify that he had intervened on behalf of Liddy when Magruder wanted to fire Liddy. Strachan said he refused.

He also denied testimony by Dean that he had agreed to perjure himself to protect Haldeman and assist in coverup efforts. He did offer to make an inaccurate public statement about his role, but not to testify falsely under oath, he said. Haldeman, he said, told him to tell the grand jury the "absolute truth."

Strachan did not contradict Dean's testimony that the President had known about the Watergate coverup. When asked by Sen. Joseph M. Montoya (D N.M.) if he thought Dean would lie about telling Nixon of the coverup, Strachan answered: "My opinion would be that John Dean would be telling the truth."

Methods of Operation. Charles W. Colson, former special counsel to the President, "emerged, remarkably, from having one staff assistant to having a fairly substantial staff—maybe 20 people," said Strachan. "He seemed to be involved in almost every major decision."

Colson's office, Strachan continued, "was referred to as the Office of Dirty Tricks." It was a "subject of some concern," he said.

Strachan described Haldeman as having a telephone system on which his aides could, if requested, push a button and monitor his conversations without being detected by the person on the other end of the line. This is the way he learned of an April 4, 1972, meeting between Haldeman and John N. Mitchell to which, Strachan said, Haldeman took a "talking paper" prepared by Strachan containing the $300,000 intelligence budget.

Haldeman, Strachan said, was a "well-organized individual" who "had a well-deserved reputation as a very, very tough staff man, and there were constant pressures to perform well, and I worked very hard."

Witness July 24

John D. Ehrlichman told the Senate select Watergate committee that he approved a "covert operation" that resulted in the 1971 break-in at the office of Daniel

Ellsberg's psychiatrist, but insisted that he did not mean to approve a burglary.

The former domestic affairs adviser to the President, who resigned April 30, further told the committee July 24 that both he and President Nixon believed the break-in was well within the President's constitutional powers to protect national security. The Ellsberg break-in was one of the factors that resulted in the mistrial and dismissal of espionage charges against Ellsberg, a former Defense Department official, and a codefendant, Anthony Russo, at their trial in May.

Ehrlichman, one of the star witnesses at the Senate Watergate hearings, spent most of the day explaining his role in the Ellsberg break-in. In other testimony, he denied playing a role in the coverup of the Watergate break-in and engaged in peppery and often heated arguments with Committee Chairman Sam J. Ervin Jr. (D N.C.) and majority counsel Samuel Dash.

Burglary Justification. Ehrlichman testified that when he approved a September 1971 operation aimed at getting a look at Ellsberg's psychiatrist's records, he did not have burglary in mind. The burglary was carried out by G. Gordon Liddy and E. Howard Hunt Jr., members of a special investigations unit set up in the White House to stop security leaks. The unit eventually came to be known as the "plumbers." Hunt and Liddy later were convicted along with five other men for the break-in at Democratic national headquarters in the Watergate building on June 17, 1972.

John D. Ehrlichman

Dash read the witness a memorandum, dated Aug. 11, 1971, from Egil Krogh Jr. and David Young, leaders of the plumbers. Part of the memo contained a recommendation "that a covert operation be undertaken to examine all the medical files still held by Ellsberg's psychoanalyst covering the two-year period in which he was undergoing analysis." On the memo was an "E" indicating Ehrlichman's approval, with the written notation, "if done under your assurance that it is not traceable."

Ehrlichman acknowledged signing the memo, but stated that his understanding of "covert operation" was that the agents seeking the information would not identify themselves as White House employees. He said he assumed the agents (Hunt and Liddy) would get the Ellsberg medical records from nurses or nurses' aides. "I certainly did not" conceive of this as asking for a break-in, he added. Asked why he was anxious that it not be traced to the White House, he replied, "I was not keen on the concept of the White House having investigators in the field." It was not desirable from a public policy point of view, he said.

Nevertheless, Ehrlichman maintained that the burglary was legal for national security reasons. What troubled him about the burglary, he said, was not its apparent illegality, but that he had not authorized it. Ehrlichman said it was his impression that Krogh authorized the Ellsberg break-in. A previous witness, John W. Dean III, a former presidential counsel, testified that Krogh told him his authorization came from the "oval office," meaning the President.

Ehrlichman said that in March President Nixon told him the Ellsberg burglary "was an important, vital national security inquiry well within the constitutional function of the President." The President, however, said in a May 22 statement that he did not authorize the break-in, did not know about it in advance and would have disapproved it if it had been brought to his attention.

Genesis. Ehrlichman said the genesis of the Ellsberg break-in was a problem Krogh, as head of the plumbers, was having with the late FBI Director J. Edgar Hoover. This was shortly after the Pentagon Papers, which Ellsberg admitted stealing, began appearing in newspapers in June 1971.

Krogh came to him, Ehrlichman said, after publication of the papers, complaining that he was having trouble getting Hoover to move more quickly on the FBI investigation of the theft. Then Attorney General John N. Mitchell told him, Ehrlichman testified, that a top man in the FBI had put in a routine request that Ellsberg's father-in-law, Louis Marx, be questioned regarding the theft, but that Hoover, a friend of Marx, had denied the request and planned to demote the official.

Ehrlichman said Mitchell interceded on the official's behalf, but there was no chance the FBI would probe the Pentagon Papers leak. From these facts, said Ehrlichman, it was decided that the plumbers unit would follow up the Ellsberg leads.

Difference with Mitchell. Ehrlichman disagreed with Mitchell's testimony that public knowledge of the Ellsberg break-in before the 1972 elections would have caused Nixon to "lower the boom" on his assistants, resulting in loss of the presidency. Mitchell had described the break-in as one of several White House "horror stories." *(Mitchell testimony, p. 180)*

Ehrlichman, on the other hand, testified that Hunt and Liddy did not do something so irrational that it would have been seriously embarrassing to Nixon. "I think it is clearly understood that the President has the constitutional power to prevent the betrayal of national security secrets," he said, "and that is well understood by the American people, and (if) an episode like that is seen in that context, there shouldn't be any problem."

Then what, Dash asked Ehrlichman, did the President mean in his May 22, 1973, statement when he said he had ordered Ehrlichman to prevent information about the plumbers from becoming known during the Watergate investigation in 1972?

"That relates to some of the subject matters that I am at this point not able to talk to the committee about," replied Ehrlichman. At another point, Ehrlichman declined to answer questions about whether he authorized any wiretaps while at the White House, claiming national security as his reason for not answering. He was the first witness to decline to answer questions for national security reasons.

Wiretaps. Ehrlichman said he had incomplete knowledge of wiretapping carried on at White House orders. He said he was unaware of any wiretaps made at the President's request concerning leaks of U.S. positions on the strategic arms limitation talks (SALT). Ehrlichman said he had some awareness of presidentially authorized wiretapping concerning national security and of taps requested by national security adviser Henry A. Kissinger.

A former assistant attorney general, Robert C. Mardian, had testified the previous week that logs and other wiretap materials from Kissinger-ordered eavesdropping on 17 newsmen and National Security Council employees were removed from the FBI in 1971 and kept in Ehrlichman's office. Ehrlichman said that the materials were kept in his filing cabinet until he left the White House, but that he did not read them or know what they contained until recently. Mardian had testified that he was ordered by Nixon to give the tapes to Ehrlichman, but the former White House aide said he had no knowledge of the President's order. *(Mardian testimony, p. 190)*

Kalmbach. Ehrlichman denied testimony by Herbert W. Kalmbach, Nixon's personal lawyer, that Kalmbach's activities as a fund-raiser for the seven Watergate defendants were legal and proper and that Ehrlichman had encouraged him to continue in that role. Kalmbach stated that in July 1972 he had grown worried about his role as a money-raiser for the defendants and had sought assurances from Ehrlichman. He told the committee he looked Ehrlichman in the eye when he asked him to say whether his activities, carried out under Dean's directions, were proper. *(Kalmbach testimony, p. 193)*

Ehrlichman said he could not recall any such conversation with Kalmbach and added that he never would have asked Kalmbach to do anything shady or illegal. He acknowledged meeting with Kalmbach July 26, 1972, in Washington, but said he was "mortally certain" Kalmbach did not ask him to vouch for his activities.

Clashes with Committee. Ehrlichman argued heatedly with Ervin about the chairman's interpretation of a taped telephone conversation between the witness and Kalmbach before Kalmbach's April 19 appearance before federal Watergate prosecutors. Ervin insisted the tape indicated that it was Ehrlichman alone who had given Kalmbach assurances to continue the fund-raising, but Ehrlichman argued that Ervin was taking the conversation out of context. He said there were references in the conversation to the fact that he (Ehrlichman) had been assured by Dean and Mitchell that what Kalmbach was doing was urgent and proper.

Ervin and Ehrlichman also argued over whether Nixon had the power to authorize the Ellsberg break-in, as Ehrlichman claimed. Ervin insisted such an action violated the Fourth Amendment to the Constitution, but Ehrlichman said national security considerations, plus congressional mandates, provided the authority without violating the Fourth Amendment.

The hearing-room audience repeatedly applauded Ervin's remarks and wisecracks and laughed at some of Ehrlichman's answers. The audience had begun regularly giving Ervin standing ovations when he enters the hearing room for the morning and afternoon sessions.

Ehrlichman also clashed with Dash over definitional matters and Ehrlichman's tendency to answer questions before Dash had propounded them. At one point they disagreed over whether Ehrlichman administered the plumbers in a "literal sense" or an "actual sense."

In claiming innocence of any Watergate coverup role, Ehrlichman said he did not know until March 1973 that Hunt was demanding money to keep silent about his part in the break-in, and he denied Dean's testimony that he had ordered Dean to try to get the Central Intelligence Agency to help out in the coverup.

Concerning the break-in itself, Ehrlichman said he first learned of it June 17, 1972, when a Secret Service official telephoned him at Cape Cod, Mass., where he was vacationing. He said he learned of Hunt's and Liddy's involvement in the break-in during subsequent meetings with Dean, Mitchell and others, but he did not tell the President what he knew at a June 20 meeting. That meeting concerned only legislative affairs in the fields of welfare reform and busing, he testified.

Antipathy to Dean. In his 30-page opening statement, Ehrlichman hit hard at Dean, implying the former presidential counsel had misled the President and himself about White House involvement in the Watergate break-in and coverup. *(Excerpts of text, p. 221)*

Ehrlichman said he asked Dean to inform him about "significant changes or new events in the Watergate case" so that he could deal with the new issues. He said he was busy with domestic policy issues during the latter half of 1972, and only "about one half of one per cent (of his time) was spent on politics and the campaign."

Dean, Ehrlichman said, met with him only 22 times between the break-in and election day (Nov. 7, 1972). Nine of those 22 meetings were held in the first two weeks after the break-in, and fewer than 14 dealt with Watergate, Ehrlichman said.

"John Dean said one thing in his testimony falser than all the other falsehoods" when he said Watergate was the major issue at the White House between June 17 and Sept. 15, 1972, Ehrlichman stated. "I do not suggest

Strachan's Advice to the Young

Gordon C. Strachan, former assistant to White House staff chief H.R. Haldeman, was asked by Sen. Joseph M. Montoya (D N.M.) July 23 about his motivation for coming to work in the White House.

For one thing, Strachan said, he found New York City "a fascinating place to practice law but a disastrous place in which to live." He had been, for two years, a member of the firm in which President Nixon and John N. Mitchell were partners.

"And were you really thrilled and enthused about your assignment here in Washington when you first came here?" Montoya asked.

"Oh, definitely," replied Strachan, who turned 30 on July 24. "To be 27 years old and walk into the White House and seeing the President on occasion, and Dr. Kissinger, and it's a pretty awesome-inspiring (sic) experience for a young man."

Montoya said he was receiving quite a bit of mail from youths concerned about the future of the country and dubious about public service as a career. What advice, he asked, would Strachan offer these young people?

"Well," Strachan responded, "it may not be the type of advice that you could look back and want to give, but my advice would be to stay away."

"I think you have answered it very well," said Montoya.

that we were all just too busy to have noticed. We did notice, and we kept informed through John Dean on the assumption that he was giving us complete and accurate information."

At another point, in departing from his prepared text, Ehrlichman said he was busy on non-Watergate matters from June to September 1972, "but that John Dean never found things so quiet and planned the most expensive honeymoon in the history of the White House staff." This was a reference to testimony by Dean that he borrowed $4,850 in campaign money to pay for his honeymoon.

Witness July 25

Former presidential adviser Ehrlichman contradicted previous testimony by John W. Dean III that he had relayed an offer of executive clemency for the seven Watergate defendants from President Nixon.

Dean, former counsel to the President, had testified in June that he met with Ehrlichman and another former White House aide, Charles W. Colson, on Jan. 3, 1973, and that executive clemency was discussed. According to Dean, Colson urged that one of the defendants, E. Howard Hunt Jr., be promised clemency. On Jan. 4, Dean said, Ehrlichman told him that "he had given Colson an affirmative regarding clemency for Hunt." Dean went on to say that there was another meeting Jan. 5 in Ehrlichman's office at which Colson said he had given Hunt's lawyer, William O. Bittman, "general assurance" of clemency for Hunt rather than a "specific commitment." *(Dean testimony, p. 152)*

Ehrlichman testified on July 25 that Nixon had told him in July 1972 that there would be no clemency for anyone convicted in the Watergate scandal and that he had given no such assurance to Colson. Ehrlichman said Dean was "spinning a tale" about the clemency offer and later agreed with Sen. Edward J. Gurney (R Fla.) that Dean "told an untruth" regarding the clemency offer.

According to Ehrlichman, executive clemency was "obviously at the forefront of everyone's mind" in the Jan. 3 meeting as a potential danger. He said he could not recall who brought it up, but that Colson was disturbed about his friend Hunt. Hunt was about to go to trial in the Watergate break-in case and his wife had been killed the previous month in a plane crash.

Ehrlichman said Colson wanted to express his continued concern about Hunt but was afraid to meet with him personally. It was agreed that Colson would express his sympathy through Bittman, Ehrlichman said, adding that he told Colson there could be no executive clemency.

According to the witness, Colson assured him at a later meeting, possibly Jan. 5, that he (Colson) had not made any promise of executive clemency in his meeting with Bittman, despite Bittman's hints at it.

Ehrlichman charged that Dean had given two false versions of the alleged promise of executive clemency. One version, which Ehrlichman referred to as an "out-of-town tryout in the papers," had Ehrlichman obtaining the President's approval in the midst of the Jan. 3 meeting, he said. But Ehrlichman told the committee the President's logs show no meeting between him and the President that day. The other version, according to Ehrlichman, was the one Dean told the committee. That "won't wash" either, he said, explaining that the only meeting he had with the President Jan. 4 was attended by two other White House officials, H. R. Haldeman and Dr. Henry Kissinger, and that clemency was not discussed.

'Deep Six.' Ehrlichman also denied Dean's testimony that he once ordered Dean to "deep six"—throw in the Potomac river—a briefcase and shred documents found in Hunt's safe after his arrest in the Watergate break-in. Dean testified that he convinced Ehrlichman that the order was wrong and that they eventually agreed that certain of Hunt's materials, including the briefcase, would be turned over to the FBI and that "sensitive documents" would be given to the then acting FBI director, L. Patrick Gray. The documents included a psychological profile of Daniel Ellsberg, the leaker of the Pentagon Papers; fake State Department cables indicating that President Kennedy had ordered the murder of the late South Vietnamese President Ngo Dinh Diem, and the results of a White House probe into the Chappaquiddick incident in which Sen. Edward M. Kennedy's (D Mass.) friend, Mary Jo Kopechne, was killed.

"I did not say 'deep six' the papers," Ehrlichman told the committee, adding that never in his life had he proposed to anyone to shred papers. His method was to burn them, he said. Ehrlichman conceded that he was concerned that the papers would be leaked to the press if turned over to the FBI, but said he never ordered their destruction.

Ehrlichman said he was present when Dean handed Gray the papers, "and I probably chimed in on the subject of leaks." But the "sense of the conversation," he related, was that the purpose of Gray's taking personal possession of the papers was to prevent the FBI from leaking them. Ehrlichman said he first learned the papers had been destroyed when he talked to Gray April 15, 1973.

Judge Byrne. The witness was questioned closely about the offer of the FBI directorship he allegedly made to the federal judge in the Ellsberg trial, W. Matthew Byrne Jr. Questions had been raised whether the offer to Byrne during the trial was unethical and compromising. Ehrlichman defended his actions, saying he was ordered by the President to inquire if Byrne was interested in the post. He maintained that nothing in the legal canons of ethics was violated by his actions.

Ehrlichman said he told Byrne before the first of their two meetings in April that he wanted to talk to him about a non-judicial federal post. Byrne assured him, he said, that it was all right to discuss the matter even though the trial was in progress. Later, when they met at San Clemente, Calif., Ehrlichman first mentioned the FBI job, he said, and Byrne expressed a "very strong interest" in it. Ehrlichman said their second meeting was held at the request of the judge and that Byrne repeated his interest in the post.

To skeptical questioning by Sen. Daniel K. Inouye (D Hawaii), Ehrlichman insisted that his motive in contacting Byrne was not to influence him toward helping get a conviction in the Ellsberg trial. Ellsberg subsequently had all charges against him and another defendant dismissed for other reasons. Ehrlichman said he was surprised that the press and public reacted to his overtures to Byrne as an attempt to influence him.

Hoover Retirement. In other testimony, Ehrlichman said the Nixon administration should have retired the late FBI Director J. Edgar Hoover early in the first term. According to his July 24 testimony, Hoover refused to have the bureau question Louis Marx, Ellsberg's father-in-law and a friend of the director, about Ellsberg's role in the theft and publication of the Pentagon Papers.

Hoover was sincere and patriotic, but fixed in his views, Ehrlichman said. "The administration would have been better off if Mr. Hoover had been retired" before the Marx episode, he said.

Break-in Authority. The hearing July 25 began and ended with a debate between Committee Chairman Ervin and Ehrlichman and his attorney, John J. Wilson. The issue was the President's power to order the break-in of the office of Ellsberg's psychiatrist if done in the interests of national security.

Ehrlichman maintained the President had that power, even though he testified Nixon did not order the break-in. Wilson said the Supreme Court had not decided the matter, but that Congress had given Presidents sweeping powers to root out subversives imperiling national security.

Ervin countered that no law authorized the President to order an illegal act and that the Constitution specifically forbade "unreasonable" searches and seizures. Furthermore, said Ervin, it was Ellsberg who was being investigated, not his psychiatrist.

Ervin for the first time admonished the hearing-room audience July 25 not to show any emotion toward witnesses, committee members or staff. The audience July 24 had repeatedly applauded Ervin's points in questioning witnesses and had laughed or groaned at some of Ehrlichman's responses.

Witness July 26

The Senate select Watergate committee voted unanimously July 26 to go to court to seek a declaratory judgment against President Nixon so that it could gain access to tape recordings and other documents its members believed were relevant to their inquiry. The committee acted after Chairman Ervin read aloud a letter from the President, dated July 25, in which Nixon refused to honor committee subpoenas issued July 23. *(Text of letter, p. 220)*

In an unprecedented public vote, all six senators present approved a motion by Vice Chairman Baker to go to U.S. District Court in Washington and to "take such steps as may be necessary" to secure the materials. Sen. Herman E. Talmadge (D Ga.), who was absent when the vote was taken, later informed the committee of his concurrence in its action.

Conflict with Dean. Meanwhile, John D. Ehrlichman continued his testimony. He repeated his disavowal of any role in the coverup of the break-in at Democratic national headquarters in the Watergate office building. He contradicted testimony by John Dean that Dean never made an investigation for the President that cleared White House employees of complicity in the break-in. *(Dean testimony, Weekly Report p. 152)*

Dean had testified that the first time he had heard of the so-called "Dean report" was after the President mentioned it at a news conference Aug. 29, 1972. But Ehrlichman told the committee that Dean had reported regularly to him on his investigation of potential White House involvement in the break-in and that Ehrlichman had imparted the results of Dean's probe to the President. Ehrlichman said he was "getting nothing but reassurances" from Dean of non-involvement by the White House staff.

Ehrlichman stated that Dean had very good sources of information in the Watergate grand jury room and apparently among the federal prosecutors and that often the White House had 24 to 36 hours of advance notice of new developments in the case. He said Dean also was sitting in on FBI interviews with White House staff members.

Ehrlichman said he considered a meeting among himself, Dean and then Attorney General Richard G. Kleindienst on July 31, the "point of virtual finality" in Dean's probe. On that date, he said, both Dean and Kleindienst reported to him that there had been no White House involvement in the Watergate break-in.

He went to the President sometime after the meeting and informed him of Dean's findings, Ehrlichman said. Asked if that was the basis of the President's Aug. 29 statement, Ehrlichman replied that it was not entirely. He explained that after the Republican convention in August, he urged the President to tell the American people of White House innocence in the break-in.

The President questioned him closely about Dean's report, Ehrlichman testified, asking how certain he (Nixon) could be that the Dean investigation was complete and accurate. "I vouched to him" that he could say the White House alone was clear of complicity, Ehrlichman told the Senate committee. Ehrlichman added that Dean's investigation did not touch on the re-election committee but that he then felt any involvement by high officials of the re-election committee was a "manageable political liability."

Asked how he could be sure of no White House involvement when he knew money was being given to the seven indicted defendants in the Watergate case and their lawyers, Ehrlichman answered that he did not interpret the money as part of a coverup. He said he considered the fund-raising by Herbert Kalmbach "perfectly proper."

Security Plea. Ehrlichman on two occasions declined to answer committee questions about the White House "plumbers" unit, claiming he might compromise national security. The plumbers were a secret investigative unit set up at the President's order to stop leaks of sensitive documents to the press. They included among their members two men, E. Howard Hunt Jr. and G. Gordon Liddy, who later were convicted in the Watergate episode.

Asked by Baker about a paragraph missing from an Aug. 11, 1971, memorandum introduced into evidence, Ehrlichman said he would be violating the law if he revealed what was in that paragraph. He said only that it involved a 1971 investigation not related to Watergate.

Baker also asked what other problems the President referred to the plumbers besides the Pentagon Papers leak, and Erhlichman mentioned leaks concerning the strategic arms limitation talks, an Indian-Soviet treaty, and a fourth matter about which he refused to answer questions. His lawyer, John J. Wilson, then read a letter from White House special counsel J. Fred Buzhardt ordering Ehrlichman to claim executive privilege against answering questions on the matter, "identified only as a fourth instance of activities of the plumbers."

Baker responded that the committee was left in an "untenable position," because the subjects Ehrlichman would not talk about left open the possibility of suspecting that the claim of national security was aimed at covering up wrongdoing. Ehrlichman said he would tell the committee what it wanted to know if the White House released him from the executive privilege directive. Wilson, referring to "colossal" leaks from the committee, said he would ask Buzhardt for permission for his client to answer in executive session before the seven senators.

FBI Resistance. In other testimony, Ehrlichman stuck to his story that the plumbers' break-in at the office of Daniel Ellsberg's psychiatrist, Dr. Lewis Fielding, on Labor Day weekend in 1971 resulted from lack of cooperation by the FBI in probing Ellsberg.

Ehrlichman had testified earlier that the late FBI director, J. Edgar Hoover, had refused permission for bureau agents to interview Ellsberg's father-in-law, Louis Marx, as part of their probe of the Pentagon Papers theft. Sen. Lowell P. Weicker Jr. (R Conn.) told Ehrlichman that Marx had told him in a personal conversation that FBI agents interviewed him in June 1971, well before the break-in at Fielding's office. Ehrlichman said his information about FBI non-cooperation came from John Mitchell and the head of the plumbers, Egil Krogh Jr.

Ehrlichman put heavy stress on Hoover's friendship with Marx to explain his alleged non-cooperation in the Ellsberg probe. To this, Weicker answered that he knew that Hoover and Marx "first met 30 years ago in Dinty Moore's (New York) restaurant and that's the last time they ever met."

"Can I add my hearsay to this?" Ehrlichman responded. He said it was "well known" that Hoover and Marx often met at the Delmar race track in California.

Asked the purpose of the break-in, Ehrlichman said it was intended to satisfy the President, who was asking, "How could this (Pentagon Papers theft) have happened?" and was pressuring Ehrlichman to get information on Ellsberg.

"Are you saying the break-in was to satisfy the President?" Weicker asked. Ehrlichman said he had been misunderstood, that the purpose was to obtain Ellsberg's psychiatric records so that the CIA could work up a psychological profile of the man.

White House Involvement. On another subject, Erhlichman denied part of the testimony of Hugh W. Sloan Jr., Nixon's former re-election campaign treasurer. Sloan testified that he went to Ehrlichman in July 1972 to discuss his fears of possible White House involvement in the Watergate break-in. Sloan said Ehrlichman told him, "Don't tell me any of the details. I don't want to know. My position would have to be until after the election that I would have to take executive privilege." *(Sloan testimony, p. 114)*

Ehrlichman acknowledged the meeting, but said he did not know what Sloan wanted to tell him. After he said he might be involved, Ehrlichman said, "I felt it would be grossly unfair to hear him out until he had taken the advice of an attorney." Ehrlichman said that all he told Sloan was to get legal advice.

Talmadge expressed skepticism about Ehrlichman's testimony at one point, saying he had listened to him for three days and could not believe that he was not aware a coverup was under way after the Watergate break-in and still did not tell the President. The witness responded that he was present when Kleindienst told the President that the "most exhaustive" investigation in the history of the Justice Department had cleared everyone but the seven Watergate defendants of a part in Watergate.

"You didn't operate in a complete vacuum, did you?" asked Talmadge. Ehrlichman said he operated in a "maelstrom of problems," primarily domestic issues, and that he was kept busy 14 to 16 hours a day with his duties.

Ervin, as he had the day before, admonished the hearing room audience against reacting to questions, testimony or other remarks with laughter or applause. He added that the committee would "seriously consider" excluding persons who applauded or otherwise showed emotion during the hearings.

Daily Chronology

Following is a day-to-day chronology of the week's events:

JULY 19

(Earlier July 19 events, p. 204)

Phone Hoax. When the Senate Watergate hearings resumed after the lunch break, Committee Chairman Sam J. Ervin Jr. (D N.C.) announced that Treasury Secretary George P. Shultz had phoned him to say that Nixon would release tapes of his personal and telephone conversations with key figures in the committee's investigation. A few minutes later, Ervin said the call had been a hoax. *(p. 191)*

After the hoax incident, White House sources assured reporters that the President would not reverse his position as stated July 6 in a letter to Ervin. In the letter, Nixon refused to testify before the committee or to give it access to presidential papers. *(Text of letter, p. 189)*

Dean Testimony. Former White House counsel John W. Dean III appeared before the House Intelligence Subcommittee and refused to answer substantive questions relating to the Watergate affair. The subcommittee was investigating Central Intelligence Agency (CIA) involvement in the scandal. Chairman Lucien N. Nedzi (D Mich.) said after the closed session that Dean invoked the Fifth Amendment against self-incrimination 67 times. Nedzi added that his panel had reached "tentative conclusions" about who directed the alleged attempt to use the CIA to cover up the Watergate bugging, but he did not elaborate. *(CIA involvement, p. 117)*

Hoover Warning. Newspaper columnist Andrew Tully revealed that former FBI Director J. Edgar Hoover, who died May 2, 1972, had warned of potential scandal in the Nixon administration during an interview in January 1972. Tully quoted Hoover as saying, "By God, he's (Nixon) got some former CIA men working for him that I'd kick out of my office. Some day, that bunch will serve him up a fine mess."

The Nixon aides Hoover reportedly attacked included former Attorney General John N. Mitchell, former chief counsel Dean and former White House advisers John D. Ehrlichman and H.R. Haldeman—later prime targets of Watergate investigators. Hoover told the columnist he had been "forced to put the kibosh on one crazy intelligence scheme against subversives," apparently the 1970 White House domestic intelligence plan Nixon mentioned in his May 22 statement.

JULY 20

Mardian, Strachan Testimony. The Senate Watergate committee completed its questioning of Robert C. Mardian, a former Nixon re-election committee official and former assistant attorney general. Gordon C. Strachan, a former aide to Haldeman, appeared in the afternoon and read a prepared statement. It included the assertion that Haldeman, Nixon chief of staff until April 30, was informed more than two months before the June 17, 1972, break-in that the Nixon re-election committee had set up "a sophisticated political intelligence-gathering system." *(p. 210)*

Nixon Remarks. Nixon, recovered from his bout with viral pneumonia, stopped off at the White House on his way from the hospital to Camp David. "What we were elected to do, we are going to do, and let others wallow in Watergate," he told a group of staff members assembled in the rose garden to greet him. *(p. 191)*

Ehrlichman Interview. Interviewed on British Independent Television, Ehrlichman, Nixon's former domestic affairs adviser, said he was "delighted" to learn of the existence of the White House tapes and said they "certainly" should be given to the committee.

Liddy Citation. The House Intelligence Subcommittee voted to cite convicted Watergate conspirator G. Gordon Liddy for contempt of Congress after he refused to take an oath as a witness at subcommittee hearings on CIA Watergate involvement. Liddy, who had consistently refused to tell the courts or other forums anything about the Watergate affair, was serving a contempt of court sentence for refusing to answer grand jury questions about the June 17 break-in.

Illegal Contribution. Special Watergate prosecutor Archibald Cox announced that the chairman of Ashland Oil Company of Kentucky had admitted that the firm contributed $100,000 in corporate funds, solicited by Nixon fund-raiser Herbert W. Kalmbach, to the 1972 Nixon campaign. Federal law prohibits corporate contributions to political campaigns. The oil company was the second to make such a disclosure—American Airlines July 6 was the first. At that time, Cox called on other companies to volunteer information on possible campaign law violations. *(Airline contribution, p. 187)*

JULY 21

White House Mood. An article in *The Washington Post* quoted White House sources as saying Nixon and his top aides viewed the Senate Watergate hearings as a "political witch-hunt."

Taping Ends. The Post also reported that the automatic taping of conversations in the oval office and other White House rooms, started in 1971 ostensibly for historical purposes, had been halted. In his July 16 letter to the Senate committee confirming the existence of the tapes, White House counsel Buzhardt said the recording system was "still in use." The White House later confirmed the Post report.

Poll Report

President Nixon continues to be hurt in the eyes of the American public as a result of the Watergate scandal. The three latest polls indicate that both his popularity and confidence in his performance have been severely damaged. *(Earlier poll report, p. 181)*

Popularity. A Gallup Poll published July 22 showed Nixon's popularity at its lowest level since he took office. It was down 5 percentage points since the previous survey a few weeks earlier.

Gallup noted that Nixon's 28-point decline in popularity since January was the sharpest drop for a President during a six-month period since the mid-1930s. But President Johnson's lowest rating of 35 per cent in August 1968 was 5 points below Nixon at this time, Gallup reported.

Interviewers July 6-9 asked 1,544 adults: "Do you approve or disapprove of the way Nixon is handling his job as President?"

	Latest	June 22-25
Approve	40%	45%
Disapprove	49	45
No opinion	11	10

Impeachment. The same survey, published July 23, asked: "Should President Nixon be compelled to leave office?"

	Latest	June 22-25
Yes	25%	18%
No	62	71
No opinion	14	11

Nixon vs. Committee. For a Harris Survey published July 25, interviewers asked 1,484 persons July 18-22: "Do you think President Nixon was more right or more wrong to refuse to testify personally before the U.S. Senate Watergate committee?"

More right	37%
More wrong	51
Not sure	12

Another Harris question: "Do you think the President was more right or more wrong to refuse to turn over White House files to the...committee?"

More right	30%
More wrong	60
Not sure	10

JULY 22

Nixon-Ervin Conversation. According to authoritative sources at the Senate investigating committee, as quoted in *The New York Times,* Nixon was in an "emotional state" during his July 12 telephone conversation with Committee Chairman Ervin—and told Ervin he thought the committee was "out to get him." Ervin made the call to plead with the President to release White House documents the panel had requested, but Nixon refused. *(Meeting agreement, p. 179)*

Brennan on Tapes. Secretary of Labor Peter J. Brennan, speaking on ABC-TV's "Issues and Answers," said he could understand AFL-CIO President George Meany's irritation upon learning that Nixon was recording conversations in the White House. "I don't condone people taping conversations without the other person knowing about it," Brennan said.

JULY 23

Nixon Refusal. In a letter to Sen. Ervin, the President turned down the committee's request for access to White House tape recordings. To do so, he wrote, would be a violation of the constitutional doctrine of separation of powers. *(Text, p. 225)*

Ervin made public a separate, private letter Nixon sent him, saying he could see "no useful purpose" for a meeting between Ervin and himself, which he had agreed to on July 12. Nixon wrote that he was willing to go ahead with the meeting if Ervin insisted, but Ervin said he would not. *(Hearings, p. 212)*

Special prosecutor Cox, who also had requested access to the tapes, received a letter from special White House consultant Charles Alan Wright refusing the request. *(Text, p. 224)*

Subpoenas. Nixon's refusal to relinquish the disputed tapes precipitated what many persons agreed was a constitutional crisis that would end up in the Supreme Court. The Senate investigating committee decided unanimously at a noon meeting to subpoena the tapes and other White House documents relevant to its inquiry. Announcing the decision, Ervin described the Watergate affair as "the greatest tragedy this country had ever suffered." Vice Chairman Howard H. Baker (R Tenn.) expressed distress at being "on the brink of a constitutional confrontation between the Congress and the White House." *(p. 212)*

Cox announced he would seek a subpoena of tapes of eight specific White House conversations. Three subpoenas—two from the Senate committee requesting tapes and other documents and one from the prosecutor—were accepted at the White House by counsels Leonard Garment and J. Fred Buzhardt. The requests called for a response by July 26. The White House was expected to ignore or oppose the subpoenas, thereby forcing the conflict into the courts. *(p. 209)*

Strachan Testimony. Haldeman's former aide, Strachan, was questioned by the Senate committee. He said that three days after the Watergate break-in, under what he believed to be instructions from Haldeman, he destroyed documents indicating that Haldeman knew G. Gordon Liddy was conducting a political intelligence operation for the Nixon re-election committee. *(p. 208)*

JULY 24

Ehrlichman Testimony. John D. Ehrlichman, Nixon's former domestic affairs adviser, read a prepared statement to the Senate investigating committee saying he welcomed the opportunity to "refute every charge of illegal conduct on my part." During the stormy interrogation session, Ehrlichman defended the break-in at the office of Daniel Ellsberg's psychiatrist on grounds that Ellsberg may have been passing government secrets to foreign powers. *(Testimony, p. 212; text excerpts, p. 221)*

Tapes Dispute. White House deputy press secretary Gerald L. Warren told reporters there was "no question that the President has abided by court rulings in the past" and that he would do so in the future. His remarks were interpreted to mean the President expected the dispute over access to White House tapes to be settled in the courts. Attorney General Elliot L. Richardson issued a statement urging both sides to seek "some practical means of reconciling the competing public interests at stake," but saying that Nixon had acted with "substantial legal and constitutional foundation" in refusing to release the tapes.

Bellino Charge. Republican National Chairman George Bush made public three affidavits which he said contained information indicating that Carmine S. Bellino, chief investigator for the Senate Watergate committee, had recruited spies to help defeat Nixon in the 1960 presidential campaign. Bush said he was not releasing the affidavits "to justify Watergate" but in the interest of "fair play." Bellino, who worked on the 1960 campaign of John F. Kennedy, labeled the allegations "absolutely false."

Common Cause Suit. U.S. District Judge Joseph C. Waddy ordered the Finance Committee to Re-elect the President to make public "a complete and accurate" account of its receipts and expenditures in the 15-month period before the new election campaign financing law took effect April 7, 1972. The order was the result of a lawsuit filed Sept. 6, 1972, by Common Cause, the "citizens' lobby." The judge told the finance committee to release the information by Sept. 28.

JULY 25

Ehrlichman Testimony. In his second day before the Senate Watergate committee, Ehrlichman denied charges linking him to the Watergate coverup and insisted that he never had sought executive clemency for E. Howard Hunt Jr., one of the convicted conspirators. The hearings began with an hour-long debate between Ehrlichman's lawyer, John J. Wilson, and Committee Chairman Ervin on whether the President had the inherent power to break the law if he believed national security was endangered. *(Testimony, p. 215)*

Reaction. Ehrlichman's testimony on the Ellsberg case touched off a series of denials from all sides involved in the case. Interviewed in Los Angeles, Daniel Ellsberg labeled as "slanderous" and "absolutely false" Ehrlichman's charge that he turned the Pentagon Papers over to the Soviet embassy.

U.S. District Judge W. Matthew Byrne Jr. of Los Angeles, who dismissed the Pentagon Papers case May 11 because of government misconduct, issued a statement contradicting key points of Ehrlichman's testimony about the White House offering him the directorship of the FBI during the trial. Byrne said he had repeatedly told Ehrlichman he could not discuss the matter during the trial. Ehrlichman had testified that Byrne expressed a "strong interest" in the position.

Los Angeles District Attorney Joseph Busch, who was conducting a grand jury investigation of the Ellsberg burglary, said the panel's work "will not be impeded by any claim that President Nixon regarded the burglary as legally justifiable." At the White House, deputy press secretary Gerald L. Warren told reporters Nixon would stand on the position taken in the President's May 22 statement, that he did not authorize, know of in advance or condone the Ellsberg break-in. *(Text, p. 90)*

JULY 26

Subpoenas. The constitutional conflict over White House tapes appeared headed toward the Supreme Court, as Nixon rejected subpoenas from the Senate investigating committee and the special prosecutor demanding access to tapes and papers. The President's decision came in letters delivered in the morning to prosecutor Archibald Cox and the Senate committee. In his letter to the committee, which Ervin read at the start of the hearings, the President offered to consider requests for specific White House documents but refused to turn over the tapes. Ervin said the committee probably would seek a declaratory judgment to require the President to comply with the subpoenas. *(Letter text, below)*

Special prosecutor Cox moved immediately to force the issue into the courts. At his request, U.S. District Judge John J. Sirica signed a show cause order directing the Nixon administration to indicate why the tapes should not be turned over by Aug. 7. Cox said he was acting on orders of the Watergate grand jury, which was polled in the courtroom by Sirica. *(Details, p. 209)*

Ehrlichman Testimony. Former Nixon domestic affairs adviser Ehrlichman testified for a third day before the Senate investigating committee. He said the White House "plumbers" group that broke into the office of Ellsberg's psychiatrist in 1971 was formed in response to constant pressure from the President for information on Ellsberg that the FBI could not provide. *(p. 216)*

NIXON LETTER ON SUBPOENAS

Following is the text of a letter written on July 25 by President Nixon to Chairman Sam J. Ervin Jr. of the Senate Watergate committee in response to the two subpoenas served on the White House by the committee on July 23:

Dear Mr. Chairman:

White House counsel have received on my behalf the two subpoenas issued by you, on behalf of the Select Committee, on July 23rd.

One of these calls on me to furnish to the Select Committee recordings of five meetings between Mr. John Dean and myself. For the reasons stated to you in my letters of July 6th and July 23rd, I must respectfully refuse to produce those recordings.

The other subpoena calls on me to furnish all records of any kind relating directly or indirectly to the "activities, participation, responsibilities or involvement" of 25 named individuals "in any alleged criminal acts relating to the Presidential election of 1972." Some of the records that might arguably fit within that subpoena are Presidential papers that must be kept confidential for reasons stated in my letter of July 6th. It is quite possible that there are other records in my custody that would be within the ambit of that subpoena and that I could, consistent with the public interest and my Constitutional responsibilities, provide to the Select Committee. All specific requests from the Select Committee will be carefully considered and my staff and I, as we have done in the past, will cooperate with the Select Committee by making available any information and documents that can appropriately be produced. You will understand, however, I am sure, that it would simply not be feasible for my staff and me to review thousands of documents to decide which do and which do not fit within the sweeping but vague terms of the subpoena.

It continues to be true, as it was when I wrote you on July 6th, that my staff is under instructions to cooperate fully with yours in furnishing information pertinent to your inquiry. I have directed that executive privilege not be invoked with regard to testimony by present and former members of my staff concerning possible criminal conduct or discussions of possible criminal conduct. I have waived the attorney-client privilege with regard to my former Counsel. In my July 6th letter I described these acts of cooperation with the Select Committee as "genuine, extensive and, in the history of such matters, extraordinary." That cooperation has continued and it will continue. Executive privilege is being invoked only with regard to documents and recordings that cannot be made public consistent with the confidentiality essential to the functioning of the Office of the President.

I cannot and will not consent to giving any investigatory body private Presidential papers. To the extent that I have custody of other documents or information relevant to the work of the Select Committee and that can properly be made public, I will be glad to make these available in response to specific requests.

NIXON ROSE GARDEN SPEECH

Following is a transcript of the remarks President Nixon made to about 200 members of his staff on July 20 in the White House rose garden after his release from Bethesda Naval Hospital, where he had spent a week for treatment of viral pneumonia:

Thank you very much for your very warm welcome.

I had heard that while I was out at Bethesda that you were all working, and here you are outside. (Laughter)

However, I do want you to know that, after a week away from the White House, it is very good to be back, and particularly good to be back to see all of you.

As I was at Bethesda, I realized that this was the first time in 13 years I had been in the hospital except for my physical examinations. The other time was in the year 1960 when, some of you may recall, I had a knee infection and was at Walter Reed for two weeks.

I told the staff at Bethesda that I got out perhaps a day or two earlier, not because their medication, which was excellent, and their competence, which was superb, but because their spirit lifted me. And I can assure you another reason I am back a little bit early is that your spirit lifts me and I am most grateful for the fact that while I was there, a few papers used to come out, you know, the things you send out to me that I sign without looking at. (Laughter)

In any event, I do want you to know that just the thought that while I was away that the White House was going forward, that all the work was being done, that everything that needed to be done for this country was going forward as I would have wanted it to go forward, and as the people would want it to go forward, that really helped me get back. And I thank you very much for all those extra hours so many of you put in during that time.

As you can imagine, while I was there, I had a lot of chance to think, to sleep, to rest. It is a little difficult, I must say, to do some of those things when you are not used to it. I mean I am used to thinking but—(laughter)—not sleeping and resting.

Also, I had a chance to go through some of the mail Rose sent out to me, selected mail and wires from all over the country. It seems that nothing really touches people more than illness. You know, if you want to talk to somebody and you say, "How are you feeling?" they usually tell you. Then things really get going. So, as far as this was concerned, I found that I must have heard from everybody in this country who had had pneumonia, and believe me, there are a lot of them that have had pneumonia. (Laughter)

All of them touched me, but I, as usual, tried to pick one out I thought was particularly interesting. It would come from California, as you might imagine, Livermore, Calif., up north. I campaigned it many years ago, in 1950, when it was a small town. It has grown up a little now. It is from an 8-year-old and he prints it.

He writes: "Dear President Nixon: I heard you were sick with pneumonia. I just got out of the hospital yesterday with pneumonia and I hope you did not catch it from me." (Laughter and applause)

"Now you be a good boy and eat your vegetables like I had to." I hate vegetables, but I will eat them. "If you take your medicine and your shots, you will be out in eight days like I was. Love, John W. James III, 8 years old."

Well, John W. James III, I got out in seven days, so did a little bit better than he did. But perhaps my case of pneumonia was not as difficult as his. I will take his advice. I will eat my vegetables. Try now and then to take the shots—maybe not the kind of shot that he takes, but who knows—(laughter)—Walter Tkach is my adviser in that respect.

But in any event, there is one bit of advice I am not going to take, and I will not take too much of your time to tell you about that advice, because this is a very serious vein—it will be of interest to our friends in the press, to the whole nation and to the thousands who have written me, and it will disturb my very good corps of doctors who were advising me to do this, do that, and so forth and so on—that is, they said, "Mr. President, now look, you have excellent health, you have been very fortunate that you have established a modern record of 4½ years in the White House without having missed a day because of illness, but you have got to realize you are human. You can't press yourself so much, and what you have to do is to slow down a little now and take some time off and relax a little more."

I just want you to know what my answer to them was and what my answer to you is. No one in this great office at this time in the world's history can slow down. This office requires a President who will work right up to the hilt all the time. That is what I have been doing. That is what I am going to continue to do, and I want all of you to do likewise.

I know many say, "But then you will risk your health." Well, the health of a man is not nearly as important as the health of the nation and the health of the world.

I do want you to know that I feel that we have so little time in the positions that all of us hold, and so much to do. With all that we have to do and so little time to do it, at the end of the next 3½ years to look back and think: But for that day, something went undone that might have been done that would have made a difference in whether we have peace in the world or a better life at home. That would be the greatest frustration of all.

I don't say this heroically, because I know that every man who has ever been in this position feels exactly the same way and has felt as I do.

So, I want you to know when I come back from Camp David Monday morning, it is going to be full tilt all the way, and we want all of you to work that way, too.

Another bit of advice, too, that I am not going to take—oh, it really isn't advice. I was rather amused by some very well-intentioned people who thought that perhaps the burdens of the office, you know, some of the rather rough assaults that any man in this office gets from time to time, brings on an illness and, after going through such an illness, that I might get so tired that I would consider either slowing down or even, some suggested, resigning.

Well, now, just so we set that to rest, I am going to use a phrase my Ohio father used to use. Any suggestion that this President is ever going to slow down while he is President or is ever going to leave this office until he continues to do the job and finishes the job he was elected to do, anyone who suggests that, that is just plain poppycock.

We are going to stay on this job until we get the job done. (Applause)

Because after all, you see, when we put all of the events that we read about, the things we see on television, in perspective and then we think of the ages, we think of the world, and not just our own little world. We think of the nation, and not only our little part of that nation. We realize that here in this office is where the great decisions are going to be made that are going to determine whether we have peace in this world for years to come. We have made such great strides toward that goal.

It is going to determine whether there is a chance that this nation can have a prosperity without war and without inflation, something we have not had since President Eisenhower was President, and we are making progress toward the goal.

It is going to determine whether or not this nation is going to be on a course that we all worked for, a course in which, rather than having the rate of crime escalating in this nation, the use of dangerous drugs destroying our young people, that we win those battles which we have launched and carried on. It is going to determine whether programs we have to provide fair and better opportunity for all Americans are going to have a chance, whether they are carried forward.

There are these and other great causes that we were elected overwhelmingly to carry forward in November of 1972. And what we were elected to do, we are going to do, and let others wallow in Watergate. We are going to do our job. (Applause)

EHRLICHMAN'S OPENING STATEMENT

Following are excerpts from the prepared text of the opening statement made by John D. Ehrlichman, President Nixon's former domestic affairs adviser, before the Senate Watergate committee on July 24:

INTRODUCTION

At the time of my resignation I assured the President that I intended to spend such time and personal resources as I had in the statement of the truth of these matters now before this committee. As I will describe, I have willingly and fully testified before several other official inquiries.

Because I sincerely do not believe I am guilty of any wrongdoing, I have not invoked the Fifth Amendment, nor have I attempted to negotiate "immunity" for myself from anyone.

A member of this committee, Senator Inouye, suggested by a question he asked that I had invoked executive privilege in some forum and thereby had sought to avoid ansering questions. Only the President can invoke that privilege. On the occasion referred to, the President had established certain guidelines which are no longer in effect. Thus, I will try to fully answer all questions put to me by the committee within the new executive privilege guidelines.

I welcome this opportunity to lay out the facts and publicly set the record straight on a number of questions. Some have been legitimately raised; others are created by leaks to the press, falsehoods and misunderstandings.

I am here to refute every charge of illegal conduct on my part which had been made during the course of these hearings, including material leaked to the news media.

I have testified fully before three grand juries—one in this city, one in New York and one in Los Angeles. I have given my deposition in civil cases to which I am not a party. I have testified before other committees of the House and Senate. I have had an off-the-record, non-public meeting with the staff of this committee, and I have been interviewed by agents of the Federal Bureau of Investigation on a number of occasions. In addition, on request of the staff of this committee, I have made available pertinent records in my possession, including transcripts of telephone conversations and meetings which I had with various people in the course of an inquiry conducted for the President.

Finally, when requested by the staff, I supplied my complete financial records and tax returns from Jan. 1, 1969. I did this despite my attorneys' advice that the scope and authority of this committee is limited to a study of the extent to which illegal, improper or unethical activities were engaged in by persons "in the presidential election of 1972, or any campaign, canvass or other activity related to it."

DEMONSTRATIONS AND THE CLIMATE

.... Mr. Dean began his statement with a somewhat superficial but gallery-pleasing repetition of the old story about fear and paranoia in the Nixon White House. Why, Mr. Dean wondered, was there all that overplayed concern about hippies coming to Washington to march peacefully down Pennsylvania Avenue? Mr. Dean's explanation is simply that we were all suffering from advanced forms of neurosis, and nothing else—some strange White House madness. He suggests he was the only sane one in the bunch.

Since he began his statement there, let me take up that subject briefly. I submit that on this general subject there are some realities of governmental life to be weighed in your deliberations.

From its first days, the Nixon administration sought a stable peace abroad and a return of our POWs from Southeast Asia; to get these results required the President to undertake foreign policy moves and initiatives which were completely interrelated and extremely delicate. In pursuit of this result, we necessarily gave earnest attention to the staffing of critical government positions with people loyal to the President's objectives. And the problems of leaks, demonstrations, bombings and terrorism, public opinion and congressional support were understandably on the President's mind.

Today the presidency is the only place in the nation where all the conflicting considerations of domestic and international politics, economics and society merge; it is there that street violence and civil rights and relations with Russia and their effect on China and the Cambodian military situation and a thousand other factors and events are brought together on the surface of one desk and must be resolved.

Some of these events in 1969 and 1970 included hundreds of bombings of public buildings, a highly organized attempt to shut down the federal government, intensive harassment of political candidates and violent street demonstrations which endangered life and property.

Taken as isolated incidents, these events were serious. Taken as a part of an apparent campaign to force upon the President a foreign policy favorable to the North Vietnamese and their allies, these demonstrations were more than just a garden-variety exercise of the First Amendment.

Just as, and because, they affected the President's ability to conduct foreign policy, they required the President's attention and concern. Had he and his staff been ignorant of the significance of such a campaign, or merely indifferent, they would have been subject to the proper criticism of all citizens interested in securing a stable peace in Southeast Asia and the return of our POWs.

But the President did understand these events to be important in the over-all foreign policy picture, and they received balanced attention along with other events and factors.

In 1969 the President took this nation into a new international era in which the stakes were extremely high. From close observation I can testify that he is not paranoid, weird, psychotic on the subject of demonstrators or hypersensitive to criticism. He is an able, tough international politician, practical, complex, able to integrate many diverse elements and to see the interrelationships of minute and apparently disassociated particles of information and events.

WHY DIDN'T EVERYONE KNOW ALL ABOUT WATERGATE?

It has been my experience that, in the trial of a long lawsuit with a great number of witnesses, it becomes hard for the lawyers, witnesses, judge and jury to remember that anything else ever happened in the community back at the time of the disputed event except that event itself. The collapse of a tunnel, collision of the trains or breach of the contract in the case which is being tried in court always appears to have occupied the very center of the stage at the time. I sense some of that shrinkage of perspective in a few of the questions here and in some of the comments of the network people on the television.

Here is what appears to be this great big thing, a burglary, a "coverup," "horrors" all going on, and witness after witness goes over the exquisite details of a few meetings, phone calls, memos and conversations, day after day here. One begins to think, surely all of this could not possibly have passed unseen by anyone of even average awareness. How, then, could people on the White House staff have failed to know all of these so-obvious and often repeated and significant details, and failed to blow the whistle on the wrongdoers long before the ninth month?

John Dean said one thing in his testimony...falser than all the other falsehoods therein, when he said: (The Watergate) "was probably the major thing that was occurring at this point in time (in the White House between June 17 and Sept. 15, 1972)."

To demonstrate the absurdity of that important misstatement, I need only briefly develop a few facts which are perhaps a broader view of the months following June 17, 1972, than Mr. Dean is willing to take for his purposes. I would like briefly to describe the White House, my experience there, and say a few things about the presidency in order to make more understandable some of the questions before you, including access to the President, Mr. Dean's role and who reported to whom. And you need a clearer picture then you've had so far of what was really going on at the White House in June 1972 and following months.

I do not suggest that we were all just too busy to have noticed. We did notice, and we kept informed through John Dean on the assumption that he was giving us complete and accurate information.

But it is important to know that, in today's White House, there must be, and there is, a heavy delegation of responsibility and duties.

It goes to the question: How could all of this have been avoided?

And it goes to the important point that a chain of delegation is only as strong as its weakest link.

WHITE HOUSE COUNSEL 1969-1970

I came to the White House as counsel to the President from a private, civil law practice in Seattle, Wash. I took a substantial financial cut to come into the government. I came because the President asked me to, and because I became convinced that there was an opportunity to really accomplish things for the country by assisting him....

... the counsel is a vital link in a chain of delegation. In my view, one in that position must bring to the job sufficient training and experience to know what to do and when to do it.

The counsel also has always had political duties. The President is the nation's chief executive. But he is also, by long-standing tradition, his political party's leader. Any President has a political role to play, whether he is going to run for re-election or not. But if he is a candidate, then he is both an executive and a practicing politician. Every such politician wants information. And the President, in his politician role, is no different from the others. He needs and wants information about issues, supporters, opponents and every other political subject known to man.

For the year 1969, to 1970, when I left the post of counsel, I attempted to gather some purely political information for the President, as I was expected to do. Out of real concern for the proprieties, I attempted to use only conventional, non-governmental sources of information. As one might hire political aides in a political campaign, Tony Ulasewicz was hired to do this chore of information gathering. He was paid from existing Nixon political money, by check, under an appropriate employer's tax number. Among other assignments, he scouted the potential opposition for vulnerability. So far as I am aware, during my tenure as counsel, Mr. Ulasewicz conducted his assignments legally and properly in all respects.

ASSISTANT TO THE PRESIDENT

.... In early 1970 my job had changed. I left the counsel's office and became one of the several assistants to the President. My assignment was domestic affairs, and those of us working in that area were given the job of bringing to the President those presidential decisions which required his attention, along with as much information, advice and opinion as we could gather, to enable him to consider an issue broadly....

As many here know, not everyone on the executive branch in the first term shared these (presidential) goals. There were a number of hold-overs in the executive branch who actively opposed the President's policies, especially his foreign policy, but also in the area of domestic affairs, I can assure you.

These people conducted a kind of internal guerrilla warfare against the President during the first term, trying to frustrate his goals by unauthorized leaks of part of the facts of a story, or of military and other secrets, or by just plain falsehood. The object was to create hostility in the Congress and abroad and to affect public opinion. Henry Kissinger, Secretary Rogers and others were seriously concerned that this internal sabotage of administration policy could actually ruin our chances to negotiate a strategic arms limitation treaty and terminate the Vietnam situation on a stable basis, for example. A similar threat to a good result in Vietnam was posed by the combination of street demonstrations, terrorism-violence and their effect on public and congressional support for the President's policy.

THE PRESIDENT AND POLITICS

In his 1960 campaign, Mr. Nixon was involved in every minute detail. In 1968, I agreed to manage the campaign tour only after securing his promise that he would completely delegate detailed control of the advance work, logistics and schedule. And his participation in these details was minimal in 1968.

In 1972, with the foreign situation as it was, the President decided quite early that he simply could not and would not involve himself in the day-to-day details of the presidential primaries, the convention and campaign. He made a very deliberate effort to detach himself from the day-to-day strategic and tactical problems. And so the regular work of the White House relating to government and the nation's problems continued unabated. If anything, we on the domestic side were busier with the President than in other years.

In 1972, the President had to delegate most of his political role, and it went to people not otherwise burdened with governmental duties. As a result, I saw very little of the campaign activity during the spring and early summer of 1972. The President asked me to be sure that the campaign organization and the national committee said or did nothing inconsistent with administration policy. And so I had a few meetings with the CRP (Committee for the Re-election of the President) people to explain existing domestic policy....

I began to spend more time with Ron Ziegler in the late spring of 1972, helping him to understand the campaign issues, reviewing the research with him, etc. It became more important than ever for me to keep ahead of developments, and I asked Mr. Dean to inform me as early as possible of significant changes, or new events in the Watergate case, so Ron Ziegler and I could deal with new issues which would be arising in the press. It was for this purpose that I talked to Dean about Watergate in most instances.

In addition, the President formed an advisory group which met twice a week to look at the campaign in overview and discuss any needed changes. Attending these Monday and Thursday morning meetings were Clark MacGregor, John Mitchell, Bob Haldeman, Bryce Harlow, Charles Colson and I. Presumably, I was the substantive issue man in the group. Since Watergate was a campaign issue, it was discussed in these meetings; it was never a major subject of discussion, however, and if anyone in the group knew more than the others, he didn't share his secrets there....

CONCLUSION

I do not write many memoranda. Most of my staff communication in the White House took place in person or on the telephone. And my work pattern was such that I ordinarily took direct phone calls only from those with whom I share direct phone lines: the President, George Shultz, Ken Cole, Bob Haldeman and Cap Weinberger.

The committee has had the log of how I spent my office time over the years. As it shows, the vast percentage of my time was devoted to domestic policy issues. Great blocks of time were consumed by a single problem or issue. Literally half of November and half of December 1972 were devoted to a reorganization of the executive branch and many personnel changes. Much of the impounding and budget cut and veto strategy unveiled by the President in January 1973 was also developed in those two months, as a result of decisions made by the President in a series of long sessions in September, October and November 1972.

I have attempted in this statement to show you the personal context in which I worked in the White House during the last three years. I had heavy duties in a rather specific area of concern. I was not a generalist once I ceased being counsel to the President in 1970.

Nor was I anyone's Siamese twin during those years. Listening to the star witness "hyphenate" me for five days, I began to know a little of how a caboose feels. Mr. Dean repeatedly and facilely would testify—"and so I informed Haldeman-and-Ehrlichman of so-and-so"—as if that were possible to do with one call or drop-by. It could not really happen, and in virtually every case to which he referred in testimony, it did not happen.

And how much time did I actually spend with Mr. Dean learning about the break-in or keeping abreast of developments to assist Ron Ziegler on the issues, or anything else, for that matter, in the weeks following Watergate?

We invariably met either in my office, or more rarely in Mr. Haldeman's (with the exception of just three or four meetings).

The logs for these two offices demonstrate the frequency of my meetings with Mr. Dean.

Remember: Dean testified that keeping Watergate covered up was a tremendous drain of my time and told of all the conferences and meetings I was having with him about it. Let's be clear: I did not cover up anything to do with Watergate. Nor were Mr. Dean and I keeping steady company during all those weeks....

(Ehrlichman submitted a list of 22 meetings with Dean between June 17 and Nov. 7, 1972.)

It should be noted that this is the total number of our contacts on *all subjects, not just Watergate.* These were *all* contacts, including group meetings....

Now, on this Siamese twin business, Mr. Haldeman and I had vastly different duties, areas and methods of operation. On many occasions he would be away when I was in the office, and many days he was there and I was gone. He invariably traveled with the President; I did not.

I did many things with and for the President, especially in the legislative and policy area, of which Mr. Haldeman was not aware.

Similarly, I had very little knowledge of what he was doing day by day.

I had a number of talks with Mr. Dean about Watergate to keep posted on the campaign issues, which I never had occasion to mention to Mr. Haldeman, but about which I talked to others, Mr. Ziegler for example.

I simply want to make the point that Mr. Haldeman and I live very separate lives and careers in and out of the office, Mr. Dean to the contrary notwithstanding.

The vast percentage of my working time was spent on substantive issues and domestic policy. About one-half of one percent was spent on politics, the campaign and the events with which you have been concerning yourself as a committtee. That is the context in which I hope you will receive this testimony....

COX REQUEST FOR TAPES

Following is the text of the letter written July 18 by special prosecutor Archibald Cox to presidential counsel J. Fred Buzhardt requesting access to the tapes of certain presidential conversations:

Dear Mr. Buzhardt:

I am writing to request access to the recordings of certain conversations between the President and various members of the White House staff and others whose conduct is under investigation in connection with the alleged coverup of the break-in at the Democratic National Committee offices. The conversations are listed below.

May I emphasize three essential aspects of this request:

First, the request is part of an investigation into serious criminal misconduct—the obstruction of justice. The tapes are material and important evidence—quite apart from anything they show about the involvement of the President—because the conversations recorded in all probability deal with the activities of other persons under investigation. Indeed, it is not implausible to suppose that the reports to the President on these occasions may themselves have been made pursuant to a conspiracy and as part of a cover-up.

Second, furnishing the tapes in aid of an investigation into charges of criminal conspiracy plainly raises none of the separation-of-powers issues you believe to be involved in furnishing so-called "Presidential Papers" to the Select Committee. The Select Committee is seeking information—as I understand the position—solely in order to recommend legislation. Whatever fears you may entertain that furnishing the tapes in aid of the Select Committee's legislation function would set a precedent for furnishing presidential papers to other legislative committees are plainly irrelevant to my request. For my request involves only a grand jury investigation resulting from highly extraordinary circumstances. No question of precedent arises because the circumstances almost surely will never be repeated.

Third, I would urge that the tapes be furnished for use in my investigation without restriction. This procedure strikes me as the method of establishing the truth which is most fair to everyone concerned, including the President. It is proper to point out, however, that if you thought it essential to furnish the papers only to the grand jury under the rules pertaining to grand jury documents, an appropriate procedure could be devised. This is an additional circumstance distinguishing the present investigation from the situation before the Select Committee.

The particular conversations to which my present request pertains have been carefully selected as those material to the investigation, to wit:—

1. Meeting of June 20, 1972, in the President's EOB Office between the President and Messrs. Ehrlichman and Haldeman from 10:30 a.m. to 1:00 p.m. (time approximate).

2. Telephone conversation of June 20, 1972, between the President and Mr. Mitchell from 6:08 to 6:12 p.m.

3. Meeting of June 30, 1972, in the President's EOB Office between the President and Messrs. Haldeman and Mitchell from 12:55 to 2:10 p.m.

4. Meeting of September 15, 1972, in the President's Oval Office between the President and Mr. Dean from 5:15 to 6:17 p.m. Mr. Haldeman joined this meeting at 5:27 p.m.

5. Meeting of March 13, 1973, in the President's Oval Office between the President and Mr. Dean from 12:42 to 2:00 p.m. Mr. Haldeman was present from 12:43 to 12:55 p.m.

6. Meeting of March 21, 1973, in the President's Oval Office between the President and Messrs. Dean and Haldeman from 10:12 to 11:55 a.m.

7. Meeting of March 22, 1973, in the President's EOB Office between the President and Mr. Dean from 1:57 to 3:43 p.m. Mr. Ehrlichman joined this meeting at 2:00 p.m., and Messrs. Haldeman and Mitchell joined at 2:01 p.m.

8. Meeting of April 15, 1973, in the President's EOB Office between the President and Mr. Dean from 9:17 to 10:12 p.m. (you will recall that this is the conversation the recording of which I requested as early as June 11 and which you declined to furnish under the misapprehension that this was only a subsequent memorandum).

You will realize that as the investigation proceeds it may be necessary to request additional recordings.

Sincerely,
Archibald Cox
Special Prosecutor

WRIGHT LETTER TO COX

Following is the text of a letter written July 23 by Charles Alan Wright, consultant to White House counsel Buzhardt, to special prosecutor Cox:

Dear Mr. Cox:

Mr. Buzhardt has asked that I respond to your letters to him of June 20th, July 18th and July 20th in which you make certain requests with regard to tape recordings of or about conversations between the President and various members of the White House staff and others.

The President is today refusing to make available to the Senate Committee material of a similar nature. Enclosed is a copy of his letter of this date to Senator Ervin stating his position about the tapes. I am instructed by the President to inform you that it will not be possible to make available to you the recordings that you have requested.

In general the reasons for the President's decision are the same as those that underlie his response to the Senate Committee. But in your letter of July 18th you state that furnishing the tapes in aid of an investigation into charges of criminal conspiracy raises none of the separation-of-powers issues that are raised by the request from the Senate Committee. You indicated a similar position when we met on June 6th. At that time you suggested that questions of separation of powers did not arise since you were within the Executive Branch, though, as I recall, you then added that your position is a little hard to describe since, in your view, you are not subject to direction by the President or the Attorney General.

I note that in your subsequent letters, and particularly that of July 18th in which you argue that the separation-of-powers argument is inapplicable, there is no suggestion that you are a part of the Executive Branch. Indeed, if you are an ordinary prosecutor, and thus a part of the Executive Branch as well as an officer of the court, you are subject to the instructions of your superiors, up to and including the President, and can have access to Presidential papers only as and if the President sees fit to make them available to you.

But quite aside from the consideration just stated, there is an even more fundamental reason why separation-of-powers considerations are fully as applicable to a request from you as to one from the Senate Committee. It is clear, and your letter of the 18th specifically states, that the reason you are seeking these tapes is to use some or all of them before grand juries or in criminal trial. Production of them to you would lead to their use in the courts, and questions of separation-of-powers are in the forefront when the most confidential documents of the

Presidency are sought for use in the Judicial Branch. Indeed most of the limited case law on executive privilege has arisen in the context of attempts to obtain executive documents for use in the courts.

The successful prosecution of those who have broken the laws is a very important national interest, but it has long been recognized that there are other national interests that, in specific cases, may override this. When Congress provided in the Jencks Act, 18 U.S.C. (subsection) 3500 (d), that the United States may choose to refuse to disclose material that the court has ordered produced, even though in some instances this will lead to a mistrial and to termination of the prosecution, it was merely recognizing that, as the courts had repeatedly held, there are circumstances in which other legitimate national interests requiring that documents be kept confidential outweigh the interest in punishing a particular malefactor. Similarly in civil litigation the United States may feel obliged to withhold relevant information, because of more compelling governmental interests, even though this may cause it to lose a suit it might otherwise have won. The power of the President to withhold confidential documents that would otherwise be material in the courts comes from "an inherent executive power which is protected in the constitutional system of separation of power." *United States* v. *Reynolds,* 345, U.S. 1, 6 n. 9 (1953).

In your letter to Mr. Buzhardt of July 10th you quoted Mr. Richardson's statement to the Senate Judiciary Committee in which he concluded that it was the President's intention "that whatever should be made public in terms of the public interest in these investigations should be disclosed.."

That is, of course, the President's view, but it is for the President, and only for the President, to weigh whether the incremental advantage that these tapes would give you in criminal proceedings justifies the serious and lasting hurt that disclosure of them would do to the confidentiality that is imperative to the effective functioning of the President. In this instance the President has concluded that it would not serve the public interest to make the tapes available.

COX STATEMENT ON SUBPOENAS

Following is the text of the statement issued on July 23 by Cox in response to Wright's letter:

This afternoon I received from the White House a letter declining to furnish tapes of conversations on the President's telephone or in his office. Eight specific tapes were requested by me in a letter dated July 18, 1973, a copy of which is attached.

Careful study before requesting the tapes convinced me that any blanket claim of privilege to withhold this evidence from a grand jury is without legal foundation. It therefore becomes my duty promptly to seek subpoenas and other available legal procedures for obtaining the evidence for the grand jury. We will initiate such legal measures to secure the eight tapes and certain other evidence as soon as proper papers can be prepared.

The effort to obtain these tapes and other documentary evidence is the impartial pursuit of justice according to law. None of us should make assumptions about what the tapes will show. They may tend to show that there was criminal activity—or that there was none. They may tend to show the guilt of particular individuals—or their innocence. The one clear point is that the tapes are evidence bearing directly upon whether there were criminal conspiracies, including a conspiracy to obstruct justice, among high government officials.

Happily, ours is a system of government in which no man is above the law. Since Chief Justice Marshall's decision in Marbury vs. Madison in 1803, the judicial branch has ruled upon the legal duties as well as the constitutional privileges of the Chief Executive. I dispute the constitutionality of the President's claim of privilege as applied to the administration of the criminal laws, but I do not question its bona fides. In seeking and obeying a constitutional ruling with respect to these papers and records, we would promote the rule of law essential to both liberty and order.

NIXON LETTER TO ERVIN

Following is the text of a letter written July 23 by President Nixon to Sam J. Ervin Jr. (D N.C.), chairman of the Senate Watergate investigating committee, concerning the committee's request for tape recordings of presidential conversations:

Dear Mr. Chairman:

I have considered your request that I permit the Committee to have access to tapes of my private conversations with a number of my closest aides. I have concluded that the principles stated in my letter to you of July 6th preclude me from complying with that request, and I shall not do so. Indeed the special nature of tape recordings of private conversations is such that these principles apply with even greater force to tapes of private Presidential conversations than to Presidential papers.

If release of the tapes would settle the central questions at issue in the Watergate inquiries, then their disclosure might serve a substantial public interest that would have to be weighed very heavily against the negatives of disclosure.

The fact is that the tapes would not finally settle the central issues before your Committee. Before their existence became publicly known, I personally listened to a number of them. The tapes are entirely consistent with what I know to be the truth and what I have stated to be the truth. However, as in any verbatim recording of informal conversations, they contain comments that persons with different perspectives and motivations would inevitable interpret in different ways. Furthermore, there are inseparably interspersed in them a great many very frank and very private comments, on a wide range of issues and individuals, wholly extraneous to the Committee's inquiry. Even more important, the tapes could be accurately understood or interpreted only by reference to an enormous number of other documents and tapes, so that to open them at all would begin an endless process of disclosure and explanation of private Presidential records totally unrelated to Watergate, and highly confidential in nature. They are the clearest possible example of why Presidential documents must be kept confidential.

Accordingly, the tapes, which have been under my sole personal control, will remain so. None has been transcribed or made public and none will be.

On May 22nd I described my knowledge of the Watergate matter and its aftermath in categorical and unambiguous terms that I know to be true. In my letter of July 6th, I informed you that at an appropriate time during the hearings I intend to address publicly the subjects you are considering. I still intend to do so and in a way that preserves the Constitutional principle of separation of powers, and thus serves the interests not just of the Congress or of the President, but of the people.

WATERGATE COMMITTEE RESOLUTION

Following is the text of the resolution adopted unanimously by the Senate Watergate committee on July 23:

The Senate Select Committee on Presidential Campaign Activities hereby unanimously resolves:

1. That the Chairman of the Committee be and he is hereby authorized to issue a subpoena duces tecum requiring the President of the United States to make available to the Committee the electronic tapes and recorded telephone messages

recording conversations between him and any other persons relating to alleged criminal acts occurring in connection with the Presidential Election of 1972, such tapes and recordings to be identified in specific terms in such subpoena.

2. That the Chairman of the Committee is authorized and directed to issue a subpoena duces tecum requiring the President to make available to the Committee any papers in his custody or under his control which tend to prove or disprove the commission of any alleged criminal acts related to the Presidential election of 1972 which the Committee is authorized to investigate under Senate Resolution 60, such papers to be designated in the subpoena to the maximum extent possible.

MARDIAN STATEMENT TEXT

Following is the opening statement of Robert C. Mardian, a former assistant attorney general and former political coordinator of the Committee for the Re-election of the President, before the Senate Watergate committee on July 19:

My name is Robert C. Mardian. I was born in Pasadena, Calif. I graduated from law school in 1949, and from that time to 1969, except for my involvement in my family business in Phoenix, Ariz., I was engaged exclusively in the practice of law in Pasadena, Calif., either in private practice or as general counsel, from 1962 to 1969, for a financial institution.

In 1969, I was appointed general counsel for the United States Department of Health, Education and Welfare, which title I held until September 1970. During the period commencing January 1970 and until November 1970, I was also the executive director of the cabinet committee on education, which was charged with the responsibility of implementing the administration's school desegregation policies, principally in the southern states.

From November 1970 until May of 1972, I was assistant attorney general, Internal Security Division, United States Department of Justice. Commencing May 1, 1972, until the election, I was employed by the Committee to Re-Elect the President. On Nov. 10, 1972, we moved from Washington, D.C., and we have, since that time, resided in Phoenix, Ariz., where I have been engaged in business with my three brothers.

Almost from the beginning of my tenure at the Justice Department, there were rumors in the press and other public media that the attorney general, John Mitchell, would leave the Department of Justice sometime in 1971 to head the 1972 presidential campaign. There were also rumors starting in the fall of 1971 that I would be leaving the Justice Department to assist Mr. Mitchell in the campaign effort.

I do not recall discussing with Mr. Mitchell his intentions regarding the campaign until the fall of 1971. As best as I can recall, he told me that it had not been finally decided whether or not he would be heading up the campaign effort. I cannot recall discussing my possible involvement in the campaign with him until sometime in January of 1972. I had agreed with my wife, prior to that time, to leave the administration at the end of the President's first term. In anticipation of this, we took advantage of an opportunity to sell our home in McLean, Va., in January 1972 and moved into an apartment in Washington.

Although I had never discussed with Mr. Mitchell my specific role in the campaign, I agreed in February of 1972 to accept Mr. Mitchell's invitation to join the campaign organization, which I did on May 1, 1972.

I was, as has been testified to, appointed originally as a campaign coordinator, but with respect to the events which are subject of this committee inquiry, I should point out that I had not in my capacity as one of the political coordinators or otherwise been consulted, advised or favored with any information relating to the "dirty tricks" campaign which has now come to light, much less given even a hint of any proposed burglary or electronic surveillance. The fact that I was not included in the inner circles of knowledge is probably now fortunate, even though disclosures were made to me when my help was needed as a lawyer.

If I make no other point in this prefatory statement, I want it in the record that as of the morning of June 17, 1972, I was relieved of my political responsibilities to the extent possible and charged with the responsibility of acting as counsel to the committee, at least as far as Watergate was concerned. I accepted this responsibility with the understanding that I would obtain the assistance of independent legal counsel and that I would be relieved of this legal responsibility when they were sufficiently acquainted with the facts to handle this matter.

I should also like to make it clear that I was and probably still am one of the attorneys of record in the litigation pending between the Democratic National Committee and the Committee to Re-elect the President and others. Thus it was as a lawyer, not as a political associate, that those persons involved confided in me and that this was made clear to me not by implication, but by express statement. And that it was as a lawyer and not as a political protege that I agreed to maintain the fiduciary obligation not to disclose that which was confided in me. If this be the basis of the broad-brush charge of "coverup," then it is a charge that every lawyer must answer under our adversary system of criminal justice—a system that requires a lawyer to respect the confidence of his client until waived by the client no matter how helpful it might be to the lawyer to disclose.

I adhered to this principle in seeking a court ruling on the attorney-client privilege before testifying in May before the grand jury. In the light of the court's ruling on the privilege and the waivers resulting from the testimony of others, I feel no constraints now and can fully discuss the facts with which I am familiar without causing the public or the bar to feel that I have not fully adhered to the duty of a lawyer to respect his client's confidence.

I would also like to say at this point that the information that I received on the morning of June 17 and June 21 was the most shocking experience in my entire legal career. The facts thus learned thrust me into a situation which I can only compare, in terms of personal anxiety, to being caught in quicksand. Commencing the morning of June 17, 1972, information was imparted to me bit by bit, much of it contradictory, which drew me inexorably into an intolerable and, at times, unbearable situation of personal conscience—a situation in which I was precluded from acting according to the dictates of my personal desires or interests. A situation in which ultimately my only hope was the selfish one of not becoming implicated in the conduct of others who I felt it my duty to serve.

I am not at all sure of the exact sequence of events, or all the times, places and parties present, but I shall attempt to relate, as fairly and as candidly as I can, the history of Watergate as I learned it.

STRACHAN STATEMENT TEXT

Following is the opening statement of Gordon Strachan, former assistant to White House chief of staff H.R. Haldeman, before the Senate Watergate investigating committee on July 20:

Mr. Chairman and members of the committee, I am here at the request of the committee and prepared to answer, fully and truthfully, all questions related to the matters specified in Senate Resolution 60, establishing this committee's jurisdiction. As you know, I met three times in executive session with the committee and its staff in order to permit the committee to prepare for today's questioning. In addition, on four prior occasions my attorney met with committee attorneys to explain the subjects on which I could testify.

The committee voted unanimously to grant immunity with respect to this testimony, and my counsel has advised me that testimony under such a grant is a legally proper procedure intended to permit a full, candid disclosure of the truth about the Watergate matter.

I should also add that before my discussion with this committee, I had already met—voluntarily—with the Watergate prosecutors on three occasions, and my attorney met with them and their successors on four more occasions.

In short, even prior to testifying here today, I made a complete and honest disclosure to the original prosecutors, to their successors and to this committee.

Much of the information I will disclose is politically embarrassing to me and the administration. Some of it shows that I closely associated during my employment at the White House with individuals who have confessed to criminal wrongdoing.

Where other witnesses have made charges, if I know their statements are true, I am here to confirm the truth of such charges, even to the extent it might reflect adversely on me. You will find that I will readily admit today many things that anyone who is trying to cover up would quickly deny.

But where I know that the statements of a witness are false, I will deny them, not out of a motive to protect anyone—certainly not out of a motive to protect myself—for I am confident that the immunity I have been granted is genuine.

In other words, my intention to corroborate specific matters and to refute others does not stem from a desire to testify for or against anyone—nor from a desire to feign excessive remorse—but solely because I am here to tell the truth.

Inaccurate Reports. Press reports predicting my testimony here have been nothing short of incredible. My testimony before the grand jury on April 11, 1973, appeared in the nation's newspapers within a week, although grand jury testimony is required by law to be kept secret. Next, several grossly inaccurate and contradictory versions of my expected testimony before this committee were reported—although the committee's staff confirmed that the newspaper headlines were a serious distortion of the information my attorney, Mr. Bray, gave the committee. Then on the 4th of July, television, radio and newspapers reported coast to coast that I had agreed to plead guilty. Only a few correspondents even bothered to ask my attorney whether that was true. Despite Mr. Bray's denials, the story was run anyway. And finally, the day after my testimony before this committee in executive session, several inaccurate stories about my testimony appeared.

Today my testimony will, to the displeasure, I suspect, of many interested onlookers, conflict with these mistaken press reports,

Missing Links. In the 2½ months I have been unemployed, I have tried to review the information I have that can aid this committee in bringing out the full story about the Watergate matter. I believe it would be helpful if I take a moment now to supply some missing links in the testimony of other witnesses and hopefully clear up some of the confusion and contradictions —at least to the extent of my own knowledge.

I was a staff assistant to Mr. Haldeman. My office was located in the basement of the White House. One of my responsibilities during the President's re-election campaign was to serve as liaison with the Committee to Re-elect the President. It was my job to accumulate all the information I could obtain from members of the White House staff, personnel at 1701 (1701 Pennsylvania Ave., the re-election committee headquarters), the Republican National Committee and from the campaign personnel in key states and cities.

Periodically, I was to report important political matters to Mr. Haldeman. I wrote him many long reports, entitled political matters memos, describing the current status of pending political matters. He relied on me as the member of his personal staff who would obtain information on campaign matters. Either I would have the answer, or I would get it.

As to the subject of political intelligence-gathering, however, John Dean was designated as the White House contact for the Committee to Re-elect the President. I have advised the committee where the documentary proof on this point is located. As a result, my inquiries about political intelligence were slight. Mr. Haldeman seldom had me attend meetings on the subject. He rarely asked me a question about the subject, and so I seldom reported about it to him.

Nor did Mr. Dean report to me about all his activities in the area of political intelligence. When the subject of political intelligence was mentioned at a meeting I attended, or when I knew the subject was on the agenda of a meeting I was not invited to attend, I would, as the staff assistant, follow up with the principals and remind them about the subjects discussed. On those occasions when I made such follow-up inquiries with Mr. Haldeman about political intelligence operations, he responded that I should let Dean handle it. When I followed up with Mr. Dean, he rarely advised me in any detail about the status of intelligence matters. Instead, he dealt directly with Mr. Haldeman.

For example, neither Mr. Haldeman nor Mr. Dean advised me of the series of meetings with Mr. Mitchell, Dean, Liddy and Magruder. Nor was I invited to or informed about Mr. Dean's February meeting with Mr. Haldeman at which Mr. Dean says he told Mr. Haldeman that the Liddy plan was outlandish and that the White House should have no further involvement. Neither Mr. Haldeman, Mr. Dean nor, for that matter, Mr. Magruder, ever told me of any of those meetings. And I certainly did not attend any of them.

Uncomfortable Situation. Turning to my duties and reporting activities with the Committee to Re-elect the President, I found myself in an unusual and not entirely comfortable situation. I was the White House conduit for reporting the activities of 1701, including the activities of Mr. Magruder—the man who shortly before had been my boss at the White House.

Mr. Magruder's reporting practices were marked by two features. First, he considered it a burden to report through me. My role—as Mr. Haldeman intended it—was somewhat of a constraint upon Mr. Magruder's ability to have free rein at the committee, independent of the scrutiny of the White House. As a result, Mr. Magruder frequently tried to avoid the reporting system. When Mr. Magruder did report, he reported as much as possible on successful developments that reflected favorably on his campaign leadership and as little as possible on projects that were not going well. On projects that went smoothly or portrayed him in a good light, Mr. Magruder would often give a full report directly to Mr. Higby or Mr. Haldeman. On ineffective or failing projects, he would seldom do more than make brief mention to me on the general subject matter—just enough to protect himself from later criticism that he had withheld information from the White House in case the project went totally sour.

Second, he considered it a serious impairment of his status to report to me rather than to someone more senior, especially since he had previously been my boss at the White House. He asked that I deal with Mr. Reisner, his administrative assistant, whose position on Mr Magruder's staff corresponded more to my position on Mr. Haldeman's staff. I did increase my contacts with Mr. Reisner and other campaign aides, but continued to insist on dealing directly with Mr. Magruder on many projects.

Political Intelligence. With respect to the particular subject of political intelligence, Mr. Magruder has testified in very general, carefully hedged and characteristically vague terms that he assumes he either automatically sent me materials about or called me and gave me a general description of intelligence plans. Had anyone ever heard the details of prostitution, goon squads, kidnapping and wiretaps, he would be unlikely to forget it. I certainly would not forget it. Mr. Magruder never gave me that information and certainly not those details, because if he had, I would immediately have passed it on to Mr. Haldeman, I would remember it and I would be here today testifying about it.

By any standard, the meetings at which the Liddy plans were presented were classic examples of poor staff work by the committee and a waste of time. The testimony has been virtually unanimous that Mr. Mitchell and Mr. Dean were shocked by Liddy's plan; Mr. Magruder's staff man, Gordon Liddy, was apparently quite humiliated; and nothing was approved. In other words, if those meetings were routinely reported to Mr. Haldeman, as evidence of Mr. Magruder's administrative ability and judgment, the January and February meetings would not very likely inspire the confidence of Mr. Haldeman or the President.

Yet Mr. Magruder testified that "as he recalled" he returned to his office after both these embarrassing meetings and routinely called Mr. Haldeman's staff assistant, me, and told me about his blunder, presumably so that I could inform Mr. Haldeman. That testimony is difficult to reconcile with good sense. Presumably, Mr. Magruder knew that Mr. Dean would report on the meetings to Mr. Haldeman—as Mr. Dean has testified he did—why would Mr. Magruder want two people reporting the same disaster to Mr. Haldeman?

It is true, however, that Mr. Magruder called me after he returned from the March 30, 1972, meeting at Key Biscayne with Mr. Mitchell and Mr. LaRue and reported on about 30 major campaign decisions. Each of these decisions was briefly described in that rather short phone conversation. During this call, he told me, and I am repeating his words rather precisely: "A sophisticated political intelligence-gathering system has been approved with a budget of 300." Unfortunately, he neither gave me, nor did I ask for, any further details about the subject.

Soon thereafter, I wrote one of my regular "political matters" memos for Mr. Haldeman. This particular memo for early April was eight to 10 pages long with more than a dozen tabs or attachments, but it contained only one three-line paragraph on polical intelligence. That paragraph read almost verbatim as Mr. Magruder had indicated to me over the phone. I wrote in the memo to Mr. Haldeman (again this is almost a quote): "Magruder reports that 1701 now has a sophisticated political intelligence-gathering system with a budget of 300. A sample of the type of information they are developing is attached at tab 'H.' "

At tab "H," I enclosed a political intelligence report which had been sent to me from the committee. It was entitled Sedan Chair II. This report and two others somewhat like it that I had received began with a statement such as, "A confidential source reveals" or "a reliable source confidentially reports." This was followed by a summary of some political information.

In April 1972, I was mainly interested in reporting to Mr. Haldeman on those 30 campaign decisions and other relevant political items. I did not give much thought to what Mr. Magruder meant by "sophisticated political intelligence-gathering system." Nor did I give much thought to the real identity of Sedan Chair II, but I remember that the information dealt with Sen. Humphrey's Pennsylvania organization.

Break-in. However, on June 17, 1972, and afterward, as the news began unfolding about the break-in at the Democratic National Committee, I certainly began to wonder who *else* but people from 1701 could have been involved. I suspected that maybe the Watergate break-in was part of the "sophisticated political intelligence operation" Mr. Magruder had mentioned to me on the phone in early April. And worse, I feared that Sedan Chair II's so-called confidential source might really have been a wiretap, or might in some way have been connected with the Watergate break-in. I immediately tried to call Mr. Magruder so I could have a report for Mr. Haldeman. Mr. Magruder did not return my calls on Saturday, and I was not able to reach him until around noon on Sunday, when I again called him in California.

When I finally reached him and began to ask him what he knew about the Watergate break-in, he cut me off and said that he had been on the phone with Mr. Haldeman that morning and the matter was being taken care of.

I doubted that Mr. Magruder had actually spoken with Mr. Haldeman, so I called Mr. Higby, who clears most calls to Mr. Haldeman. Mr. Higby told me that Mr. Magruder had talked to Mr. Haldeman and that Mr. Ehrlichman was handling the entire matter.

I met with Mr. Haldeman on June 19 or 20 and showed him the April political matters memo that mentioned the intelligence-gathering system. After speaking to him, I destroyed that memo and Sedan Chair II, as well as several other documents I have told this committee and the prosecutors about. I also told Mr. Dean that I had destroyed a political matters memo to Mr. Haldeman showing a $300,000 intelligence budget at the committee and three confidential source memos which I said could possibly have been wiretap reports with the sources carefully camouflaged. I did not tell Mr. Dean that I had, in fact, destroyed wiretap logs, because I was not then sure what they were. I only had suspicions.

I also told the prosecutors in April of this year what specific items I destroyed, and I told them I still suspected Sedan Chair II might have been a wiretap summary. It was not until Mr. Reisner and Mr. Porter testified before this committee in June that I learned Sedan Chair II was not an illegal wiretap, but was instead an informer planted in the Humphrey camp. In fact, you will recall that Mr. Magruder's testimony has established that I never received his wiretap data. Nor could I have passed it on to others or shredded a wiretap transcript. He says he made only one copy of the Watergate wiretap log, code-named Gemstone. He testified that it was so sensitive that he would not let it out of his office.

Post-Election. Turning to matters after the election, I have told the committee that I returned approximately $350,000 in cash to Fred LaRue. I was not told by anyone, nor did I know what use was being made of this money. I had received the money from the campaign committee on Mr. Haldeman's instructions and, at that time, returning it to Mr. LaRue seemed appropriate, since he was the top official left at the committee. I took it to him in December 1972 or January 1973, after I had left the White House staff. This money was the fund I had picked up in April 1972 for the purpose of conducting White House polling. It had not been used to pay polling expenses as originally planned, and after the election I had been asking Mr. Haldeman, Mr. Dean and Mr. Higby what to do with the money.

The delivery to Mr. LaRue was made in two parts, on two occasions. In December or January, after talking to Mr. Dean, I took approximately $40,000 in two envelopes to Mr. LaRue at his apartment at the Watergate. I lived two blocks away, and the delivery was made on my way home from work.

Later I was asked to return the remainder of the money. I again called Mr. LaRue, who again asked if I could deliver it to his apartment. On this occasion, before picking up the money, Mr. LaRue donned a pair of gloves and then said, "I never saw you." I had been instructed by Mr. Dean to ask for a receipt, so I did, but Mr. LaRue refused, saying, "You will have to talk to John Dean about it."

At that point I became more than a little suspicious. Frankly, after Mr. LaRue put on the gloves, I did not know what to say—so I said nothing. Nor did I know what to do—so I left. The next day I told Mr. Dean that Mr. LaRue would not give me a receipt for the money. Mr. Dean said he would speak to Mr. LaRue about it. I don't know if he ever got the receipt, but I imagine he tried to follow up on it, because I have since learned from Mr. Dean's testimony that it was Mr. Haldeman who asked that a receipt be given.

At no time did Mr. Dean or Mr. LaRue advise me what was being done with the money or that payments were being made to the defendants. Neither of them ever asked me to do or say anything that I can interpret as being part of a coverup.

In fact, there was only one occasion when I was expressly asked to do something that I knew was improper and which I could see was aimed at a coverup. That related to my upcoming grand jury testimony of April 11, 1973, and I refused to do it.

I have not attempted in my statement to describe in detail all of the subjects that I have mentioned. I have provided the committee in executive session with a good deal more of the details surrounding these subjects, and I am ready to begin the questioning on these matters. √

WATERGATE: CONTINUED HEARINGS BY A TIRED COMMITTEE

While their other colleagues on Capitol Hill packed their bags for a month's vacation, the seven members of the Senate Watergate investigating committee agreed to stay in session and listen to some more witnesses.

The committee, with one-week breaks for Memorial Day and the Fourth of July, had been meeting steadily since the hearings began on May 17. Members and staff were tired. "The country needs a rest from Watergate, said Vice Chairman Howard H. Baker Jr. (R Tenn.).

But the desire of Baker and Chairman Sam J. Ervin Jr. (D N.C.) to join the rest of Congress in its August recess, starting Aug. 3, was a minority position. The majority of the committee wanted to finish public hearings in the first phase of its investigation—the phase dealing with the June 17, 1972, break-in at Democratic national headquarters and its subsequent coverup.

So the decision was made on July 30 to hear seven more witnesses and then go home. The committee would not lose all of its vacation. Questioning of the witnesses was expected to be completed by the end of the next week.

Witnesses. During the week ended Aug. 4, the committee concluded its interrogation of President Nixon's former top two advisers, John D. Ehrlichman and H.R. Haldeman. They were followed by Richard M. Helms, former director of the Central Intelligence Agency; other CIA officials, and, at week's end, L. Patrick Gray III, former acting director of the FBI. *(Gray testimony p. 255)*

Probably the most startling revelation of the week was Haldeman's disclosure that he had taken home and listened to some of the tape-recorded presidential conversations that the committee and the special Watergate prosecutor, Archibald Cox, had been trying without success to get their hands on. The tapes substantiated the President's position that he had no knowledge of or involvement in the coverup, Haldeman testified.

Tapes Battle. Haldeman's statement hardly satisfied the senators, who wondered why he and not they should be given access to the tapes. The day before Haldeman testified, Ervin, Baker and special prosecutor Cox had suggested they be allowed to listen to the tapes privately. Senate Minority Leader Hugh Scott (R Pa.) had suggested the same day a private inspection by a panel of two or three persons.

The feeling was widespread on Capitol Hill that Nixon should release the tapes to Cox and the committee. Some members of Nixon's staff, it was revealed, had urged him to give up the tapes. But the President held firm in his refusal not to relinquish them, and the dispute moved closer toward the courts.

Growing Tension. Frustrations over Watergate were evident in the Senate hearings, elsewhere in Congress and in the White House.

Walters' Testimony

The first witness before the Senate Watergate committee on Aug. 3 was Army Lt. Gen. Vernon A. Walters, deputy director of the Central Intelligence Agency. Walters' testimony about a series of meetings he had held with administration officials soon after the 1972 break-in amplified on his reported testimony in May before other congressional committees. And it related to several of his memos that had become public. *(Memos, p. 126; hearings, p. 117, 86, 66)*

It appeared to him, Walters said, that at a June 26, 1972, meeting with then White House counsel John W. Dean III, Dean was trying to find a way to blame the Watergate break-in on the CIA. This would have been a "disaster," Walters said, and he was prepared to resign if Dean insisted on it. Dean told him an FBI investigation of the Watergate could involve some important people in the administration, said Walters.

He insisted to Dean that the CIA was not engaged in clandestine activities in Mexico, the country through which some money used in the Watergate operation had been "laundered," Walters testified. At another meeting with Dean, he said, he denied Dean's request that the CIA pay bail and salaries to the Watergate defendants.

Walters and L. Patrick Gray III, then acting director of the FBI, met on July 12, 1972, Walters said. At that meeting, he said, Gray told him he had advised President Nixon that the investigation could lead to high administration officials and that Nixon should get rid of those implicated.

Partisanship erupted at the hearings over the introduction of a memo implicating Nixon and former Attorney General John N. Mitchell in the favorable settlement of litigation involving International Telephone and Telegraph Corporation.

Rep. Robert F. Drinan (D Mass.) became the first member of Congress to introduce an impeachment resolution against Nixon, based partly on the President's bugging of his own offices.

One of the week's ugliest events was a reference by Ehrlichman's lawyer, John J. Wilson, to Sen. Daniel K. Inouye (D Hawaii) as "that little Jap." Embarrassingly for the Nixon administration, Wilson made his remark while Japanese Prime Minister Kakuei Tanaka was in Washington on a state visit. The night before, at a dinner for Tanaka, Nixon had shown his stiffening resistance to Watergate pressures. In a toast to the prime minister, he criticized people who "spend their time dealing with the murky, small, unimportant, vicious little things."

Witness July 27

Ehrlichman indicated to the Senate Watergate committee that Nixon did not receive a full report on the break-in and coverup until April 14, when Ehrlichman himself reported on the results of his own investigation. The President's former domestic affairs adviser thus challenged testimony by John W. Dean III that Dean had given Nixon a complete report on Watergate March 21. *(Dean testimony, p. 152)*

Ehrlichman told the committee he had "great difficulty believing" Dean told the President everything on March 21. He said that at March 21 and 22 meetings with Nixon, attended by Ehrlichman and Dean, the President never mentioned what he had learned from Dean March 21.

According to Ehrlichman, the March 21 meeting among himself, Nixon and Dean, and the March 22 meeting, also attended by Haldeman and former Attorney General John N. Mitchell, dealt mainly with immunity and whether White House staff members would have to testify before the select committee. There was no discussion of Watergate as such at the meetings, said Ehrlichman.

"This really puzzles me," said Sen. Edward J. Gurney (R Fla.). He asked whether the President mentioned at the meeting what Dean said he had told Nixon March 21.

Ehrlichman answered that he did not think Dean had given Nixon the full Watergate story. Stating that Nixon, at the March 22 meeting, told Dean to write out a full statement on the Watergate affair, Ehrlichman suggested that meant either Dean had not told Nixon everything or Nixon may have been "setting a few snares on the trail and was playing it cool."

Ehrlichman testified that he was ordered by Nixon March 30 to take over the White House inquiry into Watergate because Nixon told him he was "satisfied that John Dean is in this so deeply that he simply cannot any longer have anything to do with it." Dean had testified that when the President ordered him to conduct the White House inquiry, Nixon said Ehrlichman and Haldeman were "principals" in the case.

But Ehrlichman denied that "principals" meant he and Haldeman were suspected of illegal activities. He testified that Nixon merely meant that he and Haldeman might become test cases on the issue of testimony by presidential assistants before Congress.

Ehrlichman said his inquiry for the President, which he repeatedly refused to characterize as an investigation, included talks with 10 top White House and re-election committee officials, including Haldeman; Dean; Haldeman's deputy, Gordon C. Strachan, and re-election committee lawyer Paul L. O'Brien. The report was given to the President April 14, Ehrlichman said, and Nixon ordered him to tell all he had learned to the attorney general. The bulk of his information, Ehrlichman indicated, came from O'Brien, who had conducted his own investigation for the re-election committee.

Reading from shorthand notes of his meeting with O'Brien, Ehrlichman said he was told much of the story of the pre-break-in events that already had come out in committee testimony. These events included meetings where G. Gordon Liddy, a convicted Watergate conspirator, presented his surveillance plans, and the photographing by a chauffeur for Sen. Edmund S. Muskie (D Maine) of secret Muskie campaign documents that were given to the Nixon re-election committee.

At one point, Ehrlichman said O'Brien told him that "Frankly, John Dean is the problem," and that O'Brien advised caution regarding Dean's advice to the President. Later, still reading from his notes, Ehrlichman quoted O'Brien as saying that Jeb Stuart Magruder, the deputy re-election committee director, "reaches" the President in his (Magruder's) story. Ehrlichman explained that, according to what O'Brien told him, Magruder at one point fired G. Gordon Liddy from the committee, but that Liddy then went to Strachan, who told Magruder to take Liddy back because "the President wants this project (the surveillance) to go on."

Weicker Argument. The witness got into a heated argument with Sen. Lowell P. Weicker Jr. (R Conn.) over political spying in general. Ehrlichman defended the Nixon White House's practice of spying on political opponents' drinking, sexual and social habits. He said politicians had an "obligation" to expose such activities to public knowledge.

Weicker, alternating between indignation and astonishment, asked, "Do you mean...that you consider private investigators going into the sexual habits, drinking habits, domestic problems and personal social activities" as proper subjects for investigations during political campaigns? Earlier he had referred to testimony by Anthony T. Ulasewicz, a White House investigator, who told the committee he was looking for "dirt" when he probed the backgrounds of Nixon political opponents, including Sen. Edward M. Kennedy (D Mass.) *(Ulasewicz testimony, p. 200)*

Ehrlichman replied affirmatively, adding, "You can go over here in the gallery and watch a member totter onto the floor in a condition of at least partial inebriation. I think it's important for the American people to know (that),...and if the only way it can be brought out is through his opponent in a political campaign, then I think that opponent has an affirmative obligation to bring that forward."

The tension was broken somewhat when Ehrlichman said he was sure Weicker's background was "impeccable" and the senator replied, "I'm no angel. I'm no angel."

Kalmbach Testimony. In other testimony, Ehrlichman said that he was not asking Nixon fund-raiser Herbert W. Kalmbach to perjure himself before the Watergate grand jury during a taped telephone conversation April 19. A transcript of the conversation, released during Kalmbach's appearance before the committee, had Ehrlichman asking Kalmbach to tell the grand jury that the two had discussed Kalmbach's testimony in California rather than on the telephone that day. *(Kalmbach testimony, p. 196)*

Ehrlichman said he simply meant to remind Kalmbach that they had talked in California about his grand jury testimony and that he did not want Kalmbach to omit their California conversation if the grand jury asked him about it. "I was a little concerned" he might not testify to it, Ehrlichman stated, because he himself planned to discuss the conversation if asked.

Asked how often he taped his telephone conversations, the witness said he rarely did so on routine business calls, but that after March 30, when the President ordered him to probe the Watergate affair, he began taping conversations with persons in important roles. In addition to taping the conversation with Kalmbach, who he insisted was his good friend, "I also did some checking on Haldeman," Ehrlichman testified. Haldeman and Ehrlichman were friends of long standing and the President's top advisers.

Witnesses July 30

Haldeman, the former White House chief of staff, disputed prior testimony by John W. Dean III that Nixon knew of and approved the coverup of the Watergate scandal as early as Sept. 15, 1972. Haldeman, who attended the September meeting with Nixon and the former presidential counsel and who admitted listening to a tape recording of the meeting, said he disagreed with Dean's conclusion that Nixon was aware of the coverup and was congratulating Dean on his efforts. *(Dean testimony, p. 152)*

H. R. Haldeman

Haldeman said the President did, as Dean testified, "commend Dean for his handling of the whole Watergate matter," but that "...it was a perfectly natural thing for him to do." Nixon was pleased, said Haldeman, that no one in the White House had been indicted by the Watergate grand jury and that Nixon's purpose was to give Dean "a pat on the back." "I totally disagree" with Dean's interpretation of the meeting and Nixon's remarks, Haldeman stated. *(Excerpts of opening statement, p. 244)*

The witness also disputed Dean's account of an important March 13, 1972, meeting with Nixon where, Dean alleged, the President said there would be no problem in raising $1-million for Watergate defendants and discussed executive clemency for the seven defendants.

In the two hours it took Haldeman to read his 89-page statement, he contradicted not only large portions of Dean's testimony, but also that of Jeb Stuart Magruder, the deputy director of the re-election committee, and Gordon C. Strachan, Haldeman's former assistant.

In other testimony July 30, Ehrlichman, Nixon's former domestic affairs adviser and a close friend of Haldeman, ended his appearance before the Senate select Watergate committee after nearly five full days. Under more than two hours of grilling by committee counsel Samuel Dash, Ehrlichman was forced to backtrack somewhat from his prior testimony.

Access to Tapes. With the appearance of Haldeman, the committee had before it the one-time highest-ranking member of the White House staff and a close associate of the President for 17 years. Haldeman told the committee that neither he nor Nixon had any advance knowledge of the Watergate break-in July 17, 1972, at Democratic Party headquarters, nor did they know of the coverup until March 1973.

Although Haldeman's defense of his own role and that of the President in the scandal was expected, his revelation that he had listened to a tape recording of the Sept. 15 conversation among himself, Dean and Nixon came as a shock, because he said he did not hear the tape until early July. This would have been after Dean's testimony in June and more than two months after Haldeman had left the White House.

Haldeman had stated earlier that he, like Dean and Ehrlichman, had not been allowed to copy or take notes from any of his papers in the White House while examining them. But he said he was given the tape to take to his home overnight, listened to it alone and took notes from it while it was in his possession.

Haldeman said he had authorization from the President to listen to the tape and that it was given to him by Stephen Bull, a presidential aide. He said his notes were turned over to the White House along with the tape, and that he did not know if his notes still exist.

The matter of committee access to the tapes of that conversation, and other presidential conversations, had been a sore point between the committee and the President ever since it was revealed that Nixon's oval office and Executive Office Building office were bugged, with Nixon's approval. The committee felt that the tapes of selected presidential conversations would prove or disprove Nixon's complicity in the Watergate episode and issued a subpoena for them. But the President refused to give them up, claiming the doctrine of separation of powers would be violated if he did so. *(p. 209)*

Haldeman said he also had heard a tape recording in early April of the March 21 meeting between Dean and Nixon, when Haldeman still was on the White House staff. This also was done under Nixon's authorization, he testified.

Conflicts with Dean. At the March 21 meeting, Dean had testified, he told Nixon everything he knew about the break-in and the participation of himself, Haldeman, Ehrlichman and others in the coverup. Haldeman confirmed most of what Dean said about the March 21 meeting, but added that Dean apparently was confused in his testimony about the March 13 meeting with Nixon, because Dean attributed several things to the March 13 meeting that actually occurred on March 21.

Haldeman said that Dean on March 21—not March 13—reported on a $1-million blackmail threat from defendant E. Howard Hunt Jr. He said the President did, as Dean testified, reply that there would be no problem in raising the money, but told the committee that Nixon added, "That would be wrong." Dean's testimony regarding the meeting did not include that qualifying remark by Nixon.

Haldeman told the committee his impression from listening to the March 21 tape was that the President was asking leading questions to try to bring out Dean's views, adding that this was often Nixon's way of doing things. He further contradicted Dean on the matter of executive clemency for the defendants, saying the President did not mention having discussed clemency with Ehrlichman or Charles W. Colson, another former White House aide, as Dean had stated.

Testimony Ordered. The witness was reluctant at first to discuss what he had learned from the tape recording of the March 21 meeting, saying he had been ordered by the White House not to discuss it before the committee. John J. Wilson, Haldeman's lawyer, who also served as Ehrlichman's counsel, produced a letter from J. Fred Buzhardt, a special presidential counsel.

The letter informed Wilson that his client could testify to portions of meetings with the President that he attended, but that if asked to testify about meetings he did not attend, but learned of solely through tape recordings, he was not to talk. The President cited executive privilege under the separation of powers principle as the reason for limiting Haldeman's testimony, Wilson quoted Buzhardt as writing.

The committee recessed to consider the matter, and moments later Chairman Ervin informed Wilson and Haldeman that the committee had voted to overrule the claim of executive privilege and commanded Haldeman to testify on what he had heard on the tape. Apparently Haldeman had anticipated the committee's ruling, because he read a prepared "addendum" concerning the March 21 meeting before resuming reading from his longer statement. *(Text, p. 253)*

Coverup Acknowledged. Of the Watergate scandal in general, Haldeman said he believed no one in the White House was connected to the break-in, but added: "It now appears there was a coverup.... The critical question becomes who committed these acts, who directed them and who was aware of them. I committed no such acts, directed no such acts and was aware of none until March of this year. I am convinced the President was not aware of such acts until March of this year."

He said the specifics of Watergate were not the principal focus of White House attention until March. It was "a matter which arose only occasionally and only briefly" before that time, he said. He maintained that since it had not been foremost in Nixon's mind until March, it could not have been important to himself until that time because, as the President's chief of staff, his daily interests coincided with those of the President.

Haldeman said he was not familiar with all of Herbert W. Kalmbach's disbursements of leftover 1968 primary campaign funds, but admitted having a hand in disbursements regarding Donald H. Segretti, the 1970 Alabama gubernatorial campaign and White House polling. Kalmbach, Nixon's former personal attorney and campaign fund-raiser, had testified that he understood Haldeman approved all disbursements of 1968 funds he held in trust for Nixon. *(p. 193)*

Segretti is a California lawyer under indictment in Florida for campaign sabotage. Haldeman said he approved, on the basis of recommendations by Strachan and Dwight Chapin, another of his aides, certain 1972 campaign activities by Segretti. He equated the activities with those of Democratic prankster Dick Tuck, whose "stock in trade," he said, "was embarrassing Republican candidates."

But Haldeman said specific boundaries were drawn for Segretti's activities. His "pranksterism" was not to include heckling of candidates, bombing or burning of candidates' headquarters and harassment of candidates' wives and families, all of which Haldeman maintained were conducted against the President by his Democratic opponents in 1972. Haldeman did not give any specifics, but added that some of the things he mentioned might not have occurred with the knowledge of Nixon's opponents.

He said there was nothing wrong with Segretti's activities as originally conceived, although he did not specify what those activities were except to say that Segretti was not to engage in illegal acts. Noting it had been alleged that Segretti was responsible for defaming Sen. Hubert H. Humphrey (D Minn.) and Sen. Edmund S. Muskie (D Maine), Haldeman offered an apology if the allegation was true. *(1972 Almanac p. 92)*

Wallace Candidacy. Regarding the Alabama gubernatorial campaign of 1970, Haldeman said he approved a large contribution to George C. Wallace's Democratic primary opponent in the hope that Wallace might be defeated. He said he acted on the advice of Nixon's political advisers who, he said, told him that if Wallace were re-elected, he could become a third-party candidate for President in 1972. That, in turn, might have resulted in chaos if the 1972 election were thrown into the House of Representatives for a decision on the winner, Haldeman said he was told.

Haldeman said a $350,000 fund was set aside in the White House for political polling purposes, but he "never at any time saw or handled the currency." The committee heard earlier testimony that the fund eventually wound up in the hands of the defendants and their lawyers. Haldeman said Dean worked out a transfer of the money to the re-election committee and that Dean never told him that the purpose "was to buy the Watergate defendants' silence or that it was in any way illegal or improper."

Concerning the re-election committee itself, Haldeman said it operated autonomously of the White House. He said he was the basic contact between the committee and the President, but that Strachan handled day-to-day liaison matters. He said he personally exercised no authority over the committee except regarding advertising and promotion, two of his specialties before joining the White House staff. Haldeman had been a vice president of the J. Walter Thompson advertising firm and was in charge of its Los Angeles office.

Dean's Responsibility. Echoing Ehrlichman's testimony, Haldeman insisted that Dean was investigating the Watergate episode for the President and that Dean's assurances of no White House involvement in the affair formed the basis of Nixon's statement on Aug. 29, 1972.

"There is absolutely no question in my mind" that Dean was conducting the White House investigation, Haldeman told the committee. Dean sat in on FBI interviews and read FBI investigative reports, Haldeman said, adding that Dean often told him and Ehrlichman the status of his investigation. He apparently did not keep fully or accurately posted, Haldeman said. "Thus it now appears we were badly misled...."

On other matters, Haldeman said he never asked the Central Intelligence Agency to participate in the Watergate coverup, as had been alleged. He also denied ever having a discussion with Magruder in which Magruder told him about the coverup.

The witness also denied Strachan's testimony that he ordered Strachan to destroy documents relating to the electronic surveillance of Democratic headquarters. "I have no recollection of giving Mr. Strachan any instructions to destroy any materials," Haldeman testified.

Strachan had testified that one of those documents concerned a "talking paper" about a $300,000 intelligence budget that Haldeman took to a meeting with the re-election committee director, John N. Mitchell, on April 4, 1972. Haldeman said there was no discussion of intelligence at the meeting and that he could recall no such document.

Ehrlichman Testimony. Ehrlichman's exchanges with counsel Dash were often bitter and heated. On two occasions Dash accused Ehrlichman of "making speeches" instead of answering. Ehrlichman responded at one point: "You have a way of assuming your questions, Mr. Dash, with facts that are only in your knowledge."

During Ehrlichman's testimony, Committee Vice Chairman Howard H. Baker Jr. (R Tenn.) and minority counsel Fred D. Thompson accused Dash of asking improper questions and interrupting the witness' answers. It was the most obvious public display of partisan disagreement on the committee. Baker said the disagreement might have been evidence that "the committee is tired."

But in answer to Dash's questions, Ehrlichman revised some of his earlier testimony. He said he was in error regarding a meeting with Nixon June 20, 1972, at which he had testified earlier that the only subjects of their discussion were welfare reform and busing. He had said he never discussed Watergate with the President at that time. However, he said July 30 that the talk also dealt with government wiretapping and therefore might have touched on Watergate.

Ehrlichman also retreated on the subject of the break-in at the office of Daniel Ellsberg's psychiatrist. He had maintained throughout his testimony that the break-in was legal and that the President had told him so in March. But in answer to Dash's questions, he said the President never gave him a "legal opinion" on it in March. The President said he felt the break-in was "important (and) necessary" and that he could not criticize the burglars, Ehrlichman testified.

Also in regard to the Ellsberg break-in, Ehrlichman, who claimed he learned of it after it took place, said he did not consider telling the President about it. It would have "unduly taxed his consideration," and he could not have done anything about it, he said. Nixon issued a statement May 22 saying the break-in was illegal and that he would have disapproved it had he known of it in advance. *(p. 90)*

Ehrlichman was asked to comment on a sworn statement by Clark MacGregor, who succeeded Mitchell as re-election committee chairman, that was made public July 29. In the statement, MacGregor said he was "lied to" by administration officials about Watergate.

The witness disagreed with MacGregor, saying there was ample evidence available to him on Sept. 13 based on an earlier briefing by Attorney General Richard G. Kleindienst, but that MacGregor declined to make a statement on Watergate. *(MacGregor statement, box, p. 236)*

Ehrlichman also was asked about the so-called La Costa meeting in February 1973, at which several White House aides, including himself, Dean and Haldeman, gathered in California to discuss strategies for the Senate Watergate hearings. He agreed with much of Dean's testimony about the meeting, including a discussion of tactics to counter the Senate hearings. Ehrlichman referred to them as "dilatory tactics." He said it was felt the committee was critical of Nixon and that Ervin was a "partisan" figure. The group certainly did not feel the inquiry would be "benign," he testified.

Ehrlichman also revealed that Assistant Attorney General Henry E. Petersen, who was in charge of the Watergate probe for the Justice Department, had advised President Nixon on April 15 to fire Haldeman and himself, but not Dean. He said Petersen told the President there was no legal liability on Ehrlichman's or Haldeman's part, but that they should be let go for appearances' sake. According to Ehrlichman, Petersen recommended that Dean be kept on at the White House until the Justice Department's case against the counsel was completed.

Ehrlichman said Nixon chose not to take the advice, and on April 16 dictated to Ehrlichman two letters of resignation for Dean. Dean testified that he refused to sign either and told the President he would not resign unless Haldeman and Ehrlichman also did so.

By April 27, Ehrlichman said, he and Haldeman had agreed that the best course for them to follow was to ask for leaves of absence, and Nixon agreed to this. But he and Haldeman changed their minds on April 29 and handed in their resignations, effective April 30. Dean was fired April 30.

Witness July 31

Chairman Ervin charged H. R. Haldeman and the White House with collaboration in the preparation of Haldeman's testimony before the Senate select Watergate committee.

Ervin's accusation stemmed from Haldeman's testimony July 30 and 31 concerning tape recordings of meetings between Nixon and former presidential counsel John Dean on Sept. 15, 1972, and March 21, 1973. Dean testified that he told Nixon everything about the Watergate break-in and coverup at the March 21 meeting, but that he believed as a result of the Sept. 15 meeting that Nixon already was aware of the coverup.

Haldeman shocked the committee July 30 by saying that he had listened to tapes of the March 21 meeting in April and of the Sept. 15 meeting in July, the latter after his departure from the White House. Nixon had refused to release the tapes to the committee or to special prosecutor Archibald Cox.

Haldeman's statements July 30 came from prepared testimony late in the day. The July 31 session was the first chance the committee had to interrogate him.

Ervin drew from Haldeman and his lawyer, John J. Wilson, the admission that Wilson had checked with the White House before Haldeman prepared an addendum to his lengthy statement on the March 21 meeting. "What's wrong with that, Mr. Chairman?" Wilson asked.

"That's what we call in North Carolina 'colludin' together,' " Ervin replied. "The clear indication is that the White House counsel wanted Mr. Haldeman to reveal his interpretation of the tapes to the public."

Haldeman answered that he gave his testimony only after the committee had overruled his objections that he could not discuss what he had learned from the tapes because of an order by the President. Ervin, noting that Haldeman had prepared an addendum on the conversation, replied, "This is what I would call a powder puff objection."

Later, Daniel K. Inouye (D Hawaii), also referring to the addendum, said Haldeman appeared "overly eager" to testify on the March 21 meeting. Haldeman answered that he actually had two addenda ready, one in case his objection was overruled and one if it was not.

Asked by Ervin why he felt he had to check with the White House on the propriety of discussing the taped conversation, Haldeman replied that he wanted to be sure the testimony did not conflict with presidential guidelines on executive privilege. He said a ruling on his testimony was requested July 29, but that the White House never was told what he would say about the meeting.

In answer to a question from Herman E. Talmadge (D Ga.), Haldeman said he was permitted to hear the Sept. 15 tape not as a potential witness before the committee, but as a former presidential aide. But, asked Talmadge, "Why could you as a private citizen listen to it?" The former White House chief of staff said that was a question he could not answer, "except that I did it as a means of reporting to the President." In earlier testimony, Haldeman had said he was authorized by the President to listen to tapes of the two meetings.

Haldeman answered questions in a soft-spoken courteous manner at opposite extremes from the snapping, almost contemptuous tones employed by his friend and predecessor before the committee, John D. Ehrlichman.

Details on Tapes. He offered the committee more details on how he received the tapes and what he did with them. Haldeman said he could not recall whether he or the President initiated the request that he listen to the tape of the Sept. 15 meeting, which Haldeman had attended in its entirety. He said merely that the President told him to listen to the tape and give him a report.

Haldeman said he listened to the tape between July 9 and 11. This was before former White House aide Alexander P. Butterfield revealed on July 16 that the tapes existed. *(Butterfield testimony, p. 192)*

The tapes were delivered to him, Haldeman said, in a guest office he was using in the Executive Office Building, and he took them home overnight to play them. Asked why the tape of the Sept. 15 meeting was selected, Haldeman said the President and he had not listened to it, and "obviously it was of considerable importance," because their recollections of the meeting differed from Dean's.

The tapes were given to him he said, by Stephen Bull, a White House aide. Asked how he could explain that he was allowed to take the tapes home, Haldeman replied that he was acting on the President's orders, that it was not generally known the tapes existed and that no one thought it ever would be known.

He said he had "several other tapes" of other meetings in his possession at that time, but did not identify them. Haldeman explained that he did not listen to the other tapes, because he had not been at the meetings they related to.

He said he listened to the Sept. 15 tape only once and took notes on what he heard. Then he reported the content of the tapes to the President via special presidential counsel Buzhardt, he said. He never made a written report to Nixon and he no longer had his notes, having turned them over to the White House, he added.

Regarding the March 21 tapes, Haldeman said he listened to them in his White House office, again on orders from the President. He put the date of that occurrence as after April 15, and said he did not believe it had anything to do with the President's April 17 statement in which Nixon said major new developments in the Watergate case had come to him on March 21. *(p. 18)*

Ervin said Haldeman's testimony about the two meetings was "counterfeit evidence," because he had heard the tapes and the committee had not. But in answer to

Stevenson Attack on Nixon

In a Senate speech July 30, Adlai E. Stevenson III (D Ill.) accused President Nixon of breach of contract with the Senate, betrayal of the Senate's trust, obstruction of justice and "covering up the coverup" of Watergate.

Stevenson based his attack on testimony and correspondence of Attorney General Elliot L. Richardson during Richardson's confirmation hearings in May. Stevenson quoted from repeated assurances from Richardson that Nixon had promised him "absolute authority," which he in turn had passed on to special prosecutor Archibald Cox.

It was on Nixon's word and Richardson's assurances, Stevenson continued, that the Senate confirmed Richardson. But Nixon broke his word by denying Cox access to Watergate-related White House tapes, he said. *(Confirmation story, p. 96; subpoenas, p. 209)*

"I am sickened by the President's disdain for the orderly processes of the law," said Stevenson. "He does not seem to care about his own solemn assurances. They are made one day and are inoperative the next."

Stevenson accused Nixon of forcing confrontations with the legislative, executive and judicial branches. "By placing himself above the law and beyond accountability for his own words and actions," Stevenson charged, "he threatens the Congress with the choice of either confessing the bankruptcy of the system, by doing nothing, or of commencing impeachment proceedings. If the President had an honorable alternative—truth, vindication and a quick conclusion for this unhappy chapter—the public has a right to assume he would take it."

Richardson Rebuttal. The attorney general issued a statement the same day in which he said that Stevenson's speech "indicates that he completely, and unfortunately, misunderstands the charter for the special prosecutor and the elaboration of his authority and responsibilities that were discussed in full during my confirmation hearings."

The charter, according to Richardson, not only gave Cox full access to documentary evidence; it gave him authority "to contest the assertion of executive privilege or any other testimonial privilege." Both in his confirmation testimony and in the description of the prosecutor's duties, Richardson said, it was made clear that some documents might be withheld on these grounds.

Cox, he said, has "full authority to challenge the claim of executive privilege in any form he chooses," as well as the right to appeal any court decisions.

Sen. Lowell P. Weicker Jr. (R Conn.), who claimed it was "grossly unfair" for Haldeman to testify about something the committee could not listen to, Ervin said he would admit Haldeman's testimony because it was the best the committee could get at that time. He added, however, that in view of the President's remark in a letter to the committee July 23, that various people could have different interpretations of the conversations, he would be "scrupulous" in accepting Haldeman's version. *(Letter text, p. 225)*

Committee Vice Chairman Baker added that a byproduct of Haldeman's testimony was to increase further the need for the committee to have access to the tapes.

Helms Meeting. The witness also was questioned closely on a meeting he had June 23, 1972, with then CIA Director Richard Helms and the deputy director, Gen. Vernon L. Walters. Walters had charged that he was "ordered" by Haldeman to meet with former acting FBI Director L. Patrick Gray and to tell Gray the FBI's investigation of Watergate might uncover secret CIA activities and to limit the bureau's probe.

Haldeman testified that the purpose of the meeting, as explained to him by Nixon, was to see if there was any CIA involvement in Watergate and to tell the CIA that the FBI had expressed concern to the President that the CIA might be involved. Haldeman said Dean had told Nixon of the bureau's concern.

Then why, asked committee counsel Samuel Dash, did Walters say he had been ordered to see Gray? "This seems to be a difficult problem to get across," Haldeman began, and explained that the President was concerned that a full FBI probe might uncover CIA activities not related to Watergate. He said Nixon wanted Walters to meet with Gray to make sure that the bureau's probe did not mix into CIA matters.

Democratic Violence. Haldeman also was questioned about allegations in his July 30 prepared statement that Nixon's campaign opponents engaged in activities such as bombing and burning the President's campaign offices, violently demonstrating against the President, harassing his wife and family and damaging property.

Asked to detail his charges, Haldeman said they all had been "documented," but did not mention by whom. He gave specifics of only two incidents. One was a Nixon appearance in Los Angeles. Haldeman said the entire block around the Century Plaza hotel was cordoned off by police against violent demonstrators who destroyed property and stabbed a policeman. The other incident, Haldeman said, included the bombing and burning of two Nixon campaign offices in California and Arizona.

Asked to document his charge that Nixon's opponents were responsible for the demonstration, Haldeman cited only the Los Angeles demonstration where, he said, Sen. George McGovern's (D S.D.) headquarters gave out handbills noting the time and place of the anti-Nixon rally.

Ervin stated that investigative agencies had no evidence to back Haldeman's assertions. He produced a letter to Dash from John H. Davitt, chief of the Justice Department's internal security section. The letter, dated June 8, said that Justice and FBI files had no information about criminal acts allegedly directed against Republicans in 1972 by Democrats.

Haldeman also testified on a number of other topics. He denied having any detailed knowledge of the so-called White House plumbers; of Tom Charles Huston's intelligence-gathering plan; of Jeb Magruder's intention to testify falsely before the Watergate grand jury, or of $350,000 from a special White House fund that would go toward buying the silence of Watergate defendants.

Speedup. In order to speed up the first phase of the hearings, which the committee hoped to complete by Aug. 10, members began on July 31 to limit their questions to rounds of 10 minutes apiece and to answer Senate roll calls on an individual basis rather than in a group as they had earlier. The committee also decided to begin 30 minutes earlier each day and to recess for lunch for 90 minutes instead of two hours.

Witness August 1

A White House memo introduced in the Watergate hearings Aug. 1 contained a warning that other documents might "directly involve the President" in the favorable settlement of antitrust actions against International Telephone and Telegraph Corporation (ITT). The papers "would lay this case on the President's doorstep," the memo claimed.

The memo, dated March 30, 1972, was written by former White House aide Charles W. Colson to former chief of staff H. R. Haldeman. It dealt with strategies surrounding the nomination of Richard G. Kleindienst as attorney general.

The memo also appeared to indicate that former Attorney General John N. Mitchell had lied under oath to the Senate Judiciary Committee during 1972 confirmation hearings for Kleindienst, his successor. The nomination had encountered trouble when it was alleged that the Justice Department had settled its suit against ITT in exchange for an ITT pledge of $400,000 to the 1972 Republican national convention, then scheduled for San Diego, Calif. *(Nomination hearings, 1972 Almanac p. 207)*

The memo, citing another earlier memo dated before the ITT settlement, referred to a "$400,000 arrangement with ITT." It said the earlier memo put Mitchell "on constructive notice at least of the ITT commitment,...facts which he has denied under oath."

The March 30 memo expressed concern about the whereabouts of copies of the earlier memo, saying it could be "lying around somewhere at 1701." This was White House shorthand for the Nixon re-election committee, located at 1701 Pennsylvania Ave., in Washington.

The memo was introduced by committee counsel Samuel Dash, in the context of questions he had been asking Haldeman about the witness' assertions that he would always inform the President of potentially embarrassing developments. Dash noted that the memo was dated five days before Haldeman met with Nixon to discuss the Kleindienst nomination, and asked Haldeman if he had discussed the contents of the memo with the President.

Haldeman answered that he could not recall if he had and that he was not familiar with the memo. He said he recalled a lot of problems concerning the

Kleindienst nomination, but that he "was not a principal in efforts" to have the nomination confirmed.

Sen. Edward J. Gurney (R Fla.) heatedly objected to discussing the memo, arguing that because Colson's testimony had been delayed until the second phase of the hearings, it was not fair to question Haldeman about it. Gurney also objected that he had not seen the memo before Dash read from it.

Dash answered that it had been received the night before from a secretary being interrogated by a committee staff member. Gurney continued to argue that Colson should be called immediately to testify, but Chairman Ervin cut him off, saying the committee already had voted twice on a list of witnesses for the conclusion of phase one of the hearings, and Colson's name was not among them. Dash then moved on to other areas. *(Memo text, p. 268)*

Weicker Questioning. Haldeman completed his testimony after more than two full days at the witness table, still unshaken despite tough grilling, especially from Weicker of Connecticut. In a concluding statement, the witness spoke of the high standards Nixon set for the White House staff and of his "deep regret and sorrow that in a few instances there was a failure" to live up to them.

Weicker's questioning concentrated on Haldeman's interpretation of a series of memos, most of which had been given the committee by an earlier witness, John W. Dean III, the former presidential counsel.

One was a memo to Haldeman from a White House aide, Ronald H. Walker, dated Oct. 14, 1971. It dealt with a scheduled presidential appearance in Charlotte, N.C. Walker wrote that 100 to 200 anti-Nixon demonstrators were expected. "They will be violent," he wrote, "they will have extremely obscene signs.... It will not only be directed toward the President, but also toward (evangelist) Billy Graham." Haldeman acknowledged to Weicker that he had written "good" in the margin beside the statement about the violent demonstrators and the obscene signs and "great" after the reference to Graham.

What mentality, Weicker angrily asked, was there in the White House that referred to violence and obscenity directed against the President as good or great? Haldeman said the reason he reacted with those words was that previous anti-Nixon demonstrators had been ignored and that he hoped the press and television would publicize the Charlotte activities before the American people.

Another memo, dated Feb. 10, 1973, was from Haldeman to Dean. It began, "We need to get our people to put out the story on the foreign or communist money that was used in support of demonstrations against the President in 1972. We should tie all 1972 demonstrations to McGovern and thus to the Democrats as part of the peace movement." It went on to say, "The investigation should be brought to include the peace movement, which leads directly to McGovern and Teddy (Edward M.) Kennedy (D Mass.)."

Haldeman accepted responsibility for the memo but asserted that someone else must have written it. He emphasized that he wanted to develop the "facts" of Democrats being a party to anti-Nixon demonstrations, but Weicker concentrated on the first sentence of the memo.

Haldeman did not, he charged, really want to develop facts "because you said, 'We need to get our people to put out the story....' " Haldeman answered that it was his understanding that there were facts to support his statement. Where were the facts? asked Weicker. "I don't know," replied Haldeman, adding that he understood Dean had them. "This type of business... is a disgrace," charged Weicker.

While Weicker's questioning was sharp, he lost his temper only once. This was in reference to Haldeman's

MacGregor Deposition

Clark MacGregor, President Nixon's 1972 campaign manager from July 1 through the election, disagreed sharply with John D. Ehrlichman, the President's domestic affairs adviser, over Ehrlichman's willingness to disclose information about Watergate.

"I don't recall that Ehrlichman was a champion of disclosure during this particular period," said MacGregor in the July 20 sworn statement, made available to the press on July 27. He said that Ehrlichman had not told him about such matters as the burglary of Daniel Ellsberg's psychiatrist's office, a meeting between Ehrlichman and former acting FBI Director L. Patrick Gray III or meetings with Central Intelligence Agency officials.

"It appears as though John Ehrlichman had a great deal of information which was available for disclosure which was unknown to me and thus, of course, it is utterly ridiculous for John Ehrlichman, who had a great deal of information I didn't have, to be calling on me to disclose information that I didn't possess but which was known to him."

MacGregor, a former representative from Minnesota (1961-1971) and former chief of congressional liaison for the White House, gave the deposition in connection with civil suits arising from the June 17, 1972, break-in at Democratic national headquarters. After the Nov. 7 election, MacGregor became a vice president of United Aircraft Corporation. He remained in Washington.

In his five days of testimony before the Senate Watergate committee, Ehrlichman portrayed himself as a man who wanted to lay out the facts on Watergate. In a deposition given in May in the civil litigation, he said that after MacGregor had replaced John N. Mitchell as campaign director, he (Ehrlichman) had proposed a "definitive statement" on Watergate. "I urged that we make a vigorous effort to determine whether anybody else might be involved at that time," he said. "For reasons that I can't assign, that was not done, and the matter went by the board."

If such a suggestion had indeed been made, MacGregor told attorneys for the Democratic National Committee in his deposition, "it was really playing back to me what I had been saying right along."

MacGregor was asked if he thought he had been lied to by presidential advisers. He replied: "It seems obvious now that I was being misled, deceived and, in the phraseology of one story in *The New York Times*, 'lied to repeatedly.' "

allegations that Communists were involved in the 1972 presidential campaign. Referring to Bernard L. Barker, a convicted Watergate conspirator who testified that he also believed Communists took part in McGovern's campaign, Weicker shouted at Haldeman: "Mr. Barker is in jail today because somebody sold him a story" about Communists in McGovern's campaign. *(Barker testimony, p. 85)*

The Connecticut senator, in bringing up the two memos, also was attempting to counter Haldeman's opening and subsequent testimony that the Democrats in general and Nixon campaign opponents in particular were responsible for demonstrations and certain illegal acts against the President. But Haldeman consistently refused to identify any Democrat with particular acts, insisting the information was documented somewhere. Asked specifically by Weicker what acts he could ascribe to Sen. George McGovern (D S.D.), Haldeman said he could not answer. Haldeman denied that the White House ever paid people to demonstrate against Nixon.

Weicker's barrage of memos also included another from Haldeman to Dean, dated Feb. 9, 1973. In it, Haldeman suggested that Pepsico board chairman Donald Kendall, a Nixon backer, be ordered to fire Cartha DeLoach, a former top FBI official who went to work for Pepsico, if DeLoach refused to tell the White House what he knew about alleged wiretapping activities against Nixon in 1968. How, Weicker asked Haldeman, could he order the firing of DeLoach? "Do you have some hold over Mr. Kendall?"

Haldeman responded that Mitchell had a personal relationship with Kendall and that "this was a question of applying additional pressure on Mr. DeLoach."

"Oh, I see," said Weicker. "We now have the White House reaching down through you and saying to citizens of this country, if they don't do what is asked of them, they will be fired."

Haldeman replied without a trace of emotion: "That is the suggestion there. Obviously, there is no ability on our part to carry it out."

"Well, you took a good swing at the pitch," retorted Weicker.

Weicker brought up another memo, this one from Jeb Magruder, then a White House aide, to Haldeman, dated Jan. 21, 1970. It concerned a plan to monitor the news media. Haldeman acknowledged his written notation at the end: "I'll approve whatever will work—and am concerned with results—not methods."

Weicker asked: "Don't you feel that might have been in the psychology which led to the excesses we've had described to this committee?"

Haldeman disagreed, saying the notation referred only to the memo's contents, not to general policy.

Candidate Surveillance. In other testimony, Haldeman denied any knowledge of White House surveillance of Sen. Kennedy, although he acknowledged there was some concern in the executive mansion about the senator's anti-war activities. A previous witness, Anthony T. Ulasewicz, had testified that he investigated Kennedy for the White House. *(p. 200)*

Haldeman did concede, however, that he found no fault with investigating the backgrounds of opposition candidates. Asked about Ulasewicz's testimony that he sought to dig up "dirt" about Nixon political opponents, Haldeman said, "It's important to know the facts about an opponent, whatever they may be."

More on Tapes. Haldeman also added to earlier testimony about the tapes of Sept. 15, 1972, and March 21, 1973, conversations between Dean and Nixon that he had listened to. He said there was no connection between his listening to the Sept. 15 tape in early July and the revelation a few days later by a former White House aide that the tapes of presidential conversations existed. He denied erasing or altering the Sept. 15 tape when he had it in his home.

Asked about his July 31 testimony that he had more than the Sept. 15 tape in his possession, Haldeman said he was given three reels for each of three different dates, but that he did not listen to them because they involved conversations to which he was not a party. He also said he had the presidential telephone tapes for those three days but, for the same reason, did not play them. Haldeman said he could not recall what dates they applied to.

Sen. Daniel K. Inouye (D Hawaii), referring to testimony of another witness that the tapes were kept in order to provide a historical record of the Nixon administration, elicited from Haldeman the remark that the President never intended to release them to the public, even after he left office. Then how, asked Inouye, could Haldeman account for the testimony that they were for historical purposes? They were for the President's private records, Haldeman replied.

Other Testimony. In other testimony, Haldeman said he could not recall ever requesting the Internal Revenue Service (IRS) to do audits of Nixon's opponents or trying to prod the IRS into being more responsive to White House requirements, as had been charged. He said, however, that the IRS bureaucracy was anti-Nixon.

Haldeman also was asked about the so-called "enemies" lists introduced by Dean. Haldeman said inclusion on the list meant simply that that person would not be given White House courtesies, such as invitations to functions. He denied any knowledge of FBI or IRS checks of the people on the lists. He hedged on whether he had ordered the FBI to probe CBS newsman Daniel Schorr, saying he asked merely for the bureau's file on Schorr, not a background check. Haldeman maintained that the FBI keeps files on all well-known persons.

John J. Wilson, Haldeman's peppery counsel, interrupted questioning of the witness six times, claiming the questions were irrelevant. On two occasions, Chairman Ervin ruled in his favor.

At the end of Haldeman's testimony, Wilson charged that Inouye had injured his client "by a blow below the belt" and asked to enter a motion. Ervin did not allow the motion, saying Wilson could complain to the committee in writing about Inouye, who was not present at the time.

While Wilson's complaint was not made public, it was believed that he referred to Inouye's comment about former presidential aide John Ehrlichman, another client of the lawyer, and his attempt to question Haldeman about 1962 campaign practices. During Ehrlichman's testimony, Inouye was heard to mutter, after questioning the witness, "What a liar." At the Aug. 1 session, Inouye tried to question Haldeman about his role in the 1962 Nixon gubernatorial campaign in California and illegal practices by the Nixon organization during that campaign. But Ervin said the matter was irrelevant.

During the luncheon recess Aug. 1, Wilson referred to Inouye as "that little Jap." *(Box, next column)*

Lawyer vs. 'That Little Jap'

After the morning session of the Aug. 1 Senate Watergate hearings, a reporter asked John J. Wilson, attorney for former White House chief of staff H. R. Haldeman, if he thought Haldeman had been fairly questioned by Sen. Lowell P. Weicker Jr. (R Conn.).

"Oh, I don't mind Sen. Weicker," the 72-year-old Washington lawyer replied. "What I mind is that little Jap." He referred to Sen. Daniel K. Inouye (D Hawaii), who is of Japanese ancestry.

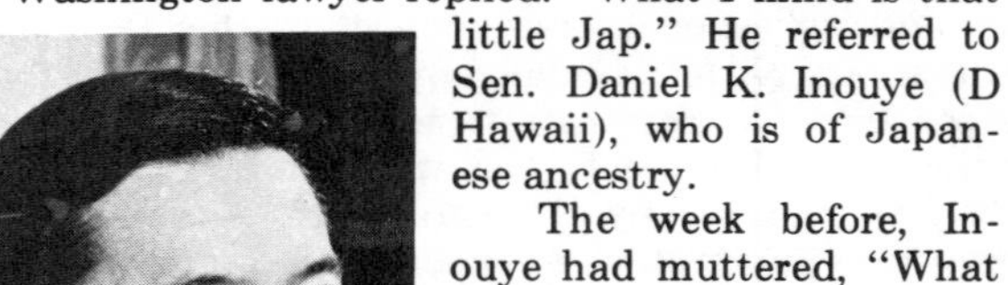

Sen. Daniel K. Inouye

The week before, Inouye had muttered, "What a liar," after he questioned another former White House aide, John Ehrlichman. He apparently thought his microphone had been turned off. Wilson represented both Ehrlichman and Haldeman.

"That's just the way I speak," Wilson told reporters later. "I consider it a description of the man—I wouldn't mind being called a little American."

"I don't think it's necessary to comment," said Inouye. "I think his statement speaks for itself."

Witnesses Aug. 2

Former CIA Director Richard M. Helms told the committee there was no agency involvement in the Watergate break-in, "no involvement whatsoever."

Helms, who left the agency earlier in the year to become ambassador to Iran, virtually shouted the point home: "The message doesn't seem to get across," he said. "The agency had nothing to do with the Watergate break-in. Can all the newsmen in the room hear me now?"

In other testimony, Helms revealed that one of the convicted Watergate burglars, Eugenio R. Martinez, was on the CIA payroll at the time of the break-in on June 17, 1972. He said Martinez was then receiving a retainer of $100 a month for information on Cuban exiles who arrived in Florida. Martinez's retainer was cut off immediately after the FBI informed the CIA of his arrest, said Helms.

It had been revealed previously that two other convicted burglars, Bernard L. Barker and Frank A. Sturgis, were contract employees of the agency at the time of the Bay of Pigs operation in 1961.

Following Helms to the witness table was Gen. Robert E. Cushman, the Marine Corps commandant and former deputy director of the CIA under Helms. Cushman corroborated and expanded on Helms' testimony regarding the loan of CIA equipment to another convicted Watergate conspirator, E. Howard Hunt Jr.

Post-Break-in Meeting. Helms' testimony dealt mainly with his role in a meeting June 23, 1972, just after the break-in, in the office of former White House aide John D. Ehrlichman. Present at the meeting were Helms' deputy, Lt. Gen. Vernon Walters, who succeeded Cushman, former White House chief of staff H. R. Haldeman, and Ehrlichman.

According to Helms, Haldeman, who did most of the talking at the meeting, told him the White House was "Taking a lot of flak" over the break-in and the Democrats were trying to capitalize on it. Haldeman asked, Helms related, whether the CIA was involved. Helms said he assured him the agency was not.

Haldeman, Helms said, told Walters to meet with L. Patrick Gray III, acting FBI director, and tell him the bureau's probe might run into CIA operations in Mexico and that he (Gray) should "taper off." At a later point in his testimony, Helms quoted Haldeman as using the word "restrain" in reference to the FBI investigation.

Helms testified that he did not know what CIA operation in Mexico Haldeman was talking about. But, he said, it was possible something was going on in that country that he did not know about, so he did not question Haldeman's assertion. Helms testified that Haldeman "used no language saying stop" in reference to the FBI's investigation.

Asked why Walters was assigned to meet with Gray, rather than Helms, who was the director, the witness replied, "I was being talked around." He said any sensible person would have wondered why Walters was chosen to contact Gray, and that he did wonder about it. He said he surmised that for some reason Haldeman wanted Walters to do the job, and that it was not a point worth arguing about.

Helms testified that he had talked with Gray on June 22 and assured the acting FBI director that the CIA was not involved in the Watergate break-in. It was at that point that Helms shouted the denial.

Fred D. Thompson, committee minority counsel, noted a contradiction between Helms' testimony and his previous testimony before the Senate Armed Services Committee on the June 23 meeting. Helms had told the Armed Services Committee that there was no discussion of the Watergate break-in at the meeting. He told Thompson, however, that his recollection about the break-in discussion came after he had talked to Walters and reviewed a Walters memo on the subject of the meeting.

Helms said he instructed Walters that, when he met with Gray, Walters should restrict his discussion to the CIA's delimitation agreement with the FBI. Under the agreement, he explained, whenever one agency conflicted with the other's operation, it would notify that agency so any problem could be resolved.

Bail Request. In answer to other questions, Helms discussed Walters' meetings with former presidential counsel Dean. Dean had testified that he was instructed by Ehrlichman to try to get Walters and the CIA to agree to provide bail money to the seven Watergate defendants and the salaries of the defendants until they got out of jail. Helms said he told Walters not to cooperate in any way. Walters, Helms said, rejected Dean's overtures.

On the subject of the Watergate break-in itself, in which five of the seven conspirators were caught, Helms called it "amateurish in the extreme." Break-ins and bugging operations, he said, "are very difficult activities, and those who do it have to be trained up to the minute."

Asked why he did not tell the President about Dean's requests for CIA assistance, which Helms described as "feelers," he said he wanted to keep the agency as far from the White House as possible on the requests and added that Dean's requests never were direct.

Psychological Profile. Helms also testified about the CIA's help in preparation of a psychological profile on Daniel Ellsberg, who gave the Pentagon Papers to *The New York Times.* He said he agreed to have the CIA do the profile at the request of David Young, a White House aide working for Ehrlichman. Helms said two profiles were prepared on Ellsberg by CIA specialists from information provided by Young. He said Young found neither profile satisfactory, and the CIA specialists began complaining to Helms that the information Young provided was inadequate.

Ehrlichman, in his testimony, said the office of Ellsberg's psychiatrist was burglarized in order to get material for a psychological profile on Ellsberg. Helms said he did not know anything about the September 1971 Ellsberg break-in until this year, and that the agency does not require psychological records of a person to do a profile on him. The agency usually works from public sources, he explained.

Helms conceded that the CIA developed film taken by Hunt at the time of the Ellsberg break-in, but that the agency did not know what the photographs related to when they developed the film. The agency kept in its files only Xerox copies of the photographs, he said.

Equipment Loan. Cushman said the loan of CIA equipment to Hunt began with a phone call from Ehrlichman on July 7, 1971, when Ehrlichman asked Cushman to meet with Hunt. Cushman had known Ehrlichman since 1960 when he served as a military aide to then Vice President Nixon and Ehrlichman was working on Nixon's presidential campaign.

The meeting with Hunt took place July 23, 1971, Cushman said. He said the conversation was tape recorded, because he wanted a record of it and Hunt requested a private meeting. A transcript of the meeting, introduced in evidence, showed that Hunt told Cushman he was on a "highly sensitive mission" to get information from "an individual whose ideology we aren't entirely sure of."

Cushman said he authorized the agency's technical services division to provide Hunt, a former CIA employee, with fake identification, a wig and a voice-altering device, and that he arranged for the material to be delivered to a "safe house" in Washington. Cushman said he did not question Hunt about why he wanted the material because he assumed it would be for a "one-time interview."

According to Cushman, Hunt later secured other agency equipment, including a tape recorder, a camera enclosed in a tobacco pouch and false identity papers for G. Gordon Liddy, another Watergate conspirator.

Cushman testified that all this was unknown to him until the technical services division began complaining about Hunt's repeated requests. He said he did not know what the equipment was used for, but when Hunt next requested a New York City office and telephone, he decided to draw the line. After checking with Helms, Cushman said he called Ehrlichman and told him the agency would no longer honor Hunt's requests. The only other Hunt request Cushman personally denied was for a CIA secretary stationed in Paris, he testified.

Cushman, agreeing with Helms, said that to the best of his knowledge, the equipment and material given Hunt were not used in the Ellsberg break-in.

Other Testimony. In other testimony, Cushman said that in January he deleted Ehrlichman's name from a memo explaining the genesis of Hunt's visit to him in July 1971. He said an original memo he wrote on the subject, dated Jan. 8, 1973, contained the names of Ehrlichman and Dean and that of former White House aide Charles W. Colson as the person who originally asked him to meet with Hunt. He could not recall who originally contacted him, he said. A second memo on the subject, dated Jan. 10, 1973, deleted all the names.

Cushman explained that when Ehrlichman and Dean saw the first memo, they called him, insisting that neither of them initiated the meeting. Ehrlichman said he was out of town on July 7, Cushman testified. He said that in order to avoid embarrassing anyone, and because he was no longer at the CIA and did not have ready access to the tape of the Hunt meeting which mentioned Ehrlichman, Cushman wrote the second memo without mentioning who initiated the meeting.

The memo, he said, was requested by a high-ranking CIA official, William E. Colby, for use by the Justice Department. Cushman said he sent it to Ehrlichman at Colby's request.

Daily Chronology

Following is a day-to-day chronology of the week's events:

JULY 26

(Earlier July 26 events, p. 220)

Nixon Tapes. The Senate Watergate investigating committee moved to force Nixon to comply with subpoenas of certain tapes and documents. The President had refused to disclose the tapes, claiming separation of powers and executive privilege. The committee voted unanimously to go to U.S. District Court to seek the recordings. Special prosecutor Archibald Cox also obtained a show-cause order from U.S. District Court Judge John J. Sirica directing Nixon to explain by Aug. 7 why he should not be compelled to release the tapes to Cox.

With a major constitutional battle in sight, White House deputy press secretary Gerald L. Warren announced Nixon would abide by a "definitive" Supreme Court decision. Committee Chairman Ervin defended the lawsuit as "essential if we are to determine whether the President is above the law." *(p. 208)*

Ehrlichman Testimony. In his third day of testimony before the Senate committee, former White House domestic adviser John D. Ehrlichman said that the "plumbers" group that investigated document leaks also was engaged in another probe that had to be kept secret for national security reasons. *(Ehrlichman testimony, p. 216)*

Ehrlichman also conceded, under grilling by Sen. Lowell P. Weicker Jr. (R Conn.), that he had abandoned L. Patrick Gray III when Gray's FBI nomination ran into difficulty in the Senate. Weicker referred to a transcript of a telephone call between Ehrlichman and John Dean in which Ehrlichman said of Gray and his troubles: "Well, I think we ought to let him hang there. Let him twist slowly, slowly in the wind."

Ellsberg Rebuttal. In a Los Angeles news conference, Daniel Ellsberg said that John D. Ehrlichman made "false and slanderous" allegations in hinting that Ellsberg might have given the Pentagon Papers to the Soviet embassy in Washington.

Meanwhile, Los Angeles District Attorney Joseph Busch said the grand jury inquiry into the break-in at the office of Ellsberg's psychiatrist would not be "impeded by any claim that President Nixon regarded the burglary as justifiable."

Liddy Silence. A contempt of Congress citation against convicted Watergate conspirator G. Gordon Liddy was delayed by younger members of the House Armed Services Committee, who asked for more time to study Liddy's legal defense of his refusal to testify before the committee's Intelligence Subcommittee.

Laird Advice. Melvin R. Laird, counselor to the President, hinted to newsmen that he had advised Nixon to release the tapes sought by the Senate investigating committee and special prosecutor Cox. But he said his recommendations were based on political considerations only and that his advice on procedures in the Watergate probe was "not always followed."

Baker Finances. Sen. Howard H. Baker Jr. (R Tenn.) released a list of previously undisclosed contributors to his 1972 re-election campaign. Baker, vice chairman of the Senate Watergate committee, collected $264,000 and spent about $80,000 before a new federal law requiring full disclosure took effect April 7, 1972. He disclosed his pre-April-7 records to the Associated Press after the wire service reported that he had $185,000 cash on hand from undisclosed sources when the new law took effect.

JULY 27

Ehrlichman Testimony. In his fourth day before the Senate investigating committee, Ehrlichman contradicted the charge by Dean that Nixon had been personally involved in the Watergate coverup. Ehrlichman testified that Nixon did not get a thorough briefing until April 14, when Ehrlichman told him about the coverup. The witness also suggested that the coverup had been engineered to disguise the involvement of John N. Mitchell. *(Ehrlichman testimony, p. 230; Dean testimony, p. 151; Dean statement excerpts, p. 163)*

Poll Report

As Watergate investigations progress, confidence in the Nixon presidency decreases, according to the latest Harris Survey. But a tiny plurality thinks he should remain in office even if he ordered a coverup. *(Previous poll report, p. 218)*

In the poll, conducted among 1,485 households July 18-22, Harris found the overall rating of Nixon was not at an all-time low (that was in March 1971). But personal confidence in the President was. These were the questions and the responses:

"In view of what has happened in the Watergate affair, do you think President Nixon should resign as President or not?"

	July	June	May
Should resign	22%	22%	14%
Should not resign	66	62	75
Not sure	12	16	11

"If it is proven that President Nixon ordered the coverup of White House involvement in Watergate, after Republican agents were caught there, do you think he should resign or not?"

	July	June
Should resign	44%	46%
Should not resign	45	40
Not sure	11	14

"How would you rate President Nixon on inspiring confidence personally in the White House—excellent, pretty good, only fair, or poor?"

	July	June	May
Good/excellent	21%	24%	32%
Only fair/poor	69	65	57
Not sure	10	11	11

"How would you rate the job President Nixon is doing as President—excellent, pretty good, only fair, or poor?"

	July	June	February
Good/excellent	42%	48%	60%
Only fair/poor	54	49	39
Not sure	4	3	1

Baker vs. Kennedy. Persons in the same Harris sample who voted in the 1972 election were also asked their preference for President in a trial heat between Sen. Howard H. Baker Jr. (R Tenn.), vice chairman of the Senate Watergate committee, and Sen. Edward M. Kennedy (D Mass.).

Baker	45%
Kennedy	44
Not sure	11

Subpoenas. Nixon's July 26 promise to abide by any "definitive" Supreme Court ruling on the release of White House tapes and documents was interpreted differently by special prosecutor Archibald Cox and Charles Alan Wright, a White House special counsel. Cox said at a press conference that he would treat any Supreme Court decision as "definitive." Cox indicated that he thought his chances of obtaining the tapes were better than those of the Senate committee. Wright asserted at a White House press conference that some rulings by the Supreme Court are "less than definitive."

Newsman Break-in. Marvin Kalb, a CBS correspondent who covers the State Department, said his office had been illegally entered and ransacked on July 9. The Associated Press reported that Kalb's telephone might also have been tapped in 1969-70 as part of the Nixon administration's efforts to stop security leaks to newsmen. Secretary of State William P. Rogers called Kalb to apologize. Kalb was on the list of White House "enemies." *(Reporter wiretaps, p. 155; "enemies" list, p. 153)*

Weicker Charge. Sen. Lowell P. Weicker Jr. (R Conn.), a member of the Senate Watergate investigating committee, accused Nixon of attempting to institute "a presidency rather than a democracy." Speaking at a National Press Club luncheon, Weicker said, "Those who directed the improprieties and illegalities of Watergate apparently did so on the knowledge that even if caught, no accounting would be called for by the American people."

Republican Concern. The Associated Press reported that Nixon's Republican allies in Congress had been using private channels to warn Nixon that his refusal to release tapes and documents might pose political problems. Sen. Robert Dole (Kan.), former Republican national chairman, said that "with the exception of a very few, Republicans in the Senate and Republicans in the House feel the tapes should be released."

Nixon Snub. Former Virginia Gov. Mills E. Godwin (D 1966-70), the Republican gubernatorial nominee, told reporters that he did not want Nixon's help in his 1973 campaign. He did, however, welcome the support of Vice President Agnew.

Laird, Harlow Advice. Rep. Gerald R. Ford (R Mich.) told newsmen that Nixon withheld tape recordings sought by special prosecutor Cox and the Senate investigating committee against the advice of two of his chief counselors, Melvin R. Laird and Bryce Harlow. Nixon spent 10 to 12 hours over the weekend listening to the tapes, Ford said. Ford added he thought the President was on "good ground" legally in his refusal to release the tapes, but "politically, it was not a good move."

Baker Remarks. Sen. Baker said he hoped the first phase of the hearings would end by the Aug. 3 recess. "The country needs a rest from Watergate," he said.

Bellino Suspension. Twenty-two Republican senators called for the suspension of Carmine S. Bellino, chief investigator for the Senate Watergate committee. Bellino, a John F. Kennedy campaigner, was accused of attempting to hire men to bug Richard Nixon's Washington hotel room during the 1960 presidential campaign. Bellino denied that he had in any way participated in political bugging.

JULY 28

MacGregor Deposition. President Nixon's former campaign director, Clark MacGregor, said he was "misled, deceived and...lied to repeatedly" by White House and Nixon campaign aides over the Watergate affair. *(Box, p. 236)*

Campaign Finances. *The Washington Post* reported that the Finance Committee to Re-elect the President had been working with special prosecutor Cox to urge corporations to disclose illegal donations to the Nixon campaign. Kenneth W. Parkinson, a committee counsel, drafted 30 letters to persons who had donated more than $1-million. *(Illegal airline contribution, p. 187)*

FBI Rebuttal. A former associate director of the FBI denied that the bureau failed to zealously investigate the Pentagon Papers case. W. Mark Felt refuted in *The Washington Post* John D. Ehrlichman's Senate testimony on the probe. He defended the FBI probe as "a vigorous, widespread investigation...accorded extraordinary priority and manpower."

JULY 29

Tapes Dispute. Chairman Ervin and Vice Chairman Baker of the Senate investigating committee appeared on CBS' "Face the Nation" to urge that they and special prosecutor Cox be allowed privately to inspect tape recordings of Nixon's conversations in the Watergate affair. They disagreed, however, on whether sensitive material dealing with a secret "plumbers" probe should have been excised from documents given to the committee.

Sen. Hugh Scott (R Pa.) suggested on ABC's "Issues and Answers" that the tapes be inspected by a "panel of two or three citizens of the highest public repute."

White House Retaliation. Katharine Graham, publisher of *The Washington Post*, said the licenses of two television stations her company owned in Florida were challenged because of the Post's role in uncovering the Watergate scandal. She said then Deputy Attorney General Richard G. Kleindienst had threatened the paper with criminal prosecution at the time that it published portions of the Pentagon Papers. Graham denied a personal bias against Nixon. *(Press fairness. p. 51)*

JULY 30

Hearings Extended. The Senate Watergate committee voted to extend its hearings beyond the Aug. 3 congressional recess, lengthen the hours of testimony and include a Saturday session. Seven more witnesses were scheduled: H. R. Haldeman, Richard G. Kleindienst, Henry E. Petersen, L. Patrick Gray, Gen. Vernon A. Walters, Richard Helms and Gen. Robert E. Cushman Jr.

Tapes Controversy. The White House rebuffed proposals for a compromise in the struggle over access to the Senate and special prosecutor of presidential tapes and documents. Gerald L. Warren, deputy press secretary, said that "the President has made his position clear on this matter" and that there had been no change in his position. Charles A. Wright, White House legal consultant who is arguing the President's case, told *The New*

York Times that he knew of no compromise between Nixon and the committee that would cancel the litigation.

Sen. Adlai Stevenson III (D Ill.) mounted a challenge to Nixon's right to withhold the tapes. In a harsh speech on the Senate floor, Stevenson accused Nixon of "placing himself above the law" and reneging on his pledge to grant full authority to special prosecutor Cox.

Stevenson's charges were answered by Attorney General Elliot L. Richardson, who issued a statement pointing out that during his confirmation hearings he had made clear that executive privilege might prevent the prosecutor from obtaining some documents. Richardson told newsmen that Cox had been given "all powers vested in the attorney general." *(Box, p. 234)*

Ehrlichman Testimony. Former president domestic adviser John D. Ehrlichman finished his five-day testimony before the Senate committee by reaffirming that he and Nixon acted within the law and refuting former White House aide Gordon C. Strachan's warning to young people to "stay away" from Washington. *(Testimony, p. 233)*

Haldeman Testimony. H. R. Haldeman, former White House chief of staff, testified that he had no knowledge of the break-in, suggesting that John W. Dean III and John N. Mitchell should share the blame. He also volunteered that he had listened to tape recordings of conversations between Dean and Nixon and that the tapes supported Nixon's account of ignorance of the coverup. *(Testimony, p. 231)*

Presidential Popularity. A Harris Survey showed that public confidence in Nixon was steadily eroding. His over-all rating on the job had slipped to 54 to 42 per cent negative, and 22 per cent of the persons polled between July 18 and 22 thought Nixon should resign over the Watergate affair. *(Box, p. 240)*

Mitchell, Stans. Federal prosecutors scored former Attorney General Mitchell and former Commerce Secretary Maurice H. Stans for demanding a double standard of justice in claiming that Watergate publicity necessitated dismissal of charges against them. The accusations by assistant U.S. Attorney James W. Rayhill were made in answer to motions filed in New York City by Mitchell and Stans. They were indicted along with Harry L. Sears and financier Robert L. Vesco in connection with a secret $200,000 contribution by Vesco to Nixon's campaign fund. *(p. 71, 56)*

Talmadge Trip. Herman E. Talmadge (D Ga.), a member of the Senate Watergate committee, was flown for a 1973 winter vacation by a major government contractor, *The Washington Star-News* reported. Rockwell International picked up the tab for Talmadge's trip and Rep. Olin E. Teague (D Texas) also benefited from Rockwell's largess, the newspaper reported.

JULY 31

Tapes Controversy. Former White House chief of staff Haldeman continued his Senate testimony about contents of taped conversations between Nixon and John Dean amid charges by Chairman Ervin that the White House and Haldeman were collaborating to "leak" Haldeman's testimony. *(Testimony, p. 231)*

The White House stuck to its view that it maintained control over the tapes. Deputy press secretary Gerald L. Warren restated the administration's position, while conceding that Haldeman and two White House aides, Stephen P. Bull and J. Fred Buzhardt, had listened to the tapes. "The question of access has been decided by the President based on the President's judgment of who could best assist him in determining the facts of the Watergate matters without jeopardizing the confidentiality of the tapes," Warren said.

Impeachment Move. Rep. Robert F. Drinan (D Mass.) introduced a resolution to impeach Nixon, saying he was moved to act by the "recent disclosure that President Nixon conducted a totally secret air war in Cambodia for 14 months prior to April 30, 1970." Drinan also cited Nixon's secret taping of oval office conversations, funds impoundment and establishment of the "plumbers" as reasons to impeach the President. *(Box, this page)*

Liddy Silence. The House Armed Services Committee voted unanimously to cite G. Gordon Liddy, convicted Watergate conspirator, for contempt of Congress. Liddy July 20 refused to answer questions before the Armed Services Intelligence Subcommittee, claiming his rights would be jeopardized by "prejudicial publicity in the media" if he invoked the Fifth Amendment. Liddy also had refused to be sworn in as a witness before the Senate Watergate investigating committee.

Wallace Probe. The Alabama attorney general said he would revive his investigation of possible election fraud in the 1970 gubernatorial race. Bill Baxley cited

Drinan Impeachment Resolution

Rep. Robert F. Drinan (D Mass.) introduced a resolution (H Res 513) July 31 for the impeachment of President Nixon for "high crimes and misdemeanors." It appeared to be regarded as premature by many members of the House and Senate, who said they awaited the conclusion of Senate Watergate hearings. *(Impeachment background, p. 55)*

Drinan, a Roman Catholic priest and former law school dean, cited these reasons for introducing the resolution, the first introduced against Nixon in either house:

- Secret bombing of Cambodia, financed by money obtained from Congress "under false pretenses and spent in an unconstitutional manner."
- Nixon's taping of conversations in his offices without the knowledge of other persons being taped.
- Refusal to spend appropriated funds, despite court rulings against the administration on impoundment.
- Establishment of a "super-secret security force within the White House."

evidence that Nixon's campaign money was channeled into the campaign of incumbent Albert Brewer, the Democratic opponent of Gov. George C. Wallace, in an attempt to weaken Wallace as a 1972 presidential threat. About $400,000 was brought into the campaign with the avowed purpose of beating Wallace, a secret transaction made apparently in violation of state elections law, Baxley said.

Talmadge Vacation. Herman E. Talmadge (D Ga.) said he went on an expense-paid vacation to Bimini with a government contractor because the contractor, Al Rockwell Jr., was a friend of his. Talmadge said he did not sit on any committees with direct power over National Aeronautics and Space Administration (NASA) authorizations, which affect Rockwell as head of the third largest contractor for NASA.

Nixon Counterattack. The President moved toward an open counterattack on his Watergate critics, deploring people who "spend their time dealing with the murky, small, unimportant, vicious little things." Nixon said that "we...will spend our time building a better world." His comments were made during a toast at a state dinner for Japanese Prime Minister Kakuei Tanaka.

AUG. 1

Haldeman Testimony. In his third day of Senate Watergate committee testimony, former White House chief of staff Haldeman conceded he wrote "good" and "great" on a 1971 memo predicting violence at a Nixon rally in Charlotte, N.C. Accused by Sen. Lowell P. Weicker Jr. (R Conn.) of trying to blame the Democrats for violent demonstrations against the President, Haldeman said he had been trying to develop facts on information that foreign money was used to support anti-Nixon demonstrations in 1972. *(Testimony, p. 235)*

ITT Settlement. The Senate committee released a 1972 White House memo warning of the existence of other internal memos that would link Nixon and John Mitchell to settlement of the International Telephone and Telegraph Company antitrust case. Samuel Dash, chief counsel of the committee, said the memo appeared to show "an act of perjury on the part of Mitchell." *(Colson role, p. 235, 144)*

Civil Suit. *The Washington Post* reported that the Democratic National Committee was reconsidering an out-of-court settlement of its $3.2-million civil suit against the Committee for the Re-election of the President. Democratic sources said Arnold Picker of United Artists Corporation, who had raised funds to keep the suit going, favored settlement. When former Nixon campaign director Mitchell met with Democratic Chairman Robert S. Strauss in April, Strauss turned down a $525,000 settlement offer. *(p. 110)*

Kopechne Probe. White House aides ordered secret inquiries into the 1969 party at Chappaquiddick, Mass., and the subsequent car accident involving Sen. Edward M. Kennedy (D Mass.) and Mary Jo Kopechne. Sources told *The Washington Post* that Anthony T. Ulasewicz, a former White House secret investigator, authorized by Haldeman and John D. Ehrlichman, concocted a plan to lure friends of Kopechne to a New York apartment, seduce and secretly photograph them to gain information by blackmail. Other probes reportedly were ordered on Rose Kennedy, Dick Dixon, Sen. John V. Tunney (D Calif.), House Speaker Carl Albert (D Okla.) and Rep. Richard H. Poff (R Va.). *(Chappaquiddick probe, p. 156)*

Justice Guidelines. Attorney General Elliot L. Richardson told *The Washington Post* in an interview that he would issue comprehensive guidelines to require the keeping of "appropriate internal records" of all third-party contacts with the Justice Department, in an effort to prevent the inhibiting of investigations—such as the scandals arising out of the ITT and Watergate cases.

Rapprochement. The Post also quoted Gen. Alexander M. Haig Jr., the new White House chief of staff, as conceding that a White House rapprochement with the press and Congress had been hampered by Watergate. Haig said that communication with the public and Congress would improve when the President made his Watergate defense and resumed holding news conferences. Haig denied that the White House was planning a hard line against critics. *(White House staff, p. 130)*

Rebozo Probe. Quoting sources close to the Senate Watergate committee, ABC News reported that the committee had subpoenaed close associates of President Nixon's friend, Bebe Rebozo. Records kept in Rebozo's Key Biscayne, Fla., bank were also subpoenaed, ABC said.

Liddy Silence. G. Gordon Liddy, convicted Watergate conspirator, asked that a U.S. court of appeals reverse his contempt citation for refusing to testify before the Watergate grand jury. *(p. 12)*

AUG. 2

Helms Testimony. Richard Helms, former director of the Central Intelligence Agency (CIA), told the Senate Watergate investigating committee that 10 days after the break-in, John Dean asked the CIA to pay bail for the suspects and put them on the CIA payroll during their jail terms. Helms said he told Gen. Vernon A. Walters, deputy director, to resist White House pressure to involve the CIA in the coverup. Helms testified that six days after the Watergate arrests, he and Walters met with then White House chief of staff H. R. Haldeman, who was worried that an FBI probe of the break-in might compromise CIA operations. *(Testimony, p. 238; earlier Helms testimony, p. 66)*

McGovern Leak. *The Washington Post* revealed a plan to leak a story that Sen. George McGovern fathered an illegitimate child in the 1940s. H. R. Haldeman, then White House chief of staff, suggested the plan in a memo early in 1973, according to the Post. The story was to be leaked in a manner to suggest that Nixon and his aides had refrained from using it during the campaign. The Post confirmed the existence of a birth certificate for a child born in Fort Wayne, Ind., listing "George S. McGovern of Mitchell, S.D.," as the father, but the child's mother denied that McGovern was the father.

HALDEMAN'S OPENING STATEMENT

Following are excerpts from the prepared text of the opening statement of H. R. Haldeman, former White House chief of staff, before the Senate Watergate committee on July 30:

SECURITY PROBLEMS

.... It has been alleged that there was an atmosphere of fear at the White House regarding security matters. I can state categorically that there was no climate of fear at all. There was, however, a healthy and valid concern for a number of matters in the general area of national security and for a number of other matters in the general area of domestic security. This was a rational concern and it was of sufficient import to require that considerable thought be given to steps to combat the actual problems and potential dangers that existed.

With regard to leaks of information, especially in the national security area, it became evident in 1969 that leaks of secret information were taking place that seriously jeopardized a number of highly sensitive foreign policy initiatives that had been undertaken by the administration, including the ending of the war in Vietnam, the Middle East crisis, nuclear arms limitation and the establishment of new relationships among the great powers. These initiatives were closely interrelated; leaks about any one of them could seriously endanger all of them; and such leaks were taking place.

In order to deal with these leaks, a program of wiretaps was instituted in 1969 and continued into early 1971. The President has stated that each of these taps was undertaken in accordance with procedures that were legal at the time and in accord with long-standing practice in this area. This program was authorized by the President of the United States, and the wiretaps were determined by coordination between the director of the FBI, the President's assistant for national security affairs and the attorney general.

In 1970 the domestic security problem reached critical proportions as a wave of bombings and explosions, rioting and violence, demonstrations, arson, gun battles and other disruptive activities took place across the country—on college campuses primarily—but also in other areas.

In order to deal with this problem, the President set up an interagency committee consisting of the directors of the FBI, the CIA, the Defense Intelligence Agency and the National Security Agency. This committee was instructed to prepare recommendations for the President—which they did. The report they submitted included specific options for expanded intelligence operations, and Mr. Huston, the White House staff man for this project, was notified by a memorandum from me of the approval of the President.

As has been reported, Director Hoover expressed opposition to parts of this program, and as a result, the agencies were subsequently notified that the approval had been rescinded. This approval was withdrawn before the plan was implemented, so the net result was that it never went into effect.

Instead of this program, an Intelligence Evaluation Committee was created in December of 1970 that included representatives of the White House, CIA, FBI, NSA and the Departments of Justice, Treasury and Defense and the Secret Service. The mission of this committee was to improve coordination among the intelligence community and to prepare evaluations and estimates of domestic intelligence.

In mid-1971, *The New York Times* started publication of the so-called Pentagon Papers, which had been stolen from the sensitive files of the Departments of State and Defense and the CIA and which covered military and diplomatic moves in a war that was still going on. The implications of this security leak were enormous, and it posed a threat so grave as to require, in the judgment of the President and his senior advisers, extraordinary action. As a result, the President approved creation of the special investigations unit within the White House, which later became known as the plumbers. John Ehrlichman was responsible for supervision of this group. Mr. Krogh and Mr. Young of the Domestic Council and National Security Council staffs were the two principal staff members. While I was aware of the existence and general purpose of this unit, I was not familiar with any of its specific activities or assignments.

Also in mid-1971, to deal with the general problem of leaks throughout government departments and agencies—the President directed me to set up a program of spotting these leaks and reporting them to the department head involved. He announced this in a cabinet meeting and dubbed me with the dubious honor of lord high executioner. The purpose of this program was to make department heads throughout the government conscious of the leak problem and aware of their responsibility to deal with it in their departments. This involved no investigations on the part of the White House.

1968 SURPLUS FUNDS

During the interim period between the 1968 elections and the start of the 1972 campaign, Herbert Kalmbach was custodian of a large cash fund which I understand was a surplus from the 1968 primary elections. In addition, he undertook to raise funds from supporters of the President to aid congressional and senatorial candidates in the 1970 elections. Also, in 1971 Mr. Kalmbach raised a substantial fund as the "start up" for the 1972 campaign.

I am not familiar with all the specifics of sources, amounts or disbursements of these funds, although Mr. Kalmbach did keep me periodically posted on his activities in this area. As he has indicated, he looked to me—as well as to other people from time to time—for direction or approval as to the disbursement of the 1968 surplus funds.

I requested or approved use of these funds for such purposes as the continuing polling that we did during that period; for campaign support to a candidate for governor in Alabama, and for funding Donald Segretti. It is my understanding that these funds were also used for other purposes, such as the funding of Mr. Ulasewicz' operations, with which I was not familiar.

The Alabama campaign funds were in support of the candidate for the Democratic nomination for governor who was opposing former Gov. George Wallace. It was the belief of some of the President's friends and advisers on the southern political scene that Mr. Wallace might very well become a third-party candidate in 1972 and thus raise again the potential problem of an indecisive election that might be turned to the House of Representatives. They felt that the best way to avoid this eventuality was to defeat Gov. Wallace in his bid for the gubernatorial nomination in Alabama. This was the reason for providing campaign financial support to his opponent.

SEGRETTI

Early in the pre-campaign period, I agreed with an idea that was suggested to set up a man functioning independently of the White House, the committee to re-elect and the national committee for the purpose of generating for our side the same kind of campaign activities that were so ably carried out over the years for Democratic candidates and in 1972 for Senator McGovern by Dick Tuck, a man who has been widely praised by political writers as a political prankster, whose basic stock in trade is embarrassing Republican candidates by activities that have been regarded as clever and acceptable parts of our political tradition.

The repertoire of the political prankster includes such activities as printing up embarrassing signs for the opponent, posing in trainman's clothes and waving the campaign train out of the station, placing an agent on the opponent's campaign train to produce witty newsletters mocking the candidate, distributing opposition signs at rallies for use by members of the crowd, encouraging band leaders to play rival songs at rallies and so forth.

The activities we had in mind, and for which we drew careful boundaries, specifically excluded anything remotely connected with the Watergate type of activity.

Moreover, the pranksterism that was envisioned would have specifically excluded such acts as the following: violent demonstrations and disruption, heckling or shouting down speakers, burning or bombing campaign headquarters, physical damage or trashing of headquarters and other buildings, harassment of candidates' wives and families by obscenities, disruption of the national convention by splattering dinner guests with eggs and tomatoes, indecent explosure, rock throwing, assaults on delegates, slashing bus tires, smashing windows, setting trash files under the gas tank of a bus, knocking policemen from their motorcycles.

I know that this committee and most Americans would agree that such activities cannot be tolerated in a political campaign. But unfortunately the activities I have describe are all activities which took place in 1972—*against* the campaign of the President of the United States by his opponents. Some of them took place with the clear knowledge and consent of agents of the opposing candidate in the last election; others were acts of people who were clearly unsympathetic to the President but may not have had direct orders from the opposing camp.

So far there has been no investigation of these activities and very little publicizing of them, either those which were directly attributable to our opponent or those which certainly served our opponent's interest but did not have his sanction.

There is no question that the 1972 campaign was not a classic in decorum—for either side. In any event, having agreed to the suggestion of a "Dick Tuck for our side," I was told by Dwight Chapin and Gordon Strachan that they had a former college friend they felt would be a good man for this project. They may have told me that his name was Don Segretti, but it would have meant nothing to me. I have never met or had any personal communication with Mr. Segretti.

I agreed that if this man wanted to take on this activity, Herbert Kalmbach should arrange for his compensation and expenses from the 1968 campaign fund surplus.

It was my clear understanding that Segretti would act independently and on his own initiative within the broad guidelines outlined above. It was also my clear understanding that he was to engage in no illegal acts. Mr. Strachan has told me that he was so advised and that he understood that. I had no specific knowledge of Segretti's activities or the details of how or with whom he worked. I do not believe that there was anything wrong with the Segretti activity as it was conceived. I have only limited knowledge, and that acquired only lately, as to how it was actually carried out.

If, as alleged, he or those under his direction were responsible for the letter which falsely defamed Senators Muskie and Humphrey, then, on behalf of everyone associated with the Nixon campaign, I would like to and do apologize to both of those men. That act was clearly outside the bounds within which he was to work.

$350,000

.... Prior to the April 7 (1972) date on which the new campaign spending legislation took effect, it was agreed by Mitchell, Stans, I believe Mr. Kalmbach and me that $350,000 of the 1968 surplus cash funds should be set aside to cover possible needs for special private polling by the White House apart from the regular polls conducted by the committee. This was in anticipation of a possibly hard-fought, close election.

I understand from Gordon Strachan that he received the cash from Hugh Sloan on April 6. He, in turn, arranged to have this cash held in a safe deposit box or safe by another individual outside the government. It is my understanding from Strachan that this transfer was made immediately and the entire $350,000 was placed in safekeeping outside the White House.

I did not feel we should keep such a large amount of cash at the White House, nor did I feel it was a good idea for it to be in the physical custody of a member of the White House Staff, which was why these arrangement were made. I never at any time saw or handled the currency, and I must rely on Strachan's reports to me as to how it was handled.

I have been informed by Strachan that there was one withdrawal in April or May of 1972 of $22,000 to pay for some advertising not directly related to the election campaign. This was at the request of Dick Howard of Chuck Colson's office. I think Strachan said the money was delivered directly to the advertising agency.

The balance of $328,000 was not used. I instructed Strachan after the election in November to turn over the unused funds to the committee, since the White House had no further need for them. I told him to work out with John Dean the means of doing this. Strachan has informed me that the funds were turned over in January 1973, although he incurred some difficulty in doing so after he took possession of the funds....

In December I became aware, probably via Dean, that there was some difficulty in turning over the cash to the committee, presumably because it posed reporting problems.

At a later time, Dean mentioned to me the committee's need for funds for legal and family support for the Watergate defendants. I suggested to Dean that he try to work out a way of solving both the problems of our desire to deliver funds to the committee and the committee's need for funds.

Dean later told me that he had worked this out and that part of the cash, I believe $40,000, could be delivered immediately to the committee via Fred LaRue. He had Strachan do this, I am told, and several days thereafter, Dean had Strachan deliver the balance to LaRue.

To sum up, after my original instruction to Strachan to transfer the money to the committee, my involvement in the transfer of the funds was entirely through John Dean. He told me of the problem in transferring the $350,000 to the committee. He told me he had worked out the problem. He told Strachan how, when and to whom to make the transfer. He told me the transfer had been made.

He did not, at any time in this sequence, advise me or imply that the transfer itself or the purpose of the transfer was to buy the Watergate defendants' silence or that it was in any way illegal or improper....

I have no recollection of any knowledge of the reported transaction on Nov. 28 when Dean had Fred Fielding of his office pick up $22,000 in cash from Mr. Stans, ostensibly for the purpose of replacing the $22,000 that had been expended from the $350,000 in April.

I do recall that one of Dean's problems in the process of transferring the $350,000 to the committee was the fact that $22,000 had been disbursed. So it is quite possible that he did have it replenished prior to having the cash turned over to LaRue, but I don't believe that he ever reported this fact to me.

In fact, Gordon Strachan's report to me in April of 1973 was that the $22,000 had not been replaced and that he had delivered only $328,000 to Mr. LaRue and not the full $350,000. However, Strachan also told me after his grand jury appearance that he had told them he had delivered $350,000. I said that was contrary to what he had told me and he said he had made a mistake at the grand jury. I urged him to correct it, if that was the case. He told me later he had called Mr. Silbert about the mistake and was told he could correct it before the grand jury. When he appeared at the court house to do so, the U.S. attorneys would not let him do it, and instead warned him he had committed perjury, was in serious trouble, should start preparations to go to jail and should hire a lawyer.

WATERGATE

I had no knowledge of or involvement in the planning or execution of the break-in or bugging of the Democratic National Committee headquarters.

To the best of my knowledge, I did not see any material produced by the bugging of the Democratic headquarters.

After the June 17 break-in, I asked Gordon Strachan whether he had had any knowledge of such an operation. He said he had not; but that he realized in thinking back that there had been three "intelligence reports" received by him identified by the code name Sedan Chair and that said something to the effect that "confidential sources report that..." He said he did not at the time know the identify of the confidential sources. He realized after the June 17 break-in, thinking back, that these reports *could* have been based on the Watergate or some other wiretap source.

I have absolutely no recollection of seeing any such report, and it is quite likely that I did not see it even if it was included in a Strachan transmission to me; since I rarely, if ever, read through or even looked at all of the materials that he sent into me in these reports.

I do not recall ever seeing any material identified by the name Gemstone.

I have no recollection of giving Mr. Strachan instructions to destroy any materials, nor do I recall a later report from Strachan that he had done so or that the files were clean.

Mr. Strachan has made clear in his testimony that he destroyed materials *not* because he thought the contents concerned criminal activity, but because he felt if they ever became public they would be politically embarrassing. He confirmed that he has reread the contents many times and that they did not suggest any illegality or criminal activity; they suggested matters which, if they became public, would be embarrassing.

I should point out that on two occasions in April 1973—once to me before his grand jury appearance and the other to John Ehrlichman—Strachan listed the areas of what he considered to be tough questions or trouble spots. On neither of these occasions did he mention to either of us that he had been instructed to destroy any materials or make sure files were clean.

I think the effort to bring in my April 4 meeting with John Mitchell as in some way significant with regard to intelligence is a little far-fetched. By his testimony, Strachan doesn't know what was discussed at that meeting—all he says is that, in routine fashion, he put an item on the talking paper regarding the adequacy of intelligence. As a matter of fact, the meeting with Mr. Mitchell that day was in connection with a meeting of Mitchell and me with the President. My notes taken at the meeting with the President indicate the discussion covered the ITT-Kleindienst hearings and a review of Mitchell's plans for assigning regional campaign responsibilities to specific individuals. They indicate no discussion of intelligence.

DEAN INVESTIGATION

John Dean, in his Camp David report...says that when he arrived in Washington on Sunday afternoon, June 18 (1972), he realized that the President would have to know everything that he could find out. He realized at that point that he would be asked to assemble all of the facts so that the White House could be fully informed as to what had transpired and how it would affect the President; but having been on an airplane for approximately 25 hours, he did nothing further that evening.

The next morning, after reading all of the news accounts of the Watergate incident, he spoke with John Ehrlichman, who instructed him to get the facts together and report to him. He then called the attorney general to get what facts he knew. He called Gordon Liddy and met with him. Dean asked Liddy if anyone at the White House was involved, and he told him no.

During the days and weeks that followed, Dean discussed the incident with everyone who he thought might have any knowledge or involvement.

The source of these facts is John Dean's report, or the start of it, which he wrote at Camp David in March of this year.

There is absolutely no question in my mind, or, I'm sure, in the minds of anyone at the White House, or at the Justice Department, that John Dean was in fact conducting an investigation for the White House regarding the Watergate as it might involve the White House. It is inconceivable to me that there could be any doubt in Dean's mind.

Dean moved in immediately after the incident as sort of the Watergate project officer in the White House. This was in keeping with our usual procedure; the responsibility was his, and he had the authority to proceed. Dean kept Ehrlichman and me posted from time to time on developments and, through us, the President. He apparently did not keep us fully posted, and it now appears he did not keep us accurately posted.

The President, Ehrlichman and I were very much involved in many other vital matters through this entire period, and we made no attempt to get into the details of, or in any way take over, the Watergate case.

The view of all three of us through the whole period was that the truth must be told, and quickly; although we did not know what the truth was. Every time we pushed for action in this direction, we were told by Dean that it could not be done. His concern, as I understood it, was that the case was complex, it involved rights of defendants and other legal complexities, the facts were not clear, and that nothing should be done publicly.

As long as we were confident that the facts as he told us were correct, we had to agree with this, since there was no proof of any involvement of higher-ups at the committee, and any premature speculation regarding any such involvement would have been unfair and damaging. Especially since the top officials at the committee had denied any involvement.

Thus, as it now appears, we were badly misled by one or more of the principals and even more so by our own man, for reasons which are still not completely clear.

At no time did I give Dean any instructions to cover up anything in this case. I did, however, occasionally receive his verbal reports of the facts and his intended actions and relayed these to the President. None of these reports concerned a cover-up.

I had no personal motivation to cover up anything, because I had no personal involvement and I knew the President had no involvement. I understood and believed that no one else in the White House was involved in the Watergate planning and break-in, and I still understand and believe that. It was obvious that some people at the committee were involved, but I had no idea who, or how far up, and I still don't—because I don't know now whom to believe. I may add that until the recent period, both John Mitchell and Jeb Magruder denied any Watergate involvement.

The President raised questions as to the facts of Watergate from time to time during the period of June through the election. His interest consistently was to get the facts and get them out. He had some concern, especially in the early stages, regarding the possibility of compromising national security and an interest, therefore, in seeing that the investigation was thorough with regard to Watergate, but that it was limited to Watergate and not extended into earlier unrelated national security activities of some of the people involved.

Throughout this period, Dean assured us that there was absolutely no evidence that anyone in the White House had been involved in Watergate in any way. He was sitting in on FBI interviews; reviewing FBI reports; he was in constant communication with officials of the Justice Department and the re-election committee; and was clearly staying closely in touch with all facets of the investigation and related matters.

On or about Aug. 27, the President instructed me to ask Mr. Ehrlichman to give Pat Buchanan the information that

Buchanan would need for preparing the President's briefing book for an upcoming press conference on any questions that might arise regarding the Watergate. I passed this request on to Ehrlichman and assumed that he carried it out. On August 29, the President had a press conference at which he stated the Dean investigation indicated that no one in the White House or in the administration presently employed had been involved in Watergate. I was not at all surprised to hear the President say this at the press conference, since it was thoroughly consistent with everything that Dean had told me, and I therefore find it hard to understand why Mr. Dean professes to have had such great surprise when he heard this statement.

COVERUP

In these hearings and in the general discussion of Watergate, the word "coverup" has come to have a broad and very ill-defined meaning. As John Dean said, the coverup had a broad range. Anything that might cause a problem came within the coverup.

Definition by usage has now come to connote illegal or improper activities—although some steps were taken to contain the Watergate case in several perfectly legal and proper aspects.

One, as the President has stated, was to avoid the Watergate investigation possibly going beyond the facts of the Watergate affair itself and into national security activities totally unrelated to Watergate.

Another was to avoid or at least reduce adverse political and publicity fallout from false charges, hearsay, etc., arising from various activities in connection with Watergate, such as the Justice Department investigation, the Democratic National Committee suit, the Common Cause suit, the Patman hearings and the Ervin Committee hearings.

A third was concern for distortion or fabrication of facts in the heat of a political campaign that would unjustly condemn the innocent or prevent discovery of the guilty.

The containment effort, as I would use the term, did not contemplate or involve any acts in obstruction of justice. To the contrary, while hoping to contain the Watergate inquiry to the facts of Watergate, there was a concurrent effort to try to get the true facts of Watergate and get them out to the public. The President frequently cautioned against any coverup of the Watergate or even the appearance of a coverup.

On the basis of testimony now before this committee, it appears that there was also an effort to cover up as well as to contain. This coverup appears to have involved illegal and improper activities, such as perjury, payments to defendants for their silence, promises of executive clemency, destruction of evidence and other acts in an effort to conceal the truth regarding the planning and commission of crimes at the Watergate.

The critical question then becomes the determination of who committed these acts, who directed them, who was aware of them.

I committed no such acts and directed no such acts, and I was aware of no such acts until March of this year, when the President intensified his personal investigation into the facts of the Watergate. I am convinced that the President had no awareness of any such acts until March of this year.

The question is asked: "How could the President *not* have known?" Very easily. Reverse the question. How could the President *have* known?

Only if he were directly involved himself or if he were told by someone who was either directly involved or had knowledge. The fact is that the President was not directly involved himself and he was not told by anyone until March, when he intensified his own investigation. Even then, he was given conflicting and unverified reports that made it impossible to determine the precise truth regarding Watergate or the coverup and, at the outset at least, he was relying primarily on one man, John Dean, who has admitted that he was a major participant in the illegal and improper coverup, a fact unknown to the President until March 1973.

Any attempt on my part at this time to try to identify those who participated in, directed or knew of the illegal coverup would of necessity be based totally on hearsay.

CONTAINMENT

There was a concern at the White House that activities which had been in no way related to Watergate or to the 1972 political campaign, and which were in the area of national security, would be compromised in the process of the Watergate investigation and the attendant publicity and political furor. The recent public disclosure of the FBI wiretaps on press and NSC personnel, the details of the plumbers operations, etc., fully justifies that concern.

As a result of this concern and the FBI's request through Pat Gray to John Dean for guidance regarding some aspects of the Watergate investigation, because of the possibility of CIA involvement, the President directed John Ehrlichman and me to meet with the director and deputy director of the CIA on June 23 (1972). We did so and ascertained from them that there had not been any CIA involvement in the Watergate affair and that there was no concern on the part of Director Helms as to the fact that some of the Watergate participants had been involved in the Bay of Pigs operations of the CIA. We discussed the White House concern regarding possible disclosure of non-Watergate-related covert CIA operations or other non-related national security activities that had been undertaken previously by some of the Watergate participants, and we requested Deputy Director Walters to meet with Director Gray of the FBI to express these concerns and to coordinate with the FBI so that the FBI's area of investigation of the Watergate participants not be expanded into unrelated matters which could lead to disclosures of earlier national security or CIA activities.

Walters agreed to meet with Gray as requested. I do not recall having any other communication or meeting with Walters, Helms or Gray on this subject. I did not, at this meeting or at any other time, ask the CIA to participate in any Watergate coverup, nor did I ever suggest that the CIA take any responsibility for the Watergate break-in. I believe that the action I took with the CIA was proper, according to the President's instructions, and clearly in the national interest.

There were a number of newspaper stories and allegations raised during the period following the Watergate break-in that posed new questions regarding the facts of Watergate or related matters. Whenever any such questions arose, the President would again ask that the facts be ascertained and made known publicly as completely and quickly as possible, but there always seemed to be some reason why this could not be done. There was no effort on my part to direct any personal attention or take any personal action on these matters, because the FBI and the Justice Department were responsible for and were conducting an extremely extensive investigation, and because Mr. Dean was responsible for White House liaison with all aspects of the investigation. I knew John Dean to be an extremely capable, thorough, hardworking and intelligent man, and I had full confidence, as did the President at that time, that Mr. Dean was in fact carrying out this responsibility diligently and thoroughly.

There is another aspect to the containment area. It must be recognized that this was the period of a political campaign. There were a number of attacks on the administration, the President and the re-election committee arising out of Watergate and allegations in connection with it. These attacks were, of course, not helpful to the re-election cause, and there was a continuing effort to avoid any false accusations or allegations from being made in the public press and to answer any that were.

There was also frequent discussion of the need for counterattack—the need to point out that while Watergate was not in any way an acceptable or excusable action, it also was not the only improper action by the two sides in that particular election campaign. I have cited earlier some examples of activities that were carried out against the President's re-election effort. Many of the campaign strategists felt that Watergate was getting all of the attention and the improper activities on the other side were being ignored.

While there was no effort and no intent to try to impede the legitimate investigation of the facts regarding Watergate and any other criminal or improper activities, there was a concern about the exploitation of unproved charges and the sensationalizing of required appearances by various people for depositions in the civil suit, etc.

DEFENSE FUNDS

I was told several times, starting in the summer of 1972, by John Dean and possibly also by John Mitchell that there was a need by the committee for funds to help take care of the legal fees and family support of the Watergate defendants. The committee apparently felt obliged to do this.

In March 1973, Dean told me that at some point in 1972, he, at Mitchell's suggestion, had asked me if it would be okay for him to contact Herb Kalmbach to ask him to raise some such defense funds. He says I agreed. He also says that he checked Ehrlichman on the same point. I do not recall such a request. I should also point out that at some times Dean has said that he checked with both Ehrlichman and me on this point, and at other times he has said only that he checked with Ehrlichman.

Later in March 1973, Dean raised the point that there was a potential problem with relation to the funds for defendants. He described this as a possible political embarrassment and indicated that it might even become a legal problem. The problem would arise if it was determined that these funds had been used to induce the defendants to refuse to testify.

I emphasized my clear understanding that the purpose of the funds, as described to me by Dean, was for legal fees and family support; and that I had understood from Dean that both Mitchell and Dean felt this was a proper and important obligation to the defendants.

Since all information regarding the defense funds was given to me by John Dean, the counsel to the President, and possibly by John Mitchell, and since the arrangements for Kalmbach's collecting funds and for transferring the $350,000 cash fund were made by John Dean, and since John Dean never stated at the time that the funds would be used for any other than legal and proper purposes, I had no reason to question the propriety or legality of the process of delivering the $350,000 to the committee via LaRue or of having Kalmbach raise funds.

I have no personal knowledge of what was done with the funds raised by Kalmbach or with the $350,000 that was delivered by Strachan to LaRue.

It would appear that, at the White House at least, John Dean was the only one who knew that the funds were for "hush money," if, in fact, that is what they were for. The rest of us relied on Dean and all thought that what was being done was legal and proper. No one, to my knowledge, was aware that these funds involved either blackmail or "hush money" until this suggestion was raised in March of 1973.

MAGRUDER

To the best of my recollection, I had no meetings or discussions with Jeb Magruder regarding Watergate after our phone call of June 18, 1972, which has already been reported, until Feb. 14, 1973. A review of my log confirms that I had no meetings at all with Magruder in 1973 until Feb. 14.

We did meet on Feb. 14 for about an hour and a quarter at Mr. Magruder's request in my office. The purpose of the meeting was to discuss his plans for the future. He felt that the Watergate matter was now settled as far as he was concerned, that his work at the inaugural committee was done and that it was time for him to make his future plans. He said he was interested in the possibility of running for office in California and he was also interested in the possibility of returning to a government post in Washington. He was especially interested in a White House position in connection with the bicentennial. I advised him that there was no possibility of a presidential appointment or a White House position until all of the Watergate matters had been cleared up, including the Senate hearings, which were, at that time, about to get under way.

I believe that, at this time, he had just returned from a trip to California, where he had taken soundings as to the political possibilities and his job opportunities. I urged him, if he was interested in California politics, to go to work in private business out there and get himself re-established in the state and then to go into politics at a later point. I recommended that he not consider coming back into the federal government, because if his interests were in California he now had the need to re-establish himself there. All of this was in the nature of political advice to a man who indicated his interests in running for political office.

He said, however, that all of the people he had talked with in California had urged him to go back into government for a while; that he had strong family reasons for wanting to stay in Washington, because his children were well established in the schools here; and that he had lost some of his interest in running for office in California and was more interested in the idea of staying in Washington. Since the presidential appointment or White House post was out of the question, I suggested that he look into other government possibilities and that he work with Jerry Jones and the White House personnel office in that regard.

I met with Magruder again on March 2 (I believe again at his request) at my office, with John Dean also present, for about an hour. At this meeting, we reviewed the same general subjects we had discussed on Feb. 14, and I gave him a list of jobs in the government that had been developed by the personnel office. He expressed interest in one of the jobs on the list, a post at the Department of Commerce, and he subsequently did take that post.

I don't recall any discussion of any of the particulars of the Watergate matter or the so-called coverup—other than what I have already indicated regarding his feeling that the matter was now behind him.

I feel certain that there was no such discussion, because, had he told me the kinds of things that he has indicated to this committee that he told me regarding perjury, etc., I would have remembered them clearly and would have done something about them.

Mr. Magruder has stated that he met with me in early January of 1973, before the inaugural, although he was unable to specify a date.

Mr. Dean, on the other hand, has indicated in his testimony that I met with Mr. Magruder in late January.

I do have a vague feeling that I talked with Magruder or at least knew about his plans prior to his trip to California, which I believe was in early February. I cannot recall any specific conversation or meeting....

Magruder's recollection of the substance of the alleged January conversation in many respects is very much along the lines of my recollection of our conversation on Feb. 14, and I have the feeling that we are dealing here with a simple error in recollection of specific dates, which is certainly understandable.

At no meeting with Magruder did he raise with me a monologue as he has described laying out the true facts, or claiming that he had committed or was going to commit perjury or that there had been any other illegal coverup activities undertaken in connection with the Watergate investigation....

On April 14, 1973, I phoned Magruder at the President's request and asked him to meet with Ehrlichman that day. I have turned over to the committee a tape recording of this conversation. At the time we talked, Magruder had already decided to tell the full truth and in fact, I believe, had done so in a meeting with the U.S. attorneys. During the phone conversation, Magruder said that his testimony had not implicated me. He also said that one of the problems he was facing was that he had committed perjury when he testified before the grand jury and the trial. I responded that I did not know anything about that, and he replied that even if I didn't, he did. He did not contradict me, thus showing that, at that point in time at least, I did not know he had perjured himself.

SEPT. 15 MEETING

I was in meetings with the President all afternoon on Sept. 15, 1972. At the end of the afternoon, the President had John Dean come in. This was the day that the indictments had been brought down in the Watergate case, and the President knew John Dean had been concentrating for a three-month period on the investigation for the White House. I am sure, therefore, that the President thought it would be a good time to give Dean a pat on the back.

There was no mood of exuberance or excitement on the President's part at the time the indictments were brought down. He does not take joy from the misfortunes of other people, and I don't think he found it very pleasant that the people had been indicted. Naturally, however, it was good news as far as the White House and the administration were concerned that when the indictments were brought down, after a thorough investigation, it had been established there was not any involvement by anyone in the White House. This confirmed what Mr. Dean had been telling us, and we had been reporting to the President over the period of the past three months.

As was the case with all meetings in the oval office when the President was there, this meeting with Mr. Dean was recorded. At the President's request, I recently reviewed the recording of that meeting (at which I was present throughout) in order to report on its contents to the President. I should interject here that I also reviewed the recording of the March 21 meeting of the President, Mr. Dean and myself for the same purpose, and I have made reports to the President on both of those meetings. I have not at any time listened to any other recordings of the meetings in the President's office or of the President's phone calls.

The President did *not* open the meeting of Sept. 15 with the statement that "Bob has kept me posted on your handling of the Watergate" or anything even remotely resembling that. He said, "Hi, this was quite a day, you've got Watergate on the way," or something to that effect. Dean responded that it had been quite a three months and then reported to the President on how the press was handling the indictments and, apparently, a Clark MacGregor press conference.

The discussion then covered the matter of the new bug that had recently been discovered in the Democratic National Committee and the question of whether it had been planted by the DNC and the matter of Mr. Nixon's campaign being bugged in 1968 and some discussion of whether to try to get out evidence of that. There was some discussion about Judge Richey hearing the civil case and a comment that he would keep Roemer McPhee abreast of what was happening. I don't recall any comment about the judge trying to accommodate Dean's hopes of slowing down the suit, but there was some discussion about the problem of the civil case depositions interfering with the criminal prosecution—apparently as a result of a conversation between Judge Richey and Assistant U.S. Attorney Silbert.

Dean indicated that the indictments meant the end of the investigation by the grand jury and now there would be the GAO audit and some congressional inquiries, such as the Patman committee, but he assured the President that nothing would come out to surprise us. In other words, there was apparently no information that would be harmful that had not been uncovered already. The President did at that point commend Dean for his handling of the whole Watergate matter, which was a perfectly natural thing for him to do. Dean reported that he was keeping a close eye on possible campaign law violations by the opposition; said there were some problems of bitterness at the re-election committee between the finance committee and political group, and said he was trying to keep notes on people who were emerging out of all this that were clearly not our friends.

There was, as Mr. Dean has indicated, quite a lengthy discussion of the Patman hearings and the various factors involved in that. There was some discussion of the reluctance of the IRS to follow up on complaints of possible violations against people who were supporting our opponents, because there are so many Democrats in the IRS bureaucracy that they won't take any action.

There was a discussion of cleaning house after the election, moving quickly to replace people at all levels of the government. The meeting closed, as I recall, with a fairly long philosophical discussion.

I totally disagree with the conclusion that the President was aware of any type of coverup, and certainly Mr. Dean did not advise him of it at the Sept. 15 meeting.

SENATE COMMITTEE

On Feb. 7, 1973, the Watergate case moved into a new phase with the establishment of the Senate select committee. The announcement of the plans for the Senate probe was the reason for holding a weekend meeting Feb. 10 and 11 in southern California with Mr. Ehrlichman, Mr. Dean, Mr. Moore and myself. These meetings have been thoroughly reported, and I would concur in Mr. Moore's description of them as sort of brainstorming sessions regarding the whole range of questions of strategy regarding the Senate hearings, a review of possible problems and general discussion of how to deal with a number of new factors.

It was obvious that the Senate hearings would generate massive publicity. In calling and hearing a wide range of witnesses one at a time on national television, there would be a lot of charges and hearsay with no opportunity to answer them, in the same news cycle at least, and there was of course the real concern that the committee hearings might evolve into a very partisan exercise.

There was a freewheeling discussion of these various possibilities and problems and of ways and means of trying to deal with them or counteract them.

I feel that Mr. Dean in his statement to the committee has, in a number of instances, substantially misinterpreted the intent or implications of things that might have been said at the meeting.

Also I believe he has overlooked one of the principal purposes of the meeting, which was a discussion at great length of how to develop some way to learn the entire Watergate story—including the other activities that were by then bunched together as Watergate—and get it out in its totality and accurately. This was considered as one of the best ways to counteract the potential of adverse publicity arising from a drawn-out public hearing. The feeling was that putting all of the facts out, in one place, at one time, would give the American people a more accurate picture of the truth than would the drawn-out process of hearing one witness at a time over an extended period.

Another objective, which was the President's objective, was to try to work out ways and means by which the facts of Watergate or any testimony that could be provided by anybody in the White House who had any knowledge which would be of interest to this committee could be provided in the most complete form but without getting into the problem of the separation of powers and executive privilege.

I don't recall any discussion of the question of raising money, but I am sure that if there were any, it was in the form that Mr. Moore described; that is, a very incidental item occupying only a few minutes in a series of meetings that lasted for many hours. It was not a principal point of discussion. There was no discussion of a coverup of Watergate during these meetings.

Dean put into evidence...an agenda he says was requested by me for a meeting with the President as a follow-up to La-

Costa (sic) on Feb. 19 or 20. He seems to feel that this is a very significant document that is self-explanatory as evidence of a continuing coverup. I completely fail to see it that way.

There were five items on the agenda. First, a meeting of Sen. Baker with the President, which it was my understanding Sen. Baker had requested and which seems to me to be perfectly natural as one step to be taken in working out the various problems regarding White House staff appearances at the Senate committee hearings, etc. Second, the question of submitting Maurice Stans' name for confirmation to the Senate for a post requiring such confirmation. This was a step designed to deal with two questions: first, to give Mr. Stans the opportunity to re-enter government at a suitably high level, and secondly, to provide him with the opportunity in a very short period of time to appear publicly and, under questioning, to clear up all charges regarding his role in the Watergate, if any, and to give him a chance to, as he requested of this committee, get back his good name. Third, a question of whether Magruder could have a White House job. At that time I had already told Magruder that that would not be possible, but I think the point here was to check that decision with the President to be sure he concurred. Fourth, the question of Buchanan sitting in on the hearings as a watchdog of the press—an idea that Dean says I suggested, although it is my recollection he suggested at the LaCosta meeting. In any event, this was certainly not a coverup move, but exactly the opposite. Fifth, the question of the attorney general meeting with the President. That, too, was a logical step, because we were into the matter of executive privilege, and the question of White House staff members going to the hearings was important for the President to discuss with the attorney general. As it concurrently or shortly thereafter developed, Mr. Baker requested that Mr. Kleindienst be his contact with the administration.

In the latter part of February, as the questions of executive privilege and other matters dealing with the Senate Watergate inquiry intensified, the President saw that this was involving a substantial amount of time of a number of people in the White House and particularly seemed to be involving Ehrlichman and me in more expenditure of time than the President felt was productive. Consequently, he met with John Dean at the end of February regarding the matters of executive privilege, the Senate hearings and so forth, and he gave instructions to me, and I am sure to others, that all Watergate matters were to be handled by Dean at the White House and by Kleindienst at the Justice Department and that no one else was to devote time to the subject and that no one else was to get into the matter with the President. He was trying to avoid everyone getting into the act, wasting time and diverting attention—which is a real danger when a highly publicized and volatile matter such as this comes up.

This decision of the President's led to the series of meetings that he had with Mr. Dean starting Feb. 27 and running through March 21. Meetings that were primarily concerned, at the outset, I believe, with executive privilege matters. That continued to be a major point, but as that three-week period went on, the President's concern did grow regarding conflicting Watergate stories, and from what he indicated to me, he was intensifying pressure on Dean to find a way to get the full story out. Dean at this point was clearly in charge of any matters relating to the Watergate. He was meeting frequently with the President, and he still indicated that he was positive there was no White House involvement. During this time, the Gray hearings also became a matter of focus, and the executive privilege question arose in connection with them, too. I have the feeling that during this period the President was gradually getting more of a feel of the possibility that there might be some problems involved in the Watergate matter that he had not even dreamed of and that that led to the meeting of March 21, in which John Dean was going to give the President the full story.

I should point out one question that Mr. Dean raised regarding a comment made by the President in his meeting of Feb. 27. He said the President told him he wanted Dean to handle the Watergate matter as it was taking too much of Ehrlichman and Haldeman's time and they were principals in it. Dean indicates that he did not understand what it was that the President meant by the statement that Haldeman and Ehrlichman were principals. If this statement was made, I think it is quite clear in the context in which that meeting was held. At that time the major issue was whether the President would permit his principal aides to be called up to the Senate committee to testify. At that time the President considered it inconceivable that anyone would think that the White House counsel would be called to testify and, therefore, was not even considering the possibility of Mr. Dean going before the Senate hearings. He was concerned about the question of Haldeman and Ehrlichman being called. In that sense, I was a principal in the matter of executive privilege. It is significant that the President, according to Dean's report, also emphasized that he would never let Ehrlichman and Haldeman go to the Hill, and I think it is in that connection that he would look at us as principals.

MARCH MEETINGS

The March 13 meeting Mr. Dean had with the President shows on the President's log as having run from 12:42 to 2, an 80-minute meeting, approximately. The President's log also shows that I was in that meeting for 12 minutes, from 12:43 to 12:55. Mr. Dean has testified that this was a long meeting, mainly regarding the Gray hearings and Dean's invitation to appear there. He says that *toward the end* of the conversation, they got into a discussion of Watergate matters and the question of money demands being made by the defendants. He says that it was during this conversation that Haldeman came into the office for a brief interruption but that Haldeman then stayed on. It was then, Dean says, that he told the President there was no money to pay the individuals; the President asked how much it would cost; Dean estimated a million dollars; the President said that was no problem and looked over at Haldeman and repeated that statement. Dean then goes on to describe a conversation regarding executive clemency and then back to the question of money, ending with a laugh from me at Dean's comment that next time he would be more knowledgeable.

The log, however, shows that I was in for 12 minutes at the beginning of the meeting and not at the end.

I have no notes on the March 13 meeting, and I have no recollection of that meeting at all. I do not recall going into the President's office and interrupting the meeting with John Dean, but I am sure that I did if the log so indicates. However, I seriously doubt that the conversation John Dean has described actually took place on March 13. I doubt it because of the difference in timing as shown in the President's log, but I also doubt it because a discussion of some of those matters actually occurred during a meeting on March 21.

There is also a logistic problem regarding the meeting of March 21, since Dean has stated that I was only in that meeting for the last five minutes or so when the President called me in to suggest that a meeting be set up with John Mitchell. My log indicates that I was in a meeting with the President from 11:15 to 11:55 on the morning of March 21. I do recall that meeting, and I recall being in it for substantially more than the five minutes that Mr. Dean remembers.

I was not present for the first hour of the meeting, but I did listen to the tape of the entire meeting—including that portion before I came in.

While I am free to testify to everything which I can recall heppening during the time I was present, the President has directed that I not testify as to any facts which I learned solely by listening to the tape of this meeting.

My counsel will present a letter in this respect, and I shall obey the decision of the committee as to its ruling thereon. Depending on that decision, I shall issue an appropriate addendum to this statement concerning the March 21 meeting.

(The committee rejected the President's order, and Haldeman read from the addendum. The text is below, after his opening statement.)

Mr. Dean, Mr. Ehrlichman and I met with the President later that afternoon of the 21st. That meeting dealt with the questions of the grand jury, the Senate committee and executive privilege in connection with gathering the facts and getting them out. I think there was some discussion of Ehrlichman's theory that everybody should go to the grand jury, and Dean's reaction that that would be fine as long as we had immunity. Mr. Ehrlichman, as I recall, very strongly shot down that thought from Dean, saying it didn't make any sense at all. Dean has testified that he argued that the way to get the truth out would be to send everybody to the grand jury with immunity. That in itself is rather indicative of the different attitudes. Mr. Ehrlichman was arguing for going to the grand jury *without* immunity in order to get the truth out. Mr. Dean was arguing for going to the grand jury *with* immunity to get the truth out.

I recall an incident after that afternoon meeting that Mr. Dean also recalls, but he says it took place before and sees it a little bit differently. I remember that Dean and Ehrlichman and I were standing on top of the steps of the EOB outside the President's office. Dean said, sort of thoughtfully, that maybe the solution to this whole thing was to draw the wagons around the White House and let all the chips fall where they may, because that wouldn't hurt anyone in the White House, nobody here had a problem—but his question was: What would that do in the way of creating problems for Mitchell and Magruder? The significance of that comment was that it still seemed to be clear in Dean's mind that the problem didn't lie in the White House.

The next step was the meeting of Mitchell, Ehrlichman, Dean and myself the next day with the President.

The four of us met first in the morning in my office and had some discussion of Dean's report to the President, although not in any detail. Most of the discussion was regarding approaches to dealing with the situation rather than a review of the facts...

Mitchell turned the discussion to the problem of executive privilege, and he argued very strongly that the position the President had taken and was maintaining regarding executive privilege appeared to the public to be a coverup on the part of the President and that it was bad politics, bad public relations and a bad idea. Dean at that meeting again argued his idea of everybody going to the grand jury with immunity in order to get the facts out.

That was the day the news report was received regarding Pat Gray accusing Dean of having been a liar in some report he had given to the FBI. That interrupted the meeting and there was some discussion about it.

We met in the afternoon in the EOB office with the President, and that too was a discussion of how to handle the situation rather than any further exploration of facts. At that meeting, the grand jury argument was ruled out. Ehrlichman again opposed the idea of going to the grand jury with immunity, and the more discussion there was, the more it seemed that it wasn't a practical thing and probably not within our control anyway.

Mitchell very strongly recommended that the President drop his claim of executive privilege, contending that was a bad position for him to be in. That view, for the time of that meeting at least, prevailed, and the decision that came out of the meeting was for the President to waive executive privilege and to permit all White House staff people to go to the Senate committee and testify fully in open hearing. But it was felt that before that was done, and in order to avoid the problem that had been discussed earlier of the committee hearings resulting in the facts coming out piecemeal, one witness at a time, and being the subject of a major news story, there should first be a complete report put out by the White House prepared by Dean covering all of the facts so that what all of us would say would already by known in one place rather than having bits and pieces come out over a period of time.

So, as I recall, Dean was told at that meeting on the afternoon of March 22 to prepare a full written report for public release regarding the facts as they were known to him and as they in any way involved anyone in the White House. We talked about including in that, even though it wasn't related to the Watergate, all of the facts on the Segretti matter so that any question that might arise on that would also be answered.

There was also at that meeting a question of the Senate committee rules and how the committee was going to operate. The President had expected Kleindienst to be in contact with Sen. Baker, the vice chairman of the committee, regarding these matters. We weren't sure whether he had been or not and the President picked up the phone during the meeting and called Kleindienst to talk to him about maintaining the contact with Sen. Baker.

John Dean was asked how long it would take him to write a report, and he said it would probably take two days. He was told to go ahead with that process, and the meeting ended on the note that the way this would be handled was that all of us would go the Senate committee without any claim of executive privilege but that first there would be a complete report put out publicly.

Through this period of time, I still had full confidence in John Dean, and I think the President did. He had not in any way hit himself except on the indirect point that there was a possible circumstantial chain of evidence leading to a charge of obstruction of justice which he reported as being more a problem of appearance than of legality. If it was his intention to impress the President, Ehrlichman and me with the fact that he and the two of us were heavily involved in a coverup program of illegal activities, he did indeed fail to do so, and it is my very clear impression that that was not his intent at that time. He did start dropping some indications that Magruder, at least, and possibly Mitchell, had serious legal problems, and the President did become concerned about the problem of Watergate and the new information that had been brought to his attention. That was the reason for his decision that afternoon, and for some changes in his decision over the following week, regarding the White House staff going to the Senate committee without executive privilege; but more importantly, regarding the assignment to John Dean to prepare a full and complete report on all of the facts of the matter. After the March 22 meeting in the afternoon, the President left for Key Biscayne. The rest of us remained in Washington. I went to Key Biscayne the next morning to join the President for the weekend. John Dean went home to write his report, but found that he was besieged by reporters as a result of the Pat Gray allegation that he had lied, and so the President, in talking to him on the phone the next day, suggested that he go to Camp David, where he would be free from the press and would have an uninterrupted opportunity to get his report prepared. I am convinced that there *was* a discussion of Dean writing a report and that when we left the meeting on the afternoon of the 22nd, it was clear in all of our minds that that was Dean's assignment and that he was expected to do so over the next couple of days.

CAMP DAVID

Over the weekend that Dean was at Camp David, I had several phone conversations with him. There was a story that Dean and Magruder knew about the bugging, and that was a matter of concern to Dean with which he was dealing. He had obviously been working on the report he was supposed to be preparing, and perhaps talking to people. He seemed now to feel that Magruder was definitely involved. He gave that indication, which he had given before, on the phone. He was not at all sure about whether or not Mitchell was involved.

On the 26th, I had a long phone call with Dean. It is interesting, because he said there was no communication on that day of any significance.

I had called Dean to ask if he would have any problem if the President announced that he was requesting that Dean be called to the grand jury without immunity, and I specified that, because in the earlier discussions Dean had made the point of immunity. Dean said, "No, I would have no problem with that." Then he said, "I have been working on this whole thing and trying to analyze what our problems are."

He said there is a problem with Magruder regarding the planning meetings, because apparently he has testified as to the number of meetings and the content of the meetings, and his testimony was different than what mine would be if I went to the grand jury now. He said there was only one meeting, and it was for the purpose of discussing campaign spending laws; while, in fact, there were two meetings and they were for the purpose of discussing intelligence presentations by Liddy.

He said, in looking over this whole thing, there are several areas of concern. One is the blackmail area. Blackmail started way back. (This was the first time he spelled this out to me.) Mitchell was hit by Parkinson or O'Brien, who were hit by Bittman, who was hit by Hunt, who had been hit by the defendants saying that they needed money, and if they didn't get it they were going to cause trouble. It wasn't spelled out much more than that, I don't think.

Mitchell told Dean (this is Dean now recounting to me what his report apparently was showing) to tell Haldeman and Ehrlichman to get Kalmbach to raise the money, and Dean did. Kalmbach raised about $70,000, which he gave to LaRue.

Then we got to the question of the $350,000, and there was a problem there, because the $22,000 was spent out of that, and there was a problem of how to return it and account for the missing $22,000.

Then there was the problem of blackmail to the White House directly. He said there were two instances of that. One—Mrs. Hunt called Colson's secretary and said something about a demand for money. The other was Hunt's that preceding week.

Regarding clemency, he said Colson talked to Bittman. He didn't make any commitment but told him he would help.

He referred to a letter McCord had written to Caulfield requesting a meeting. Mitchell told Dean to have him see him and find out what he was up to.

Another problem area was Dean's delay in turning over the evidence in Hunt's safe to the FBI. Another was a call Liddy had made to Krogh. Apparently he had been given a brushoff by Krogh, and that had made Liddy mad.

Following that phone call, the President dropped his plan to announce that Mr. Dean would be requesting an appearance immediately before the grand jury in order to lay out all the facts as he knew them. The problem was that Dean hadn't really sorted out the facts at that point and it wasn't appropriate for him to go to the grand jury.

Dean has said in his testimony that there was no discussion in the March 26 phone call of his going to the grand jury—yet that was the reason for the call.

In one of the phone calls from Camp David, I believe on the 27th, Dean told me he had talked with Paul O'Brien, who had told him Magruder had said that he had gone ahead with the Watergate operation on orders from Strachan, who said Haldeman had ordered it because the President wanted it done. This is the same report that Dean testified he had given to me in early February. Another confusion in dates—but an important one.

By the 30th, Dean had not delivered any report, and he said he hadn't been able to write one; and the President stopped dealing with Dean. In effect, he had stopped dealing with him after the 23rd.

I don't believe my attitude toward Dean had changed at that point. I was puzzled, and maybe Dean was reading some puzzlement; but I had been in frequent communication with him in quite lengthy phone conversations while he was at Camp David—contrary to the implication he has created that he was practically incommunicado while he was up there. I had the feeling that he was telling me quite openly what the problems were and what he was trying to work out.

On the 30th of March, the President made the announcement that nobody in the White House would go to the Senate hearings but that all members of the White House staff would, of course, appear before the grand jury, if called, and would cooperate fully.

APRIL

Also on the 30th, the President put Mr. Ehrlichman officially on the Watergate investigation and told him to develop the facts in the case and try again to get to a final conclusion.

From April 1 to 7 I was in San Clemente with the President. Despite Mr. Dean's statement that during that period, he, under advice of counsel, endeavored to avoid any contact with Haldeman, Ehrlichman or Mitchell, we talked on the phone daily. The main problem he seemed to have during that period was the continuing one with Mitchell regarding the discrepancy on the number of meetings.

It is my understanding that Dean hired a lawyer, Mr. Shaffer, about March 30. He had indicated earlier that he might do this so he—and, through him, the President—could consult an attorney familiar with criminal law on the implications of some of the concerns Dean was developing. He told me that his lawyer had told him he should not write anything down about the Watergate case, and, if he had written anything down, he should not show it to anyone and he should not talk to Mitchell or Magruder. He did not mention to me that his lawyer had told him not to talk to me or Ehrlichman and he did, in fact, continue to talk to me, at least.

He told me his lawyers had met privately with the U.S. attorneys on April 4. He told me again on April 7 that his lawyers had met with the U.S. attorneys on April 6. This despite the fact that in his testimony he has said that his lawyers were meeting with the prosecutors, but this was unknown to Haldeman or Ehrlichman.

He further said that the U.S. attorneys had told his lawyers (and he believed that this was the straight information, because this was an eyeball-to-eyeball meeting) that the U.S. attorneys were only interested in the pre-June-17 facts. They had no concern with post-June-17. They only wanted Dean as a witness. They did not consider him a target of their investigation. They did not consider Haldeman as a target and probably would not even call him as a witness. Liddy had told them everything, but his lawyers didn't know it; and Liddy completely cleared the White House; that is, in telling them everything, Liddy had confirmed that nobody in the White House had had any involvement.

We returned to Washington on April 8. During that week, Ehrlichman continued his investigation—and on Saturday the 14th, reported his conclusions to the President in the form of a verbal statement of his theory of the case based on all of the information he had acquired—still, of necessity, mostly by hearsay.

There were several meetings with Dean that week, and I recall a continuing concern on Dean's part regarding the discrepancy with Mitchell and the planning meetings. I don't recall any major changes in Dean's view of the facts from what he had reported on the phone earlier.

By the end of the week, both Dean and Ehrlichman had come to the view that Mitchell had approved the Watergate plan, and there was some discussion that, if that were the fact, and if Mitchell decided to step forward and say so, it would be a major step in clearing up the Watergate mystery. This was not discussed in any context of asking Mitchell to do this as a scapegoat or to divert attention from others—but as a major step in bringing out the truth.

Over the weekend, both Magruder and Dean met with the U.S. attorneys in private sessions and gave their full accounts of the Watergate. These meetings were reported to the President on Sunday the 15th by Attorney General Kleindienst and Assistant Attorney General Petersen. Their report was not very surprising to the President, since it confirmed, with minor variations, the theory that Ehrlichman had given him on Saturday.

Because the Dean and Magruder testimony seriously implicated John Mitchell, Kleindienst removed himself from responsibility on Watergate, and the President put Petersen in full charge.

By the end of April, it had become apparent to me that, because of the increasing intensity of charges and rumors in which my name was raised and the need for me to appear before the grand jury and this committee, it was no longer possible for me to perform my White House duties effectively. After some discussions regarding leave of absence versus resignation, I concluded I should resign, and the President agreed. I resigned on April 30.

I said then that I was confident that when the full truth was known, it would be clear I had had no knowledge of or involvement in Watergate or any "coverup" and I had not failed to meet the very high standards of integrity which President Nixon had properly expected of everyone on his White House staff and which I have always held for myself.

I have that confidence in full measure today and welcome the opportunity to help in the process of making the truth known.

ADDENDUM

MARCH 21 MEETING

I was present for the final 40 minutes of the President's meeting with John Dean on the morning of March 21. While I was not present for the first hour of the meeting, I did listen to the tape of the entire meeting. Following is the substance of that meeting to the best of my recollection.

Dean reported some facts regarding the planning and the break-in of the DNC (Democratic National Committee) and said again there were no White House personnel involved. He felt Magruder was fully aware of the operation, but he was not sure about Mitchell. He said that Liddy had given him a full rundown right after Watergate and that no one in the White House was involved. He said that his only concerns regarding the White House were in relation to the Colson phone call to Magruder, which might indicate White House pressure, and the possibility that Haldeman got some of the "fruits" of the bugging via Strachan since he had been told the "fruits" had been supplied to Strachan.

He outlined his role in the January planning meetings and recounted a report he said he made to me regarding the second of those meetings.

Regarding the post-June 17 situation, he indicated concern about two problems, money and clemency. He said that Colson had said something to Hunt about clemency. He did not report any other offers of clemency, although he felt the defendants expected it. The President confirmed that he could not offer clemency, and Dean agreed.

Regarding money, Dean said he and Haldeman were involved. There was a bad appearance which could be developed into a circumstantial chain of evidence regarding obstruction of justice. He said that Kalmbach had raised money for the defendants; that Haldeman had okayed the return of the $350,000 to the committee, and that Dean had handled the dealings between the parties in doing this. He said that the money was for lawyers' fees.

He also reported on a current Hunt blackmail threat. He said Hunt was demanding $120,000 or else he would tell about the seamy things he had done for Ehrlichman. The President pursued this in considerable detail, obviously trying to smoke out what was really going on. He led Dean on regarding the process and what he would recommend doing. He asked such things as—well, this is the thing you would recommend? We ought to do this? Is that right? And he asked where the money would come from? How it would be delivered? And so on.

He asked how much money would be involved over the years, and Dean said probably a million dollars—but the problem is that it is hard to raise. The President said there is no problem in raising a million dollars, we can do that, but it would be wrong. I have the clear impression that he was trying to find out what it was Dean was saying and what Dean was recommending. He was trying to get Dean's view, and he was asking him leading questions in order to do that. This is the method the President often used when he was moving toward a determination.

Dean also mentioned his concern about other activities getting out, such as the "Ellsberg" break-in, something regarding Brookings, the other Hunt activities for Colson on Chappaquiddick, the Segretti matter, use of Kalmbach funds, etc.

When I entered the meeting, there was another discussion regarding the Hunt threat, and the President again explored in considerable depth the various options and tried to draw Dean out on his recommendation.

The meeting then turned to the question of how to deal with the situation, and the President mentioned Ehrlichman's recommendation that everybody should go to the grand jury. The President told Dean to explore all of this with Haldeman, Ehrlichman and Mitchell.

There was no discussion while I was in the room, nor do I recall any discussion on the tape on the question of clemency in the context of the President saying that he had discussed this with Ehrlichman and with Colson. The only mention of clemency was Dean's report that Colson discussed clemency with Hunt and the President's statement that he could not offer clemency and Dean's agreement—plus a comment that Dean thought the others expected it.

Dean mentioned several times during this meeting his awareness that he was telling the President things the President had known nothing about.

I have to surmise that there is a genuine confusion in Mr. Dean's mind as to what happened on March 13 vs. what happened on March 21, because some of what he describes in quite vivid detail as happening on March 13, did, in fact, happen on March 21. The point about my laughing at his being more knowledgeable next time, and the question that he says he raised on March 13 regarding the million dollars are so accurately described, up to a point, as to what really happened on March 21 that I believe he is confused between the two dates.

Mr. Dean's recollection that the President had told him on March 13 that Ehrlichman had discussed an offer of clemency to Hunt with him and he had also discussed Hunt's clemency with Colson is at total variance with everything that I have ever heard from the President, Ehrlichman or Colson. I don't recall such a discussion in either the March 13 or the March 21 meeting.

Now to the question of impression. Mr. Dean drew the erroneous conclusion that the President was fully knowledgeable of coverup at the time of the March 13 meeting in the sense (1) of being aware that money had been paid for silence and that (2) the money demands could reach a million dollars and that the President said that was no problem. He drew his conclusion from a hypothetical discussion of questions, since the President told me later that he had no intention to do anything whatever about money and had no knowledge of the so-called coverup.

I had no difficulty accepting the President's version, based on years of very close association with President Nixon and on hundreds of hours meeting with him. Having observed the President all those years, in many different situations, it was very clear to me on March 21 that the President was exploring and probing; that he was surprised; that he was trying to find out what in the world was going on; he didn't understand how this all fit together and he was trying to find out. He was pushing hard for that kind of information about Mr. Dean.

The President further was concerned about how this ought to be dealt with, and he was interested in getting views from Ehrlichman, Dean, Haldeman and Mitchell, because he felt that those views might be enlightening as to what the true situation was. For that reason he asked that a meeting be held with the four of us in the immediate future, and such a meeting was scheduled for the next day. ✓

WATERGATE: COMMITTEE HEARS 33RD WITNESS, RECESSES

The Senate Watergate committee recessed its hearings Aug. 7 after zeroing in for two days on the Justice Department and FBI's early handling of the case. The stories told by its final two witnesses, Assistant Attorney General Henry E. Petersen and his ex-boss, former Attorney General Richard G. Kleindienst, were unstartling. Nevertheless they admitted fascinating insights into two areas: the inside workings of a department whose halting progress in the Watergate investigation had been widely criticized, and the severe tensions the probe induced within the top ranks of the Nixon administration. *(Testimony, p. 260)*

With a final ripple of his now-famous eyebrows, Committee Chairman Sam J. Ervin Jr. (D N.C.) unceremoniously gaveled the hearings closed at 4:45 p.m. Tuesday after finishing with Petersen, the committee's 33rd witness. Seven more witnesses were due to appear beginning Sept. 10 before the panel moved beyond the first phase: the break-in itself.

The conflict between the legislature and executive branches of government seemed to be advancing inexorably toward a constitutional crisis which many observers warned could juggle the balance of authority between the branches of government. Speaking generally on the moral issues of Watergate in an address before the American Bar Association Aug. 5, Nixon Supreme Court Justice appointee Harry A. Blackmun warned that the "very glue of our ship of state seems about to become unstuck." The observation seemed to apply with special aptitude to the tapes controversy.

The White House position grew increasingly obdurate as the week progressed. In a CBS television interview Aug. 3, White House chief of staff Alexander M. Haig Jr. argued that selective release of tapes of White House conversations sought by the committee would encourage Watergate defendants to insist on complete disclosure so as to exonerate themselves of perjury charges.

Then, on Aug. 7, White House lawyers filed a 34-page brief with Federal Judge John J. Sirica opposing the subpoena filed by special prosecutor Archibald Cox for the tapes and related documents. Nixon's lawyers argued that the President had a right to withhold the tapes in order to safeguard the confidentiality of presidential communications—even if they dealt with a criminal plan—and that under the separation of powers doctrine the court had no business enforcing the subpoena. The committee filed its own suit Aug. 9.

Four Versions on Notification

The question of what President Nixon knew about the Watergate coverup and when he learned it is one that committee Vice Chairman Howard H. Baker Jr. (R Tenn.) asked repeatedly during the hearings. It never was finally settled. As the committee recessed for a month-long vacation, there were four versions of when Nixon first got word of the coverup:

Nixon: "Until March of this year, I remained convinced that the...charges of involvement by members of the White House staff were false. However, new information then came to me which persuaded me that there was a real possibility that some of these charges were true, and suggesting further that there had been an effort to conceal the facts...." *(Statement issued April 30)*

Dean: On March 21, "I began by telling the President that there was a cancer growing on the presidency" and "then proceeded to tell him some of the highlights that had occurred during the coverup." *(Statement to the committee June 25)*

Ehrlichman: The former domestic adviser to the President said he gave Nixon a complete report on the coverup April 14, based on his inquiry that began March 30. "I have great difficulty believing" Dean's testimony that he gave the President a complete report March 21, Ehrlichman said. *(Testimony July 27)*

Kleindienst: "I would say that the information, the nature that I described with (Nixon on April 15) would have come to his attention contemporaneously. If Mr. Ehrlichman is talking to Magruder all afternoon the day before, I would just assume, although he didn't say, that Mr. Ehrlichman would have made a report like this to the President. But I would gather from my meeting with the President that he had no such knowledge until immediately prior to my meeting." *(Testimony Aug. 7)*

Petersen and Kleindienst. Assistant Attorney General Petersen, 52, was a registered Democrat who described himself as "non-partisan." His ex-boss, Kleindienst, who described himself as "a hard-nosed 50-year-old geezer", was a creature of Republican politics. He had directed the 1964 presidental campaign of fellow-Arizonian Barry Goldwater and had been national field director for Richard Nixon's 1968 campaign.

Both witnesses made persuasive cases for the propriety of their handling of Watergate, if not entirely for their effectiveness. However, Petersen bitterly disputed the decision to hand the investigation over to a special prosecutor, arguing that the switch reflected unjustly on the integrity of the Justice Department. Given time, he said, the original prosecution team "could have made the case."

So far as the President was concerned, perhaps the most damaging testimony offered by the two witnesses was their agreement that neither had received instruc-

Summary of Nixon's Reply in Court Test Over Tapes

Following is the text of the summary of President Nixon's reply to special prosecutor Archibald Cox's subpoena seeking taped conversations in the Watergate case. The Nixon brief was filed Aug. 7 in U.S. district court in Washington, D.C.

The present proceeding, though a well-intentioned effort to obtain evidence for criminal prosecutions, represents a serious threat to the nature of the presidency as it was created by the Constitution, as it has been sustained for 184 years, and as it exists today.

If the special prosecutor should be successful in the attempt to compel disclosure of recordings of presidential conversations, the damage to the institution of the presidency will be severe and irreparable. The character of that office will be fundamentally altered and the total structure of government—dependent as it is upon a separation of powers—will be impaired.

The consequence of an order to disclose recordings or notes would be that no longer could a President speak in confidence with his close advisers on any subject. The threat of potential disclosure of any and all conversations would make it virtually impossible for President Nixon or his successors in that great office to function. Beyond that, a holding that the President is personally subject to the orders of a court would effectively destroy the status of the executive branch as an equal and coordinate element of government.

There is no precedent that can be said to justify or permit such a result. On the contrary, it is clear that while courts and their grand juries have the power to seek evidence of all persons, including the President, the President has the power and thus the privilege to withhold information if he concludes that disclosure would be contrary to the public interest.

The breadth of this privilege is frequently debated. Whatever its boundaries it must obtain with respect to a President's private conversations with his advisers (as well as to private conversations by judges and legislators with their advisers). These conversations reflect advisory opinions, recommendations, and deliberations that are an essential part of the process by which presidential decisions and policies are formulated. Presidential privacy must be protected, not for its own sake, but because of the paramount need for frank expression and discussion among the President and those consulted by him in the making of presidential decisions.

The privilege with regard to recordings was not waived by the decision of the President, in the interest of having the truth about Watergate come out, to permit testimony about portions of those conversations by persons who participated in them. Testimony can be limited, as recordings cannot, to the particular area in which privilege is not being claimed. Nor does the privilege vanish because there are claims that some of the statements made to the President by others in these conversations may have been pursuant to a criminal conspiracy by those other persons. That others may have acted in accordance with a criminal design does not alter the fact that the President's participation in these conversations was pursuant to his constitutional duty to see that the laws are faithfully executed and that he is entitled to claim executive privilege to preserve the confidentiality of private conversations he held in carrying out that duty.

In the exercise of his discretion to claim executive privilege the President is answerable to the nation but not to the courts. The courts, a co-equal but not a superior branch of government, are not free to probe the mental processes and the private confidences of the President and his advisers. To do so would be a clear violation of the constitutional separation of powers. Under that doctrine the judicial branch lacks power to compel the President to produce information that he has determined it is not in the public interest to disclose.

The issue here is starkly simple: will the presidency be allowed to continue to function?

---

tions from Nixon on or after March 21 to report new facts to him, as Nixon had maintained.

Nixon seemed about ready to reply. As the hearings recessed he was huddling with top advisers and speechwriters at his Camp David retreat in Maryland's Catoctin Mountains, preparing his long-promised statement on the Watergate hearings.

Witnesses Aug. 3

L. Patrick Gray III told the Senate select Watergate committee that he destroyed Watergate-related documents because he felt that was what John D. Ehrlichman and John W. Dean III, then White House aides, wanted him to do. *(Excerpts of Gray's testimony, p. 264)*

"I distinctly recall Mr. Dean saying that these files were 'political dynamite' and 'clearly should not see the light of day,' " Gray testified. "It is true that neither Mr. Ehrlichman nor Mr. Dean expressly instructed me to destroy the files. But there was, and is, no doubt in my mind that destruction was intended. Neither Mr. Dean nor Mr. Ehrlichman said or implied that I was being given the documents personally merely to safeguard against leaks.... The clear implication of the substance and tone of their remarks was that these two files were to be destroyed and I interpreted this to be an order from the counsel to the President of the United States (Dean) issued in the presence of one of the two top assistants to the President of the United States."

Gray, who resigned from the FBI April 27 when it became known he had destroyed the documents, had been acting director of the bureau for one year and was President Nixon's nominee for director. The destruction of the documents—fake State Department cables implicating President Kennedy in the 1963 murder of President Diem of South Vietnam—took place in December 1972, six months after Gray's meeting with Ehrlichman and Dean. The two presidential aides left their posts April 30.

Gray's testimony came in a prepared statement it took him two hours to read. The committee recessed before questioning him. Gray, a lawyer, called his acceptance of the documents "a grievous misjudgment" which was compounded when he destroyed them.

The documents were from the White House safe of E. Howard Hunt Jr., one of seven men convicted in the Watergate burglary of June 17, 1972. They were prepared by Hunt in 1971 while he was a member of a secret White House unit called the plumbers, which was set up originally to stop the leaks of sensitive documents to the press and others.

Hunt Papers. A retired Navy captain, Gray had held several high-level governmental jobs before becoming acting director of the FBI upon the death of J. Edgar Hoover on May 2, 1972. The meeting at which he took possession of the Hunt documents was in Ehrlichman's office June 28, 1972. Gray told the committee he went there to discuss leaks of information about the FBI's Watergate probe and was surprised to find Dean there. Although disagreeing on details, Gray, Dean and Ehrlichman all testified that Gray was not specifically ordered to destroy the documents. *(Dean, Ehrlichman testimony, p. 152, 230)*

L. Patrick Gray III

As Gray told it, Dean handed him two file folders, telling him that they contained classified papers with "national security implications or overtones" and that they had nothing to do with Watergate. Gray said he asked whether the documents should become part of the bureau's Watergate file, and that Dean said no, "but that he wanted to be able to say, if called upon later, that he had turned all of Howard Hunt's files over to the FBI."

Gray told the committee he took the papers to his apartment, later moved them to his office and then to his home in Stonington, Conn., and finally burned them during Christmas week with other household trash. Before burning them, however, Gray said he looked at one of the files and found that it contained what appeared to him to be genuine copies of top secret State Department cables on the Diem assassination.

Also testifying Aug. 3 was Lt. Gen. Vernon A. Walters, the deputy director of the Central Intelligence Agency, who discussed his meetings with Gray and Dean about the FBI's Watergate investigation. His testimony was similar to that of former CIA Director Richard M. Helms, Walters' boss at the time. Walters' testimony differed somewhat from Gray's, but primarily on relatively minor points. *(Helms' testimony, p. 238)*

Walters Memo. In other testimony, Gray revealed that Walters gave him a memo on July 12, 1972, indicating that Hunt and another Watergate conspirator, G. Gordon Liddy, had received CIA help at an earlier time. It had been charged that he purposely surpressed information about the memo. Gray said that was "nonsense," and that the fact that it was found in his safe after he left the bureau was proof that he did not consider it important enough to hide from authorities. Gray said he did not recall ever seeing the memo until federal prosecutors showed it to him this spring.

Ehrlichman's recollection about two telephone conversations with Gray on April 15 differed from Gray's. Ehrlichman told the committee he called Gray on Nixon's orders to find out what had happened to the Hunt files. Nixon had learned of the existence of the files earlier that day, Ehrlichman said.

The former domestic adviser to the President quoted Gray as telling him that he would deny having received the documents because he had destroyed them and that Ehrlichman would have to back up his story. Ehrlichman said he was shocked at what Gray told him and, after telling the President what Gray said, called Gray back to emphasize that he would not support the story.

According to Gray's version of the calls, the first one had Ehrlichman simply informing him that Dean had been talking to the prosecutors. Gray said the second call contained his admission that he had destroyed the documents.

"I know that Mr. Ehrlichman has testified that in these conversations I told him I would deny receiving the files and asked him to support me in that denial. "I have absolutely no recollection of such an exchange...," Gray said, adding that the conversations may have been taped.

Mexican Activities. Walters confirmed earlier testimony by Helms that former White House chief of staff H. R. Haldeman ordered him June 23, 1972, to meet with Gray and tell him unspecified CIA activities in Mexico might be uncovered if the FBI pursued an all-out Watergate investigation in that country.

Walters said he went to Gray the same day and told him, without mentioning his source, that the White House wanted Gray to "taper off" the bureau's probe in Mexico. Walters, like Helms, said Haldeman was very close to the President and it was possible that he knew something about the CIA's Mexican operations that the two top CIA officials did not know.

Walters said that within the next few days he confirmed that the agency's Mexican operations would not be compromised by a full FBI Watergate investigation there, and tried to get the point across to both Gray and Dean. But, according to Walters, Dean kept insisting that the CIA was involved in Watergate and made repeated overtures to Walters about having the agency provide bail money and salaries for the five men arrested at the Democratic Party headquarters in the Watergate building. *(Dean, Walters meetings, p. 229)*

Gray, in his version of the June 23 meeting with Walters, said it was his impression that Walters was stating a CIA position, rather than a message from the White House. Another difference between Gray and Walters was Walters' contention that in the meeting Gray's problem was how to "low key" the FBI's investigation.

Gray, however, stated that while he may have used words to that effect, it would only have been to let Walters know that the bureau would handle any CIA aspect in Mexico with kid gloves. Gray said the bureau's Watergate probe in Mexico was slowed until July 6, when he got confirmation in writing from Walters that no CIA operation there would be affected.

The Mexican aspect of the Watergate investigation involved tracing the source of four checks totaling $89,000 and drawn on a Mexican bank. The money wound up in the Miami bank account of Bernard L. Barker, one of the Watergate burglars.

Potential Damage. Gray also disputed Walters' version of a July 12 conversation with Gray in which Walters said Gray discussed talking to the President about the Watergate investigation. According to Walters, Gray told Nixon July 6 that the investigation would reach high on his staff and that he should get rid of those implicated.

Gray's version of the July 6 conversation with the President had him telling Nixon that Walters and he "feel that people on your staff are trying to mortally wound you by using the CIA and FBI and by confusing the question of CIA interest in, or not in, people the FBI wishes to interview." Gray said the President paused a moment and said, "Pat, you just continue to conduct your aggressive and thorough investigation."

Witness Aug. 6

Gray agreed, under questioning by Herman E. Talmadge (D Ga.), that President Nixon should have realized as early as July 1972 that the possibility of a Watergate coverup existed in the White House.

In his prepared testimony of Aug. 3, Gray said he told the President July 6, 1972, that he and Lt. Gen. Vernon A. Walters, deputy director of the CIA, believed that persons on Nixon's staff were trying to "mortally wound" the President by confusing the question of CIA interest in persons the FBI wanted to investigate in its Watergate probe.

Although he said he mentioned no names to the President on that occasion, Gray said Aug. 6 that he had in mind Nixon's domestic adviser, John D. Ehrlichman, and his counsel, John W. Dean III. In following up on Gray's prepared testimony, this exchange occurred between Talmadge and Gray.

Talmade: "Did you think that your conversation with the President on July 6, 1972, was sufficient to adequately put him on notice that the White House staff was engaged in obstructing justice?"

Gray: "I don't know that I thought in terms of obstruction of justice, but I certainly think there was, it was adequate to put him on the notice that the members of the White House staff were using the FBI and the CIA."

Talmadge: "Do you think it adequate, do you think a reasonable and prudent man on the basis of the warning that you gave him at that time, would have been alerted to the fact that his staff was engaged in something improper, unlawful and illegal?"

Gray: "I do because frankly I expected the President to ask me some questions for two weeks after that...." Gray went on to explain that the President never told him anything except to pursue his investigation. On the 12th and 28th of July, Gray said, he asked Walters if the President had spoken to him about their concern. When Walters answered no, Gray said he felt he and the general had been "alarmists" in their concerns about White House involvement in the coverup.

Gray's Recollection. Gray's recollection of the July 6 call from the President differed from Nixon's. In his May 22 statement on the Watergate affair, the President characterized it in these terms:

"During the conversation, Mr. Gray discussed with me the progress of the Watergate investigation, and I asked him whether he had talked with General Walters. Mr. Gray said that he had, and that General Walters had assured him that the CIA was not involved. In the discussion, Mr. Gray suggested that the matter of Watergate might lead higher. I told him to press ahead with his investigation." *(Text of Nixon's May 22 statement, p. 90)*

Gray also testified Aug. 6 that he got no orders from Nixon after March 21 to report progress of the FBI's investigation directly to the President. Gray also said he got no requests for information from Ehrlichman, who earlier testified that he took over the Watergate probe for the White House on March 30.

Blackmun: 'Grave Damage'

Supreme Court Justice Harry A. Blackmun Aug. 5 told 750 members of the American Bar Association (ABA) and their families that the Watergate scandal had created an atmosphere whereby the "very glue of our ship of state seems about to come unstuck."

Blackmun told the assembled lawyers and judges there was a fear that "grave damage" had been done to the democratic process because of the scandal. "The pall of Watergate, with all its revelations of misplaced loyalties, of strange measures of the unethical, of unusual doings in high places, and by lawyer after lawyer after lawyer, is upon us," he said.

Appointed to the court in 1970 by President Nixon and generally considered a member of the court's conservative wing, Blackmun noted that every administration in recent times had been affected by scandals—large and small. "One senses a laxness in public life that 20 years ago, if indulged in, could not be politically surmounted," he said.

Speaking before the bar association's annual prayer breakfast, Blackmun chose as his text the Old Testament book of Nehemiah, which describes the rebuilding of the walls of Jerusalem in 446 B.C. against what seemed to be overwhelming odds. "One may say that our Jerusalem is in ruins," he said. One might question, he added, whether American society's "foundations are eroding, and whether the walls, after all, are only rubble.

"Perhaps we need to make our own solitary inspection of the walls," he concluded, "to plan; to cooperate; to resolve that it is worth doing; to provide leadership; to engage, if necessary, in activity that simultaneously is both defensive and constructive; to rededicate—or should I say dedicate—ourselves to what this bar association and this nation stand for."

The justice received a standing ovation.

The subject was raised by Sen. Lowell P. Weicker Jr. (R Conn.), who noted that the President, in his April 30 Watergate statement, said that new information came to him March 21. "As a result, on March 21," Nixon said, "I personally assumed the responsibility for coordinating intensive new inquiries into the matter, and I personally ordered those conducting the investigations to get all the facts and to report them directly to me...." *(Text of Nixon's April 30 statement, p. 34)*

No Orders. Asked by Weicker whether he ever got any orders from the President after March 21, Gray said, "No sir. I received no such order from anybody." Gray testified that the only call he got from Nixon on March 21 was "in the nature of a buck-up call" because of the criticism he had been receiving during his confirmation hearings for the post of FBI director. Gray said the President told him there always would be a place for him in the Nixon administration and "there'll be another day to get back at our enemies."

In other testimony, Gray told of a meeting April 26 in which Assistant Attorney General Henry Petersen

(Continued on p. 260)

Watergate Box Score: Over 20 Investigations...

By early August, Watergate had triggered eight civil suits, seven congressional inquiries, six grand jury investigations, three trials and numerous federal agency investigations. Still more actions were planned.

CONGRESSIONAL

• The House Banking and Currency Committee on Oct. 3, 1972, voted to reject a probe of Nixon campaign finances. *(1972 Almanac p. 91)*

According to House committee sources, Chairman Wright Patman (D Texas) directed the staff to stay on top of the case for possible future hearings.

• Sen. Edward M. Kennedy (D Mass.), chairman of a Senate Judiciary subcommittee, reported on Jan. 22 the results of a staff investigation of Watergate.

• Sen. Sam J. Ervin Jr.'s (D N.C.) Senate Select Committee on Presidential Campaign Activities opened hearings on Watergate May 17.

• The full Senate Judiciary Committee heard Watergate-related testimony during the confirmation hearings of L. Patrick Gray III for FBI director and of Elliot L. Richardson for attorney general. *(p. 90, 62; 1972 Almanac p. 92)*

• The House and Senate Armed Services Committees and the Senate Appropriations Committee held extensive hearings on CIA involvement in the Watergate coverup. *(p. 68)*

Planned. In an interview published in *The New York Times* June 16, Rep. Peter W. Rodino Jr. (D N.J.), chairman of the House Judiciary Committee, said he was planning a broad investigation into Justice Department and FBI operations as a result of Watergate. *(p. 147)*

Possible. Rep. Wilbur D. Mills (D Ark.), chairman of the House Ways and Means Committee and the Joint Committee on Internal Revenue Taxation, said June 27 he had directed the staff of the Joint Committee to begin preliminary checks into charges that the Internal Revenue Service was used for political purposes. *(p. 153)*

GRAND JURIES

Washington, D.C. The original Watergate grand jury was first impaneled June 5, 1972, in Washington as a regular monthly jury. It began its investigation of the Watergate break-in immediately after the crime had occurred. After handing down the indictments of the original seven defendants on Sept. 15, 1972, the jury reconvened on March 26, 1973, to consider new charges.

Although still in session, the jury was to be joined on Aug. 13 by a special grand jury requested by Watergate special prosecutor Archibald Cox to probe new areas. The new jury was to consider charges of campaign corruption, focusing on illegal contributions by corporations, extortion by federal officials, conspiracy and obstruction of justice.

New York City. A federal grand jury in New York City on May 10 indicted four men, including two former Nixon cabinet officers, on charges of conspiring to arrange a secret $200,000 contribution to the 1972 campaign. Indicted were former Attorney General John N. Mitchell, former Commerce Secretary Maurice H. Stans, New Jersey financier Robert L. Vesco (who made the contribution) and New Jersey attorney Harry L. Sears. Mitchell, Stans and Sears pleaded not guilty on May 21. A bench warrant was issued for the arrest of Vesco, who was believed to be out of the country. *(p. 89, 56)*

Los Angeles. A federal grand jury in Los Angeles on June 7 opened an investigation into the break-in at the office of Pentagon Papers defendant Daniel Ellsberg's psychiatrist. *(p. 137, 121)*

Orlando, Fla. A federal grand jury in Orlando, Fla., on May 4 indicted Los Angeles attorney Donald H. Segretti and Tampa accountant George Hearing on charges of distributing a bogus letter under the letterhead of 1972 Democratic presidential candidate Edmund S. Muskie. Hearing pleaded guilty to one count of a two-count indictment and was sentenced on June 15 to a maximum of one year in prison. Segretti, who pleaded innocent on May 17, was scheduled for trial in Tampa the week of Oct. 8. *(p. 147, 69, 54, 25)*

Houston. A federal grand jury in Houston, Texas, was investigating a $100,000 contribution made by Gulf Resources and Chemical Corporation to the Nixon campaign. Part of the money allegedly went through Mexico into the Miami bank account of convicted Watergate conspirator Bernard L. Barker and was used to help finance the Watergate bugging. *(p. 117, 87)*

Anne Arundel County. A grand jury in Anne Arundel County, Maryland, on June 13 indicted Blagden H. Wharton, a Maryland banker and 1972 Republican campaign official, on four counts of violating state election laws by falsifying campaign contribution reports on a dinner held for Vice President Agnew in May 1972. *(p. 149, 140, 121)*

CIVIL SUITS

Democrats. Three days after the Watergate break-in, then Democratic Chairman Lawrence F. O'Brien announced a $1-million invasion-of-privacy suit against the Nixon re-election committee. On Sept. 11, 1972, the Democrats announced they would file an amended complaint that would add to the defendants finance chairman Stans, re-election committee treasurer Hugh W. Sloan, finance committee counsel G. Gordon Liddy and former part-time White House consultant E. Howard Hunt Jr., as well as the five men arrested on June 17. The Democrats also raised the damages sought from $1-million to $3.2-million and charged the defendants with political espionage dating back to March 1972. However, a federal district judge dismissed the five from the suit on Sept. 20. *(1972 Almanac p. 90)*

...Lawsuits, Trials—and Several More Threatened

The Democrats doubled the damages sought to $6.4-million and added Jeb Stuart Magruder and Herbert L. Porter, two former officials of the re-election committee, as defendants, on Feb. 28.

The Washington Post reported April 18 and Aug. 1 discussions of an out-of-court settlement of the suit. *(p. 19)*

Republicans. Two days after the Democrats added Stans to their suit, Stans and re-election committee chairman Francis I. Dale on Sept. 13, 1972, filed a $2.5-million abuse of process suit against the Democrats, charging them with using the courts "as an instrument for creating political headlines." *(1972 Almanac p. 91)*

The next day, Stans filed a $5-million libel suit against O'Brien on grounds that O'Brien on Sept. 11 had falsely accused him of political espionage. *(p. 19; 1972 Almanac p. 91)*

McCord. Convicted conspirator James W. McCord Jr. on April 20 filed a $1.5-million cross claim against the President's re-election committee and three campaign officials: Magruder, Liddy and E. Howard Hunt Jr. McCord claimed the defendants had entrapped him in activities that resulted in his conviction. *(p. 20)*

Common Cause. The so-called citizens' lobby filed suit Sept. 6, 1972, to compel the President's re-election finance committee to make full disclosure of its income and expenditures before April 7, 1972, the date such disclosures became mandatory. On July 24 a U.S. District Court judge in Washington, D.C., ordered the committee to comply. *(p. 147, 21, 19)*

McCarthy. The California Committee for Eugene McCarthy on May 18 filed suit in San Francisco Superior Court against officials of the Nixon campaign and others, charging that a bogus letter had been sent out under the committee's letterhead during the 1972 California primary campaign. Named in the suit were Segretti, former Nixon lawyer Herbert W. Kalmbach, Stans, Mitchell, the President's re-election committee and 15 others. *(p. 87)*

Halperin. Morton H. Halperin, a former consultant to the National Security Council, on June 14 filed suit in U.S. District Court in Washington, D.C., for the bugging of his telephone from 1969 to 1971 for as long as 25 months. Halperin, a senior fellow at the Brookings Institution, named as defendants national security adviser Henry A. Kissinger; former White House aides H. R. Haldeman and John D. Ehrlichman; White House chief of staff and former Kissinger deputy Alexander Haig; John Mitchell; former FBI official William C. Sullivan; former acting FBI Director William D. Ruckelshaus; the Chesapeake and Potomac Telephone Company, and unnamed agents of the FBI and other government agencies. *(p. 141)*

Oliver. Democratic party official R. Spencer Oliver, whose telephone at Democratic National Committee headquarters was tapped, on June 15 filed a $5-million suit against Nixon campaign officials and others.

FEDERAL INVESTIGATIONS

Justice Department. Watergate special prosecutor Archibald Cox inherited the original Justice Department investigation of Watergate. A Cox spokesman told Congressional Quarterly that the Cox team was dealing directly with the FBI and was receiving "full cooperation."

GAO. The General Accounting Office had been investigating Watergate since August 1972, when it released a report citing Republicans for apparent violations of the campaign spending law—which the GAO helps police. By the beginning of August 1973, the GAO had referred seven Watergate-related reports to the Justice Department for action out of a total of 21 reports of apparent election law violations. *(p. 90, 84)*

BAR ASSOCIATION

The State Bar of California was planning an investigation of Nixon and five California lawyers for possible disciplinary action, *The San Francisco Examiner* reported July 29. The lawyers named were Ehrlichman, Kalmbach, Segretti, former White House aide Gordon C. Strachan and former Nixon re-election committee official Robert C. Mardian.

TRIALS

For all the legal maneuvering that surrounded Watergate, it had produced only three trials by the summer of 1973.

- Two of the seven men tried on criminal charges in the Watergate break-in, McCord and Liddy, were convicted Jan. 30, 1973, in U.S. District Court in Washington, D.C. The other five pleaded guilty.
- Bernard L. Barker, one of the convicted conspirators, was convicted in Florida Nov. 1, 1972, on a charge that he had misused a notary public seal to indicate that a campaign check was endorsed in his presence. Barker received a 60-day sentence, which was suspended on the condition that he surrender his notary's license.
- The President's re-election finance committee June 20 was found guilty of concealing a $200,000 cash contribution from indicted financier Robert L. Vesco. A U.S. District Court judge in Washington fined the committee $3,000. It was the second conviction for the Nixon campaign organization and the second under the Federal Election Campaign Act of 1971. The finance committee had been fined $8,000 on Jan. 26 after pleading no contest to charges of not reporting to the GAO cash sums given by treasurer Hugh Sloan to G. Gordon Liddy.

(Continued from p. 257)
said the two of them were "expendable." The conversation took place in the office of former Attorney General Richard G. Kleindienst a day before Gray resigned as acting FBI director. (Gray's nomination as director was withdrawn April 5 at his own request.)

At the late April meeting, Gray related, he told Kleindienst that he had informed Weicker about his destruction of the papers from E. Howard Hunt's safe and that Kleindienst told him he would probably have to resign as acting director. Gray said he disagreed, pointing out that the Hunt papers did not relate to the Watergate scandal.

Expendable. While Kleindienst went to another room to call Nixon, Gray said Petersen told him, "Pat, I'm scared...because it appears that you and I are expendable and Haldeman (H.R. Haldeman, the White House chief of staff) and Ehrlichman are not." Gray said that Kleindienst returned just as Petersen was advising him to get a lawyer. Kleindienst, Gray related, told him the President wanted him to continue as acting director. But, said Gray, after thinking about it over night, he decided the next day to resign.

Under further questioning, Gray said he did not agree with Petersen that they were expendable, but that he decided to take his advice anyway and seek legal counsel.

Hunt Documents. Gray was asked by several committee members to expand on the meeting June 28, 1972, where he took possession of the Hunt papers from Dean in Ehrlichman's presence.

Asked why he did not tell them to destroy the documents, as he assumed they wanted him to do, Gray said the matter never entered his mind. "I was not about to question orders" from the counsel to the President or the President's top assistant, he said. He went on to explain that on the basis of his 26 years in the Navy he regularly followed orders from superiors and, using military jargon, said he had "no need to know" what was in the files or why he was being asked to take possession of them. "I carried out my orders and I destroyed them," he said.

Gray could not explain to the committee why he waited six months to burn the papers or why they would have been potentially embarrassing to the Nixon administration since they dealt with Kennedy-era policies. He said he did not know at the time he had the papers that two wastebaskets under his desk at the bureau were "burn baskets" and that he knew from the start that he would burn the papers at his home in Stonington, Conn.

Richard Kleindienst

He said he did not feel at the time that he was committing an illegal act by burning the papers because he was told they had no connection with Watergate. Asked if he had been overawed by the White House staff in doing their bidding, Gray replied that he always had a "deep and abiding respect" for the office of the presidency and believed that the people who worked for the President were "above reproach."

"At no time did I ever think the people I dealt with were trying to sweep me into the very conspiracy I was trying to investigate," he said. Earlier he referred to it as running into a "buzz-saw."

Gray admitted having given Dean various FBI documents concerning the Watergate investigation, but he said he did so in the belief that Dean, as presidential counsel, was in charge of the White House's Watergate probe and was reporting directly to Nixon. Dean denied during his testimony that he conducted a Watergate investigation for the White House. *(Dean testimony, p. 152)*

Gray's repeated assertions that the FBI's investigation of Watergate was "terriffic," "fine" and "exhaustive" was received skeptically by the committee and counsels. Gray was asked about a story written by James W. McCord Jr., one of the seven convicted Watergate burglars, that appeared in the August *Armed Forces Journal.* McCord wrote that FBI agents were hampered in their investigation by unnamed persons.

Gray asserted that McCord's article was unfair. Asked by Sen. Edward J. Gurney (R Fla.) why, if the bureau's investigation was so good, it did not lead beyond the seven defendants, Gray said he did not know. "I've asked myself that many times," he told the committee, explaining that he at first thought the FBI agents might somehow have been "awed" by the important people they interviewed or that they did not ask the right questions. But, he said, "One must conclude... that what was told the agents was not true."

Witnesses Aug. 7

The Senate select Watergate committee recessed its hearings for a month Aug. 7 after hearing from former Attorney General Richard G. Kleindienst and Assistant Attorney General Henry E. Petersen. Petersen, as chief of the Justice Department's criminal division, was in over-all charge of the Watergate probe from the break-in June 17, 1972, until a special prosecutor was appointed in May 1973.

When Chairman Sam J. Ervin Jr. (D N.C.) banged his gavel at 4:45 p.m. and announced the hearings were in recess "until the call of the chair," the committee had just heard from Petersen, its 33d witness since testimony began May 17.

The committee recessed without completing the first phase of its hearings, which was to concentrate on the break-in itself, as distinguished from other campaign activities such as financing and alleged "dirty tricks." The first phase will be completed after seven witnesses appear when hearings resume Sept. 10.

Kleindienst and Petersen asserted in separate appearances that neither was directed personally by President Nixon at any time between March 21 and April 15 to report all the facts about Watergate to him. The President said in an April 30 statement that he ordered "those conducting the investigations to get all the facts and report them directly to me" on March 21.

The only other known probe during this period was one conducted for the White House by its former domestic affairs chief, John D. Ehrlichman. But Ehrlichman testified that he did not begin until March 30, and referred to his work as an "inquiry" rather than an investigation because he questioned only about 10 persons.

Henry E. Petersen

"Exactly who was it in the city of Washington who received (the President's) orders?" asked Sen. Lowell P. Weicker Jr. rhetorically. Both Kleindienst and Petersen speculated Nixon was referring to Ehrlichman in his March 21 directive, although neither could explain the nine-day gap between the directive and Ehrlichman's taking over the White House investigation.

The two witnesses, whose testimony generally coincided, differed somewhat on their recollection of the President's reaction when informed on April 15 that the break-in and coverup reached higher than the seven conspirators convicted in January.

They said they told Nixon that the federal investigation implicated Ehrlichman, White House chief of staff H. R. Haldeman, presidential counsel John W. Dean III, former Attorney General John N. Mitchell and others.

Kleindienst told the committee the President was "dumbfounded." He gave the impression of a man who either was receiving the information for the first time or who just had received it "contemporaneously" from another source, he said. Kleindienst said Nixon appeared upset and troubled at the news.

Nixon Calm. Petersen, on the other hand, testified that Nixon appeared concerned, but "calm" at the news. "I remember I remarked to Kleindienst how I admired his calm," Petersen said.

With Kleindienst's testimony on the point, the committee had heard three versions of when Nixon first got the news of high administration involvement in the Watergate affair. Dean testified that he gave the President the complete story March 21, and Ehrlichman said he gave Nixon similar results from his "inquiry" April 14. *(p. 152, 230; box, p. 254)*

White House Interference. Kleindienst said that when he learned of the call, he told Ehrlichman that he should never again interfere with his department and that if he wanted to communicate anything to a departmental employee, he should work through the attorney general. Kleindienst said he threatened to resign if the President ruled that Ehrlichman could give orders to Justice Department officials. But, said the witness, Ehrlichman agreed and the problem never arose again.

Petersen confirmed prior testimony, however, that Stans was given special consideration in that his testimony was taken outside the grand jury. Petersen defended the move as proper, if not customary, saying it was done "to avoid publicity."

Kleindienst also said he discussed executive clemency with Dean and Ehrlichman after the Watergate defendants were convicted. He said the question came up at a luncheon, but that no names were mentioned. The discussion dwelt on "technical" aspects of clemency, he said, including probation reports, eligibility and circumstances for clemency. Ehrlichman pursued the subject, he said.

No Evidence. Petersen and Kleindienst said they had no evidence of high official involvement in the Watergate affair until the early morning hours of April 15, when they met with the federal prosecutors who in turn had just learned of it from Dean and Jeb S. Magruder, the deputy director of the re-election committee. The two carried their information to Nixon later in the day.

Petersen said he had a "visceral reaction" early in the criminal proceedings that someone was giving false testimony, but no hard evidence. He said some witnesses may have lied two or three times before the grand jury and at the Watergate trial. The assistant attorney general, who is believed the first career Justice Department lawyer to rise to that post, said the government's strategy was to convict the seven defendants and then grant them immunity from further prosecution in order to compel them to testify about the possible involvement of higher ups.

Petersen angrily responded to suggestions by Ervin that the government's Watergate probe was less than adequate. Shouting, "I've got to get something off my chest," Petersen said he "resented" the appointment of a special Watergate prosecutor. The case was "snatched from under us" at the Justice Department, he said, when it was 90 per cent completed and that "we would have convicted those people" if prosecutor Archibald Cox had not been appointed after demands by the Senate. "I've been here too long and its been a terrible year," he concluded. But later he conceded that "larger interests" than convictions required Cox's appointment and that if he had been a senator he would have voted for a special prosecutor.

Petersen gave the impression of a blunt, uncompromising adviser to the President. At one point he explained that he had been in the Justice Department for 26 years, "too long to jeopardize my reputation for anyone."

He said that he advised the President April 15 to fire Haldeman and Ehrlichman. Although he could not guarantee at that time that they would be prosecuted, Petersen said he felt their continued presence in the White House would be "an embarrassment." At the same time, Petersen testified that he recommended Nixon not fire Dean because the counsel was cooperating with federal prosecutors.

Advice Accepted. On April 30, after "a longer period than I would have liked," Petersen said, Nixon accepted the resignations of his top two advisers and fired Dean.

At another time, Petersen related, the President ordered him not to follow up on the discovery that two Watergate conspirators had been involved in the 1971 burglary of Daniel Ellsberg's psychiatrist. He quoted Nixon as saying, when he raised the matter of the burglary: "I know about that. That's a national security matter. You stay out of it."

But, said Petersen, he and Kleindienst felt that the information had to be given to the judge presiding in Ellsberg's Pentagon Papers trial. They agreed, the witness said, to resign if Nixon refused to let them inform the judge about the break-in, but that Nixon agreed with their request.

Petersen also said Nixon once offered to let him hear a tape of a presidential conversation with Dean on April 15, but that he refused.

Wife's Role. In other testimony, Petersen credited his wife with playing an unwitting role in the President's staff shakeup of April 30. He said he had told Nixon at one point that his wife was asking whether the President was involved in the Watergate affair and that he told the President he would "waltz it over to the House of Representatives" if he found out Nixon was indeed involved. Impeachment proceedings begin in the House.

Petersen said his remarks appeared to affect Nixon "quite strongly" and that on April 30, after the staff resignations were announced, Nixon called him and said: "You can tell your wife that the President has done what needed to be done."

Ervin announced at the start of the day that the committee would postpone its lawsuit to compel the President to produce tapes of certain conversations until it can study Nixon's brief against production of the tapes for Cox. *(Brief, p. 255)*

Poll Report

An Aug. 6 Harris poll revealed that while a majority of those polled wanted to give President Nixon the benefit of the doubt over Watergate, they questioned whether or not the President could actually continue to govern the country properly.

By 56 to 35 per cent, those polled agreed with the statement that "with most of his second term to go," it is best to give the President "the benefit of the doubt in the Watergate bugging and cover-up."

By 54 to 38 per cent, a majority also agreed with Nixon's statement that "it is more important for him to spend time working for the country than to be trying to find out what happened in the Watergate affair."

But the same people polled by Harris also agreed by 55 to 32 per cent that "President Nixon does not inspire confidence as a President should." In May, the split on that question was 43 to 44 per cent.

A substantial majority—69 to 21 per cent—also felt that "dirty campaign tactics exist among most Republicans and Democrats, and the Nixon campaign people were no worse than the Democrats, except they got caught at it."

Daily Chronology

Following is a day-to-day chronology of the week's events:

AUG. 2

(Earlier Aug. 2 events, p. 243)

ITT Case. Sen. John V. Tunney (D Calif.) urged the Justice Department to reopen its antitrust action against International Telephone and Telegraph Corp. in the wake of the Aug. 1 disclosure of a memo indicating White House interference in the case. *(Colson ITT memo, p. 235)*

Civil Suits. U.S. District Court Judge John J. Sirica hinted that he will order the Democrats' civil suit postponed indefinitely if more indictments are returned in the Watergate case. Sirica said to proceed with a civil suit would jeopardize a defendant's right to a fair trial, should he be indicted later. A settlement in the $6.4-million suit would not be precluded by the postponement of the case. *(p. 110)*

McCord, FBI. James W. McCord Jr., convicted Watergate conspirator, revealed that if the FBI had searched his home and car soon after his arrest in the break-in, they would have found a $18,000 cache and enough evidence to break the case. McCord, who made his revelations in an article in *Armed Forces Journal,* said he destroyed documents relating to the planning of the bugging and said he thinks the FBI was blocked from conducting a thorough inquiry. *(McCord testimony, p. 80)*

Helms Testimony. Former Central Intelligence Agency Director Richard M. Helms testified before the Senate Watergate committee that, although he knew five of the Watergate conspirators had worked for the CIA, he did not conduct an internal investigation. Helms denied that the CIA had anything to do with the break-in and said he was not aware of domestic intelligence against Americans. Helms testified that he told Lt. Gen. Vernon A. Walters, CIA deputy director, to resist requests from then-White House aide John W. Dean III to raise bail money for the Watergate defendants. *(Helms testimony, p. 238)*

Cushman Testimony. Another Helms aide, Gen. Robert E. Cushman testified before the Senate investigating committee that the CIA had loaned equipment to E. Howard Hunt, since convicted in the Watergate break-in. Hunt's requests had begun with a phone call from former White House domestic adviser John D. Ehrlichman, and the CIA subsequently resisted aiding Hunt because the agency had not been informed of Hunt's reasons for borrowing the equipment. *(Cushman testimony, p. 239)*

Bellino Controversy. Sen. Sam J. Ervin Jr. (D N.C.) chairman of the Senate investigating committee, asked Senators Herman E. Talmadge (D Ga.), Daniel K. Inouye (D Hawaii) and Edward J. Gurney (R Fla.) to serve on a special subcommittee to investigate the Watergate committee's own investigator, Carmine S. Bellino. Bellino, a John F. Kennedy worker, had been accused of bugging the hotel room of then-vice-president Nixon during the 1960 campaign.

AUG. 3

Ellsberg Profile. *The New York Times* published a copy of a CIA psychological assessment of Daniel Ellsberg. The study concluded that Ellsberg was motivated by "what he deemed a higher order of patriotism" in releasing the Pentagon Papers to the press. Helms told the Senate Watergate committee that the White House had been disappointed over the Ellsberg study and had required the CIA to conduct a second study. No details of the contents of the second study were revealed.

Gray Testimony. L. Patrick Gray III, former acting FBI director, told the Senate investigating committee that he examined papers removed from the safe of E. Howard Hunt Jr. before burning the documents with his Christmas trash. Gray reversed himself after having said in April that he did not read the documents. Gray called his role in document destruction a "grievous misjudgment" that left him with a "sense of shame." *(Gray testimony, p. 255)*

Wilson Apology. Sen. Inouye said that John J. Wilson, attorney for Ehrlichman and H. R. Haldeman, had sent him a letter apologizing for referring to him as "that little Jap." *(Box, p. 238)*

Walters Testimony. Gen. Walters testified before the Senate committee that Haldeman ordered him to cite unspecified intelligence activities as a reason for inhibiting the Watergate probe in Mexico. Walters corroborated Helms' Aug. 2 testimony, but was later disputed by Gray. *(Walters testimony, p. 256)*

Haig on Tapes. Alexander M. Haig Jr., White House chief of staff, told CBS' "60 Minutes" that he opposed selective release of the secret Nixon tapes because Watergate defendants would insist on complete disclosure to exonerate themselves of perjury charges. Haig also felt that some of Nixon's quotes might do "severe damage, not only to the individual, but even more importantly, to the institution of the presidency itself."

Nixon Statement. Gerald L. Warren, deputy press secretary, said it would be reasonable to expect a Nixon statement on Watergate within two weeks, assuming the Senate Watergate committee concluded the first phase of its hearings.

Bar Discipline. A national lawyers' organization set up a special committee to bring disciplinary proceedings against attorneys involved in the Watergate scandal. The committee is headed by John G. Banomi of New York City.

Mitchell, Stans. The attorney for Maurice H. Stans, former secretary of commerce indicted for helping conceal a campaign contribution made by financier Robert L. Vesco, pleaded that Stans be granted mercy. Stans' attorney, Walter J. Bonner, said that Stans was facing eight different court cases. U.S. District Court Judge Lee P. Gagliardi told defense attorneys in New York for Stans and John N. Mitchell, former attorney general, to be ready for trial Sept. 11, although he was seriously considering their request for a delay. *(Indictment excerpts, p. 71)*

Army Intelligence. An investigator for Sen. Lowell P. Weicker Jr. (R Conn.) turned up documents showing that in 1972 U.S. Army intelligence units in Europe wiretapped, photographed and infiltrated a group of supporters of Sen. George McGovern. Weicker ordered the material turned over to the Senate Watergate investigating committee, the Armed Services Committee and a constitutional rights subcommittee. The Army had been ordered to cease civilian spying in 1970.

Nader Speech. Consumer advocate Ralph Nader called for Nixon to resign for "condoning the coverup" and continuing to keep needed evidence from the courts. Nader was speaking before the International Platform Association in Washington.

Inouye Remark. Sen. Daniel K. Inouye's (D Hawaii) "what a liar" remark, muttered into a live microphone during the testimony of John D. Ehrlichman might have really been "what a lawyer." Inouye said a Canadian broadcast team recorded the phrase and indicated that Inouye said "lawyer." *(Box, p. 238)*

Tapes Controversy. Samuel Dash, chief counsel of the Senate investigating committee, said the committee had decided against intervening in the suit brought by special prosecutor Archibald Cox to obtain the tapes. *(Tapes conflict, p. 209)*

AUG. 4

Kopechne Impact. A poll indicated that more Americans think the drowning of Mary Jo Kopechne from an accident in Sen. Edward M. Kennedy's (D Mass.) car was more "morally reprehensible" than the Watergate bugging. The telephone poll was conducted by Kevin P. Phillips and Albert Sindlinger, favorite poll-taker for the White House.

Mansfield Advice. Senate Democratic leader Mike Mansfield (Mont.) advised Nixon to hold an informal meeting with the seven members of the Senate investigating committee. Mansfield told a United Press International interviewer that judgment should not be passed on Nixon's actions until he responds.

AUG. 5

Blackmun Speech. Supreme Court Justice Harry A. Blackmun addressed the moral issues of Watergate, telling an American Bar Association audience that the "very glue of our ship of state seems about to become unstuck." He urged the lawyers to remove the "taint and corruption in our public life." *(Box, p. 257)*

Taldmage on Impeachment. Sen. Herman E. Talmadge (D Ga.) told CBS-TV that the Senate investigating committee had found no evidence to justify impeaching Nixon. He said much of the suspicion around Nixon would be lifted if Nixon would release the tapes. Talmadge also said the committee may release an interim report by early fall before completing all three phases of the hearings. *(Presidential impeachment, p. 55)*

Justice on Subpoenas. Assistant Attorney General Robert G. Dixon Jr. said he could find no legal precedents that would require Nixon to turn over White House tapes, even if they could be used as evidence in criminal prosecutions. The Justice Department official declined to discuss the Senate and special prosecutor's subpoena directly. *(Tapes conflict, p. 251)*

Violence Study. *The Washington Post* reported that civil disorder and political violence—according to statistics—did escalate during 1969 and 1970, the years Nixon used to justify what he termed domestic intelligence operations. *(Memos, p. 122)*

AUG. 6

Nixon Counterattack. Presidential assistant Patrick J. Buchanan said in a CBS-TV interview that Nixon would respond to Watergate charges within a week to 10 days after the Senate committee hearings recess.

Gray Testimony. Former acting FBI Director L. Patrick Gray testified that in July 1972 he hinted to Nixon that White House staff members were using the FBI and CIA to "confuse" the Watergate probe, but said Nixon asked him no questions about it. Gray also said that, on March 23, Nixon called to "buck up" the embattled candidate, whose confirmation was stalled in the Senate. Ehrlichman had testified earlier that the

White House had abandoned Gray by March 6. *(Gray testimony, p. 255)*

Harris Poll. An analysis of the public mood showed that most people want to give Nixon the benefit of the doubt in the Watergate scandal, but they believe he has lost much credibility. The Harris survey figures were 55 to 32 that Nixon "does not inspire confidence as a President should," but 69 to 21 that both Democrats and Republicans engaged in dirty campaign tactics, and the Nixon people were no worse at it—they just were caught. *(Box, p. 2196; earlier poll report, p. 240)*

Gutter Politics. George Bush, Republican national chairman, said on NBC television that he disagreed with John D. Ehrlichman's rationalization of investigating the drinking and sex habits of political opponents. *(Ehrlichman testimony, p. 230)*

Dairy Donations. Dairymen, Inc., a cooperative that contributed to Nixon's 1972 campaign urged the President to turn over memos or tapes relating to the 1971 dairy price supports decision. Ralph Nader is also seeking the documents in connection with a lawsuit stemming from the dairy price hike.

Bar Speech. Robert W. Meserve, outgoing president of the American Bar Association, deplored Watergate and public apathy toward it as "a threat to our liberties and to our very sense of decency," in a speech before the ABA convention in Washington.

AUG. 7

Hearings. The Senate select Watergate committee recessed its hearings until Sept. 10 after listening to testimony from former Attorney General Richard G. Kleindienst and Assistant Attorney General Henry E. Petersen, head of the criminal division. Testifying separately, each said they got no instructions from President Nixon on or after March 21 to report new facts directly to him as Nixon said he had ordered. Each testified they never uncovered anything that lead them to believe the President was involved in the Watergate break-in or coverup. *(Testimony, p. 261)*

Court Case. White House lawyers told a federal judge that the courts could not force the President to hand over tape recordings of his conversations to special Watergate prosecutor Archibald Cox. In a 34-page brief handed over to Judge John J. Sirica, Nixon's attorneys argued that the President had a right to withhold the tapes and other documents sought—even if they dealt with a criminal plan—in order to safeguard the confidentiality of presidential communications. *(Excerpts from brief, p. 255)*

McGovern Funds. The FBI said that it was conducting an investigation of financial aspects of Sen. George S. McGovern's (D S.D.) presidential campaign in Connecticut at the request of Cox. The special agent in charge of the bureau's New Haven office termed it a "preliminary and limited investigation" stemming from allegations brought to Cox's attention by an unnamed citizen.

Ervin Committee. The Senate select Watergate committee voted to delay filing its lawsuit seeking tapes of certain presidential conversations until it had a chance to study the White House's brief against the Cox suit, Chairman Sam J. Ervin (D N.C.) announced.

AUG. 8

Ervin Committee. Sen. Herman E. Talmadge (D Ga.), a member of the Senate select Watergate committee, suggested that the panel be split into two subcommittees in order to speed up its work. He said a decision on splitting the committee will be made when it returns to work in September.

Bar Investigation. The Massachusetts Bar Association announced it has been informally investigating Charles Colson, former presidential aide, and Gerald Alch, former lawyer for convicted Watergate burglar James McCord, regarding their roles in the scandal. A bar spokesman said formal proceedings would not begin until the findings of the Senate committee and the special prosecutor are announced.

AUG. 9

Committee Suit. The Senate select Watergate committee filed suit in federal district court in Washington, D.C., seeking an order forcing President Nixon to turn over tape recordings of certain presidential conversations. The committee said any presidential claim of confidentiality concerning the tapes had been breached. This was an apparent reference to former White House aide H. R. Haldeman's testimony that he had listened to two of the tapes.

GRAY'S OPENING STATEMENT

Following are excerpts from the prepared text of the opening statement of L. Patrick Gray III, former acting director of the Federal Bureau of Investigation (FBI), before the Senate Watergate committee on Aug. 3:

My prepared statement will cover two areas believed to be of prime interest to the committee—the CIA dimension and the Howard Hunt files. I cannot possibly review the entire Watergate investigation in the time available and I do not believe the committee expects me to launch into such a review.

THE CIA DIMENSION

At the time of the Watergate break-in I was on the West Coast visiting FBI field offices and meeting a commitment to make a commencement address at Pepperdine University Law School in Santa Ana. I returned to Washington on the evening of June 20 and received a phone call from John Ehrlichman the next morning. Mr. Ehrlichman informed me that John Dean would be handling an inquiry into Watergate for the White House, that I should deal directly with John Dean concerning the investigation and that Mr. Dean was expecting a call from me. Mr. Ehrlichman and I then discussed the matter of procedural safeguards against leaks and I told him that we were handling this case as a major special with all of our normal procedures in effect. I also indicated to him that we were going to conduct an aggressive and vigorous investigation and would probably be interviewing people at the White House.

BRIEFING BY BATES

On Thursday, June 22, 1972, after being briefed by Mr. Charles W. Bates, Assistant Director, General Investigative Division, regarding the latest development in the Watergate case and undoubtedly as a result of information developed at the briefing, I telephoned Director Helms of the CIA. I told him of our thinking that we may be poking into a CIA operation and asked if he could confirm or deny this. He said he had been meeting on this every day with his men, that they knew the people, that they could not figure it out but that there was no CIA involvement.

I met again with Mr. Dean at 6:30 p.m. the same day to again discuss the scheduling and interviews of White House staff personnel and to arrange the scheduling of these interviews directly through the Washington field office rather than through FBI headquarters.

At this meeting I also discussed with him our very early theories of the case; namely that the episode was either a CIA covert operation of some sort simply because some of the people involved had been CIA people in the past, or a CIA money chain, or a political money chain, or a pure political operation, or a Cuban right wing operation, or a combination of any of these. I also told Mr. Dean that we were not zeroing in on any one theory at this time, or excluding any, but that we just could not see any clear reason for this burglary and attempted intercept of communications operation.

I believe that it was at this meeting on June 22 that I told him of our discovery of a bank account in the name of Bernard Barker, who was arrested in the Watergate burglary, and the fact that a $25,000.00 check associated with Kenneth Dahlberg and four checks drawn on a Mexican bank payable to Manuel Ogarrio, in the total amount of $89,000.00, were deposited in the Barker account. I do not have a clear memory of telling him about my telephone call earlier in the day to Director Helms regarding the question of CIA involvement. It is likely that I would have discussed the Helms call with him in connection with our discussion of the theories of the case, since Mr. Helms had informed me that there was no CIA involvement.

On Friday, June 23, 1972, Mr. Bates met with me again to brief me on recent developments. I telephoned Mr. Dean following my meeting with Mr. Bates. I am quite certain that this call again involved the Barker bank account and the Ogarrio and Dahlberg checks. Either in this call or in the meeting of the preceding evening Mr. Dean first raised with me the idea that if we persisted in our efforts to investigate this Mexican money chain we could uncover or become involved in CIA operations. I remember telling Mr. Dean in one of these early telephone calls or meetings that the FBI was going to pursue all leads aggressively unless we were told by the CIA that there was a CIA interest or involvement in this case.

At 1:35 p.m. on Friday, June 23, 1972 Mr. Dean telephoned me and said that General Walters, Deputy Director, CIA, would be calling for an appointment that afternoon and I should see him. Mr. Dean said, "He has something to tell you."

I met with General Walters at 2:34 p.m. on Friday, June 23, 1972. He informed me that we were likely to uncover some CIA assets or sources if we continued our investigation into the Mexican money chain. I understood his statement to mean that if the FBI persisted we would uncover CIA covert operations and that the CIA had an interest in Messr. Ogarrio and Dahlberg and in the $114,000.00 involved. He also discussed with me the agency agreement under which the FBI and CIA have agreed not to uncover and expose each other's sources. I had not read this agreement and still have not, but it was logical to me at the time and I did not question General Walters.

I undoubtedly said to General Walters that we will handle this in a manner that would not hamper the CIA, and that I would have to make a determination as to how the FBI would proceed with our investigation in this area.

I knew from Mr. Dean's earlier telephone conversation with me on this day that General Walters would be coming to see me, but I have no recollection or memory whatsoever of General Walters informing me at this meeting that he was coming to me after talking to the White House, or that he had talked to the White House at all. I understood him to be stating a CIA position not a White House message.

At this point I would like to comment on General Walters' memorandum of this meeting, which I understand to be in evidence before this committee. With respect to General Walters' statement in paragraph 2 of his memorandum that "his (Gray's) problem was how to low key this matter now that it was launched", I may have said words to this effect to let him know that we would handle the CIA aspects of this matter with kid gloves. I can state categorically, however, that any sentiment of that kind expressed by me was an effort by me to abide by the CIA-FBI agreement and related solely to the possibility of exposing CIA covert activities in the pursuit of our investigation into Mexico. This sentiment, if expressed, could in no way have related to any effort by me or the FBI to "low key" the Watergate investigation generally.

In fact, the FBI did not low key the Watergate investigation generally and instructions were issued at the outset of the investigation and regularly thereafter to ensure that this case was handled as a major case under the immediate supervision of the special agent in charge of each field office to which investigative leads were referred by the Washington field office or any other field office setting out leads to be pursued.

REPORT TO DEAN

On the afternoon of Friday, June 23, 1972 I again telephoned Mr. Dean on two occasions, once at 3:24 p.m. and once at 3:47 p.m. I cannot be absolutely certain that the names Ogarrio and Dahlberg were mentioned in connection with the CIA situation. It is my best recollection, however, that they were and I undoubtedly told him that we would continue our peripheral investigation because of the apparently inconsistent reports I had received from Helms and Walters. He requested that we not conduct any interviews that would expose CIA sources in connection with our investigation into the source of the $114,000.00 in checks that were deposited in Mr. Barker's bank account. Again I told Mr. Dean that we would hold off temporarily with interviews of Ogarrio and work around this problem to determine what we were encountering.

On Tuesday morning, June 27, 1972 I met with Mr. Bates and Mr. Mark Felt, acting associate director, to receive a briefing on the latest developments. While they were in the office Mr. Dean called. The call involved establishing the chain of custody for the contents of Howard Hunt's safe and his providing us with photographs of certain White House staff members to aid us in identifying an individual who had been with Mr. Hunt at the Miami Playboy Club in December of 1971. In this conversation I also told Mr. Dean that if Mr. Dahlberg continued to evade us he would be called before the Grand Jury. Although I cannot pinpoint the exact telephone conversation I believe that by this date Mr. Dean had requested that Mr. Dahlberg not be interviewed because of alleged CIA interest in him.

In this same conversation, I also told Mr. Dean that it was extremely important that the FBI continue its aggressiveness until we determine the motive, reasons, and identify of all persons involved. I said that I might be called upon at a later date to testify before congressional committees and we could not have the FBI accused of not pursuing this case to the end.

Following the briefing by Mr. Felt and Mr. Bates and as an outgrowth of it, I telephoned Director Helms of the CIA and asked him to tell me specifically if the CIA had any interest in Mr. Ogarrio that would prevent us from interviewing him and also asked that he and General Walters meet the following day at 2:30 p.m. in my office with me, Mr. Felt, and Mr. Bates to review our respective positions in this investigation. Director Helms told me that he would have to check to determine whether the CIA had any interest in Mr. Ogarrio and would call me later. I advised Mr. Felt of this meeting and asked that he notify Mr. Bates. Director Helms called me back later that afternoon, told me the CIA had no interest in Mr. Ogarrio and confirmed our meeting for the next day.

Just seven minutes after Director Helm's call to me, Mr. Dean called me (3:47 p.m.) and although I cannot be absolutely certain, I believe this was a call again requesting me to hold off interviewing Mr. Ogarrio and Mr. Dahlberg because of CIA interest in these men. I cannot recall if I told him that I had just talked to Director Helms who informed me that CIA had no interest in Mr. Ogarrio and that I was going to order that Mr. Ogarrio be interviewed. I seem to remember that Mr. Dean said to me that these men have absolutely nothing to do with Watergate, but I cannot remember whether he said this to me in this conversation or in earlier conservations.

On Wednesday, June 28, 1972 at 10:25 a.m., Mr. Dean telephoned me and talked about rumors of leaks from the FBI, the material from Hunt's safe previously delivered to the FBI, rumors of a slow-down in the FBI, and leaks from the FBI concerning the tracing of the $114,000.00. Once again I believe there was some discussion about Ogarrio and Dahlberg and it is my recollection that I was asked if I had ordered the interviews of Ogarrio and Dahlberg. I replied that I had either ordered or was going to order the interview of Ogarrio. In this discussion, I may have told Mr. Dean that I had arranged to meet with Director Helms and Deputy Director Walters at 2:30 p.m. that afternoon to try to get this CIA situation resolved, but I cannot be positive that I did.

At 10:55 a.m. on this same day Mr. Ehrlichman called me. I was not available, but I returned his call at 11:17 a.m. His first words, issued abruptly, were "cancel your meeting with Helms and Walters today, it is not necessary." I asked him for his reasons and he simply said that such a meeting is not necessary. I then asked him point blank who was going to make the decisions as to who is to be interviewed. He responded, "you do."

I then telephoned Director Helms to tell him that I was cancelling our meeting. I also advised Messrs. Felt and Bates of the cancellation, but stated that the three of us would meet. In this same conversation with me, Director Helms requested that we not interview active CIA men Karl Wagner and John Caswell. I passed this information to Mr. Felt and instructed that these men not be interviewed. Before orders could get to the field, however, Mr. Caswell had already been interviewed.

At 3:58 p.m., June 28, Mr. Dean called and I was not available. I returned the call at 4:35 p.m. and I believe now that this call involved a request by Mr. Dean to hold up on the interview of Miss Kathleen Chenow for alleged reasons of national security until she returned from her vacation in England. I'm sure I said we would hold up for the time being but she would have to be interviewed soon. I can recall saying that we will interview her in England unless she returns from vacation at an early date. Mr. Dean gave me her address in England in this conversation, I believe, and I passed it along in a call to Mr. Felt in which I instructed him to temporarily discontinue leads to interview and investigate Miss Kathleen Chenow in England.

At 8:15 a.m. on Thursday, June 29, 1972, I issued orders to cancel the interview of Mr. Ogarrio and to instruct Minneapolis field division to make no further attempts to interview Mr. Dahlberg but to continue to obtain records of his long distance calls. I am fairly certain that I did so as the result of a telephone call I received from Mr. Dean at home, prior to my departure to Dulles Airport for an inspection trip to San Diego and Phoenix. He again urged that these interviews be held up for national security reasons or because of CIA interest. I called Mr. Felt, or his office, and gave these cancellation orders. On my own initiative I also ordered that George Munro, CIA Station Chief at Mexico City, not be interviewed because I noted in one of the many reports that crossed my desk that he was CIA station chief in Mexico City.

In San Diego, on Friday, June 30, I received a call from Mr. Felt. He informed me that assistant United States attorney Silbert wanted the FBI to interview Mr. David Young, Mr. Ogarrio and Miss Chenow and that our Washington field office recommended interviews of Mr. Mitchell, Mr. Young and Miss Chenow. I instructed Mr. Felt to tell Mr. Dean that we were going to interview Mr. Mitchell, Mr. Young, Miss Chenow, and any others that we must interview, and I also told him to give to Mr. Dean the message from assistant United States attorney Silbert just as we received it.

WALTERS MEMO

On Wednesday, July 5th at 5:54 p.m. I telephoned General Walters. My contemporaneous notes on this call read as follows:

"7-5-73 WED

5 55 P

"TCT General Walters
"(Dick Walters)

"1. "I will need a request in writing rather than the verbal request to refrain from interviewing Ogarrio and Dahlberg because of CIA interest

"2. Position of developing investigation indicates there is CIA involvement in that some of these men have been used by CIA in part & there is indication some are currently being used; there is the dollar chain either CIA or political; I do not want to uncover and surface a CIA national security operation in pursuing these leads, but I must for the record have in writing from CIA a request to refrain on the basis of national security matters or I must proceed.

"3. He stated that he would respond not later than 10 a.m. tomorrow.

"4. I said that I would order the interviews if I did not have the writings by 10 a.m.

"Gave above info to JWD 6:00 P
WMF TO
CWB 6:10 P"

At this point I would like to comment on General Walters' memorandum of this phone call which I believe is in evidence before this committee.

With respect to General Walters' statement that I told him that "the pressures" on me "to continue the investigation were great" I am quite certain that I did not so express myself. It is entirely possible, however, that on the limited question of the alleged impact of the investigation on CIA national security matters, the only topic General Walters and I were discussing, I may have expressed the thought that the leads to Messr. Ogarrio and Dahlberg were clear and that their interviews were a necessity which only the clearest expression of national security interest should prevent and that the FBI, for the sake of its own integrity, would refrain from conducting the interviews only if we received such a written request from the CIA.

With respect to General Walters' statement that "he (Gray) had talked to John Dean", while I have no specific recollection of telling General Walters that I had talked to John Dean it is entirely likely that I did tell General Walters that I had informed Mr. Dean that the FBI was going to interview Messrs. Ogarrio and Dahlberg unless we had a writing from the CIA requesting that we not do so.

On Thursday, July 6, 1972, I met with General Walters in my office. I remember that he delivered to me the writing that I requested and I remember that it indicated the CIA had no interest in Ogarrio or Dahlberg. After reading the document, I concluded that there was no reason for us to not interview Messrs. Ogarrio and Dahlberg. When General Walters departed my office at about 10:25 a.m. or 10:30 a.m., I ordered the interviews of Ogarrio and Dahlberg immediately.

My recollection of the conversation with General Walters at this meeting differs with his in several respects.

My principal recollection is his preoccupation with the fact that he was unable to give me a writing stating that there was a CIA interest in Ogarrio and Dahlberg and his telling me that he would resign if he were asked or directed to give me such a writing. He reported this thought to me several times during our conversation.

I, too, was concerned and disturbed at the contradictory reports I had been receiving from Director Helms, Mr. Dean and General Walters with respect to CIA interest and at the abrupt cancellation by Mr. Ehrlichman of the meeting I had scheduled with Director Helms and General Walters on June 28. I undoubtedly so expressed myself to General Walters.

My recollection is that he and I then engaged in a general discussion of the credibility and position of our respective institutions in our society and of the need to ensure that this was maintained. Toward the end of the conversation, I recall most vividly that General Walters leaned back in the red overstuffed leather chair in which he was sitting, but his hands behind his head and said that he had come into an inheritance and was not concerned about his pension, and was not going to let "these kids" kick him around any more.

We stood up together as he prepared to leave. I cannot recall which one of us suggested that we ought to call the President to tell him of this confusion and uncertainty that had been encountered in determining CIA interest or no CIA interest. I believe it was General Walters who suggested it first, because I can firmly recall saying to him, "Dick, you should call the President, you know him better than I." I believe he said, "No, I think you should because these are persons the FBI wishes to interview." We did not settle on who, if anyone, would make such a call and General Walters left.

After General Walters left the office I sat at my desk quietly and mulled over our conversation. I was confused, uncertain, and uneasy. I was concerned enough to believe that the President should be informed.

I decided to call Clark MacGregor to request that he inform the President of what I would tell him. I decided on Mr. MacGregor because I knew he was close to the President and had his confidence.

At 10:51 a.m., Thursday, July 6, 1972, I spoke to Mr. MacGregor at San Clemente, California via White House switchboard and I told him that Dick Walters and I were uneasy and concerned about the confusion that existed over the past two weeks in determining with certainty whether there was or was not CIA interest in people that the FBI wishes to interview in connection with the Watergate investigation. These of course are not my exact words but they do express the thoughts that I conveyed to him.

I asked if he would please inform the President and it is my best recollection that he said he would handle it.

CALL FROM NIXON

Thirty-seven minutes later, at 11:28 a.m. on Thursday, July 6, 1972, the President called me. He expressed his congratulations to the FBI and asked that I express his congratulations to the agents in San Francisco who successfully terminated a hijacking there the previous day. I thanked the President and then said to him, and to the very best of my recollection these are the words:

"Mr. President, there is something I want to speak to you about.

"Dick Walters and I feel that people on your staff are trying to mortally wound you by using the CIA and FBI and by confusing the question of CIA interest in, or not in, people the FBI wishes to interview.

"I have just talked to Clark MacGregor and asked him to speak to you about this." There was a slight pause and the President said, "Pat, you just continue to conduct your aggressive and thorough investigation."

Following this conversation I experienced no further concerns of this kind. I believed that if there was anything to the concerns I expressed to the President or to Mr. MacGregor that I would hear further in the matter. I did not. Frankly, I came to the conclusion that General Walters and I had been alarmists, a belief I held for many months.

OTHER CIA CONTACTS

The only other CIA contacts I can recall at this time are as follows:

A) On October 18, 1972 Director Helms visited me. He said he had come by to see me as a courtesy before he went to see the attorney general. He said that one of his lawyers had met with assistant United States attorney Silbert the previous week. Mr. Helms also told me that CIA was to provide documented answers to questions of the assistant United States attorney. He did not tell me what the subject matter or nature of the questions was and I did not ask him, feeling that CIA business was not my business. In fact, I had a hard time trying to figure out why he came to see me because his conversation was so general and non-specific. I assumed, of course, that the questions had to do with Watergate and CIA's role in Watergate, if any; however, I did not question Director Helms about this and he did not offer to enlighten me.

B) General Walters came to see me again on February 21, 1973 at 9:00 a.m.

My notes of this meeting show that the topics discussed involved national security projects of great sensitivity. If the committee wants to hear about this meeting, I respectfully request that my testimony be taken in executive session.

C) General Walters came to see me again on Thursday, April 12, 1973 at 10:37 a.m. on one of the national security projects we discussed in the meeting of February 21, 1973. If the committee wants to hear about this meeting I respectfully request that my testimony be taken in executive session.

THE HOWARD HUNT FILES

Prior to a meeting I had with Mr. Dean and Mr. Ehrlichman in Mr. Ehrlichman's office on the evening of June 28, 1972, I had no knowledge from any source whatever of the existence of these particular files or of the information and instructions I was to receive that evening.

I arrived at Mr. Ehrlichman's office at about 6:30 p.m. that evening for the purpose of discussing with him the many rumors and allegations concerning leaks of information from the FBI regarding the Watergate investigation. One of his secretaries told me to go right on into his private office. Mr. Dean was in the office talking with Mr. Ehrlichman. I remember being surprised at Mr. Dean's presence because I had not known that he would be at the meeting.

After the usual greetings were exchanged, Mr. Ehrlichman said something very close to, "John has something that he wants to turn over to you." I then noticed that Mr. Dean had in his hands two white manila legal size file folders. It is my recollection that these folders were not in envelopes at this time.

Mr. Dean then told me that these files contained copies of sensitive and classified papers of a political nature that Howard Hunt had been working on. He said that they have national security implications or overtones, have absolutely nothing to do with Watergate and have no bearing on the Watergate investigation whatsoever. Either Mr. Dean or Mr. Ehrlichman said that these files should not be allowed to confuse or muddy the issues in the Watergate case.

I asked whether these files should become part of our FBI Watergate file. Mr. Dean said these should not become a part of our FBI Watergate file, but that he wanted to be able to say, if called upon later, that he had turned all of Howard Hunt's files over to the FBI.

I distinctly recall Mr. Dean saying that these files were "political dynamite," and "clearly should not see the light of day."

It is true that neither Mr. Ehrlichman nor Mr. Dean expressly instructed me to destroy the files. But there was, and is, no doubt in my mind that destruction was intended. Neither Mr. Dean nor Mr. Ehrlichman said or implied that I was being given the documents personally merely to safeguard against leaks.

As I believe each of them has testified before this committee the White House regarded the FBI as a source of leaks. The clear implication of the substance and tone of their remarks was that these two files were to be destroyed and I interpreted this to be an order from the Counsel to the President of the United States issued in the presence of one of the two top assistants to the President of the United States.

It is my recollection that I asked for large brown envelopes in which to place the files. I believe that Mr. Dean stepped briefly into the outer office to obtain the envelopes and placed each file in a separate brown envelope in Mr. Ehrlichman's inner office and handed them to me.

Although my memory is not perfectly clear on this, I believe Mr. Dean then left Mr. Ehrlichman's office and I stayed for 5 or 10 minutes to discuss the rumors and allegations of leaks from the FBI. These were the same rumors that had been rampant in the first week of the investigation. I believe that I told Mr. Ehrlichman that I had spoken to all of the agents assigned to the case and was quite confident that these leaks had not come from the FBI.

I then left Mr. Ehrlichman's office with the two manilla envelopes containing the files, went to my car, placed the files in my briefcase, and proceeded to my apartment. I placed the files on a closet shelf under my shirts. After two or three weeks I took them into the office and placed them in my personal safe.

To the best of my recollection I removed the files to my home in Stonington, Connecticut, in late September or early October 1972 and placed them in a chest of drawers in the area just outside my bedroom. I intended to burn them but I did not get around to doing so until after my illness, hospitalization, and convalescence in the latter half of November and December.

I distinctly recall that I burned them during Christmas week with the Christmas and household paper trash that had accumulated immediately following Christmas. To this point I had not read or examined the files. But immediately before putting them in the fire I opened one of the files. It contained what appeared to be copies of "Top Secret" State Department cablegrams. I read the first cable. I do not recall the exact language but the text of the cable implicated officials of the Kennedy administration in the assassination of Presi-that the conversations may have been recorded without my knowledge.

On Monday, April 16, 1973 at 10:54 a.m., assistant attorney general Petersen came to see me. He said that Mr. Dean told the prosecutors he had turned over two of Hunt's files to me. I denied that I had received them. Mr. Petersen went on to say that Mr. Dean had said these two files had nothing to do with Watergate. He also said that Mr. Dean told the prosecutors that Mr. Ehrlichman had said to him, "Dean, you drive across the bridge each day, throw them in the river."

I was extremely troubled at my denial to Mr. Petersen. I slept little, if any, that night.

On Tuesday, April 17, 1973 at approximately 9:00 a.m., I placed a call to Mr. Petersen on my private line. He was not in and I left word. He called me back and, at my request, we met in my office later in the morning. I started our meeting by admitting that Dean had given me two white manila files in Ehrlichmans' office. He asked if I had them and I told him I had burned them. He asked if I knew what was in them. I told him I had not read the files. He said the assistant United States attorneys will want you before the Federal Grand Jury. I told him I would go willingly and "tell it to them straight".

On Wednesday, April 25, 1973 I telephoned Senator Weicker asking to meet with him. For a week I had thought about this matter and of Senator Weicker's staunch and valiant support of me and his warm friendship. I had a duty to tell him of these two files, yet my shame was so deep that it was hard to pick up the phone and call.

Senator Weicker and I met twice that day in my office and again the next day. I told him the manner in which I had received the files, that I had not read them, and that I had torn them in half and thrown them in my burn wastebaskets under my desk in my office on July 3, 1972, after returning from a visit to the San Diego and Phoenix field divisions. We discussed this subject at great length and he questioned me intensively on the entire matter. I persisted in my assertions to him that I had not read them, and that I had thrown them in my burn wastebaskets in my office on July 3, 1972.

I really cannot explain why I failed to tell Senator Weicker all the facts at this time and made the misstatements to him concerning the date I destroyed the files and my knowledge of what one of them contained. A sense of shame is all I can remember. I suppose I felt, in some irrational way, that I would look better in his eyes if I had destroyed them promptly and never looked at them. I have subsequently revealed all the facts of the matter to Senator Weicker, the staff of this committee, the prosecutors and the Grand Jury.

COLSON MEMO TO HALDEMAN

Following is the text of a memorandum written March 30, 1972, from Charles W. Colson, then a special counsel to President Nixon, to H.R. Haldeman, then White House chief of staff. The memo was made public at Senate Watergate committee hearings on Aug. 1. It relates to Senate Judiciary Committee hearings in 1972 on the nomination of Richard G. Kleindienst as attorney general. At issue was an allegation that an antitrust case against the International Telephone and Telegraph Corporation (ITT) had been decided in the corporation's favor by the Justice Department after ITT had pledged $400,000 to help finance the Republican national convention, then scheduled for San Diego, Calif. (Story, p. 235)

Memorandum For: H.R. Haldeman March 30, 1972
From: Charles Colson
Subject: I.T.T.

There are four points in the analysis you outlined to MacGregor and me this morning with which MacGregor, Wally Johnson and I disagree:

(1)

Mitchell, Kleindienst or Mardian dealing with Eastland and MacGregor presumably dealing with the other members of the committee guarantees a divided approach. One or the other has to call the shots. Kleindienst has already this morning told MacGregor that he, MacGregor, should not deal with any of the other Republican Senators (Scott, Cook, etc.) but rather should deal only through Hruska. In the kind of day-to-day operation this is, that is simply an untenable arrangement.

I know you and the President are concerned that all of us are taken away from other more important matters. You should be, however, equally concerned that Mitchell in the last 30 days has done little with respect to the campaign and that may be a more serious loss than MacGregor's time and mine.

(2)

On the one hand, you have the assessment of Kleindienst, Mardian and Mitchell as to what will happen in the committee and on the floor. On the other hand, you have the legislative assessment of MacGregor, Colson and Johnson which is very different, (Johnson spent from 1968-1970 as minority counsel of this same committee and has been involved in all of the confirmation battles of this Administration either from the committee end or from the Justice Department end. He left the committee to go to Justice in 1970. MacGregor spent 10 years in Congress. I spent 5 years as a senior Senate assistant and 9 years in law practice, involving very considerable contact with the Hill. The Justice team simply has not had the same experience.)

Admittedly it is all opinion at this point, but Johnson, MacGregor and I unanimously do not believe that Kleindienst can be confirmed by June 1. Johnson does not feel he can be confirmed at all and on this point I am at least doubtful. I emphasize that this is an opinion and a judgment call. Lots of things could happen. We could get a big break in the case; the media could turn around and become sympathetic to Kleindienst; the Democrats could decide that they are better having him in the job than beating him. Obviously there are many unforeseen possibilities, but as of now that is our best assessment. I would think that whatever decision we make now should be based on the most knowledgable—and I would add the most detached—assessment of our legislative prospects.

Wally Johnson has done a detailed analysis of the various procedural moves that are likely to be made in committee or on the floor. He is not shooting from the hip. He has analyzed it and a senate vote in his judgment cannot be achieved by June 1; the Democrats will only let it come to a vote if they have votes to reject Kleindienst, which is the least desirable outcome. Neither Johnson, MacGregor or Colson are prepared to predict whether we can hold the votes necessary to confirm him should the nomination in fact get to a vote.

(3)

Assuming MacGregor, Johnson and Colson are correct, then setting June 1 as our deadline date merely puts the hard decision off to a time when it will be considerably more volatile politically than it is today. Kleindienst's withdrawal will then be an admission of defeat but it will come two months closer to the election. In June Kleindienst will be a hot issue for the Democratic convention. Confirmation of Kleindienst's replacement will also be vastly more difficult in June than it would be now. Obviously this again is opinion.

(4)

The most serious risk for us is being ignored in the analysis you gave us this morning—there is the possibility of serious additional exposure by the continuation of this controversy. Kleindienst is not the target, the President is, but Kleindienst is the best available vehicle for the Democrats to get to the President. Make no mistake, the Democrats want to keep this case alive—whatever happens to Kleindienst—but the battle over Kleindienst elevates the visibility of the I.T.T. matter and, indeed, guarantees that the case will stay alive. It may stay alive in any event and, hence, the key question not addressed in your analysis is whether pendency or withdrawal of Kleindienst nomination serves to increase the Democrats' desire to continue. That is the hardest call to make but for the following reasons it may be the most important point to make.

Neither Kleindienst, Mitchell nor Mardian know of the potential dangers. I have deliberately not told Kleindienst or Mitchell since both may be recalled as witnesses and Mardian does not understand the problem. Only Fred Fielding, myself and Ehrlichman have fully examined all the documents and/or information that could yet come out. A summary of some of these is attached.

(1)

Certain I.T.T. files which were not shredded have been turned over to the S.E.C., there was talk yesterday in the committee of subpoenaing these from I.T.T. These files would undermine Griswold's testimony that he made the decision not to take the appeal to the Supreme Court. Correspondence to Connally and Peterson credits the delay in Justice's filing of the appeal to the Supreme Court in the Grinell case to direct intervention by Peterson and Connally. A memo sent to the Vice President, addressed, "Dear Ted," from Ned Gerrity tends to contradict John Mitchell's testimony because it outlines Mitchell's agreement to talk to McLaren following Mitchell's meeting with Geneen in August, 1970.

It would carry some weight in that the memo was written contemporaneous with the meeting. Both Mitchell and Geneen have testified they discussed policy only, not this case, and that Mitchell talked to no one else. The memo further states that Ehrlichman assured Geneen that the President had "instructed" the Justice Department with respect to the bigness policy. (It is, of course, appropriate for the President to instruct the Justice Department on policy, but in the context of these hearings, that revelation would lay this case on the President's doorstep.) There is another internal Ryan to Merriam memo, which is not in the hands of the S.E.C.; it follows the 1970 Agnew meeting and suggests that Kleindienst is the key man to pressure McLaren, implying that the Vice President would implement this action. We believe that all copies of this have been destroyed.

(2)

There is a Klein to Haldeman memo, date June 30, 1971, which of course precedes the date of the I.T.T. settlement, setting forth the $400,000 arrangement with I.T.T. Copies were addressed to Magruder, Mitchell and Timmons. This memo put the A.G. on constructive notice at least of the I.T.T. commitment at that time and before the settlement, facts which he has denied under oath. We don't know whether we have recovered all the copies. If known, this would be considerably more damaging than Rieneke's statement. Magruder believes it is possible, the A.G. transmitted his copy to Magruder. Magruder doesn't have the copy he received, he only has a Xerox of the copy. In short, despite a search this memo could be lying around anywhere at 1701.

(3)

The Justice Department has thus far resisted a request for their files, although their files were opened to Robert Hammond, one of Turner's deputies and a holdover who is now a practicing Democratic lawyer in Washington. Hammond had access to several memos that could be embarrassing. Whether he kept them or not is unknown, but it is probable that he recalls them. One is a memo of April, 1969, from Kleindienst and McLaren to Ehrlichman responding to an Ehrlichman request with respect to the rationale for bringing the case against I.T.T. in the first place. There is a subsequent April, 1970, memo from Hullin to McLaren stating that Ehrlichman had discussed his meeting with Geneen with the A.G., and suggesting to McLaren that Mitchell could give McLaren "more specified guidance."

There is another memo of September, 1970, from Ehrlichman to the A.G. referring to an "understanding" with Geneen and complaining of McLaren's actions. There is a May 5, 1971, memo from Ehrlichman to the A.G. alluding to discussions between the President and the A.G. as to the "agreed upon ends" in the resolution of the I.T.T. case and asking the A.G. whether Ehrlichman would work directly with McLaren or through Mitchell. There is also a memo to the President in the same time period. We know we have control of all the copies of this, but we don't have control of the original Ehrlichman memo to the A.G. This memo would once again contradict Mitchell's testimony and more importantly directly involve the President. We believe we have absolute security on this file within Justice, provided no copies were made within Justice and provided there are no leaks. We have no idea of the distribution that took place within Justice.

(4)

Merriam's testimony will of necessity involve direct contact with Jack Gleason. I can't believe that after Merriam's testimony, Gleason will not be called as a witness. ✓

AGNEW REVEALED AS TARGET OF FEDERAL INVESTIGATION

Vice President Spiro T. Agnew, one of the few major administration figures to survive without a taint of the Watergate scandal, was informed Aug. 2 that he is under federal investigation on charges of bribery, extortion and tax fraud. The charges were reported to relate to the award of state contracts during Agnew's two years (1967-1968) as governor of Maryland, and to the award of federal building contracts in Maryland since he became vice president in 1969.

Agnew met with President Nixon for almost two hours Aug. 7, and on the following day told a press conference that he was defending himself, instead of "spending my time looking around to see who's supporting me." The White House refused to comment on the charges.

Vice President Agnew

On Aug. 6, as *The Wall Street Journal* was printing its editions containing the first major story on the Agnew investigation, Agnew released a brief statement: "I have been informed that I am under investigation for possible violations of the criminal statues. I will make no further comment until the investigation has been completed, other than to say that I am innocent of any wrongdoing, that I have confidence in the criminal justice system of the United States and I am equally confident that my innocence will be affirmed."

The Knight newspaper chain on Aug. 8 reported that Agnew had received $50,000 from private contractors after he became vice president. *The Los Angeles Times* the same day quoted a source close to the investigation as saying that an indictment of Agnew was expected within weeks.

In response to these allegations which Agnew denied and labeled "damn lies," the vice president called an afternoon press conference on Aug. 8. Saying that he had no intention of being "skewered" by "defamatory statements...leaked to the news media by sources that the news reports refer to as close to the federal investigators," Agnew responded to questions from a packed auditorium of newsmen. He labeled the allegations which went beyond the bare statement that he was being investigated as "false and scurrilous and malicious." He said he had "no expectation of being indicted" and that he had given no consideration to leaving the post of vice president, even temporarily.

He indicated a willingness to cooperate with the investigators, who had begun their inquiry early in 1973 concerning reported kickbacks to Baltimore County officials by contractors and architectural firms. Agnew served as Baltimore county executive from 1962 until he moved to the governor's mansion in 1967. There were "highly unprecedented constitutional questions" which were involved in such an investigation, Agnew noted, but he said he would make available whatever—including "my own body for interrogation"—was needed and whatever was considered advisable by his legal counsel. ✓

'Fallen on Evil Times....'

At least three earlier vice presidents have been touched by scandal during their time in office, but none of them were forced out of office because of the alleged indiscretions. No impeachment proceedings were brought against any of them.

Aaron Burr, vice president to Thomas Jefferson, ran into the most serious trouble of any vice president to date, when he killed Alexander Hamilton in a duel in 1804, after Hamilton described Burr as a "dangerous man...who ought not to be trusted with the reins of government." Burr was indicted for murder in both New York and New Jersey. The indictments were later dropped. Burr returned to his duties as vice president and presiding officer of the Senate, receiving considerable criticism in the process.

Senator William Plumer of New Hampshire wrote that it was the "first time (God grant that it be the last) that ever a man indicted for murder presided in the American Senate. We are indeed fallen on evil times.... The high office of President is filled by an infidel, that of Vice-President by a Murderer."

After leaving the vice presidency in 1805, Burr became involved in a plot to invade Mexico. Betrayed by a one-time friend, he was tried for treason and found not guilty.

Credit Mobilier. Ulysses S. Grant's vice president, Schuyler Colfax, was implicated in the Credit Mobilier scandal after Colfax had been dumped from the Grant ticket when Grant decided to run for re-election in 1872.

The Credit Mobilier was a dummy corporation set up by several members of Congress to pocket $23-million in appropriations intended to be used for the building of the Union Pacific Railroad.

As an owner of Credit Mobilier "stock," Colfax was implicated in the scandal. Questions were also raised about a $1,000 campaign contribution to Colfax from George F. Nesbitt, a printer who held valuable contracts with the Post Office Department while Colfax was a member of Congress and chairman of the House Committee on Post Offices and Post Roads.

Borrowed Funds. Daniel Tompkins, governor of New York and later vice president under James Monroe, borrowed considerable sums during his governorship to pay soldiers under his command in the War of 1812. He failed to keep adequate records of the money borrowed—both from the state and the federal treasuries, and ended up apparently in default to both. His accounts were later balanced by the state legislature and Congress, but he was defeated when he ran, while still vice president, for another term as governor.

Only one vice president has ever resigned. John C. Calhoun, who served as vice president with John Quincy Adams and Andrew Jackson. He resigned late in 1832 to return to the Senate during a nationwide controversy over protective tariffs and states rights.

$10-MILLION TO PROTECT NIXON'S OTHER WHITE HOUSES

Since Jan. 1, 1969, it has cost the American taxpayer at least $10-million to ensure the safety and comfort of President Nixon and his family while they are at the Western White House, the Florida White House, or the residences of their daughters, according to figures released Aug. 6 by the White House and the General Services Administration (GSA).

Of this amount, $6-million has been spent by the military, primarily for installing and operating communications systems. About 10 per cent of this total, Deputy White House Press Secretary Gerald L. Warren said Aug. 6, would be removed when Nixon left office.

The remaining $4-million includes GSA expenses related to repairing, furnishing, improving and securing the presidential homes and grounds at San Clemente and Key Biscayne, and to acquiring, maintaining, improving and operating the various necessary support offices and facilities. It also includes security-related measures taken at the Grand Cay home of Robert Abplanalp, a friend whom Nixon frequently visits, and at the daughters' homes.

Obviously intended to be the definitive statement of government expenditures at Key Biscayne and San Clemente, the Aug. 6 announcement was designed to end the inquiry begun in May when the White House said that $39,525 had been spent at San Clemente. By the end of June this figure had been twice revised and stood at $703,367; the comparable figure for Key Biscayne was set at $597,907. These totals, amounting to $1.3-million, stood virtually unchanged in the Aug. 6 report, which provided additional figures reflecting expenditures for offices and general administrative support for the President in California and Florida.

Public reaction had been vigorous and widespread to the disclosure that public funds had been spent for such apparently non-security-related items as furnishings for the President's den in San Clemente, weed removal, a new heating system for the San Clemente residence, and flagpoles. A House appropriations subcommittee June 27 heard GSA officials defend the expenses as necessary.

Apparently unsatisfied, the House Government Operations Committee Aug. 2 subpoenaed records of all federally financed improvements on private property owned or used by Chief Executives since Roosevelt. The day before, the House had approved language in an appropriations bill which declared that no further improvements should be made at public expense on the Key Biscayne or San Clemente residences without consultation with Congress.

Military Spending. The $6-million figure for military spending included $2-million for Key Biscayne and $3.7-million for San Clemente. One-time spending amounted to $730,000 for Key Biscayne—including a helicopter landing pad, a shark net, and communications equipment; at San Clemente this figure jumped to $1-million. Recurring annual costs to the military were given as $330,000 for Key Biscayne and $677,000 at San Clemente.

Protection and Support. Press treatment of the matter had been "confusing...and grossly unfair to the President," said GSA Administrator Arthur F. Sampson

GSA Spending for Nixon Residences

(Jan. 1, 1969-June 30, 1973)*

(figures in thousands)

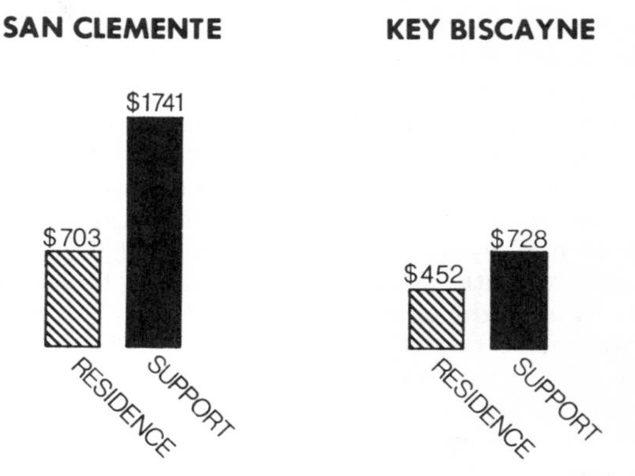

**Except that San Clemente figures apply only through May 31, 1973.*

SOURCE: GSA Summary of Expenditures, August 6, 1973.

Aug. 6. GSA released a 70-page summary of its $3,690,902.80 in spending at San Clemente, Key Biscayne, Grand Cay, Bethesda, Md., Atlantic Beach, Fla., Virginia Beach, Va., New York City and Cambridge, Mass.

At San Clemente, Sampson said, only $68,148.07 had been spent on the President's house by the government, less than 2 per cent of the total GSA figure; at Key Biscayne, some $137,482.13—or 10 per cent of the total—was spent on the house, but $130,000 of this was for bullet-proof doors and windows.

Sampson did not include in these figures federal funds spent on the grounds surrounding both residences: $635,219.13 at San Clemente and $315,226.12 at Key Biscayne. "Virtually all of the money spent on the private grounds...at San Clemente was for security needs such as walls, lighting and alarm systems," he said. Substantial amounts of this total, however, were spent to repair damage done in the installation of security equipment. Such items included $76,000 spent in 1970 to repair and replace landscaping and a sprinkler system damaged by construction work; earlier more than $6,000 had gone to remove and replace damaged plantings, and more than $2,700 to repave the roadway and driveway damaged by construction. In 1970 $7,515 was spent to repair roadways again damaged by construction and in 1971 it cost $6,276.63 to repair the driveways again.

Landscaping has security implications, too. Dry weeds are fire hazards, and so the government spent $9,910 to have them removed from San Clemente. Unpruned trees also present safety problems and so $2,500 had been spent to prune them while about $5,500 was spent to plant some new trees and relocate others.

Sampson said that the flagpoles at Key Biscayne and San Clemente, the furniture for the President's office in San Clemente, and all other installations at the two residences would be removed by the government when they were no longer needed, provided that the cost of removal was not prohibitive. ✓

THE 34TH WATERGATE WITNESS: NIXON RESTATES HIS CASE

To many it seemed anticlimactic. Instead of adding new information to that already accumulated during eight weeks of Senate Watergate committee hearings—and wave upon wave of sensational White House secret-baring—President Nixon in his Aug. 15 response to the testimony for the most part only repeated earlier claims of non-involvement. Nixon declared he was telling "the simple truth" and asked the public to let him return to running the country.

"We must not stay so mired in Watergate that we fail to respond to challenges of surpassing importance to America and the world," the President said near the end of his nationally televised speech. "We cannot let an obsession with the past destroy our hopes for the future."

At another place Nixon directed a pointed barb toward Congress, blaming preoccupation with Watergate for lack of attention to legislative programs. "Legislation vital to your health and well-being sits unattended on the Congressional calendar," Nixon told the viewers.

Early reaction to Nixon's statement was mixed.

In working on his speech with advisers earlier in the week at Camp David, Md., the President seemed to face a clearly defined challenge: to win back the confidence of the American people, who had elected him less than 10 months earlier by the third largest electoral vote in history. Nixon's public support had fallen dizzily since the beginning of the Watergate hearings: a late public opinion poll showed that had the election been held in late July or early August 1973, former opponent George McGovern might have defeated him. *(Box, p. 274)*

By choosing national television as a vehicle for his statement, Nixon had decided to employ a tactic he had used before: to go over the heads of Congress and the press and appeal directly to the public. But the tactic had two edges. In using television, Nixon would be appearing in the same forum, on the same video screen that 33 Watergate committee witnesses had already flashed across, each with his own version of events. Each had offerred his own rationale, and each had asked for belief, even though some of their statements were completely incompatible.

Thus, in a sense, the President would be the 34th witness, and instead of seven men, an unseen grassroots panel would be deciding his credibility in a most profound way.

Nixon's approach to them came in several parts.

First, he surprised some observers who had been predicting an attack on the Watergate committee by offering only oblique criticism. While complaining that the committee had become "increasingly absorbed in an effort to implicate the President personally" in Watergate, Nixon asserted, "I do not question the right of a Senate committee to investigate charges made against the President to the extent that this is relevant to their legislative duties." And, he said, it was the duty of the committee—along with the courts—to decide who told the truth during the hearings.

Nixon also repeated an earlier position that "because the abuses occurred under my administration and in the campaign for my re-election, I accept full responsibility for them." Looking directly at the camera he added, "I regret that these events took place."

It was a brisk, business-like apology, but an apology nonetheless. Having said that, the President briefly reiterated earlier statements in which he had maintained his own innocence.

And he repeated arguments already made by White House lawyers, that releasing tapes of his private conversations with White House aides in order to prove his truthfulness would violate the presidential privilege of confidentiality. This principle "is absolutely essential to the conduct of the presidency, in this and future administrations," Nixon claimed, and to violate it "would cripple all future presidents by inhibiting conversations between them and those they look to for advice." *(Tapes controversy, p. 255)*

Nixon said he recognized that the term Watergate had taken on a number of definitions, including abuse of the political process, and of investigational authority in the name of national security. However, he stated an argument similar to that of Watergate witness Jeb Stuart Magruder, that those transgressions had arisen from the same devotion to a "higher morality" that had been invoked by liberal political activists in the 1960s.

"That attitude can never be tolerated in this country," Nixon said. "...The notion that the end justifies the means proved contagious. Thus it is not surprising, even though it is deplorable, that some persons in 1972 adopted the morality that they themselves had rightly condemned and committed acts that have no place in our political system."

Saying that those acts should be punished, Nixon called for "a renewed respect for the mutual restraints that are the mark of a free and civilized society."

The President admitted that "instances have now come to light in which a zeal for (national) security did go too far, and did interfere impermissibly with individual liberty." However, he cautioned against an over-reaction that would place unreasonable limits on the President's duty to protect the nation's security.

In a more detailed statement released in conjunction with the speech, Nixon corrected his May 22 declaration that he had not learned of the break-in at the office of Pentagon papers figure Daniel Ellsberg's psychiatrist until after Nixon had begun his own investigation March 21. He actually learned of the burglary March 17, Nixon said. However, he did not explain exactly how he found out, nor did he say why he had erred on May 22, other than to suggest an oversight. The point was but one of a number of questions he left untended.

Summary of Cox Argument for Tapes Subpoena

Following is the text of the summary of Watergate Special Prosecutor Archibald Cox's memorandum filed in U.S. District Court in Washington on Aug. 13 in support of his suit to compel President Nixon to turn over to the grand jury investigating the Watergate affair recordings of certain taped conversations relating to the case.

The 68-page memorandum responded point-by-point to the Aug. 7 White House reply to the Cox subpoena in which President Nixon was held "answerable to the nation but not to the courts." (Nixon Aug. 7 reply, p. 255)

Arguments in the case to obtain release of the tapes and documents were scheduled to begin in U.S. District Court in Washington on Aug. 22.

I

The President has an enforceable legal duty not to withhold material evidence from a grand jury. The grand jury occupies a fundamental position in the administration of public justice. There is no exception for the President from the guiding principle that the public, in the pursuit of justice, has a right to every man's evidence. These propositions were recognized as early as 1807 in *United States* v. *Burr*, 25 Fed. Cas. 30 (No. 14,692d) (C.C.D. Va. 1807). They have critical importance in a grand jury inquiry into gross misconduct by high officials in the Executive Offices of the President.

The decision in *United States* v. *Burr* is but a specific application of two historic constitutional principles: (1) even the highest executive officials are subject to the rule of law, which it is emphatically the province and duty of the courts to declare; and (2) the rights and obligations of the President and other high executive officers are defined and judicial orders are entered on the premise that these officials, rather than interpose their naked power, will obey the law's explicit and particularized commands. Accordingly, the Court of Appeals for this Circuit, like every other Federal court, has rejected the claim that absolute executive privilege flows from the constitutional separation of powers. It has ruled that it is for the Judiciary—not the Executive—to determine what materials may be held confidential because of a particular exigency and what evidence must be produced. *Committee for Nuclear Responsibility, Inc.* v. *Seaborg*, 463 F2d 788, 792-94 (D.C. Cir. 1971).

The subpoena was properly directed to the President, and the Court has power to enforce it. Counsel's claim that the President, because of his great powers, has immunity from orders enforcing legal obligations is inconsistent with our entire constitutional tradition. The President cannot be limited by judicial intrusion into the exercise of his constitutional powers under Article II. Here, however, the grand jury is not seeking to control the President in the exercise of his constitutional power to withhold the evidence sought by the subpoena merely by his own declaration of the public interest. The grand jury is seeking evidence of criminal conduct that the respondent happens to have in his custody—largely by his personal choice. All the Court is asked to do is hold that the President is bound by legal duties in appropriate cases just as other citizens—in this case, by the duty to supply documentary evidence of crime. In the language of the authoritative precedents, this is a "ministerial duty."

Contrary to counsel's argument, enforcement of the subpoena would not create the threat of "potential disclosure of any and all conversations" (Brief in Opposition 2-3), nor does our submission suggest that every participant in a Presidential conversation would have to speak "in continual awareness that at any moment any Congressional committee, or any prosecutor working with a grand jury, could at will command the production of the verbatim record of every word written or spoken" (Brief in Opposition 16-17). Not only are the facts of the case much narrower, but a settled rule of evidence protects a broad range of Presidential papers and conversations against disclosure *when the Court decides*—after *in camera* inspection when necessary—that the public interest in the secrecy of the particular items outweighs the need for the evidence in the administration of justice.

II

The present case does not fall within the traditional rule of executive privilege as administered by the courts. Counsel for respondent wisely refrain from pressing such a claim. Under the usual rule, the Court—not the President—determines whether particular documents are privileged by weighing the need for the evidence against any governmental interest in secrecy. Here, the only possible governmental interest in secrecy is encouraging openness and candor in giving advice and promoting the free flow of discussion in deliberations upon executive policy by assuring a measure of confidentiality. Preservation of secrecy is unwarranted in the present case for two independent reasons. First, the interest in confidentiality is never sufficient to support an official privilege where there is reason to believe that the deliberations may have involved criminal misconduct. Second, under the particular circumstances of the present case, the need of the grand jury for the critically important evidence provided by the recordings upon a question of wrongdoing by high officials and party leaders easily outweighs the slight risk to the freedom of executive discussions. There will be few occasions upon which a grand jury will have similar cause to believe there may be material evidence of the criminality of high officials in the papers and documents in the Executive Office of the President. The aides of future Presidents are not likely to be timid because of this remote danger of disclosure. If there be some small risk of greater reticence, it is not too great a price to pay to preserve the integrity of the Office of the President.

III

Even if the tape recordings might once have been covered by a privilege, any such claim to continued secrecy has been waived by the extensive testimony, given with respondent's consent, publicizing individual versions of the conversations. In his public statement of May 22, 1973, respondent announced that "Executive privilege will not be invoked as to any testimony concerning possible criminal conduct, in the matters presently under investigation, including the Watergate affair and the alleged cover-up." In accordance with that statement, Dean, Mitchell, Ehrlichman and Haldeman already have testified extensively before the Senate Committee and/or in other proceedings concerning the conversations specified in the subpoena. Haldeman even was allowed access to various tapes after he left government office and gave testimony based upon his listening to the tapes denied the grand jury. Respondent and his counsel themselves have made comments for publication upon the content of the conversations. Under familiar legal principles those disclosures waive any right to further confidentiality. Not even a President can be allowed to select some accounts of a conversation for public disclosure and then to frustrate further grand jury inquiries by withholding the best evidence of what actually took place.

NEXT QUESTION FOR WATERGATE PANEL: HOW TO PROCEED?

While members of the Senate Select Committee on Presidential Campaign Activities were home testing the political waters or just relaxing during the August congressional recess, the committee's 70-member staff was pushing hard to get things in shape for the senators' return in September. Still unanswered were several questions of how the committee would proceed upon its return.

Next on the committee's agenda was the completion of the first phase of its hearings—the Watergate affair—and phases two and three—political espionage (so-called "dirty tricks") and campaign financing.

With the ground work already laid for phase one, the staff was busy putting together evidence and background on the latter two segments of the investigation. This included a grueling pace of two or three interviews a day with potential witnesses, field investigations and laborious reading of records and documents.

"The committee has a sense of urgency now to get its public business over," Rufus L. Edmisten, the deputy chief counsel, told Congressional Quarterly. Two-to-14 hour days and six-day weeks were commonplace for the staff, he said.

Edmisten said the seven committee members were beginning to feel pressures from their constituents to resolve the Watergate affair and get on to other Senate business. As a result, he said, the staff was "extremely busy" preparing a status report on phases two and three so the committee members could make some basic decisions when they return on how to proceed. Among the major decisions that awaited the committee's return were when to resume the hearings, whether they will be televised, how much time to devote to each of the two remaining phases, whether the committee should issue an interim report and whether it should split into subcommittees in order to speed its work.

September Hearings. The hearings probably would resume in the second week of September, Edmisten said. Seven witnesses remained on the committee's list before it could wind up phase one of the hearings, but he thought it possible that only one—former White House aide Charles W. Colson—would be heard publicly.

The other six were E. Howard Hunt Jr., one of the seven convicted Watergate burglars; Egil Krogh Jr. and David Young, the two men who headed the plumbers, a White House contingent responsible for the 1971 break-in at the office of Daniel Ellsberg's psychiatrist; Paul O'Brien and Kenneth Parkinson, lawyers for the Committee for the Re-Election of the President who allegedly were involved in distribution of silence money to the Watergate defendants, and William O. Bittman, Hunt's lawyer, who, according to testimony, received and distributed money for the defendants and their lawyers.

Colson faced questions on allegations that he discussed executive clemency for the defendants with the President, but his testimony was expected to deal mostly with phase two of the hearings—political espionage.

Television. Even if the committee opened the hearings to the television cameras, it remained up to the networks to decide whether they would continue the same kind of daily coverage, rotated between the networks.

Nixon Drop In Polls

President Nixon's approval rating has dropped to the lowest point for any president in 20 years, according to the latest findings of the Gallup poll, published August 14.

31 per cent of the persons interviewed approved of the way the President is handling his job. 57 per cent disapproved. The approval percentage dropped nine points since the last survey, published July 22, and 37 percentage points since January of this year. *(Previous poll reports, p. 262, 240, previous Gallup poll report p. 218)*

Interviewers Aug. 3-6 asked 1,435 adults, "Do you approve or disapprove of the way Nixon is handling his job as President?" The results:

	Latest	July 6-9
Approve	31%	40%
Disapprove	57	49
No Opinion	12	11

President Nixon's latest rating puts him lower in public approval than President Lyndon B. Johnson's lowest point, 35 per cent, reached in August 1968. The last time the presidential approval rating was as low as 31 percent was President Harry S. Truman's 31 per cent in January 1953.

But the current Nixon low is not a record. In the Gallup poll released December 31, 1951, during the Korean war, only 23 per cent of the American people approved of the way Truman was handling his job. Despite Nixon's precipitous decline in the polls, Gallup found that only 26 per cent of Americans believe the President should be compelled to leave office. Another poll, conducted during the last week of July and the first week of August by Oliver Quayle for NBC News, showed similar results to Gallup.

Cited as key factors by Gallup in the President's decline in the polls were concern over high prices, the bombing in Cambodia, and Watergate.

Gallup found that 73 per cent of the American public felt Nixon was involved in or had knowledge of either the Watergate bugging itself or the alleged coverup. Only 15 per cent felt he had no knowledge of either the bugging or the coverup. Twelve per cent had no opinion.

Among his results, Quayle found that if a rematch were held between President Nixon and Sen. George S. McGovern (D S.D.), last year's Democratic presidential nominee, McGovern might win. Quayle asked his respondents: "Suppose another election were being held right now and the candidates were again Richard Nixon, the Republican, and George McGovern, the Democrat. As of now, would you be for Nixon or McGovern?" The results: McGovern 51 percent, Nixon 49 percent.

AGNEW RELEASES RECORDS

Declaring that "I have nothing to hide," Vice President Spiro T. Agnew Aug. 14 consented to a federal prosecutor's request to turn over personal records sought in an investigation of charges of bribery, extortion, conspiracy and tax fraud during Agnew's term as governor of Maryland and while vice president. *(p. 270)*

In a letter to Maryland U.S. Attorney George Beall, Agnew also offered to meet Beall for "a personal interview so that I may answer any questions you may have."

Beall had written Agnew's Washington lawyer, Judah Best, Aug. 1, advising him that Agnew was under investigation and asking the vice president to turn over several documents, including bank records and income tax returns dating back to Jan. 1, 1967. While agreeing to turn over his personal records, Agnew refused to acknowledge that Beall or "any grand jury have any right to records of the vice president."

"Nor do I acknowledge the propriety of any grand jury investigation of possible wrongdoing on the part of the vice president so long as he occupies that office," wrote Agnew.

Richardson Meeting. *The New York Times* reported Aug. 16, and the justice department confirmed, that Attorney General Elliot L. Richardson had met with Agnew Aug. 6 to "supplement" information about the investigation.

Citing sources close to the investigation, the Times said Richardson had discussed the following elements of the investigation: that a Baltimore engineering consultant had paid the vice president $2,500 in 1971 for help in getting someone a job in the General Services Administration; that several Maryland businessmen told investigators they paid Agnew associates for state and government contracts and believed that "some of the money" was "funneled" to Agnew, and that three of the associates told prosecutors they had turned over some of the money to Agnew.

Text of Letter

Dear Mr. Beall:

In your letter of August 1st you request that I make certain of my personal records available to you. I am prepared to do so immediately.

The records you request have been assembled and are at my offices. You and any of your assistants may inspect them there at any time you may desire. My staff have been instructed to give you the fullest cooperation. Should you wish, they will prepare copies for you of any of the records. And you may, of course, compare the copies with the originals to verify their accuracy.

You understand that, by making these records available to you I do not acknowledge that you or any grand jury have any right to records of the Vice President. Nor do I acknowledge the propriety of any grand jury investigation of possible wrongdoing on the part of the Vice President so long as he occupies that office. These are difficult constitutional questions which need not at this moment be confronted.

As I advised you many months ago, I wish in no way to impede your investigation. I have done nothing wrong. I have nothing to hide. And I have no desire save that justice be done speedily and efficiently. Accordingly, the records you request are now available to you.

My desire to cooperate in your investigation does not stop here. I am eager to be of any help I can. Specifically, should you wish, I shall be glad to meet with you and your colleagues for a personal interview so that I may answer any questions you may have.

Very Truly Yours,
S/Spiro T. Agnew

AUG. 15 WATERGATE TEXT

Following is the prepared text of President Nixon's Aug. 15 television address on the Watergate affair:

Now that most of the major witnesses in the Watergate phase of the Senate Committee hearings on campaign practices have been heard, the time has come for me to speak out about the charges made and to provide a perspective on the issue for the American people.

For over four months, Watergate has dominated the news media. During the past three months, the three major networks have devoted an average of over 22 hours of television time a week to the subject. The Senate Committee has heard two million words of testimony.

This investigation began as an effort to discover the facts about the break-in and bugging at the Democratic national headquarters and other campaign abuses.

As the weeks have gone by, it has become clear that both the hearings themselves and some of the commentaries on them have become increasingly absorbed in an effort to implicate the President personally in the illegal activities that took place.

Because the abuses occurred under my Administration, and in the campaign for my re-election, I accept full responsibility for them. I regret that these events took place. I do not question the right of a Senate Committee to investigate charges made against the President to the extent that this is relevant to their legislative duties.

However, it is my constitutional responsibility to defend the integrity of this great office against false charges. I also believe that it is important to address the overriding question of what we as a nation can learn from this experience, and what we should now do. I intend to discuss both of these subjects tonight.

The record of the Senate hearings is lengthy. The facts are complicated, and the evidence conflicting. It would not be right for me to try to sort out the evidence, to rebut specific witnesses, or pronounce my own judgments about their credibility. That is for the Committee and the courts.

I shall not attempt to deal tonight with the various charges in detail. Rather, I shall attempt to put the events in perspective from the standpoint of the Presidency.

On May 22nd, before the major witnesses had testified, I issued a detailed statement addressing the charges that had been made against the President.

I have today issued another written statement, which addresses the charges that have been made since then as they relate to my own conduct, and which describes the efforts that I made to discover the facts about the matter.

On May 22, I stated in very specific terms—and I state again to every one of you listening tonight—I had no prior knowledge of the Watergate operation; I neither took part in nor knew about any of the subsequent cover-up activities; I neither authorized nor encouraged subordinates to engage in illegal or improper campaign tactics.

That was and is the simple truth.

In all of the millions of words of testimony, there is not the slightest suggestion that I had any knowledge of the planning for the Watergate break-in. As for the cover-up my statement has been challenged by only one of the thirty-five witnesses who appeared—a witness who offered no evidence beyond his own impressions, and whose testimony has been contradicted by every other witness in a position to know the facts.

Tonight, let me explain to you what I did about Watergate after the break-in occurred, so that you can better understand the fact that I also had no knowledge of the so-called cover-up.

From the time when the break-in occurred, I pressed repeatedly to know the facts, and particularly whether there was any involvement by anyone at the White House. I considered two things essential:

First, that the investigation should be thorough and above-board; and second, that if there were any higher involvement, we should get the facts out first. As I said at my August 29 press conference last year, "What really hurts in matters of this sort is not the fact that they occur, because overzealous people in campaigns do things that are wrong. What really hurts is if you try to cover it up." I believed that then, and certainly the experience of this past year has proved it.

I knew that the Justice Department and the FBI were conducting intensive investigations—as I had insisted that they should. The White House Counsel, John Dean, was assigned to monitor those investigations, and particularly to check into any possible White House involvement. Throughout the summer of 1972, I continued to press the question, and I continued to get the same answer: that there was no indication that any persons were involved other than the seven who were known to have planned and carried out the operation, and who were subsequently indicted and convicted.

On September 12 at a meeting that I held with the Cabinet, the senior White House staff and a number of legislative leaders, Attorney General Kleindienst reported on the investigation. He told us it had been the most extensive investigation since the assassination of President Kennedy, and that it had established that only those seven were involved.

On September 15, the day the seven were indicted, I met with John Dean, the White House Counsel. He gave me no reason whatever to believe that any others were guilty; I assumed that the indictments of only the seven by the Grand Jury confirmed the reports he had been giving to that effect throughout the summer.

On February 16, I met with Acting Director Gray prior to submitting his name to the Senate for confirmation as permanent Director of the FBI. I stressed to him that he would be questioned closely about the FBI's conduct of the Watergate investigation, and asked him if he still had full confidence in it. He replied that he did; that he was proud of its thoroughness, and that he could defend it with enthusiasm.

Because I trusted the agencies conducting the investigations, and because I believed the reports I was getting, I did not believe the newspaper accounts that suggested a cover-up. I was convinced that there was no cover-up, because I was convinced that no one had anything to cover up.

It was not until March 21 of this year—that I received new information from the White House counsel that led me to conclude that the reports I had been getting for over 9 months were not true. On that day, I launched an intensive effort of my own to get the facts and to get them out. Whatever the facts might be, I wanted the White House to be the first to make them public.

At first I entrusted the task of getting me the facts to Mr. Dean. When, after spending a week at Camp David he failed to produce the written report I had asked for, I turned to John Ehrlichman and the Attorney General—while also making independent inquiries of my own. By mid-April I had received Mr. Ehrlichman's report, and also one from the Attorney General based on new information uncovered by the Justice Department. These reports made it clear to me that the situation was far more serious than I had imagined. It at once became evident to me that the responsibility for the investigation in the case should be given to the Criminal Division of the Justice Department. I turned over all the information I had to the head of that department, Assistant Attorney General Petersen, a career government employee with an impeccable non-partisan record, and instructed him to pursue the matter thoroughly. I ordered all members of the Administration to testify fully before the Grand Jury.

With my concurrence, on May 18 Attorney General Richardson appointed a Special Prosecutor to handle the matter, and the case is now before the Grand Jury.

Far from trying to hide the facts, my effort throughout has been to discover the facts—and to lay those facts before the appropriate law enforcement authorities so that justice could be done and the guilty dealt with.

I relied on the best law enforcement agencies in the country to find and report the truth. I believed that they had done so—just as they believed that they had done so.

Turning Over the Tapes

Many have urged that in order to help prove the truth of what I have said, I should turn over to the Special Prosecutor and the Senate Committee recordings of conversations that I held in my office or on my telephone.

However, a much more important principle is involved in this question than what the tapes might prove about Watergate.

Every day a President of the United States is required to make difficult decisions on grave issues. It is absolutely necessary, if the President is to be able to do his job as the country expects, that he be able to talk openly and candidly with his advisers about issues and individuals. This kind of frank discussion is only possible when those who take part in it know that what they say is in strictest confidence.

The Presidency is not the only office that requires confidentiality. A Member of Congress must be able to talk in confidence with his assistants. Judges must be able to confer in confidence with their law clerks and with each other. For very good reasons, no branch of Government has ever compelled disclosure of confidential conversations between officers of other branches of Government and their advisers about Government business.

This need for confidence is not confined to Government officials. The law has long recognized that there are kinds of conversations that are entitled to be kept confidential, even at the cost of doing without critical evidence in a legal proceeding. This rule applies, for example, to conversations between a lawyer and a client, between a priest and a penitent, and between a husband and a wife. In each case it is thought so important that the parties be able to talk freely to each other, that for hundreds of years the law has said that these conversations are "privileged" and that their disclosure cannot be compelled.

It is even more important that the confidentiality of conversations between a President and his advisers be protected. This is no mere luxury, to be dispensed with whenever a particular issue raises sufficient uproar. It is absolutely essential to the conduct of the Presidency, in this and future Administrations.

If I were to make public these tapes, containing blunt and candid remarks on many different subjects, the confidentiality of the Office of the President would always be suspect. It would make no difference whether it was to serve the interests of a court, of a Senate Committee or the President himself—the same damage would be done to the principle, and it would be irreparable. Persons talking with a President would never again be sure that recordings or notes of what they said would not suddenly be made public. No one would want to advance tentative ideas that might later seem unsound. No diplomat would want to speak candidly in those sensitive negotiations which could bring peace or avoid war. No Senator would want to talk frankly about the Congressional horse-trading that might get a vital bill passed. No one would want to speak bluntly about public figures, here and abroad.

That is why I shall continue to oppose efforts which would set a precedent that would cripple all future Presidents by inhibiting conversations between them and those they look to for advice. This principle of confidentiality of Presidential conversations is at stake in the question of the tapes. I must and shall oppose any efforts to destroy this principle, which is so vital to the conduct of the Presidency.

Turning now to the basic issues which have been raised by Watergate, I recognize that merely answering the charges that have been made against the President is not enough. The word "Watergate" has come to represent a much broader set of concerns.

To most of us, "Watergate" has come to mean not just a burglary and bugging at party headquarters, but a whole series of acts that either represent or appear to represent an abuse of trust. It has come to stand for excessive partisanship, for "enemies lists," for efforts to use the great institutions of Government for partisan political purposes.

National Security

For many Americans, the term "Watergate" also has come to include a number of national security matters that have been brought into the investigation, such as those involved in my efforts to stop massive leaks of vital diplomatic and military secrets, and to counter the wave of bombings and burnings and other violent assaults of just a few years ago.

Let me speak first of the political abuses.

As I know from long experience, a political campaign is always a hard, tough contest. A candidate for high office has an obligation to his party, to his supporters, and to the cause he represents. He must put forth his best effort to win. But he also has an obligation to the country to conduct that contest within the law and within the limits of decency.

No political campaign ever justifies obstructing justice, or harassing individuals, or compromising those great agencies of Government that should and must be above politics. To the extent that these things were done in the 1972 campaign, they were serious abuses. I deplore them.

Practices of that kind do not represent what I believe Government should be, or what I believe politics should be. In a free society, the institutions of Government belong to the people. They must never be used against the people.

In the future, my Administration will be more vigilant in ensuring that such abuses do not take place, and that officials at every level understand that they are not to take place.

I reject the cynical view that politics is inevitably or even usually dirty business. Let us not allow what a few overzealous people did in Watergate to tar the reputation of the millions of dedicated Americans who fought hard but clean for the candidates of their choice in 1972. By their unselfish efforts, these people make our system work and keep America free.

I pledge to you tonight that I will do all that I can to ensure that one of the results of Watergate is a new level of political decency and integrity in America—in which what has been wrong in our politics no longer corrupts or demeans what is right.

Let me turn now to the difficult questions that arise in protecting the Nation's security.

It is important to recognize that these are difficult questions and that reasonable and patriotic men and women may differ on how they should be answered.

Only last year, the Supreme Court said that implicit in the President's constitutional duty is "the power to protect our Government against those who would subvert or overthrow it by unlawful means." How to carry out this duty is often a delicate question to which there is no easy answer.

For example, every President since World War II has believed that in internal security matters the President has the power to authorize wiretaps without first obtaining a search warrant.

An Act of Congress in 1968 had seemed to recognize such power. Last year the Supreme Court held to the contrary. My Administration is of course now complying with that decision. But until the Supreme Court spoke, I had been acting, as did my predecessors—President Truman, President Eisenhower, President Kennedy and President Johnson—in a reasonable belief that in certain circumstances the Constitution permitted such measures to protect the national security in the public interest.

Although it is the President's duty to protect the security of the country, we must be extremely careful in the way we go about this—for if we lose our liberties we will have little use for security. Instances have now come to light in which a zeal for security did go too far, and did interfere impermissibly with individual liberty. It is essential that such mistakes not be repeated. But it is also essential that we do not over-react to particular mistakes by tying the President's hands in a way that would risk sacrificing our security, and with it all of our liberties.

I shall continue to meet my Constitutional responsibility to protect the security of this Nation so that Americans may enjoy their freedom. But I shall and can do so by Constitutional means, in ways that will not threaten that freedom.

As we look at Watergate in a longer perspective, we can see that its abuses resulted from the assumption by those involved that their cause placed them beyond the reach of those rules that apply to other persons and that hold a free society together.

That attitude can never be tolerated in this country. However, it did not suddenly develop in 1972. It became fashionable in the 1960s, as individuals and groups increasingly asserted the right to take the law into their own hands, insisting that their purposes represented a higher morality. Then, their attitude was praised in the press and from some of our pulpits as evidence of a new idealism. Those who insisted on the old restraints, and who warned of the overriding importance of operating within the law and by the rules, were accused of being reactionaries.

That same attitude brought a rising spiral of violence and fear, of riots and arson and bombings, all in the name of peace and justice. Political discussion turned into savage debate. Free speech was brutally suppressed as hecklers shouted down or even physically assaulted those with whom they disagreed. Serious people raised serious questions about whether we could survive as a free democracy.

The notion that the end justifies the means proved contagious. Thus it is not surprising, even though it is deplorable, that some persons in 1972 adopted the morality that they themselves had rightly condemned and committed acts that have no place in our political system.

Those acts cannot be defended. Those who were guilty of abuses must be punished. But ultimately, the answer does not lie merely in the jailing of a few overzealous persons who mistakenly thought their cause justified their violations of the law.

Rather, it lies in a commitment by all of us to show a renewed respect for the mutual restraints that are the mark of a free and civilized society. It requires that we learn once again to work together, if not united in all of our purposes, then at least united in respect for the system by which our conflicts are peacefully resolved and our liberties maintained.

If there are laws we disagree with, let us work to change them—but let us obey them until they are changed. If we have disagreements over Government policies, let us work those out in a decent and civilized way, within the law, and with respect for our differences.

We must recognize that one excess begets another, and that the extremes of violence and discord in the 1960s contributed to the extremes of Watergate.

Both are wrong. Both should be condemned. No individual, no group and no political party has a corner on the market on morality in America.

If we learn the important lessons of Watergate, if we do what is necessary to prevent such abuses in the future—on both sides—we can emerge from this experience a better and stronger Nation.

Challenge of Surpassing Importance

Let me turn now to an issue that is important above all else, and that is critically affecting your life today and will in the future.

After 12 weeks and 2 million words of televised testimony, we have reached a point at which a continued, backward-looking obsession with Watergate is causing this Nation to neglect matters of far greater importance to all of the American people.

We must not stay so mired in Watergate that we fail to respond to challenges of surpassing importance to America and the world. We cannot let an obsession with the past destroy our hopes for the future.

Legislation vital to your health and well-being sits unattended on the Congressional calendar. Confidence at home and abroad in our economy, our currency and our foreign policy is being sapped by uncertainty. Critical negotiations are taking place on strategic weapons and on troop levels in Europe that can affect the security of this Nation and our allies long after Watergate is forgotten. Vital events are taking place in Southeast Asia which could lead to a tragedy for the cause of peace.

These are matters that will not wait. They cry out for action now. Either we, your elected representatives here in Washington ought to get on with the jobs that need to be done—for you—or every one of you ought to be demanding to know why.

The time has come to turn Watergate over to the courts, where the questions of guilt or innocence belong. The time has come for the rest of us to get on with the urgent business of our Nation.

Last November, the American people were given the clearest choice of this century. Your votes were a mandate, which I accepted, to complete the initiatives we began in my first term and to fulfill the promises I made for my second term.

This Administration was elected to control inflation—to reduce the power and size of Government—to cut the cost of Government so that you can cut the cost of living—to preserve and defend those fundamental values that have made America great—to keep the Nation's military strength second to none—to achieve peace with honor in Southeast Asia, and bring home America's prisoners of war—to build a new prosperity, without inflation and without war—to create a structure of peace in the world that would endure long after we were gone.

These are great goals, worthy of a great people. I would not be true to your trust if I let myself be turned aside from achieving those goals.

If you share my belief in these goals—if you want the mandate you gave this Administration to be carried out—then I ask for your help to ensure that those who would exploit Watergate in order to keep us from doing what we were elected to do will not succeed.

I ask tonight for your understanding, so that as a Nation we can learn the lessons of Watergate, and gain from experience.

I ask for your help in reaffirming our dedication to the principles of decency, honor and respect for the institutions that have sustained our progress through these past two centuries.

I ask for your support, in getting on once again with meeting your problems, improving your life and building your future. ✓

SUPPLEMENTARY STATEMENT

Following is the text of a Presidential statement on Watergate released as President Nixon began his Aug. 15 television address.

On May 17th the Senate Select Committee began its hearings on Watergate. Five days later, on May 22nd, I issued a detailed statement discussing my relationship to the matter. I stated categorically that I had no prior knowledge of the Watergate operation and that I neither knew of nor took part in any subsequent efforts to cover it up. I also stated that I would not invoke Executive Privilege as to testimony by present and former members of my White House staff with respect to possible criminal acts then under investigation.

Thirty-five witnesses have testified so far. The record is more than 7,500 pages and some two million words long. The allegations are many, the facts are complicated, and the evidence is not only extensive but very much in conflict. It would be neither fair nor appropriate for me to assess the evidence or comment on specific witnesses or their credibility. That is the function of the Senate Committee and the courts. What I intend to do here is to cover the principal issues relating to my own conduct which have been raised since my statement of May 22, and thereby to place the testimony on those issues in perspective.

I said on May 22nd that I had no prior knowledge of the Watergate operation. In all the testimony, there is not the slightest evidence to the contrary. Not a single witness has testified that I had any knowledge of the planning for the Watergate break-in.

It is also true, as I said on May 22nd, that I took no part in, and was not aware of, any subsequent efforts to cover up the illegal acts associated with the Watergate break-in.

In the summer of 1972, I had given orders for the Justice Department and the FBI to conduct a thorough and aggressive investigation of the Watergate break-in, and I relied on their investigation to disclose the facts. My only concern about the scope of the investigation was that it might lead into CIA or other national security operations of a sensitive nature. Mr. Gray, the Acting Director of the FBI, told me by telephone on July 6th that he had met with General Walters, that General Walters had told him the CIA was not involved, and that CIA activities would not be compromised by the FBI investigation. As a result, any problems that Mr. Gray may have had in coordinating with the CIA were moot. I concluded by instructing him to press forward vigorously with his own investigation.

Early Reports

During the summer of 1972, I repeatedly asked for reports on the progress of the investigation. Every report I received was that no persons, other than the seven who were subsequently indicted, were involved in the Watergate operation. On September 12, at a meeting attended by me, and by the Cabinet, senior members of the White House staff and a number of legislative leaders, Attorney General Kleindienst reported on the investigation. He informed us that it had been the most intensive investigation since the assassination of President Kennedy, and that it had been established that no one at the White House, and no higher-ups in the campaign committee, were involved. His report seemed to be confirmed by the action of the Grand Jury on September 15th, when it indicted only the five persons arrested at the Watergate, plus Messrs. Liddy and Hunt.

Those indictments also seemed to me to confirm the validity of the reports that Mr. Dean had been providing to me, through other members of the White House staff—and on which I had based my August 29 statement that no one then employed at the White House was involved. It was in that context that I met with Mr. Dean on September 15, and he gave me no reason at that meeting to believe any others were involved.

Not only was I unaware of any cover-up, but at that time, and until March 21st, I was unaware that there was anything to cover up.

Then and later, I continued to have full faith in the investigations that had been conducted and in the reports I had received, based on those investigations. On February 16, I met with Mr. Gray prior to submitting his name to the Senate for confirmation as permanent Director of the FBI. I stressed to him that he would be questioned closely about the FBI's conduct of the Watergate investigation, and asked him if he still had full confidence in it. He replied that he did; that he was proud of its thoroughness, and that he could defend it with enthusiasm.

My interest in Watergate rose in February and March as the Senate Committee was organized and the hearings were held on the Gray nomination. I began meeting frequently with my counsel, Mr. Dean, in connection with those matters. At that time, on a number of occasions, I urged my staff to get all the facts out, because I was confident that full disclosure of the facts would show that persons in the White House and at the Committee for the Re-election of the President were the victims of unjustified innuendoes in the press. I was searching for a way to disclose all of the facts without disturbing the confidentiality of communications with and among my personal staff, since that confidentiality is essential to the functioning of any President.

March 21

It was on March 21st that I was given new information that indicated that the reports I had been getting were not true. I was told then for the first time that the planning of the Watergate break-in went beyond those who had been tried and convicted, and that at least one, and possibly more, persons at the Re-election Committee were involved. It was on that day also that I learned of some of the activities upon which charges of cover-up are now based. I was told then that funds had been raised for payments to the defendants, with the knowledge and approval of persons both on the White House staff and at the Re-election Committee. But I was only told that the money had been used for attorneys' fees and family support, not that it had been paid to procure silence from the recipients. I was also told that a member of my staff had talked to one of the defendants about clemency, but not that offers of clemency had been made. I was told that one of the defendants was currently attempting to blackmail the White House by demanding payment of $120,000 as the price of not talking about other activities, unrelated to Watergate, in which he had engaged. These allegations were made in general terms, they were portrayed to me as being based in part on supposition, and they were largely unsupported by details or evidence.

These allegations were very troubling, and they gave a new dimension to the Watergate matter. They also reinforced my determination that the full facts must be available to the grand jury or to the Senate Committee. If anything illegal had happened, I wanted it to be dealt with appropriately according to the law. If anyone at the White House or high up in my campaign had been involved in wrongdoing of any kind, I wanted the White House to take the lead in making that known.

When I received this disturbing information on March 21st, I immediately began new inquiries into the case and an examination of the best means to give to the grand jury or Senate Committee what we then knew and what we might later learn. On March 21st, I arranged to meet the following day with Messrs. Haldeman, Ehrlichman, Dean, and Mitchell to discuss the appropriate method to get the facts out. On March 23rd, I sent Mr. Dean to Camp David, where he was instructed to write a complete report on all that he knew of the entire Watergate matter. On March 28th, I had Mr. Ehrlichman call the Attorney General to find out if he had additional information about Watergate generally or White House involvement. The Attorney General was told that I wanted to hear directly from him, and not through any staff people, if he had any information on White House involvement or if information of that kind should come to him. The Attorney General indicated to Mr. Ehrlichman that he had no such information. When I learned on March 30th that Mr. Dean had been unable to complete his report. I instructed Mr. Ehrlichman to conduct an independent inquiry and bring all the facts to me. On April 14, Mr. Ehrlichman gave me his findings, and I directed that he report them to the Attorney General immediately. On April 15th, Attorney General Kleindienst and Assistant Attorney General Petersen told me of new information that had been received by the prosecutors.

By that time the fragmentary information I had been given on March 21st had been supplemented in important ways, particularly by Mr. Ehrlichman's report to me on April 14th, by the information Mr. Kleindienst and Mr. Petersen gave me on April 15th, and by independent inquiries I had been making on my own. At that point, I realized that I would not be able personally to find out all of the facts and make them public, and I concluded that the matter was best handled by the Justice Department and the grand jury. On April 17th, I announced that new inquiries were underway, as a result of what I had learned on March 21st and in my own investigation since that time. I instructed all Government employees to cooperate with the judicial process as it moved ahead on this matter and expressed my personal view that no immunity should be given to any individual who had held a position of major importance in this Administration.

My consistent position from the beginning has been to get out the facts about Watergate, not to cover them up.

On May 22nd I said that at no time did I authorize any offer of Executive clemency for the Watergate defendants, nor did I know of any such offer. I reaffirm that statement. Indeed, I made my view clear to Mr. Ehrlichman in July 1972, that under no circumstances could Executive clemency be considered for those who participated in the Watergate break-in. I maintained that position throughout.

Ellsberg

On May 22nd I said that "it was not until the time of my investigation that I learned of the break-in at the office of Mr. Ellsberg's psychiatrist, and I specifically authorized the furnishing of this information to Judge Byrne." After a very careful review, I have determined that this statement of mine is not precisely accurate. It was on March 17th that I first learned of the break-in at the office of Dr. Fielding, and that was four days before the beginning of my own investigation on March 21st. I was told then that nothing by way of evidence had been obtained in the break-in. On April 18th I learned that the Justice Department had interrogated or was going to interrogate Mr. Hunt about this break-in. I was gravely concerned that other activities of the Special Investigations Unit might be disclosed, because I knew this could seriously injure the national security. Consequently, I directed Mr. Petersen to stick to the Watergate investigation and stay out of national security matters. On April 25th Attorney General Kleindienst came to me and urged that the fact of the break-in should be disclosed to the court, despite the fact that, since no evidence had been obtained, the law did not clearly require it. I concurred, and authorized him to report the break-in to Judge Byrne.

In view of the incident of Dr. Fielding's office, let me emphasize two things.

First, it was and is important that many of the matters worked on by the Special Investigations Unit not be publicly disclosed because disclosure would unquestionably damage the national security. This is why I have exercised Executive Privilege on some of these matters in connection with the testimony of Mr. Ehrlichman and others. The Senate Committee has learned through its investigation the general facts of some of these security matters, and has to date wisely declined to make them public or to contest in these respects my claim of Executive Privilege.

Second, I at no time authorized the use of illegal means by the Special Investigations Unit, and I was not aware of the break-in of Dr. Fielding's office until March 17, 1973.

Many persons will ask why, when the facts are as I have stated them, I do not make public the tape recordings of my meetings and conversations with members of the White House staff during this period.

I am aware that such terms as "separation of powers" and "Executive Privilege" are lawyers' terms, and that those doctrines have been called "abstruse" and "esoteric." Let me state the common sense of the matter. Every day a President of the United States is required to make difficult decisions on grave issues. It is absolutely essential, if the President is to be able to do his job as the country expects, that he be able to talk openly and candidly with his advisers about issues and individuals and that they be able to talk in the same fashion with him. Indeed, on occasion, they must be able to "blow off steam" about important public figures. This kind of frank discussion is only possible when those who take part in it can feel assured that what they say is in the strictest confidence.

The Presidency is not the only office that requires confidentiality if it is to function effectively. A Member of Congress must be able to talk in confidence with his assistants. Judges must be able to confer in confidence with their law clerks and with each other. Throughout our entire history the need for this kind of confidentiality has been recognized. No branch of Government has ever compelled disclosure of confidential conversations between officers of other branches of Government and their advisers about Government business.

The argument is often raised that these tapes are somehow different because the conversations may bear on illegal acts, and because the commission of illegal acts is not an official duty. This misses the point entirely. Even if others, from their own standpoint, may have been thinking about how to cover up an illegal act, from my standpoint I was concerned with how to uncover the illegal acts. It is my responsibility under the Constitution to see that the laws are faithfully executed, and in pursuing the facts about Watergate I was doing precisely that. Therefore, the precedent would not be one concerning illegal actions only; it would be one that would risk exposing private Presidential conversations involving the whole range of official duties.

Need for Confidence

The need for confidence is not something confined to the Government officials. The law has long recognized that there are many relations sufficiently important that things said in that relation are entitled to be kept confidential, even at the cost of doing without what might be critical evidence in a legal proceeding. Among these are, for example, the relations between a lawyer and his client, between a priest and a penitent, and between a husband and wife. In each case it is thought to be so important that the parties be able to talk freely with each other, that they need not feel restrained in their conversation by fear that what they say may someday come out in court, that the law recognizes that these conversations are "privileged" and that their disclosure cannot be compelled.

If I were to make public these tapes, containing as they do blunt and candid remarks on many subjects that have nothing to do with Watergate, the confidentiality of the Office of the President would always be suspect. Persons talking with a President would never again be sure that recordings or notes of what they said would not at some future time be made public, and they would guard their words against that possibility. No one would want to risk being known as the person who recommended a policy that ultimately did not work. No one would want to advance tentative ideas, not fully thought through, that might have possible merit but that might, on further examination, prove unsound. No one would want to speak bluntly about public figures here and abroad. I shall therefore vigorously oppose any action which would set a precedent that would cripple all future Presidents by inhibiting conversations between them and the persons they look to for advice.

This principle of confidentiality in Presidential communications is what is at stake in the question of the tapes. I shall continue to oppose any efforts to destroy that principle, which is indispensable to the conduct of the Presidency.

I recognize that this statement does not answer many of the questions and contentions raised during the Watergate hearings. It has not been my intention to attempt any such comprehensive and detailed response, nor has it been my intention to address myself to all matters covered in my May 22nd statement. With the Senate hearings and the grand jury investigations still proceeding, with much of the testimony in conflict, it would be neither possible to provide nor appropriate to attempt a definitive account of all that took place. Neither do I believe I could enter upon an endless course of explaining and rebutting a complex of point-by-point claims and charges arising out of that conflicting testimony which may engage committees and courts for months or years to come, and still be able to carry out my duties as President. While the judicial and legislative branches resolve these matters, I will continue to discharge to the best of my ability my Constitutional responsibilities as President of the United States. ✓

INDEX

A

Abplanalp, Robert, 109, 271
Adams, Sherman, 44-45, 53
Advertising, 172
AFL-CIO. *See* American Federation of Labor-Congress of Industrial Organizations.
Agnew, Spiro T.
Attacks media, 51
Bribery probe, 270, 275
Criticizes Senate hearings, 132, 139-140
Election reform, 73, 75
Fundraising dinner
GAO report, 174, 186
Irregularities, 115, 121, 135, 140
Grand jury probe, 149, 258
Harris poll, 29
Martha Mitchell remark, 146
Republican Party, 38
Supports Nixon, 22, 27, 141
White House staff reorganization, 130
Aiken, George D. (R Vt.), 28, 73-74
Airlines. *See* Finances, Republican Campaign.
Airplane Crash, Chicago, 105
Albert, Carl (D Okla.), 77, 130, 243
Alch, Gerald
Bar association probe, 264
CIA coverup role denied, 54
McCord attorney
Contradicts McCord, 83-85, 90
Defense, 10
McCord testimony, 64
McCord May 18 statement, 94-95
McCord memo, 57-59, 80, 82
Alioto, Joseph L., 148
Allen, Robert H., 7
Ambassadors. *See* White House. Wiretapping.
American Airlines, 186-187, 218
American Bar Association. *See* Bar Associations.
American Broadcasting Company. *See* Television.
American Civil Liberties Union, 150, 180, 189
American Federation of Labor-Congress of Industrial Organizations, 54, 153
American Motors Corporation, 201
American Telephone and Telegraph Company. *See* Telephone Companies.
Americans for Democratic Action, 87
Anderson, Jack, 9, 20, 22, 144
Anderson, John B. (R Ill.), 27-28, 138
Andreas, Dwayne, 5, 133-134
Antiwar Movement *(see also* Ehrlichman, John D. Haldeman, H.R.), 136
Armed Forces *(see also* Defense Department)
Civilian espionage, 263
Dean documents, 122-125
FBI newspaper break-in, 107
Haig appointment, 53, 105
Nixon property expenditures, 271
Armstrong, Anne, 14
Arnold, Byron, 30
Ash, Roy L., 42, 108
Ashland Oil Company, 218
Attorney, Office of U.S., 89-90
Attorneys, Discipline of *(see also* Bar Associations) 259, 263-264

B

Babcock, Tim, 201
Baker, Howard H. Jr. (R Tenn.)
Alch questioning, 85
Biography, 6
Committee procedures
Conflicts with other probes, 47-48
Decorum, 48
First-round statement, 63-64
Immunity debate, 47
Length of hearings, 229, 241
Dean documents, 122-125
Dean leaks, 149
Dean questioning, 176
Dean-White House conflict, 151
Democratic finances, 135, 146
Ehrlichman questioning, 216-217, 233
Ellsberg probe, 138
Election reform, 116
Haldeman, statement on, 12
Magruder motives, 136
Mitchell questioning, 183-184
Nixon, assessment of, 150
Nixon tapes controversy *(see also* Executive Privilege)
Access sought, 195-196, 203, 208-209, 211-219
Requests private listening, 241, 229
Personal finances, 240
Popularity, 29, 240
Porter questioning, 118
Presidential testimony, 65, 159, 176
Weicker smear reaction, 159
Wiretapping exchange, 82
Bailey, F. Lee, 83, 197
Bailey, Shirley, 72
Baldwin, Alfred C. III, 4-5, 10, 84-85
Banking Committee Probe. *See* Committees, House.
Banomi, John G., 263
Bar Associations
American Bar Association, 27, 67, 264
Blackmun speech, 254, 257, 263
California Bar Association, 174, 259
Massachusetts Bar, 264
New York City Bar, 27
Barkan, Alexander E., 153
Barker, Bernard L.
CIA background, 238
Break-in role
Conviction blame, 237
Criminal trial, 9-11
Executive Clemency *(see also* Executive Clemency), 202
Funding, *(see also* Finances, Republican Campaign), 87, 117, 133, 135, 264-266
Houston probe, 258
Immunity, 12, 65
Indictment, 4
McCord memo, statement, 57-59, 94-95
Senate testimony, 84-86, 90
Chilean Embassy plot, 117, 127
Ellsberg break-in witness, 118-119
Florida trial, 5, 116, 121, 259
Jail transfer, 105
Barker, Robert W., 133-134
Barrett, John, 64
Barrick, Paul E., 141-142
Bates, Charles W., 264-265
Baxley, Bill, 242-243
Bayh, Birch (D Ind.), 43
Bay of Pigs. *See* Cuba.
Beard, Dita, *(see also* International Telephone and Telegraph Corp.), 120, 144
Begich, Nick (D Alaska), 84
Belknap, William W., 55
Bellino, Carmine S., 219, 241, 262
Bennett, Donald V. (Gen.), 88, 91-94, 123
Berentson, Buehl, 38
Bernstein, Carl, 51
Berrigan, Daniel and Philip, 120
Biden, Joe (D Del.), 98
Biester, Edward G. (R Pa.), 69
Bittenbender, Gary, 58
Bittman, William O.
Alch Testimony, 84
Conspirator payments, 195, 197, 199-201
Executive clemency role, 215
McCord memo, testimony, 57-59, 64, 94-95
Black Panthers, 104, 119
Blackmun, Harry A., 254, 257, 263
Block, Herbert A., 51
Blount, William, 55
Boggs, Hale (D La.), 84
Bonner, Walter J., 263
Boorstin, Daniel J., 169-173
Bratt, Harry M., 198
Bremer, Arthur H., 150
Brennan, Peter J., 219
Brezhnev, Leonid I., 145, 148
Brill, Theodore T., 9
Brinegar, Claude S., 31, 52
Brock, Bill (R Tenn.), 29
Broder, David, 51, 171
Brooke, Edward W. (R Mass.), 29, 43, 62
Brookings Institution *(see also* Halperin, Morton, Mitchell, John N.), 120, 141, 155, 163, 180.)
Brown, Clarence J. (R Ohio), 69
Brown, Edmund G., 30
Buchanan, James, 74
Buchanan, Patrick J., 42, 153, 205, 263
Buckley, James L. (R N.Y.), 29
Bugging. *See* Espionage. Domestic Intelligence. Wiretapping.
Bull, Stephen, 231, 234, 242
Burgener, Clair W. (R Calif.), 69
Burr, Aaron, 270
Busch, Joseph, 56, 219, 240
Bush, George
Asks CRP funds, 87
Gutter politics remark, 264
Republican strength assessment, 23
Senate hearings, 132, 139, 189
Watergate comments, 12, 20
Businessmen's Educational Fund, 153
Butler, M. Caldwell (R Va.), 69
Butterfield, Alexander P., 191-194, 202-203, 234
Butz, Earl L., 60-61, 65
Buzhardt, J. Fred
Appointment, 46, 57, 60
Assistant named, 130
Biography, 61
Dean files, 151
Nixon tapes
Disclosure, 192-193, 203
Halted, 218
Listening role, 242
Subpoenas, 212, 224-225
White House counterattack
Anti-Dean, Mitchell memo, 157-159, 162-163, 181-182
Briefing on Nixon May 22 speech, 88-89
Plumbers letter, 216
Byrd, Robert C. (D W.Va.)
Impeachment opinion, 90
Nixon Apr. 30 speech reaction, 27
Special prosecutor, 32, 96, 98
Watergate impact, 33
Byrne, W. Matthew Jr.
Ellsberg trial *(see also* Pentagon Papers.)
Asks affidavits, 29
Charges dismissed, 46, 70-71, 121
CIA role, 59
Fabricated cables, 53
Files theft, 20
Halperin suit, 141
Nixon May 22 statement, 91-94
Ruckelshaus wiretap statement, 69-70
White House intervention, 30-32
FBI conflict
Directorship offer, 24, 29, 32, 177, 219
Ehrlichman Senate testimony, 215

C

Cabinet, 44-45, 53
Caddy, C. Douglas, 195
Califano, Joseph A. Jr., 87
California Bar Association. *See* Bar Associations.
California Committee for Eugene McCarthy. *See* McCarthy, Eugene.
California Fund. *See* Finances, Republican Campaign.
Campaign Spending. *See* Election Reform.
Campbell, Donald E., 89, 104, 120, 177-178
Cannon, Howard W. (D Nev.), 112
Carey, Hugh L. (D N.Y.), 33
Casey, William, 21, 67, 71, 86-87, 177
Cashen, Henry C., 144
Castro, Fidel, 127
Caudle, T. Lamar, 44-45
Caulfield, John J.
IRS misuse, 87, 157, 177
Kennedy surveillance, 155
Leaks probe, wiretap, 155
Resignation, leave, 65, 104
Watergate coverup role
Executive clemency, 68, 80, 87, 89-90
Implicated by McCord, 63-65, 80, 82-83, 94-95
White House memo, 162
Center on Corporate Responsibility, Inc., 186, 203-204
Central Intelligence Agency (CIA)
Hoover opinion of aides, 217
Hunt Kennedy probe, 177
National security, 104, 121, 125
Pentagon Papers case
Byrne dismissal, 70-71
Cushman testimony, 107
Ellsberg profile, 217, 239, 262
Hearings on involvement, 89
Memos, 54, 59
Richardson confirmation role, 98
Staff
Officials' testimony. *See* Helms, Richard M., Cushman, Robert E., Walters, Vernon A.
Schlesinger appointment, 46, 57, 61
Watergate involvement pressure
Bugging motives memos, 117, 120, 126-129

Central Intelligence Agency (CIA)
Caulfield testimony, 84
Congressional probes, 258
Conspirator backgrounds, 4, 40
Conspirator payments, 186,
Cushman testimony, 238-239, 262
Dean silence, 217
Domestic scandals covered, 66-67, 85-87, 89-90, 103
Ehrlichman role denial, 99-102, 107
Gray testimony, 256, 264-267
Haldeman role denial, 137, 99-102, 107
Haldeman testimony, 232, 235, 244, 247-248
Helms defense, 102-103, 238-239, 243, 262
Liddy silence, 218
McCord role, (*see also* McCord, James W.) 54, 80, 82, 160-161
McGregor deposition, 236
Mardian testimony, 201
Memos doctored, 239
Nixon May 22 statement, 79-80, 91-94
Nixon knowledge, 158
Plumbers aid, 149
Walters memos, 110, 126-129, 256, 266-267
Walters testimony, 256, 229, 263
White House denials, 162
Chambers, Arden, 119, 141-142
Chapin, Dwight L.
Biography, 38-39
Campaign espionage role, 8-9, 188, 232
Demonstrator reaction, 155
Resignation, 56
Sabotage funding, 197
Watergate coverup role, 31, 116
Chase, Samuel, 55
Chennault, Anna, 9
Chenow, Kathleen, 266
Chesapeake and Potomac Telephone Company. *See* Telephone Companies.
Chile, 117, 119, 127, 129
Chotiner, Murray, 178
Christopher, Warren, 67-68
Chrysler Corporation, 202
Civil Aeronautics Board, 187
Civil Suits. *See* Common Cause. Democrats. Halperin, Morton. McCarthy, Eugene.
Civil War Sudy, 15
Clawson, Ken, W., 8
Clay, Richard, 72
"Cleo," Pirham, 129
Cleveland, Grover, 55
Clifford, Clark, 175
Colby, William E.
Appointment, 46, 60-61
Chilean break-in, 129
CIA memos altered, 239
Ehrlichman meeting, 101
Cole, Kenneth R., 42, 130, 144, 223
Collins, George W. (D Ill.), 84
Colson, Charles W.
Biography, 38-39
Bremer break-in plot, 150
Chappaquiddick probe, 177
CIA memo doctored, 239
Counter-demonstrations, 119
Domestic security meetings, 223
Enemies list, 153
Executive clemency
Denial, 161
Ehrlichman testimony, 215, 231
Hunt attempts, 52-53, 150, 152, 154
Nixon annoyance, 164, 168
Fabricated cables, 31
Haiphong publicity, 23
ITT intervention, 144, 235-236, 243, 268-269
Massachusetts Bar inquiry, 264
Pentagon Papers case
Brookings firebomb plot, 155, 161
FBI interview, 47, 64-65
Grand jury testimony, 137
Plumbers role, 100, 149
SEC appointment role, 90, 144
Staff, 212
Watergate coverup
Advance knowledge alleged, 26, 148
Alerts Nixon, 21
Budget approval pressure, 136
Bugging planning role, 125
Dean, Ehrlichman roles, 112
Dean suspicions, 155
Denies Nixon knowledge, 178
First implicated, 12
Hunt flight plan, 137-138
Sabotage against Democrats, 188
Selected Senate witness, 57
Weicker smear, 159
White House memo, 162
Columbia Broadcasting System. *See* Television.
Commerce Department, 105, 133
Committee, Fair Campaign Practices. *See* Campaign Practices Committee.
Committee for the Re-election of the President. *See* Nixon Re-election Committee.
Committees, House
Armed Services. *See* Intelligence Subcommittee, House.
Banking and Currency
Democrats issue report, 5
Money trust study, 15
Nixon concern, 164
Nixon funds probe rejected, 258
Stans Meeting, 141
Government Operations, 271
Historical investigations, 15
Interstate and Foreign Commerce
Investigations Subcommittee, 90, 144, 177
ITT file removal probe, 90
Judiciary, 28, 147, 161, 258
Post Office, 107
Republican research, 69
Un-American Activities, 190
Ways and Means, 153
Committees, Joint
Executive Privilege and Government Secrecy, 66, 69, 161
Internal Revenue Taxation, 153, 177, 258
Committees, Senate
Appropriations (*see also* Intelligence Operations Subcommittee)
Cox staff, 198
SEC Vesco probe, 67
Armed Services
Army spying, 263
Embassy break-in, 89
Haig appointment, 105, 130
Pressure on CIA to coverup Watergate, 66-67, 85-86, 90, 100, 117, 238
Campaign abuses, 76
Foreign Relations
CIA domestic involvement, 86, 89, 102-103
ITT in Chile, 117, 129
Government Operations, 19, 203
Historical investigations, 15-16
Judiciary
Cox independence, 89
Dean executive privilege, 163, 167
Election reform, 74
Gray confirmation hearings, 11, 165-166, 258
Kleindienst strategy memo, 235
Richardson confirmation hearings, 56, 62, 96, 98
Separation of Powers subcommittee, 103
Special prosecutor, 32, 67-68, 86, 155
Watergate Subcommittee, 258
Rules, 112, 144
Select Watergate Subcommittee. *See* Senate Watergate Subcommittee.
Subcommittee on bugging (1965), 106-107
Common Cause
Civil suit
Defendants named, 19, 21
Nixon-Dean discussion, 158, 164
Overview, 259
Republican funds disclosure efforts, 147, 187, 219
Sloan secret fund deposition, 50
Enemies List, 153
Nixon election reform proposals, 73
Communist Party, U.S.A., 122-125
Congress
Conspiracy laws, 157
Enemies list, 153
White House relations (*see also* Impeachment)
Haig statement, 243
McGovern views, 147
Mansfield statement, 263
Nixon meetings, 131
Staff relations, 130-131
Tapes impact, 191, 241, 224-225
Watergate impact, 33, 90, 127, 258
Connally, John B.
Appointment, 46, 60
Business resignations, 65
Gulf inquiry, 87
Harris poll , 29
Party shift, 56-57
Connolly, Joseph J., 198
Conspiracy, 157
Conspirator Payments. *See* Finances, Republican Campaign Hunt, E. Howard. Kalmbach, Herbert W. White House.
Constitution
Dean-Nixon logs, 120
Dean questioning by Ervin, 159
Election reform, 74-76
Historical perspectives, 171-173
Impeachment, 55
Nixon files dispute, 179, 184, 186, 189-190
Presidency
Resignation, 175
Subpoena, 103, 161, 151
Conyers, John (D Mich.), 153
Cook, G. Bradford
Colson appointment pressure, 90, 144
Resignation, biography, 67-68
SEC Vesco Case, 86
Vesco indictment excerpts, 71-72
Cook, Dick, 164
Coolidge, Calvin, 44
Corruption
History, 15-16, 44-45
Poll, 104
Vice-presidents, 270
Corrupt Practices Act, 187
Costa Rica, 72
Cotton, Norris (R N.H.), 28
Council for Livable World, 153
Cox, Archibald
Agnew dinner, 174
Biography, 96
Campaign finances
Airline contributions, 187
McGovern funds, 264
Oil contribution, 218
Republican cooperation, 241
Vesco case, 90, 106
Conflicts with other probes
Dean evidence folder, 149
Democrats' civil suit, 204
Justice Department, 104, 177
Nixon independence, 89, 107, 120
Second grand jury, 204
Senate hearings, 99, 110-111, 118, 120-121
Senate Watergate TV, 121, 132, 132, 137-138, 140
White House logs, 147-148
ITT probe authority, 137
Special prosecutor, Watergate
ACLU criticism, 150
Authority, 234, 242, 258
Confirmation, 63, 85, 96, 98
LaRue guilty plea, 161
Nixon support, 94
Presidential subpoena, 148
Staff, 198, 202
TV report rebuttal, 178
Weicker smear, 151, 159
Tapes, Records dispute
Access request, 203, 273
Issues, 209
Lawsuit, 208, 212, 219-224, 241
Listening request, 229
Nixon response, 220, 254-255, 264
Senate parallel, 263
Crane, Philip M. (R Ill.), 69
Credit Mobilier, 15, 270
Crime Control, Omnibus and Safe Streets Act, 141
Cuba, 10, 85, 102, 127
Curtis, Carl T. (R Neb.), 27-28, 189
Cushman, Robert E. (Gen. USMC)
CIA aid to Hunt, 100-101, 107
Pentagon Papers probe, 52, 54, 56, 59
Senate Armed Services testimony, 85
Senate Watergate testimony, 238-239, 262

D

Dahlberg, Kenneth H., 5, 127-128, 135, 265-267
Dairy Funds. *See* Finances, Republican Campaign.
Dale, Francis I., 11, 259
Dane, Maxwell, 153
Danielson, George E. (D Calif.), 33
Dash, Samuel
Appointment, 3-4, 48
Biography, 7
Butterfield questioning, 192-193
Committee friction, 46-47
Cox hearings suspension request, 99, 118
Cox tapes suit, 263
Dean-Nixon meetings, 110, 120
Dean questioning, 156
Documents dispute, 188
Ehrlichman questioning, 213-214, 231, 233
ITT memo, 235-236
Magruder questioning, 136
Mitchell questioning, 179-181, 185
Nixon property, 178
White House memo release, 63
Davidoff, Sidney, 153
Davis, Richard J., 198
Davitt, John H., 235
Dean, John W. III
Agency misues, 186
Biography, 38-39
CIA pressure, 217, 229, 239, 264-265
Conspirator bail requests
Haldeman statement, 247-248
Helms testimony, 238-239, 243, 262
Strachan testimony, 210
Criminal prosecution faced, 106, 149, 178
Democrats' civil suit, 204
Documents
Authenticity, 137
Content hinted, 118
Copying restrictions, 151, 175, 189
Removal from White House, 54
Texts, 122-125
Turned over to Sirica, 50, 66-67, 99
White House release to Senate, 157
Ellsberg probe role, 91-94, 137, 147-148
Finances, personal use, 145, 149-150, 215
Gray abandonment, 240
Haldeman discrepancies, 231-232, 242

Dean, John W. III
Hoover assessment, 217
Immunity
Cox evidence, 149
Delay, 107
Federal prosecutors', 47
Limited use, 132, 138, 140
Resignation clause, 154
Role in Senate testimony, 156
Sought by Senate, 47, 53, 67
ITT file removal, 90
Justice Department probe, 233
Nixon Watergate notification, 254
Nixon-Dean meetings
Analysis, 150
Cox log request, 147-148
No Nixon rebuttal, 178
Tapes *(see* Executive Privilege)
Testimony, 152, 154
Perjury, 212
Resignation
Announcement, 24-25, 27-28, 56
FBI files supervision, 30
Nixon statement, 36-37
Personal trust fund, 145
Senate testimony, 154
Successor, 60
Senate Watergate probe
Brezhnev delay, 145
Buzhardt memo, 162-163
Cox limiting efforts, 111, 121, 137-138
Denounced by Scott, 150
Ehrlichman testimony, 208, 213-216, 222-223, 230-231
Evidence doubted, 57
Gray testimony, 255-256, 260, 264-268
Implicated by McCord, 63-64
Kalmbach testimony, 193, 195
Kleindienst, Petersen testimony, 261
La Rue testimony, 199
Leaks, 145, 148-150
Limiting testimony statement, 64
Magruder testimony, 132
Mardian testimony, 200-201
Mitchell testimony, 179-184
Moore testimony, 179, 184-185, 205-207
Named witness, 57
Nixon property, 178
Public testimony, 151-161, 174-177
Statement excerpts, 163-168
Strachan testimony, 227-228
Tapes impact, 191-193, 203
Undercover election activities, 125-126, 134
Vesco case role, 71, 87, 177
Watergate coverup
Asks FBI reports, 148, 113
Bugging planning, 136
CIA involvement efforts, 66-67, 100-102, 117, 126-129
Colson describes role, 112
Conspirator payments, 20, 150, 116, 121, 133
Dean role reported, 31, 87
Disclosure, 25
Ehrlichman role, 150
Hunt clemency, 137-138
Haldeman, Colson bugging roles, 139, 148, 150
McCord clemency, 68, 82-84, 89, 95, 105
News source, 51
Nixon knowledge, 47, 72, 52-53
Nixon meetings, 110, 120-121, 145, 150
Nixon memos, 139
Nixon May 22 statement, 79-80, 91-94, 276-279
Magruder scapegoat fears, 137
Role in resignation, 24-25, 27-28, 56
Sloan silence pressure, 116
Undercover recruiting, 65
White House inquiry, 11, 17-18, 66, 68, 152

Defense Department, 56, 58, 61
Defense Fund, Watergate conspirators *(see also* Finances, Republican Campaign. Dean, John W. III. Kalmbach, Herbert W.), 185, 188
Defense Intelligence Agency, 79-80, 91-94, 122-125, 244
Dellums, Ronald (D Calif), 153
DeLoach, Cartha, 156, 165, 237
Democratic National Committee. *See* Democrats.
Democrats
Civil suits
Cox seeks delay, 204
Delay, 107
Ehrlichman, depositions, 110, 125, 120-121
Haldeman deposition, 110, 113, 137
Harmony perjury alleged, 119
Mardian statement text, 226
1962 election rigged poll, 30
Nixon-Dean discussions, 158, 168
Overview, 11, 17-19, 258-259
Strauss break-in statement, 120, 160
Ziegler records subpoena, 188
Demonstrators, violence, 243, 235-236
Finance records subpoena, 135
Election reform, 73, 75-76
Presidential impeachment, 115
Watergate break-in
Authorization, 125-126, 148
CIA memos, 126
Conspirators, 3
Dean testimony, 153-155
Espionage plans, 112-114
Forewarning, 138
Liddy funding, 136
Mitchell briefing, 132
O'Brien fears, 160
Strachan Haldeman briefing, 146, 148
Wiretap logs, 35-36, 120
Watergate impact
Congressional race, 136
House, 77-78
Strauss counterattack, 106
Democracy. *See* Historical Antecedents.
Demonstrators, 154-155
DeMotte, Clifton, 9
Dennis, David W. (R Ind.), 69
Dent, Harry, 153, 177
Diem, Ngo Dinh *(See also* Destroyed Documents. Gray, L. Patrick III), 22 31, 52, 180
Dixon, Dick, 243
Dixon, Robert G. Jr., 112, 263
Document Destruction
Finance records, 134-135, 140
Hunt papers
Ehrlichman testimony, 215
Gray role, 22-23
Gray testimony, 255-256, 260, 262-263, 267-268
Liddy information, 64, 219
Watergate bugging files
LaRue testimony, 199
McCord FBI laxity charge, 262
Mardian testimony, 201
Strachan role, 212, 219
Wiretap reports, 154-155, 158, 228
Dogole, S. Harrison, 153
Dole, Robert, (R Kan.), 26, 69, 116, 241
Domestic Intelligence *(see also)* Central Intelligence Agency. Federal Bureau of Investigation. Investigations, White House.
Budget, 232
Ellsberg break-in impact, 138
Haldeman testimony, 235, 244
Hoover interview, 217-218
Republican campaign, 154
Special unit
Dean files, 99, 118, 121-125, 137
Dean testimony, 159
FBI probe, 119
Judge approached, 147
McClosky impeachment rationale, 161
Nixon statement, 79-80, 91-92
Student informer use, 138-139
White House document disclosure, 157
Watergate impact, 152
Dorsen, David M., 117
Doyle, Dane and Bernbach, 153
Doyle, James, 198
Dreyfus Corporation, 153
Drinan, Robert F. (D Mass.), 229, 242
Drug Control. *See* Justice Department
Duncan, Walter T., 7
Dyson, Charles, 153

E

Eagleton, Thomas F. (D Mo.), 86-87, 160-161
Eastern Airlines, 187
Eastland, James O. (D Miss.), 62, 268
Eavesdropping. *See* Wiretapping.
Ehrlichman, John D.
Biography, 38-39
Chappaquiddick blackmail plot, 243
CIA coverup role
Pressure alleged, 66-67, 126-128, 239
Denial, 99-102, 107, 149
Criminal investigation, 178, 105
Dean discrepancies, 174-175
Disbarment effort, 174, 259
Domestic intelligence, 121, 147
Eagleton medical records, 86
Ellsberg probe
Aid to Hunt, 107, 145, 160
Break-in planning, 139-141
Brookings plot, 155
Byrne FBI offer, 24, 29, 32, 177
Dean trust, 137
Employs Young, 52
FBI interview, 31-32, 34
Halperin wiretap, 141, 191, 259
Reporter wiretaps, 66, 70
Richardson call, 98
White House probe, 30, 52, 56, 79
Executive clemency, 152, 160, 179-180, 188
Executive privilege, 149
Gray testimony, 255-256, 260, 267-268
Gutter politics scored, 264
Haldeman relationship, 223
Haldeman statement, 244
Hearings strategy, 155, 233
Helms testimony, 238-239
Hoover assessment, 217
Inouye remark, 237
IRS misuses, 87, 153
ITT settlement role, 144
Kalmbach personal loan, testimony, 189, 195-196, 203
Kleindienst, Petersen testimony, 260-261
MacGregor deposition, 236
Moore testimony, 185, 205-206
Named Senate witness, 57
Nixon abandonment, 148
Nixon tapes controversy, 218, 224
Nixon Watergate notification, 254
Resignation
Announcement, 24-25, 27-28, 36-37
Congress impact, 33, 78
Dean testimony, 154
FBI supervises files, 30
Impact on White House staff, 42, 56, 60-61, 108
Nixon acceptance, 35
Nixon meeting, 26
Replacement, 121, 130
Securities and Exchange Commission intervention, 144
Senate Watergate probe
Interview, 189
Statement, 221-224
Testimony, 212-220, 229-233, 239-240
Vesco role, 24-25
Watergate coverup
Watergate coverup
Anxiety, 21-22
Bugging planning, 189
CIA meetings, 117
Civil suit deposition, 110, 120-121, 125-126
Colson links to Dean, 112
Conspirator payments, 138, 150, 166-167, 188-189
Dean report denied, 155
Dean account, 25, 50, 150, 164-168
Denies wrongdoing, 31, 68, 177
Document destruction role, 22
Hunt clemency, 52-53, 137-138, 150
Implicated, 31
Indictment predicted, 106
Liddy payment, 116
McCord clemency, 89, 83
Mitchell testimony, 181
Suspension urged, 160
White House memo, 162-163
Eisenhower, Dwight D., 44-45, 74
Eisenhower, Julie Nixon, 174, 178
Election Reform
History, 74, 171
House proposals, 78
Nixon commission proposals, 67-69, 73, 75-76, 93-94
Reform suggestions, 73-75
Senate action, 112, 144
Sloan views, 115
Elections *(see also* Espionage)
Campaign spying, 114, 120, 146
Finances *(see also* Finances, Republican Campaign)
Common Cause records subpoenas, 147
Fair Campaign Practices report, 105
Foreign donations, 139
Humphrey primary, 69, 137
McCarthy civil suit, 87
Montoya, 161, 177
Republican spending, 133
Senate subpoenas of Democrats' records, 146
Stans statement, 142-143
Historical perspectives, 171
McGovern wrongdoing denial, 160
Watergate impact
CIA memos, 126-129
Mitchell silence, 182-183
Wiretapping, 120
Electronic Surveillance. *See* Wiretapping. Espionage.
Ellsberg, Daniel *(see also* Pentagon Papers.)
Break-in
CIA memos, 54, 59
CIA, White House roles, 100-101, 152
Coverup attempts, 64-65, 47
Ehrlichman testimony, 212-214, 219, 240
Files theft, *(see also* Investigations, Federal Grand Jury), 20 107, 118-119, 121
Haldeman role, 105
Krogh role, 52
LaRue testimony, 199
Nixon statements, 91-94, 279
Richardson role, 96
Government secrecy testimony, 66, 69
Pentagon Papers trial
CIA memos, 59
Dismissal of charges, 46, 70, 121, 155

Ruckelshaus wiretap memo, 70
Personality profile, 215, 239, 262
Soviet papers acquisition, 240, 219
White House probe
Basis of dismissal of charges, 30-32
Hunt hush money, 145, 160
Wiretapping, 191
Ellsberg, Patricia, 31-32
Embassy Wiretapping. *See* Wiretapping.
Employment Vacancies, White House (*see also* White House), 26.
Environmental Protection Agency, 25, 45.
Erickson, William, 67
Ervin, Joseph Wilson, 84
Ervin, Sam J. Jr. (D N.C.)
Bellino probe, 262
Biography, 6
Committee funding, 23
Executive Privilege
Early statements, 19, 167, 159
Nixon files, testimony dispute, 179-186, 188-190, 202
Nixon records request, 225-229
Nixon tapes access, 232-235, 233, 239, 241
Nixon tapes refusal letters, 186, 191, 195-196, 203, 211, 219-220
Nixon telephone call, 218
Presidential power, 216
Telephone hoax, 191, 217
White House 'colludin' (should be 'canodelin'), 233-235, 242
Haldeman assessment, 12
Justice Department probe, 87-89
Senate Watergate probe
Alch questioning, 84-85
Brezhnev delay, 145, 148
Campaign records destruction, 134-135
Closes hearings, 254, 264
Cox probe conflicts (*see* Cox, Archibald)
Dean documents, 99, 118, 151, 175
Dean leaks, 145, 149
Democrats funds records, 146
Ellsberg probe, 138
Evidence, 105
Disbarment information, 174
Domestic intelligence papers, 157
Ehrlichman questioning, 214
FBI data, 164
Gurney exchange, 135, 140
Liddy ruling, 32, 114
McCord testimony, 84-85, 64
McGovern testimony offer, 160
Moore questioning, 192
Nixon-Dean conflict, 151
Nixon records subpoena, resolution, 208-212, 218-220, 225
Opens hearings, 62-63, 69
Petersen questioning, 261
Presidential subpoena, 103, 176
Scored by Butz, 65
Stans Vesco prejudice, 133-134
Wilson conflict, 219
Special prosecutor authority, 62
Espionage
Alioto charges, 148
1960 campaign, 219, 241
1968 campaign, 164
1972 campaign
Abductions, call girls, 136
Allegations, 8
Army role, 263
"Black advance," 201
California fund, 21
CIA memos, 126-127
Cox probe, 146
Democratic conduct, 160
Ehrlichman testimony, 230
Financing, 21, 133, 140, 180, 188
Haldeman testimony, 244-245
Government agency plan, 89
Greenspun burglary, 82
Humphrey infiltration, (*see also* Muskie, Edmund), 114, 146, 160-161
Nixon May 22 statement, 91-94
Opinion poll, 263-264
Sedan chair, 160-161
Segretti role, 202
Strachan role, 208, 210, 212, 227-228
Student use, 9, 22, 122, 144
Weathermen, 121
Wiretaps authorization, 121
Weicker smear, 151, 159
Evans, Daniel J. (R Wash.-Gov.), 29
Evans, Rowland, 134
Executive Clemency
Dean-Nixon meetings, 119, 231
Denials, 91-94, 192-193
Hunt attempts
Colson disclosure, 150
Dean testimony, 152
Ehrlichman role denial, 179-180, 188, 215, 219
Hunt promise, 202
Nixon discussion, 165-166, 168
Kleindienst testimony, 261
McCord offer
Alch testimony, 84
Caulfield testimony, 82-83, 89
Dean linked, 105
McCord testimony, 63-64, 80, 87, 94-95
Executive Privilege
Ehrlichman, 189, 216-217
Immunity, 53
IRS suit, 203-204
Mitchell interpretation, 167, 183-184
Nixon records, tapes dispute
'Colludin' ('canoodelin') charge, 233-234, 242
Cox letter, Wright reply, 224-225
Ehrlichman interview, 218
Haig statement, 254, 263
Haldeman testimony, 229, 231-235, 237, 250-253
Issues, 209
Laird advice, 240
Lawsuits, 208, 216, 219-220
Nixon stand, 209
Nixon response to Cox, 254-255, 264
Nixon letters, 220, 225
Nixon stand, 209
Nixon statements, 219, 272, 275-280
Petersen listening offer, 261
Phone hoax, 217, 191
Senate denial response, resolution, 209, 225-226
Supreme Court role, 239, 241
White House, Cox court memos, 254-255, 264, 273
Pre-election concern, 164
Sloan position, 116
White House guidelines
Allowing testimony, 50
Baker criticism, 148
Early position, 12, 17-18, 19, 47
Nixon-Dean logs, 120
Nixon May 22 statement, 80
Presidential subpoena, 103, 151, 176, 190

F

Fair Campaign Practices Committee, 105
Federal Aviation Administration, 191
Federal Bureau of Investigation (*see also* Investigations, FBI)
Congressional probes, 147, 258
Domestic espionage plan, 89, 121-125
Ellsberg trial
Byrne offer, 177
Colson interview, 47
Ehrlichman interview, 34
Reporter wiretaps, 66
Ruckelshaus statement, 69-70
Secret White House probe, 30, 46, 70, 241
Executive privilege guidelines, 47
Gray resignation. *See* Gray, L. Patrick III.
Halperin suit, 141
Kelley appointment, 121
Ruckelshaus appointment, 25, 43
Schorr probe, 157
Violence files, 235
Watergate probe
Buzhardt memo, 162-163
Document destruction, 215
Files availability, 47-48, 164
Gray warning, 66
Kleindienst, Petersen testimony, 261
Mexican bank inquiry, 67, 256
White House pressure, 247-248
White House misuse, 139, 158, 165, 237
Federal Election Campaign Act
Agnew dinner, 186
GAO charges, 5, 8, 25
Humphrey donation, 69, 137
Senate hearings, 63
Stans statement, 142-143
Vesco role, 31, 140, 150, 259
Federal Grand Jury. (*See* Investigations, Federal Grand Jury.)
Federini. (*See* Sturgis, Frank)
Feld, Bernard T., 153
Felt, W. Mark, 241, 265
Fensterwald, Bernard W., 14, 83-85 90, 106-107
Fernandez, Pablo, 105
Fielding, Fred F., 87, 154
Figueres, Jose, 72
Finances, Republican Campaign (*see also* Nixon Re-election Committee. Election Reform.)
Agnew dinner
GAO report, 174
Indictment, 149
Irregularities, 115, 121, 135, 140
Conspirator payments
Ehrlichman denial of wrongdoing, 214, 216
Haldeman-Dean discrepancy, 231
Kalmbach testimony, 192-193, 195-197
LaRue testimony, 199-201
Civil suits, 219, 259
Corporate donations
American Airlines, 186-187, 202
Ashland, 218
Cox cooperation, 241
Dairy funds, 119, 139, 264
Dean personal use, 145, 149-150
Disbursements, 114-116
Donation to William Mills, 84, 90
Espionage, 232
Foreign donations, 133, 139
Gulf inquiry, 87
Irregularities, various, 25, 117
IRS asked to seize assets, 188
Mexican bank inquiry
Early developments, 100-102, 117, 126-127
Gray, Walters testimony, 256, 264-266
Stans defense, 133
Nixon property, 178, 271
Secret funds
California fund, 21
Early developments, 3-4, 73
Haldeman deposition, 110-112
Indictment, fine, 4-5
Senate subpoenas, 140
Sloan deposition, 50
Records subpoenas, 128-129, 147
Senate Watergate probe
Disbursements revealed, 132-135, 139-143
Document destruction, 134-135
GAO dispute, 140
Stans statement, 141-143
Smith donation, 119
Stone contribution, 202
Teamsters fundraising role, 178
Wallace probe, 242-243
Vesco donation
Charges filed, 31, 25
Conviction, 140, 150, 259
Cox probe, 146
Indictments, 46, 71-72
Pleas, 46, 65
Finch, Robert, 42
Flanigan, Peter, 153
Force, Helen, 72
Ford, Gerald R. (R Mich.), 27, 77, 131, 241
Frenzel, Bill (R Minn.), 69
Frey, Louis Jr. (R Fla.), 69
Froehlich, Harold V. (R Wis.), 69
Fulbright, J. W. (D Ark.), 68, 175

G

Gagliardi, Lee P., 112, 137, 263
Gallup Poll. (*See* Polls.)
Gardner, John W., 19, 73
Garment, Leonard
Appointment, 24-25, 36-37, 42, 130
Briefing, Nixon May 22 statement, 88-89
Biography, 43
Camp David meeting, 26
Domestic intelligence, 157
Election reform, 73
Executive privilege, 73
Resignation letters draft, 168
Special prosecutor suggestion, 67
Tapes subpoena, 212
Gayler, Adm. Noel, 88, 91-94, 123
Gemstone. (*See* Operation Gemstone)
Geneen, Harold S., 144
General Accounting Office. (*See* Investigations, GAO)
General Services Administration, 271
Glanzer, Seymour, 89, 104, 120, 177-178
Gettys, Tom S. (D S.C.), 33
Gleason, Jack, 177
Globe Security Systems, 153
Godwin, Mills E., 241
Goldwater, Barry (R Ariz.), 14, 26-27 69, 86
Gonzalez, Virgilio R., 4, 9-12, 105, 202
Gorton, George K., 22-23, 41
Government Services Administration, 109
Governors, Watergate Impact, 29, 120
Graham, Billy, 236, 243
Graham, Katharine, 241
Gravel, Mike (D Alaska), 98
Gray, L. Patrick III
Confirmation hearings, 11, 163, 165-166, 240
Document destruction, 22-23, 31, 215
Indictment evidence, 178
Resignation, 22-23, 42-43, 56, 121
Senate Watergate probe
Haldeman testimony, 235
Named witness, 57
Statement text, 264-268
Testimony, 229, 255-257, 260, 262-263
Walters testimony, 229
White House coverup pressure
Allegations, 66, 86, 100-102
CIA memos, 110, 126-129
Cushman, Helms testimony, 238-239
FBI reports access, 165, 148
McCord memo, 57-58
MacGregor deposition, 236
Misled by Dean, 163
Nixon knowledge, 65, 79, 93, 104
Post-burglary warning, 66
Volunteers testimony, 139
Greenspun, Hank, 82
Gregory, Thomas J., 10

Gross, H.R. (R Iowa), 115
Guido, Kenneth Jr., 21
Gulf Resources and Chemical Corp. (*see also* investigations, Federal Grand Jury), 65, 87, 117
Gun Control, 114
Gurney, Edward J. (R Fla.)
Bellino probe, 262
Biography, 6
Criticism of hearings, 99, 107, 118
Dean questioning, 158, 161, 176
Ehrlichman questioning, 230
Ellsberg probe, 138
Executive clemency, 215
ITT memo protest, 236
Kalmbach questioning, 196
Moore questioning, 192
Nixon assessment, 164
Nixon friends funds, 178
Stans questioning, 135, 140
Guthman, Ed 153

H

Haig, Alexander M. Jr.
Appointment, 24
Army conflict, 105, 110, 121, 130-131
Biography, 53
Congressional rapprochement, 243
Halperin suit, 141, 259
Special prosecutor suggestion, 67
White House duties, 108
Haiphong Publicity, 22, 64
Haldeman, H.R.
Biography, 38-40
Campaign sabotage
Advance break-in knowledge, 136, 148
Authorization, 188
Dean assessment, 154-155
Ehrlichman statement, 223
Funding (*see also* Finances, Republican Campaign), 8, 13, 133
Gemstone memos, 114
Kennedy, 155-156
McGovern illegitimate child plot, 243-244
1962 Nixon campaign, 30
Scope, 32
Segretti, 202
Wiretap contents, 120, 156
Campaign spending, 133
CIA coverup pressure
Allegations, 66-67, 86, 89
Denial, 99-102, 107
Intelligence plans, 112
Criminal investigation, 178 (*see also* Ellsberg, Daniel)
Ellsberg probe, 91-94, 105, 137
Executive clemency, 215
Executive privilege impact, 149
Halperin suit, 259
Hoover assessment, 217
Intelligence files, 212
ITT memo, 235
Kennedy-Kopechne probe, 243
National security, 141, 210
Resignation
Announcement, 24-25, 27-28,36-37
Congress impact, 33, 78
Dean Testimony, 154
FBI file supervision, 30
Haig replacement, 53
Nixon meeting, 26
Nixon TV speech, 35
White House staff impact, 42, 56, 60-61
Senate Watergate probe
Buzhardt memo, 162-163
Dean contradictions, 174-175
Helms, Cushman testimony, 238-239
Implicated by Magruder, 132, 136-137
Moore statement, 205-206
Named witness, 57
Nixon abandonment, 148
Nixon tapes controversy, 194, 209, 224
Odle testimony, 63
Squelching efforts, 155
Statement text, 244-253
Strachan role, 219, 227-228
Testimony, 229, 231-237, 242-243
Watergate role
CIA pressure, 117, 126-218
Dean account, 25, 50, 139, 150
Dean inquiry, 230
Dean testimony, 152, 158-159, 163-168
Defendants' payments, 138, 150, 166-167
Denial, 146
Deposition on Nixon concern, 110, 113, 137
Document destruction, 155
Implicated, 31
Indictment predicted, 106
Kleindienst, Petersen testimony, 261
Mitchell role, 177, 181
Nixon May 22 statement, 79-80
Nixon meetings, 158-159
Sloan perjury attempts, 118
Strachan role, 146, 148, 178
White House staff
Organization role, 108, 212, 223
Suspension urged, 160, 233
Halperin, Morton
Enemies list, 153
Ruckelshaus statement, 70
Wiretapped, 132, 141, 191, 259
Harding, Warren G. *See* Teapot Dome.
Harlow, Bryce, 223, 241
Harmony, Sally, 57, 112, 114, 119-120
Hart, Gary, 112
Hart, George L., 150
Hart, Philip A. (D Mich.), 32, 56, 62
Hartford Fire Insurance Co. *See* International Telephone and Telegraph Corp.
Hastings, James F. (R N.Y.), 69
Hayes, Rutherford B., 74
Health, Education and Welfare Department, 42-43
Hearing, George, 69, 147, 258
Helms, Richard M.
Caulfield letter, 80, 82
CIA memos, 126-128
Dean documents, 122-125
Ehrlichman, Haldeman pressure, 101-103, 117
Gray visit, 267
Haldeman testimony, 235
McCord memo, 58
Nixon May 22 statement, 91-92
Senate testimony
Other, 85-86
Select Watergate, 229, 238-239, 243, 262
White House coverup pressure, 66, 68, 89, 101-103
Hersh, Seymour, 129
Heymann, Philip B., 107, 198
Hickel, Walter J., 131, 174
Higby, Lawrence M., 155-156, 194, 197, 228
Historical Antecedents, 15-16, 44-45 55, 169-173, 270
Hitt, Robert J., 84, 115
Hoback, Judy, 141-142
Hoffa, James R., 68, 178
Holton, Linwood (R Va.-Gov.), 120
Hoover, Herbert, 55
Hoover, J. Edgar
Domestic intelligence plans
First disclosed, 70, 80, 88-89, 91
Haldeman statement text, 244
Opposition, 119, 121-125
Students, 138-139
Ellsberg probe, 213, 215-218
1968 campaign spying, 164
White House FBI misuse, 158
House of Representatives
Election reform, 73-76
Impeachment
Drinan resolution, 229, 243
McCloskey effort, 110, 115, 119, 121, 161
Poll, 104, 136
Powers, 55, 103
Proceedings, 132, 140
Republican Conference, 138
Watergate impact, 77-78
Howard, W. Richard, 119, 209
Hughes, Harold E. (D Iowa), 98
Hughes, Howard, 82
Hughes, Phillip S., 14, 140
Humphrey, Hubert H. (D Minn.)
Campaign donations, 69, 137
Campaign sabotaged
Allegations, 65
Phony letter, 25, 232
"Sedan Chair," 114, 146, 160-161, 210
Enemies list role, 153
Popularity poll, 149
Records subpoena, 146
Hundley, William G., 20, 177, 189
Hungate, William L. (D Mo.), 19
Hunt, Dorothy
Death, 40, 105, 215
McCord memo, 58
Money conduit, 14, 40, 195, 197
Ulasewicz testimony, 200
Hunt, E. Howard
Biography, 38, 40
Blackmail attempts
Dean requests, 132, 145, 150, 165-166, 179
Haldeman testimony, 231, 251-253
Mirchell denial, 181
Moore testimony, 184-185
Other conspirators, 188
CIA aid, 161, 238-239, 256, 266-267
Document destruction, 22, 215
Democrats civil suits, 258
Ellsberg break-in
Barker role, 85
Burglary role, 29, 52-53
CIA cooperation, 54, 56, 107, 128-129
CIA memos, 54, 59
Dean testimony, 155
Ehrlichman testimony, 213
Grand jury probe, 118-119
Plumbers, 30-23, 216
Nixon May 22 statement, 91-94
White House backing, 50
Executive clemency
Attempts, 52-53, 84, 150, 152
Colson denial, 161
Dean-Nixon meetings, 154, 160, 165-166, 168
Ehrlichman role, 179-180, 188, 215, 129
Flight plan, 112, 137-138
Other defendants, 202
Indicted, 1-10, 4, 12
ITT affair, 144
Jail transfer, 105
Kennedy probe, 177
McCord suit, 20
Mexican bank inquiry, 256
Phony cables
Authorization, 53-54
Colson confirmation, 31
Mitchell silence, 180
Destruction, 215, 255-256, 260, 262-263, 267-268
Undercover activities
Assassination plot, 139
Bremer break-in plot, 150
Code name, 195
McCord memo testimony, 57-59, 64, 94-95
Moore statement, 207
Hunt, John E. (R N.J.), 69
Huston, Tom Charles
Buzhardt memo, 162-163
Intelligence plan
Disclosure, 89, 121, 124-125, 188
Haldeman denial, 235, 244
Hutchinson, Edward (R Mich.), 69
Hyde, Eveline M. 119, 141-142

I

Immunity
Cox view, 111, 121, 149
Dean
Attempts, 53, 107, 132, 138, 140
Role in testimony, 119, 156, 167
Gray, 139
Magruder, 107, 132, 138, 140
Nixon-Dean-Ehrlichman meeting, 230
Other conspirators, 12, 65, 68, 178
Prosecutors' recommendations, 178
Richardson remarks, 62
Vesco attempt, 65
Impeachment (*see also* House)
Cox study, 148
Drinan resolution, 229, 242
Historical background, 55
Intelligence unit role, 161
McCloskey effort, 110, 115, 119, 121
McCord memo, 58
Mansfield warning, 180, 188
Poll, 149
Resignation, 175
Talmadge statement, 263
Inouye, Daniel K. (D Hawaii)
Bellino probe, 262
Biography, 6
Buzhardt memo, 157-160
Democrats, 85
Ehrlichman questioning, remark, 215, 263
Enemies list, 175
Haldeman questioning, 237
LaRue questioning, 201
Nixon tapes, 202, 233
Wilson insult, 229, 238, 263
Intelligence Evaluation Committee, 91-94, 107, 244
Intelligence Operations Subcommittee, Senate
Bugging motives memos, 117, 120, 126-129
CIA pressured by White House
Allegations, 66, 68, 86, 89-90, 100
White House memo impact, 160-161
Colson role, 149
Ellsberg break-in, 112, 137, 140-141
Gray warning, 104
Haldeman, Ehrlichman testimony, 99-102, 107
Kennedy probe, 177
Intelligence Subcommittee, House
Dean silence, 217
Intelligence plan, 188
Krogh silence, 203
Liddy silence, 218, 240, 242-243
Young silence, 204
Interagency Committee on Intelligence, 124
Interagency Group on Domestic Intelligence and Internal Security. *See* Domestic Intelligence.
Internal Revenue Service
Audit harassment
Dean testimony, 151
Enemies list, 153
Haldeman testimony, 237
Nixon concern, 164
Reporters (*see also* Press), 145, 157, 177
Congressional probes, 153, 177, 258
Joint security agency, 124-125
Republican campaign finances (*see also* Finances, Republican Campaign), 188
Tax exemption suit, 186, 203-204

International Telephone and Telegraph Corporation
Antitrust action urged, 262
Colson settlement role
Background, 90, 144
Memo impact, 229, 235-236, 243
Memo text, 268-269
Cox inquiry authority, 137, 146
Kleindienst role denial, 26
Liddy, Beard activities, 120, 180
SEC file removal, 90
Senate inquiry, 117, 128
Intra Bank. *See* Vesco, Robert L.
Investigations, FBI
Ellsberg
Byrne ruling, 46, 70
Ehrlichman, Hunt, Liddy roles, 24, 139, 213, 215-218
Soviet papers copies, 120
Wiretaps, 191
Kennedy, Kopechne, 156
National security
Dean documents, 119
Kissinger wiretaps *(see also* Kissinger, Henry A. National Security), 107
Newspaper break-in, 107, 119
Nixon May 22 statement, 79-80, 91-94
Republican finances, 119
Watergate
CIA memos, 110, 117, 120, 126-129
Conflicts with other probes, 47-48
Dean role, 148, 158, 216, 232
Ehrlichman testimony, 214
Gray warnings, 65-66, 104
Haldeman testimony, 235
Helms testimony, 243
Leaks, 128; role, 4.,
Liddy perjury payment, 118
McCord laxity charge 260, 262
Mardian testimony, 201
Schultz phone hoax, 191
Segretti-Hunt calls, 9
Senate report, 165
White House resistance, 11, 67, 100-103, 117
Investigations, Federal Grand Jury
Agnew dinner
Hearings, 115, 121, 135, 140
Indictment, 149
Overview, 258
Elections, Second, 204
Ellsberg break-in
Burglary authorization, 50
Busch statement, 219
CIA, Hunt role, 107
Cox cooperation, 118-119
Ehrlichman, Colson testify, 137
Ellsberg testimony, 121
Hunt cables, 53
Krogh, Young silence, 132, 137
Impaneled, 56
White House pressure, 219, 240
Florida, 54, 69, 147, 258
General history, 54
Houston, 87, 117, 258
Vesco
Cook role, 67
Indictments, 46, 56, 71-72
Nixon concern, 164
Overview, 258
Pretrial publicity, 148, 188
Secret contribution, 21-22, 54
Stans Senate appearance, 112, 132-134, 137
Trial date, 107
Vesco subpoena *(see also* Vesco, Robert L.), 50, 65, 89
Watergate *(see also* Sirica, John J. Immunity. Perjury)
ACLU criticism, 150
Break-in, 3-4, 12
Conflict with other probes *(see also* Cox, Archibald), 47-48
Conspirator payments, 107, 110, 117-118
Coverup fund, 26-27
Dean role, 66-67, 158, 167-168, 216
Dean offer, 106, 139
Executive privilege, 47, 149
Gray volunteers testimony, 139
Immunity, 12
Indictments report, 31, 104, 106 178
Kalmbach perjury, 230-231
McCord memo, 57-59
Overview, 258
Porter perjury, 178
Private testimony, 156
Presidential subpoena, 103, 106
Prosecutors' withdrawal, 177
White House restraints, 105
Investigations, General Accounting Office
Agnew dinner, 174, 186
Conspirator payments, 87, 138
Foreign coverup funds, 139
Irregularities, 4-5
Mills donation, 84, 90
Post-election report, 138
Republican finances, overview, 259
Sloan charged, 25
Vesco donation, 7-8, 31, 259
Investigations, Historical, 15-16
Investigations, House. *See* Committees, House.
Investigations, Senate. *See* Committees, Senate.
Investigations, Justice Department
Ellsberg
Break-in planning, 30, 139-140
Hunt silence money, 145, 160
Learned of incident, 189
Nixon role, 147-148, 261
IRS misuse, 186
Kennedy, Kopechne, 156
Republican finances, 143
Vesco. *See* Finances, Republican Campaign.
Watergate
Cox probe, 259
Criticized by Ervin, 87-89
Ehrlichman testimony, 217
Nixon influence, 115
Petersen role, 156
Segretti role, 9
Senate probe, 52, 160
Investigations, White House
Plumbers *(see also* Ehrlichman, John D. Krogh, Egil Jr. Young, David)
Break-in scope, 120
Buzhardt memo, 162-163
CIA pressured, 149
Dean testimony, 155
Ehrlichman, Haldeman evidence, 105, 101-102
Ellsberg break-in role, 53
Haldeman statement, 244
Huston description, 119, 121
Nixon May 22 statement, 79-80
Richardson confirmation role, 98
Wiretapping, 47, 69-70, 141
Watergate
Dean role, 230-234
Dean testimony, 152, 154-155
Dean-Nixon phone call, 139
Dean-Nixon meetings *(see also* Executive Privilege), 66, 68, 110, 120-121
Nixon involvement denial, 11
Nixon April, May statements, 17-18, 34-35, 91-94

J

Jackson, Andrew, 74
Jackson, Henry M. (D Wash.)
Aide on enemies list, 153
Campaign sabotaged *(see also* Espionage), 9, 25
Records subpoenaed, 146
Schlesinger statement, 80
Wiretap inquiry, 203
Jefferson, Thomas, 208-209
Johnson, Andrew, 55, 74
Johnson, Lyndon B.
Various matters, 68, 74, 96
White House tapes, 192-193, 204
Johnson, Wallace H. Jr., 148
Jones, Jerry, 90, 144
Jones, Thomas V., 195, 197
Justice, Code, 157
Justice Department *(see also* Investigations, Justice Department)
Congressional probe, 258
Campaign contributions, 7-8
Ellsberg case
Burglary files release, 32, 56
Dismissal, 70-71
Liddy, Hunt documents, 155
New guidelines, 243
Intelligence Evaluation Committee, 91-94, 107
IRS Suit, 203-204
ITT antitrust suit. *(see also* International Telephone and Telegraph.)
Mitchell's tenure, 63, 68, 138
Narcotics control, 124-125
National security, 69, 91-94, 107, 235
Nixon tapes subpoenas, 263
Staff
House probe, 147
Kleindienst resgination, 26
Richardson appointment, 36-37, 42-43, 62
Richardson confirmation, 90, 96, 98
Special prosecutor impact, 89, 96-98, 120, 261
Vesco case, *(see also* Vesco, Robert L. Investigations, Federal Grand Jury), 25, 21, 240
Watergate impact
ACLU criticism, 150
Cox reports, 118
Immunity delay, 62, 107, 111, 121
Petersen defense, 254-255
Strachan delay, 148
White House pressure, 129

K

Kalb, Marvin, 241
Kalmbach, Herbert W.
Biography, 38-40
Conspirator payments
Allegations, 87, 133, 152, 176
Ehrlichman role, 188, 214, 216
Haldeman testimony, 232
La Rue, Ulasewicz testimony, 199-201
Mitchell testimony, 181
Segretti payments, 9
Corporation donations, 187, 202, 218
Criminal probe, 138, 178
Disbarment effort, 174, 259
Ehrlichman personal loan, 189
McCarthy suit, 87, 259
Perjury request, 230-231
Republican finances misuse
California fund, 21
Dean role, 162
Coverup fund, 26-27
Federal probe, 65
Haldeman statement, 244-245
Senate Watergate probe
Named witness, 57
Statement, 204-205
Testimony, 192-193, 195-197, 203
Keating, William J. (R Ohio), 69
Kefauver, Estes (D Tenn.), 16, 68
Kehrli, Bruce A., 32, 64, 69, 209
Kendall, Donald, 237, 165
Kelley, Clarence M., 121
Kennedy, Edward M. (D Mass.)
Chappaquiddick aftermath, 215, 263, 243
Enemies list, 153
Hunt probe, 9, 22, 177
Mitchell questioning, 182
Political espionage, 230, 236
Popularity, 29, 240
Richardson confirmation, 62
Watergate impact, 144
White House surveillance, 155-156 212, 237
Kennedy, John F. *(see also* Document Destruction, Hunt, E. Howard Jr.)
Cox solicitor general, 96
Fabricated cables, 22, 31, 53, 180
History of caucus room, 68
Taped conversations, 203
Kennedy, Robert F., 68
Kennedy, Rose, 243
Kissinger, Henry A.
Demonstrations impact, 223
Executive clemency meeting, 215
Foreign aid briefing, 78
Security leaks
Employed Young, 52
Halperin suit, 132, 141, 259
Source, 87
Wiretapping of aides, 69, 107, 120, 214
Watergate remarks, 21
Klein, Herbert, 121, 130-131, 160
Kleindienst, Richard G.
Attorney general hearings, 182
Beard ITT memo, 144
Colson ITT memo, 235
Ellsberg break-in, 92
Kennedy probe, 156
Resignation, 24-28, 36-37, 56
Threatens Washington Post, 241
Vesco case, 31
Watergate coverup
Buzhardt memo, 162
Ehrlichman testimony, 216
Gray testimony, 260
Investigation statements, 9, 11, 22
Mardian testimony, 201
Nixon meetings, 164, 167-168
Nixon notification, 161, 254
Suspension urged, Haldeman, Ehrlichman, 160
Testimony, 254, 260-261, 264
White House pressure on FBI, 128-129
Kopechne, Mary Jo, 156, 243, 263
Kraft, Joseph, 155
Kreindler, Peter M., 198
Krogh, Egil Jr.
Biography, 52
Congressional silence, 203
Ellsberg Break-in
Dean account, 147-148, 155
Ehrlichman testimony, 213-217
Grand jury silence, 132, 137, 174, 186
Implicated, 31-32, 50
Memo, 140
Nixon May 22 statement, 79-80, 91-94
Responsibility, 52
confirms role, 89, 98
Richardson confirmation
Soviet papers copies, 120
Plumbers resignation, 54, 56

L

Lacovara, Philip A. 198
Labor Department, 178
Laird, Melvin R.
Appointment, 110, 130-131, 121
Earlier Housecleaning offer, 22, 42
Nixon questioning, 174, 177
Tapes release advice, 240-241
Lambert, Samuel M., 153
Lambert, William, 31
Landau, Jack C., 68
Landgrebe, Earl F. (R Ind.), 115
Lankler, Alexander M., 115, 121, 149, 174

LaRue, Frederick C.
Break-in knowledge, 134
Bugging planning, 125-126
Campaign spy, 210
Cash transfers, 14, 228, 245
Conspirator payments, 21, 107, 116, 121
Colson role, 26
Dahlberg check, 135
Guilty plea, 161
Liddy role, 181, 183, 185
Implicated, 31
Silence money, 160, 193, 195
Senate witness, 57
Testimony, 197, 199, 201, 203-204
Las Vegas Sun (*see also* Press), 82
Lasky, Victor, 115
Lawrence, John F., 13
Lawyers. *See* Bar Associations.
Leaks, (*See also* Investigations), 11, 20-22, 53, 91-94, 101
LeBlanc, Norman P., 106
Leeper, Paul, 57, 64, 69
Lehigh Valley Cooperative Farmers, 119
Liddy, G. Gordon
Biography, 38, 40
Burglary involvement, 29, 52, 30, 61
CIA memos, 59
Civil suits, 20, 47, 119, 258
Criminal indictment (*see also* Immunity) 4, 9-11
Dean testimony, 155
Ehrlichman testimony, 213
Ellsberg break-in (*see also* Investigations, White House)
LaRue testimony, 199
Nixon approval alleged, 120
Nixon May 22 statement, 91-94
Plumbers, 31, 216
ITT role, 120, 180
Political intelligence, 219, 230
Refuses testimony
Contempt of Congress, 218, 240, 242-243
Federal grand jury, 12
Senate committee, 57, 114, 120
Undercover activities
Bugging plans, 125-126, 136-137
Buzhardt memo, 162-163
Call girls plot, 136, 154
CIA pressure, 256, 266-267
Conspirator payments, 133-134
Document destruction, 134-135, 140
Gemstone, 112-114
Greenspun burglary plan, 82
LaRue, Mardian testimony, 199, 201
Magruder assessment, 118, 212
Mitchell testimony, 180-181, 183-185
Moore statement, 206-207
Nixon scapegoat, 152, 162-163, 167-168
Odle testimony, 64
Reporter wiretaps, 32
Stans statement, 143
Lie Detector, 84-85, 90
Lincoln, Abraham, 176
Lindsay, John, 153
Lipset, Harold K., 19
Loeb, John L., 69, 137
Los Angeles Times (*See also* Press), 13, 153
Lott, Trent (R Miss.), 69
Lowenstein, Allard, 153
Lucey, Patrick J. (D Wis.-Gov.), 120
Lynn, James T., 60-61

M

McBride, Thomas F., 118, 198
McCandless, Robert C., 20, 203
McCarthy, Eugene, 87, 259, 153
McCarthy, Joseph R., 16, 68
McClellan, John L. (D Ark.), 66, 68, 90, 104, 149
McCloskey, Paul N. (R Calif.)
Impeachment attempts, 110, 115, 119 121
Senate information, 161
Nixon Committee donation, 134
White House staff remark, 130
McCord, James W.
Biography, 38, 40
CIA defense, 53-54, 89, 160,
Civil suits, 20, 259
Criminal trial
Convicted, 4, 911, 203
Letter, 152, 154
New trial motion, 150
Sentencing postponed, 132, 137
Testimony, federal grand jury, 14
Executive clemency
Dean role, 68, 105
Offer, 87, 89-98
FBI probe criticism, 262, 260
Senate Watergate probe (*see also* Alch, Gerald. Immunity)
Baldwin recruiting, 85
May 18 statement, 94-95
Memo, 57-59
Nixon blame, 120
McGovern, George
Campaign sabotaged
Army role, 263
Bugging, 125-126
Illegitimate child allegation, 243-244
Infiltration, 160-161, 212
Nixon committee donation, 134
Spying, 32, 112, 114, 155
Democrats' tactics, 160
Demonstrations memo, 236-237
Finances, 146, 264
Nixon Apr. 30 speech, 27
Popularity, 149
Watergate impact, 12, 147
MacGregor, Clark
Coverup ignorance, 137, 156
Deposition, 236, 241
Ehrlichman concern, 22
Ehrlichman meetings, 223
Haldeman remarks, 233
Intelligence memos, 114
Press criticism, 13
Secret fund, 8
McGrory, Mary, 153
McIntyre, Thomas J. (D N.H.), 130
McMinoway, Michael W., 146, 160-161
McPhee, H. Roemer, 186
Magruder, Jeb Stuart
Biography, 38, 40
Civil suits, 20, 259
Criminal probe (*see also* Immunity. Investigations. Federal Grand Jury)
Evidence, 106, 178
Government witness, 79, 104
Perjury, 152, 166
Testimony, 10
White House coaching, 158
Coverup role
Break-in knowledge, 134
Buzhardt memo, 162-163
Colson implicated, 26
Commerce funds memo, 133
Conspirator payments, 116-118, 121
Dean testimony, 154, 158-159
Ehrlichman role, 110, 113, 230
Gemstone, 112, 114, 120
Haldeman role, 113, 146, 231-232, 248-249
Implicated, 31
LaRue role, 197, 199
McCord statement, 64, 95
Mardian discrepancies, 201
Mitchell, Dean roles, 17, 179-183
Motives, 136
Spying, 125-126, 188
Stans complicity, 132, 134-137, 141, 143
Strachan account, 210, 227-228
Haiphong publicity, 22
Immunity
Attempts, 107, 132, 138, 140
Cox limiting efforts, 111, 121, 137-138
Nixon campaign role, 67-68
Resignation, rehiring, 23, 56, 105
Senate witness, 57, 132, 135-137, 141
Wallace drive, 115-116, 121-122
Mail Tampering, 107, 121-122, 124
Mallory, King, 90, 144
Mankiewicz, Frank, 160-161
Mansfield, Mike (D Mont.)
Criticism of media, 51
Congress-White House relations, 130, 263
Electoral reform, 73-74
Impeachment, 55, 180, 188
Leaks, 150
Marchetti, Victor, 58
Mardian, Robert C.
Disbarment effort, 174, 259
Ellsberg break-in, 120
ITT affair, 120
Watergate break-in
Conspirator payments, 116
Discovery, 134
McCord memo, 58
Planning role, 162, 181, 185, 199
Senate testimony, 200-201, 204, 208, 214, 218
Statement, 226
Wiretaps, 70, 120, 214
Maroulis, Peter, 197, 199, 201
Marriott, J. Willard Sr., 105
Martinez, Eugenio R.
CIA background, 238
Ellsberg break-in, 118-119
Executive clemency, 202
Watergate break-in, 4, 9-12, 105
Mathias, Charles McC. Jr. (R Md.), 12
Marx, Louis, 213, 215-218
Media. *See* Press. Television.
Merriam, William R., 144
Merrill, William, 198
Meserve, Robert W., 27, 67, 264
Mexican Bank Inquiry. *See* Investigations, FBI.
Miami Herald (*see also* Press), 178
Mills, Wilbur D. (D Ark.), 77-78, 153, 177, 258
Mills, William O. (R Md.), 84, 90, 115
Mitchell, John N.
Biography, 38-39, 41, 43
Civil suits, 87, 243, 259
Ellsberg break-in, 136, 217
Hoover assessment, 217
ITT link, 229, 235-236, 243
Political intelligence
Alioto charges, 148
Campaign role, 63, 68, 223, 226
Dean memo testimony, 154-155, 157
Planning role, 110, 113, 125
Wiretapping, 32, 120, 141, 191
Vesco case
Dismissal asked, 242
First linked, 7, 24-25, 31
Indictment, 46, 56, 71-72, 89
Lebanese Bank deal, 30-31
Overview, 258
Pretrial publicity, 148, 188, 203
Trial date, 107, 263
Vesco's assessment, 65
Watergate coverup
Alch testimony, 83-84
Authorization alleged, 10, 12, 17, 20, 82
Break-in statements, 4, 89
CIA memos, 128
Concealed funds, 8, 116
Conspirator payments, 107, 150, 166-167
Criminal evidence, 106, 178
Dean leaks, testimony, 145, 152, 154-155
Ehrlichman discrepancies, 213, 230, 240
Gemstone, 112, 114
Haldeman testimony, 242, 246, 249-253
Implicated by Stans, Magruder, 132-133, 135-137, 141
Kleindienst, Petersen testimony, 261
LaRue testimony, 197, 199
Mardian contradictions, 200-201
Moore statement, 205-207
Nixon tapes, role, 177, 224
Planning role, 64, 120-121, 125-126
Strachan testimony, 210
Testimony, 179-186, 188-189
White House counterattack, 151, 162-163, 157
Mitchell, Martha
Baldwin guard, 85
Public statements, 13, 19, 48, 146
Speechwriter money, 115
Mittler, Austin, 94
Money Trust Investigation, 15
Montoya, Joseph M. (D N.M.)
Biography, 6
Campaign funds, 161, 177
Dean questioning, 156, 161
Nixon-Ervin meeting, 189
Strachan questioning, 212, 214
Moore, Richard A.
Buzhardt memo, 163
Conspirator payments, 150, 166
Dean-Nixon meetings, 165, 179, 192
Duties, 42
Names witness, 57
Statement, 205-207
Testimony, 179, 184-185, 189, 192, 202-203
Morin, Charles H., 144
Morton, Rogers C.B., 84, 115, 132, 139
Moss, John E. (D Calif.), 27, 55
Mott, Stewart Rawlings, 153
Munro, S. Sterling Jr., 153
Muskie, Edmund S. (D Maine)
Campaign sabotaged
Bugging plans, 125-126
Disclosures, 8-9, 32, 69, 155
Ehrlichman testimony, 230
Grand jury probe, 258
Infiltration, 212
Haldeman apology, 232
Phony letter, 8-9, 25, 32, 69
Spying, 134, 155
Enemies list, 153
Nixon Apr. 30 speech reaction, 27
Popularity, 149
Records subpoenaed, 146
Thurmond outburst, 66

N

Nader, Ralph, 132, 263-264
Narcotics Control Bureau. *See* Justice Department.
National Aeronautics and Space Administration, 243
National Association of Attorneys General, 139-140
National Broadcasting Company. *See* Television.
National Education Association, 153
National Labor Relations Board, 178
National Security (*see also* Investigations, White House. National Security Council. Pentagon Papers.)
CIA memos, 110, 117, 126-129
CIA pressured by White House, 102, 104
Dean documents, 122-125
Ellsberg-break-in, 212-217, 219, 261
Historical perspectives, 173
Huston memos, 119-121
McCord conviction, 203
Nixon aides' remarks, 88
Nixon May 22 speech, 79, 89-94, 102
National Security Act, 66, 103
National Security Agency, 79-80, 91-94, 122-125, 244
National Security Council (*see also* Kissinger, Henry A.)
Laird duties, 130

National Security Council
Wiretaps
Authorization, 68-69
Ehrlichman rationale, 214
Ellsberg dismissal, 191
Haldeman justification, 102
Halperin suit, 132, 141, 259
Kissinger disclaimer, 107
Mardian, logs, 120, 191
Young role, 31, 52, 105
National Transportation Safety Board, 105
Neal, James F., 107, 198
Nedzi, Lucien N. (D Mich.)
CIA coverup role, 86, 112, 141
Dean testimony refusal, 217
Ellsberg break-in, 140-141
Haldeman involvement, 112, 137
Intelligence plan, 188
Nelson, Jack, 13
Newman, Paul, 153
Newsday *(see also* Press), 157
Newspapers. *See* Press.
Newsweek. *See* Press.
New York Daily News. *(see also* Press), 178
New York Times *(see also* Press)
Criticism, 51
Editorial, 81
Subpoenaed, 13
Wiretapped, 32, 47
Nixon, Donald, 72
Nixon, Edward, 7, 22, 164
Nixon Foundation, 109
Nixon Inaugural Committee, 105
Nixon Re-election Committee *(see also* Finances, Republican Campaign)
Chain of command, 106
Civil suits
Cox seeks delay, 204
Ehrlichman deposition, 110, 125
Haldeman deposition, 110, 113, 137
Harmony perjury, 119
McCarthy, 87, 259
Mardian statement, 226
MacGregor deposition, 236
Oliver, 147, 259
Overview, 19-20, 259
Perjury, 110, 119
Postponement, 262
Records subpoena, 188
Settlement effort, 226
Demonstrators, 154
Domestic security, 223
Finance violations, 4-5, 87, 150, 245
Mail tampering, 107
Republican National Committee, 87
Vesco case, 7-8, 24-25, 140, 150
Vesco indictments, 71-72
Watergate break-in
CIA memos, 126, 128-129
Coverup reported, 31
Criminal trial, 9-11
Dean testimony, 154
Democrats forewarned, 138
Ehrlichman testimony, 230
First implicated, 4
Gemstone, 112, 114
Haldeman, Strachan roles, 178, 219
Magruder, Stans roles, 132-137, 139-143
Mitchell testimony, *(see also* Mitchell, John N.), 180
Odle testimony, 63-64
Officials to testify, 57
Porter perjury, 117-118
White House links, 154-156, 227-228
Nixon, Richard M. *(see also* Presidency)
Agnew, 27, 141, 270
Bar probe, 259
Campaign finances *(see also* Finances, Republican Campaign), 100-101, 117, 139, 229
Civil suits, 204, 259
Critics *(see also* Congress. Press), 66, 180, 189, 241
Demonstrators, 155, 236, 243
Domestic intelligence
Dean documents, 121-125
Federal judge pressure, 147
Haldeman role, 112
Hoover opposition, 119
May 22 speech, 107, 188
Election reform, 67-69, 73-76, 105
Ellsberg break-in
Authorization, 30, 120, 152, 155
Ehrlichman testimony, 233
Krogh role, 147-148
May 22 statement, 219, 220
Executive clemency *(see also* Executive Clemency)
Dean meetings, 119
Hints, 63-64, 87
Hunt attempts, 150, 152, 154, 160-161
McCord offer, 80, 82-84, 89-90
Executive privilege
Baker statement, 148
Congressional subpoena, 65, 103, 148, 161, 186
Ehrlichman, Haldeman impact, 149
Grand jury subpoena, 107
Guidelines, 17-18
Percy statement, 161
Tapes, records. *See* Executive Privilege
Godwin snub, 241
Illness, 179, 218, 220-221
Impeachment speculation
Background, 55
Byrd reaction, 90
Cox study, 148
Drinan resolution, 229, 242
House discussion, 132, 140
McCloskey attempt, 110, 115, 119, 121
Mansfield warning, 180, 188
Public opinion, 149
ITT link, 229, 235-236, 243
Past scandals, 30, 45
Political retaliation, 150
Property, 109, 178, 271
Public opinion. *See* Polls.
Republican Party, 38, 49, 67-69, 89
Resignation speculation
Asked *(see also* McCloskey, Paul), 87, 120, 146
Daughter's remarks, 174, 178
Nader speech, 263
Percy, 161, 175
Polls, 176, 218, 240, 242
Refusal, 191
Security leaks, 120
Senate Watergate probe *(see also* Executive Privilege)
Baker propriety, 160
Brezhnev delay, 145, 148
Buzhardt memo, 157-158, 162-163
Dean evidence, 145, 151
Dean testimony, 152, 154-156, 158-161, 163-168
Ehrlichman testimony 212-224, 229-233, 239-240, 243
Ervin meeting *(see also* Ervin, Sam J. Jr.), 184
Files dispute, 202
Gurney clarification, 90, 107, 118
Haldeman testimony, 231-238, 242-253
Kalmbach statement, 204-205
Magruder testimony, 132, 134
Mitchell testimony, 179-180, 182-183, 188
Moore testimony, 179, 184-185, 189, 205-207
Talmadge focus, 104-105
Testimony sought, 159, 174, 177-178, 186
Special prosecutor, 32, 34, 89, 120
Staff *(see also* White House)
Aides' resignations, 24, 50
Apr. 22 speech, 27-29, 34-37, 160
Cabinet meetings, 131
Dean tapes, 139
Ehrlichman, Haldeman suspensions, 160
Hickel criticism, 174
Krogh, 52
Reorganization, 42, 60-61, 130-131
Vacancies, 105, 108
Watergate coverup *(see also* Dean, John W. III, Ehrlichman, John D. Haldeman, H.R. Mitchell, John N. White House.)
Alch vendetta charge, 84
Approval alleged, 52-53
Apr. 30 statement, 34-37
Aug. 15 speech, 272, 274-280
Cabinet meeting statement, 20
CIA role, 85-87, 89-90, 101-103
Dean evidence, 42, 66, 68, 72
Dean memos, 139
Dean probe, 110, 120-121, 145, 148
Grand jury leaks, 22
Gray warning, 65, 104, 148, 229
Haldeman defense, 249-251
Liddy authorization, 201
McCord blame, 57-59, 120
Magruder denial, 141, 134-135
May 22 statement, 79-80, 88-94, 99, 161
Mitchell remarks, 177, 180
Notification, 106, 254, 256-257, 260-261, 267
Outside counsel, 179
Porter loyalty, 118
Responsibility denial, 11
Statement preparation, 254-255, 262, 263
Stevenson attack, 234, 242
Tanaka-dinner remarks, 229, 243
Watergate impact
Congress, 77-78, 180, 263, 130-131
Credibility, 149, 176, 262, 264
Faith in system, 147
Popularity, 104, 111
Presidency, 86
Re-election, 110, 112
Nofziger, Lyn, 115-116, 153
Nolan, Ramon, 139
Northrop Corporation, 195
Novak, Robert, 134
Nye Munitions Inquiry, 16

O

O'Brien, Lawrence
Break-in, 4, 11, 17-18
Civil suit *(see also* Democrats), 258
Colson role, 136, 148
Fear for life, 160
Forewarned, 138
Various plots, 125, 154-155
O'Brien, Paul
CIA link, 58
Conspirator payments, 166, 195
Coverup role, 230
Mardian talks, 201
Odle, Robert C. Jr.
Gemstone papers, 114
Implicated, 4
Resignation, 56
Senate witness, 57, 63-64, 69
Ogarrio, Manuel, 265-267
Oliver, R. Spencer, 4, 125, 147, 259
O'Neill, Thomas P. Jr. (D Mass.), 27, 55, 77-78
Operation Gemstone *(see also* Wiretapping)
Bugging transcripts, 136-137
Details, 63, 112, 114
Strachan role, 212
Opinion Research Corporation. *See* Polls.
Organized Crime Control Act, 54
Ostrow, Ronald J., 13

P

Packard, David L., 60
Packwood, Robert W. (R Ore.), 12, 26
Panama, 139
Papers. *See* Pentagon Papers.
Paper Shredder. *See* Document Destruction.
Parker, Douglas M., 209
Parkinson, Kenneth W.
Campaign funds, 14, 31, 241
McCord memo, 58
Mardian talks, 201
Patman, Wright (D Texas), 258
Peck, David, 67
Pecora Stock Exchange, 16
Pell, Claiborne (D R.I.), 144
Pentagon, 68
Pentagon Papers *(see also* Ellsberg, Daniel. National Security.)
Ellsberg break-in
Authorization, 152
Barker testimony, 85
Buzhardt memo, 163
CIA involvement, 54, 56, 100-101, 239
Cox inquiry, 118-119, 146
Ehrlichman role, 139-141, 177, 215-219, 233
Files theft, 20, 52-53
Grand jury probe, *see* Investigations, Federal Grand Jury
House subcommittee probe, 203-204
Hunt role, 107, 145
Justice Department knowledge, 189
Krogh, 52, 174, 186
Linked to White House probe, 30, 119
MacGregor deposition, 236
Mitchell silence, 180
Nixon May 22 statement, 91-94
Nixon planning dispute, 147-148
Richardson impact, 89, 96
White House coverup, 47, 56, 64-65, 105
Ellsberg investigation
CIA role, 59, 66-68
FBI thoroughness, 241
Justice Department hindered, 261
White House probe, 30, 80, 91-94, 155
Soviet copies, 119-121, 240
Trial
CIA memos, 54, 59
Byrne dismissal, 46, 65, 66, 70
Ehrlichman FBI interview, 31-32
Watergate affidavits, 29
Wiretaps
Reporters, 32, 66, 141, 155
Ruckelshaus statement, 69-70
Pepsico, 237
Percy, Charles H. (R Ill.)
CIA hearings, 86, 103
Harris poll, 29
Special prosecutor, 27-28, 32
Watergate remarks, 86, 161, 175
Perjury
Agnew dinner, 174, 186
Dean, warning 176, 212
Harmony, 114, 119
Kalmbach intent, 196, 230-231
McCord new trial, 137, 150, 152, 154
Magruder, 152, 166, 181, 235
Mitchell, ITT, 235
Porter, 110, 117-118, 178
Sloan, 110, 114, 116, 118
Tapes impact, 263
Vesco defendants, 71
Persons, Wilton B., 53
Petersen, Henry E.
Ellsberg break-in, 32, 53, 92
Watergate probe
Advises firings, 160, 233
Dean impropriety, 156, 161
Dean-Nixon meeting, 167-168
Duties, 20, 22-23, 27-28
Senate testimony, 254, 260-262, 264
Special prosecutor, 261
White House interference, 129
Philippines. *See* Finances, Republican Campaign.
Picker, Arnold M., 153, 243
Picker, David, 153
Picker, Ruth, 153
Pierson, John, 38

Plumbers, *See* Ehrlichman, John D. Krogh, Egil Jr. Investigations, White House. Young, David.
Poff, Richard H. (R Va.), 243
Police, District of Columbia, 57, 64
Political Enemies List, 151, 153, 158, 175
Politics. *See* Historical Antecedents.
Polls
April-May, 23-24, 29, 50
June
House races, 136
Nixon popularity, 104, 112, 176
Nixon coverup role, 149
Press fairness, 141
July, 181, 218, 240, 242
August, 262, 264, 274
1962 gubernatorial, 30
Porter, Herbert L.
Cash fund, 114
Civil suit, 259
Conspirator payments, 133-134
Criminal charges, 178
Implicated, 11, 31
Perjury, 110, 117-118
Senate witness, 57, 121
Stans statement, 143
Precision Valve Corporation, 109
Presidency
Election reform, 73-75
Historical perspectives, 169-173
Resignation, 175
Subpoena, testimony, 103, 159, 190, 209
President, Committee for the Re-election of the. *See* Nixon Re-election Committee.
Press (*see also Las Vegas Sun, Los Angeles Times, Newsday, Newsweek, New York Times, Time, Wall Street Journal, Washington Post, Washington Star-News.)*
Enemies list, 153
Historical perspectives, 172-173
Leaks, 134, 159
Newsmen's subpoenas, 13, 103
Surveillance
Break-in, 107, 119
Haldeman plan, 237, 250
Halperin suit, 141
Kraft, 155
Reporter list, 150
Wiretaps, 32, 47, 65, 102
Tax audits, 145, 157
Trial prejudice role, 110-111, 119
Watergate coverage, 13, 51, 81, 141
Prisoners of War, 104
Prosecutor, Special Vesco, 50, 65
Prosecutor, Special Watergate (*see also* Cox, Archibald)
Approved, 11
Candidates, 67
Cox appointment, 63, 96, 98
Guidelines, 86, 96-98
Historical precedents, 45, 67-68
Justice Department resentment, 261
McCord conviction dispute, 203
Republican support, 12
Richardson confirmation role, 30, 32, 56, 62
Senate resolutions, 27-28, 34, 62
White House suggestions, 67
Prostitutes. *See* Espionage.
Proxmire, William (D Wis.), 51, 67, 130
Public Broadcasting System. *See* Television.
Public Opinion. *See* Polls.

R

Radical Groups, 119-120, 136
Rand Corporation, 129
Rayhill, James W., 242
Reagan, Ronald, 29, 148
Rebozo, C. G., 109, 157, 178, 243
Reed, Clarke, 38
Reedy, George, 74
Reisner, Robert
Gemstone role, 112, 114, 120
Humphrey campaign role, 114, 146
Liddy bug plan, 181
Odle testimony, 63
Republicans (*see also* Elections. Finances Republican Campaign)
Agnew dinner, 115, 121, 135
Bush remarks, 139
Civil suits, 18-19, 110, 120-121, 259
Connally shift, 56-57
Coverup, 127
Election reform, 73, 75-76
Fund-raising, 38, 49
House impact, 77-78, 90, 136
Mitchell status, 182
Nixon re-election funds, 87
Nixon tapes, 241
Watergate protest, 25-26
Weicker smear, 151, 159, 177
Reston, James, 51
Reuss, Henry S. (D Wis.), 188
Richardson, Elliot L.
Appointment, 24, 26-28, 36-37
Biography, 42-43
Confirmed, 90, 96, 98, 104
Election reform, 73, 75
Ellsberg break-in, 53, 89
Haig appointment, 105
Justice Department
Conflicts, 160
Guidelines, 243
Leaks, 107
New inquiry, 118
Nixon confidence, 49
Publicity, 178
Tapes lawsuit, 219
Special prosecutor (*see also* Cox, Archibald)
Charter proposal, 86
Cox appointment, 63, 87, 99
Cox independence, 89, 97, 120
House views, 28
ITT probe, 137
Statements, 56, 62, 65
Stevenson attack, 234, 242
White House role, 30, 67, 94
Richardson, Laurance B., 72
Richey, Charles R.
Civil suits, 9, 13, 19, 107
IRS probe, 186, 203-204
Republican cooperation, 186
Rietz, Kenneth
Biography, 41
Infiltrators, 134
Resignation, 22, 38, 56
Rinaldo, Matthew Jr. (R N.J.), 69
Rinehart, Jonathan, 187
Ripon Society, 27
Rockefeller, Nelson A., 29
Rockwell International, 242-243
Rodino, Peter W. Jr. (D N.J.), 147, 258
Rogers, William P.
Congressional briefing, 78
Demonstrators, 223
Kalb break-in, 241
White House offer, 22, 26
Rogovin, Mitchell, 21
Romney, George, 26
Rothblatt, Henry, 10, 197, 202
Ruckelshaus, William D.
Biography, 43
FBI directorship, 25, 42
Wiretapping, 66, 69-70, 141, 259
Russo, Anthony J.
Charges dropped, 46, 70, 121, 191
CIA memos, 59
Ruth, Henry S. Jr., 198

S

Sabotage (*see also* Espionage. Operation Gemstone), 30, 32, 63, 91-94
St. Clair Inquiry, 15
St. Louis Post-Dispatch, 146
Sampson, Arthur, 271
Sandwedge Plan, 162
Scandals, *See* Historical Antecedents.
Schell, Orville H. Jr., 27
Schlesinger, James R.
Appointment, 46, 57, 60, 89
Biography, 61
Ellsberg break-in, 54, 56
Watergate coverup
Alch testimony, 84
CIA memos, 117, 120, 126-129
McCord revelations, 57-59, 80
White House zeal, 90
Schorr, Daniel, 153, 159, 237
Schultz, George P., 191, 195-196, 200, 217
Schweiker, Richard S. (R Pa.), 26
Scott, Hugh (R Pa.)
Call for leadership, 69
Criticism of media, 51
Dean denunciation, 150
Election reform, 73, 75, 144
Nixon tapes, 229, 241
Special prosecutor, 12
Watergate impact, 131
Sears, Harry L.
Charges, Vesco, 46, 56, 71-72, 89
Delay sought, 263
Overview, 7, 107, 258
Publicity, 188, 203
Seattle Post-Intelligencer, 147
Secrecy in Government (*see also* Central Intelligence Agency. Investigations, White House. National Security), 79
Secret Service, 194-196
Securities and Exchange Commission
Colson role, 90, 144
Cook resignation, 67
ITT file removal, 90
Smith fraud suit, 119
Vesco case
Background, 7, 21
Casey-Vesco meeting, 21
Indictments, 46, 56, 71-72
Mitchell intercession, 30-31, 177
Sedam, J. Glenn Jr., 4
"Sedan Chair," (*see also* Espionage)
Disclosure, 114, 146, 160-161
Strachan testimony, 210, 228
Segretti, Donald H., (*see also* Espionage)
Biography, 38-39, 41
Disbarment effort, 174, 259
Political Sabotage
Authorization, 202
Civil suit, 87
Cox probe, 146
Funding, 21, 197, 142
Haldeman testimony, 232, 244-245
Indictment, 25
Innocence claimed, 69
Probe, 258
Various activities, 8-9, 39, 188
Senate (*see also* Committees, Senate. Congress)
Impeachment role, 55
Nixon meeting, 180
Nixon records, 209
Richardson confirmation, 90, 96, 98
Special prosecutor, 28, 30
Senate Select Committee on Presidential Campaign Activities. *See* Senate Watergate Subcommittee.
Senate Watergate Subcommittee
Army spy probe, 268
Audience participation, 216-217
Bellino, 219, 262
Brezhnev delay, 145, 148
Campaign finances
Conspirator payments, 116-118, 121, 203-204
Donors list, 147
Personal bank records, 150
Stans testimony, 132-135, 139-143
Weicker smear, 159
Caucus room history, 68
CIA role, 80, 82, 89-90
Conflicts with other probes
Civil suits, 19
Cox. *See* Cox, Archibald.
Dean probe, 110
Disbarment information, 174
Grand juries, 46-48, 99
Impeachment effort, 161
Justice Department, 32, 52, 62, 177
Vesco case, 112
White House, 148, 185
Criticism of proceedings
Agnew, Morton, 132, 139
Bush, 132,
Butz, 65
Gurney, 99, 107, 118
McGovern, 147
Mansfield, Scott, 150
Nixon Aug. 15 speech, 272, 274-280
Talmadge, 104-105
Dean revelations
Baker assessment, 150
Buzhardt memo, 162-163
Evidence doubted, 57
Files, 66-67, 99, 118-119, 122-125
Leaks, 137, 149
Testimony, 151-161, 174-176, 163-168
Election reform, 144
Executive clemency
Caulfield role, 68, 82-83
McCord offer, 64, 94-95, 89-90
Executive privilege (*see also* Executive Privilege)
Ehrlichman use, 189
Flight records, 19
Nixon-Dean logs, 120-121
Nixon May 3 guidelines, 47
Nixon questioning, 174
Presidential subpoena, 12, 103
Funding doubled, 23
Gray, 65, 255-257, 260, 262-268
Gurney money, 178
Haldeman statement, 249-250
Hearings
Expanded, 138, 146
Extended, 229, 241
Recessed, 254, 260, 264
Procedures, 48, 50, 140
Speedup, 235, 264
Weicker smear, 177
Historical perspectives, 172-173
Hunt, 160
Immunity
Dean, 47, 132, 138, 140
Liddy refusal, 68, 114, 120, 242-243
Magruder, 132, 138, 140
Strachan, 148, 178
Waiting period, 62, 107
Young, 178
McGovern testimony offer, 160
Mitchell testimony, 148, 179-186, 188-189
Partisan division, 233
Plumbers secrecy, 216-217
Presidential testimony (*see also* Executive Privilege), 151, 174, 177
Rebozo records, 243
Second phase focus, 178
Talmadge on impeachment, 263
White House strategy, 155, 233, 249-250
Witnesses, 57, 110
Shaffer, Charles N., 139, 149-150
Separation of Powers. *See* Executive Privilege.
Shankman, Bernard, 57-59, 94-95
Sharp, Morell E., 147
Sheehan, Neil, 31, 141
Sheppard, Roy H., 67
Shoffler, Carl M., 64
Shredder. *See* Document Destruction.
Shriver, Sargent, 87
Silbert, Earl J.
Appointment, 9-10
Ellsberg file memo, 20, 32
Mexican bank inquiry, 117
Special prosecutor conflict, 89, 104, 120, 177
Sirica, John J.
ACLU motion, 150
Civil suit, 262
Criminal trial, 9-11

Dean evidence
Cox folder, 149
Files acquisition, 50, 66-67, 99, 118
Files texts, 122-125
Senate use, 157
Federal grand jury, 12
LaRue guilt, 161
McCord evidence, 40, 84, 132, 137
McCord memo text, 57-59
Second grand jury, 204
Senate probe
Cox limit efforts, 111, 121, 137-138
Immunity, 107, 132, 138, 140
Liddy silence, 68
Young immunity, 178
Tapes controversy *(see also* Executive Privilege)
Nixon position, 254-255, 264
Show cause order, 209, 239
Sloan, Hugh W. Jr.
Buzhardt memo, 162
Campaign funds
Agnew dinner, 174
Conduit role, 114-116, 118, 122
Criminal charge, 10, 31
GAO probe, 5, 25
Haldeman statement, 245
"Laundered" checks, 135
Mills gift, 84
Smith donation, 119
Stans statement, 141-142
Civil suits, 47, 50, 65, 258
Ehrlichman conflict, 217
Liddy bug plan, 181
Perjury, 110, 114
Senate witness, 57
Smith, C. Arnholdt, 87, 119
Smith, Howard W. (D Va.), 77
Smithsonian Institution, 169
Socialist Workers Party, 204
Sonnenfeldt, Helmut, 69
Soviet Union, 119-121, 219, 240
Spater, George A., 186-187
Staggers, Harley O. (D W.Va.), 144
Stans, Maurice H. *(see also* Finances, Republican Campaign)
Biography, 38-39, 41
Campaign finances
Conspirator payments, 193-195
Corporation soliciting, 202
Disbursements, 114-116
Document destruction, 134-135, 140
GAO dispute, 140
Implicated by Magruder, 141
Mexican bank deposit, 128
Senate witness, testimony, 57, 132-135, 139-143
Civil suits, 19, 21, 87, 258-259
Committee salary, 138
Vesco role
Charges, finance committee, 5, 31
Charges, Vesco, 46, 56, 65, 71-72
First linked, 7-8, 10-11, 14, 21-22
Mercy asked, 242, 263
Overview, 89, 107, 258
Pretrial publicity, 188, 203
SEC intervention, 67-68
Senate conflict, 112, 132-134, 137
State Department
Fabricated cables
Disclosure, 54, 177, 180
Gray destruction, 215, 255-256, 260, 267-268
Joint intelligence agency, 124-125
Steelman, Alan (R Tex.), 33
Stein, Howard, 153
Stevens, Ted (R Alaska), 130
Stevenson, Adlai E. III (D Ill.), 62, 234, 242
Stone, W. Clement, 202
Strachan, Gordon C.
Biography, 38, 41
Break-in knowledge, 136
Bugging transcripts, 137, 154-156
Buzhardt memo, 162
Cash fund, 110, 112, 133
Conspirator payments, 21, 87, 199, 201
Criminal evidence, 178
Disbarment effort, 174, 259
Document destruction, 154-155, 158
Ehrlichman testimony, 230, 242
Haldeman role, 146-148, 231-232, 244-245
Immunity, 148
Implicated, 9, 31, 188
Liddy role, 126
Media funds, 115
Nixon records subpoena, 209
Resignation, 56
Senate statement, 226-228
Senate testimony, 210, 212, 214, 218-219
Strategic Arms Limitation Talks, 32, 92, 213-214
Strauss, Robert S.
Civil suits, 18-19, 243
Election reform, 73
Home break-in, 120, 160
National security, 106
Students *(see also* Espionage), 9, 22
Sturgis, Frank
Break-in role, 4, 9-12, 105
Chilean break-in, 129
CIA background, 238
Executive clemency, 202
Subpoena *(see also* Executive Privilege), 103
Suicides, 84
Sullivan, William C.
Ellsberg wiretaps, 70, 141, 158, 191
Halperin suit, 259
Nixon meeting, 165
Sunday Times of London *(see also* Press), 47
Supreme Court
Congressional subpoenas, 103
Nixon records case, 208-209, 239-241
Wiretap case, 68
Symington, Stuart (D Mo.)
CIA hearings, 66-67, 85-87, 89
Haig appointment, 105, 130
Watergate remark, 106
Szulc, Tad, 141

T

Talmadge, Herman E. (D Ga.)
Bellino probe, 262
Biography, 6
Committee procedures, 104-105, 111, 135, 264
Ehrlichman questioning, 217
Gray questioning, 257
Impeachment statement, 263
Junket, 242-243
Kalmbach questioning, 197
Mitchell questioning, 182-183
Nixon tapes, 216, 234
Perjury warning, 85
Tapes, records dispute *(see also* Executive Privilege)
Butterfield disclosures, 191-194, 202-203
Collusion charge, 233-234
Copying restrictions, 189
Cox changes, 241
Early efforts, 179, 186, 188-191, 195-196
Ehrlichman appraisal, 218
Ervin letter, 186
Haldeman testimony, 232-235
Lawsuit resolution, 225-226, 262, 264
Nixon Aug. 15 speech, 272, 274-280
Nixon-Ervin phone call, 218
Nixon letters, 189-190, 220, 225
Phone hoax, 191, 200, 217
Subpoena, 208-212, 218-220
Talmadge statement, 263
Television coverage
Agnew objection, 27
Cox limit efforts, 121, 132, 137-138, 140
Curtailed by networks, 119
Grand jury role, 99
Tapman, Kenneth C., 65
Taxes, *See* Internal Revenue Service.
Teague, Olin E. (D Texas), 242
Teamsters Union, 178
Teapot Dome, 15-16, 44-45, 68
Telephone Companies, 141, 203, 259
Television *(see also* Press)
Enemies list, 153
Hearing coverage
Cox limiting efforts, 16, 111, 121, 140
Historical precedents, 172-173
Network rotation, 119
Nixon role, 120
Kalb break-in, 241
Monitoring plan, 237
Poll, 141
Schorr probe, 157
Status report, 178
White House pressure, 241
Thomas, Helen, 146
Thompson, Fred D.
Appointment, 3, 48
Biography, 7
Butterfield questioning, 192, 194
Dean questioning, 160
Ehrlichman questioning, 233
Helms questioning, 238
Liddy probe, 114
Thrower, Randolph W., 177
Thurmond, Strom (R S.C.), 66
***Time* Magazine,** 13
Timmons, William E., 4, 130, 164
Title Insurance and Trust Company, 109
Titus, Harold H. Jr., 79, 104, 117
Tkach, Walter R., 179
Tolson, Clyde, 165
Torrijos, Omar, 139
Townsend, Lynn A., 201
Transportation Department, 52, 104, 177
Treasury Department, 195
Treese, James T., 116
Trials, Criminal. *See* Investigations, Federal Grand Jury.
Trials, Civil. *See* Common Cause. Democrats. Republicans.
Truman, Harry S
Defense committee, 16
Impeachment resolution, 55
Presidential resignation, 75
Scandals, 44-45
Separation of powers, 186, 190
Tuck, Dick, 232, 244-245
Tully, Andrew, 217
Tunney, John V. (D Calif.), 32, 98, 243, 262
Tyler, Harold R. Jr., 67
Tyler, John, 55

U

Udall, Morris K. (D Ariz.), 78
Ulasewicz, Anthony T.
Clemency offers, 89
Political spying
Conspirator payments, 193, 195, 197
Haldeman statement, 244
Ehrlichman statement, 222-223, 230
Kennedy probe, 156, 237, 243
Testimony, 82-84, 199-200, 203
Underwood, Edwin H., 109
United Artists Corporation, 153, 243
United Auto Workers, 153
United Press International, 146
United States Intelligence Board, 123
Urech, Arthur M., 87

V

Vandenberg, Arthur, 175
Vaughan, Harry, 44-45
Velde, Harold H., 190
Vesco, Robert L.
Campaign role
Concealed funds, 31, 150
Mitchell, Stans meetings, 7-8, 21-22
Conspiracy law, 157
Grand jury probe
Bench warrant, 89
Extradition, 132
Immunity, 50, 65, 90
Indictment, 46, 56, 71-72, 140
Mitchell business help, 30-31, 177
Mitchell, Stans, Sears trial date, 107
Overview, 258
Pretrial prejudice, 188, 203
SEC suit, 67-68, 86-87
White House aid, 25
Watergate documents, 106
Vietnam, 91-94
Violence *(see also* Central Intelligence Agency. Domestic Intelligence. Ehrlichman, John D. Haldeman, H.R., 263
Vorenberg, James, 99, 107, 146-147, 198
Voting Rights Act, 138

W

Waddy, Joseph C., 219
Waggonner, Joe D. (D La.), 77, 115
Walker, Ronald H., 236
Wallace, George C.
Bremer break-in plot, 150
Campaign, presidential, 115-116, 121-122, 232, 242-243
Finance records, 146
***Wall Street Journal*,** 13, 81, 270
Walters, Vernon A.
Bugging memos, 117, 120, 126-129
CIA pressure, 66-67, 100-102, 107
Conspirator help, 256, 266-267, 262
Dean role, 162
Haldeman testimony, 235
Helms testimony, 238, 243
Nixon May 22 statement, 79
Testimony, 229, 256, 263
Ware, John (R Pa.), 33
Warren, Gerald
Coverup denial, 53, 119, 161
Document copying, 189
Domestic spy memos, 137
Ellsberg break-in, 219-220
Haldeman, Ehrlichman blame, 148
Nixon-Dean meetings, 120
Nixon property, 109, 271
Nixon resignation denial, 174
Records, tapes access, 209, 219, 239, 241
White House staff
Duties, 177
Reorganization, 105, 108, 131
Washington Post
Editorial, 81
Ellsberg-Watergate link, 69
Espionage reported, 8
Pulitzer prize, 51
Subpoenaed, 13
TV license, 241
Wiretap reports, 32, 47
***Washington Star-News*,** 13, 81
Watergate *(see also* Democrats. Wiretapping.)
Break-in
Advance knowledge links, 152, 156
Arrests, 3-4
CIA early role, 90, 160
Financing, 87
Special prosecutor guidelines, 97
White House meeting, 100
Song, 19
Weathermen *(see also* Radical Groups), 119-121
Weicker, Lowell P. Jr. (R Conn.)
Army spying, 263
Biography, 7
Brezhnev delay, 145, 148
Burglary of safe, 19

Weicker, Lowell P. Jr. (R Conn.)
Caulfield questioning, 83
Criticizes administration, 12, 241
Domestic intelligence, 138-139
Ehrlichman questioning, 217, 230, 240
Gray questioning, 257, 268
Haldeman questioning, 236-237, 243
Kalmbach questioning, 196
Kleindienst, Petersen questioning, 261
Mitchell questioning, 182-183, 185
Nixon files, tapes, 202, 235
Presidential testimony, 176
Ulasewicz questioning, 200
White House smear, 151, 159, 177
Weinberger, Caspar W., 60-61
Western Airlines, 187
Wharton, Blagden H., 149, 174, 258
White House *(see also* Investigations, White House. National Security. Nixon, Richard M.)
Agency misuse
Congressional probe, 258
Enemies list, 153, 158
FBI, 139, 157, 165, 237
IRS, 164, 177, 186, 203-204
Kleindienst, Petersen testimony, 261
Schorr probe, 157, 237
Tax audits, 157, 237
Billy Graham rally memo, 236
Byrne FBI offer, 219
Campaign links, 227-228
Campaign sabotage, 180
CIA pressure
CIA memos, 110, 117, 126-129
Colson testimony, 149
Helms disclosures, 102-103
Hunt role, 100-101, 161
McCord memo, 54, 57-59
Mexican bank, 100-102, 117
Watergate coverup, 66, 85-87, 89, 158
Conspirator payment fund, 235, 244-245
Dean counterattack
Buzhardt memo, 151, 157-159, 161-163, 181-182
Dean inquiry *(see also* Dean, John W. III), 151, 157, 246-248, 251-253
Ellsberg profile, 239, 262
Executive clemency *(See also* Executive Clemency), 87
Executive privilege (*See also* Executive Privilege), 47, 103
Intelligence operations
Dean documents, 122-125, 157
FBI probe, 119
Huston plans, 85, 119, 121
Justice Department, 62
Kennedy probe, 155-156, 237, 243
Leaks, 155
Nixon May 22 statement, 91-94, 121
Security, 104
Nixon property, 109, 271
Nixon tapes, files *(see also* Executive Privilege)
Brennan reaction, 219
Cox suit response, 264
Drinan impeachment move, 229, 242
Haldeman testimony, 231
Halt, 218
Lawsuit statement, 208-209
Ziegler comment, 203
Plumbers *(see also* Investigations, White House), 213, 216-217
Polling funds, 232
Political reprisals
Enemies list, 151, 153, 158, 175
Gray call, 257
Reporter list, 150
Tax audits, 151
Weicker smear, 151, 159, 177
Senate Watergate probe
Baker liaison, 160
Interference, 155, 185
Nixon appearance, files, 103, 179, 186, 188-190
Special prosecutor *(see also* Cox, Archibald), 67, 120
Staff
Aides resign, 36-37, 42, 56
Buzhardt, 46, 57
Climate, 222-223
Connally, 46, 57
Garment, 24-25, 42-43, 130
Haig, 53, 105, 121, 130-131
Klein, 121, 130-131
Laird, 110, 121, 130
Reorganization, 60-61, 130-131
Vacancies, 105, 108
Watergate impact, 218
Wright, 130
Ziegler, 130-131
Watergate coverup
Aides' roles, 111-112
Criticism of Washington Post, 13
Dean intimidation, 47, 72
Dean report denial, 154-155
Dean tapes, 139
Foreign funds, 139
Gray warning, 66
Haldeman testimony, 232
Hunt role, 112, 132, 137-138, 145
Klein remarks, 160
Mitchell motives, 181
Moore disclosures, 192, 205-207
Nixon Apr. 17 statement, 17-18
Nixon-Dean meetings, 110, 192-193
Nixon May 22 statement, 79, 89-94
Strachan role, 178
Watergate impact
Congress, 77-78, 127, 144, 243
Disclosure asked, 86
Grand jury procedures, 156
Impeachment. *See* Impeachment.
Scapegoating, 154
Wiretapping, 22, 154-156, 213-214, 244
Wilkins, Roger, 51
Williams, John J. (R Del.), 27-28
Wilson, Charles H. (D Calif.), 107
Wilson, John J.
Clients, 21, 146
Executive privilege, 149
Inouye slur, 229, 238, 263
National security, 216-217, 219
Strachan briefing, 148
Tapes controversy, 231-233
Wilson, Woodrow, 176
Wiretapping *(see also* Democrats. Espionage. Investigations, White House.)
Campaign, Democratic, 120, 125-129
Campaign, Republican
Authorization, 121, 213-214
Democrats forewarned, 138
Liddy plans, 154, 180-181, 183-184
McCord case, 83, 95
Strachan testimony, 210
Transcripts, 136-137
Ulasewicz, 82-84, 199-200
Civil suits. *See* Democrats.
Congressional inquiry, 203
Document destruction, 154-156, 158, 228
Ellsberg, 46, 69-71, 141, 191
Embassies, 80, 82-84, 89, 117
Historical perspectives, 170
Justice Department, 138
National security
Cambodia role, 68
Dean documents, 122, 124-125
Halperin suit, 132, 141
Huston memos, 121
Kalb, 241
Kissinger aides, 69, 102, 107
Kraft, 155
Nixon role, 91-94, 120, 164
Reporters, 32, 47, 65, 102
Ruckelshaus statement, 69-70
Presidential, 203-204
Wong, Alfred C., 195
Woodcock, Leonard, 153
Woods, Rose Mary, 147
Woodward, Robert, 51
Wright, Charles A.
Appointment, 130
Nixon tapes, 209, 219, 224, 241-242

Y

Young, David
Biography, 52
Ellsberg break-in, 139-140, 213
Ellsberg probe, 31-32, 105, 239, 91-94
Grand jury silence, 132, 140
Hunt cables, 54
Immunity, 178
Resignation, 56
Young, Milton R. (R N.D.), 26
Young Socialist Alliance, 204

Z

Ziegler, Ronald L.
Biography, 38, 41
Civil suit, 188
Dean probe
Duped by Dean, 156, 163, 176
Inconsistencies, 11, 68, 139
'Inoperative' remark, 17
May 22 statement, 88
Media criticism, 13
Nixon meeting, 26-27
Domestic security, 223
Ellsberg break-in, 56
Executive clemency, 87
Executive privilege, 103, 106
Nixon silence, 86, 165, 178
Tapes controversy, 203
White House changes
Cabinet meetings, 131
Connally appointment, 57, 60
Duties, 121, 130-131, 177
File supervision, 30
Haig appointment, 53
Nixon illness, 179
Nixon resignation, 174
Packard meeting, 60
Workload, 42

OTHER CQ PUBLICATIONS

HARD COVER BOOKS

Congress and the Nation
Volume I: 1945-1964 $27.50
Volume II: 1965-1968 $35.00
Volume III: 1969-1972 $35.00

This 4,300 page, three-volume resource brings detail and perspective to the important issues and events in national affairs since World War II, spanning six Presidencies and twenty-eight years. Carefully organized and indexed for reference. Volume I: 1945-1964 (1965) 2,000 pages, 8½" x 11", hard cover; Volume II: 1965-1968 (1969) 1,100 pages, 8½" x 11", hard cover; Volume III: 1969-1972 (1973) 1,200 pages, 8½" x 11", hard cover.

Congressional Quarterly's Guide to the Congress of the United States $35.00

The definitive reference on Congress—its origins, history and development. Explains how Congress works, its powers, the pressures upon it, and prospects for change. Carefully organized and indexed for reference. September 1971. 984 pages, 8½" x 11", hard cover.

America Votes 9 $22.50

A handbook of American election statistics. Official results for the 1970 vote in each state for Senator, Representative and Governor, with vote totals, percentages and pluralities. Compiled and edited by Richard M. Scammon, Director, Elections Research Center. July 1972. 470 pages, 8½" x 11", hard cover. Also available: America Votes 8 ($20.00)

PAPERBACKS

Future of Social Programs $4.00

Comprehensive review of national efforts to solve the problem of poverty in America. Covers Johnson's war on poverty, Nixon's family assistance proposals, federal hunger programs and OEO, income redistribution and social security financing. August 1973. 92 pages, 8½" x 11", paper.

Energy Crisis in America $4.00

Comprehensive background on the energy crisis that is now a fact of life for millions of Americans. Gasoline prices, Alaska pipeline dispute, strip mining, new energy sources, pollution technology, environmental problems, legislation from 1969-72. March 1973. 93 pages, 8½" x 11", paper.

Congressional Districts in the 1970s $10.00

Complete demographic profiles of all 435 congressional districts based on the 1970 census. Includes maps for each state and largest cities, and background report on political process of redistricting in each state. Statistical data on each district. March 1973. 236 pages, 8½" x 11", paper.

Congressional Roll Call 1972 $8.00

A chronology and analysis of votes in the House and Senate, 92nd Congress, 2nd Session. Reports the vote of each Representative and Senator for every roll-call vote taken during 1972. Indexed, March 1973. 192 pages, 8½" x 11", paper. Also available: *Congressional Roll Call 1971* ($8.00) and *Congressional Roll Call 1970* ($8.00).

Crime and the Law $4.00

The fight by federal forces to control public problem number one in America. Crime facts and figures, urban crime, organized crime and white collar crime, penal and court reform, political response of the administration, Congress and the courts. July 1971. 96 pages, 8½" x 11", paper.

Current American Government (CQ Guide) $3.00

Updated and published twice each year, in January and August, to serve as an up-to-date handbook on recent significant developments in the legislative, executive and judicial branches of American government. Spring edition (January) and fall edition (August). 144 pages, 8½" x 11", paper. Annual subscription for both spring and fall editions is $6.00.

Standing order. **Includes future paperback titles which will be mailed upon publication.**

Dollar Politics $4.00

The issue of campaign spending. How funds are raised and spent; wealthy candidates and richest givers; Campaign Spending Act of 1971; 1972 spending data. January 1972. 96 pages, 8½" x 11", paper.

Education for a Nation $4.00

Financing education in the U.S. Nixon record on education. Education for Jobs. School busing. Lobbying and education. September 1972. 108 pages. 8½" x 11", paper.

Man's Control of the Environment $4.00

Ecological problems facing America: population explosion, land use, air and water pollution, solid waste disposal, pesticides, electric power problems, coastal pollution, noise pollution, politics of pollution, state actions, international vs. national interests. August 1970. 96 pages, 8½" x 11", paper.

The U.S. Economy: Challenges in the 1970s $4.00

Federal economic policy: 1945-1968. Nixon economic policy: 1969-1972. Economic issues during the 1970s. Congressional powers. Trading with foreign and communist nations. December 1972. 124 pages, 8½" x 11", paper.

Nixon: The Fourth Year of his Presidency $4.00

Reviews 1972 administration actions on the economy, foreign affairs, the budget, nominations and appointments, regulatory agencies. Texts of messages, statements and news conferences. January 1973. 224 pages, 8½" x 11", paper. Also available: *Nixon: The Third Year; Nixon: The Second Year; Nixon: The First Year* at $4 each.

Politics in America 1946-1970 $4.00

The politics and issues of the years since World War II including the 91st Congress and 1970 elections. Results of 6 presidential and 13 congressional elections. Fourth edition: September 1971. 160 pages, 8½" x 11", paper.

The Power of the Pentagon $5.00

Examination of Congress's relationship with the military, problems within the ranks, quest for answers. Includes case studies. July 1972. 118 pages, 8½" x 11", paper.